HUMAN RELATIONS

The Art and Science of Building Effective Relationships

Vivian McCann Hamilton

PEARSON

Prentice
Hall

UPPER SADDLE RIVER, NEW JERSEY 07458

Library of Congress Cataloging-in-Publication Data

Hamilton, Vivian.
　　Human relations : the art and science of building effective relationships / Vivian Hamilton.
　　　p. cm.
　　Includes bibliographical references and index.
　　ISBN 0-13-193064-8
　　1. Interpersonal relations.　　2. Interpersonal communication.　　I. Title.
　　HM1106.H35 2007
　　302—dc22

2006038394

VP/Editorial Director: Leah Jewell
Executive Editor: Jeff Marshall
**AVP/Director of Production
　and Manufacturing:** Barbara Kittle
Assistant Managing Editor: Maureen Richardson
Production Liaison: Nicole Girrbach-Ramirez
Production Editor: Shelley L. Creager
Manufacturing Manager: Nick Sklitsis
Manufacturing Buyer: Sherry Lewis
Cover Director: Jayne Conte
Cover Design: Bruce Kenselaar
Cover Illustration/Photo: Jose Ortega/Stock
　Illustration Source, Inc.

Director, Image Resource Center: Melinda Patelli
Manager, Rights & Permissions: Zina Arabia
Manager, Visual Research: Beth Brenzel
Manager, Cover Visual Research & Permissions:
　Karen Sanatar
Image Permission Coordinator: Annette Linder
Composition/Full-Service Project Management:
　Techbooks
Printer/Binder: Edwards Brothers, Inc.
Director of Marketing: Brandy Dawson
Sr. Marketing Manager: Jeanette Moyer

Photo Credits: *Page 64: Figure 2.10:* Markus Boesch/Getty Images, Inc. - Allsport Photography; *p. 186: Figure 6.1:* Acey Harper/Getty Images/Time Life Pictures; *p. 206: Figure 6.5;* Getty Images, Inc.; *p. 228: Figure 7.4:* Evan Agostini/Getty Images, Inc.; *p. 231: Figure 7.6:* Copyright © Mark Peterson/CORBIS. All Rights Reserved; *p. 369: Figure 11.2a:* Phillip V. Caruso/Picture Desk, Inc./Kobal Collection; *Figure 11.2b:* Evan Agostini/Getty Images, Inc.

Pearson Education Ltd.
Pearson Education Singapore Pte. Ltd.
Pearson Education Canada, Ltd.
Pearson Education—Japan

Pearson Education Australia Pty. Limited
Pearson Education North Asia Ltd.
Pearson Educación de Mexico, S.A. de C.V.
Pearson Education Malaysia Pte. Ltd.

1 0 9 8 7 6 5
ISBN 0-13-193064-8

CONTENTS

4 Emotions, Stress, and Human Relations   107

PART TWO: External Influences on Human Relations

5   The Role of Perception in Human Relations   149

6 Social Influence in Our Relations with Others

7 Prejudice: Foundations, Causes, Effects, and Remedies

PART THREE: Principles of Effective Communication

8   Listening   247

PREFACE

Relationships are the very foundation of our lives. Whether personal or professional, our ability to understand and communicate effectively with the people in our lives can make the difference between a satisfying, fulfilling life, and one filled with tension and frustration. What does it take to build effective relationships? Certainly good communication skills are a critical component. We also need some basic psychological principles to help us understand how and why people in similar situations often have very different interpretations and responses. And in our increasingly diverse society, we cannot ignore the impact of cultural norms on the effectiveness of our interactions with others. Studying one or two of these topics alone, though, is not enough.

This book aims to break new ground in the study of human relations by integrating these three key components of successful relationships. First, some basic psychological principles are presented to help the reader understand both internal and external influences on our thoughts, feelings, and behaviors. With this as a foundation, development of basic communication skills in the second part of the book goes beyond the standard one-size-fits-all perspective. Instead, the reader learns to consider the psychological influences on the individual with whom he or she is communicating, and tailor these communication skills accordingly. Multicultural findings and issues are included throughout the book, so that the reader emerges with skills and understanding that are widely effective in our multicultural world.

The subtitle of the book reflects the importance of both science and art in the development of good interpersonal relations. Every effort has been made to include the most rigorous scientific findings in psychology and communication, so that the foundation provided is based on solid and credible research. This research provides the context for artful application of the communication skills and principles which follow. Numerous examples and activities are included in each chapter so that the reader can see how principles apply differently in different situations and with different people, and can practice various applications of the skills to their lives in personal and professional settings. The ability to adapt one's communication skills to a variety of different situational and cultural contexts is indeed an art, and recognition of the importance of context is a key feature of this book.

ORGANIZATION

Part One lays the foundation for the study of human relations, and examines internal influences on our thoughts, feelings, and behaviors. Chapter One discusses the importance of context, and introduces several dimensions of culture which form a framework for understanding the diverse people of our world. Chapter

Two examines various aspects of the self and how it develops in childhood as well as throughout stages of adult life. Chapter Three offers an overview of major personality theories, with an eye towards how these various perspectives can help us better understand others' behaviors as well as our own. Chapter Four studies the role of emotions and stress in our relationships, including common irrational beliefs which influence emotions and how these beliefs can be overcome.

Part Two examines external, or sociocultural influences on our relations with others. Chapter Five introduces perception in human relations, including cognitive biases, physiological and cultural factors which influence perception, as well as an overview of how memory influences perception. Chapter Six offers an in-depth look at conformity, principles of compliance, and obedience to authority. Chapter Seven focuses on prejudice, including its foundations in group formation, ethnocentrism, and stereotypes, as well as causes and consequences of prejudice and discrimination, and how to work towards overcoming them.

Part Three encompasses communication principles and skill-building. Chapter Eight begins with development of the relational climate, and studies elements of listening, barriers to effective listening, and a variety of authentic listening styles. Chapter Nine presents basic skills and strategies in verbal and nonverbal communication, with four principles of communication as the framework: language must be clear, responsible, culturally sensitive, and congruent. Chapter Ten examines various myths about conflict, as well as various personal conflict styles; it also includes ways to reduce defensiveness in oneself and others, and the win-win (or integrative) approach to conflict resolution.

Part Four takes a broader look at human relations in our personal and professional lives. Chapter Eleven includes key concepts in intimate relationships, such as love, attraction and mate selection, and key components in healthy long-term relationships. Chapter Twelve focuses on surviving and thriving in the workplace, with information on leadership, motivating people, creativity, and the role of work in a meaningful life. Gender and cultural issues and variations are included in every chapter, based on current research.

PEDAGOGY

Over fifteen years of experience teaching college students has taught me that information is only useful when students perceive it as engaging and relevant to their lives, so I've written the book in the same voice students hear from me in class. My goal is always to balance academic rigor with friendliness and accessibility, so many examples are included based on what students have shared, as well as my own life. I also firmly believe that students like to be challenged, as long as they perceive a way to meet that challenge, and this belief has guided development of the book as well. Although the tone is conversational, I tried hard not to oversimplify either the language or the concepts.

Numerous pedagogical features are integrated into the textbook in order to help students develop a strong working knowledge of each concept. First, *preview questions* at the beginning of each section signal the main issues addressed in that section, and also provide a running outline for the material. Second, a number of *critical thinking questions* are integrated into each chapter, strategically placed to help students analyze and apply concepts as they are learning about them. These questions encourage specific application of topics and issues to the readers' own lives, as well as connections between concepts, so that they develop a deeper understanding both of the concepts and of their relevance. Third, each chapter contains several *interim summaries,* which summarize the concepts included in that particular section. This feature helps students digest those concepts prior to moving on to new material. The interim summaries are also tied to the preview questions that appeared at the beginning of that section. At the end of each chapter, several *class-tested activities* are provided that help the student apply chapter concepts, practice communication skills, or gain additional insight into their own relations with others. Each activity is keyed to a particular section within the chapter, with notations suggesting at what point an activity should be completed for optimal learning and understanding. Finally, *figures and tables* provide graphic synopses of key concepts. *Key terms* appear in bold text, with boxed definitions of each term in the margin nearby. A list of key terms is provided at the end of each chapter, and a complete *glossary* is included in the back of the book.

SUPPLEMENTS

Ancillary materials for this text include:

Instructor's Resource Manual with Test Item File. The Instructor's Resource Manual includes key learning objectives, self-contained class lectures and activities for each chapter, discussion ideas, and an annotated list of additional resources, including video clips and other outside resources such as texts, journals, and websites; all resources are organized by chapter-section, in an effort to better focus content and ease the process of lecture preparation for instructors. The Instructor's Resource Manual with Test Item File will be available as a print item, or for download via the Prentice Hall eCatalog. TestGen software will also be available, as both a physical item and an eCatalog download. [IRM/TIF ISBN: 0131930664 & TestGen ISBN: 0131930656]

PowerPoint Lecture Slides with Classroom Response System Questions. These slides are not only intended to be the basis for class lectures, but also for class discussions. The incorporation of the CRS questions into each chapter slideshow facilitates the use of 'clickers'—small hardware devices similar to remote-controls, which process student responses to questions, and interpret and display results in real time. CRS questions are a great means to engage students in learning and precipitate contemplation of text concepts. The slides also feature prominent figures and tables from the text. The PowerPoint Lecture Slides with Classroom Response System Questions will be available for download via the Prentice Hall eCatalog. [ISBN: 0131930672]

ACKNOWLEDGMENTS

This book would not have been conceived of nor completed were it not for the strong and ongoing support of many important people in my life. In graduate school and my early career, De Gallow, Tom Crawford, Ross Conner, Sergio Lopez, and Peter Wilson all believed in me and gave me opportunities to grow and create. When I first conceived of this book, Marianne Taflinger was integral in helping me get it off the ground. At Portland Community College, I am indebted to my generous colleagues who reviewed earlier drafts of the manuscript, class-tested it with their students, and offered valuable insights, ideas, and general support and goodwill: they are Marlene Eid, Cynthia Golledge, Wayne Hooke, Lauren Kuhn, Richard Lazere, and Tani McBeth. Christy Bowker was not only an excellent research assistant, but provided thoughtful feedback on the manuscript as well. Special thanks also to several people who played key roles in turning the manuscript into the book: Sheryl Rose for her careful and thoughtful copy-editing; John Nebraska for his funny, creative, and on-target original cartoons; and Shelley Creager for her close attention to detail, her accessibility, and the grace with which she managed the production of this book. And Jeff Marshall, my editor at Prentice-Hall, has got to be the best editor on the planet for his savvy guidance, his unflagging enthusiasm and support, and his collaborative approach to the development and publishing of this book.

I was extremely fortunate to have many outstanding reviewers provide feedback on drafts of the manuscript. Their thoughtful perspective, careful attention to detail, and astute suggestions were invaluable, and truly made this a much better book. They went "above and beyond," and I am deeply indebted to each of them. They are:

Robert E. Beneckson, Miami-Dade College
Jayne P. Bowers, Central Carolina Technical College
Dale V. Doty, Monroe Community College
Leila Harclerode, Hudson Community College
Karl N. Kelley, North Central College
Carrie Lane, University of Texas, Arlington
Gary T. McElroy, Appalachian State University
Samuel Pierce, Chemeketa Community College
Gregory Pool, St. Mary's University
Jacqueline Pope-Tarrence, Western Kentucky University
Diane Wentworth, Fairleigh Dickinson University
Lynn Wilijanen, Wor-Wic Community College

On a personal level, I have been blessed to have a few very special individuals in my life. Mom and Dad always believed in me, and made great sacrifices to provide whatever support and resources necessary to explore the (many) paths that interested me. Rusty Hamilton was there through some of the most challenging times of my life, and provided steady support as I learned and grew through them. Lauren Kuhn has been a constant source of true friendship, encouragement and honest feedback. And my beloved Shawn has renewed and enriched my life beyond measure, and his generous and insightful spirit inspires me every day.

Finally, I am indebted to the many students I have had the pleasure of teaching and learning with throughout my career. Their interesting and diverse selves have stimulated, challenged, and enhanced my worldview and my life.

I have learned from all of you, and for that I thank you. Now let's celebrate!

FOUNDATIONS OF HUMAN RELATIONS

CHAPTER 1

WHY STUDY HUMAN RELATIONS?

PREVIEW QUESTIONS

(1) How important is good human relations in our personal lives?

(2) How important is good human relations in our work lives?

(3) Are good human relations simply good communication skills?

Effective interpersonal skills is the single factor most responsible for success or failure in business and in personal relationships. This is surprising to most people, perhaps because it contradicts some popular myths of our society. One of the most popular of these myths is "Love conquers all," which implies that if two people love each other enough, they can overcome any problems that might arise. That sounds logical enough, and it also appeals to our idealistic sense of love. Unfortunately, research demonstrates that it simply isn't true— love, by itself, *doesn't* conquer all. The divorce rate in America remains at about 50%. Couples who divorce didn't start out loving each other any less than couples whose marriages succeed, and sometimes even continue to love each other despite a divorce; the difference between them is often rooted in their communication skills. Howard Markman, a leading expert in the field of couple communication, has determined that communication skills account for more than 60% of the level of satisfaction and happiness in married couples' relationships. Even more astounding is relationship expert John Gottman's research, which can predict with greater than 90% accuracy whether a relationship will succeed or fail *based on observing the partners' patterns of communication with each other*. Later in this book, we will explore this research in more detail.

Another popular myth is that, in the working world, the most qualified person gets the job. We tend to think that "most qualified" means the person with the most experience in that type of work, or with the most skills in that area. Surprisingly, research shows this

1

isn't true either. The National Association of Colleges and Employers conducts annual surveys of employers to find out what factors influence them when they hire recent college graduates. Interpersonal skills, including communication, teamwork, and relating well to others, top the list and are considered even more important than analytical skills, computer skills, or GPA (NACE, 2003).

These findings provide a strong rationale for developing good interpersonal skills. Do good human relations, then, result from acquiring good communication skills? On the surface, this may seem to be a logical conclusion, and there are certainly many books and courses built around development of communication skills. *Seven Steps to Improving Your Relationship*, *50 One-Minute Tips to Better Communication*, and *A 30-Minute Guide to a Better Relationship* all promise better relationships for readers who follow the step-by-step guidelines. In reality, though, skills by themselves are not enough, because no two people, relationships, or situations are the same. We don't live in a "one-size-fits-all" world, and indiscriminately applying communication rules or tools is only going to result in the occasional success. *Human relations are more accurately thought of as an art — an art in which development of good skills is an important component.* The skills alone, though, are of little use without an understanding of the **context**, or in other words, the personalities, cultural backgrounds, and situational factors involved in each interaction.

> **Context** The personalities, cultural backgrounds, and situational factors involved in each interaction.

WHAT IS CONTEXT?

PREVIEW QUESTIONS

(1) How does context affect our everyday lives?
(2) What types of context are important in human relations?
(3) Why do we need to understand context to be effective in our relations with others?

This issue of context is important, so let's look at a few examples, starting with context in skills that many people already have. For example, most people know how to cook. Granted, some are better than others, but most people know something about cooking. In fact, it is sometimes said, "If you can read, you can cook," implying that cooking is simply following the directions in a recipe; sometimes the recipe is even accompanied by a beautiful, mouth-watering photo, so how can you go wrong? Well, just as step-by-step guidelines to better relationships tend to be oversimplified, most of us have probably realized that making a recipe turn out like the photo is often far more complicated than it looks! And even after we've developed our art to the point where our dish looks as good as the picture, there is still more to consider.

For example, one dish by itself rarely constitutes a full meal, especially when you are having guests for a special occasion. The type of occasion, your culture, and your guests all might influence the combination of dishes you put together for your meal. For a Fourth of July party, you might barbecue your entree, serve it with beans and a cold salad, and have homemade ice cream with fresh berries for dessert. At Thanksgiving, many people choose to roast a turkey, serve it with mashed potatoes and gravy, cranberries, and a fruit salad, and perhaps bake an apple pie for dessert—that is, if they've mastered the challenge of making a good piecrust! And These holiday traditions are distinctly American. A person from another country may not be familiar with these traditions and could thus expect or prepare something very different, illustrating the importance of culture in context. And what if your guests were vegetarian or had other dietary needs such as low fat or no sugar? Clearly, simply knowing how to cook is not enough. To be successful, you would want to consider contextual factors such as your guests' preferences, the occasion, cultural influences, and your own strengths and weaknesses in cooking.

We can also look at the issue of context in a sport, such as football. Knowing how to throw a good spiral pass, make a great catch, or throw a block isn't enough to win a game. First, consider your teammates—your skills must fit well with theirs. If you are used to being a wide receiver, but someone else on the team has that spot, you might need to modify your skills so that you can be a tight end instead. Then consider the other team. If they have a great passing game but a weak running game, you'll want to put extra coverage on their receivers and work on breaking through the line to sack the quarterback. Third, think about the particular game. Is it preseason, so you don't have much to lose by trying out some new plays, or is it the conference championship? Is it raining, in which case you might need to plan more running plays than pass plays? Is it the beginning of the second quarter or the final minute of the fourth quarter? That might determine whether you kick a field goal or go for the touchdown. Once again, simply knowing the skills isn't enough. To succeed in football, you must also know the context, which in this case includes your team, the other team, the particular game, and your own strengths and weaknesses.

 Think of a skill that you know well and list some of the ways that context is important in mastery of that skill.

Now that we understand the importance of context in activities we already know, let's consider how it applies to a human relations activity. One important aspect of human relations is listening. In this book you will learn about several different styles of listening, including offering advice, giving support, asking questions, and analyzing the situation. Each of these listening styles can be useful, depending on several factors. One factor to consider is the person you're listening to: Does she need advice, or analysis, or should you ask questions designed to help her sort through the situation on her own? Another important consideration is the situation. Perhaps you recently listened to someone else who was in the same situation. Should you use the same listening style? Not necessarily, because even if the situation is the same, the people involved are different. You must also consider yourself. What are your experiences with this person and with this situation? And what do you know about your own strengths and weaknesses in listening? Clearly, there is much more to effective human relations than just acquiring the skills. This is where the "art" of human relations becomes important, as you work at becoming more proficient in knowing what skills to use and when and how to use them.

One additional type of context that is integral to any modern study of human relations is recognition of the ever-increasing diversity in American culture and society, and awareness of its influences on our relations with others. Our cultural backgrounds play a significant role in the beliefs, expectations, and interpretations that color our interactions with others. For example, in Western society we value assertiveness in communication; in other words, we tend to believe that we should express ourselves directly. To do otherwise is to "beat around the bush," a tactic that many people find frustrating. In some cultures, though (such as Japan), this same directness is considered rude and offensive. In these cultures it is more respectful to politely hint at your meaning, so the listener can make the connection on her own and thus "save face" by not having to have the message "spelled out" for her (Hall, 1959). Knowing these various cultural expectations would be another factor to consider in choosing the best listening style.

An understanding of these different cultural norms is necessary in order to correctly interpret others' behavior when we are interacting with them. Therefore, we will begin our study of human relations with a general overview of the meaning of culture, along with the most common ways of categorizing culture. Then, research findings that illuminate cultural similarities and differences will be woven into each chapter, so that your study of human relations truly reflects a realistic, multicultural perspective of modern American society.

PSYCHOLOGY, SCIENCE, AND HUMAN RELATIONS

PREVIEW QUESTIONS

(1) What is psychology, and how does it help us develop better human relations?
(2) What makes psychology a science?
(3) How do we best define human relations?

Clearly, effective human relations involves much more than simply mastering a set of communication skills. Effective application of the skills relies on a deep understanding of the context, and the field of study best suited to helping us develop such an understanding is **psychology**, which is the scientific study of human thoughts, feelings, and behaviors. Psychology takes into account both internal (personality) and external (social and cultural) factors that influence a person, so it can provide us with the solid foundation we need to become effective, or artful, in applying the communication skills that we will develop.

> **Psychology** The scientific study of thoughts, feelings, and behaviors.

We should also note the scientific nature of psychology. Contrary to the popular opinion that psychology involves an intuitive understanding of people, psychology is more accurately considered a science. As such, the psychological principles we include as our basis for understanding people in this book will rely on scientific, or **empirical evidence**. Empirical evidence is based on data that has been collected through precise measurement under carefully controlled conditions. It is essential to understand the

> **Empirical evidence** Based on data that has been collected through precise measurement under carefully controlled conditions.

difference between empirical evidence and personal experience, or anecdote. In a nutshell, personal experience is just that—one person's experience or observations. Empirical evidence, on the other hand, is the equivalent of the combined experiences or observations of many people. Furthermore, these combined experiences or observations have been collected and measured using scientific methods that help eliminate bias, which in turn gives us even more confidence in the findings. So, it follows that in our study of why people do what they do, we have a better chance of drawing an accurate conclusion if we rely on empirical evidence, rather than on our own or another person's more limited experience.

Throughout the course of this book we will explore some basic principles of psychology that help us understand why people act, think, and feel in certain ways. As we study each concept, we will apply it to our own patterns of thoughts and behaviors—to enhance our self-awareness—as well as to patterns of our friends, family members, and the general population. Then, armed with this new understanding, we will learn a broad array of communication skills, and actively explore how application of these skills will vary depending on the person with whom we are interacting and the specific situation. By the time you complete this book, you will see a significant improvement in your relations with others, both personally and professionally.

For our purposes, then, we will define **human relations** as the ability to interact effectively with diverse others in a variety of situations. Developing this ability is a *process*—just as artists work throughout their lives to improve their art, we must make a commitment to work continually to improve our art, the art of human relations. Actually, the process began informally many years ago, when as a young child you began observing and interacting with your environment. As you grew into adulthood, you continued to hone your abilities based on your experiences and your instincts. That background will serve you well as you now begin your formal study of human relations, where you will uncover new knowledge to add to your experience, so that you can continue to improve your interpersonal effectiveness.

> **Human relations** The ability to interact effectively with diverse others in a variety of situations.

Interim SUMMARY #1

Effective human relations is at the core of successful relationships in both our personal and professional life. Although interpersonal skills, such as communication, listening, and conflict resolution skills, are important components of human relations, they are only effective when they are applied in the context of the person, the culture, the relationship, and the situation. Thus, a broad understanding of personality and social and cultural influences must be developed as well. These psychological concepts provide the foundation on which we build effective and artful human relations.

Before reading the next section, turn to the end of this chapter and complete Activity 1.1, which will give you an opportunity to assess your current strengths and weaknesses in your relations with others.

CULTURE: A UNIFYING THEME

PREVIEW QUESTIONS

(1) What is culture? Name at least six different examples of culture.

(2) What are values? Do they affect culture?

(3) What factors influence development of a particular culture and its values?

(4) To what extent can we determine a person's culture from his or her physical appearance?

We hear more and more about culture these days, but what exactly does it mean? Many people think of nationality when they hear someone refer to culture or cultural differences; for example, you might think of Americans, Japanese, Egyptians, or Irish. Ethnicity is another term that people equate with culture, especially in describing cultural differences in our own country. We might refer to African Americans, Native Americans, or Latinos, just to name a few. But did you know that age is also a type of culture? We hear about the "Greatest Generation," the "Me Generation," "Gen X," and most recently "Gen Y," referring (in order) to the World War II generation, people who grew up in the 1970s and 1980s, people who grew up in the 1990s, and today's teens. And indeed, research has found differences among these groups in terms of their perception of the world and their place in it (e.g., Sheehy, 1995). Similarly, gender, sexual orientation, physical ability/disability, religion, educational level, and even things such as interests and hobbies can all be included in the broad category of culture. We'll dig deeper into these and other aspects of culture shortly, but first, let's start with a definition of culture. Figure 1.1 shows the diversity of ethnic groups and cultures in the United States.

What Is Culture?

Many different definitions of culture have been proposed—in fact, if you pick up five different textbooks, you'll probably find five different definitions of culture. Don't let this confuse you, though, because the variety of definitions simply reflects the complexity of the nature of culture as well as the different disciplines that have studied it—anthropology, sociology, history, political science, and of course psychology. Many of the definitions put forth can be pulled together into a single idea, which we will use as our definition of culture: A **culture** is a set of values, shared by a group of people, which shape and influence the norms, attitudes, beliefs, expectations, perceptions, and behaviors of the group members. With this definition as our guide, let's examine the concepts of culture and values more closely.

> **Culture** A set of values, shared by a group of people, which shape and influence the norms, attitudes, beliefs, expectations, perceptions, and behaviors of the group members.

Earlier, we mentioned nationality as an example of culture, and indeed it can be. Many cross-cultural studies have examined behaviors and values using nationality as the basis for comparison. Our personal experiences support this notion as well. If you visit a foreign country, you will find that residents of that country do some things differently than the residents of your own country. In France, for example, it is not

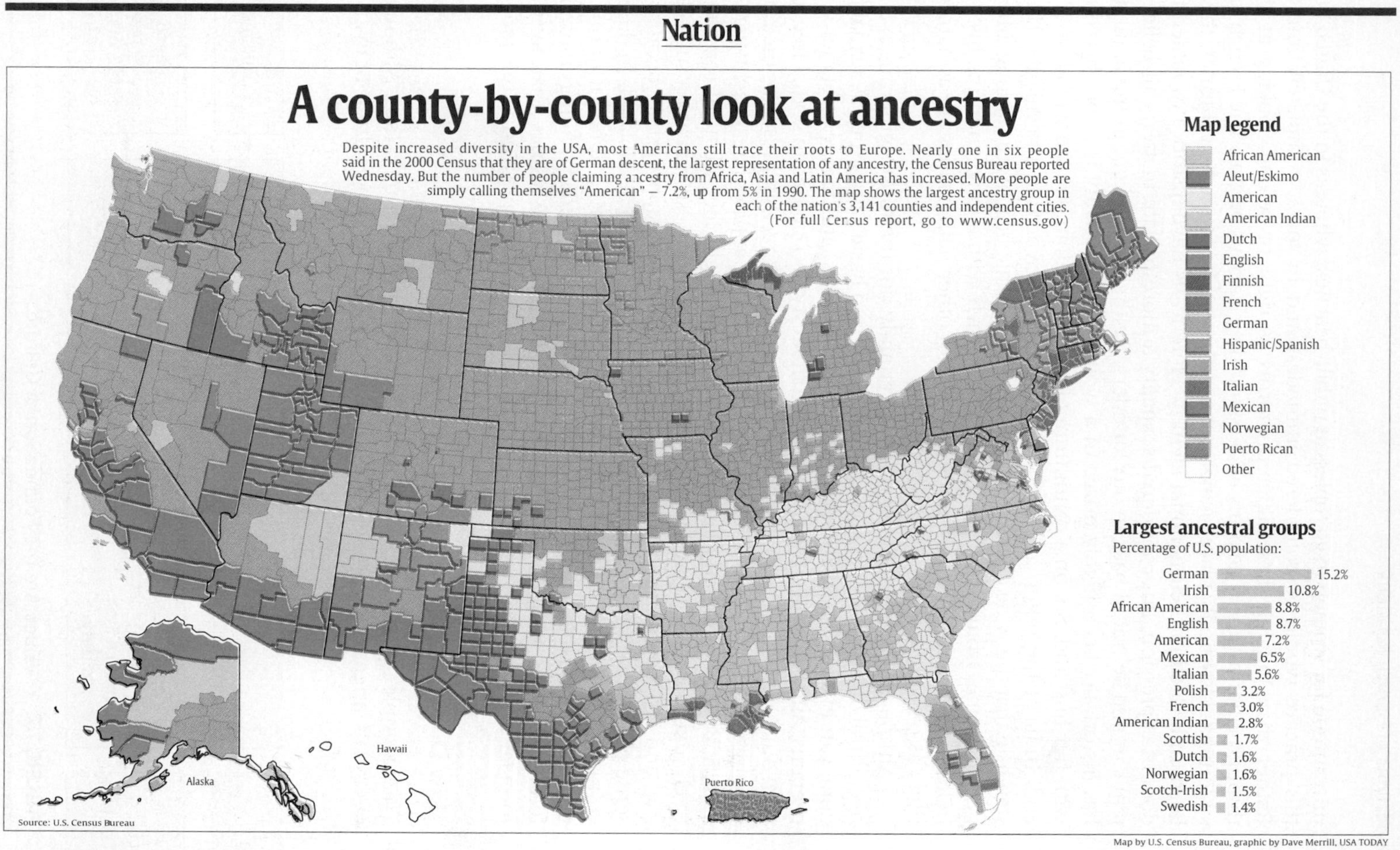

A county-by-county look at ancestry

Despite increased diversity in the USA, most Americans still trace their roots to Europe. Nearly one in six people said in the 2000 Census that they are of German descent, the largest representation of any ancestry, the Census Bureau reported Wednesday. But the number of people claiming a ancestry from Africa, Asia and Latin America has increased. More people are simply calling themselves "American" — 7.2%, up from 5% in 1990. The map shows the largest ancestry group in each of the nation's 3,141 counties and independent cities.
(For full Census report, go to www.census.gov)

Map legend

- African American
- Aleut/Eskimo
- American
- American Indian
- Dutch
- English
- Finnish
- French
- German
- Hispanic/Spanish
- Irish
- Italian
- Mexican
- Norwegian
- Puerto Rican
- Other

Largest ancestral groups
Percentage of U.S. population:

Group	Percentage
German	15.2%
Irish	10.8%
African American	8.8%
English	8.7%
American	7.2%
Mexican	6.5%
Italian	5.6%
Polish	3.2%
French	3.0%
American Indian	2.8%
Scottish	1.7%
Dutch	1.6%
Norwegian	1.6%
Scotch-Irish	1.5%
Swedish	1.4%

Puerto Rico

Hawaii

Alaska

Source: U.S. Census Bureau

Map by U.S. Census Bureau, graphic by Dave Merrill, USA TODAY

FIGURE 1.1 | Diversity in the United States

Source: USA TODAY, July 1, 2004, p. 7A. Reprinted with permission.

7

uncommon for women to go topless at public beaches, whereas in the United States this practice would be considered immodest and in India, completely immoral. Rather than judging these different norms as right or wrong, looking at them through cultural lenses helps us understand their various origins. The French value system has historically placed a high value on sexual freedom; for centuries, this has been embedded in their national identity. Americans have historically valued freedom of expression, but considered sexuality a more private matter; this belief system can also be traced back to our founders. By the same token, in India, modesty has historically been highly prized in a woman and sexuality is to be shared only with her husband. So, on a continuum of sexual freedom, France would be at one end, India at the other, and the United States somewhere in the middle. Understanding that the wide degree of diversity in acceptable beachwear among different peoples comes from different value systems—each with a long, enduring history—helps us accept that the beliefs and practices of other nationalities are as natural to them as ours are to us.

Although the issue of toplessness is certainly not the most significant example of cultural diversity, it does serve to illustrate how a basic value, such as sexual freedom, can influence a person or group's norms, beliefs, attitudes, expectations, perceptions, and behaviors. If we *value* sexual modesty (as opposed to sexual freedom), then our *belief* would be that people should wear clothing that preserves their modesty, which in turn would affect our *expectations* of appropriate beachwear. Our *attitude* would be similarly influenced, in that we might feel offended (or, alternatively, excited) if we come in contact with someone who isn't wearing such clothing, and we would *perceive* that behavior as wrong or inappropriate, because our sense of "normal" or the social norm of our culture would be violated. In different cultures we will find different value sets, which in turn drive different norms, beliefs, attitudes, expectations, perceptions, and behaviors. Understanding cultural differences begins with identifying and understanding the values that form the foundation of that culture. Figure 1.2 shows a flowchart representing this model.

How Do We Define Values?

The example of Figure 1.2 also illustrates a basic point about values. Although in everyday language we sometimes say that a person "has good values" or even that

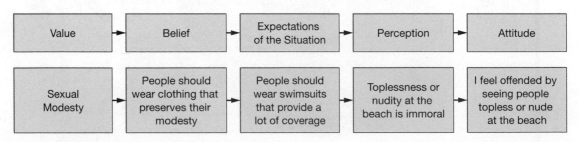

FIGURE 1.2 | Values Are the Foundation of Culture

someone "has no values," in reality everyone has values. *Values are simply the beliefs that guide us*—when we think someone has "good values," it's probably because their values match our own. When we think someone has "bad values" or "no values," it's usually because we disagree with their beliefs and behaviors. Our values are deeply embedded in us, and thus tend to prompt judgments like right or wrong, good or bad. And while we are certainly entitled to our own personal values and beliefs, we must remember that everyone else is, too.

So, when thinking about values from a psychological point of view, we must start by defining **values** as guiding principles. With this in mind, the challenge in identifying the value underlying someone's behavior is to figure out what positive outcome

> **Values** Guiding principles.

the person seems to be aiming for. If the behavior is very different from our own, this can be a daunting task. Fortunately, though, it is a skill that improves with practice. Also, becoming familiar with the value systems of different peoples around the world—which we will start doing in the next section—will provide you with a base from which to draw ideas and possibilities.

For now, let's try a few examples. Consider someone who has a habit of lying. Although our gut reaction might be to think that person has "bad values," we need to think instead about what outcome the person seems to be striving toward. It would probably be inaccurate to say that the person's goal is to lie to you or mislead you. Think about it: How many people do you suppose really get up every morning thinking, "I'm going to lie and mislead people as often as possible today!" Instead, that person probably just values something else more highly than honesty, such as harmony. So, if he finds himself in a position where telling the truth is likely to lead to conflict or to upset someone, he might tell a lie in order to avoid the conflict and keep the peace. Understanding this motivation doesn't mean you have to accept his behavior as "okay" or that you have to sacrifice your own values. It can be immeasurably helpful, though, in working through the differences between the two of you. As you will learn in more detail in Chapter 10, conflict resolution begins with values identification.

Here is another example. Perhaps you value stability or intelligence. These are positive qualities, and at first it might be difficult to understand people who don't seem to share these values. We need to remember, though, to look for what they might be valuing *more* than these things. Someone who jumps from job to job or relationship to relationship, for instance, might value excitement over stability. Or someone who dates a person who isn't very smart doesn't do so because he values ignorance, but perhaps because he values a different quality more highly, such as compassion or athleticism. At first, it can seem difficult to find positive values behind a behavior that doesn't fit our own value system, but with practice it does get easier.

Critical Thinking QUESTION Take a moment and consider someone's behavior that has puzzled you. What value might be driving that behavior? Remember to frame the value as a positive outcome, rather than in negative terms (such as excitement rather than instability).

A culture, then can be defined by its values. Furthermore, as mentioned at the beginning of this section, culture can be associated with nationality, ethnicity, gender, sexual orientation, age, religion, geographical region, and personal interests, just to name a few. How do these different cultures end up with different value systems? That is the question we will address next, but first, turn to Activity 1.2 at the end of this chapter to identify your own values.

The Origins of Culture

We humans are curious creatures, and often wonder why people do what they do. This question applies to cultural differences as well, when we find ourselves intrigued by the different values and behavior patterns around the world. Cross-cultural researchers have suggested a handful of factors that may be at the heart of cultural norms. Moreover, it has been argued that they all boil down to one basic need: the need for survival.

Earlier, we identified historical traditions as one influential factor in cultural values. In other words, cultural norms tend to get passed down through generations of a culture and thus can be very slow to change. "Culture . . . is also the crystallization of history in the minds, hearts, and hands of the present generation," says cross-cultural researcher Geert Hofstede (2001). So, our search for understanding how and why different cultures developed different norms often requires us to trace a culture back to its very beginning. In doing so, the most fruitful line of investigation has turned out to be the survival challenges faced by that particular group; in other words, *most cross-cultural researchers believe that a culture's values grow out of whatever behavior patterns are necessary to survive and thrive in that culture.* People living in a geographic region with few natural resources, for example, may have to work more collaboratively to locate and utilize those resources than people living in a region of abundance. This need for collaboration would foster values such as harmony and interdependence, rather than individual achievement and independence. Research on wealth and cultural values supports this hypothesis: As cultures become wealthier, with greater and easier access to resources, they also become more independent.

Population density is another example: People living in crowded areas may need a greater degree of social structure to maintain order. This need for order, in turn, may lead to development of strict hierarchies within the culture as a means of enforcing the rules necessary to maintain the structure and order. People living in sparsely populated areas, on the other hand, can more easily make and live by their own rules, since there aren't many other people around who may disagree.

Critical Thinking
QUESTION Can you think of an example of a crowded region that has strict social structure and hierarchical status groups?.

Climate is a third factor that affects the values and practices of a culture, and in a general sense it is similar to the issue of resources. Essentially, it is argued that very hot and very cold climates present a greater survival challenge than do moderate climates, both in the accessibility of natural resources and in the need for

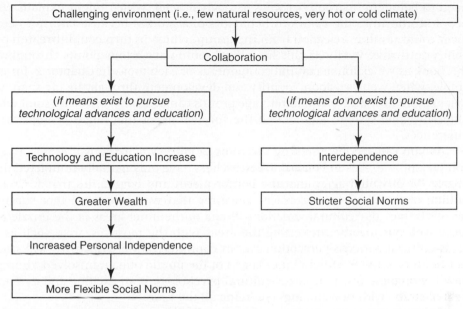

FIGURE 1.3 | A Model of Cultural Development

technology to survive in the difficult climate. Thus, groups living in the climate extremes are more likely to start out collaboratively, working together to meet the challenges. Then the greater need for technology tends to promote more educated populations, technology and education together tend to increase wealth, and ultimately these groups may end up more independent than interdependent, as they were when they started out (see Figure 1.3).

Thus, the values, norms, and behavior patterns of a culture begin to develop as a result of the particular challenges present in the environment and how they are resolved so that the people of the culture can survive and thrive. Then, over time, the development of various technologies, greater wealth, and contact with other cultures combine to present new survival challenges, thus requiring modification of the survival strategies, or culture, of the group. We will connect these general origins of cultural norms to some specific cultural differences in the next section.

It is fairly easy to see how survival factors such as availability of resources, population density, and climate can influence the value system of a large group of people who share a geographical region. But can we also explain cultural differences based on nongeographical factors such as age, gender, and even educational level in terms of survival needs? The answer to that question is the current focus of ongoing research into cultural similarities and differences. It should be noted, however, that humans are social animals. As such, our survival needs are not just biological in nature, but social as well, because our chances of survival improve when we belong to a group. The group can help us get what we need to survive and can help protect us from external threats. Thus, the need to belong to a group becomes a survival need, which might explain why people conform to the values or behaviors of a group—because failure to conform could result in rejection from the group, which in turn could threaten our ability to thrive. We'll test this line of reasoning at various points throughout this book as we examine cultural components of each topic. In Chapter 2, for example, when we learn about identity and development through the life span, we will explore how and why different age groups can be characterized by somewhat different value systems and look at the survival needs that might prompt these differences.

As you can see, determining the roots of cultural variations presents a very complex puzzle, and cross-cultural researchers have only partially completed that puzzle. Most would agree that the corner pieces and boundaries that form the outline of the puzzle are in place—meaning that we understand that survival needs "frame" our cultural variations. Some of the inner areas of the puzzle are fairly well put together, reflecting the areas with the most research, such as in cross-cultural patterns perception and in communication, which we will study in Chapters 5 and 9. Other "inner" parts of the puzzle remain unsolved, though, pending ongoing research. Cross-cultural psychology is an exciting and dynamic field of study, with new findings emerging all the time.

Culture permeates our lives and the choices we make as we pursue our individual goals. Culture influences, for example, whether a person pursues a college education or how much time a person spends with family. It also influences the degree and type of sacrifices that we're willing to make for our families, our

We need a bigger stage.

Copyright © John Nebraska.

FIGURE 1.4 | We often take our own cultural norms for granted, and don't even notice them until they come into contact with norms from another culture that are different.

jobs, and our other interests. For example, if you were offered a big promotion at your job that would double your income, but that required you to move to a different country, what would you do? Would the answer be different if your significant other had a great job where you currently lived, or if you had children involved in activities at their school? If your culture places a high value on career advancement and status, you would probably jump at the chance. If your culture valued family stability more, you'd probably turn down the offer.

This powerful role that culture plays in our everyday lives often goes unseen. Culture seems to be an invisible force, something so very basic to our existence that we are unaware of its influence until we come into contact with someone whose culture is different from our own. (see Figure 1.4) We see or hear of someone whose action seems very different from what we would do in that particular situation, and we wonder why. Is their behavior a result of some individual personality difference, or is it rooted in some aspect of their group's culture? In a quest for the answers to these questions, cross-cultural researchers have identified several different dimensions, or categories, that we can use to compare and contrast the many different cultures of our world. Let's take a closer look at these dimensions now so that we can use them in later chapters as a basis for comparison in our study of human relations.

 *Critical Thinking* QUESTION Think about your own culture and identify one important element of it—it might be your age, gender, ethnicity, religion, or race. Next, think about how this element of your culture— and thus your identity— has influenced your life in terms of your choices, opportunities, or goals. What is one specific life outcome that you can link directly to your culture? That is, name one specific way that this element of your culture helped lead you to where you are now. If you are comfortable sharing that information, compare your answer to that of one of your classmates or friends.

Interim SUMMARY #2

Culture is a key component of context in human relations. Culture is defined as a shared value system that shapes the attitudes, beliefs, expectations, perceptions, and behaviors of group members. Values themselves are simply guiding principles. The key to identifying the values underlying a person's behavior is to figure out what positive outcome the person seems to be working toward.

Most researchers agree that a group's cultural norms develop as a result of its particular survival challenges, such as scarce natural resources, population density, or climate. Whichever strategies turn out to be most effective at mastering these challenges become embedded in the culture of that group and are passed down through successive generations. Because humans need others for survival, smaller social groups based on such factors as age, gender, and education can also be considered cultural groups. Our culture exerts a powerful influence on our daily lives, our choices, and our relations with others.

DIMENSIONS OF CULTURE

PREVIEW QUESTIONS

(1) What are the four main dimensions used to compare cultures, and what does each one include?
(2) Name a few characteristics of each dimension of culture.
(3) What two dangers must we be aware of in comparing national cultures?

One of the challenges facing cross-cultural researchers has been how to quantify, or compare, different cultural values without showing bias toward one or the other. A second challenge has been how broad or narrow to make the cultural groups under scrutiny, with research ranging from broad-based studies comparing one nation to another, to more narrowly focused studies comparing the culture of one college or career, for example, to another. Our study of human relations will include as much credible and reliable cross-cultural information as we can, but for organizational purposes, we need to start on a broad scale to provide some basic foundations. So, because many cross-cultural studies have used nationality as the basis for comparison, we will begin there. The dimensions of culture laid out in this section will use nationality as examples and cite research from studies of more than 50 nations (Hofstede, 1980, 2001) that show where various nations stand on each dimension.

Although this is a useful starting point, we must be aware of two dangers in comparing national cultures. The first is the danger of stereotyping, which would happen if we were to assume that just because a national culture has a certain value, every person who lives in the culture shares that value. Instead, we need to remember that data on national culture, like any other data, reflect the *average* for that nation—some individuals show more of the characteristic and some show less. This ties into the second danger, which is to assume that the national culture explains all cultural differences between you and another person. Remember that national culture is only one type of culture to which each of us belongs. Just like the United States is often referred to as a "melting pot" of various cultures, so each one of us is an individual "melting pot" that reflects a unique blend of the various cultures to which we belong. Thus, your own individual "cultural profile" would include such things as your nationality, gender, age, ethnicity, religion, hobbies, and so forth. The bottom line is that when we see someone who seems to be exhibiting a different cultural norm than our own, national culture is but a starting place in our quest for understanding—other cultural explanations may also apply, and it's important to consider as many as we know. Now, with these things in mind, what are the best dimensions on which we can compare cultures?

Individualism–Collectivism (IC) A value system based on the relative importance of the individual versus the group or family.

Individualism–Collectivism

The most common dimension used to compare one culture to another is **individualism–collectivism (IC),** which refers to the relative importance of the individual versus the group or family, or in other words, how closely connected an individual is to his or her social groups. This dimension can be characterized on a continuum, with individualism on one end and collectivism on the other.

| Individualism | Collectivism |

Cultures that place a higher value on the individual are called *individualist* cultures, and cultures that place a higher value on the group or family are called *collectivist* cultures.

Let's look at a few examples. The first social group we typically experience is our family. Before reading further, stop for a moment and name the persons you think of when you think of your family. How many people are on your list? For most of us, family includes a mother and/or a father, any brothers or sisters we have, and possibly grandparents. If you are married and/or have children of your own, you would include them in your family group. But what about extended family members such as aunts, uncles, and cousins, or godparents, or in-laws? How many of them (if any) did you think of when you thought of your family? And are there other people with whom you don't share blood ties, but whom you consider family? The answers to these questions often reveal the degree to which a person's culture is individualistic or collectivistic: People in individualist cultures are more likely to live in nuclear families (comprised only of parents and siblings), whereas people in collectivist cultures are more likely to live in extended families or even tribes.

Interestingly, a majority of the world's people live in collectivist cultures (Hofstede, 2001), and the collectivist value is reflected in their family group (see Table 1.1). In such groups people maintain very close ties with grandparents and other elders throughout their lives, and family rituals such as marriages, baptisms, and especially funerals are attended faithfully by everyone, no matter how "inconvenient" it might be in time or distance. Elder members of the family are revered, and after

---

TABLE 1.1 | A Sample of Individualism–Collectivism Rankings

High Individualism	United States, Australia, Great Britain, Canada, Netherlands, New Zealand
Moderate Individualism	Italy, Belgium, Denmark, Sweden, France, Ireland, Norway, Switzerland, Germany, South Africa, Finland
Middle Rankings	Austria, Israel, Spain, India, Japan, Argentina
Moderate Collectivism	Iran, Jamaica, Brazil, Arab countries, Turkey, Uruguay, Greece, Philippines, Mexico, Yugoslavia, Portugal, East Africa, Malaysia, Hong Kong, Chile
High Collectivism	Singapore, Thailand, West Africa, El Salvador, South Korea, Taiwan, Peru, Costa Rica, Pakistan, Indonesia, Colombia, Venezuela, Panama, Ecuador, Guatemala

* Note: Hofstede did not have access to data from Russia and China; thus, they are not included on this list.

their deaths their graves are carefully tended by the remaining family members. Their memories are held close and often called to mind, with the concepts of past, present, and future intertwined. As one researcher of Chinese culture described it, "Descent is a unity, a rope which began somewhere back in the remote past and which stretches to the infinite future . . . the individual alive is the personification of all his forbears and of all his descendants yet unknown" (Baker, 1979, pp. 26–27).

Just as an individual's identity is closely connected to the family group in collectivist cultures, so are finances and other resources shared. For example, in a large extended family of modest financial means, all of the adults—including aunts, uncles, cousins, and so forth—might work to contribute to the funding for one younger family member to go to college. The expectation would be that upon graduation and securing a well-paying job, that family member would share his or her earnings with the family. This collectivist principle of "all for one and one for all" can be linked to the general wealth and resources of a nation or region: Generally, collectivist countries tend to have less wealth than individualist countries (Hofstede, 1991). As mentioned earlier in our discussion of survival needs, the accepted explanation for this correlation is that when resources are more scarce, people are more likely to work together to survive and thrive. Thus, the relationship between an individual and his or her group in a collectivist culture is one of *interdependence*. According to a study of more than 50 countries (Hofstede, 2001), Latin American and Asian countries are the most collectivistic.

By contrast, the relationship between an individual and his or her group in individualistic countries is one of *independence*, rather than interdependence. Individuals grow up in small nuclear families and are typically encouraged to "stand on their own two feet." Traditionally, children might have had a paper route or set up lemonade stands to earn "their own money"; today, these earlier traditions have been replaced by jobs in fast-food restaurants or other retail establishments where teens can easily find employment. Rather than use the funds to contribute to the family finances, earnings are more often used for what the individual earner desires. When a person turns 18, he or she is often encouraged to leave the family home and live independently; similarly, young adults pursuing a college education often rely on their own earnings combined with whatever grants and loans are available. A sense of achievement and success is felt by individuals and their parents when young people are able to "make it on their own."

This value on independence affects older adults in individualist cultures as well. When elders become unable to fully care for themselves, they often move (or are moved) into convalescent facilities; few adults want or are able to take on the responsibility of caring for an older parent. Even those who might want to personally care for an aging parent may not be able to, because they are probably working full-time to take care of themselves. Examples of individualistic countries include North America, Australia, and most western European countries.

In the individualist culture of the United States the needs and goals of the individual typically take precedence over the needs and goals of the social groups (the family, the workplace, the neighborhood, the school, etc.) to which an individual belongs. These priorities usually become apparent when we are faced with a decision that involves choosing between what we want as an individual and what would be best for one of our social groups. In these cases, we often hear advice like, "Do what's best for *you*," or, "If you don't look out for yourself, no one will." These common phrases underscore the American value on individualism. So, for example, a person might leave one job without much notice for a higher paying job or leave a marriage that is unhappy.

Remember, though, that on an individual level, all members of a nation do not exhibit the exact same degree of individualism or collectivism—the nation's scores reflect the national average, around which individual members vary, based on other cultural groups to which they belong. Right now, you might be asking yourself, "Am I more individualist or collectivist?" On one hand, you might value your independence and enjoy pursuing your own goals, but on the other hand, you might be feeling more closely connected to your family than the typical individualist. If this is the case, you are not alone. Remember that individualism and collectivism are rarely "black and white" classifications; instead, we use the continuum to allow each of us to identify our own degree of individualism or collectivism. One person might be strongly individualist, another only moderately so; and the same goes for collectivists. In addition, our degree of individualism or collectivism may vary somewhat according to the particular setting or situation: We might be more collectivistic with our families than with our co-workers, for example. Thus, we might be more willing to sacrifice our time or other resources for a family member than for a work colleague or supervisor. Our personal level of individualism or collectivism would take into account our overall patterns across our various relationships and life situations.

To test your own level of individualism or collectivism, complete the questionnaire and reflection questions in Activity 1.3, then turn to Activity 1.4 and complete part 1 of that exercise.

There are advantages and drawbacks to both the individualist and the collectivist value systems. People in individualist cultures enjoy more personal choice in their relationships, jobs, and interests, but too much focus on pursuing one's own desires often results in a trail of broken or lost relationships. Perhaps the most obvious example of this is the divorce rates in individualist North American and western European countries, which approach or exceed 50%. Collectivist cultures enjoy much greater loyalty in family and social groups, but extreme closeness can be oppressive. Privacy and opportunities are limited—Hofstede (1991) cites one African student who, upon arriving at a Belgium university and being given her own room, commented that it was the first time she had ever been alone for any length of time.

Individualism–collectivism is the dimension that has been most widely used in cross-cultural research; because of the abundance of research findings on this dimension, it is the one that we will reference most often in this text.

Power Distance ✕

A second dimension of culture is **power distance (PD)**, which examines how a culture deals with the basic issue of human inequality (Hofstede, 2001; Mulder, 1977). Societies that hold equality as an ideal also recognize that it can never completely

> **Power Distance (PD)**
> Examines how a culture deals with the basic issue of human inequality.

High power distance cultures Stricter hierarchies with greater distance between each level.

Low power distance cultures De-emphasize hierarchies and strive to reduce distance between the various levels.

become a practical reality. Even if great pains were taken to equalize the distribution of resources, inequalities in physical and mental capabilities would quickly enable some to dominate over others. The question, then, becomes: Will a society create mechanisms to reinforce dominance, or will it choose to downplay the inevitable dominance? **High power distance cultures** have stricter hierarchies with greater distance between each level, whereas **low power distance cultures** deemphasize hierarchies and strive to reduce distance between the various levels.

Essentially, power distance identifies the value of inequality in a society. High power distance cultures see inequality as a valuable means of maintaining social order and thus place a high value on it. From this perspective, because humans are dominance-oriented creatures, establishing strict hierarchies creates a system of controls and reduces chaos. Inequality is accepted, and those with power are seen as deserving of the power. Low power distance cultures value equality rather than inequality, conceding that inequality is a necessary evil, but not necessarily liking it. In these cultures, although hierarchies may be accepted as the most efficient way of maintaining social order, those with power are not considered superior. Power is more arbitrary and more achievable. As you might guess, low power distance countries have much greater social mobility, meaning that a person born into a lower class has greater opportunity to achieve higher status than a similar person in a high power distance culture.

Hofstede's international research reveals some interesting cultural differences in power distance among nations. With individualism–collectivism, large regions tend to clump together (western European countries individualistic, Latin American and Asian countries collectivistic), but differences in power distance are much more globally scattered. The lowest power distance countries, for example, are Austria, Israel, the Scandinavian countries, New Zealand, and Ireland. The United States and Canada are moderately low in power distance, as are Australia, Argentina, Costa Rica, Japan, and most of the remainder of western Europe. Whereas most Latin American and Asian countries are moderately or strongly high in power distance, one surprising finding is that France—in contrast to the rest of western Europe—is among the high power distance countries.

Once again, we can look to a combination of survival needs and historical precedent to explain this. In terms of survival needs, the greatest challenge faced by people in colder climates was harsh environmental conditions, which promoted their coming together in urban areas as well as developing technology to master the environment. Urbanization tends to promote both education and social mobility, which are associated with low power distance. The greatest challenge for people in more tropical climates was not environmental conditions, but competition for resources, which promoted the development of high power distance norms to control potential aggression. This explains the general tendencies of North America and northern/western Europe to cluster in low power distance cultures, and for much of Latin America, Asia, and East Africa to cluster as high power distance cultures. To explain the anomaly of France as a high power distance culture, Hofstede points out France's long and enduring history of aristocracy and strict class boundaries that, until the relatively recent revolution of 1789, remained firmly entrenched. Two hundred years may seem like a long time, but it takes more time than that to reverse patterns that took 2000 years to develop.

Power distance affects human relations in a variety of ways, beginning in the family and the educational system. Children in high power distance cultures are taught to obey their elders without question, and this deference to elders continues throughout their lifetime. Teachers are treated with great respect both in and out of the classroom and are seen as imparters of great wisdom. Communication in the classroom is mostly one-way, with students speaking only when asked. Low power distance cultures, on the contrary, encourage children to speak their mind early on and to become independent decision makers. This value extends into the classroom, where students are expected to question ideas and think critically about them. Understanding these differences can help us avoid misinterpretation of others' behavior in terms of deference versus challenge. Rather than immediately thinking a person is out of order for acting in a manner that doesn't fit our own power distance culture, we should first consider the possibility that the person's own cultural norms are rooted in a different value system (see Table 1.2).

 *Critical Thinking* QUESTION   Can you think of teachers you have had that seemed to be "high PD" or "low PD"? How did their expectations fit with your own? How did any discrepancy between your style and your teacher's style affect your learning and general experiences in the classroom?

Before continuing to the next section, turn to Activity 1.4 and complete part 2 to assess your own cultural level of power distance.

TABLE 1.2 | Key Features of High and Low Power Distance Cultures

HIGH PD CULTURES	LOW PD CULTURES
Parents teach children obedience.	Parents treat children as equals.
Children should work hard.	Children should enjoy leisure.
Teachers are gurus.	Teachers and students are treated as equals.
Subordinates at work expect to be told.	Subordinates expect to be consulted.
Managers feel underpaid and dissatisfied.	Managers feel adequately paid.
White-collar jobs are valued over blue-collar jobs.	Manual work has the same status as clerical work.
There is more corruption in the political system.	Scandals end political careers.
The use of force is the essence of power.	The use of force reveals failure of power.

Source: Adapted from Culture's Consequences, *by G. Hofstede, 2001, Thousand Oaks, CA: Sage.*

Uncertainty Avoidance

How do you feel when you are faced with uncertainty? Do you feel anxious and a bit threatened, or does the lack of clear direction seem interesting to you, something to be explored? The answer to this question is at the heart of the third dimension we can use to compare cultures: **uncertainty avoidance (UA)**, or "the extent to which the members of a culture feel threatened by uncertain or unknown situations" (Hofstede, 2001). Uncertainty is a basic fact of life that people in all cultures face, but interestingly, the way it is perceived varies significantly. **High uncertainty avoidance** cultures see uncertainty as an ongoing threat to be resisted, whereas **low uncertainty avoidance** cultures are more comfortable with uncertainty, and thus don't feel anxiety about it nor the need to avoid it. Essentially, for people of high uncertainty avoidance cultures, uncertainty makes the world a scary place, which in turn provokes anxiety.

> **Uncertainty Avoidance (UA)** The extent to which the members of a culture feel threatened by uncertain or unknown situations.

> **High uncertainty avoidance culture** Perceive uncertainty as an ongoing threat to be resisted.

> **Low uncertainty avoidance cultures** Perceive uncertainty as normal and non-threatening.

Fortunately for their health, open expression of emotions is acceptable in high UA cultures, and this is indeed one way that the anxiety is reduced. Second, high UA cultures place a high value on staying busy, which helps channel anxious energy into productive directions. Third, high UA cultures cope with uncertainty by creating stability in as many ways as possible, such as by creating rules and rituals that prescribe concrete ways to react in the face of uncertainty, and by resisting change. Low UA cultures don't feel particularly bothered by uncertainty and therefore, don't feel the same anxiety when they encounter it that their high UA counterparts do. Consequently, they experience less stress and place higher value on control of one's emotions than on expression of them. Low UA cultures also don't feel the need to stay busy and are less resistant to change and other new ideas (see Table 1.3 for key features of UA).

At the heart of these differences seems to be a basic issue of trust and optimism versus suspicion and pessimism. High UA cultures don't blithely trust that everything will turn out fine, and instead prefer clear structure and concrete answers. Law and order are highly valued in these cultures. Low UA cultures feel a

TABLE 1.3	Key Features of High and Low Uncertainty Avoidance Cultures
LOW UA	**HIGH UA**
Lower stress	Motivated to stay busy
Suppressed emotions	Freely expressed emotions
Openness to change and risks	Cautious approach to risk
Difference triggers curiosity	Difference triggers sense of danger
Comfortable with uncertainty	Need for clarity and structure
Belief in personal control over outcomes	Belief that external forces control outcomes

great deal of optimism and trust in the future and thus are able to approach uncertainty with curiosity rather than anxiety. New and different ideas are seen as a novelty, which provokes interest rather than suspicion. An interesting correlate of these two very different approaches to uncertainty is the issue of empowerment: People in low UA cultures feel very capable of influencing their lives and the world around them—perhaps this sense of empowerment makes it easier to accept change and diversity. Conversely, people in high UA cultures feel a sense of powerlessness regarding their fate and the happenings in their lives, which in turn may help explain the strong need for stability.

Countries high in uncertainty avoidance include the Latin American countries, Japan, Middle Eastern countries, and southern European countries, while low uncertainty avoidance countries are Malaysia, India, Indonesia, Great Britain, Ireland, Australia, New Zealand, the United States, and Canada. Clearly, the degree of warmth of climate does not influence uncertainty avoidance, because both cold and warm climates are included in both lists. Instead, the best explanation for variance in uncertainty avoidance is probably rooted in historical and religious traditions: Countries with closer ties to Great Britain tend to cluster with it in low uncertainty avoidance. Also, the degree of unpredictability of life conditions, such as threats from neighboring countries (for examples for centuries Japan faced threats from nearby China, and Middle Eastern countries have traditionally been embroiled in battles with each other), arguably may have led to the perception of life as threatening.

Understanding the diverse ways in which cultures cope with uncertainty is crucial to our study of human relations, and we will return to this dimension as we study topics such as emotions, communication, and work environments later in the book. For now, though, there are a couple of differences to be aware of. First, remember that individuals from high uncertainty avoidance cultures appear more reactive to unexpected events, more cautious in approaching new situations, and more resistant to change and new ideas. People from low avoidance uncertainty cultures aren't going to be very bothered by unexpected events and may actually seek new ideas and change. Also, because of the strong need for certainty among high uncertainty avoidance cultures, in school these individuals tend to want to know the right answer, seeing things in more "black and white, right or wrong" terms, and expect a learning environment that is highly structured and led by an all-knowing teacher. Students from low uncertainty avoidance cultures want to explore various possibilities for answers through lively discussion, prefer open-ended assignments to clearly structured ones, and will tolerate a teacher who admits not knowing all the answers.

Before reading the next section, turn again to Activity 1.4 and complete part 3 to determine your own cultural level of uncertainty avoidance.

Masculinity–Femininity

The final dimension on which we can compare cultures is that of **masculinity–femininity (MAS)**, which deals with the degree of differentiation between the roles of men and women in a

> **Masculinity–Femininity (MAS)** The degree of differentiation between the roles of men and women in a culture.

Sex The *biological* differences between men and women.

Gender The *social* or *cultural* differences between masculinity and femininity.

Masculine culture Expects a high degree of separation between men's and women's role.

Feminine culture Expects and accepts overlapping roles for men and women.

culture. In order to fully understand this concept, we must begin with some basic information about sex and gender. **Sex** refers to the biological differences between men and women, whereas **gender** refers to the social or cultural differences between masculinity and femininity. Even though you might have heard these two terms used interchangeably (or, more often, "gender" used to refer to both), it is important to use the terms correctly, because they refer to two very different concepts. Sex differences are, in most cases, obvious and irrefutable: Only women can bear children, and only men can beget them. *Male* and *female* are the terms used to distinguish between the two. Gender differences, on the other hand, can vary considerably among different cultures, with the traditional female role referred to as *femininity* and the traditional masculine role as *masculinity;* these are the differences that we will explore in this section.

Think for a moment about what psychological characteristics you typically associate with being masculine and which ones you typically associate with being feminine. For most people, emotionally tough, assertive, independent, competitive, and achievement-oriented are some of the qualities most commonly associated with masculinity. Feminine characteristics tend to include cooperative, nurturing, supportive, emotionally sensitive, and relationship-oriented. Although these distinctions between masculinity and femininity are almost universally accepted, what differs among various cultures is the degree of separation between the two sets of roles. In other words, some cultures expect men to fulfill the masculine role, and women to fulfill the feminine role, without either of them crossing over into the territory of the other. This high degree of separation is what defines a **masculine culture**. Other cultures prefer more flexibility and encourage both men and women to fulfill both roles; this lack of separation is what defines a **feminine culture**.

On first learning about masculine and feminine cultures, many people get confused and think that masculine cultures value independence and other masculine characteristics, but not feminine characteristics, whereas feminine cultures value cooperation and other feminine characteristics, but not masculine characteristics. This is not the case. *Remember, when we talk about cultural masculinity–femininity, we're referring to the degree of separation between the two sets of role behaviors: Masculine cultures keep the two roles separate, and feminine cultures overlap them.* So, in a masculine culture, men would be expected to be high achievers in the workplace in order to financially support the family, whereas women would be expected to be supportive and nurturing wives and mothers. This exemplifies a traditional separation of masculine and feminine roles. In a feminine culture, both men and women can follow their own paths toward career achievement and/or nurturing relationships, depending on their own strengths and interests.

Japan, much of western Europe, the United States, and Australia are masculine cultures, with the national value systems emphasizing the traditional division between the sexes. On the feminine end of the spectrum are the

Scandinavian countries (Sweden, Norway, Denmark, and Finland), along with France, Israel, Spain, and Portugal. Researchers have been unable to identify any factors that clearly explain whether a country develops a feminine or masculine culture: Factors such as population size, wealth, and even religion don't seem to explain masculinity–femininity. Perhaps the most intriguing theory has to do with climate and its relationship to whether a culture is historically a hunter-gatherer society or an agricultural one. Hunter-gatherer societies tend to be more feminine, and, interestingly, only survive today in very cold and very warm regions. Agricultural societies flourish in more moderate climates. Anthropologist Mary Bateson (1994) suggests that agriculture creates competition for land and resources, which fosters a more competitive, masculine society. Hunter-gatherer cultures, conversely, must cooperate for survival; hence, their development of feminine cultures. Her position is supported by a study published in the *Journal of Cross-Cultural Psychology*, which contends that survival challenges in very cold and very hot climates require a father to invest more time and effort in the care of the family (Van de Vliert, Schwartz, Huismans, Hofstede, & Daan, 1999).

Regardless of the origin of a culture's masculinity–femininity, this dimension of culture, like the others, is very firmly rooted in historical traditions. For example, the symbolic personalities of some Western countries over the past few centuries illustrate these gender differences: If you grew up in the United States, you are probably familiar with Uncle Sam, just as the British are familiar with John Bull which is their equivalent. The French equivalent is a female figure known as Marianne, which is consistent with France's identity as a feminine culture. Also, the fact that the Latin American countries range from very masculine (such as Mexico) to very feminine (such as Costa Rica) can likely be traced to the various early civilizations of these regions. The very masculine Aztec culture influenced Mexico and the historically Aztec regions, whereas the more feminine Incan and Mayan cultures provided the foundation for Costa Rica and its surroundings, as well as the Yucatan peninsula and the Peruvian region. These long-standing historical traditions help us understand why cultural norms are so slow to change. For example, even with the broad influence of feminism in the United States and its accompanying emphasis on equality, U.S. culture remains rooted in masculine traditions, with the expectation of a clear division between men's and women's roles.

The degree of masculinity–femininity of a culture informs human relations in a multitude of ways, and as we progress through the other chapters of this book, we will discuss each one in the context of each chapter's topic. For now, though, we can identify some general differences. In masculine cultures, for example, money and material objects tend to rank highest in overall importance, and status is derived from wealth, whereas in feminine cultures emphasis is placed instead on quality of life and relationships. Masculine cultures tend to define a person in terms of achievements and career: Two adults, meeting for the first time, typically open a conversation with a question like "What do you do?" or "Where do you work?" In our masculine culture, it would seem odd indeed if the first question were "What is your family like?" One humorous example of the emphasis on power in masculine cultures is a study in Europe indicating that car buyers in masculine cultures were more interested in bigger engines than were buyers in feminine cultures (Hofstede, 2001)!

Masculinity–femininity also influences expectations of school, sex, and the workplace. Masculine cultures prefer teachers who are very smart, whereas feminine cultures prefer their teachers to be friendly. Similarly, performance and grades are considered most important in masculine schools, whereas social skills are paramount in feminine schools. Along the same lines, sex in masculine cultures is about performance, rather than about relating to one's partner, as it is in feminine cultures. The traditional double standard—men are supposed to be studs and women are supposed to be chaste—thrives more in masculine cultures, whereas sex is more openly discussed and accepted by both sexes in feminine cultures. More open-mindedness toward sexual orientation also prevails in feminine cultures.

The differential value placed on achievement versus relationships by masculine and feminine cultures influences workplace norms as well. Managers in masculine cultures are supposed to be decisive, whereas their counterparts in feminine cultures are expected to pay attention to feelings and make decisions by consensus. Also, when a European commission study gave respondents a (hypothetical) choice between earning more money or working fewer hours, workers in masculine cultures chose the higher earnings; workers in feminine cultures chose the reduced workloads. Finally, Hofstede (2001) reports that job applicants from masculine cultures tend to "oversell" themselves, packing their resumes with achievements and presenting a high degree of confidence in interviews. Applicants from feminine cultures, conversely, are more modest both on their resumes and in interviews. This is useful information for employers in both types of cultures. See Table 1.4 for a summary of MAS differences.

Now, turn to Activity 1.4 and complete part 4 to determine your cultural level of masculinity–femininity.

All these dimensions of culture are part of a learned value system that begins in the family. Family values are reinforced and perpetuated by social institutions such as schools, churches, the government, and the media. When the messages coming from all these various sources are "in sync" with one another, they play a

TABLE 1.4 | Key Features of Masculine and Feminine Cultures

MASCULINE CULTURES	FEMININE CULTURES
Importance of challenge and recognition at work	Importance of cooperation at work
Higher job stress	Lower job stress
Centrality of work in life	Centrality of relationships in life
Values of mastery, ambition, independence	Values of well-being, service
Children taught to fight back	Children taught to avoid aggression
Importance of money and things	Importance of quality of life

Source: Adapted from Culture's Consequences, *by G. Hofstede, 2001, Thousand Oaks, CA: Sage.*

powerful role in the development of an individual's value system. However, the mere fact that there are several influencing institutions allows for the possibility of divergent or conflicting messages—and this is why, within most national cultures, there exist a variety of subcultures. In the family and/or social group (which could include race, neighborhood, religious group, etc.) in which you grew up, if the value system was different from the national culture, your own placement on one or more of these four cultural dimensions could be markedly different from that of the United States (or your country of origin) as a whole. The same goes for every other person you meet: Just knowing their country of origin may not be enough to understand their cultural value system. The best we can do, in most cases, is to just keep these various cultural value systems in mind when we encounter persons whose behavior seems different from our own, and to assume that their behavior makes as much sense in their culture as ours does in our own.

Finally, with regard to all four of these dimensions, researchers note that even as countries evolve and change, drastic differences in a nation's placement on each dimension is highly unlikely. Instead, there will probably be some very gradual shifts, but the relative standing of each nation in relation to the others will probably remain fairly stable. Thus, these dimensions, along with the placement of the various countries on each one, are expected to remain important to our understanding of human behavior in an increasingly multicultural world.

Interim SUMMARY #3

Cross-cultural researchers have identified four dimensions on which cultures can be compared. Individualism–collectivism (IC) refers to the relative importance of the individual versus the family member and is the dimension that has been used most often to compare cultures. Individualist cultures value independence and personal achievement, whereas collectivist cultures value interdependence and the needs of the group. The power distance (PD) dimension deals with the value of inequality in a culture, with high PD cultures imposing stricter hierarchies and greater distance between levels and low PD cultures preferring as much equality as possible.

The third dimension of culture, uncertainty avoidance (UA), measures the way a culture perceives change and the unknown: High UA cultures see uncertainty as a threat that must be resisted, and low UA cultures see uncertainty and change as interesting. Finally, the dimension of masculinity–femininity (MAS) assesses the degree of differentiation between the expected roles of men and women in the culture. High MAS cultures expect male and female roles to be separate and distinct, and low MAS cultures prefer the two sets of roles to overlap.

Although international research has determined the placement of more than 50 countries on these four dimensions, it is critical for us to remember that everyone—including ourselves—is a blend of numerous cultural influences, only one of which is nationality. Nationality is a useful starting point in our search for intercultural understanding, but it must not be relied on exclusively.

CHAPTER TERMS

Context
Psychology
Empirical evidence
Human relations
Culture
Values
Individualism–Collectivism
Power Distance

High power distance
  cultures
Low power distance
  cultures
Uncertainty
  Avoidance
High uncertainty
  avoidance cultures

Low uncertainty
  avoidance cultures
Masculinity–Femininity
Sex
Gender
Masculine culture
Feminine culture

ACTIVITY 1.1

ASSESSING YOUR CURRENT HUMAN RELATIONS ABILITIES

INSTRUCTIONS: *This exercise will help you evaluate your current strengths and areas for improvement in your relations with others. For each of the following questions, first rate yourself on a scale of 1–5 (1 = lowest and 5 = highest), then provide the additional information.*

1. Overall, how well would you say you *understand* people? 1   2   3   4   5

    The person(s) I understand the most is/are _____.

    I least understand _____, and/or people when _____
    (Name of person)

    _____.
    (Particular situation, setting, or characteristic)

2. Overall, how well would you say you *get along with* people? 1   2   3   4   5

    The person(s) I get along with best is/are _____.

    I get along the worst with _____, and/or people when
    (Name of person)

    _____.
    (Particular situation, setting, or characteristic)

3. Overall, how effectively do you *communicate* with people? 1   2   3   4   5

    The person(s) I communicate with best is/are _____.

    I communicate the least effectively with _____, and/or people
    (Name of person)

    when _____.
    (Particular situation, setting, or characteristic)

4. Overall, how effectively do you *resolve conflict* with people? 1   2   3   4   5

    The person(s) I resolve conflict with best is/are _____.

    I have the most problems resolving conflict with _____, and/or
    (Name of person)

    when _____.
    (Particular situation, setting, or characteristic)

5. How often do you feel understood by others? (1 = never, 5 = always)
   1   2   3   4   5

   The person(s) who best understand(s) me is/are _____.

   I feel the least understood by _____, and/or when
   _____(Name of person)
   _____.
   (Particular situation, setting, or characteristic)

6. Finally, think about your general interpersonal skills. What are your best qualities (which enhance your human relations)?

   _____

   _____

   _____

   What are your weakest areas (which detract from your human relations)?

   _____

   _____

   _____

7. a. Now, get a "second opinion" on question 6: Ask a person who knows you well what he or she thinks are your best and weakest areas in your relations with others.

   Best: _____

   _____

   _____

   Weakest: _____

   _____

   _____

   b. Compare your answers to question 6 to what you learned in question 7. What thoughts do you have about the similarities and differences?

   _____

   _____

   _____

8. Reflect on the answers you gave to each of the questions in this exercise and look for patterns that may lend insight into your human relations. Overall, what is working well for you, and with whom or in what settings? What presents your biggest challenges in terms of personal characteristics, people, or situations?

   _____

   _____

   _____

ACTIVITY 1.2

VALUES IDENTIFICATION EXERCISE

INSTRUCTIONS: *This activity will help you prioritize your values. Part 1 lists some terminal values, or values that refer to overall life goals. In part 2 you will find instrumental values, or values that refer to types of behavior that we strive for or prefer. For each list, choose the values that are most important and least important to you and rank that list from 1 to 18. Your number 1 should be your highest value on that list, number 2 your second highest, and so forth, down to number 18, which is your least important value.*

PART 1: TERMINAL VALUES

_____ A Comfortable Life (a prosperous life)

_____ An Exciting Life (a stimulating, active life)

_____ A Sense of Accomplishment (making a lasting contribution)

_____ A World at Peace (free of war and conflict)

_____ A World of Beauty (beauty of nature and the arts)

_____ Equality (equal opportunity for all)

_____ Family Security (taking care of loved ones)

_____ Freedom (independence, free choice)

_____ Happiness (contentedness)

_____ Inner Harmony (freedom from inner conflict)

_____ Mature Love (sexual and spiritual intimacy)

_____ National Security (protection from attack)

_____ Pleasure (an enjoyable, leisurely life)

_____ Salvation (saved, eternal life)

_____ Self-Respect (self-esteem)

_____ Social Recognition (respect, admiration)

_____ True Friendship (close companionship)

_____ Wisdom (a mature understanding of life)

PART 2: INSTRUMENTAL VALUES

_____ Ambitious (hard-working, aspiring)

_____ Broadminded (open-minded)

_____ Capable (competent, effective)

_____ Cheerful (lighthearted, joyful)

_____ Clean (neat, tidy)

_____ Courageous (standing up for your beliefs)

_____ Forgiving (willing to pardon others)

_____ Helpful (working for others' welfare)

_____ Honest (sincere, truthful)

_____ Imaginative (daring, creative)

_____ Independent (self-reliant, self-sufficient)

_____ Intellectual (intelligent, reflective)

_____ Logical (consistent, rational)

_____ Loving (affectionate, tender)

_____ Obedient (dutiful, respectful)

_____ Polite (courteous, well-mannered)

_____ Responsible (dependable, reliable)

_____ Self-Controlled (restrained, self-disciplined)

PART 3: SUMMARY AND ANALYSIS

1. What are your top three terminal values? Your top three instrumental values?

   _____

   _____

   _____

2. It is thought that we have the best chance of achieving our terminal values when we act in ways consistent with these goals, or in other words, when the behaviors we say we value (our instrumental values) really reflect our most common behaviors. For each of your top three instrumental values, give an example that illustrates how frequently you act consistently with this value.

   _____

   _____

   _____

3. Overall, what insights did you gain from this activity?

   _____

   _____

   _____

Source: Rokeach, 1967.

──── ACTIVITY 1.3 ────

ARE YOU AN INDIVIDUALIST OR A COLLECTIVIST?

INSTRUCTIONS: *For each of the following 11 statements, rate how strongly you agree or disagree with the statement using the following 7-point scale:*

1	2	3	4	5	6	7
Strongly Disagree	Disagree		Neutral	Agree		Strongly Agree

_____ 1. I would not let my cousin(s) use my car (if I have one).

_____ 2. It is enjoyable to meet and talk with my neighbors regularly.

_____ 3. I would not discuss newly acquired knowledge with my parents.

_____ 4. It is not appropriate for a colleague to ask me for money.

_____ 5. I would not let my neighbors borrow things from me or my family.

_____ 6. When deciding what kind of education to have, I would pay no attention to my uncles' advice.

_____ 7. I would not share my ideas with my parents.

_____ 8. I would help, within my means, if a relative told me he or she were in financial difficulty.

_____ 9. I am not interested in knowing what my neighbors are really like.

_____ 10. Neighbors should greet each other when we come across each other.

_____ 11. A person ought to help a colleague at work who has financial problems.

Source: Deborah Cai and Edward L. Fink, "Conflict Style Differences Between Individualists and Collectivists" *Communication Monographs* 69, pp 67–87. Copyright 2002 Reprinted by Permission of Taylor & Francis and the authors.

SCORING

To score your questionnaire, first reverse your scores for items 1, 3, 4, 5, 6, 7, and 9. This means that if you scored the item 1, change it to 7, or 7 becomes 1. Similarly, if you scored it 2, change it to 6, or change 6 to 2. Finally, if you scored it 3, change it to 5, or change 5 to 3. If you scored it 4, that remains the same. (If you'd like to know why certain scores are reversed, ask your instructor!)

Next, total all your scores, using the new numbers for the items whose scores were reversed. You should end up with a number between 7 and 77. Lower scores indicate more individualism. Higher scores indicate greater collectivism.

APPLYING AND COMPARING YOUR SCORE

On the following continuum, place an X to indicate where you scored.

|---|
7   21   35   49   64   77
High Individualism   High Collectivism

━━ QUESTIONS FOR REFLECTION ━━━━━━━━━━━━━━━━━━━━━━━

1. What is your initial reaction to your score? Are you surprised? How does your actual score compare to what you thought your score would be?

_____

_____

_____

2. What factors (e.g., parents or family, peers, your educational system, religion, nationality) have most influenced the development of your belief system concerning individualism–collectivism?

_____

_____

_____

_____

3. How does your score compare to the scores of some of the other students in your class? In small groups, discuss the similarities and differences in your scores, along with how your individual cultural backgrounds influenced your scores.

_____

_____

_____

Source: Scale by Cai & Fink, 2002; used with permission.

ACTIVITY 1.4

ASSESSING YOUR OWN DIMENSIONS OF CULTURE

PART 1: INDIVIDUALISM–COLLECTIVISM (IC)

1. Based on your IC score from Activity 1.3, place an X on the following scale to indicate your placement.

|--|

Individualist   Collectivist

2. List two or three examples of your own behavior patterns or values that explain the placement you selected on the IC continuum.

_____

_____

_____

PART 2: POWER DISTANCE (PD)

3. Based on your understanding of the PD dimension and the common behavioral patterns that characterize each value system, where would you place yourself on the PD scale? Place an X on the following scale to indicate your answer.

|--|

High PD   Low PD

4. List two or three examples of your own behavior patterns or values that explain the placement you selected on the PD continuum.

_____

_____

_____

PART 3: UNCERTAINTY AVOIDANCE (UA)

5. Based on your understanding of the UA dimension and the common behavioral patterns that characterize each value system, where would you place yourself on the UA scale? Place an X on the following scale to indicate your answer.

   |---|
   High UA   Low UA

6. List two or three examples of your own behavior patterns or values that explain the placement you selected on the UA continuum.

   _____

   _____

   _____

PART 4: MASCULINITY–FEMININITY (MAS)

7. Based on your understanding of the MAS dimension and the common behavioral patterns that characterize each value system, where would you place yourself on the MAS scale? Place an X on the following continuum to indicate your answer. (Remember that high MAS refers to separation between gender roles and low MAS refers to equal roles, rather than to the traditional masculine or feminine behavior patterns.)

   |---|
   High MAS   Low MAS
                                                                    (High femininity)

8. List two or three examples of your own behavior patterns or values that explain the placement you selected on the MAS continuum.

   _____

   _____

   _____

PART 5: REFLECTIONS

9. Which of these four dimensions seems to have the most impact on your life? Explain your answer.

   _____

   _____

   _____

THE SELF IN HUMAN RELATIONS

Make it thy business to know thyself, which is the most difficult lesson in the world.

—CERVANTES (*DON QUIXOTE*)

Who are you? If you had to answer that question not just once, but 20 times, what words or phrases would you use? How would you describe yourself so that your completed list was both accurate and thorough? Before continuing, take a moment and turn to Activity 2.1 at the end of this chapter, which gives you the opportunity to try this self-assessment, known as the Twenty Statements Test. Then, return to this page and read on to learn some of the ways that psychologists study a topic that many people find fascinating: the self.

THE FIRST STEPS: DEFINING AND UNDERSTANDING THE SELF

PREVIEW QUESTIONS

(1) What is our self-concept, and what purpose does it serve? How is it influenced by culture?

(2) What is self-esteem, and what are its functions?

(3) How does self-esteem develop, and to what extent does it change over time? How powerful is it?

(4) What is self-efficacy, and what benefits does it provide?

Learning to interact effectively with others must begin with an exploration into the **self**. The self is the sum total of who and what you are. It exists both in our conscious awareness and in our unconscious. In other words, most psychologists agree that we are conscious of some aspects of our self, but that other aspects are hidden from our awareness.

> **Self** The sum total of who and what you are, both consciously and unconsciously.

Precisely which aspects reside in each area—the conscious or the unconscious—varies from person to person, and can also change as a result of our experiences and efforts.

Another way to think about the self is in terms of our identity. Questions such as "Who am I?" and "How or where do I fit in?" are at the core of our conscious sense of self, or our identity. As we examine these interesting questions, we will first learn about three basic frameworks psychologists use to understand and measure various aspects of the self. They are self-concept, self-esteem, and self-efficacy.

Self-Concept

We study several aspects of the self to improve our relations with others. The first is **self-concept**, or "the relatively stable set of perceptions" you have about yourself (Adler & Towne, 2003). If you completed the Twenty Statements Test in Activity 2.1, then the list you developed should be a pretty good representation of your self-concept. For example, are you athletic, intelligent, responsible, witty, quiet, compassionate, or brave? Some of those words might describe you well; others might not seem like you at all. Or perhaps your list was built around your important relationships or roles and included words like son or daughter, sister or brother, mother or father, friend, student, coach, and so forth. The words we typically use to describe ourselves tend to reflect our self-concept (see Figure 2.1).

> **Self-concept** The relatively stable set of perceptions you have about yourself.

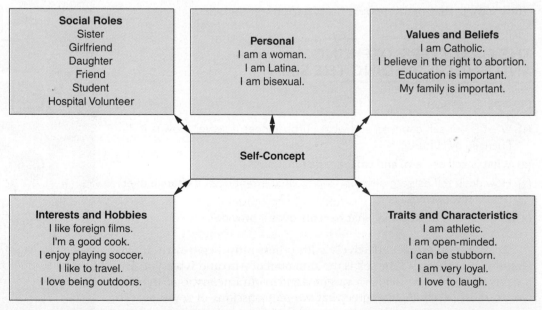

FIGURE 2.1 | Example of Self-Concept

Functions of the Self-Concept Overall, our self-concept serves as an organizer of information about the self. As such, it influences the way we take in and process new information. This interpretive function of the self-concept takes two forms. The first form is **self-verification**: We tend to seek and retain information that confirms or verifies our self-concept. According to this theory (Swann, 1997), we need our self-concept to remain consistent over time; this consistency gives us a sense of stability, or a kind of mental anchor. The anchor, in turn, helps us feel more confident about the judgments and assessments we make of ourselves and our experiences. For all the stability it lends, though, it also carries a serious limitation: Research has found this need for consistency can cause us to reject new information about the self that contradicts the current self-concept. For example, a person might have been a poor reader earlier in his life and have developed a self-concept that included this idea of himself as a poor reader. If, over time, his reading ability improved, the feedback he received about that improvement might be rejected, since it contradicts his idea of himself as a poor reader. As a result, he would continue to see himself as a poor reader, which could limit his perception of his choices in life. We'll explore this issue of obsolete information in more detail a little later in this chapter.

> **Self-verification** The human tendency to seek out and retain information that confirms or verifies our self-concept.

The second way our self-concept influences our interpretation of information is through our need for **self-enhancement**. In other words, we have a basic human need to feel good about ourselves (Greenwald, 1980). Although this might seem surprising to you if you've been paying attention to all the media reports of poor self-esteem in America, hundreds of studies provide solid evidence that we have a strong tendency to develop and maintain a positive sense of self. We achieve that goal by gravitating toward environments that support these positive evaluations, perhaps because they involve things we are good at (Steele, 1988). Concurrently, we tend to avoid environments that promote negative self-feelings. For example, if you are good at art but struggle with science, you are more likely to take art classes than science classes when you choose your electives. And finally, when we compare ourselves to others, we tend to pay more attention to the qualities we think are our strongest, which of course results in fairly favorable comparisons (Beauregard & Dunning, 1998). We don't do this intentionally; it is just natural for us to notice things that are more important to us. Taken together, these strategies work well for most people to keep our sense of self more positive than negative.

> **Self-enhancement** The basic human need to feel good about ourselves.

Possible Selves Another interesting aspect of our self-concept is something that social psychologist Hazel Markus calls "possible selves." **Possible selves** are visions, both positive and negative, of who and what we might become someday (Markus & Nurius, 1986). Thus, they encompass our fondest dreams and our greatest fears, and they serve as motivators toward our dreams and away from our fears. For example, you might be in school as a way of trying to fulfill your possible self of being successful and independent, or as a way of trying to avoid your possible self of being unemployed. Research suggests that possible selves provide us with a type of "blueprint" for our future (Ruvolo & Markus, 1992).

> **Possible selves** Visions, both positive and negative, of who and what we might become someday.

An interesting example of the value of possible selves is provided by Mark Lenzi, the 1992 Olympic gold medalist in diving. He was originally a wrestler; but when watching the 1984 Olympics, he decided that he had the capability to be an Olympic-caliber diver. This possible self propelled him forward into his training as a diver and ultimately to his gold medal in the sport (Horowitz & Bordens, 1995).

 *Critical Thinking* QUESTION What are some of your possible selves? Identify at least one positive possible self and one negative possible self. How do these possible selves influence your behavior?

 Culture and Self-Concept   Research in the last decade has determined that culture has a significant impact on our self-concept. In Chapter 1, we learned about individualism–collectivism (IC) as a dimension of culture. Can you think of how this dimension might affect the way a person perceives herself? If you're thinking that individualists probably see themselves as more independent from others, while collectivists see themselves more in terms of their important social groups, you would be off to a good start. Just as individualists' values center around independence, so are their self-concepts independent. From early childhood, individualists are encouraged to be unique, and in describing themselves, individualists strive to show how they are unique (Markus, 1990). This is in direct contrast to collectivists' value system, where the emphasis is on blending in with the group, typified by the saying, "The nail that sticks up shall get pounded down" (Matsumoto, 2000). Thus, collectivist values center around *inter*dependence, and their self-concepts are interdependent. The collectivists' sense of self is connected to and overlaps with the people in their lives, and they place a high value on the ability to develop and maintain harmonious relationships (see Figure 2.2).

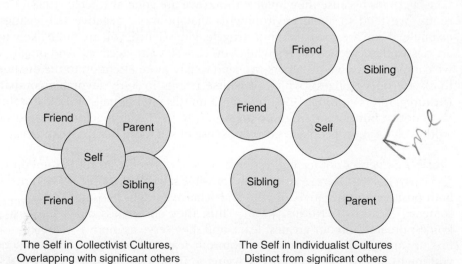

The Self in Collectivist Cultures, Overlapping with significant others

The Self in Individualist Cultures Distinct from significant others

FIGURE 2.2 | The Self in Individualist and Collectivist Cultures

In keeping with these contrasting value systems, individualists' self-concepts tend to rely primarily on personality traits (such as athletic, intelligent, responsible) whereas collectivists are more likely to describe themselves in terms of the social groups to which they belong (such as family, friendships, school) (Markus & Kitayama, 1991). In fact, up to 80% of collectivists' self-descriptors relate to their social groups (Matsumoto, 2000); a typical collectivistic self-description might be daughter, friend, student, and so on. Also, collectivists' self-concepts are more context-specific: They see their personality traits as dependent on the situation. If you ask a group of people to rate on a scale of 1–5 the degree to which they are loyal, for example, the individualists in the group would consider that a straightforward question, but the collectivists would think it was too vague and would want to know "loyal to whom?" because it seems obvious to them that a person might be more loyal to a family member than to a stranger.

Interestingly, this cultural difference in the basis for our self-concept also seems to play a role in the actual function of the self-concept. In the previous section, we noted that the self-concept has a self-enhancement function; the newest research in this area, though, is beginning to reveal that this finding may be unique to individualistic cultures. For example, one large study that included students in the United States as well as students in Japan noted a difference in the way students responded to feedback. When these students were told they had failed at a task, the American students tended to shift their focus to an easier task as a means of regaining their positive self-perception. The Japanese students returned to the failed task and worked harder at it as a means of self-improvement (Kitayama, Markus, Matsumoto, & Norasakkunkit, 1997). This research supports other emerging evidence that collectivist cultures may value self-improvement over self-enhancement, and that collectivists' self-concepts function to improve the self rather than to enhance it.

Self-Esteem

The second framework psychologists use to understand the self is **self-esteem**, which essentially reflects how we feel about ourselves, or the degree to which we are satisfied with our self-concept. Self-esteem, then, is the emotional component of the self, in contrast to the self-concept, which is the cognitive component. In general, self-esteem can be thought of as a continuum with "positive" and "negative" at the polar ends (see Figure 2.3).

> **Self-esteem** How we feel about ourselves, or the degree to which we are satisfied with our self-concept.

Some psychologists characterize self-esteem as the difference between your self-concept and your *ideal self* (Rathus & Nevid, 1995). For example, perhaps you

---

FIGURE 2.3 | The Self-Esteem Continuum

|—————————————————————————————————————|
Negative Self-Esteem   **Positive Self-Esteem**

Where on this continuum is your self-esteem?

have always valued spontaneity and thought that being spontaneous was a good way to go through life. Spontaneity was part of your ideal self. With that as a guiding principle, you have always tried to be spontaneous, and you have been fairly successful at it. Spontaneity is now a part of your self-concept, and it enhances your self-esteem because it is something that you value. Lately, however, you've noticed that your spontaneity is starting to interfere with getting your schoolwork finished on time—instead of studying, you've been going out with friends at the last minute, and your grades are slipping. This is a problem for you, because your ideal self also includes being a good student. At this point, you may start to become dissatisfied with the spontaneous aspect of your self-concept, which would lower your self-esteem—until and unless you either modify your ideal self or change your behavior.

Functions of Self-Esteem Self-esteem seems to function as a means of giving us feedback about two important aspects of life: a sense of belonging and a sense of meaningfulness. Let's examine these functions in more detail.

Sociometer theory, developed by psychologist Mark Leary and his colleagues (Leary, Tambor, Terdal, & Downs, 1995), provides the best explanation to date for how self-esteem helps us measure our sense of belonging. This theory argues that self-esteem acts as a gauge, or monitor, that measures the level of acceptance a person feels from his or her social environment. Much like the fuel gauge of a car, which gives feedback to the driver about how much fuel remains and when the tank is dangerously low, the sociometer gives feedback—in the form of self-esteem—to a person about how functional, supportive, or successful his relations are with important social groups such as family, friends, co-workers, and so on. When these relations are positive and functioning optimally to help the individual survive and thrive in his environment, the sociometer sends information about these positive relations through the mechanism of positive self-esteem. But when relations are difficult or strained, or the individual is not feeling supported or accepted in his environment, the sociometer alerts him to this danger through the mechanism of lower self-esteem.

> **Sociometer theory** Self-esteem acts as a gauge, or monitor, that measures the level of acceptance a person feels from his or her social environment.

Furthermore, it is thought that each of us has not just one, but a set of sociometers. To explain this, Leary continues with the automobile analogy. A car does not have one single gauge that gives the driver feedback about the overall level of the car's current functioning, because it is a complex machine. Instead, it has a fuel gauge, an oil gauge, a temperature gauge, and so on. Similarly, we humans are complex organisms and rely on a variety of social relationships in pursuit of a healthy life. For example, most of us seek a long-term mate, and many people want children with whom they hope to have good relationships. In addition, we want friends to hang out with, coworkers that we enjoy, and so forth. Rarely will all these relationships be uniformly positive or negative; it is more likely that some will be working well at a given time, while others may not be as ideal at that time. Consequently, we need a separate sociometer for each type of relationship. It follows, then, that a positive relationship with our mate and our friends might promote high self-esteem in those areas, but at the same time if our relationship with our children or coworkers is having problems, we could have low self-esteem in that area.

Self-esteem also serves as a measure of our sense of meaning in life (Brown, 1998). Sometimes referred to as mastery (although not in the sense of being good at something), meaning is thought to be gained when we are fully immersed in a project or activity and enjoying the process to the fullest. In these instances, the outcome of the project or activity—specifically if it is a success or not—is less relevant than the joy we experience in the process. Learning to enjoy what we do, or "the journey," so to speak, is an important key to developing self-esteem.

Critical Thinking **QUESTION** Think about your most important relationships and how well they are currently functioning. If they are functioning well, is your self-esteem also fairly positive? If they are experiencing difficulties, have you noticed your self-esteem being negatively affected? Overall, does the sociometer theory seem to explain your current level of self-esteem?

Development of Self-Esteem   Our self-esteem is strongly influenced by feedback from others. Beginning early in life, we receive signals from our environment that

left off

tell us if we are good or bad. Carl Rogers, one of the most popular psychologists of our time, called positive feedback **positive regard**. According to Rogers, there are two types of positive regard. The first type is **unconditional positive regard**, which is what we often think of as unconditional love. For example, if a child steals her sister's toy and breaks it, a parent might let the child know that this behavior is unacceptable and wrong, but at the same time would let the child know that she is loved. Essentially, unconditional positive regard involves separating the behavior from the person: It is a message that says "You are okay, but what you did is not okay." Children who receive unconditional positive regard, according to Rogers, develop positive self-esteem.

Positive regard Positive feedback, good feelings, and acceptance.

Unconditional positive regard Giving positive regard and acceptance at all times and in all situations.

On the other hand, **conditional positive regard** gives a child the message that when he does something wrong, he is no longer worthy of love. For example, if a boy throws a temper tantrum, and his parents put him in his room, tell him he is a "bad boy," and follow by giving him the silent treatment and

Conditional positive regard Giving positive regard and acceptance only in certain conditions.

disapproving looks, the child gets the message that he is a bad person because he did a bad thing. According to Rogers, this type of message gives a child a feeling of hopelessness, a feeling that wrongdoing makes you a bad person in a rather permanent sense. This, not surprisingly, lowers self-esteem.

As we grow up and become adults, significant others in our lives continue to contribute to our self-esteem. Both peers and authority figures are constantly giving us a wide variety of feedback (both verbal and nonverbal). The more we value that person's opinion of us, the more power he or she has over our self-esteem. For example, if the person you love most tells you that you are beautiful, in time you will probably start to believe it, even if you've never really considered yourself to be beautiful. Assuming you value beauty, your self-esteem will probably rise. Conversely, if a teacher or other authority figure tells you that you are stupid, that will probably have a powerful negative effect on your self-esteem.

This power over others' self-esteem goes both ways. Just as those whom you love or respect have power over your self-esteem, you have power over the self-esteem of others who love or respect you. It is very important to be aware of this, because we send signals to others that we may be unaware of, but that have an effect on them. These signals have been referred to as "ego boosters" and "ego busters" (Adler and Towne, 1996). Part of our goal in improving our human relations is to increase our awareness of the ego boosters and ego busters we send.

To learn more about how these factors figure into your own life, turn to Activity 2.2 at the end of this chapter.

What Self-Esteem Can and Cannot Do   Self-esteem has become a very popular concept in Western culture over the past few decades, because research has linked it to a wide range of positive life outcomes including success in relationships, school, and career. As sometimes happens with exciting new research findings, though, the power of self-esteem became exaggerated to the point that many saw (and continue to see) positive self-esteem as a magic ticket to a better life and a better society. A comprehensive review of self-esteem research recently published by the American Psychological Society (Baumeister, Campbell, Krueger, & Vohs, 2003) put self-esteem back into perspective by more accurately identifying what self-esteem can and cannot do. It does seem to promote happiness, increase a person's persistence, and make one more likely to speak up in groups. Surprisingly, though, it does not lead to better school performance; in fact, the reverse may be true, in that better school performance increases self-esteem. Moreover, it does not influence relationship success, nor does low (or high) self-esteem cause violence. Figure 2.4 summarizes some myths and facts about self-esteem.

FIGURE 2.4 | Myths and Facts About Self-Esteem

Does self-esteem improve school performance?   No. In fact, the opposite is true: Doing well in school tends to improve self-esteem.

Does self-esteem improve social relationships?   No. People with high self-esteem claim to have better relationships, but empirical research does not support that claim. Self-esteem appears to have no impact on relationship quality or longevity.

Do people with high self-esteem make better leaders?   Yes and no. Self-esteem has both benefits and drawbacks to leadership. On one hand, people with high self-esteem are more assertive and thus more likely to express their viewpoints, even if it involves criticism. On the other hand, people with high self-esteem show more bias toward their own group members, and thus may be more prone to exhibiting prejudice and discrimination.

Does high self-esteem prevent children from experimenting with risky behaviors, such as drinking, smoking, drugs, and sex?   No. In fact, the opposite may be true. Some research indicates that children with high self-esteem are more comfortable experimenting with new things.

Does high self-esteem promote health?   Sometimes. High self-esteem does reduce the risk of bulimia in women. Low self-esteem predicts depression and even physical illness in certain circumstances.

These important findings challenge a lot of popular beliefs in our culture and have the potential of improving the effectiveness of efforts to help people overcome various problems. Rather than trying to boost people's self-esteem, it appears that our efforts ought to be focused instead on providing honest and accurate feedback along with specific skills development. In other words, honesty seems to be more important than false positive information in helping people make improvements in their lives.

 Can you recall a specific time when you thought someone was giving you feedback that was overly positive, possibly in an attempt to make you feel better about yourself? How effective was it? Did it actually boost your self-esteem? If not, what effect did it have?

Stability of Self-Esteem　Another line of research in the area of self-esteem has examined its stability: Is a person's self-esteem stable over time, or does it fluctuate up and down as a result of positive and negative events? Interestingly, research has found support for both of these propositions. On one hand, a recent analysis of 50 studies indicates that although self-esteem fluctuates in childhood, it becomes more stable throughout adolescence and remains relatively stable throughout adulthood (Trzesniewski, Donnellan, & Robins, 2003). On the other hand, a number of studies have demonstrated that a person's self-esteem rises when the person receives praise or achieves success on a difficult task, and falls in the face of failure. What are we to do with these seemingly contradictory findings? Rather than assuming that one or the other must be correct, it might prove more enlightening to consider how the two might work together.

An effort to reconcile these findings starts with recognition of two different types or levels of self-esteem. **Trait self-esteem** is the term used to denote an individual's general pattern of self-esteem over a lifetime. **State self-esteem** is the type of self-esteem that is vulnerable to momentary fluctuations. With that in mind, it is possible that each of us has a baseline level or internal "set point" for self-esteem; for some of us, that level is higher or lower than for others, but we all have this baseline level, which is our trait self-esteem. When we encounter an uplifting, or alternatively, a disappointing event, which affects our self-esteem, our state self-esteem fluctuates up or down, but then returns fairly quickly to its baseline level or trait level of self-esteem. In this way, the two types of self-esteem co-exist.

> **Trait self-esteem** An individual's general pattern of self-esteem over a lifetime.

> **State self-esteem** The type of self-esteem which is vulnerable to momentary fluctuations.

This idea is not inconsistent with the sociometer theory proposed earlier in this chapter: Even though we have a different sociometer for each set of relationships, these sociometers work together to keep us constantly informed of our overall "average" level of self-esteem.

Finally, research suggests that a variety of possible selves may contribute to the stability of our self-esteem. This is because our possible selves contribute to our self-complexity, which in turn helps buffer the effects of a negative experience (Linville, 1985, 1987). For example, a woman who thinks of herself as a mother, a wife, an accountant, a gardener, and an artist could experience a career loss without as much damage to her overall self-esteem as might a woman who only considered herself an accountant and a wife. In fact, one study indicates that her self-complexity may not only protect her from damage to her self-concept, but may actually help prevent stress-related illnesses (Linville, 1987).

Culture and Self-Esteem   The path to positive self-esteem is not the same for all people. Our values play a critical role in our self-esteem, because they dictate what is important to us. And as we have learned, our culture influences our values, which in turn motivate us to act in a way that is consistent with those values, which is how we develop self-esteem.

Culture $\longrightarrow$ Values $\longrightarrow$ Behavior $\longrightarrow$ Self-Esteem

So, for individualists, the path to self-esteem involves personal achievement, independent thinking, and being true to oneself. For collectivists, self-esteem is achieved and maintained by thinking and acting in ways that support the health and happiness of one's important social groups. For both cultures, then, feeling good about oneself is derived from acting in ways that support cultural norms. Self-esteem is also related to overall well-being, and research has uncovered some fascinating differences in the paths used by individualists and collectivists toward well-being. We will examine this topic in Chapter 4.

Self-Efficacy: Where Self-Concept and Self-Esteem Intersect

The third concept that helps psychologists understand the self is **self-efficacy**, or the extent to which we believe we are capable of achieving our goals. This concept

> **Self-efficacy** The extent to which we believe we are capable of achieving our goals.

has connections to both self-concept and self-esteem. As we have learned, self-concept reflects what we think about ourself, and self-esteem reflects how we feel about ourself. Self-efficacy, in some ways, bridges the gap between these concepts, in that our belief that we can achieve a goal has both cognitive and emotional components. In other words, it is influenced by both our thoughts and our emotions.

Self-efficacy can be global (general) or specific: We can have strong confidence in our ability to achieve any goal we set for ourselves, or our confidence can be confined to only one or a few specific types of goals. Included in the concept of self-efficacy is the knowledge of what actions we need to take to achieve the desired outcome, along with the ability, desire, and motivation to carry out those actions. Albert Bandura, the psychologist who first theorized about self-efficacy, referred to it as "a person's estimate that a given behavior will lead to certain outcomes . . . (and) the conviction that one can successfully execute the behavior required to produce the outcomes" (Bandura, 1977, p. 193). For example, you might believe that if you study hard you will do well in school. If you think that your study time is limited by your work schedule, though, your self-efficacy regarding doing well in school would be lowered. In other words, high self-efficacy includes knowing what you need to do *and* being able to do it.

Benefits of Self-Efficacy   Many psychological researchers have tested the theory of self-efficacy and found it to have numerous benefits. In fact, high self-efficacy beliefs contribute to better grades and achievement of academic goals (Multon, Brown, & Lent, 1991). In addition, self-efficacy seems to positively affect mental and physical health. Studies report lower levels of depression, more success in programs geared toward losing weight or giving up smoking, and overall better physical health (Holden, 1991; O'Leary, 1992) among people with high self-efficacy beliefs. This research dovetails nicely with research reported earlier in this chapter about the myths of self-esteem: The true key to improvement in many areas lies not in hearing people *tell* you that "you can do it," but in having an accurate sense of exactly what you need to do, along with the confidence that you are indeed capable of doing it.

How Does Self-Efficacy Develop?   As do most aspects of our self, self-efficacy begins to develop in childhood and continues to be influenced by our experiences throughout our lives. Bandura suggested that parents could help their children build self-efficacy beliefs by teaching them to set high but achievable goals. In this way, the child must stretch a little to accomplish the goal, but learns that she is capable of stretching and that stretching will lead to goal achievement. This is the basic principle of self-efficacy in action. Furthermore, research has demonstrated that this type of experience can increase self-efficacy at any point in life. For example, one study noted that women who participated in a self-defense class felt less vulnerable to threats and better able to defend themselves afterwards, thus increasing their self-efficacy in that area (Ozer & Bandura, 1990). So, it seems that at any point in our life, we can increase our self-efficacy by setting goals that are high enough so that we feel good when we achieve them, but not so high that we are setting ourselves up for failure.

Messages that we receive from others can have an effect on our self-efficacy as well. For example, African Americans who report having faced racial discrimination have lower self-efficacy beliefs (Hughes & Demo, 1989). This finding helps explain the much-reported phenomenon of lower academic achievement among African American students: If you are not given equal opportunities to achieve, then your ability to learn about your own capabilities for achievement would logically be limited.

Culture and Self-Efficacy   Cross-cultural research has discovered some interesting variations about how self-efficacy develops, as well as its consequences, in different types of cultural groups. In fact, self-efficacy seems to be more highly valued in individualistic cultures than in collectivistic cultures. Here's why: In individualistic cultures, the self is perceived primarily as an independent being, with the ultimate goal of personal achievement or excellence. In this type of culture, social situations tend to be perceived as opportunities to achieve by doing something to control or influence the situation or the group (Kitayama, 2000). Taking on a leadership role or mastering a situation are valued as indicators of personal achievement and independence, or autonomy. Thus, self-efficacy is an important goal, and it is achieved by mastery, which typically results from successful control or influence over a situation or group.

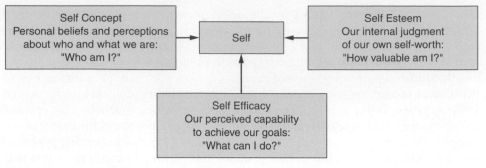

FIGURE 2.5 | Key Elements of the Self

Collectivistic cultures, through the perception of the self as an interdependent being, tend to value relations with others more highly than personal achievement or efficacy. Thus, social situations are perceived as opportunities to develop or strengthen relationships, which involve adjusting to the situation or group, rather than influencing or mastering it. This adjustment, or conformity, strengthens group solidarity and harmony, which is of supreme value in collectivist cultures. It stands to reason, then, that self-efficacy, while not unimportant, would certainly be less important in the collectivist society.

Finally, the cultural dimension of uncertainty avoidance also influences self-efficacy. International research indicates that people in low uncertainty avoidance cultures tend to feel less threatened by change and more personally able to influence the outcomes of their lives (Hofstede, 2001), thus affecting self-efficacy. A study of schoolchildren in low and high uncertainty avoidance cultures provided support for this finding. Children in low uncertainty avoidance cultures felt greater control and more optimism about their academic abilities (Oettingen, 1995). Figure 2.5 summarizes the key elements of the self we have been discussing.

Critical Thinking QUESTION

Identify at least one area in which you have high self-efficacy and another in which you have lower self-efficacy. What is one specific thing you could do to improve your self-efficacy in your low area?

Interim SUMMARY #1

Improving our human relations begins with an understanding of our self and its various aspects. Our self-concept refers to our perception of ourself, which typically contains some accuracies and some inaccuracies. It influences our interpretation of our experiences through the processes of self-verification and self-enhancement. Self-concept is also rooted in our cultural values: Individualists tend to have independent self-concepts; collectivists' self-concepts rely more heavily on interdependence with important social relationships. Possible selves are the various images that might come to mind as we envision our future. They include the best ideas about what we might or could become, as well as any fears we have about negative paths we could take.

Self-esteem is our subjective evaluation of our self-concept, or the degree to which we are satisfied with ourselves. Its basic functions seem to be to provide feedback about our connectedness to others and about the degree of meaning we are experiencing in life. Although self-esteem certainly feels good and promotes happiness, persistence, and assertiveness, it does *not*—contrary to popular opinion—influence interpersonal relationship success or the degree of violence a person exhibits toward others. In general, self-esteem is stable over time, with certain events causing temporary fluctuations up or down, followed by a return to one's average level.

Self-esteem begins to develop in childhood via the messages we receive from influential others in our environment about whether we are good or bad. It is also influenced by our culture: Individualists develop higher self-esteem through achievement, whereas collectivists' self-esteem comes primarily from supporting the betterment of one's social group.

Self-efficacy is the degree of confidence we have about our ability to achieve a particular goal. It involves both knowing what we need to do as well as having the skill and resources to do it. Like other aspects of the self, self-efficacy begins to develop in childhood and continues throughout life as we take on new situations and achieve our goals. Individualists value self-efficacy more highly than collectivists, because it is more closely linked to the individualist value system, which prizes achievement. Individualists, then, are more likely to perceive social situations as opportunities to exert influence or control, which boosts self-efficacy. Collectivists tend to value adjustment or conformity in social situations, rather than power or control.

DEVELOPING SELF-KNOWLEDGE

PREVIEW QUESTIONS

(1) What is self-knowledge, and how is it important?

(2) Describe four ways self-knowledge can be improved. Give an example of each.

Self-knowledge refers to the conscious knowledge you have about your motivations, beliefs, expectations, values, strengths, and weaknesses. In other words, self-knowledge can be thought of as the accuracy of your self-concept.

For example, Kristie is aware that she is a shy person. Shyness is part of her self-concept. Others also see her as shy, so in this respect her self-concept is accurate. However, people who know Kristie well also know that when a friend is in trouble, Kristie will move heaven and earth to help out, even if it requires that she "come out of her shell" to do so. This characteristic is something that Kristie is unaware of—it is part of her

> **Self-knowledge** The conscious knowledge you have about your motivations, beliefs, expectations, values, strengths, and weaknesses.

self, but she is not conscious of it, so it is not part of her self-knowledge. Becoming more aware of this would increase the accuracy of her self-concept and, in turn, her ability to interact effectively with others. The more accurate your self-knowledge, the more insightful you can be about your influences on others and their influences on you.

Development of self-knowledge, then, involves a commitment to continually examine the accuracy of our self-concept. And since our self-concept consists of our perceptions about ourself, it follows that it is subject to distortions: As much as we'd like to believe that our perceptions are completely accurate, the truth is that sometimes they are not. Psychological research has identified a plethora of factors that distort the accuracy of our perceptions, making them either more positive or more negative than they ought to be. You'll be learning about many of them as you continue through this book; for now, let's examine a few that especially influence our self-concept.

Social Comparison

Self-knowledge can be improved in several ways. **Social comparison** involves evaluating yourself based on how you think you compare to others. This theory was first proposed by Leon Festinger almost 50 years ago, and it continues to play an important role in our self-concept. For example, time spent studying is often considered to be a key to doing well in school. Sam believes he is a hard worker when it comes to studying, because he studies about 10 hours per week. This worked well for him in high school; he graduated with a 3.7 grade point average. Now he is in college, and his grade point average is 2.5. He doesn't know why it has slipped, because he spends just as much time studying as he did before. His frustration over his grades is starting to influence his relations with his instructors. He feels resentment toward them because he isn't getting the grades he feels he deserves.

> **Social comparison** Evaluating yourself based on how you think you compare to others.

Social comparison could help him improve his self-awareness, or the accuracy of his self-concept, as he asks around and finds out that the better students at his college study about 20 hours per week. In his new environment (college), the definition of "hard worker" is different from what it was in his former environment (high school). Social comparison has helped him to become more self-aware, which will help him improve his study habits. In turn, his resentment at his instructors fades away, because he has uncovered the real reason for his lower grades.

This example also illustrates how social comparison can lead to distorted perceptions and, consequently, an inaccurate self-concept. When Sam compares himself to others at a much higher or much lower grade level, his social comparison is going to yield inaccurate results. One way this often manifests itself in our culture is through perfectionism. When we compare ourselves to impossibly high standards, we are setting ourselves up for failure, which in this case is an inaccurate self-concept.

For example, many women in American culture feel pressured to live up to standards of beauty and body image set forth by the supermodels we see on magazine covers. Almost any woman who compares herself to this standard is likely to perceive herself as less attractive than she really is, because when she looks in the mirror she is not likely to see herself as "in the same league" as these supermodels.

Her self-esteem may suffer as her distorted perceptions affect her emotions and her sense of worthiness. To counteract this danger, she needs to objectively evaluate the appropriateness of her comparison. In this case, she is comparing herself to a person who is known first and foremost for beauty. Second, she should remind herself that models have access to the best makeup artists available, and also that print ads are always retouched to hide imperfections and improve the model's overall look. With this information in mind, hopefully she will be able to dismiss the model as a valid source of comparison.

Culture and Social Comparison Cross-cultural researchers have uncovered some interesting differences between individualists and collectivists in terms of social comparison. First, collectivists engage in social comparison more often than their individualist counterparts; this, perhaps, is not surprising given the increased group focus of collectivist culture. Furthermore, in making social comparisons, collectivists are more likely to make upward comparisons—in other words, to compare themselves to those who are doing better than they are, whereas individualists tend more to make downward comparisons (Chung & Mallery, 2000). These divergent approaches have very different implications for the self-concept: Individualists who compare downward are going to judge themselves favorably as a result, which is consistent with the individualistic emphasis on personal excellence. Collectivists, in making upward comparisons, do so to benefit the entire group.

Regardless of whether you are an individualist or a collectivist, when using social comparison in an attempt to evaluate yourself objectively, it is important that you compare yourself to others who are similar to you. For example, Sam was initially comparing himself to high school students, which resulted in an inaccurate assessment. When he began comparing himself to college students in his major, who were his new peers, his comparison was more useful. If he had compared himself to his cousin, a medical student, his comparison probably would have been inaccurate.

To improve your self-knowledge by testing the accuracy of your self-concept through social comparison, turn to Activity 2.3 at the end of this chapter.

Self-Perception Theory

Another way to improve the accuracy of our self-concept, or our self-knowledge, is through **self-perception**. This theory proposes that we make assumptions about ourselves based on our own observations of our behavior, thoughts, and feelings (Bem, 1972). Research suggests that this is true. One study asked people to act outgoing and talkative during an interview; later, these people rated themselves as more outgoing and more talkative than they did prior to the interview (Schlenker, Dlugolecki, & Doherty, 1994). In other words, we take cues about who we are from observations of our own behavior. As one cartoon put it, a robin singing cheerily in a tree concluded, "I don't sing because I am happy; I am happy because I sing."

> **Self-perception** Assumptions about ourselves based on our own observations of our behavior, thoughts, and feelings.

For example, Terry has begun to notice that she isn't taking as much care with her appearance as she usually does. She used to wash and blow-dry her hair every morning, make sure her clothes were neat and clean, and wear makeup. Lately, she has been leaving the house with wet hair, sometimes in rumpled clothes, and not wearing any makeup at all. Looking in the mirror one day at work, she notices the change and wonders about it. As she thinks about it, she realizes that she used to really value her job and enjoy it, which motivated her to look her best for work every day. Lately, work has become less challenging, the new boss doesn't seem to recognize her capabilities, and she realizes she just isn't enjoying her job anymore. Self-perception theory, the process of drawing conclusions about yourself based on your own observations of your behavior, has helped increase her self-awareness in terms of her job satisfaction.

Discussing Observations and Ideas with Others

A third way to improve self-knowledge is to discuss your observations and ideas with others. The mere act of talking something out can often help you clarify your ideas; in fact, many types of counseling rely on this premise. Research indicates that schools are finding this method useful, too. Studies of student learning find that students retain much more of what they learn when they discuss the concepts with other students.

Discussing ideas and observations is helpful in two ways. First, putting something into words often forces you to be more specific about what you mean, in order to make sense of it. As your ideas become more focused, your awareness deepens, which can produce powerful insights into issues that might be confusing you. Second, discussing ideas and observations with others gives you a chance to get feedback from them. Feedback can help you know whether your observations match others' observations, or can shed light on whether others see you as you see yourself.

For example, Eric notices that he has been sleeping a lot lately and that he is having trouble concentrating. He reads in his psychology textbook that these are two common symptoms of depression. Other symptoms, he reads, include a loss of pleasure in everyday activities and a depressed mood almost every day over a period of time. He wonders if he is suffering these other symptoms, too, and if he has a clinical depression. He discusses it with his wife, who tells him that she has noticed that he isn't finding pleasure in anything anymore, and that he has also seemed more negative and depressed almost every day for the past few months. She offers some examples of things they have recently done that Eric used to enjoy, but that didn't lift his spirits when they did them recently. As she talks, Eric realizes that she is right. His wife's observations and feedback helped him to increase his self-knowledge and motivated him to see a therapist to get some help.

Although discussing our observations and ideas about ourself with others can improve our self-knowledge, we must also be aware that it carries with it the potential for distorted feedback and subsequent distortions in our self-concept. If the feedback we receive is inaccurate, but it comes from a source we value and trust, we may accept that feedback as reliable, which can distort our self-concept.

Sometimes distorted feedback comes in the form of obsolete information: If a parent, peer, or other authority figure has historically seen you as unreliable, for example, their own unconscious need for consistency may cause them to fail to notice changes you have made in this area. As a result, they may continue to give you messages (verbally or nonverbally) that transmit their perception of you as unreliable. This can influence you to discount your own sense of improvement in this area and continue to see yourself as unreliable when in fact you are not.

Distorted feedback can emerge from a variety of other situations as well. Sometimes people simply don't pay close attention; other times they may have a motive (often unconscious) to give you feedback that isn't accurate. Regardless of the intentions, though, this distorted feedback can have a powerful effect on our self-concept.

 Consider the feedback you have recently received from others, either in your personal life or at work. Are you aware of any distorted or obsolete information that you may not have noticed at the time? If so, do you need to modify your self-concept to compensate for the distortion?

The Johari Window

A fourth way of developing greater self-knowledge is to construct a Johari Window. Named for its creators, Joe Luft and Harry Ingham, the **Johari Window** is a graphic depiction of your relationships with others. As previously mentioned in this chapter, part of who we are is in our conscious, and part of it is in our unconscious. In addition, some of who we are is known to others, and some is kept privately to ourselves. The Johari Window is a visual representation of how much of your self is known to you and how much of your self is known to others. There are four areas in the Johari Window (see Figure 2.6):

> **Johari Window** A visual representation of the parts of yourself that are known to you and known to others.

The Open area, which represents all that you know about yourself that is also known to others

The Hidden area, which represents all that you know about yourself that is private and not known to others

The Blind area, which represents the part of yourself that others can see, but that you are not aware of

The Unknown area, which represents the part of yourself that is hidden from others and also hidden from yourself

FIGURE 2.6 | The Johari Window

	Known to Self	Unknown to Self
Known to Others	Open	Blind
Unknown to Others	Hidden	Unknown

FIGURE 2.7 | The Johari Window in a Close Relationship

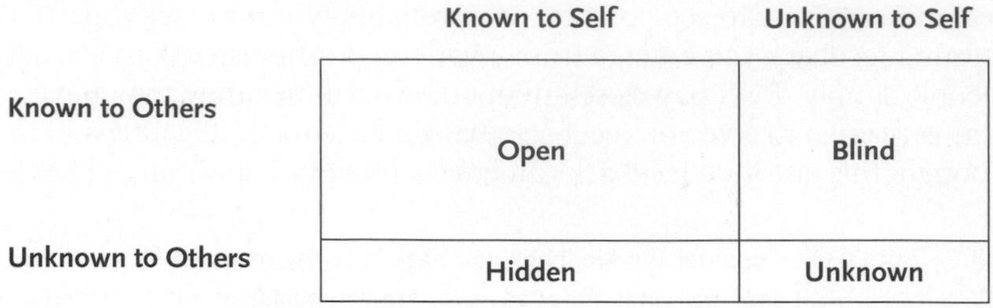

	Known to Self	Unknown to Self
Known to Others	Open	Blind
Unknown to Others	Hidden	Unknown

Our Johari Window varies somewhat from relationship to relationship. For example, your relationship with your significant other or your best friend might have a very large Open area on its Johari Window (see Figure 2.7). Conversely, your relationship with someone you recently met may have a very small Open area (see Figure 2.8). As that relationship develops, the Open area will probably grow, as you become closer to that person and tell her more about yourself. Thus you will probably learn more about yourself by listening to her feedback to you, which will reduce the size of your Blind area. In fact, this is one way you can use the Johari Window: to assess an important relationship.

Typically, the strongest and most lasting relationships have large Open areas; trust is a strong relationship foundation, and being open with the other person and listening to feedback helps build trust. Drawing a Johari Window to represent a current relationship may reveal some important clues that can help you analyze the relationship. For example, you might become aware that you are keeping many parts of your self hidden from the other person, in which case you might want to consider why you are doing this, and whether continuing this pattern is healthy for the relationship.

You can also use the Johari Window to evaluate your awareness of the general degree to which you are open with people in your life. For example, you might consider your interactions with the people at work or the people at school in a general sense. Creating a Johari Window that represents your interactions in these situations can lend insight into your effectiveness in your human relations and help you decide what, if any, modifications you would like to make to increase your effectiveness.

FIGURE 2.8 | The Johari Window Early in a Relationship

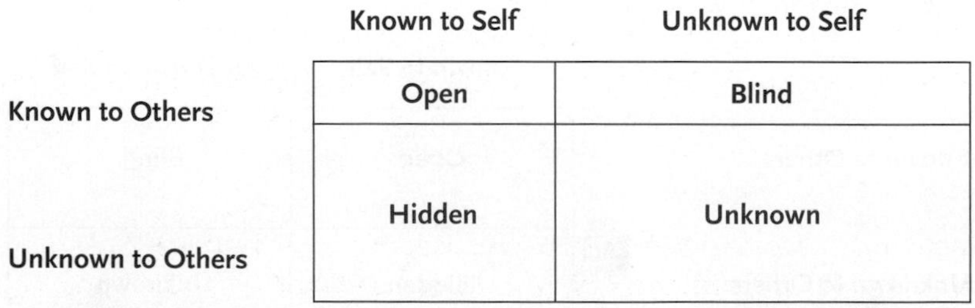

	Known to Self	Unknown to Self
Known to Others	Open	Blind
Unknown to Others	Hidden	Unknown

As you study the examples of Johari Windows in Figures 2.6, 2.7, and 2.8, think about what the various Johari Windows in your life look like and how you would like to change them.

In using the Johari Window to increase your self-knowledge, it is important to understand some strategies for decreasing the size of the two areas not known to you: the Blind area and the Unknown area.

A strategy that is useful for reducing the size of the Blind area is to ask for and be open to feedback from others. This has already been discussed as a way of improving self-knowledge; it is important to point out here, though, that people who ignore or consistently reject feedback from others have trouble reducing the size of their Blind area. Keep this in mind and think carefully before asking for honest feedback from those who are close to you. Be sure that you're ready to hear something that you might not really enjoy hearing—it might be difficult or even painful—and be prepared to take it in the spirit in which it is intended. Also, be sure the other person knows that you want honest feedback, rather than simply to hear something that will make you feel good. Later in this book, we'll learn some effective strategies for responding nondefensively to criticism (Chapter 10).

To reduce the size of your Unknown area, try Activity 2.4 at the end of this chapter (Johnson, 1997). As you progress through this course, you will continue to develop and improve your self-knowledge, which will decrease the size of your Unknown area and ultimately improve your human relations.

Interim SUMMARY #2

Self-knowledge is our conscious knowledge of ourselves, including our strengths and weaknesses. The accuracy of our self-concept and our overall self-knowledge can be increased by several methods. These include social comparison, self-perception, discussing observations and ideas with others, and exploration of the Johari Window. Some of these methods, however, carry the potential for distorted feedback, which can lead to distorted self-perceptions.

SELF-PRESENTATION: HOW (AND HOW MUCH) WE SHOW OURSELVES TO OTHERS

PREVIEW QUESTIONS

(1) What is the difference between our public and private selves?

(2) What is self-monitoring? In what ways is self-monitoring beneficial, and how can it hinder our relations with others?

The Public Self and the Private Self

In constructing our Johari Window, it becomes apparent that we have both a public self and a private self. The part of our self that is known only to us is the **private self**. For example, we might

Private self The part of our self that is known only to us.

keep some of our wildest dreams and hopes to ourselves, revealing them either not at all or only to our closest friends. Also, the way we behave when we are alone at home may be different from the way we behave when others are home with us. These are examples of the private self. The **public self** is the image we present to the world.

> **Public self** The image we present to the world.

Before we continue with this discussion, skip to the end of the chapter and complete the first part of Activity 2.5. Then return to this page and continue reading this section.

Self-Monitoring

Our public self may vary with different situations. This is because, in our busy lives, we often play several roles. For example, you may act differently when you are in your student role than you would when you are in your role as a parent or babysitter. Similarly, most people show a different side of themselves to their significant other or best friend than they do to a work colleague or a salesperson in a store. Does this mean we are phony? Not usually. For most people, it simply means that we utilize different parts of our self, or different public selves, in different situations. We are engaging in what is known as **self-monitoring** (see Figure 2.9). Interestingly, some people do this much more than others. Activity 2.5 gave you an opportunity to determine the degree to which you engage in self-monitoring.

> **Self-monitoring** We utilize different parts of our self, or different public selves, in different situations.

Research suggests that there are benefits and drawbacks to self-monitoring. High self-monitors are able to readily adjust their behavior to any given situation (Snyder, 1987). This makes them more socially skilled than low self-monitors. This can be very helpful in adapting to a new job, a new role, or a new relationship. In fact, research examining cross-cultural adaptation indicates

Copyright © John Nebraska.

FIGURE 2.9 | To what extent do you present different sides of yourself at work and at play?

that the ability to self-monitor helps a person adapt to new cultural situations or demands, such as a new job in a different country or culture (Montagliani & Giacalone, 1998). However, high self-monitors may have less intimate social relationships (Snyder and Simpson, 1985), and, in individualistic cultures, may tend to judge others on a more superficial basis (Jamieson, Lydon, Stewart, & Zanna, 1987).

Low self-monitors are more likely to act in a way that is consistent with their true thoughts and feelings (McCann & Hancock, 1983). They are less interested in presenting "the proper image" and "fitting in" than high self-monitors; it is more important to low self-monitors to be true to themselves than to please others. Therefore, they may come across as stubborn and insensitive (Brehm & Kassin, 1996). Interestingly, research suggests that self-monitoring scores tend to decrease with age (Reifman, Klein, & Murphy, 1989).

 *Critical Thinking* QUESTION What reasons can you think of that might explain the relationship between age and self-monitoring?

Cross-cultural research indicates different patterns of self-monitoring between individualists and collectivists. First, individualists are *more* likely to self-monitor than collectivists (Gudykunst, Yang, & Nishida, 1987), a finding that runs contrary to what we might expect. After all, shouldn't individualism, which encourages each of us to "be ourselves," reduce self-monitoring, and collectivism, which emphasizes harmony, promote self-monitoring? In explaining why this is not the case, we must look at the mental processes at the heart of self-monitoring. These mental processes are different for high self-monitors than for low self-monitors. A high self-monitor imagines what a *prototypical person would ideally do* in that situation, and then adjusts his or her behavior to fit that image. A low self-monitor thinks about what *he or she would usually do* in that particular situation and adjusts accordingly. Thus, since collectivists' self-concept is so context-specific anyway (as we noted in the beginning of this chapter), it cannot be characterized as self-monitoring. Individualists, on the other hand, are more likely to engage in self-monitoring, because self-monitoring involves acting in a manner that is outside their self-concept.

For example, an individualist's self-concept might include being talkative, but in a formal situation—such as attending a fancy dinner with the parents of her fiancé—this individualist might adjust her behavior to be more restrained, which she deems appropriate to do in this type of situation. In this case, she is a high self-monitor. A collectivist wouldn't have a broad characteristic like "talkative" as part of her self-concept, but instead might consider herself talkative with peers, more formal or restrained with elders. So, when she behaves with more restraint in a formal situation—like the fancy dinner with the future in-laws—she is not acting in a manner that is outside her self-concept; thus she would be considered a low self-monitor.

Overall, neither very high self-monitoring nor very low self-monitoring is without disadvantages. Probably the best way to integrate this concept into your human relations is to be aware of your level of self-monitoring and consider its effectiveness up to this point. If you are at one extreme end or the other on the self-monitoring scale, you may need to consider the effects of your behavior and some possible strategies for modification.

Now that you have read this section, return to Activity 2.5 and complete the "Reflections" portion of the activity.

Interim SUMMARY #3

In studying the self, it is important to note that we present ourselves differently in different social situations. The public self refers to the image we present to the world, whereas the private self may be revealed only to our closest friends and relatives. Self-monitoring refers to the degree to which each individual adjusts his or her behavior to fit the situation, or in other words, to what extent one's public self might look different in different environments. There are both benefits and drawbacks to self-monitoring.

THE SELF THROUGHOUT ADULTHOOD

PREVIEW QUESTIONS

(1) According to Erikson, what three challenges do adults face as they progress through their adult lives? What is the key to resolving each challenge successfully?

(2) What did Levinson's work contribute to our understanding of adult life stages?

(3) How did Sheehy conceptualize adulthood, and what are the stages of adult life in her model?

Another important component in understanding people is to understand how the stage of life they are in influences their behavior, goals, and reactions to others. This is a relatively new area of study for psychologists. For many years, the study of human development was limited to the childhood and adolescent years, with the assumption that these formative years set a pattern that would persist throughout adult life. As we will see, though, adults pass through various stages in life, just as children do, that present distinctly different challenges and opportunities. These stages influence not only one's course in life, but one's relations with others. To learn about this, we will look at the work of three researchers who have contributed much to our understanding of adult developmental stages: Erik Erikson, Daniel Levinson, and Gail Sheehy.

Erikson's Theory

Erik Erikson is one of the most prominent names in the study of human development. He studied child development, but then began to observe adult development as well, becoming the first to suggest that adulthood is a dynamic period full of changes. His theory of development (1963) was the first to span the entire life cycle. It included eight stages each person passes through in the normal course of life. The first five stages involve the childhood and adolescent years, with the last three stages devoted to adulthood. We will focus our attention on the three adult stages.

To understand Erikson's theory, we must first look at his background as a psychologist. He was trained as a psychoanalyst; one of his mentors was Anna Freud

(Sigmund Freud's daughter and a respected psychoanalyst in her own right). For psychoanalysts, personality and development grow out of conflict. Erikson's theory was grounded in this conflict perspective. He believed that each stage of our development involved facing a particular conflict or crisis—a crossroads, so to speak. Each of these crises offered a choice between two possible directions: One direction required taking some risk to meet the challenge, and the other involved avoiding the risk and consequently failing to meet the challenge and pass successfully into the next stage. Erikson theorized that, in either case, we pass to the next stage, but if we fail to meet the challenge of a particular stage, the challenge of each subsequent stage becomes more difficult to master.

Stage One: Intimacy vs. Isolation The first of Erikson's adult stages encompasses the twenties and thirties and is called Early Adulthood. The crisis at this stage is **intimacy vs. isolation**. Erikson theorized that the major developmental task of Early Adulthood is to establish and maintain an intimate relationship with a life partner. As with all of Erikson's stages, successfully meeting this challenge depends on having met the previous developmental challenges—in this case, the previous challenge is the challenge of adolescence, which Erikson believed was establishing an identity. The essence of identity is a strong sense of who you are (a sense of self, psychologists would say) and a confidence in that identity. This identity is necessary to establish true intimacy with another person.

> **Intimacy vs. isolation**
> Erikson's first stage of adult development, which is to establish and maintain an intimate relationship with a life partner.

Let's examine this a little more closely. In adolescence, a person is concerned with the question "Who am I?" Answering this question and discovering one's identity involves some exploration, which can seem threatening or risky. Erikson believes that a person must take these risks to find his true identity. The alternative is role confusion, or never knowing exactly who you are or where you fit in. The other key idea in establishing one's identity is separation from parents. As we grow up, our identities are often provided by our family, and who we are is directly connected to the family identity. Erikson maintains that for a person to establish his own **identity**, you must become individuated from the secure base of the family and have the courage to find and become your own unique person. (Clearly, this theory is based on an individualistic set of values; in collectivist families, identity is much more connected to the family, as we have learned.)

> **Identity** The unique sense of self which requires individuating from the family.

Once this identity is established, the young adult is ready to face the challenge of intimacy vs. isolation. Intimacy, according to Erikson, involves both physical and emotional closeness. *In addition to sharing a sexual relationship, true intimacy involves genuine caring and concern about your partner's needs.* Inherent in this idea is honesty and trust: Intimate partners must have the ability to be honest with each other about their feelings, trusting that their partner will understand and respond honestly. With a clear sense of identity firmly in place, a person can be secure and comfortable in taking the risk of trusting another person to this degree. If the identity was not forged in the previous stage, Erikson believed that a person wouldn't be able to establish true intimacy due to *the fear of losing one's sense of self in the relationship*. This lack of intimacy was what Erikson called isolation. People who are isolated might be in committed relationships like marriage, but wouldn't be able to give freely of themselves or care as deeply for their partners as a person who has established a strong identity. As a result, the relationship wouldn't be as fulfilling as it could be.

Stage Two: Generativity vs. Stagnation   Erikson's second adult stage, Middle Adulthood, encompassed the forties and fifties. Erikson called this stage **generativity vs. stagnation**. The major developmental task of this stage is to nurture the next generation, or to raise children in a way that helps them master their environments and establish their own identities. For Erikson, a natural outgrowth of mastering the intimacy vs. isolation stage was to marry and have children; it followed, then, that raising the children in a productive and healthy environment would be the next step in the life cycle. Of course, not everyone who establishes an intimate relationship has children, but Erikson believed that there were other ways to contribute to the growth of the next generation. He did believe, though, that caring for these younger ones in some way fulfilled a basic need for all adults and was necessary to achieve generativity.

> **Generativity vs. stagnation** Erikson's second stage of adult development, which is to nurture the next generation, or to raise children in a way that helps them master their environments and establish their own identities.

Critical Thinking
QUESTION   What ways can you think of for an adult without children to make positive contributions to the next generation?

However, marrying and having children does not guarantee generativity. Just as Erikson believed that identity establishment was crucial to developing intimacy, he also believed it necessary to generativity. Adults with a fragile sense of self might view children as a threat to their stability, and therefore refrain from investing themselves completely in the children's growth process. Stagnation was Erikson's alternative to generativity. He believed that adults who did not meet the challenge of contributing to the next generation would experience frustration and a lack of fulfillment, and lacking momentum, would have difficulty forging ahead in life.

Stage Three: Integrity vs. Despair   The final stage of adulthood according to Erikson, Late Adulthood, takes place in the sixties and beyond. **Integrity vs. despair** presents the challenge of looking back on one's life and feeling a sense of satisfaction at a life lived well. People who feel integrity are confident that the choices they made were consistent with their identity and values, and thus they are able to face the end of life peacefully. People who look back on their life and see a series of missed opportunities, wishing they had done things differently, feel despair, according to Erikson. This

> **Integrity vs. despair** Erikson's third stage of adult development, which is the challenge of looking back on one's life and feeling a sense of satisfaction at a life lived well.

TABLE 2.1 | Erikson's Adult Life Stages

Early Adulthood	Intimacy vs. Isolation	Goal: To establish and maintain an intimate relationship with a life partner
Middle Adulthood	Generativity vs. Stagnation	Goal: To nurture the next generation
Late Adulthood	Integrity vs. Despair	Goal: To reflect on one's life and come to terms with both the joys and the disappointments

despair promotes a sense of fear and anxiety about the end of life, because the person feels unresolved about the way life was lived. Table 2.1 summarizes Erikson's stages of adult life.

In sum, Erikson made a great contribution to psychology by his recognition that personality and development continue to evolve throughout the lifespan. His theory presents a broad framework that can serve as a guide to understanding adults at different stages of life. Critics of Erikson's lifespan theory point out that he based his theory solely on his own clinical observations, which by nature are biased—in other words, when observing others it is sometimes easy to see what we expect to see. Still, Erikson's lifespan theory continues to hold a prominent place in the study of adulthood, and as we will see shortly, it is supported by more recent work.

Levinson's Theory

In the 1970s, a Yale University researcher, Daniel J. Levinson, began what was to become a landmark study in the search to understand adult development. In the book *The Season's of a Man's Life* (1978), Levinson and his colleagues sum up their research on men's adult development.

Levinson and his colleagues gathered together 40 men of varying backgrounds, from blue-collar workers to business executives to novelists, and conducted an intensive series of interviews, asking each man to reflect upon the different time periods in his life and the major issues he remembered facing at that time. From the biographies that were constructed out of the interviews, Levinson's team identified what they saw as the typical progression of male adulthood. They concluded that a man's life was made up of a cycle of stable periods, with transitional periods in between each stable period. In the transitional periods, men were contemplating their recent stable period, exploring ideas of what should come next, and preparing to move ahead.

For example, Levinson believed that the first major adult stage for men occurred between the ages of 17 and 22, called the **early adult transition**. During this time, the young man is completing the major task of adolescence—forming an identity—and

Early adult transition According to Levinson, completion of the major task of adolescence—forming an identity—and working toward becoming an independent, self-reliant person.

working toward becoming an independent, self-reliant person. The transition is complete and early adulthood begins when he commits himself to a place in the world, such as to a job and/or a life partner. According to Levinson, this usually happens in the early twenties, and then for seven or eight years he enjoys a period of relative stability. The **age 30 transition** is the next phase in the cycle, a period of four to five years when he questions the choices he has made so far, considering what modifications he might make to build a more stable and fulfilled life. The early and middle thirties are characterized by another stable period, a time of *settling down and strengthening the commitments he has made.* During this time he *builds his relationships with family and experiences professional growth as well.*

> **Age 30 transition** According to Levinson a period of four to five years when a man questions the choices he has made so far, considering what modifications he might make to build a more stable and fulfilled life.

Around the age of 40, Levinson found, most of the men in his study experienced the next transitional phase, which Levinson termed the **midlife transition.** Like the age 30 transition, this is characterized by a period of reflection and questioning regarding the life choices he has made so far, but in this phase there is an increased awareness of his mortality and the fact that his time on earth is limited. This new awareness adds a sense of urgency to this transitional phase, as he reflects on the dreams he had for himself and compares them to his accomplishments. As a result, he must come to terms with the loss of some of these dreams. Levinson found that 80% of the men in his study experienced a real crisis during this time as they struggled with this issue.

> **Midlife transition** A period of reflection and questioning regarding the life choices he has made so far.

The next phase in the cycle is another stable period in which the man enters middle adulthood. Levinson ended his study in this phase, but speculated that the rest of the lifespan would continue in a similar pattern of stable periods and transitions. Like Erikson's and other psychoanalytic theories, Levinson's theory is grounded in the idea of conflict: Each transitional stage presents a conflict or crisis in which the man must choose between taking some risk to move forward and grow, or staying in the safety of his current patterns and stagnating.

Levinson's theory has received much attention, because it was the first comprehensive attempt at empirical research in the area of adult development. It has been criticized, though, for its assumption that women's lives progress in the same fashion as men's lives; although more recent research shows some similarities, marked differences are present as well. Also, we must be cautious in making broad assumptions about the general population based on a small sample of just 40 people. In addition, some psychologists believe that the "midlife crisis" that Levinson found so prevalent among the men in his study is an exaggeration, and that most people do not experience a "crisis" as such.

Sheehy's Theory

Social scientist and journalist Gail Sheehy has been studying the life stages and cycles of American men and women for more than 25 years. Through observations, surveys, interviews, and extensive analysis of demographic and census data, she has developed a lifespan theory of development that adds an important dimension to existing work in the field. That dimension is culture. Influenced by the work of anthropologist Margaret Mead, Sheehy's theory recognizes the role of age in life stages, but believes that *our cultural and societal environment interacts with age to produce unique goals and interests for different cohorts at the same chronological age.*

Let's explain that a little further. A **cohort** is defined as a group of people born at about the same time in history, so that they share common experiences in society at about the same time and age. Theoretically, this produces similar reactions among them. For example, people born in the early 1900s experienced World War I and the Great Depression relatively early in their lives. These events shaped their expectations about the world

> **Cohort** A group of people born at about the same time in history, so that they share common experiences in society at about the same time and age.

and their role in it. Subsequently, when World War II began, they experienced it differently than did people who were born after the Great Depression. Our past experiences influence the way we perceive current experiences; thus, although several cohorts may experience the same historical event, they could all perceive and respond to it differently due to the cohort effect. As Sheehy puts it, "The playing field is quite different for each generation when its young members start their journey into adulthood. The point where you and your friends come in on your culture's history has influenced your choices and attitudes . . . profoundly influencing which tasks of development you accomplish early, which you postpone, and which you will have to catch up on" (1995, p. 23).

The proliferation of technology in recent years, combined with the relative peace enjoyed by the United States, has produced revolutionary changes in the adult life cycle, according to Sheehy. Specifically, the lifespan is lengthening: A woman who reaches the age of 50 today, free of heart disease and cancer, can expect to live to 92. Similarly, today's healthy 65-year-old men can expect to see 81 (Sheehy, 1995). The prospect of a significantly longer, healthier life is changing the way Americans live their lives at all ages. Sheehy's latest work, *New Passages* (1995) illustrates the effects these changes are having on each cohort.

Critical Thinking
QUESTION   Think about your own generation as a cohort. What cultural or societal events or conditions have been influential in your overall worldviews, beliefs, and ideals as a cohort? What is your prediction about how these forces will influence the choices and direction your cohort makes as you collectively progress through your lifespan?

Early Adulthood   Sheehy's first adult stage, the **Tryout Twenties**, is characterized by a feeling of freedom to "try out" different roles in life, both occupationally and in close relationships. Gone is the settling down that formerly characterized the twenties; in its place is a sometimes paralyzing recognition of the many choices in life, combined with a new sense of awareness of the dangers of the world. These factors together are producing a generation that feels a lack of security in the future, according to Sheehy's research. Young adults in their twenties today are seeing their parents struggle

> **Tryout Twenties** A feeling of freedom to "try out" different roles in life, both occupationally and in close relationships.

with downsizing; in addition, Sheehy notes a heightened awareness of AIDS, environmental issues, and interracial violence in their own cities and neighborhoods. On the brighter side, more people in this generation will earn college degrees than any of their predecessors. Many are staying in school longer, while simultaneously aware that there won't be an automatic job waiting for them when they graduate. Because of the lengthening time span during which young adults choose their paths in life, Sheehy terms this first stage of adulthood "Provisional Adulthood."

Turbulent Thirties A time in which young adults are juggling multiple roles, often including raising children, building a career, and maintaining an intimate relationship with a partner.

"First Adulthood" begins with the **Turbulent Thirties**, typified by a race to catch up on all the things that got put on hold during the Tryout Twenties. During this time, many young adults are starting families while at the same time building careers, not to mention trying to maintain an intimate relationship with a partner. Sheehy notes that the current generation of thirtysomethings grew up in the prosperous 1980s, swept along in the tide of materialism and fast money that prompted real temptation to live in the moment. The approach of the thirtieth birthday acted for many as a wake-up call signaling a sudden awareness of the passing of time. The Turbulent Thirties, more than any other period in adulthood, involves a juggling act as these young adults struggle to fill multiple roles and to do so successfully.

Flourishing Forties Characterized by the recognition that 40 doesn't feel old, which prompts middlescence.

The next decade of the life cycle, the **Flourishing Forties**, often begins with confusion for adults in this stage today, says Sheehy. Previously, 40 was the age that signified the beginning of the end—the crossing over of the boundary from young to old. Today's fortysomethings grew up with that perception. Thus, it comes as quite a shock when they reach 40 and notice that they still feel thirtysomething. Many work out regularly, and the emphasis on physical fitness adds to the feeling of youth. Add to this the fact that approximately 12,000 people in the United States are turning 40 each day (Sheehy, 1995), which tends to normalize the experience, a phenomenon capitalized on by advertisers who market endless kinds of products designed to enhance the youthful outlook and persona of today's fortysomethings. The result is a dramatic change in perspective. This group doesn't feel 40, and refuses to slide peacefully into "old age."

Sheehy also points out that this group grew up in what she dubs "the Vietnam era," with the mind-set that anything was possible. They took on big issues and believed in their ability to make a difference. They grew up believing that life would get better and better, which in many ways it has for this group. These early experiences shaped the way they perceive life and their roles in it, as illustrated by a resistance to the traditional age-40 persona. As they progress into their forties, however, the realization of the passage of time slowly creeps in, prompting a reassessment of their lives (see Table 2.2).

Middlescence A time of reflection on life so far and reassessment of goals, values, and identity. Signals the transition from First Adulthood to Second Adulthood.

Sheehy calls this phase **middlescence**, based on its similarity to adolescents' identity-establishment phase. And just like its teenage counterpart, middlescence isn't easy. Any kind

TABLE 2.2 | Sheehy's Life Stages

Tryout Twenties	Characterized by a feeling of freedom to "try out" different roles in life, both occupationally and in close relationships.
Turbulent Thirties	A time in which young adults are juggling multiple roles, often including raising children, building a career, and maintaining an intimate relationship with a partner.
Flourishing Forties	Characterized by the recognition that 40 doesn't feel old, which prompts middlescence.
Middlescence	A time of reflection on life so far and reassessment of goals, values, and identity. Signals the transition from First Adulthood to Second Adulthood.
Flaming Fifties	A time to build on and enjoy pursuit of the new goals set during middlescence.
Serene Sixties	Characterized by a sense of inner harmony, usually a result of a sense of living in a manner consistent with one's ideal self.
Sage Seventies	Successful 70-somethings stay mentally and physically in shape and continue to find missions in life.
Uninhibited Eighties	Characterized by direct expression of thoughts and opinions, and feeling as if there is no reason to hold back.
Noble Nineties	A time of generosity of mind and spirit, and ability to forgive.
Celebratory Centenarians	Typically mentally active and engaged in life, optimistic, and with a good sense of humor.

of growth involves breaking through some barriers, and middlescence is no exception. Recognition of mortality may be the biggest barrier: Before these adults realize the opportunities presented by this phase, they must come to terms with what Sheehy calls the "little death" of their First Adulthood. For some, this involves giving up on some of the dreams they've carried around for years, stubbornly believing there was still plenty of time to accomplish them—the man who always dreamed of being a professional athlete, for example, must accept in his forties that that particular dream isn't going to come true. Similarly, the woman who put off having children, thinking that with the new technological advances in fertility there was still time, must accept by her mid-forties that the odds are highly against her conceiving a child.

Giving up these dreams often provokes what Sheehy calls a *meaning crisis*, in which the adult is forced to reassess what he or she has accomplished to this point and think seriously about how fulfilling those accomplishments have been. As a result of this reassessment, many adults in this phase realize that in their first adulthood they were presenting somewhat false selves, designed more to please others or fit society's expectations than to fulfill their own innermost needs. Recognition of this seems to free these adults to dream again and make some changes in how they want to live the next part of their lives, or in Sheehy's words, their "Second Adulthood."

Middle Adulthood "Second Adulthood" is a brand-new concept that has resulted from the societal and technological changes that were mentioned previously. Recognizing the opportunities this presents and reinventing their identities in a way that is more consistent with their ideal selves prompts an invigorated approach to the later decades of life as these adults pass into what Sheehy calls the **Age of Mastery**. The new goals this involves for these late-forties adults seem to revolve around whatever has been missing for that particular person up to this point. For example, the woman who married early and had children often sees Second Adulthood as her opportunity to go back to school or establish a career. Men who followed the traditional path and have been concentrating on being a good provider often turn their attention to their families and friends, trying to reconnect and establish some close relationships. The key here, says Sheehy, is to "find your passion and pursue it."

> **Age of Mastery** Characterized by renewed vigor and purpose, from about ages 45–65.

> **Flaming Fifties** A time to build on and enjoy pursuit of the new goals set during middlescence.

The next decade, the **Flaming Fifties**, is a time for building on and enjoying the pursuit of the new goals set during middlescence. Today's adults in this group came of age in the 1950s, when conformity and obedience were at a peak. "In their day, grass was mowed, coke was a cold drink, and pot was something a girl asked for at her bridal shower—preferably in stainless steel" (Sheehy, 1995, p. 29). Almost half of the women in this group were married by the age of 19, and in the prosperous postwar period their husbands had secure jobs. Having missed the real identity-choosing opportunity of adolescence, many of these early-marrying couples ended up divorced by age 40. The result: an early middlescence, especially for the women who, having married right out of high school, had no job skills. They made it through, though, and now feel that they are in the best time of their lives. Women in their fifties experience a growth in self-confidence and well-being. "I can now live by my own rules and stop trying to please everyone," report almost half the women surveyed by Sheehy when asked about the best part of being over 45.

The passage into the fifties is more difficult for the men currently in this stage, though, and isn't looked upon as optimistically as it is by their female counterparts. Shaped by society to pride themselves on their physical strength and ability to support a family, many of these men struggle with the realities of their aging bodies and unexpected loss of jobs due to corporate downsizing. Lacking the support systems that have been such a fundamental part of women's lives, these men often feel a lack of control over their lives and frustrated at the unfairness of it— after all, they grew up in a time when if you worked hard, your job was secure until you chose to retire. The frustration is often compounded by the contrasting success of the women in their lives. The key to overcoming the negativity of this time and finding new optimism in the future seems to be changing the focus from *competing* to *connecting,* according to Sheehy's research. Men who can learn to look for happiness in other, non-work-related aspects of their life come through this phase the happiest and healthiest. Fathers often accomplish this by establishing new, closer bonds with their children. Married men focus on spending more time with their wives. Making this change is easier for educated, white-collar men than it is for blue-collar men who are more steeped in traditional cultural norms, but the good news, Sheehy reports, is that blue-collar workers tend to follow the same trends as white-collar workers, but about five years later.

 As you read about these stages of Sheehy's model, do you notice any similarities to Levinson's model? Explain.

Adults in their **Serene Sixties** today report feeling about 10 years younger than they really are, a phenomenon that is shared by today's adults in their forties and fifties as well. No longer are the sixties considered the final decade of life, nor are most sixtysomethings in poor health: Sheehy reports that "only 10% of Americans 65 and over have a chronic health problem that restricts them from carrying on a major activity" (Sheehy, 1995, p. 351). This group of pacesetters is also enjoying a healthy

> **Serene Sixties** Characterized by a sense of inner harmony, usually a result of a sense of living in a manner consistent with one's ideal self.

economic status, experiencing an increase in median income (adjusted to 1992 dollars) from 1974 to 1992 of 15–27%, the highest of any age group. Additionally, only 12% fall into the poverty range, a decrease from 35% in the 1960s. The chief goal for this group is a sense of inner harmony, usually satisfied by the feeling of having become authentic or having lived in a way consistent with the pursuit of one's ideal self. Following Erik Erikson's lead, Sheehy calls this the Age of Integrity.

The good health and economic prosperity of adults in their Serene Sixties today is prompting a renewed dedication to enjoying life and what it has to offer. The most successful adults in this stage are, essentially, learning that it is okay to "play." Some are enjoying vacations, others are taking up artistic pursuits, and still others are finding joy in exploring new intimate relationships. These adults have also learned the importance of coming to terms with old wounds and are thus seeking out long-lost ex-friends or family members and reconciling. Although many of these adults looked forward to retirement, some are finding after a few years of it that they are bored; therefore they are getting involved in some type of structured work by either rejoining the workforce or volunteering in some way.

Late Adulthood The Serene Sixties gives way to the **Sage Seventies**. Sheehy notes that these adults grew up in the aftermath of the Great Depression and came of age during World War II. Having survived much hardship, they developed resilience, a characteristic that serves them (and any others who are fortunate to claim it) well. Their early life experiences taught them to see life

> **Sage Seventies** Successful 70-somethings stay mentally and physically in shape and continue to find missions in life.

as a series of missions, and that mind-set still shapes their outlook toward life. To be happy in this stage, adults need to find something to keep living for. For some it is grandchildren, for others it may be a social or environmental cause close to their heart, or other important work they are engaging in. The nature of the mission is irrelevant, but there must be a mission, an important reason to keep living.

FIGURE 2.10 | Successful aging involves staying both physically and mentally active, and continuing to pursue your passions.

This supports Sheehy's thesis that in aging you have two choices: Either sit back and let it overcome you, or take control of your life and choose to meet the challenge of each new passage. Physical and mental exercise keeps people sharp enough to meet this challenge and able to progress from the Sage Seventies into the Uninhibited Eighties, the Noble Nineties, and for some, to become a Celebratory Centenarian (see Figure 2.10).

Sheehy concludes her report of the life cycle with a few observations about centenarians, summarized from various studies. They are typically intelligent, interested in current events, and healthy. They tend to get up early in the morning, drink coffee, and while they don't pay strict attention to their diets, generally eat food high in protein and low in fat. They are usually religious, optimistic, and have a good sense of humor. "Life seems to have been a great adventure," Sheehy says to sum up their outlook on life (1995, p. 427).

Interim SUMMARY #4

Erikson's theory set the stage for the division of adulthood into three general phases. Levinson's work generally supported Erikson's theory, at least to the mid-forties age range where Levinson terminated his study. Sheehy's work supports both of these theories in a general sense, from the search for identity and intimacy, to the pursuit of generativity and integrity. Her work also is somewhat similar to Levinson's idea that the adult life cycle is characterized by a series of stable periods punctuated by reassessments. Sheehy's work breaks new ground, though, in two ways. It is the most detailed and demographically inclusive study of its kind to date, in that it includes adults from all regions of the United States, blue-collar and white-collar alike. Also, her keen observation of the general shift in typical age-related stages (e.g., that identity-seeking is continuing into the twenties, intimacy-seeking isn't happening until the thirties, and today's fiftysomethings are what fortysomethings used to be) lends new insight into our understanding of adulthood today.

Turn now to Activity 2.6 and see how life stage theories improve your understanding of some of the key people in your life.

CHAPTER TERMS

Self
Self-concept
Self-verification
Self-enhancement
Possible selves
Self-esteem
Sociometer theory
Positive regard
Unconditional positive
  regard
Conditional positive
  regard
Trait self-esteem

State self-esteem
Self-efficacy
Self-knowledge
Social comparison
Self-perception
Johari Window
Private self
Public self
Self-monitoring
Intimacy vs. isolation
Identity
Generativity vs.
  stagnation

Integrity vs. despair
Early adult transition
Age 30 transition
Midlife transition
Cohort
Tryout Twenties
Turbulent Thirties
Flourishing Forties
Middlescence
Age of Mastery
Flaming Fifties
Serene Sixties
Sage Seventies

ACTIVITY 2.1

THE TWENTY STATEMENTS TEST

INSTRUCTIONS: *Fill in the spaces with 20 different words or phrases you would use to complete the statement. If you get stuck, consider your traits, relationships, roles, jobs, hobbies, values, strengths, and weaknesses.*

1. I am _Responsible_.
2. I am _Honest_.
3. I am _Focused_.
4. I am _Loyal_.
5. I am _trustworthy_.
6. I am _Dependable_.
7. I am _____.
8. I am _____.

9. I am _____.

10. I am _____.

11. I am _____.

12. I am _____.

13. I am _____.

14. I am _____.

15. I am _____.

16. I am _____.

17. I am _____.

18. I am _____.

19. I am _____.

20. I am _____.

REFLECTIONS

A. How difficult was it to fill in all 20 spaces? At what point did you start to have trouble?

_____

_____

_____

B. Randomly choose 3 numbers between 1 and 20, then cross off the words above that correspond to those numbers. Now, imagine that you do not possess those qualities. Imagine how that might come about, and how it would affect you. Write your thoughts and reactions to that in the following space.

_____

_____

_____

_____

_____

_____

_____

_____

_____

_____

— ACTIVITY 2.2 —————————————————————————
EGO BOOSTERS AND EGO BUSTERS IN YOUR LIFE

PART 1: INTROSPECTION

A. Think of a recent "ego boosting" message you received from someone you love or respect. What was it? How and why did it affect your self-esteem? Do you think the other person was aware of its effect on you?

_____

_____

_____

_____

_____

B. Think of a recent "ego busting" message you received from someone you love or respect. What was it? How and why did it affect your self-esteem? Do you think the other person was aware of its effect on you?

_____

_____

_____

_____

_____

PART 2: INTERVIEW AND ANALYZE

A. Talk to a close friend, work colleague, or loved one and ask him or her to tell you of a recent "ego booster" message he or she received from you. In the following space, summarize the message. Then consider whether you gave the message deliberately or not. Were you aware of its effects on the other person? How do you feel now that you know the effects?

_____

_____

_____

_____

B. Talk to a close friend, work colleague, or loved one and ask him or her to tell you of a recent "ego buster" message he or she received from you. In the following space, summarize it. Then consider whether you gave the message deliberately or not. Were you aware of its effects on the other person? How do you feel now that you know the effects?

_____

_____

_____

_____

_____

PART 3: FUTURE APPLICATIONS

In the following space, reflect on what you have learned from this activity. In the future, what (if any) changes will you make in your human relations based on what you have learned in this activity?

_____

_____

_____

_____

_____

_____

Source: Adapted from Adler & Towne, 1996.

ACTIVITY 2.3

IMPROVING SELF-KNOWLEDGE THROUGH SOCIAL COMPARISON

GOAL: _To consider the accuracy of your self-concept by comparing yourself to similar others in terms of each descriptor._

PART 1: YOUR SELF-CONCEPT

Begin by referring back to Activity 2.1 and identifying the five most important aspects of your self-concept. Write them here.

1. _____
2. _____
3. _____
4. _____
5. _____

PART 2: SOCIAL COMPARISON

In the first blank space of each item, write in the word you chose in part 1 that corresponds to each number. For example, in part 1, if you chose the word "athletic" for the first word of your self-concept, write that word in comparison 1. Then go on to test out the accuracy of each aspect of your self-concept by comparing yourself to other people you know well: the second blank space of each item should name the person to whom you are comparing yourself, and the third blank space should describe what you notice in that comparison.

1. I think that I am _____. As I compare myself to
_____ on this characteristic, I notice _____
_____
_____.

Based on this comparison, I can conclude that my self-awareness in terms of
this characteristic is *as accurate/not as accurate* (circle one) as I thought it was.

2. I think that I am _____. As I compare myself to
_____ on this characteristic, I notice _____
_____
_____

Based on this comparison, I can conclude that my self-awareness in terms of
this characteristic is *as accurate/not as accurate* (circle one) as I thought it was.

3. I think that I am _____. As I compare myself to
_____ on this characteristic, I notice _____
_____
_____.

Based on this comparison, I can conclude that my self-awareness in terms of
this characteristic is *as accurate/not as accurate* (circle one) as I thought it was.

4. I think that I am _____. As I compare myself to
_____ on this characteristic, I notice _____
_____
_____.

Based on this comparison, I can conclude that my self-awareness in terms of
this characteristic is *as accurate/not as accurate* (circle one) as I thought it was.

5. I think that I am _____. As I compare myself to
_____ on this characteristic, I notice _____
_____
_____.

Based on this comparison, I can conclude that my self-awareness in terms of
this characteristic is *as accurate / not as accurate* (circle one) as I thought it was.

PART 3: CONCLUSIONS

In the following space, write your reflections on what you have learned about the
accuracy of your self-concept. Also, describe one way in which you can use your
new insight(s) to improve your relations with others.

_____

_____

_____
_____
_____
_____
_____
_____
_____
_____
_____

ACTIVITY 2.4

FREE ASSOCIATION AND THE UNKNOWN

PART 1: FREE ASSOCIATION

Following is a list of 18 words. As you read each word, write down the first word that comes to mind in the space next to the word.

Tool _____   Season of the year _____

Color _____   Musical instrument _____

Human _____   Weapon _____

Food _____   Vacation _____

Fruit _____   Legendary figure _____

God or goddess _____   Animal _____

Retreat _____   Article of clothing _____

Geographic location _____   Piece of furniture _____

Hero or heroine _____   Protect _____

PART 2: INTROSPECTION AND FEEDBACK

Study the words you wrote. What themes are apparent in your responses? Do you notice anything that indicates something about yourself that you weren't aware of, such as a goal, fear, or value? If you are comfortable showing your responses to others, let someone else (or a few other people) look at your responses, and see if they notice any themes.

_____
_____
_____
_____
_____
_____
_____
_____

PART 3: CONCLUSIONS

In the following space, write the themes that you or others noticed in your responses. Describe your feelings and thoughts about anything new you discovered about yourself by doing this exercise.

_____

_____

_____

_____

_____

_____

_____

_____

_____

Source: Reaching out: Interpersonal Effectiveness and Self-Actualization, by D.W. Johnson, 1997, Needham Heights, MA: Allyn and Bacon.

ACTIVITY 2.5

INSTRUCTIONS: *For each of the following questions, answer* True *or* False.

_____ 1. I find it hard to imitate the behavior of other people.

_____ 2. At parties and social gatherings, I do not attempt to do or say things that others will like.

_____ 3. I can only argue for ideas that I already believe.

_____ 4. I can make impromptu speeches even on topics about which I have almost no information.

_____ 5. I guess I put on a show to impress or entertain others.

_____ 6. I would probably make a good actor.

_____ 7. In a group of people, I am rarely the center of attention.

_____ 8. In different situations and with different people, I often act like very different persons.

_____ 9. I am not particularly good at making other people like me.

_____10. I'm not always the person I appear to be.

_____11. I would not change my opinions (or the way I do things) to please someone or win their favor.

_____12. I have considered being an entertainer.

_____13. I have never been good at games like charades or improvisational acting.

_____14. I have trouble changing my behavior to suit different people and different situations.

_____15. At a party I let others keep the jokes and stories going.

_____16. I feel a bit awkward in company and do not show up quite as well as I should.

_____17. I can look anyone in the eye and tell a lie with a straight face (if for a right end).

_____18. I may deceive people by being friendly when I really dislike them.

Scoring: Give yourself 1 point for each *True* answer you gave for items 4, 5, 6, 8, 10, 12, 17, and 18. Then, give yourself 1 point for each *False* answer you gave for items 1, 2, 3, 7, 9, 11, 13, 14, 15, and 16. Add up your total number of points. This total represents your self-monitoring score. The average score for North American college students is between 10 and 11.

My score is _____.

Reflections: (Complete this section only after finishing the section on public and private selves.) Based on this activity and what you have learned about self-monitoring, how satisfied are you with your level of self-monitoring? What changes (if any) will you make in your self-monitoring behavior based on what you have learned?

_____

_____

_____

_____

_____

_____

_____

_____

Source: Snyder and Gangestad (1986). On the nature of self-monitoring: Matters of assessment, matters of validity *Journal of Personality and Social Psychology.* Copyright © 1986 by the American Psychological Association. Reproduced with permission.

ACTIVITY 2.6

LIFE STAGES AND THE ADULTS IN YOUR LIFE

INSTRUCTIONS: *Choose four adults in your life who are at least 10 years apart from each other in age (you may include yourself if you wish). Then consider which life stage theory best explains each adult. Give some examples to support your ideas.*

Person #1: Name _____

In the following space, answer these questions:

■ What seem to be the main themes in this person's interests, goals, and behavior at this stage in his or her life?

_____

_____

■ What life stage theory seems to best fit this person? Give some examples
that support your belief.

_____

_____

_____

_____

_____

_____

_____

_____

_____

Person #2: Name _____

In the following space, answer these questions:

■ What seem to be the main themes in this person's interests, goals, and behavior at this stage in his or her life?

_____

_____

■ What life stage theory seems to best fit this person? Give some examples
that support your belief.

_____

_____

_____

_____

_____

_____

_____

_____

_____

Person #3: Name _____

In the following space, answer these questions:

- What seem to be the main themes in this person's interests, goals, and behavior at this stage in his or her life?

  _____

  _____

  _____

- What life stage theory seems to best fit this person? Give some examples that support your belief.

  _____

  _____

  _____

  _____

  _____

  _____

  _____

  _____

Person #4: Name _____

In the following space, answer these questions:

- What seem to be the main themes in this person's interests, goals, and behavior at this stage in his or her life?

  _____

  _____

  _____

- What life stage theory seems to best fit this person? Give some examples that support your belief.

  _____

  _____

  _____

  _____

  _____

  _____

  _____

How Personality Influences Human Relations

Personality is the glitter that sends your little gleam across the footlights and the orchestra pit into that big black space where the audience is.

—MAE WEST

"**B**ecause I want to find out what makes people tick."

"So I can better understand why people (including myself) do what they do."

If these statements sound familiar, it may be because they are the answers students frequently give when asked why they are taking a psychology course. After all, isn't that what psychology is supposed to be all about? Well, as any psychologist will tell you, the more you learn about psychology, the more you realize how complex these goals are. A good place to begin, though, is to learn some of the most influential theories of personality.

Before we continue, it is important to clarify the meaning of the word *theory,* because its meaning in everyday language is often quite different from the scientific meaning. In everyday language, we often use the word *theory* to refer to an untested idea or someone's own explanation of why or how something happened. "It's just a theory," we might say, meaning that it's just one person's opinion, and it may be right or wrong—in other words, it probably isn't very reliable. This everyday use of the word *theory* is very different from the scientific use of the word, and it is important to understand why. As scientists, psychologists use the word *theory* to refer to a set of beliefs that has been tested a number of times and is considered valid. So, when we refer to "theories of personality" in this text, we are discussing the most influential explanations of "what makes people tick."

In psychology, **personality** refers to a person's pattern of thoughts, feelings, and behaviors that are consistent over time and across situations.

CHAPTER 3

> **Personality** The unique pattern of thoughts, feelings, and behaviors in an individual that is consistent over time and across situations.

For example, imagine that you meet someone named Jorge at a party, and you find him to be outgoing, relaxed, and to have a good sense of humor. Would it be correct, then, to use these words to describe Jorge's personality? Based on having met him only one time, you couldn't know for sure: For these characteristics to be an accurate description of Jorge's personality, they must apply to him in most situations over much of his life. And most of us have been at parties where we've acted in a way that may not be consistent with how we usually act! Psychologists have been studying personality for more than one hundred years, and several major schools of thought have emerged that try to explain how personality develops. These personality theories can be useful in helping us understand some of the internal reasons for why people do what they do, which is an important component in laying the foundation for good human relations.

THE PSYCHOANALYTIC PERSPECTIVE

PREVIEW QUESTIONS

(1) According to psychoanalytic psychologists, what shapes our personality?

(2) What are the three forces of personality according to Freud? What role does each force play, and how do they work together?

(3) What are defense mechanisms, and how do they influence our personality?

(4) How does the psychoanalytic perspective give us insight into our relations with others?

Sigmund Freud was the first psychologist to attempt the challenging task of formulating a personality theory. Born in Austria in 1856, Freud trained as a medical doctor. As a practicing neurologist, he became increasingly fascinated with the intricacies of the human mind, and he devoted the rest of his life to the study of the human personality. As you may know, some of Freud's work is controversial today (many psychologists believe that Freud placed undue emphasis on sexual urges, for example), but his view of the structure of personality remains influential, and that is what we will discuss here.

> **Psychoanalytic theory** The theory which suggests that our personality is shaped by an ongoing internal struggle between two or more conflicting needs.

Freud founded what is known as the **psychoanalytic theory** of personality. Psychoanalytic theorists believe that our personality is shaped by an ongoing internal struggle between two or more conflicting needs. For Freud, the struggle was between three forces: (a) the desire to satisfy our most basic urges, (b) the need to adhere to society's laws and rules, and (c) the goal of living within one's own personal moral code. Obviously, these three needs aren't always compatible with one another. What we want to do doesn't always fit within the laws and rules of our society, and even when these first two needs are compatible, we must also decide whether it meets our own individual sense of what is right and wrong. Each decision we make, according to psychoanalysts, brings us into contact with these often-conflicting forces, and as a result we sometimes choose to satisfy one need at the expense of one or both of the others. In general, psychoanalytic theorists believe that we can understand why people do what they do by analyzing the processes by which they resolve this conflict.

The Mind as an Iceberg

You may be wondering how it can be possible for every action we take, every decision we make to be preceded by a consideration of all three forces. If we're always focusing on trying to resolve the conflict, how is there time for anything else? The answer to this question lies in the fact that, for psychoanalytic theorists, much of our personality resides in our unconscious. In other words, we are usually not aware of the internal struggle. In fact, Freud saw the mind as an iceberg (Figure 3.1). The tip of the iceberg, or the small portion that can be seen above the water, is the part Freud thought is our **conscious**, or *awareness*. The large majority of an iceberg is underwater, and this Freud thought was comparable to the large portion of our mind that we are not aware of, or our **unconscious**. Sometimes the uppermost area of what lies underwater is somewhat visible,

> **Conscious** The portion of our mind that we are aware of at any given time.

> **Unconscious** The large portion of our mind including thoughts, feelings, memories, and expectations, that we are not aware of.

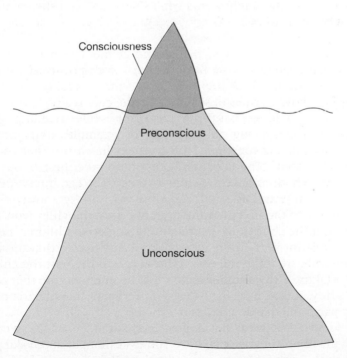

FIGURE 3.1 | Freud's Iceberg Model

Preconscious The part of the unconscious that can be brought into consciousness by focusing on it.

and this Freud called the **preconscious**, or the part of the unconscious that can be brought into consciousness by focusing on it. The preconscious can be useful when we try to analyze some aspect of our personality or behavior that is puzzling to us. Keep this iceberg model in mind as you think about the following information and apply it to your own life.

The Three Components of Personality

The Id To better understand the general psychoanalytic model, let's apply it to the specific components of the structure of personality. Freud believed that the personality was made up of three elements: the id, the ego, and the superego. The id is the most basic element of personality, and it operates on *the pleasure principle*. In other words, the id is the part of personality concerned with satisfying our basic instincts and urges. For example, when we are hungry, the id is interested only in getting food, and getting it right now, regardless of any obstacles that may be in the way. Not surprisingly, the id is the only element of personality present at birth. Consider an infant: When she is hungry, she demands to be fed; when she is tired, she falls asleep; and when she has to go potty, she goes—regardless of whether the timing is convenient or not. She has no consideration of the needs of her mom or dad, no awareness of whether her needs are realistic or not—she simply wants what she wants, and she wants it immediately. That is the id at work.

Id The part of personality concerned with satisfying our basic instincts and urges.

The Ego Around 1 year of age, the second element of personality begins to emerge. The **ego** operates on the *reality principle* and is concerned with meeting the needs of the id in a way that is realistic, or fits with the laws or rules of society. For the ego, reality involves satisfying the id (maximizing pleasure) while avoiding getting hurt (minimizing pain). Take, for example, two young toddlers playing together. One of them has a toy that the other one wants. The id's urge is simply to take the toy, but since these children have developed an ego, the ego intervenes in the id's urge and asks, "If I take the toy, can I get away with it?" The ego wants to satisfy the id, but wants to make sure the child won't get caught and punished. If the child is accustomed to taking other children's toys and not getting in trouble for it, then the ego will probably decide that the risk is minimal, and the child will take the toy. If, however, in the past the child has been punished for taking away another child's toy, he might decide that although the id wants the toy, it isn't a realistic desire in terms of maximizing pleasure and minimizing pain, and decide not to take the toy.

Ego The part of personality concerned with meeting the needs of the id in a way that is realistic, and fits with the laws or rules of society.

This id vs. ego struggle is not limited to children. As adults, we face similar struggles all the time. For example, have you ever thought about skipping class or calling in sick to work when you weren't sick? If you gave any thought to the consequences, that was your ego at work. Also, the preceding paragraph describes the ego functioning in a healthy manner, doing what it is ideally designed to do. It doesn't always work the way it is supposed to, though. Have you ever had a desire for something, but knew you'd probably get caught and experience some type of pain or punishment for satisfying your desire—but you did it anyway? Most of us have been in this situation, and it exemplifies the ongoing nature of the internal struggle that psychoanalysts believe is the foundation of personality. We don't always have the strength to give up what we want, even if we know it will cause problems for us later. We will return to this dilemma shortly, but first we must discuss the third element of personality.

The Superego The third and final element of personality is the superego. The superego functions on the *morality principle* and is concerned with making sure the id and the ego function in a way that is consistent with the person's own moral code. Most of us are already familiar with this concept—we call it our conscience. The superego begins to develop around 5 years of age. This is the time when children begin to be able to internalize the concepts of right and wrong for their own sake, rather than for the sake of avoiding punishment. For example, imagine that the two toddlers playing in the previous example are now 9 years old. One child might still have something that the other one wants, but if the superego is in place, the child may refrain from taking it, since that would be "wrong." In this instance, the child's decision isn't so much concerned with getting caught—perhaps there is no one nearby and he knows he could get away with it—but he chooses not to take the toy because of his own sense of right and wrong. If he were to violate it, he would feel guilty, and the superego's motivation is to avoid guilt.

> **Superego** The part of personality concerned with making sure the id and the ego function in a way that is consistent with the person's own moral code.

With the emergence of the superego, the ego's job becomes more complicated. Not only must the ego try to keep the id happy without breaking any laws or rules of society, but now the ego must also keep the peace with the superego. This is sometimes a very difficult task, and maintaining a healthy balance between the structures of personality is one of the keys to psychological health, according to psychoanalytic psychologists. As you might guess, this additional task of the ego is more difficult than it sounds: It involves paying attention to each force and satisfying each need, without putting too much or too little emphasis on any one of them. That is why the ego is sometimes referred to as the *executive* or the *manager* of the personality. Table 3.1 summarizes the three components of the personality.

TABLE 3.1 | Summary of the Components of Personality

Id	Pleasure Principle	Maximize pleasure
Ego	Reality Principle	Avoid pain or punishment
Superego	Morality Principle	Avoid guilt

How the Components Work Together   By the time we become adults, most of us have developed a pattern of responding to these conflicting forces, and that pattern helps explain why we do what we do, or our personality (according to this theory). Let's look at a few examples of how different people might tend to resolve their ongoing internal struggle, and how being able to recognize this helps us understand and predict others' behavior.

Tanya is a 21-year-old college student who also works full-time. She was raised in a family that had a very strict sense of right and wrong. In fact, she learned that no matter what, you must never go against your own moral code. Part of the moral code that her family instilled in her involves always helping others, or being "a good Samaritan." Based on that moral code, Tanya thinks she should always stop to help someone whose car has broken down on the road. Almost every day on her way to work, Tanya sees a stalled or broken-down car on the side of the road. Up until now, she has always stopped to offer assistance. As you might imagine, this sometimes causes her to be late to work. Also, the city is becoming more dangerous, and news reports indicate that it isn't always safe for a young woman to offer someone assistance on the side of the road. If Tanya continues to stop and help anyway, putting her job in jeopardy (and perhaps even her life), psychoanalysts would say that she has an overdeveloped superego, and that it is interfering with healthy functioning. Ideally, her ego would be able to find a balance between satisfying her own needs (the need to stay alive and to keep her job so she can pay for the basic necessities of life) and satisfying the needs of her moral code. As things are, though, it would be useful for people who know Tanya to recognize her superego-driven pattern of decision making, so they can better understand why she does things differently than they might do.

A second example involves Dave, a 30-year-old accountant. Dave was the youngest of five children in his family, and it seemed as though there was never quite enough to go around. He felt he often ended up with hand-me-downs, or what was left after everyone else got what they wanted. Wanting a better life for himself, he took out student loans to pay for his education, earned his degree in accounting, and landed a well-paying job with a large firm. He has always felt that if you want something, you'd better go after it, because no one else is going to help you get it. He also feels that, after all those years of school, he deserves a nice wardrobe and a new BMW. Unfortunately, his salary can't cover his student loan payments, car payments, and the expenses of his fancy new lifestyle. He decides to give himself a small loan from the company—since he is an accountant, he can fix the books so that the missing money will be undetected until he can pay it back. This works so well that he gives in to the temptation to "borrow" the company's money a few more times when he needs it, even though he hasn't paid any of it back yet. Deep down inside, he knows that what he is doing is wrong, but he gives in to the temptation anyway. Can you guess what element of personality is ruling Dave's life? He is pursuing pleasure, while violating society's laws against theft and his own moral code. Clearly, Dave's id is ruling his life. We might guess that in other, perhaps less important decisions, Dave also has a tendency to give in to his id. This would be important information for people who know Dave, so that they can understand and sometimes even predict his behavior.

Critical Thinking QUESTION What suggestions can you make that might help Dave achieve a better balance among the three elements of his personality? In other words, how could he satisfy his id without going outside of society's rules or his own moral code?

Defense Mechanisms

How do you feel when you are faced with a difficult decision that requires you to choose among your id, ego, and/or superego? Most of the time, this type of dilemma causes a person to feel anxiety. If you call in sick to work in order to go skiing, will you get caught? And how will you feel later, knowing that you may have caused problems for your coworkers? Because many of our decisions are made unconsciously, though, Freud speculated that much of this anxiety may be developing on an unconscious level as well. Curiously, however, most of us tend to function pretty well in spite of it, so Freud theorized that we must often be resolving it on that same unconscious level. Furthermore, he identified a number of strategies our unconscious uses to resolve this anxiety. He called these strategies **defense mechanisms**. Let's take a closer look at some of the defense mechanisms, along with how they operate. As you read through them, keep in mind that they are, by definition, in the unconscious: These are not processes a person would be aware of.

Rationalization involves creating a rational explanation or justification for our behavior to avoid any worries about punishment or feelings of guilt. For example, if you did decide to call in sick to work so you could go skiing (choosing your id over your ego or superego), you might rationalize it to yourself by deciding that you really need a "mental health day," or that you rarely call in sick so this one time won't really matter.

Repression occurs when we completely suppress a feeling that is unacceptable. For example, a woman who gave up her career to be a stay-at-home mom may be jealous of her daughter's successful career. In the mother's mind, jealousy of her child's achievement is not something a loving and supportive mother should ever feel, so these feelings are buried deep in her unconscious.

Displacement operates when we have a feeling or reaction to someone that could cause us harm if we acted on it, so instead we act it out toward a nonthreatening or safe target. Imagine that one of your teachers said something to you that made you angry. Retaliating to that teacher directly could cause you problems, because the teacher has power over your grade in the class, so instead you go home and pick a fight with your roommate.

Projection is when we have an unacceptable impulse or thought, but instead of seeing it in ourselves, we think we see it in others. For example, a married man who believes in monogamy but finds himself strongly attracted to other people would be projecting if he thought other married men had trouble being faithful to their partners.

Defense mechanisms Strategies our unconscious uses to resolve anxiety.

Rationalization Creating a rational explanation or justification for our behavior.

Repression Completely suppressing a feeling which is unacceptable.

Displacement Redirecting a negative feeling toward a "safe" target.

Projection Having an unacceptable impulse or thought, but instead of seeing it in ourselves, we think we see it in others.

Reaction formation
Acting in a way that is completely opposite to an unacceptable thought or impulse.

Regression Psychologically retreating to an earlier, less mature time.

Sublimation Channeling an unacceptable feeling or urge into a positive, or more socially acceptable direction.

Reaction formation occurs when we act in a way that is completely opposite to an unacceptable thought or impulse. Imagine a person raised in an environment where homosexuality is unacceptable. If this person has strong homosexual feelings, he might instead date many women to create an image of himself as a "playboy."

Regression involves dealing with a difficult situation by regressing, or psychologically retreating to an earlier, less mature time. For example, an adult who deals with conflict by throwing a temper tantrum or crying helplessly might be engaging in repression if it helps him or her avoid difficult feelings or reality.

Sublimation is when we channel an unacceptable feeling or urge into a positive or more socially acceptable direction. For example, a person who feels extremely angry at his child might work out vigorously, channel his energies into work, or fanatically support a local charity.

Once again, it is important to note that these defense mechanisms operate on an unconscious level as a means of reducing anxiety. In some cases, though, a person can become aware of her own use of some defense mechanisms, either through therapy or through use of some of the strategies for increasing self-knowledge that we discussed in Chapter 2. Also, as we become more familiar with these defense mechanisms and the various ways they manifest themselves, we become better able to detect them in others' behavior. This gives us an additional tool to apply when we are trying to figure out why someone is doing something that seems irrational, dysfunctional, or problematic in some other way (see Figure 3.2).

Copyright © John Nebraska.

FIGURE 3.2 | What defense mechanism seems to be operating for George?

To apply the psychoanalytic theory to your own life and your relations with others, turn now to Activity 3.1.

Interim SUMMARY #1

Several major psychological theories strive to explain how internal forces drive our behavior. Psychoanalytic theory, originated by Freud, asserts that much of our behavior is driven by forces that are largely unconscious. Our id operates on the pleasure principle, our ego on the reality principle, and our superego on the morality principle. Healthy personalities pay attention to all three of these forces and strive to keep them relatively balanced.

As we unconsciously resolve numerous dilemmas each day, anxiety is produced by our ego as it recognizes that not all needs can be met all the time. Defense mechanisms resolve this anxiety by unconsciously distorting reality so that unacceptable thoughts and impulses are reconfigured into a more acceptable form.

THE BEHAVIORIST PERSPECTIVE

PREVIEW QUESTIONS

(1) According to behavioral psychologists, what shapes our personality?

(2) What is classical conditioning, and how does it affect our behavior and our human relations?

(3) What are the basic principles of operant conditioning, and how does it influence our behavior and our relations with others? Comparatively, how effective are rewards and punishments in shaping behavior?

(4) What is observational learning, and what does it add to our understanding of how we acquire behaviors?

> Give me a dozen healthy infants, well-formed, and my own specified world to bring them up in and I'll guarantee to take one at random and train him to become any type of specialist I might select—doctor, lawyer, artist, merchant, chief, and yes, even beggerman and thief, regardless of his talents, penchants, tendencies, abilities, vocations, and race of his ancestors. There is no such thing as an inheritance of capacity, talent, temperament, mental constitution, and behavioral characteristics (Watson, 1924, p. 104).

This provocative statement summarizes the next theory of personality that we will consider. By the 1900s, the psychoanalytic perspective had become very popular, but one of the primary criticisms of the theory was that it was difficult to measure reliably. In other words, how can we be sure that people have an id, ego, or superego if these components are not visible? The psychoanalytic idea of the unconscious seemed to make sense to a lot of people, but from a strict scientific perspective, if you can't see it, you can't measure it, and if you can't measure it, it isn't scientific. And if this fledgling field of psychology was to be accepted as credible, it must follow scientific principles. Therefore, the **behaviorists**

> **Behaviorist theory** The theory which suggests that our personality is shaped exclusively by our experiences.

argued that personality could only be described through observable behaviors, and thus, personality is simply the sum total of the reactions a person has learned to exhibit in certain situations.

In the behaviorists' view, we are all born as a "blank slate," and the person that each of us becomes is strictly the result of the environmental forces that act upon us. Have you ever heard people debating the issue of nature versus nurture: Are we who we are because of our nature (genetics), or because of our environment (learning)? If you have, then this theory the behaviorists proposed would come down firmly on the side of environment. This view suggests that each of our behaviors develops because of some type of response it produces in our environment—in other words, we are what we learn.

This concept is a radical departure from other psychological schools of thought. It suggests that we are passive creatures in our environment, and that we have no free will or choice in what we do and who we become. Instead, we are programmed by our environment. Behaviorists refer to this programming, or learning, as **conditioning**. According to behaviorists, there are two general types of conditioning, or learning, that shape our behavior and, consequently, our personalities.

Conditioning Learning from our experiences.

Classical Conditioning

The first type of learning studied by behaviorists is called **classical conditioning**, which essentially is a type of learning by association. Interestingly, it was discovered by accident by a Russian scientist named Ivan Pavlov. Pavlov was conducting a laboratory study of digestion, and as part of the study he was tracking the salivation of dogs. When he wanted the dogs to salivate, he put a small amount of meat powder on their tongues. This produced an instinctive response not unlike what happens when we smell or see our favorite food—the dogs' mouths would water (salivation). This is a normal response to food. Something unexpected happened, though: Pavlov began to notice that the dogs sometimes salivated when he didn't want or expect them to, and he didn't know what was causing it.

Classical conditioning A type of learning that relies on associating a neutral stimulus with a natural, biological stimulus.

As he began to observe the dogs more closely, he noticed that their salivation seemed to occur when they saw or heard something that preceded their daily feeding—when they heard the footsteps of the person who fed them, for example. This was interesting, Pavlov thought. It appeared that the dogs were associating the sound of the footsteps with food, and more importantly, that their instinctive response to food was being transferred to a noninstinctive stimulus (the footsteps). The dogs had learned that one stimulus (for example, the footsteps) was likely to lead to a second, more meaningful stimulus (food), and having associated the two stimuli, they were producing a learned response (salivation).

Upon noticing the association the dogs appeared to be making, Pavlov wondered if it had happened by chance, or if he could make it happen again under more controlled circumstances. Could it be possible to teach a dog to salivate at, say, the sound of a musical tone? And so he began a new experiment, first by sounding a musical tone and then checking to see if the dog salivated. Not surprisingly, there was no salivation at this point, since the tone was not meaningful to the dog. The tone was chosen as the neutral stimulus. The next step involved trying to teach the dog to associate the tone with food by sounding the tone and immediately giving the dog some meat powder. Pavlov did this several times in a row, and eventually when Pavlov sounded the tone, the dog salivated—*even when he did not get any meat powder.* Pavlov was thrilled. He had discovered an important learning process, which has come to be known as classical conditioning.

Unconditioned stimulus (US) A stimulus which produces a natural, biological response with no prior learning.

How the Process Works   Let's look more closely at how this type of learning, or conditioning, occurred. (see Figure 3.3 for an illustration of this process.) At first, the dog salivated only when he received food. This is a normal, instinctive response; there is no learning involved in this. This is a key point: *Classical conditioning occurs only with involuntary responses,* such as salivation, eye-blinking, or, as we will see later, fear. So, at this point, we call the food the **unconditioned stimulus (US)**, and we call the salivation the **unconditioned response (UR)**. They are unconditioned because they are instinctive; they are not learned. The learning process begins when a **neutral stimulus (NS)**, such as the sound of the tone, is paired with the unconditioned stimulus (food). During this phase of the learning process, the sound of the tone must be immediately followed by the arrival of food, and this pairing must happen several times in a row. Eventually, the dog learns to associate the sound of the tone with food, and he will salivate simply upon hearing the tone. At this point, the stimulus that was previously the neutral stimulus (the tone) becomes the **conditioned stimulus (CS)**, and the salivation that follows it becomes the **conditioned response (CR).** Learning, or classical conditioning, has occurred

Unconditioned response (UR) A natural, biological response to a stimulus with no prior learning.

Neutral stimulus (NS) A stimulus which is not meaningful.

Conditioned stimulus (CS) A previously neutral stimulus that has become associated with an unconditioned stimulus.

Conditioned response (CR) A learned response to conditioned stimulus.

Critical Thinking **QUESTION** What similar examples from your own life can you think of, especially if you have a pet?

Another powerful example of classical conditioning in action is an experiment conducted by John Watson in the early days of behaviorist study. The subject of Watson's study was a little boy named Albert. At the beginning of the study, Watson let Albert play with a harmless white rat. Albert exhibited no fear of the rat and played with him comfortably. Then, while little Albert was playing with the rat, Watson stood behind Albert and loudly hit a steel rod with a hammer. Not surprisingly, the sound startled Albert and caused him to cry (this reaction was an involuntary, *unconditioned* response to an *unconditioned* stimulus, because it is *instinctive* for a small child to be frightened at a loud sound). Watson repeated his actions, hammering the steel rod each time Albert

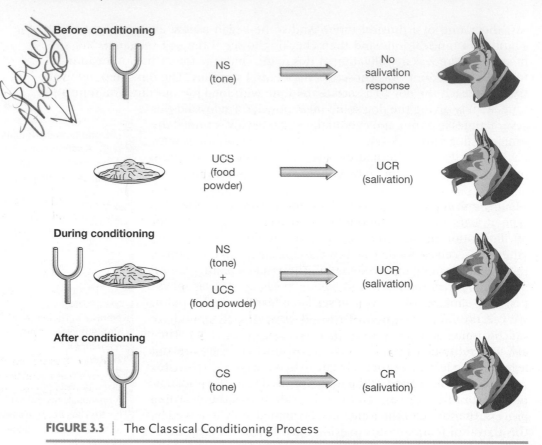

Before conditioning

NS (tone) ⟹ No salivation response

UCS (food powder) ⟹ UCR (salivation)

During conditioning

NS (tone) + UCS (food powder) ⟹ UCR (salivation)

After conditioning

CS (tone) ⟹ CR (salivation)

FIGURE 3.3 | The Classical Conditioning Process

began to play with the rat. By pairing the unconditioned stimulus (the loud noise) with the neutral stimulus (the rat), Watson was conditioning the child to associate the rat with fear. After this occurred several times, Albert began to show fear of the rat even when the steel rod was not being banged by the hammer. What began as an unconditioned response (fear) to a loud noise became a conditioned response when it came as a result of exposure to the rat. Through classical conditioning, little Albert learned to fear rats.

Watson didn't stop there. Through a phase of classical conditioning called **generalization**, little Albert also learned to be afraid of rabbits and even dogs. Generalization is when the response occurs upon exposure to a stimulus that is similar to the original conditioned stimulus, or in other words, when the scope of the conditioned stimulus broadens so that the response occurs more frequently. In this example, little Albert originally showed no fear of rats, but learned to fear them when they were associated with a loud noise. To a small boy,

Generalization When a conditioned response occurs upon exposure to a stimulus that is similar to the original conditioned stimulus.

a large white rat is similar in appearance to a small white rabbit (they are both furry, white, with similar shapes), so little Albert's conditioned fear was generalized to a rabbit and eventually to a dog.

Today, the psychological community has clear ethical standards that must be met by all research studies. Watson's study would never meet today's standards, because teaching a child to be afraid of animals is clearly unethical. This example, though, dramatically illustrates how irrational fears, or **phobias**, can develop.

Phobias Irrational fears.

What Watson should have done was to reverse the procedure. **Extinction** is the phase of classical conditioning that involves eliminating the conditioned response. This is accomplished by repeated exposure to the conditioned stimulus *without* pairing it with the unconditioned stimulus, so that the conditioned response becomes extinct. Pavlov accomplished this with his dogs by sounding the tone a number of times without following it with an offer of food. As a result, the dogs eventually forgot that the tone was an indicator that food was coming, and they no longer salivated at the sound of it. Later, after this extinction had occurred, once in a while the dogs would unexpectedly salivate at the sound of the tone, in what is known as **spontaneous recovery**, but it happened less and less frequently and eventually disappeared.

Extinction The phase of classical conditioning that involves eliminating the conditioned response.

Spontaneous recovery Occasional, unpredictable recurrence of a conditioned response that has become extinct.

In the case of little Albert, a simple reversal of the process probably would not have been enough for his conditioned fear to become extinct. As you may know, phobias can be very powerful and difficult to eliminate. Watson probably would have had to recondition little Albert to like rats by starting an entire new classical conditioning procedure.

Classical conditioning can be useful in our human relations when we use it to help us understand others' behavior that seems surprising or unusual to us. For example, people who have what seems to be an irrational fear of something (such as driving, crowded places, or even intimacy) may have developed that fear through classical conditioning earlier in life if they had a bad experience associated with the object of their fear. In the same way, a person could develop strong positive associations to certain situations or types of people.

Critical Thinking QUESTION

Consider how classical conditioning may have facilitated the development of one of your current relationships, either personally or professionally. Hint: Think about first impressions of people, and how we sometimes meet someone who reminds us of someone else.

To examine how classical conditioning plays a role in your relations with others, turn to Activity 3.2.

Operant Conditioning

Classical conditioning explains some of our behavior, but as you now know, it is limited to behavior that involves involuntary responses. What about the many behaviors we exhibit that are voluntary, such as going to school or doing the laundry? According to behaviorists, these voluntary behaviors are also learned, by a process called **operant conditioning**. Operant conditioning relies on the **law of effect**, which states that behaviors followed by positive consequences are more likely to be repeated, and behaviors followed by negative consequences are less likely to be repeated. As you might guess, operant conditioning works based on what we typically think of as reward and punishment.

Operant conditioning A type of learning based on associating behaviors with the consequences they have previously produced.

Law of effect Behaviors followed by positive consequences are more likely to be repeated, and behaviors followed by negative consequences are less likely to be repeated.

Reinforcement A consequence that increases the likelihood of the behavior being repeated.

Positive reinforcement A consequence that increases likelihood of a behavior by adding something pleasant.

Negative reinforcement A consequence that increases likelihood of a behavior by taking away or avoiding something unpleasant.

Reinforcement   *Reinforcement* is the term behaviorists use for what we think of as rewards. In operant conditioning, there are two types of reinforcement: positive reinforcement and negative reinforcement. Contrary to what you might assume, though, negative reinforcement is not the same as punishment. Instead, think of **reinforcement** as anything that increases the likelihood of the behavior being repeated. Since punishment decreases the likelihood of a behavior being repeated (in theory, anyway), punishment cannot qualify as a type of reinforcement. We'll talk about punishment more in a moment, but first let's make the distinction between positive reinforcement and negative reinforcement.

First, keep in mind that all reinforcement increases the likelihood of the behavior being repeated. Then, think of **positive reinforcement** as adding something pleasant (or positive) that increases the likelihood of the behavior being repeated, and **negative reinforcement** as taking away something unpleasant (or negative) that increases the chance of the behavior being repeated. For example, if you offer someone $10 to do your laundry each week, you are giving something positive (money) that you expect will increase the likelihood of the person continuing to do your laundry. Other examples of this basic "reward" principle abound. Perhaps you know of a movie rental store that offers you a free rental after you have rented 10 movies, or a pizza place that offers you a free pizza after you buy 10 pizzas. These marketing gimmicks work based on the principle of positive reinforcement: The movie rental stores and pizza places are adding something pleasant (the free movie or pizza) that increases the likelihood of your repeating the behavior (shopping at their store). An even more common example of positive reinforcement is the paycheck that we get for working: We continue to go to work, even when we would rather do something else, because we know we will be "rewarded" with money. Examples of positive reinforcement abound in our human relations. How many different rewards (either tangible or intangible) can you think of that you get from your relationships? Conversely, in what ways do you "reward" people in your work or personal relationships?

 *Critical Thinking* QUESTION Identify three aspects of your relationships that have been shaped by positive reinforcement.

Now let's consider negative reinforcement. A good example of this principle involves taking medicine. Imagine that you have a bad cold. You try a new kind of cold medicine, and it makes you feel much better. Chances are, the next time you have a cold, you'll take that same medicine again, right? That is because something unpleasant (negative) was taken away (the cold symptoms), which will probably result in your repeating the behavior (taking the same medicine next time). Examples of negative reinforcement can also be seen in relationships when we do something to avoid or reduce someone's anger, disapproval, or other negative feeling toward us. This ultimately strengthens our avoidance behavior, because each time we do it, we avoid the negative experience of the other person's anger. We can even see negative reinforcement at work in studying for exams: If you are feeling worried about an upcoming test, and you overcome the worry by studying for the test, then you are removing the unpleasant worry by studying, which should increase the likelihood of your studying the next time you feel worried about a test (Figure 3.4).

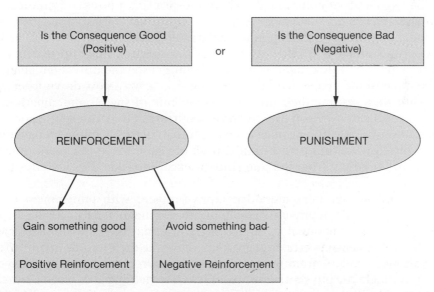

FIGURE 3.4 | Positive Reinforcement, Negative Reinforcement, or Punishment? Use this flowchart to help you figure out whether a behavior is a result of positive reinforcement, negative reinforcement, or punishment.

Critical Thinking
QUESTION
What examples can you find in your own life—either at work or at home—of negative reinforcement?

Punishment   Punishment has the opposite effect. **Punishment** is anything that decreases the chances of the behavior being repeated. Examples of punishment are

> **Punishment** Anything that decreases the chances of the behavior being repeated.

easy to find, but remember that, because we're dealing with operant conditioning, punishment (and reinforcement) only applies to voluntary behavior. For example, if you get a speeding ticket on the freeway, you will probably be less likely to speed in the near future. What other examples of punishment come to mind?

B. F. Skinner, the founder of operant conditioning, suggested that punishment is the most widely used form of behavioral control in Western society (1953). Does that mean it is the most effective? Skinner, and most other psychologists as well, thought not. Although punishment may be an effective way to stop a behavior immediately (such as when a child is about to do something that may cause him bodily harm), it has not been found to be an effective way of changing behaviors in the long run.

Problems with Punishment   In fact, punishment often does more harm than good. One problem with punishment is that it doesn't teach an alternative, more acceptable behavior. Consider the child whose parent spanks her for throwing a temper tantrum while she is playing with several other children. The spanking isn't teaching the child a better option for playing nicely with her friends. By contrast, paying closer attention to the child and providing positive reinforcement when she exhibits good behavior is more likely to have a lasting effect (not to mention a more beneficial one) on the child's behavior.

A second problem with punishment is that it often ends up teaching the person to avoid getting caught, rather than eliminating the unwanted behavior. For example, some people who get speeding tickets may slow down for a short while, but then resume their previous higher rate of speed, remembering this time to keep a closer eye on their rear-view mirror, so they can spot a police car in time to slow down and avoid getting caught. Similarly, a young teenager who gets punished when her parents find a pack of cigarettes in her room probably won't learn anything from the punishment except to hide the cigarettes better next time.

The third and perhaps most dangerous problem with punishment is that when the punishment is physical (a spanking, for example), it may actually demonstrate that when someone does something you don't like, you should respond with physical violence. As children grow up, they take their lessons in how to deal with various situations from their parents or caregivers. If these important role models routinely use physical punishment when something goes wrong, the child may learn that hitting or spanking is the normal way to deal with people when there is a problem to be resolved. Research over the past 25 years has powerfully demonstrated this effect (see, for example, Bandura and Walters, 1959; Patterson, Chamberlain, & Reid, 1982; Widom, 1989).

All in all, most experts do not consider punishment the most effective means of changing behavior in most situations. Instead, it is recommended that people look for positive behaviors and reinforce them, so that they increase in frequency, thus reducing and perhaps even eliminating the need for punishment.

Now, turn to Activity 3.3 at the end of this chapter to explore how operant conditioning plays a role in your own family or work environment.

So far, we have two contrasting explanations for why people do what they do. Psychoanalytic theorists believe that our personality is a result of the way our unconscious resolves internal conflicts, and behaviorists believe that personality is a result of what we have learned via external programming from the various forces in our environment. The next theory we will discuss—social learning theory—shares the behaviorist belief that our environment influences our behavior, but suggests that our individual thought processes have some influence on our responses.

Observational Learning

In 1961, an experiment at Stanford University produced startling results that provided the foundation for a new personality theory. Psychologist Albert Bandura was conducting an experiment with preschool children and toys. He divided the children into two groups. Children in the first group began by working on an art project, each doing so individually while alone in the room. While the child was engaged in this, an adult in another part of the room was playing with some toys, including Tinkertoys, a mallet, and a Bobo doll (a large inflatable doll, weighted on the bottom so that it stands up). After a few minutes of playing with the Tinkertoys, the adult picked up the mallet, went over to the Bobo doll, and attacked it, beating it with the mallet, hitting and kicking it, all the while shouting, "Punch it in the nose," and "Kick it hard," and other aggressive phrases. Children in the second group merely worked alone in a room on an art project without having an adult in the same room acting aggressively toward a Bobo doll.

Next, the child was taken to a room filled with interesting toys and allowed to play with them. After a few minutes, an adult came in and told the child that these were the best toys and they must be saved for the other children. At that point the child was taken to a third room that contained some different toys, including a Bobo doll and a mallet. The child was left alone in the room to play, while being secretly observed through a two-way mirror by Bandura. The reactions of children in the first group varied considerably from those of children in the second group.

Children in the first group, who had been exposed to the adult yelling at and beating on the Bobo doll mimicked the adult's behavior. Many of them acted out their frustration by beating the Bobo doll and shouting the same phrases they had heard the adult shouting at the doll. By contrast, children who had not observed an adult attacking the doll played quietly with the other toys, even though they experienced the same frustration as the first group of children. Children in the first group had learned to act out their frustration and to do it by aggressively beating the doll—and they had learned this merely by observation.

This experiment, now considered a classic, confirmed Bandura's belief that not all learning is based on the trial-and-error principles of classical or operant conditioning. **Observational learning**, also known as modeling, is the process by which we learn behaviors by watching others engage in them. Indeed, suggested Bandura, efficiently interacting with others and the world requires that we take many cues or lessons from observing others' actions and words. Think of the many things we learn by watching others, ranging from simple behaviors like how to put on a hat, to social norms like which piece of silverware to use for different foods, to basic belief systems regarding religion, politics, or social issues. In fact, many of our prejudices are learned by observation, an issue we will address in Chapter 7.

> **Observational learning**
> The process by which we learn behaviors by watching others engage in them. Also known as modeling.

Critical Thinking **QUESTION** Can you think of three behaviors or attitudes you have learned by observation?

What Individual Factors Influence Our Responses? This modeling process is a type of learning that relies on mental activity, a cornerstone of social learning theory. This is where the social learning theorists disagree with the early behaviorists. Behaviorists did not acknowledge the role of the mind in learning; they focused strictly on behavior as a result of environmental stimuli. Social learning theorists argue that some behaviors can be learned through mental activity only, such as in modeling. They also believe that although environmental forces certainly provide stimuli, our individual responses to these stimuli may differ based on our own experiences. There are two primary factors that influence our experiences and, consequently, our responses.

One factor that influences our responses to stimuli is our *values*. Social learning theorists believe that we will respond to a stimulus only if we value it, or if it has a positive meaning to us. For example, Pavlov's dog learned to respond (salivate) to the sound of the tone because the tone was associated with meat, which the dog liked. Imagine that the dog didn't like the kind of meat that was being used—he wouldn't salivate, and classical conditioning would not occur. The early behaviorists didn't consider this, but the social learning theorists do.

Similarly, consider the primary reward system used in education: grades. Most people assume that students value high grades, and thus if a student studies hard for an exam and gets an A as a result, the student is likely to study hard the next time because the studying was positively reinforced by the A the last time. This works as long as the A is important to the student. But what if the student is carrying 15 credits, working full-time, and trying to support a family? In that situation, getting an A on a particular exam might not be as important as finishing a term paper in another class, or showing up at work to avoid getting fired. As a result, the A is not that effective as a positive reinforcement for studying in that situation, since it is not as highly valued as meeting other obligations the student has at that time.

Critical Thinking QUESTION Think of two specific differences we might expect to see in the values of individualists versus collectivists.

The second factor that influences our responses to stimuli is our *expectations about the outcome.* Let's continue with the example of grades. Imagine that we have two students who both study hard for an exam and subsequently get an A on it. The early behaviorists would suggest that both students will study hard the next time in anticipation of the A as positive reinforcement. Social learning theorists recognize another possibility, though. What if one of the students, Carly, has always gotten As when she has studied hard, but the other student, Thoa, has had less predictable experiences? In fact, Thoa has sometimes received an A when she studied hard, but sometimes received a D when she studied hard—on the other hand, she has also sometimes received an A when she hasn't studied much. Thoa would have very different expectations about the outcome of studying hard than Carly would. Thus, the A wouldn't work as well as a positive reinforcement for Thoa as it would for Carly.

To sum up, the social learning theorists agree with the early behaviorists that our environment influences our behavior, but their viewpoint is less rigid. Social learning theorists recognize the role of the mind in choosing behaviors, based on values and expectations about the outcome. Social learning theorists also believe that some behaviors can be learned simply by watching others.

Once again, there are numerous ways that this perspective can help us understand others' behavior. In the workplace, for example, why do some people meekly accept whatever the boss says, while others feel comfortable arguing or asking for explanations? Perhaps because they have been surrounded by role models who exhibited the same type of behavior they are now exhibiting, or because they highly value obedience or assertiveness. Similarly, we are often puzzled by the behavior of a friend or romantic partner in a relationship: Why, for example, do some people keep calling and leaving messages until they hear back from you, whereas others only leave one message? Social learning explanations for these different responses to the same situation could include influence of role models, the person's values, or their expectations about the outcome.

Interim SUMMARY #2

The behaviorist perspective argues that our personality is nothing more than the set of behaviors that our environment has conditioned us to exhibit. It includes both classical and operant conditioning. Classical conditioning is learning by association and happens when we associate an innocuous stimulus with a more meaningful stimulus that immediately follows it. As a result, we learn to respond to the innocuous stimulus in anticipation of the more meaningful stimulus. The salivation of Pavlov's dog to the sound of the tone and Little Albert's conditioned fear of rats are examples of classical conditioning.

Operant conditioning, a simpler concept, relies on the law of effect. Positive reinforcement occurs when we repeat a behavior because we have received a reward for it; negative reinforcement occurs when we learn that a particular behavior can help us avoid a negative consequence. In both situations, the consequence of our actions is a positive one, which should cause us to repeat the action the next time we experience that situation. Punishment is administering a negative consequence in an attempt to extinguish a behavior. Although punishment can help extinguish a behavior if it is administered effectively, it does not facilitate development of better behaviors.

Observational learning theory builds on the behaviorist perspective by demonstrating that learning can take place not just by direct experience, but by observation as well. In addition, it asserts that our values and our expectations about the outcome of a particular behavior also shape our personalities.

THE HUMANIST PERSPECTIVE

PREVIEW QUESTIONS

(1) According to humanistic psychologists, what shapes our personality?

(2) How does Carl Rogers define "fulfilling our potential," and what environmental factors do we need for this to happen?

(3) How does Abraham Maslow define "fulfilling our potential," and what environmental factors are necessary for this to happen?

(4) How does the humanist perspective help us understand ourselves and others better?

In the second half of the twentieth century, another theory emerged to explain human behavior. **Humanists** believe that we are all born with an innate drive to reach our potential as good, contributing persons to our society (contributing in whatever way suits our own strengths). This theory is essentially an optimistic one that views human nature in the best possible light; it provides a stark contrast to the conflict-driven psychoanalytic theory and the environment-driven behaviorist theory. Two psychologists typically come to mind when we think of humanist theories: Carl Rogers and Abraham Maslow.

> **Humanists theory** The theory which suggests we are all born with an innate drive to reach our potential as good, contributing persons to our society.

Carl Rogers's Self Theory

You recall our discussion of Carl Rogers in Chapter 2, which revolved around development of self-esteem. Rogers believed that self-esteem was essential to growth and fulfillment of one's potential, and he believed that positive self-esteem developed through unconditional positive regard. (You may wish to refer to Chapter 2 to refresh your memory about this.) For Rogers, fulfilling one's potential meant becoming a **fully functioning person**, or one who gets along well with others by offering unconditional positive regard and genuinely caring about them. If a person receives unconditional positive regard, he will develop good self-esteem, which will

> **Fully functioning person** One who gets along well with others by offering unconditional positive regard and genuinely caring about them.

enable him to treat other people with genuine concern and respect, even if their viewpoints differ from his own.

Rogers believed that we are born with this potential inside us. If our environment is a positive one, which fosters self-esteem, we will reach this potential and become fully functioning. If our environment impedes our progress toward this potential by only offering conditional positive regard, our self-esteem will be low, and as a result we will not be able to treat others with the respect and genuine caring they deserve. As you might guess, each of the two possible paths here tends to perpetuate itself. If we feel good about ourselves and treat others well, we will probably continue to feel good, and so on. If we have low self-esteem and treat others poorly, our self-esteem will remain low and our relations with others will continue to deteriorate.

Rogers maintained an optimistic viewpoint about the possibility of change, though. If we are in an environment that is offering conditional positive regard (causing low self-esteem), the situation can be reversed by a change in the environment. Rogers himself practiced this belief in his work with clients who came to him for psychotherapy. He believed that his role was to provide the environment of unconditional positive regard, wherein the client learned that she was a worthy person even if some of her behaviors were negative. Over time, this unconditional positive regard would increase the client's self-esteem, and she would become a more fully functioning person as a result.

> **Critical Thinking QUESTION** Give some examples of unconditional and/or conditional positive regard that you have received in your life. How did you feel as a result of these messages?

Maslow's Need Hierarchy

Abraham Maslow also believed that humans are born with an innate drive to maximize our potential. For him, though, maximizing one's potential didn't revolve around self-esteem; it revolved around what Maslow called *self-actualization*. Maslow believed that we all have unique strengths and capabilities, and to strive for self-actualization is to strive to achieve our maximum potential in these areas whether they be intellectual, athletic, artistic, self-understanding, or something else. In other words, **self-actualization** occurs when an individual has developed a complete sense of who she is and what her strengths are and routinely acts in a way that is consistent with that.

Maslow believed that in our quest for self-actualization, several other needs may impede us along the way; these levels of need form what is known as **Maslow's need hierarchy** (see Figure 3.5). The lower order needs must be fulfilled before the higher order need can be addressed, according to Maslow. The most basic needs are our *physiological or biological needs*, such as needs for food, water, air, and to maintain a comfortable body temperature (to stay warm in cold weather and cool in hot weather). When these needs are met, we then concern ourselves with meeting the next level of needs, our *safety needs*. Safety needs revolve around the need to keep ourselves safe

> **Self-actualization** When an individual has developed a complete sense of who she is and what her strengths are, and routinely acts in a way that is consistent with that.

> **Maslow's need hierarchy** A model which suggests that lower-order needs must be met before we can focus on higher-order needs.

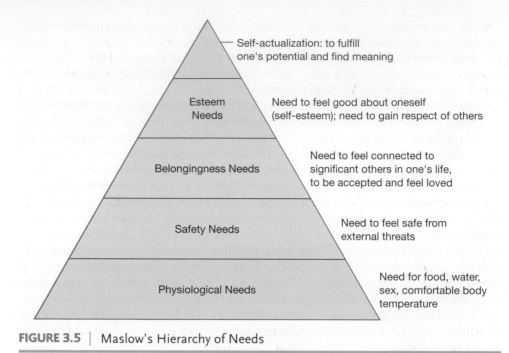

FIGURE 3.5 | Maslow's Hierarchy of Needs

from physical harm and include examples such as living in a safe neighborhood, having locks on the doors, driving a car with fully functioning brakes, and so on.

 Can you think of a situation in which someone might not be concerned with personal safety because of worry about meeting physiological needs?

The third level of needs in Maslow's hierarchy is *belongingness needs,* or the needs to feel connected to others in our social world. Humans are social creatures and need to be part of a group with whom we share certain basic beliefs and values. Belongingness needs may be satisfied by feeling connected with our family, close friends, people at work, a religious group, or any other group with whom we identify. Once these and the other lower order needs are met, we can then work on the fourth level of needs, our *esteem needs.* Esteem needs include both the need to feel good about oneself (self-esteem) and the need to be respected by significant others. There are many ways to meet these needs. For example, some people improve their self-esteem through working out, others do it by enrolling in college, and others might strive for better self-esteem by getting out of a negative job environment and into a better one. In fact, self-esteem has become such a focus in our society that bookstores abound with titles offering various ways to improve self-esteem.

Self Actualization   Finally, when all of the lower order needs are met, Maslow says that we can then strive for self-actualization, or work toward reaching our potential in some way that is meaningful to us as individuals. This can take a variety of forms, based on an individual's values and interests. For one person self-actualization might be immersing herself in her career; for another it might be achieving personal excellence in athletic or artistic pursuits; for another it could involve becoming fully developed and connected with his family in his role as father, and so forth. This is a formidable goal.

As Maslow put it, a self-actualizing person "has within him a pressure toward unity of personality, toward spontaneous expressiveness, toward full individuality and identity, toward seeing the truth rather than being blind, toward being creative, toward being good and a lot else. That is, the human being is so constructed that he presses toward . . . serenity, kindness, courage, honesty, love, unselfishness, and goodness" (Maslow, 1968, p. 155). This statement truly seems to capture Maslow's belief that we are innately driven toward self-actualization, as well as the characteristics he thought represented the pinnacle of humanity and a self-actualized life (Table 3.2).

It is also important to recognize that self-actualization manifests itself in very different ways among different individuals, based on their values and interests. In our individualistic culture, we might assume that self-actualization involves reaching one's potential in terms of career advancement, but this is not the case for everyone. Interestingly, Maslow believed that many people do not ever reach this level, because they get stalled in the fourth level. For example, someone might be feeling so good about herself and the respect she is getting from others that her motivation to climb higher toward maximizing her potential might dissolve in the waters of her positive self-esteem. If she does reach this level, there is no guarantee that she will stay there. Maslow thought that we continually move up and down on the hierarchy throughout our lives, as situations change. For example, you might have a great life, a great family, a great job, have all your needs met, and be working on self-actualization—but then you lose your job, which threatens your ability to keep your mortgage or rent paid and food on the table for your family. Suddenly, you are no longer concerned with self-actualization, self-esteem, belonging, or even safety needs—you are focusing only on the most basic physiological needs such as food and shelter.

Culture and the Hierarchy of Needs These needs that Maslow theorized about are uniquely Western needs, at least in terms of the hierarchy in which he

---

TABLE 3.2 | Characteristics of Self-Actualizing People

According to Maslow, people who are able to achieve self-actualization share some common characteristics, which include the following:

• Self-acceptance	• Democratic values and attitudes
• Independence and autonomy	• Spontaneity
• Need for privacy	• Creativity
• Resistance to conformity	• Interest in the welfare of others
• Ability to achieve deep, meaningful relationships	• Courage

arranged them. A different hierarchy was found in a recent study that included both American students and South Korean students (Sheldon et al., 2001). In this study, self-esteem was the highest-rated need, followed by autonomy (the ability to choose based on one's own interests), competence, and relatedness (in that order). Interestingly, self-actualization was much further down the list in this study, as were physical thriving (similar to physiological needs) and security (similar to safety).

Applying the Humanist Theory to Human Relations

All in all, the humanists' optimistic theory offers a refreshing alternative to the pessimistic viewpoint of the psychoanalysts and the deterministic perspective of the behaviorists. In the humanist view, our innate tendency is to grow in a positive direction that helps ourselves as well as the world around us, and positive environmental conditions help us reach that goal. People who are acting in ways that hurt others or themselves are thought to do so because of negative environmental conditions that can be changed, according to the humanists.

For example, you may notice that some people in your life routinely trust others, and other people behave with more suspicion. Carl Rogers would explain this difference by looking to these individuals' environments and the feedback they were receiving from important others. He would expect that the trusting person was experiencing an environment of unconditional positive regard, which promotes trust in others. By contrast, he would expect to find conditions of conditional positive regard in the suspicious person's background, which he would assume inhibited that person from being able to freely trust others. Maslow would be more likely to expect that the trusting person was self-actualized, whereas the suspicious person was probably working on a lower-order need.

Both these theories are useful to us. Rogers's theory will make more sense in some situations; Maslow's theory will make more sense and seem more applicable in others. Taken together, they encourage us to respond to others' difficult or perplexing behavior with compassion, and endeavor to understand how the person's environment might be restricting the innate tendency toward goodness and positive growth.

 *Critical Thinking* QUESTION Humanist theories are appealing to many people, because they seem logical and easy to relate to our own lives. What examples can you think of from your own life that can be explained by one or both of the humanist theories? Can you also think of some examples of situations or people you have heard of that don't fit one of the humanist theories?

THE TRAIT THEORIES

PREVIEW QUESTIONS

(1) According to trait theorists, what shapes our personality?

(2) How can trait theory help us understand others better and improve our relations?

write *Big five theory* ← *Big five theory*

INTROVERSION reserved, quiet, contemplative	EXTRAVERSION outgoing, friendly, sociable, talkative
NEUROTICISM anxious, moody, insecure, worried	EMOTIONAL STABILITY calm, relaxed, secure, stable
LOW OPENNESS traditional, practical, conforming, likes routine	HIGH OPENNESS imaginative, curious, likes variety, nonconforming
LOW CONSCIENTIOUSNESS indecisive, spontaneous, disorganized, unreliable	HIGH CONSCIENTIOUSNESS reliable, organized, persevering, self-disciplined
LOW AGREEABLENESS stubborn, suspicious, hostile, callous	HIGH AGREEABLENESS trusting, good-natured, helpful, accommodating

FIGURE 3.6 | The Big Five Trait Theory

Any discussion of the question "Why do people do what they do?" must include one of the oldest explanations of personality: the trait theories. Trait theories suggest that people do what they do based on **personality traits**, or characteristics that predict their behavior consistently across a wide range of situations. A number of different trait theories have been proposed, each of which used a somewhat different set of traits, but the current predominant trait theory is called the **Big Five theory**. The Big Five trait theory suggests that personality can be measured on five major dimensions. Each dimension represents a continuum, and every person falls somewhere on the continuum for that dimension (see Figure 3.6). A person's placement on each dimension is usually measured by a questionnaire, and together the placement on the five dimensions makes up one's personality.

> **Personality traits** Characteristics that predict a person's behavior consistently across a wide range of situations.

> **Big Five theory** A theory which suggests that personality can be measured on five major dimensions.

The Big Five Theory

The first dimension of the Big Five model is **extraversion/introversion**, with extraversion and introversion being the two opposite traits at each end of the continuum. Extraverted people are outgoing, friendly, and gain energy from social situations. Introverted people are more quiet and reserved, though recent research shows that sometimes introverts can be just as gregarious in social situations as extraverts; the key seems to be in the source of energy. Extraverts gain energy from social situations, whereas introverts gain energy from solitude. For example, some introverted professors are highly energetic and engaging while teaching a class, but may need some time alone later to reenergize themselves. Not knowing

> **Extraversion/introversion** A personality trait based on a person's preferences for social or contemplative environments.

about the need for solitude, many people might be fooled into thinking those professors are extraverts. Extraverted professors, by contrast, would feel energized after leading an exciting discussion. Because we usually don't know where a person gets his or her energy, it is sometimes difficult to tell an introvert from an extravert unless we know the person well.

Neuroticism A personality trait characterized by anxiety, nervousness, self-consciousness, and moodiness.

The second trait in the Big Five is known as **neuroticism**, and is characterized by anxiety, nervousness, self-consciousness, and moodiness. The opposite of neuroticism is emotional stability: These people tend to be relaxed, secure, calm, and unflappable. Research suggests that high neuroticism is associated with lessened ability to adapt to social situations (Chaikin, Derlega, Bayma, & Shaw, 1975).

This interesting study asked subjects to carry on a telephone conversation about various topics with someone they didn't know. Topics ranged from impersonal topics such as where one lived, to more intimate topics such as sexual behavior and feelings about parents. Subjects who were low in neuroticism were able to comfortably adapt to various intimacy levels, accepting whatever intimacy level was set by the telephone partner and responding in kind. High-neuroticism subjects, on the other hand, gave mid-level information about themselves regardless of the intimacy level set by the telephone partner. Researchers suggested that these high-neuroticism subjects' focus on their own reactions might be interfering with their ability to attend to environmental cues. In other words, people with higher levels of neuroticism are more sensitive and attuned to their own emotional reactions, which may distract them from environmental cues or signals and interfere with their cognitive processing.

Openness to experience A personality trait characterized by originality, imagination, independence, curiosity, and broadmindedness.

The third Big Five trait is **openness to experience**, which is characterized by originality, imagination, independence, curiosity, and broadmindedness. People low in this trait tend to be conventional, down-to-earth, and more likely to choose something familiar over something new and untried. People high in openness to experience welcome change and see it as a challenge. Research also suggests that openness to experience is related to coping strategies. A large study of people who had experienced stressful events noted that subjects high in openness to experience used humor as a coping mechanism, whereas subjects low in the trait tended to rely on faith (in God or in others) (McCrae & Costa, 1986).

Conscientiousness A personality trait characterized by dependability, efficiency, persistence, and a strong sense of order.

Conscientiousness, the fourth trait in the Big Five constellation, is characterized by dependability, efficiency, persistence, and a strong sense of order. These are the people who can be relied on no matter what. People low in the trait tend to be disorganized, irresponsible, and careless, characteristics that bode ill in the area of human relations. Research in this area indicates that conscientiousness may account for the missing link between aptitude scores and academic performance. In other words, conscientiousness may play a role in school achievement by accounting for the "will to achieve" (Digman, 1989) considered integral to success.

The final Big Five trait, **agreeableness**, plays an especially important role in human relations. People high in this trait are described as kind, sincere, courteous, helpful, patient, honest, and cooperative. They are committed to their friends, family, and the general good of society (Goldberg, 1990). People low in agreeableness tend to be argumentative, cruel, untrustworthy, and manipulative. Both agreeableness and conscientiousness have been found to correlate with psychological well-being, presumably because the positive qualities of people high in these traits foster good relationships and quality of life (McCrae & Costa, 1991). Interestingly, collectivists tend to score higher on both of these scales than do individualists (Triandis & Suh, 2002).

> **Agreeableness** A personality trait which includes behaviors such as kind, sincere, courteous, helpful, patient, honest, and cooperative.

Applying the Big Five Theory

As you might guess, certain traits tend to facilitate intimate relationships, a finding that was reported in the *Journal of Marriage and the Family* (Bouchard, Lussier, & Sabourin, 1999). The researchers assessed 446 couples on the 5 traits and compared them to adjustment and satisfaction in the marriage. Overall, personality traits accounted for almost 20% of marital adjustment for the women in the sample and 11% of marital adjustment for the men. The trait of neuroticism played the biggest role in this effect: Both women and men who scored high in neuroticism were less well-adjusted in their marriage. This makes sense: Emotional stability would help a person cope with the inevitable ups and downs of a relationship.

In addition, the men's marital adjustment was influenced by agreeableness, as well as openness and conscientiousness. For the women in the study, agreeableness contributed to marital adjustment, but openness and conscientiousness did not. It seems, then, that agreeableness is a factor for both men and women in their relationship health. Whether a person was introverted or extraverted didn't make a difference for men or women in the study.

Trait theory has also been examined quite a bit cross-culturally. A large number of studies indicate that these same five traits are indeed the major determinants of personality in collectivistic as well as individualistic cultures, although they do not predict behavior as well in collectivistic cultures as they do in individualistic cultures (Church & Katigbak, 2000). If we think about what we've learned about the basic values of these two types of cultures and how these values affect our self-concepts, this makes perfect sense: Given individualists' value on self-determination and autonomy, it stands to reason that they would act in ways consistent with their sense of self. Collectivists, by contrast, would place the needs of the group above their own, resulting at times in behavior that is less characteristic of their self-concept and more consistent with the demands of the situation.

Finally, a good deal of research has examined the development of these five traits over the lifespan. Across many cultures, extraversion, neuroticism, and openness tend to decline as a person grows from adolescence into adulthood; during the same period, agreeableness and conscientiousness increase. After about the age of 30, traits tend to remain relatively stable.

Understanding these traits and how they reveal themselves in others' behavior can be very helpful to us in our relations with others. Often, when we are first getting to know a person, his behavior and speech provides indications of how agreeable or open he is, how conscientious, or how neurotic. Similarly, we often get a feel for whether a person is frequently drawn to social situations, or if she often prefers solitude or introspection. Accurate observations can help us determine if a person is similar to us or not, and also make better predictions about how an individual might react to a certain situation. In the workplace, this type of information can be invaluable in decisions regarding hiring and assignment of job duties.

Critical Thinking QUESTION — Think of someone you know well and guess how high that person might score on each of the five traits. How does this information help you predict how the person might react in a particular situation?

PERSONALITY THEORIES: THE BIG PICTURE

As you can see, the field of personality psychology is broad and varied, ranging from optimistic to pessimistic, from unconscious motivations to behavioral explanations, from psychological needs to traits. So what is the bottom line? How are we supposed to make sense of it all?

The answer is simpler than you might think. Rather than trying to determine which theory is "the right theory," consider instead the advantages of having multiple theories to call on in our efforts to understand human nature. After all, humans are a broad and varied group of people, so it stands to reason that we need a broad and varied group of theories to understand everyone. As you go through life, there will be times when Freud's theory is the key to understanding someone you know, other times when behaviorist or social learning theory provides the insight you need, and still other times when you will call on your knowledge of humanist or trait theory to help you understand someone. The key to understanding human nature, then, begins with an understanding of each of the major theories of personality.

Interim SUMMARY #3

Humanist theory takes a benevolent approach to human nature, asserting that we are driven by a strong internal need to maximize our potential and make positive contributions to our society. Carl Rogers believed that we reach this goal primarily by receiving unconditional positive regard, which helps us develop positive self-esteem. Abraham Maslow's theory argued that we must work through a hierarchy of needs to become self-actualized.

The trait theorists believe that there are certain core personality characteristics that, once developed in each of us, remain relatively stable throughout our life and thus comprise our personality. The predominant trait theory, the Big Five theory, finds that these traits are extraversion/introversion, neuroticism, openness to experience, agreeableness, and conscientiousness.

CHAPTER TERMS

Personality
Psychoanalytic theory
Conscious
Unconscious
Preconscious
Id
Ego
Superego
Defense mechanisms
Rationalization
Repression
Displacement
Projection
Reaction formation
Regression
Sublimation

Behaviorist theory
Conditioning
Classical conditioning
Unconditioned stimulus
Unconditioned response
Neutral stimulus
Conditioned stimulus
Conditioned response
Generalization
Phobia
Extinction
Spontaneous recovery
Operant conditioning
Law of effect
Reinforcement
Positive reinforcement

Negative reinforcement
Punishment
Observational learning
Humanist theory
Fully functioning person
Self-actualization
Maslow's need hierarchy
Personality traits
Big Five theory
Extraversion/introversion
Neuroticism
Openness to experience
Conscientiousness
Agreeableness

ACTIVITY 3.1

LISTENING TO THE FORCES OF YOUR PERSONALITY
The Id, the Ego, and the Superego in Decision Making

GOAL: *To understand how you and someone close to you are influenced by your id, your ego, and your superego in decision making.*

PART 1: YOUR OWN DECISIONS

1. Think of a recent decision you made. Write a brief description of it in the following space.

   Put my math Homework away cause I cant figure it out.

2. As you reflect on that decision, answer the following questions:

   a. What was your id urging you to do?

   Figure it out anyway.

   b. What was your ego encouraging you to do?

   Put it away and work on PSY 101.

   c. What was your superego encouraging you to do?

   Read ch 3 in PSY 101, then later on on live to Kahn academy, and see if that will help me in math.

d. In the decision you made, analyze what force of your personality had the most power and explain how you know it was this force.

My I.d. Because I have been struggling w/ two sections for 2 days now.

e. Which (if any) defense mechanisms helped resolve your anxiety in this situation? Explain how.

Sublimation, Because instead of giving up. I put it away, & worked on this homework.

f. In general, what force of your personality most often rules your decisions? How well does that work for you? What adjustments could you try to make to improve the outcome of your decisions and achieve a better-balanced personality?

① superego ② seem to work real well up-until about 3 months ago. ③ Have more empathy & pick and choose my words better. when I get upset think before I speak

PART 2: OTHER DECISIONS THAT AFFECT YOUR LIFE

1. Think of someone close to you who sometimes makes choices that frustrate or anger you. Give an example of one of those choices.

① Does everything last minute. is a know it all.

2. Using your new knowledge of Freud's personality theory, analyze your friend's decision by considering what personality force seemed to be driving that decision, and why.

Id & maybe Ego. cause he is hurting and does not want to deal with the emotions, Just wants to bury them.

3. How can your new understanding of your friend's decision-making style help you in maintaining a good relationship with him or her?

Have more empathy learn to leave him alone, when he is upset or frustrated, leave the room.

ACTIVITY 3.2

CLASSICAL CONDITIONING AND YOU

GOAL: *To deepen your understanding of classical conditioning by identifying ways it has affected your own behavior and analyzing the process involved (see Figure 3.3 to review your knowledge of classical conditioning.)*

1. Think of a behavior or reaction you have in a particular relationship that you have learned through classical conditioning. (Remember, for the behavior or reaction to fit the classical conditioning model, it must be involuntary and based on an instinctive response.) Write the behavior in the following space.

_____

_____

_____

2. Now, test your idea by identifying the various stimuli and responses involved in your learned behavior. Use the diagram in Figure 3.3 to refresh your memory about the process of classical conditioning, and sketch a similar diagram in the following space that shows the following:

■ How your behavior began with an unconditioned (instinctive) response to an unconditioned stimulus

■ What neutral stimulus began to become associated with the unconditioned stimulus

■ How the neutral stimulus became the conditioned stimulus when it began producing the conditioned response when the original (unconditioned) stimulus was not present

_____

_____

_____

_____

_____

3. Has your behavior become generalized to any other stimuli? Explain.

_____

_____

_____

4. If you wanted to eliminate your behavior, how could you accomplish that? List the steps that would be involved.

_____

_____

_____

ACTIVITY 3.3

OPERANT CONDITIONING IN YOUR FAMILY RELATIONS
Summary Application Paper

For this activity, you will consider the many ways that operant conditioning has played and continues to play a role in your family relations. The best way to do this is to write a summary application paper. The first part of your paper should summarize the main concepts involved in operant conditioning. Use the relevant terms, but explain them in your own words, as you would explain them to someone who doesn't know what they mean. Be sure your summary also includes a description of how the various concepts involved in operant conditioning work together in changing behavior.

In the second part of your paper, apply the information you summarized to your own family's behavior (alternatively, you can apply it to people in your work environment or your circle of friends). Give examples that show how the various principles of operant conditioning are illustrated in the behavior of the people you are discussing. Be sure to include at least one example of positive reinforcement, one example of negative reinforcement, and one example of punishment.

Finally, analyze the effectiveness of the behaviors you have been discussing. In other words, do these behaviors contribute to the healthy functioning of your family (or work or friendships), or detract from it? Make some suggestions of how you could use operant conditioning principles to improve the functioning of these relationships.

Your paper should be about 3 pages (typed, double-spaced).

EMOTIONS, STRESS, AND HUMAN RELATIONS

There can be no knowledge without emotion. We may be aware of a truth, but until we have felt its force, it is not ours. To the cognition of the brain must be added the experience of the soul.

—ARNOLD BENNETT

In the three previous chapters, we have explored how our culture, our sense of self, our stage of life, and our personality influence our relations with others. In this chapter, we will complete our examination of internal factors in human relations by looking at how our emotions and stress influence our interactions with others.

Mark and Carmen, recent college graduates, got married last year and relocated to a new state where they both had good job offers. Last Sunday, they were supposed to go to a barbecue at the home of one of Mark's coworkers. An unexpected rainstorm hit, though, and at the last minute the barbecue was canceled. Mark was disappointed at the news, but Carmen seemed pleased. Noticing that they were reacting differently to the news but not knowing why, they each felt hurt.

Have you ever been in a similar situation, where you and someone important to you had different emotional reactions to the same event? When we're in a situation like this, it is sometimes hard to imagine how someone else could feel differently than we do. And too often, this leads to conflict in our relations with others.

How does it happen that people have different emotional reactions to the same event? Is there anything we can do to keep this phenomenon from damaging our relationships? These questions can be answered by taking a closer look at research findings in the study of emotions.

THE STUDY OF EMOTION

(1) How do our thoughts influence our emotions?

(2) What are seven irrational beliefs that commonly lead to emotional reasoning? How can they negatively affect our relations with others?

(3) What irrational beliefs affect you the most, and how can you overcome them?

For centuries, most western European and American societies have considered emotion to be a generally bothersome aspect of human nature, and one that can wreak havoc on the logical, rational thought that we so value. Perhaps for this reason, relatively little research focused on understanding emotion and its role in human behavior. Recently, though, psychologists have been recognizing the importance of understanding how emotion influences our behavior in a wide variety of contexts and situations. In fact, the current popularity of evolutionary psychology seems to provide support for the idea that our emotions not only *are not* interference, but on the contrary are actually an important contributor to our survival and growth as a species. After all, feeling instant fear at the sight of a predator does have its advantages.

What causes emotion? Recent research has offered several new insights, each of which seems to account for a small part of the answer to this complex question. For example, brain research seems to indicate that a tiny part of the brain called the amygdala is linked to our ability to accurately assess danger in a situation. Additional studies suggest that the left hemisphere of the brain is critical to positive emotions such as happiness, and the right hemisphere is associated with processing of negative emotions; happier people experience greater left hemisphere activation, whereas sad and anxious people have more activity in their right hemisphere. Other physiological explanations for emotion include skin temperature (which rises with certain emotions and falls with others) and the effects of certain brain chemicals on emotion.

Another focus of research on emotion has noted the surprising finding that our facial expressions can sometimes prompt an emotion. For example, studies that ask people to hold a pencil sideways with their teeth (which contorts the facial muscles in a way that mimics a smile) note that subjects holding the pencil this way find cartoons funnier than subjects who are holding a pencil in their lips with the tip pointing forward (which mimics frowning muscles) (Myers, 1999). A third area of research has focused on the physiological arousal (such as a pounding heart, faster and more shallow breathing, and "butterflies" in your stomach) that accompanies many emotions. Although each of these directions in emotion research is providing clues to the origins of emotion, they alone cannot account for why people often respond differently to the same situation. For example, in the example at the beginning of this chapter, why did Mark and Carmen respond differently to the news of the barbecue being canceled? For the answer to this question, we must explore the other major perspective in emotion research: cognition, or our thoughts.

How Thoughts Influence Feelings

Although different researchers in the area of emotion may have differing views on what causes emotion, almost all psychologists believe that our emotions are inextricably linked to our thoughts. How does this work? Essentially, our emotions result not from the situation we are in, but from how we *interpret* that situation. This concept can be understood more easily by breaking it down into a series of steps.

An emotion begins when we experience an **activating event**, such as interviewing for a new job, barely avoiding a car accident, seeing an attractive person, having a barbecue canceled, or any other event that is meaningful to the person experiencing it. In a process called **cognitive appraisal**, our mind evaluates the event in the context of our individual belief system, expectations, needs, and past experiences and forms an interpretation of what the event means to us. Once the interpretation is made, we often engage in some **self-talk** that reinforces the interpretation as we continue to focus on it. Thus, it is how we interpret or perceive the event that determines the emotion that results. Simply put, our thoughts influence our emotions.

> **Activating event** Event that is meaningful to the person experiencing it.
>
> **Cognitive appraisal** Interpretation of an event in the context of our individual belief system, expectations, needs, and past experiences.
>
> **Self-talk** Internal thoughts that reinforce our interpretation of an activating event.

Consider this example: You are at school and have just arrived at your second class of the day. Today is the day of the big midterm exam, and you are ready for it. You've been studying a little at a time for several weeks and have spent extra time reviewing during the past week. You know every answer on the study guide, and you are confident that you will do well. For once, the exam didn't fall on a day when you have other exams to take; you do have two more exams this week, but with this one out of the way, you'll have plenty of time to review for the others. Then, just as the professor is getting ready to pass out the exams, the fire alarm sounds! You suddenly remember hearing a couple of weeks ago that random fire drills would occur this month to test the evacuation procedures. This must be one of them, but it couldn't have come at a worse time. By the time the drill ends and everyone is back in the room, there won't be enough time for the exam, so the professor will probably postpone it. Now you'll have to keep reviewing for this exam, while trying to prepare for the other two—there's no way you'll have enough time for everything, and your grades are bound to suffer.

How would you feel in this situation? Angry? Frustrated? Depressed? If you blame the school, thinking that they shouldn't have scheduled fire drills during midterms, you might feel angry. If you blame fate, thinking that something always seems to go wrong even when you really try to organize your time, you might feel depressed. *This is how our mind influences our emotions: through the interpretations we make of the activating event.* And there is more. Imagine the student who hadn't studied for this midterm: The fire drill might activate a feeling of relief or even elation at getting a few more days to prepare. From this example, it is easy to see how people exposed to the same activating event can react with different emotions.

In our relations with others, this information can be invaluable in preventing misunderstandings. In the example of Mark and Carmen at the beginning of the chapter, they each had a different reaction to the news of the barbecue's cancelation, based on their individual cognitive appraisals. Then, as they noticed each other's different reactions, they each drew their own conclusions, again based on their own interpretations. Carmen had been pleased at the cancelation, because she thought it would give her and Mark a day at home alone, which they hadn't had in a long time. She looked forward to curling up together on the sofa, maybe watching a good movie, and just talking. When Mark acted irritated at the cancelation, she assumed that he didn't miss their one-on-one time together the way she did, and her feelings were hurt. Mark, on the other hand, had really been looking forward to an opportunity for his coworkers to get to know Carmen and vice versa—he loved her very much and felt proud to be with her, and he was thus disappointed that the barbecue was canceled. When Carmen acted happy at the cancelation, he assumed that she probably didn't want to spend time with his friends from work, and he felt hurt (see Figure 4.1).

 **Critical Thinking QUESTION** Can you think of a situation that happened in your life recently in which you reacted differently than someone else, based on your different interpretations? Did it lead to a misunderstanding? If so, how did you resolve it?

This example illustrates one way that our individual interpretations of an event can lead to a variety of emotions, which in turn may result in problems in our relations with others. Another problem that can result from the cognition-emotion connection is when our interpretations are irrational, or get blown out of proportion in some way. You might be thinking, "What, me, irrational? Never!" The truth is, though, we make several common mistakes in our interpretations—normal mistakes that are simply the result of being human. But the good news is that these common mistakes, once identified, can be corrected with a little practice.

Fantasies and Nightmares: Seven Irrational Beliefs

Emotions are a wonderful element of our humanity. By their very nature, though, they are in direct contrast to rational thinking. Because of this, we typically fall

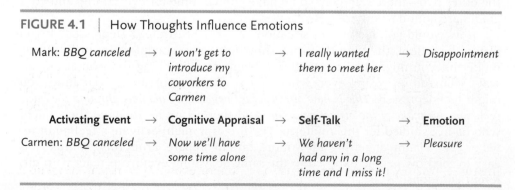

FIGURE 4.1 | How Thoughts Influence Emotions

TABLE 4.1 | Common Irrational Beliefs That Influence Emotions

Catastrophizing	Exaggerating the importance of a negative event
Overgeneralization	Exaggerating the frequency of an event, or making broad assumptions based on limited evidence
Myth of Causation	Belief that one person's emotions are the direct result of another person's actions
Need for Approval	Belief that you are okay only if everyone else approves of you
Tyranny of Shoulds	Belief that other people, or the world in general, ought to think and act in a way that fits your belief system
Perfectionism	Expecting yourself to achieve perfection in everything you do, or in many things
Myth of Helplessness	Assuming that you are stuck in a bad situation and cannot do anything about it

prey to some common irrational beliefs (Ellis, 1962; Beck, 1987) that, when tied into our emotions, can result in some real problems in our relationships. In some cases, these irrational beliefs are fantasies about the way the world (or other people, or ourselves) should be. In other cases, these fantasies become nightmares as we blow things out of proportion and self-talk ourselves into a panic. As you read the following descriptions of these common irrational beliefs, consider which ones sound like familiar patterns in your own thinking (see Table 4.1).

Catastrophizing   Have you ever had something mildly irritating happen, but you were busy or stressed out at the time so you overreacted, "making a mountain out of a molehill," so to speak? Very few people can say no to that question, which is what makes catastrophizing such a common irrational belief. **Catastrophizing** is when you exaggerate the importance of a negative event, imagining it as a catastrophe instead of evaluating its implications in more realistic terms.

> Catastrophizing
> Exaggerating the importance of a negative event.

For example, imagine that you go out to your car on the morning of the first day of school, only to find that your car won't start. This is an activating event. If you tend to catastrophize, you might interpret this as a disaster, because your belief system tells you that it's really important to be on time the first day. Your self-talk might go something like this: "Oh, no! I can't believe it! Now what am I going to do? Parking is always such a nightmare the first week of classes, so even if I do get my car started, I won't be able to find a parking place, and I'll surely be late for my first class—if I even make it at all. I might end up getting dropped from the class, which will mess up my whole schedule! At this rate, I'll never finish school, and my whole life will be ruined!"

Sound familiar? We might expect the emotions that would result from this interpretation and self-talk would be panic, anxiety, anger, or some combination of the three. And if you act on this catastrophic interpretation, you might skip school altogether and have to deal with the consequences. A more rational interpretation might go like this: "This is so frustrating, and on the first day of school! Well, like they say, stuff happens—now, what can I do about it?" That interpretation is more likely to help you take some steps to try to get the car started, or think about taking the bus or finding another way to school if the car doesn't start. Either way, you could take control of the situation and reduce the possibility of negative consequences by simply calling your professors for your first few classes and apprising them of the situation, just in case you do end up being late. With this alternate interpretation, your emotion may still be a little anxiety, but it would certainly be combined with some sense of control and confidence in your ability to handle the situation. You may even see the humor in your overreaction and laugh a little at yourself as you remember how silly your catastrophizing really was.

Overgeneralization   Like catastrophizing, overgeneralization is a form of exaggeration. But whereas catastrophizing involves exaggerating the importance of an event, **overgeneralization** involves exaggerating the frequency of an event. An overgeneralization often involves the use of the words "always" or "never."

> Overgeneralization Exaggerating the frequency of an event, or making broad assumptions based on limited evidence.

For example, Yvette and Dani have been good friends for several years. They are supposed to go to a movie Friday night that starts at 7:30. Yvette is ready at 7:00, which is the time Dani is supposed to pick her up. Yvette knows that Dani often runs late, which Yvette hates because in her view being on time is important. Yvette even offered to drive, so they would be on time, but Dani promised her she wouldn't be late. Sure enough, though, Dani didn't pick Yvette up until 7:20. The whole time she was waiting, Yvette was trying to hold in her frustration. She kept thinking, "I don't understand why Dani can't ever be on time. She knows I really want to see this movie, and I hate missing the first part. Why can't she just get her act together?" When Dani finally arrives, Yvette can't hold it in any longer and explodes: "Dani, you're always late! You are so irresponsible!"

If you were Dani, would you respond calmly and rationally, or would Yvette's outburst likely make you defensive? For most people, the answer would be the latter—who likes to be accused of being irresponsible? And what Yvette said to Dani contained not one, but two types of overgeneralization. First, she said Dani was always late. This is simply not true, even if it may seem that way. The truth is that Dani is frequently late, but there have been times when she has been punctual. By accusing her of always being late, Yvette is exaggerating the frequency of Dani's lateness in her own mind, which interferes with her ability to discuss the problem calmly with Dani. If Yvette really stopped to think about it, she would remember the times that Dani has been on time and she wouldn't be so angry. Her irrational belief (that Dani is always late) increased her anger and affected her ability to discuss the issue productively with Dani.

Yvette's accusation also contained another type of overgeneralization. She accused Dani of being an irresponsible person, when what she really meant was that Dani had been late frequently. In Yvette's mind, being on time is a type of responsible behavior, and when Dani wasn't on time Yvette made a broad assumption that if Dani was late (which to Yvette is an irresponsible behavior), she must also be irresponsible in other ways. Her accusation of irresponsibility was far too general; instead, she should have been specific and accurate in describing Dani's behavior by simply noting that she had been late on many occasions. This type of overgeneralization is similar to saying that someone is a good student when the person is actually good at math (but just average in other subjects), or thinking that you are a loser when you do poorly on one exam (but have done fine on others). The result in these various situations is the same: an emotional response blown out of proportion because of the irrational thought pattern of overgeneralization. To overcome this problem, be more specific and accurate as you observe and describe situations that affect you.

Critical Thinking
QUESTION
To what extent do you tend to overgeneralize? Do you do it more with certain people or in certain situations? Give an example that illustrates your answer.

The Myth of Causation   Another irrational belief that wreaks havoc on our emotions is the belief that one person's emotions are caused by another person's actions, when in reality emotions are caused by one's own interpretation and self-talk. This **myth of causation** essentially gives credit to (or lays blame on) someone else for your emotions, rather than taking personal responsibility for them.

> Myth of causation Belief that one person's emotions are the direct result of another person's actions.

One way this myth affects our human relations is by the way it inhibits some people from speaking the truth, for fear of hurting someone's feelings. You can probably think of several examples of this, such as when you didn't tell someone how you really felt about his behavior, or when someone asked your opinion on something and you told her something nice instead of what you really thought. Certainly in minor instances this may not lead to any long-term problems, but to maintain good human relations, honesty is important.

Imagine if one of your good friends has the habit of drinking too much when you go out together, and then insists on driving home. Many people respond to this situation by not saying anything for fear of hurting the other person's feelings, but this is a powerful example of when you're doing more harm than good by holding back. If you do decide to speak up, you might say something such as, "Since you drove us here, how about I drive us home?" Or, you could be even more direct and say, "Hey buddy, I think you've had a few too many. How about letting me drive?" In either case, if the other person becomes angry at what you say, that anger is his emotion and his responsibility—it is not your fault he became angry. You were simply trying to look out for yourself and your friend; his angry response was based on his belief system and self-talk. Another person might have responded to your statement in a different way, perhaps with serious gratitude for your friendship. In either case, you said the same thing in the same way, so how can your statement be the cause of two different reactions?

We can also use the previous example of Yvette and Dani to see the myth of causation at work. In her outburst to Dani, Yvette might have also said, "You make me so mad!" This statement implies that it is Dani's fault that Yvette is mad, when Yvette's anger is really the result of the violation of her own belief system that being on time is important. If Dani has a different belief system, then that is Dani's choice, and Yvette is only causing problems for herself and her friendship by blaming Dani for it and for her anger. Yvette would be better off recognizing Dani's pattern and adjusting her own expectations accordingly—realistic expectations can often pave the way to a less frustrating life. Or, if she really can't handle Dani's lateness, she should talk with her about it (some suggestions for handling this type of difficult situation constructively will be included in Chapters 8–10).

Falling prey to the myth of causation can have another, more insidious effect on our human relations. If a friend or coworker continually does something that bothers you, but you don't say anything about it to him because you don't want to "make him upset," what happens to your feelings? Chances are, they don't just disappear. It is more likely they will continue and perhaps even intensify as the other person's behavior continues to bother you. You may begin to feel frustrated with the other person because of his behavior. Is this rational, since you've never spoken up about it?

In addition, you may begin to dislike the person as your feelings about his behavior intensify and build (you may even begin to overgeneralize about him). The end result doesn't bode well for a good relationship. If and when the other person does find out about your feelings, he may wonder what kind of a friend you really are if you can't be honest about your feelings. Without trust, neither business nor personal relationships can thrive. The key, then, to overcoming the myth of causation is to learn to be honest about your feelings and to take responsibility for them. We will learn an excellent technique for doing this in Chapter 9.

The Need for Approval The fourth common problem in the link between thoughts and emotions is the **need for approval**, which, according to some psychologists (e.g., Ellis, 1958) is a major cause of depression and anxiety. Have you ever, for example, felt anxious or nervous about what someone would think about you? Certainly this may be a natural reaction if the other person is someone who is important to you, such as a spouse, parent, child, friend, or valued colleague. It becomes irrational, though, in a couple of cases: First, when you begin to compromise your own beliefs or principles to please the other person. Even if the other person is important to you, this may not be a wise choice.

> **Need for approval** Belief that you are okay only if everyone else approves of you.

It also becomes an irrational belief when we start to believe that everyone must like us. As pleasant as this fantasy may be, it simply isn't realistic. You are bound to meet people with whom you have nothing in common or people with whom you strongly disagree about something. If your need for their approval overrides your own belief system and sense of self, you might end up going along with their beliefs just so they will like you. This type of behavior has disastrous results in the long run, because research shows that our behavior (even if it is only on the outside) eventually has the power to change our beliefs on the inside (e.g., Zimbardo, 1972).

Overcoming this irrational belief takes time and effort. It must begin with your acknowledgement that you are indeed falling prey to it. If you are, you must next develop some self-knowledge in this area so that you can identify the situations or people with whom you are most vulnerable to the need for approval. Once you've figured that out, you can give yourself a little pep talk before going into these situations or seeing these people, reminding yourself first that in life, some people like each other and some don't. If these people don't like you, that's just the way it is; it is certainly not worth being someone you are not. After all, wouldn't you rather be around people who genuinely like you for you?

We'll offer an additional way to overcome this irrational belief (along with all the others) in just a few pages.

The Tyranny of Shoulds   Have you ever caught yourself thinking, "She should be more understanding," or "He shouldn't criticize me so much"? You might even apply this type of irrational belief to yourself: "I should be able to handle this." If these statements sound familiar, you're not alone. Ascribing to these beliefs will only cause you misery. Karen Horney (pronounced "Horn-eye"), a prominent psychoanalyst, coined the term "tyranny of the should" to reflect this type of irrational belief (Horney, 1950). Although it might be nice to imagine that the world should be just the way you think it should be, this is clearly unrealistic. By living by these "shoulds" we are only causing frustration for ourselves. We do not have control over other people or their behavior, so it makes no sense to expect that everyone will please us all the time.

Another common example of the **tyranny of shoulds** is the basic belief that if we work hard and play by the rules, life should turn out the way we want it to, whether it be in our career, relationships, or even our health. We certainly hope this is true, and we even have sayings that emphasize it, such as "what comes around, goes around," but the truth is that we

> **Tyranny of shoulds** Belief that other people, or the world in general, ought to think and act in a way that fits your belief system.

don't always get what we deserve or deserve what we get. When this happens, it is only natural that we feel disappointed, frustrated, or even angry; that emotion by itself isn't necessarily a problem. It becomes a problem if we get stuck in this emotion, holding ourselves back by continuing to ruminate over why this happened, or how it could have turned out this way. After all, we did everything we were supposed to! It is crucial to our health and well-being to learn to let go of this irrational belief, accept that bad things sometimes happen to good people, and move on.

Critical Thinking **QUESTION**   Do you know anyone who seems to be especially affected by the tyranny of shoulds? Think back to the four dimensions of cultures you learned about in Chapter 1. Which dimension seems most related to this irrational belief?

Perfectionism   The tyranny of shoulds can also lead to two related problems. The first is perfectionism. In our achievement-oriented society, with our drive toward "better—stronger—faster," **perfectionism** affects many people. When you find yourself thinking things such as "I should know how to do this," or "I should be able to handle this," you are imposing on yourself an irrational belief. Who says you should be able to? Even if you still think you should be able to, what good does it do to beat yourself up about it? Instead, either do something about it, or let it go. Accept that what you're doing isn't working and go at the problem in another way.

> **Perfectionism** Expecting yourself to achieve perfection in tasks, relationships, communication, or other goals.

For example, if you are having a problem in your biology class, and you keep telling yourself that you should be able to understand the subject, you aren't getting anywhere. Instead, take some action—starting by accepting the fact that you don't understand—and seek some tutoring or attend the professor's office hours for some help. Even if you never get the grade you think you "should" get, accept that we all have our strengths and weaknesses—maybe biology just isn't your strong point. Think about what you are good at and focus more attention on that. The emotional frustration caused by perfectionism is unnecessary stress, so don't put yourself through it (see Figure 4.2).

The Myth of Helplessness   The tyranny of shoulds also affects our relationships when we think that someone else "should" be doing something differently. For example, perhaps your employer has implemented a new policy of no eating or drinking anywhere but in the lunchroom. This may seem unreasonable to you and some of your coworkers, because many of you eat lunch while working and don't know how you'd get all your work done if you didn't. If you get trapped by the tyranny of shoulds, you might find yourself thinking, "He shouldn't have implemented such an unreasonable rule." You might feel frustrated or angry with your boss: emotions that only hurt you. If you allow these feelings to continue to burn, while just *assuming that you can't do anything about the situation,* you are accepting the **myth of helplessness**, which is the second type of problem with the tyranny of shoulds.

> **Myth of helplessness** Assuming that you are stuck in a bad situation and cannot do anything about it.

Instead of feeling helpless about the situation, consider what your options are. Perhaps a group of you could meet with your boss to air your concerns and discuss the situation. Even if this doesn't work out, you still aren't helpless. Maybe this is a good time for your boss to recognize that his demands aren't realistic if they can't be completed without working through lunch. And even if you exhaust all other options, there are other jobs out there. You could choose to find a new job, which may not be something you want to do right now, but by recognizing that you do have that choice, you are giving yourself some element of control over the situation. This will help reduce the negative feelings that result from the mistaken belief that you are helpless.

I'm just really upset that my gum lost its flavor at 6000 feet!

FIGURE 4.2 | This mountain climber is allowing perfectionism to dilute the joy and satisfaction of his accomplishment. Has perfectionism ever affected you in a similar manner?

Disputing Irrational Beliefs

In addition to helping us understand how irrational thoughts can lead to negative emotions, cognitive psychology also offers a solution to the problems caused by irrational beliefs (Beck, 1987). The key lies in recognizing the belief systems that color your interpretations and replacing the fantasies and nightmares with more accurate interpretations and self-talk. When you find yourself having a strong emotional reaction to an activating event, take a few moments to examine your self-talk, and identify which irrational beliefs are intensifying your emotional reaction. Then, consider more rational interpretations of the activating event and ceate new, more effective self-talk that supports the more rational interpretations. Table 4.2 shows an example of this process.

TABLE 4.2 | Disputing Irrational Beliefs

ACTIVATING EVENT	EMOTION	SELF-TALK	IRRATIONAL BELIEFS IN SELF-TALK	REPLACE WITH MORE RATIONAL SELF-TALK
Friend is late	Anger	People should be on time.	Tyranny of Shoulds	My shoulds are my own; other people are entitled to their own values and shoulds.
		She is always late.	Overgeneralization	She isn't always late; I just notice when she is, because I get upset.
		It makes me so mad!	Myth of Causation	It isn't her fault that I'm angry; I'm angry because I set myself up for it with unrealistic expectations that she'll just magically change.

To identify the irrational beliefs in your life and practice overcoming them, turn to Activity 4.1.

Interim SUMMARY #1

Our thoughts (cognitions) exert a powerful influence on our emotions by way of the interpretations we form of things that happen to us. This is a natural human process, but it can cause problems in our relations with others when our interpretations go astray or are irrational in some way.

Research has identified seven major irrational beliefs. They are catastrophizing, overgeneralization, causation, the need for approval, the tyranny of shoulds, perfectionism, and helplessness. When we fall into these traps, our internal self-talk leads us to see the situation from an irrational perspective, which leads to debilitative emotions. Fortunately, research has demonstrated that we can divert the process by learning to identify the irrational beliefs we tend to have, challenging them, and replacing them with more accurate interpretations. Of course, it takes time to unlearn our old, irrational behaviors and replace them with newer, more accurate interpretations and behaviors, but with practice it becomes easier and more automatic.

SOME BASIC EMOTIONS AND THEIR EFFECTS ON RELATIONSHIPS

PREVIEW QUESTIONS

(1) What is the difference between sadness and depression? How can depression be treated?

(2) Is anger always bad? Why or why not?

(3) What are four methods of handling anger, and how do you see them in your own life and relationships?

(4) What factors influence a person's happiness, and how does this information help you improve the effectiveness of your relations with others?

In the last section, we discovered how some common irrational beliefs create negative emotional states, which can cause problems in our human relations. Emotions can influence our relationships in other ways, too, and in this section we will explore the effects of sadness, anger, and happiness on human relations.

Sadness

Most of us have felt sad or "down" on occasion, typically as a result of some type of loss or disappointment. Normal sadness usually lasts a relatively short amount of time. When the feeling is intensified, sadness becomes grief. Whether the emotion is sadness or grief, though, it is often a normal and appropriate emotional response. In fact, sadness or grief at a loss can actually be adaptive, because it promotes a reflective period in which we can mourn the loss, consider its meaning, and adjust. For example, if a close friend decides to move to another state or country, it would be normal to feel sad for a time. You would probably be remembering the good times you shared with your friend and considering the changes you might make in your life that will help you adjust to his move and go on with your own life. If you continue to feel sad for months, though, and have less energy and interest in doing things you used to do without being able to break out of the cycle of sadness, you may be experiencing depression, a psychological condition that often interferes not only with your own well-being, but with the well-being of those close to you.

Are You Depressed, or Merely Sad? Depression is the most widespread psychological disorder in our society—so prevalent, in fact, that it is often called the common cold of psychological disorders. Although there can be a fine line between normal sadness and depression, the main distinguishing factors are duration and intensity: how long it lasts, and how much it interferes with normal functioning. Another distinguishing factor is general pessimism: A person experiencing normal sadness or grief can usually recognize the cause of her feelings and assume that she will eventually feel better. The depressed person, on the other hand, feels no hope of ever feeling better. Also, state self-esteem (remember that from Chapter 2) is affected in the depressed person: People experiencing normal sadness continue to see themselves as valuable individuals, but the depressed person often feels completely worthless.

Other common symptoms of depression include changes in eating or sleeping habits, crying, inability to think clearly or solve problems, loss of pleasure in activities that used to be enjoyable, and thoughts of suicide. When a person experiences several of these symptoms on a daily basis for several weeks or more, it is a good idea to seek medical or psychological advice.

Causes and Consequences of Depression Not surprisingly, depression affects our relations with others. People who are depressed report greater dissatisfaction in their marriages and generally experience lower overall marital quality. In fact, their depression influences their spouses' satisfaction with the marriage, too: Spouses of depressed persons also report lower marital quality (Coyne, 1987). Depression takes its toll on friendships and roommate situations, too. A recent study of college roommates found that roommates of depressed persons were more likely to become depressed themselves, even when other factors that might cause depression were accounted for (Joiner, 1994). Depression appears to be contagious.

What causes depression? In some cases, depression is physiological and can be treated effectively with medication. In other cases, depression is cognitive and responds well to cognitive therapies, which are similar to the process used to overcome irrational thoughts discussed earlier in this chapter. Regardless of the basis of the depression, research suggests that depression tends to be a self-perpetuating cycle. Depressed people tend to focus more on their negative characteristics and support their negative perceptions with memories of negative events; in other words, memories in depressed people are selectively attuned to the worst of times, rather than the best of times. It is easy to see how this pattern feeds on itself. On a positive note, though, there are numerous effective treatments for depression.

Treating Depression As previously mentioned, cognitive therapies are one type of treatment that can be useful in treating depression. Just as we learned how to identify our irrational thoughts to overcome problematic emotions, cognitive therapies work to help the depressed understand how their thinking affects their emotions and thus learn to adjust their emotions by adjusting their thinking. Cognitive therapists like Aaron Beck and Albert Ellis have reported excellent results with their cognitive therapies for years, and recent research demonstrates that the cognitive skills necessary to prevent or reverse depression can be learned, even by children. An impressive study of fifth and sixth graders who were at risk for depression recently demonstrated this.

This study involved an intervention program that "taught (children) to identify their pessimistic beliefs, examine the evidence for and against the beliefs, and generate more realistic alternatives" (Gillham, Reivich, Jaycox, & Seligman, 1995). At-risk children who participated in the training had lower levels of depression at the end of the trial period than did a control group of at-risk children who did not participate. What's more, the positive effects persisted during the two years that the researchers followed the children as they entered adolescence, which is a historically difficult time. By comparison, the control group children's levels of depression skyrocketed at the two-year mark. This study provides encouraging support for the effectiveness of depression intervention programs.

Low-level depression can be treated effectively with behavioral therapies, which aim to lift depression by taking action geared toward distracting a sad or depressed person from his or her depressive thoughts. One of the most common and useful recommendations is socializing. Going out with friends can often raise someone's spirits and help the person refocus on the positive. Other recommendations include seeing a funny movie or reading a good book, taking a walk or engaging in some other form of exercise, or indulging in one of your favorite preoccupations such as treating yourself to a ball game, some live music, a good meal out, or a visit to a favorite museum or gallery. Also, tackling a moderately difficult chore that you've put off for a long time can have very rewarding results to feelings of self-worth and accomplishment. Finally, doing something to help someone else tends to lift our spirits as well. All of these suggestions have been found to be effective at helping mildly depressed people lift themselves "out of the dumps."

Critical Thinking **QUESTION** List three activities you really enjoy that you could use to try to lift yourself out of a low-level depression.

Anger

Like sadness, anger is an emotion with which virtually everyone is familiar. What many people aren't familiar with is the fact that anger isn't necessarily a bad thing. In fact, anger is adaptive: It is an inner signal that something is wrong. It could mean that you have been offended or violated in some way; it could signal frustration at being blocked from a goal; it could be an indication that you are giving too much to a relationship, or conversely not being able or allowed to give enough.

Whatever the cause, anger carries with it the benefit of the physical and emotional energy needed to do something about it—and that is where most people get the idea that anger is bad, because what people do about it is often destructive. Anger, though, isn't the same as aggression. **Anger** is an emotion; **aggression** is a behavior. As with any other emotion, we have a choice regarding what behaviors we'll use to exhibit our anger: We can choose to handle it constructively or destructively, directly or indirectly.

Anger A normal human emotion that provides a signal that something is wrong.

Aggression A behavior that is destructive or hostile.

Direct Expression of Anger **Direct expression of anger** involves expressing your anger directly toward the object of your anger. There are both benefits and risks involved in expressing anger directly. One positive aspect is that direct expression of anger carries the implicit assumption that the relationship is strong enough to withstand and work through the conflict. In a way, direct (and constructive) expression of anger is a message that you trust the other person enough to deal with your anger openly. If you are able to express your anger directly and constructively, it can clear the air and strengthen the foundation of

Direct expression of anger Expressing your anger directly toward the object of your anger.

the relationship. On the other hand, direct expression of anger, even when constructive, can be risky. It takes trust, patience, and skill to deal with anger constructively and openly; if these are absent in either one of you, the relationship could be damaged by direct expression of anger.

Direct expressions of anger take two forms: *constructive* and *destructive*. Destructive means of expressing anger directly include physical aggression and verbal aggression. There are many types of verbal aggression. One common form is the evaluative judgment, or labeling. In essence, this is name-calling. Rather than telling the other person you are upset because she didn't do the dishes, you call her a slob. Rather than telling someone you are angry because he lied to you, you call him a jerk or a liar. The problem with these statements is that they are overgeneralizations, and they usually sound judgmental. Even if they seem entirely accurate to you, they are likely to promote defensiveness or anger in the other person, which will result in escalation of the conflict rather than resolution. "Kitchen-sinking" is another destructive type of direct expression of anger. This is when, in telling the other person what is bothering you, you throw in all the other things that have ever upset you about the other person ("everything but the kitchen sink," so to speak). This also escalates the conflict, rather than promotes a peaceful solution.

Constructive ways of expressing your anger directly involve describing the problem in a factual (rather than judgmental) manner and staying focused on the issue at hand (rather than kitchen-sinking). Imagine, for example, that your roommate didn't clean the kitchen when it was his turn. Rather than calling him a slob, tell him you are upset because he didn't clean the kitchen. Here, you are clearly describing the behavior (as opposed to labeling the person), and you are taking responsibility for your feelings (rather than getting trapped by the myth of causation and blaming him for your anger). Similarly, if your best friend lied to you about something, don't call her a jerk or even a liar. Instead, describe her behavior in this one situation—just because she lied this time doesn't mean she's a liar (calling her a liar implies that lying is a consistent character trait for her). The key is to separate the person from the behavior and to describe the behavior rather than making a judgment about her based on the behavior.

Tips for Direct, Constructive Expression of Anger

Timing is critical when expressing your anger directly. The age-old advice of "counting to 10" turns out to be good advice when you are angry. Remember, anger is an emotion, and when an emotion is running strong it can overpower our ability to think clearly. As a result, what might seem like a good idea in the heat of the moment may not be such a good idea when you've calmed down and your brain has returned to its normal efficiency. Think carefully before deciding what to do with your anger and how to do it. If you decide to express it directly, think in advance about what you want to say and how you want to say it.

In addition, don't ambush the other person with your anger; instead, catch them when they aren't in a rush or distracted by something else, and ask if you can talk with them about something. Do everything you can to set up your discussion for success, and you'll increase the odds of a peaceful resolution. Activities 4.1 and 4.2 at the end of this chapter will help you take the first steps toward expressing anger directly and constructively. Then, in Chapters 9 and 10, we'll learn additional techniques for handling a variety of situations effectively.

Directly expressing your anger isn't always the best way to deal with this powerful emotion. In some cases, you might decide that the risks involved in direct expression outweigh the potential benefits. If your boss is imposing what seem like irrational rules, for example, and you and your colleagues have tried to talk with her about it but it hasn't done any good, you might feel justifiably angry. Direct constructive expression of the problem hasn't worked in the past, though, and only seems to be escalating the conflict, so in this case you might decide the risk of unemployment outweighs whatever benefits may come from it. In other cases, our anger is really about a minor issue: When we recognize this happening, our anger is still justified, but it may not be important enough to bring out into the open. The old phrase "Choose your battles" often makes good sense. In either of the above situations, managing our anger indirectly may be the best choice.

Indirect Expression of Anger **Indirect expression of anger** involves channeling your anger in a direction other than toward the object of your anger. Like direct expression of anger, indirect expression can also take constructive or destructive forms. Destructive forms of indirectly expressed anger include excessive alcohol consumption, drug use, or physical violence—even if the violence is aimed at an inanimate object. This latter idea surprises many people. For years, some common recommendations for "venting" anger included such strategies as screaming into a pillow, hitting a punching bag, shouting or cursing, and throwing dishes at the wall. Experts who made these suggestions relied on a premise called **catharsis**, or the idea that releasing pent-up hostilities will return us to a peaceful state. Recent research, though, points out the potential negative effects of these techniques. Each involves aggression: Even though the aggression is not directed at another person, it is still aggression. And aggression tends to increase one's hostility, rather than drain it (Myers, 1996).

> **Indirect expression of anger** Channeling your anger in a direction other than toward the object of your anger.

> **Catharsis** The theory that releasing pent-up hostilities will return us to a peaceful state.

Anger can be indirectly expressed in a constructive manner by such means as exercise, relaxation, psychological detachment, and cognitive restructuring. Exercise and relaxation are fairly self-explanatory. Exercise carries with it added health benefits, too. Forms of relaxation include meditation and prayer. Psychological detachment involves a recognition that the issue may be out of your control, but your reaction to it isn't. Acknowledge that negativity is harmful only to yourself and try to let it go. Cognitive restructuring can help, too, by shifting your focus to the positive aspects of the situation. For example, you might realize that even though you can't control your boss' actions, you really only have to deal with her occasionally, and that most of the time you really enjoy your work. Or you might decide that you will start looking for work elsewhere and meanwhile put up with

TABLE 4.3 | Methods of Handling Anger

	DIRECT	INDIRECT
CONSTRUCTIVE	Describe problem in a factual, nonjudgmental manner; stay focused on issue; think before you speak	Exercise, relaxation, psychological detachment, cognitive restructuring
DESTRUCTIVE	Physical aggression, verbal aggression (name calling, sarcasm, etc.)	Excessive alcohol consumption, drug use, aggression at self or an inanimate object

her until you find something better. Or you could recognize that work is only one part of your life, and that the rest of it (including your family and friends) is pretty good. Any of these "cognitions" can help you put your anger in perspective and deal with it constructively. Table 4.3 summarizes methods of handling anger.

Whether you express your anger directly or indirectly, constructively or destructively (and I hope you'll choose the constructive route!), you must express it in some way. Unexpressed anger doesn't just disappear. On the contrary, it often builds. A series of little things or minor annoyances can add up; as one former student put it, "Sweep too many things under the rug and you end up with one giant dust bunny!" Left unexpressed, anger can lead to headaches, ulcers, depression, high blood pressure and increased risk of heart disease, as well as a host of other physical and mental disorders. Want to live a long, healthy life? Learn to express your anger constructively.

To explore your own reactions to anger and practice handling them constructively, turn to Activity 4.2.

Happiness

Money and Happiness "If I just had a little more money, I'd be so much happier!" Have you ever entertained this notion? If you have, you are not alone. In a recent survey of students entering college, the most sought-after goal was "being very well off financially" (Astin, 1993). Our society seems obsessed with the pursuit and acquisition of material goods. Everywhere we turn, it seems, we are bombarded by glitzy images of the glamorous lifestyles of the rich and famous and (we assume) happy. The ancient proverb, "Money can't buy happiness," while still resonating in the depths of our intuitive knowledge of life, seems largely ignored in the day-to-day bustle of our drive toward the next step on the ladder of success.

Is it working? Are we making ourselves happier by our growing achievements? Well, research does tell us that people living at or below the poverty level in our country experience less joy and feel less happiness than people who are living a more comfortable lifestyle (Myers, 1993). Does happiness rise proportionately with income, though? Let's look at some research findings that will help us answer this question.

Between 1957 and 1990, the per capita income in the United States (in today's dollars) doubled. That means that, on the average, people in our country today have twice as much money to spend as they did four decades ago. Are we twice as happy? Surveys taken in 1957 and in 1990 by the National Opinion Research Center at the University of Chicago offer this startling information: In 1990, only 1 in 3 people said that they were "very happy"—the same percentage that claimed to be "very happy" in 1957. The answer, then, is a resounding "No." People today are no happier than they were 40 years ago, despite a doubling of their income. On a more individual level, studies of lottery winners indicate that one year after their "big win," most winners report being no happier than they were prior to their win. The truth is that, once beyond the poverty level, money does not increase happiness. If money doesn't make people happier, then what does?

In his book *The Pursuit of Happiness* (1993), psychologist David Myers discusses the research findings of hundreds of studies on happiness. Myers reports that certain characteristics have been linked consistently to happiness levels in individuals.

Factors Affecting Happiness   One factor that increases happiness is *having a sense of personal control over one's life*. Control is usually measured on a continuum, where one end of the continuum represents a strong sense of internal control and the other end signifies a strong sense of external control. People who score high on the scale, or "internals" (representing internal control) would be likely to agree with such statements as, "What happens to me is my own doing"; people who are "externals" would agree that "I don't have enough control over the direction my life is taking."

Myers suggests that a person's sense of internal control can be increased by setting and achieving goals. The key to achieving long-term goals, he says, is to break them down into realistic short-term increments. For example, reading an entire 50-page chapter of a textbook may seem like a lot of reading when considered all at once; instead, break it down into five 10-page portions and read one portion a day. At the end of each day's reading, you'll feel a sense of accomplishment at achieving your objective, and at the end of the week you'll feel even better for having read the whole chapter on time. Setting realistic goals and managing your time effectively each day to work toward achieving those goals can increase your happiness by strengthening your sense of internal control.

Happy people also tend to be optimists, expecting the best instead of the worst. Optimism, in turn, is linked to success, as demonstrated by numerous studies. One such study examined the demanding field of insurance sales, which is notoriously hard on new salespeople as they inevitably face repeated rejections in their attempts to build a client base. Frustrated at the lack of payoff for their efforts, many just give up. Psychologist Martin Seligman studied a group of new insurance salespeople (Seligman & Schalman, 1986) and found that those who were optimistic tended to view rejection as a fluke, rather than a personal failing. As a result, they were more resistant to the frustration that often comes with rejection. Ultimately, the optimists sold more policies and were only half as likely to quit during their first year as their less-optimistic colleagues.

It is important to note here that optimism is beneficial only when it is tempered with a dose of realism. When taken to the extreme, optimism can actually be harmful. People who are very high on optimism, for example, are less likely to take precautions regarding their health and safety. As a result, studies show these people are more likely to be seriously injured in car accidents (they were too optimistic to wear seat belts) and less likely to take health risks such as cancer or AIDS seriously (and thus not take precautions against them).

Not surprisingly, perhaps, *happiness also comes from having close relationships with others.* In a National Opinion Research Center survey (Myers, 1993), people who reported having five or more persons with whom they shared their joys, sorrows, frustrations, and other life experiences were 60% more likely to feel "very happy" than people who didn't have anyone with whom they shared these things. It may be that the intimacy that develops from self-disclosure promotes happiness. And having what many consider to be the "ultimate" in close relationships, which is marriage or a similar lifetime partnership, improves happiness *and* health. In findings mirroring those reported earlier in this paragraph, married people reported being "very happy" 60% more often than unmarried people. Furthermore, married people tend to live longer and enjoy better health than their unmarried counterparts (Burman & Margolin, 1992).

To sum up, Myers reports a number of factors that seem to increase happiness, including personal control, optimism, close relationships, and a sense of meaning and faith. In addition, Myers notes that self-esteem, satisfying work, seven to eight hours' sleep each night, and time for personal reflection also contribute to happiness. Conversely, we know that money does not generally increase happiness; other factors not found to affect happiness include age, sex, race, and disabilities.

Before leaving the topic of happiness, one additional influence on happiness must be noted: *the effect of genetics.* By studying hundreds of sets of twins, researchers have been able to determine that happiness is highly dependent on genetic makeup (Lykken & Tellegen, 1996). Building on the twin studies, psychologists and physicians studying happiness have identified a "happiness center" in the brain's left frontal lobe. For example, studies of infant temperament have indicated that happy babies have more brain activity in their left frontal lobes than unhappy babies. So, it seems that while social and psychological factors play a definite role in happiness, some of us are biologically predisposed to experience happiness more than others.

Critical Thinking QUESTION   Overall, how happy do you generally tend to be? How does your overall happiness level affect your relations with others?

Tips for Increasing Happiness   Does that mean that, for less happy people, the situation is hopeless? Far from it, says Myers. To increase your happiness, consider these suggestions:

- Keep yourself busy with challenging but manageable tasks.
- Count your blessings. If you can't think of very many, try comparing yourself to others less fortunate than yourself.

- Actively seek out social networks that can provide you with the potential for close relationships.
- Try looking on the bright side of things. Consider ways the situation could be worse than it is, and you'll probably end up happier with what you have.
- Exercise regularly. Studies show that people with healthier bodies tend to be happier.
- Laugh! Studies show that people who can see humor in everyday situations report greater happiness.

Interim SUMMARY #2

Sadness, happiness, and anger may be the three basic human emotions that elicit the most interest. Surprisingly, perhaps, all three of these different emotions can be either facilitative or debilitative. Sadness, for example, can be an appropriate and adaptive response to a difficult situation, but if it lasts for too long can develop into depression. Depression, the most common psychological disorder in our society, is characterized by loss of interest in activities that used to provide pleasure. Psychological treatment for depression is often very effective.

Anger, another emotion often considered to be a "negative" emotion, can also be either adaptive or maladaptive. Furthermore, it is a normal human emotion. On one hand, it can be a powerful signal that something is wrong that carries with it the energy to take action. On the other hand, not knowing how to deal with anger effectively can lead to disastrous consequences. Anger can be expressed either directly or indirectly, and constructively or destructively.

Happiness is an emotion that has been the focus of much research and attention in the past decade. Although it turns out that money does not increase a person's happiness level, a sense of personal control, optimism, close relationships, and faith all are correlated with happiness. Happiness is also strongly influenced by our individual genetic makeup.

EMOTIONAL INTELLIGENCE

PREVIEW QUESTIONS

(1) What is emotional intelligence, and what are its five components?

(2) Is empathy the same as sympathy? Why or why not?

(3) How does emotional intelligence influence our relations at home and at work?

Now that we have examined a few specific emotions and their effects on our relations with others, let's look at emotions and human relations from a more general perspective. Are there some people who are just better at the emotional aspect of human relations than others? That is the question we will now address as we look at a topic that has received much attention during the last several years: the concept of emotional intelligence.

As previously mentioned in this chapter, the study of emotions was for a long time rather ignored by the psychological and medical sciences. The emphasis has traditionally been on rational thought; emotions were viewed as the opposite of rational thought and thus considered an annoyance. In recent years, though, the tide has begun to turn: Psychologists and other scientists are beginning to become aware of the important role of emotions in our thinking and in our interactions with others. Cutting-edge technology is helping us in our quest to understand emotions by allowing us to actually see what is going on inside the brain as we experience different emotions. The result is a growing understanding of how emotions work, accompanied by a simultaneous and sobering awareness of how critical this understanding is in a world that is becoming more angry, more reactive, and more aggressive.

Harvard-educated psychologist Daniel Goleman summarizes the research on emotions and their impact on human relations in his highly acclaimed book *Emotional Intelligence* (1995). Goleman notes, first, that the traditional means of measuring intelligence—the IQ score—measures only thinking ability. He suggests that IQ score has been overrated as a tool for predicting success in life, pointing out that IQ scores only account for about 20% of whether a person is successful in life. Many other psychologists agree that while IQ might get a person into a particular college or career, other factors seem more important in predicting who succeeds once they are there (Myers, 2001). But what are these other factors?

Drawing on some groundbreaking work by other well-known psychologists such as Howard Gardner, Goleman argues that there are multiple forms of intelligence, and that one such form is *interpersonal intelligence*. It is this interpersonal intelligence that determines in large part who succeeds in life and who doesn't, by essentially giving a person the skills necessary to capitalize on other abilities (such as IQ). Goleman identifies five components of this interpersonal intelligence, or what he calls **emotional intelligence**: self-awareness, emotional self-control, persistence, empathy, and social competence. Let's take a closer look.

> **Emotional intelligence** Self-awareness, emotional self-control, persistence, empathy, and social competence.

Self-Awareness

Self-awareness serves as the foundation for emotional intelligence. Goleman defines **self-awareness** as "an ongoing attention to one's internal states" (1995, p. 46). In other words, self-awareness involves consciously monitoring one's feelings as they occur. Ideally, Goleman suggests, one is able to monitor feelings objectively, almost as an unbiased observer in the mind. For example, if a close friend betrays you, you might naturally feel angry. Self-awareness would enable you to simultaneously recognize and label your anger as you are experiencing it, perhaps thinking, "I am feeling really angry about this." Self-awareness is the foundation of emotional intelligence in that we cannot hope to control our emotions if we are not aware of what they are when we are experiencing them. Thus, self-awareness is crucial to the second component of emotional intelligence, which is the ability to work through negative emotions.

> **Self-awareness** An ongoing attention to one's internal states.

Ability to Regulate Emotions

People high in emotional intelligence are able to effectively manage their emotions. It is almost impossible to predict *when* we will be struck by an emotion, but Goleman argues that we can and must learn to control the *duration* of the feeling, or how long it lasts. Emotions that go on too long become debilitating, such as depression (extreme sadness), rage (extreme anger), or mania (extreme joy). We have already discussed the problems associated with depression and rage, but one might wonder what could possibly be debilitating about extreme joy. As it turns out, the high arousal level that accompanies it seems to lead to an agitated state during which thinking processes can go awry. Thus, although a somewhat elevated mood is good for creativity and thinking, taken to the extreme it, like any other extreme mood, interferes with our functioning.

The essence of this component of emotional intelligence is **regulating emotions**. Goleman points out the difference between managing one's emotions and suppressing them: The idea is not to suppress them, for they are the very flavor of life. Instead, we should strive to keep our highs from becoming too high and our lows from being too low. By keeping our emotions balanced in this way, we can enjoy the spice they add to life without becoming disabled by them.

> **Regulating emotions** Managing the intensity and duration of feelings and the ability to delay gratification.

There is a second element of emotional regulation, and that is the ability to delay gratification. In a now-famous experiment, 4-year-old children were offered a choice: They could have one marshmallow immediately, or two marshmallows if they could wait for the experimenter to run an errand. The payoff for waiting 15–20 minutes (which must have seemed like forever to the children) was a doubling of the reward. When the experimenter left the room after explaining the choice to the child, about one-third of the children waited only a few seconds before grabbing the single marshmallow that so temptingly sat in front of them. The other two-thirds did whatever they had to do to distract themselves, covering their eyes, singing, or whatever they could think of to help themselves hold back until the experimenter returned.

What was the point of the experiment? When researchers followed these children as they grew up and graduated from high school, they discovered a significant difference between the two groups. Children who had successfully restrained the urge to grab the first marshmallow (thus delaying gratification in pursuit of a longer-term goal) were more socially competent than their less-patient counterparts. Specifically, research indicated that they were more self-assertive, motivated by challenges, self-reliant, and dependable. They were also less likely to buckle under stress. Children who had not been able to delay gratification at age 4 were less capable in their social environments as young adults. They became more upset and disabled by frustration, less trusting and more jealous, more prone to temperamental outbursts, and indecisive. Furthermore, researchers found that the ability to delay gratification also influenced academic performance. Children in the first group outscored children in the second group by more than 200 points on their SAT scores (Shoda, Mischel, & Peake, 1990).

Persistence

The third component of emotional intelligence is **persistence**, and it seems to be a natural outgrowth of the ability to regulate one's emotions. People high in emotional intelligence are able to stay focused on long-term goals, persisting through the inevitable frustrations and setbacks that may thwart a less-determined person. Goleman notes a couple of characteristics that facilitate persistence: optimism and flow. Optimism, discussed earlier in this chapter as one of the keys to happiness, seems to work in favor of goal achievement as well. By viewing frustrations and setbacks as challenges to be overcome (rather than permanent roadblocks), we can see hope in any situation and focus our efforts on finding creative ways to navigate around these temporary impediments.

> **Persistence** Continuing to work toward goals despite setbacks and frustration.

Flow, a concept first named by psychologist Mihaly Csikszentmihalyi (1997), refers to a state of being in which we feel we are one with what we are doing. Athletes refer to this state as "the zone"; others call it a "peak experience." Regardless of what we call it, it can be experienced in any kind of work or play. It is the ultimate harnessing of emotional energy to the point when we become so engrossed in what we are doing that we are no longer consciously thinking about it—we are instead part of it. At this point, our performance is excellent, exceeding our expectations, but if we stop to notice how well we are doing or consciously become aware of it in some other way, the feeling of flow is lost and with it, the level of achievement. A few examples of flow best illustrate its essence.

> "I felt like a waterfall," said gold-medalist Olympic skiier Diane Roffe-Steinrotter after her medal-winning run. She said she "remembered nothing about it but being immersed in relaxation." *(Goleman, 1995, p. 90)*

> Somehow the right thing is done without you ever thinking about it or doing anything at all. . . . It just happens. And yet you're more concentrated. *(Csikszentmihalyi, 1997, p. 87)*

An essential requirement to achieving flow is setting your goals at a challenging, but reachable level. If tasks are not challenging, Csikszentmihalyi says, we become bored, which prohibits us from engaging fully enough in the task to feel flow. Conversely, overly challenging tasks can lead to anxiety, which leads us to focus too much on the details or intricacies of the task or goal: Anxiety by its very nature prohibits the unconscious rhythm of flow. Having experienced flow even once, we are motivated further to achieve it again; thus, the internal reward it carries with it reinforces the persistence and motivation it took to achieve it the first time. In this way, emotionally intelligent people stay focused on their goal through persistence, which is facilitated by optimism and flow experiences.

 *Critical Thinking* QUESTION

Have you ever experienced flow? If so, what were you doing, and how do you think you got to that point? What concepts from Chapters 2 and 3 seem to fit well with the idea of flow?

Empathy

A fourth element of emotional intelligence is **empathy**, or the ability to feel the emotions of another person. Empathy is different from sympathy in that empathy involves sharing the other person's feelings, usually by having an understanding of what it feels like to be in that position. Sympathy is a more general sense of feeling badly about another person's situation without really imagining what it feels like. Another way to think about it is like this: Sympathy is feeling *for,* whereas empathy is feeling *with.*

> **Empathy** Feeling and understanding the emotions of another person.

The development of empathy begins very early in life when infants are nurtured emotionally by their parents and/or caregivers. A mother, for example, who picks up her crying baby while murmuring in an understanding tone, "Poor baby, I know you don't feel good, let Mommy hold you and make it better," shows empathy to the infant, which in turn promotes empathy in the child. Later, as a toddler, the child might empathize with a playmate who has fallen down and skinned her knee by going over to the playmate, patting her on the shoulder, and sharing her distress. Not surprisingly, research indicates that people with more empathy get along better with others. Also, studies measuring empathic ability suggest that women are generally more accurate than men in detecting and understanding others' feelings; we will explore this finding in more detail in Chapter 9 in our discussion of gender differences in human relations.

Special Topic
A CLOSER LOOK AT EMPATHY

Goleman's discussion of empathy focuses on the emotional component of empathy. Other researchers take a broader view of empathy that includes an additional component. Because empathy is a key aspect of good human relations, this expanded definition of empathy can be useful to us as we seek to expand our own empathic ability.

First, let us further distinguish empathy from sympathy. Empathy is different from sympathy in that empathy is a deeper emotion than sympathy. We can feel sympathy for someone's plight without knowing very much about it. We hear about a family whose home burned down, for example, and we feel sympathy for them. To empathize with them, though, involves a deeper understanding of what they are experiencing. Imagine the complex feelings involved in suddenly having nowhere to live, not having any of your own clothes to wear, and having lost all your photographs and other keepsakes; add to that the red tape typically involved in dealing with insurance (if they had any) and the immediate need to think clearly so you can find a place to live, take care of your children, and so forth. Recognizing and understanding the overwhelming nature of such a situation can help you to feel *with* them (instead of just feeling *for* them) as you feel their anguish, loss, fear, and worry about how they will put their lives back together.

True empathy includes a cognitive, or intellectual, component called *perspective-taking.* This part of empathy involves temporarily setting aside your own views on an issue to see the other person's viewpoint. For example, you and a friend might disagree on the subject of education:

You might believe that education is the best route to a better life, whereas your friend believes that education is expensive and carries no guarantee of a better job after graduation. The perspective-taking component of empathy would involve putting aside your own beliefs for a short time and truly trying to "put yourself into your friend's shoes" and understand the reasons for his beliefs.

The second component of empathy is the emotional component, wherein you allow yourself to feel what the other person is feeling. To do this, you must again put aside your own feelings for a time. Continuing with the example of a disagreement about the importance of education, you might initially feel angry and defensive when your friend disagrees with you: After all, you're putting a lot of time and money into getting an education. To experience the emotional component of empathy, you must first put this anger aside so that you can really listen to (and hear) your friend's viewpoint (the cognitive component), and then imagine how it would feel being in that position.

It is important to note that empathizing with another person does not mean that you must agree with that person. By making an attempt to truly empathize with your friend, though, you might come to understand his reasons for believing that education isn't a necessary or valuable key to a better life. Perhaps he has had friends who went to college, only to end up with huge student loan debts and working in jobs they could have had without a college degree. Understanding the reasons for his belief will help you to understand the feelings he has about education: Perhaps he feels angry when he applies for jobs that require a college degree when he is sure that he can do the job just as well without a degree. Empathizing allows you to put yourself in his shoes for a moment, giving you greater insight into his views and emotions about the issue. You may still disagree with him, but your relationship will be stronger because you haven't just heard his viewpoint, but you've actually experienced it with him.

Practicing empathy can be invaluable when we find ourselves in disagreement with someone close to us about an important issue. Too often, this situation results in conflict. Learning to empathize with the other person can reduce the conflict tremendously, thus allowing the relationship to thrive even in the face of disagreement. Sometimes, it can even dissolve the conflict if the empathy gained results in the realization that the issue has been blown out of proportion and isn't worth damaging the relationship.

To practice developing empathy in your own life, turn to Activity 4.3.

Social Competencies

The final element of emotional intelligence is something Goleman calls *social competencies*. These social competencies include the ability to organize groups, the talent to mediate conflict and negotiate solutions, the empathy necessary to make personal connections with people, and the ability to accurately analyze others' feelings, motives, and concerns. These social abilities all build on the foundations of emotional intelligence previously described: self-awareness, emotional regulation, persistence, and empathy. Taken all together, they facilitate the social competencies found in effective leaders and team players.

Interim SUMMARY #3

The concept of emotional intelligence grew out of the recognition that traditional intelligence wasn't a strong predictor of life success. Research into this relatively new concept has identified five key elements of emotional intelligence. Self-awareness is the act of paying attention to our internal states. The ability to regulate our emotions and delay gratification builds on self-awareness and also is a strong predictor of life outcomes. Persistence influences emotional intelligence through the mechanisms of optimism and flow. Empathy, or feeling with another person, facilitates life success through the strengthening of our relationships with others. Finally, social competencies include a variety of abilities that foster group and interpersonal relations.

THE ROLE OF STRESS IN HUMAN RELATIONS

PREVIEW QUESTIONS

(1) How are our bodies equipped to handle stress, and in what ways is this both helpful and harmful?

(2) What internal and external factors can help moderate the effects of stress?

(3) What strategies can help us cope with stress more effectively?

Thus far, we have seen how emotions influence our human relations through the irrational beliefs that we often have, through a few of our most common emotions, and through our emotional intelligence. Now let us turn our attention to a final aspect of how emotions influence our relations with others: when we experience stress.

Certainly, we've all experienced stressful times. Not only does stress make our lives more complicated and affect our physical and mental health, but stress takes its toll on our relationships with others. Thus, it is important to understand how stress affects our bodies and minds, and what we can do to better cope with the stress in our lives.

The Stress Response

Imagine that you are camping in the woods on a beautiful summer weekend. The warm sun is filtering through the trees as you wander along a trail, and you are filled with a deep sense of peace as you commune with nature. You round a curve and enter a small clearing. Suddenly your heart stops as you freeze in your tracks: A large bear got there before you did, and she doesn't look too happy at your invasion of her territory. What should you do?

If the familiar phrase "fight or flight" came to mind, you are right on target. This phrase, coined by researcher Walter Cannon in 1932, has become the common term for the first phase of the **general adaptation syndrome (GAS)**, which is the human body's response to stressful or threatening situations

> **General adaptation syndrome (GAS)** The human body's response to stressful or threatening situations.

(Selye, 1976). It is called an *adaptation response* because it is something our bodies and minds have developed over time as a way of adapting to or handling stress or threats. It is the same response that our primitive ancestors experienced when they crossed paths with a predator, and it must have been an effective response or else we (their descendants) wouldn't be here today.

In fact, this fight or flight response is uniquely designed to handle situations that require immediate response and are short-term, or **acute**, in nature: You either stay and fight, or run away—whether you live or die, it's over in a few moments. In today's world, though, many stressful situations are not resolved quite so quickly; in other words, they are **chronic**, or long-term. So, how does our long-established GAS work in today's world, and how effective is it in helping us cope with stress?

First, let's take a closer look at how the GAS actually works. The fight or flight response, or the **alarm phase**, is only the first phase of this three-phase system. When we are faced with a threatening or stressful situation, a number of changes occur in the body as it launches into this protective phase and prepares to combat the threat. The body releases a flood of certain hormones into the bloodstream, including epinephrine, norepinephrine, and corticosteroids. Epinephrine (also known as adrenaline) and norepinephrine promote a number of physiological changes that help the body cope effectively with the threat. For example, the heart rate and respiration increase, blood sugar levels rise, blood flow to the skin slows down while blood flow to the muscles speeds up, pupils dilate, perspiration increases, and digestion slows down. At the same time, corticosteroids are working to conserve stores of carbohydrates, reduce inflammation in case of injury, and pump up the immune system. For a more detailed picture of the body's response to stress, take a look at Figure 4.4.

> **Acute stressors** Stressful situations that require immediate response and are short-term.

> **Chronic stressors** Stressful situations not resolved quickly that are long-term.

> **Alarm phase** Fight or flight response.

Critical Thinking QUESTION

Each of the above-mentioned physiological changes produced during the alarm phase serves a specific purpose. Can you identify the purpose served by each change? For example, how does increased heart rate help the body cope effectively with a threat?

When faced with a threat, our bodies work amazingly fast and efficiently to prepare us to fight or flee from the danger. These temporary enhancements can only be sustained for a short period of time, however. If the threat continues, the alarm phase soon gives way to the **resistance phase**, which is the second stage in the GAS. During this phase, our bodies work to keep our immune systems at a peak and to repair damage while we continue to combat the threat. In this stage, our resistance levels aren't quite as high as they were during the alarm phase, but are still higher than normal.

Finally, if the threat continues to persist, our bodies can no longer sustain the enhanced levels of arousal and we enter the

> **Resistance phase** Our bodies work to keep our immune systems at a peak and to repair damage while we continue to combat the threat.

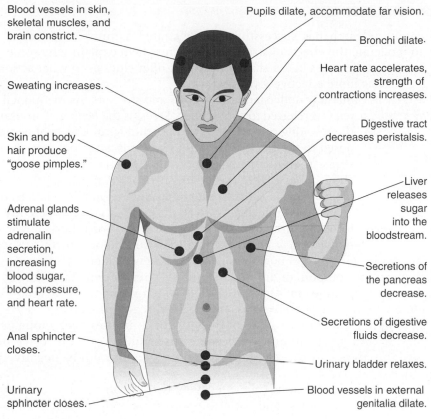

Blood vessels in skin, skeletal muscles, and brain constrict.

Sweating increases.

Skin and body hair produce "goose pimples."

Adrenal glands stimulate adrenalin secretion, increasing blood sugar, blood pressure, and heart rate.

Anal sphincter closes.

Urinary sphincter closes.

Pupils dilate, accommodate far vision.

Bronchi dilate.

Heart rate accelerates, strength of contractions increases.

Digestive tract decreases peristalsis.

Liver releases sugar into the bloodstream.

Secretions of the pancreas decrease.

Secretions of digestive fluids decrease.

Urinary bladder relaxes.

Blood vessels in external genitalia dilate.

FIGURE 4.4 | Bodily Reactions to Stress

exhaustion phase of the GAS. At this point, our resistance levels drop to a point that is below normal, because our resources have been depleted and can no longer combat the threat. As a result, we become more susceptible to a host of stress-related illnesses—and this stress-illness link isn't just a myth. Research has demonstrated connections between stress and a number of physiological and psychological conditions, including heart disease, ulcers, headaches, depression, and high blood pressure (Maier, Watkins, & Fleshner, 1994).

Clearly, our GAS is designed to help us cope effectively with **stressors** (threats) that are acute. Unfortunately, many of the stressors we face today are chronic, such as relationship conflicts, financial difficulties, stressful jobs, noise, crowding, and traffic jams. Are there any factors that can moderate, or buffer, the deleterious effects of long-term stress, or are we simply doomed to suffer the consequences of our stressful world?

Exhaustion phase Our resistance levels drop to a point that is below normal, because our resources have been depleted and can no longer combat the threat.

Stressors Stressful events or situations.

Moderators of Stress

Fortunately, research has successfully demonstrated a number of factors that seem to moderate the effects of stress. These factors help explain why some people seem to handle stress better than others, and offer clues as to what action we can take to cope more effectively with stress.

First, let us clarify our understanding of stress and stressors. As mentioned earlier, *any stressful situation* is referred to as a stressor. **Stress** is the feeling of arousal and the resulting physiological and psychological effects of being exposed to the stressor. So in other words, stressors may result in stress. It is interesting to note that people differ in their ideas about what constitutes a stressor. For example, starting a new job may be a real stressor for people who don't like change, or for a person who feels unsure about his ability to competently perform the tasks required in his new job. For others, however, a new job may be an exciting opportunity for growth or success, especially for people who get bored easily or enjoy new challenges.

> **Stress** The feeling of arousal and the resulting physiological and psychological effects of being exposed to the stressor.

An essential component in understanding stress, then, is cognitive appraisal, or the cognitive (mental) process by which we evaluate a situation to determine whether we perceive it as a potential threat. If the answer is yes, our GAS kicks in to combat the stressor. If the stressor continues over a long period of time, our GAS gives out and we become susceptible to illness. If we never perceived the stressor as a threat in the first place, we may not be negatively affected by it.

What factors, then, help us cope effectively with chronic stress? Certain personality traits, coping styles, and social support are among the factors that research has found to have a moderating effect on stress. These moderators work in a variety of ways: They can affect the appraisal process by influencing the degree to which we perceive an event to be a stressor; they can reduce the amount of stress we feel as a result of exposure to stressors; and they can reduce the impact of the stress by decreasing the link between stress and illness. Let's take a closer look at each of these stress moderators.

> **Control** The general belief that you can influence your life and your situations.

Personality Traits That Moderate Stress   A sense of **control** over your life and the stressful events that affect you can play a significant role in stress and illness. Sense of control surfaced before in this chapter in our discussion of happiness, where we found that feelings of internal control were linked to happiness. Many studies have investigated the connection between control and stress, and findings suggest strongly that people who feel more control cope more effectively with stressors and are less likely to become ill when exposed to chronic stress (e.g., Thompson & Spacapan, 1991).

> **Optimism** The tendency to focus on the positive aspects of a situation.

The second personality trait that moderates stress is another familiar concept: **optimism**. As you recall, optimism has been linked to happiness, and also to emotional intelligence. In addition, a number of studies have demonstrated a strong link between optimism and stress: Put simply, optimistic people feel less stress. For example, college students high in optimism were less likely to become ill at the end of a difficult semester (Scheier & Carver, 1985); also, optimists have been found to recover faster from heart bypass surgery than pessimists (Scheier, Matthews, Owens, Magovern, et al., 1989).

Hardiness is a third personality style that has been found to moderate the effects of stress. Conceived of by psychologist Suzanne Kobasa, **hardiness** is a personality style that consists of three components: control, commitment, and challenge. Control, as we have already noted, involves the belief that we can influence the events that happen in our lives.

> **Hardiness** A personality style that consists of three components: control, commitment, and challenge.

Commitment is the tendency to become fully involved in whatever activities or events in which we are engaged. Challenge refers to the perception that new things represent exciting possibilities, as opposed to the perception that change is somewhat unnerving. Each of these components can be measured on a continuum of low to high, and people who score high on each of these factors are said to have hardy personalities. Research indicates that hardiness increases both physical and mental health (e.g., Kobasa & Puccetti, 1983; Maddi & Kobasa, 1984).

In summary, control, optimism, and hardiness all moderate the effects of stress. Thus, people with greater tendencies toward these characteristics perceive stressors as less stressful than other people do. A sense of control alleviates stress by enabling a greater awareness of options in dealing with the stress. Optimism alleviates stress by enabling a person to focus on the brighter side of the situation and on possibilities, rather than on the darker side and potential problems. Hardiness seems to combine both of these principles into a general personality style that involves facing life head-on, with a positive outlook, eagerness, and a strong sense of self-efficacy.

Coping Styles and Stress In addition to some basic personality factors, the strategies people use in coping with stress have been found to play a significant role in physical and mental health. In general, coping strategies can be separated into two categories: problem-focused coping and emotion-focused coping. **Problem-focused coping** efforts are aimed at taking specific action geared toward reducing the threat presented by the stressor. For example, in trying to juggle a full-time job, school, and a relationship, problem-focused coping might involve constructing a schedule to help manage time better, or figuring out how to cut back in one area. **Emotion-focused coping**, on the other hand, is an attempt to regulate the emotional impact of the stress. An example of emotion-focused coping might include relaxation or anger management. Research suggests that both coping strategies can be effective in moderating stress (Folkman & Lazarus, 1980), indicating that neither strategy is necessarily better than the other in any given situation. In fact, a combination of both

> **Problem-focused coping** Taking specific action geared toward reducing the threat presented by the stressor.

> **Emotion-focused coping** An attempt to regulate the emotional impact of the stress.

strategies may be best: Take whatever action is possible to reduce the threat, and at the same time work toward reducing the negative feelings that are resulting from the stressor.

Social Support and Stress   **Social support**, defined as the awareness that one is cared for, valued, and part of a network of communication and mutual support, has been the focus of much research in stress, relationships, and physical and mental health. For adults and children alike, social support has been found to reduce the negative emotional effects of stress, and also to reduce the possibility of physical or mental illness developing as a result of chronic stress.

Social support The awareness that one is cared for, valued, and part of a network of communication and mutual support.

Consider these examples: Women with higher levels of social support experienced fewer complications in pregnancy and childbirth (Collins, Dunkel-Schetter, Lobel, & Scrimshaw, 1993); AIDS patients with more social support were less susceptible to depression (Zich & Temoshok, 1987); a long-term study of more than 7,000 people in California found that people with more social and community ties lived longer than those without such ties, regardless of health habits or socioeconomic status (Berkman & Syme, 1979); and breast cancer patients with more social support lived an average of 18 months longer than those without social support (Taylor, 1999). Indeed, social support is thought to be one of the most important indicators of physical and mental health.

Critical Thinking
QUESTION   What reasons can you think of that might explain why and how social support improves physical and mental health?

Coping Effectively with Stress

Now that we have a better understanding of how stress works and a few of the factors that significantly moderate the impact of stress, let's identify some specific strategies that we can employ to better cope with our own stressors.

First, let's apply the stress moderators we studied to our own coping strategies. Although it is true that personality factors by definition are relatively stable, there are things we can do to increase our sense of control, optimism, and hardiness. For example, people who are feeling "stuck" in a situation, without perceiving much control, can increase their sense of control by brainstorming all the different choices they could make to change the situation. Some of the choices will be things they do not want to consider, but simply recognizing that they are indeed choices can increase the perception of control they feel over the situation. And in addition, brainstorming often leads to recognition of some viable options that may have escaped recognition up to that point.

Finally, remember what you have already learned in this chapter and consider how it relates to stress. For example, the suggestion about increasing one's sense of personal control helps us cope with stress: Set challenging but realistic goals for yourself and work toward them in short-term increments to increase your chances for success. Also, stress is often caused or exacerbated by our thinking processes, so what we have learned about overcoming irrational beliefs can help us cope effectively with stress as well.

To increase optimism, research suggests making **downward comparisons**. In other words, you might think your situation is pretty awful, but think about people who are in worse situations. For example, breast cancer patients who have undergone a lumpectomy and chemotherapy report feeling better when they consider women who have had full or partial mastectomies (removal of one or both breasts) (Taylor, 1999). It is important to note here that downward social comparisons are *not* about taking any pleasure in someone else's misfortune; rather, they are simply the act of putting your own misfortune into perspective by acknowledging how it could be worse.

> **Downward comparisons** Identifying and acknowledging situations in which people are worse off than you are.

Hardiness has been shown to be amenable to change through a unique hardiness training program developed by Salvatore Maddi, one of the co-creators of the hardiness concept. In the training program, Maddi guides participants through a three-step process that includes both problem-focused and emotion-focused coping strategies. In the first phase, called **situational reconstruction**, participants imagine ways the situation could be worse, ways the situation could be better, and form an action plan that lists steps they can take to improve the stressful situation. As we can see, this phase effectively works to increase both control and optimism, while at the same time taking a problem-focused approach to coping with the stress.

> **Situational reconstruction** Imagining ways the situation could be worse, ways the situation could be better, and forming an action plan that lists steps to take to improve the stressful situation.

The second phase, called **focusing**, helps the participant learn to focus on how he or she feels about the situation, digging deep into those feelings in search of new insights that may lie at the heart of what is causing the stress. For example, you might be feeling stressed about your school schedule and the difficult exams that are coming up; focusing would help you dig into the feelings you have when you think about the situation to try to find out if there is more to the stress than you know. In this case, you may discover that what is really bothering you is fear of failing, and fear that you may never realize your career dreams. This new awareness might help you cope with your stress more effectively by understanding where the stress is really originating.

> **Focusing** Digging deep into feelings about a situation in search of new insights that may lie at the heart of what is causing the stress.

The third phase of Maddi's hardiness training program is aimed at helping participants who are in a situation that they truly cannot control. Maddi recognizes that there are indeed such situations and teaches that **compensatory self-improvement** can help us regain momentum and move forward in our lives when we are faced with an uncontrollable situation. In this phase, participants learn to identify something that may be related to the stressor that they previously ignored and take action in that related area. For example, a person who has always dreamed of being a professional basketball player may realize at some point that he simply isn't tall enough to compete

> **Compensatory self-improvement** Identifying something related to the stressor that was previously ignored, and taking action in that related area.

effectively in a professional league. In compensatory self-improvement, he may decide to pursue a career in coaching instead, or find another way to meet the needs that were at the heart of his goal to be a professional basketball player. Taken all together, the hardiness training program has been shown to effectively reduce stress (Maddi & Khoshaba, 2003).

Several other recommendations may be made in considering ways to effectively manage stress. Exercise, for example, has been shown to reduce stress (Kobasa, Maddi, & Pucetti, 1982). Also, a sense of humor appears to buffer stress. One study of college students found that students who were able to find humor in stressful situations suffered less stress from negative life events than students who could not find humor in stressful situations (Martin & Lefcourt, 1983). In keeping with the wealth of research on the benefits of social support, reaching out to friends and loved ones in times of stress is certainly a valid recommendation. Finally, there are a number of stress management programs that research has found to be effective in teaching people to better cope with stress. Typically, these programs involve three phases: They teach the participants to recognize the stressors in their own lives, work on building a variety of skills geared toward coping with the stress, and then practice the new skills and monitor their effectiveness in coping with real-life stressors (Taylor, 1995).

To examine the stress in your life, as well as how you can apply this information to better cope with it, turn now to Activity 4.4.

Interim SUMMARY #4

Stress affects our human relations in the toll it takes our physical, mental, and emotional resources: When we are stressed, we are less able to think clearly and interact effectively with others. The general adaptation syndrome (GAS) is a three-phase process our bodies use to cope with stressful situations (stressors). It works very well in situations of acute stress, but can lead to immune system breakdown and illness if the stressor persists over an extended period of time.

Research has demonstrated a number of factors that can moderate the effects of stress. Personality moderators include personal control, optimism, and hardiness. Problem-focused coping and emotion-focused coping can both be effective stress moderators. Social support is another important moderator of stress. Applying these concepts to your own stressful situations can help you reduce your stress level and keep you healthier.

CHAPTER TERMS

Activating event	Need for approval	Direct expression of
Cognitive appraisal	Tyranny of shoulds	anger
Self-talk	Perfectionism	Indirect expression of
Catastrophizing	Myth of helplessness	anger
Overgeneralization	Anger	Catharsis
Myth of causation	Aggression	Emotional intelligence

Self-awareness
Regulating emotions
Persistence
Empathy
General adaptation
  syndrome
Acute stressors
Chronic stressors

Alarm phase
Resistance phase
Exhaustion phase
Stressors
Stress
Control
Optimism
Hardiness

Problem-focused coping
Emotion-focused coping
Social support
Downward comparisons
Situational reconstruction
Focusing
Compensatory
  self-improvement

— **ACTIVITY 4.1** —

IDENTIFYING AND OVERCOMING YOUR IRRATIONAL BELIEFS

Common irrational beliefs include:

Catastrophizing
The myth of causation
The tyranny of shoulds
The myth of helplessness

Overgeneralization
The need for approval
Perfectionism

PART 1

The text discussion of these beliefs included descriptions and examples of each. Choose the four that seemed to best fit your own life and for each one, write an example of a time that you found yourself getting trapped by that irrational belief.

Example 1: _____ (name of irrational belief)

_____

_____

_____

Example 2: _____ (name of irrational belief)

_____

_____

_____

Example 3: _____ (name of irrational belief)

_____

_____

_____

Example 4: _____ (name of irrational belief)

_____

_____

_____

PART 2

Now, for each example, write your original interpretation of the event and the self-talk that led to your irrational belief, then rewrite the self-talk in a way that disputes the irrational belief and replaces it with more accurate information. For an example, refer to the section entitled "Disputing Irrational Beliefs" in this chapter.

Example 1:

Original interpretation and self-talk:

_____

_____

_____

_____

_____

Rewritten self-talk that provides a more accurate interpretation:

_____

_____

_____

_____

_____

Example 2:

Original interpretation and self-talk:

_____

_____

_____

_____

_____

Rewritten self-talk that provides a more accurate interpretation:

_____

_____

_____

_____

_____

Example 3:

Original interpretation and self-talk:

_____

_____

_____

_____

_____

Rewritten self-talk that provides a more accurate interpretation:

_____

_____

_____

_____

_____

Example 4:

Original interpretation and self-talk:

_____

_____

_____

_____

_____

_____

Rewritten self-talk that provides a more accurate interpretation:

_____

_____

_____

_____

_____

_____

_____

PART 3: REFLECTIONS

Now that you have completed this activity, what conclusions can you draw about irrational beliefs and your human relations?

_____

_____

_____

_____

_____

_____

— **ACTIVITY 4.2** —————————————————————

HANDLING ANGER CONSTRUCTIVELY

PART 1: IDENTIFICATION AND ANALYSIS

Think of three situations in which you found yourself angry. For each one, please complete the following steps:

1. Write a brief description of the circumstances.
2. Describe how you handled the situation.
3. Identify whether your reaction was constructive or destructive, and whether it was direct or indirect.
4. Consider how effective your reaction was and what you would do differently next time.

Situation #1

1. _____

   _____

2. _____

   _____

3. _____

   _____

4. _____

   _____

   _____

   _____

   _____

Situation #2

1. _____

   _____

2. _____

   _____

3. _____

_____

4. _____

_____

_____

_____

_____

_____

Situation #3

1. _____

_____

2. _____

_____

3. _____

_____

4. _____

_____

_____

_____

_____

PART 2: REFLECTIONS

Now that you have completed this exercise, what conclusions can you draw about the types of situations that typically anger you, the way you typically handle your anger, and the effectiveness of your reactions? What changes would you like to make in learning to handle your anger more constructively?

_____

_____

_____

_____

_____

_____

_____

_____

_____

_____

ACTIVITY 4.3

USING THE PILLOW METHOD TO DEVELOP EMPATHY

OVERVIEW

The Pillow Method is a technique used to gain empathy for someone else's perspective on a situation when it is different from your own and is consequently causing problems in your relationship with that person. This method involves looking at the issue from four different angles (like the four corners of a pillow) and forming a conclusion based on your new view of the whole issue.

ASSIGNMENT

College students report a great deal of insight on an issue when they write out all perspectives of the Pillow Method. Accordingly, this activity will ask you to write a paper that contains one to two paragraphs for each of the following steps of the Pillow Method. Overall, your Pillow Method paper should be about 3 pages.

1. *Background.* Identify an issue in which you and someone important to you have different and conflicting view points. Describe the situation and how it has evolved into a conflict or disagreement.

2. *Position 1: "I am right and you are wrong."* In this section, write out all of your beliefs about why you are right and the other person is wrong (this is the easy part!).

3. *Position 2: "You are right and I am wrong."* This is the hard part. Put your own beliefs aside and put yourself in the other person's shoes. Imagine how the person feels about the situation. Write down the beliefs and feelings that support why the person is right and you are wrong.

4. *Position 3: "We're both right and we're both wrong."* Now, reflect on parts 1 and 2 and consider the strengths and weaknesses of each side. Write them down in this section, making your best effort to be fair and even-handed for both sides.

5. *Position 4: "This issue has gotten blown out of proportion."* Often in a conflict situation, the very nature of the struggle results in the issue taking on a life of its own and becoming more of a problem than it deserves to be. Compared to the importance of the relationship at stake, the issue itself may need to be shrunk back to its appropriate size. Consider this as you write this section and strive to put the issue back into its proper perspective.

6. *Conclusion.* Reflect back on what you have written and consider how there is truth in all perspectives. Write about any new insights you have gained through this exercise. How do you think and feel about the issue now, and what will you do about it?

ACTIVITY 4.4
STRESS AND STRESS MANAGEMENT IN YOUR LIFE

PART 1: IDENTIFICATION

In the following space, briefly describe the situations in your life that are causing you to feel stress.

_____

_____

_____

_____

_____

_____

_____

_____

_____

_____

_____

_____

_____

PART 2: ANALYSIS

Now, review the text's discussion of stress moderators and coping styles. Consider which ones are currently playing a role in your reactions to the stressful situations in your life. For each one that is relevant to you, describe how it helps you handle your stress and consider how effectively it is working.

_____

_____

_____

_____

_____

_____

_____

_____

_____

_____

_____

_____

PART 3: LOOKING AHEAD

Finally, reflect on the available information on stress moderators and coping. Identify some concrete strategies you can use to reduce the impact of the stress in your life. In other words, make a list of ideas you have gained that can help you cope effectively with stress.

_____

_____

_____

_____

_____

_____

_____

_____

_____

_____

_____

_____

_____

THE ROLE OF PERCEPTION IN HUMAN RELATIONS

CHAPTER 5

> There is nothing either good or bad, but thinking makes it so.
>
> —WILLIAM SHAKESPEARE (*HAMLET*)

In August of 1997 Diana, Princess of Wales, was killed in an auto accident in Paris. When a group of American students was asked a few weeks later why her death had been a notable event worldwide, students differed in their responses.

> "She was such a compassionate person and a wonderful mother to her sons. She had suffered a lot during the years of her marriage to Prince Charles, and her death is made even more tragic by the fact that she was just now finding true happiness and coming into her own."

> "She lived her life in the fast lane, and died by it."

> "She was every guy's dream girl."

> "She had been out on a date with her boyfriend, a wealthy Egyptian playboy, and the driver of their car was too drunk to drive. It is rumored that their deaths were a plot by British loyalists to keep an Egyptian from gaining a link to the royal family."

> "She was a true humanitarian, giving generously of her time and celebrity to help raise money to find cures for AIDS, breast cancer, and other causes. She really cared about people, and it showed. I am struck by the fact that she and Mother Teresa died around the same time."

Five students, five very different perceptions. What, then, is the truth about why Diana's death attracted such worldwide attention?

This intriguing question provides us with an excellent example of one of the fundamental principles of social psychology: that *reality is subjective.* In other words, different people will have different perceptions of the truth in any given situation, simply because we filter our interpretation of an event or situation through our own belief systems, interests, values, expectations, and experiences.) Thus, each of the previous explanations given for the worldwide attention paid to Diana's death was the right explanation in the mind of the person who wrote it. The first explanation, for example, was written by a single mom who identified with Diana's struggles in her marriage and her devotion to her sons. The fourth explanation was written by a political science student who was fascinated with international relations, so you can see how his interests shaped his perceptions. Similarly, your own perception of an event will be shaped by your own filters. In this chapter we will explore some of the most common ways in which our differing perceptions can lead to misunderstandings and even conflict in our relations with others.

COGNITIVE BIASES THAT INFLUENCE OUR PERCEPTION

PREVIEW QUESTIONS

(1) How do our sophisticated brains set us up to make perceptual errors?

(2) Do first impressions really last? Why or why not?

(3) What are two cognitive biases that affect our perceptions and our relations with others?

(4) What is the fundamental attribution error, and how does it interfere with good human relations? How can it be overcome?

Humans have an innate need to understand and make sense out of the world. Throughout our millennia on this planet, our brains have evolved in ways that help us do this ever more quickly and efficiently. In fact, we human beings have amazing brains: We can process so much information in the blink of an eye! Unfortunately, this superfast processing speed comes with a price: the occasional mistake. In order to work so rapidly, our brains have developed a series of "mental shortcuts" that help us draw quick conclusions in a variety of situations. Although these mental shortcuts are often effective, they sometimes lead instead to a misjudgment about the person or situation.

These perceptual errors often play a key role in the judgments and conclusions we draw about people and events, so an understanding of what they are and how they operate is critical to our efforts to see others and the world more clearly. Only by learning about them, recognizing how they influence our own judgments, and continually reminding ourselves of these mental traps can we guard against them and increase our own resistance to them.

First, though, let's take a moment to focus on this need that humans have to make sense out of the world. Actually, this isn't just a human need—it is a basic survival need for all creatures with more developed brains. Think about it: To survive in any environment, a creature must be able to observe its surroundings, notice when two or more events seem related, and then construct some understanding of what causes what. In this way we are able to predict events, which is often critical to survival. Certainly, in the modern world, day-to-day survival isn't as big a concern as it was for our ancestors over the past several thousand years, but it's still a factor. For example, during hot summers, fires become more frequent and destructive in many dry wooded areas. This is probably not a news flash—most people know this, and we know it because people have observed incidences of fires and recognized a pattern of increased frequency during hot weather. Our well-developed brains allow us to make the mental connection between hot weather and forest fires, and to remember it. Thus, when the weather heats up, we can predict a greater risk of fires and take the necessary precautions.

Humans are constantly trying to figure out what causes things, whether it be a child's tendency to get an upset stomach, your pattern of headaches, or why your best friend sometimes acts grumpy. Often we are able to figure it out, which increases our confidence in our ability to see connections between events. Unfortunately, though, as our confidence increases, so does our vulnerability to these perceptual errors that are simply an outgrowth of our need to understand our world and the people in it. What are these errors? (Table 5.1 gives a summary.)

The Primacy Effect

You have probably heard about the importance of first impressions, and that is exactly what the **primacy effect** is all about. Research shows that people pay much more attention to initial information they receive about a person or situation than they do to later information. This was illustrated by a brilliantly simple experiment conducted by one of the most prominent social psychologists of the 20th century, Solomon Asch. Asch (1946) began by giving the participants in his study a list of character-

> **Primacy effect** People pay more attention to initial information they receive about a person or situation than they do to later information.

istics about a person they had never met. The list went as follows: intelligent, industrious, impulsive, critical, stubborn, and envious. Subsequent questions indicated that the participants formed a generally positive impression of this person (whom they hadn't met) based on the list. A second group of participants was given the same list, but the characteristics were in reverse order: envious, stubborn, critical, impulsive, industrious, intelligent. The list contained the exact same words, so shouldn't the second group of participants have formed the same impression of the

TABLE 5.1 | Cognitive Biases That May Lead to Misperceptions

Primacy Effect	Paying greater attention to the first information we get about a person or situation than to information that comes later
False Consensus Bias	Assuming that other people perceive and interpret things the same way we do
Confirmation Bias	Noticing and remembering information and events that support the beliefs we already have about something, while simultaneously failing to notice or remember information or events to the contrary
Fundamental Attribution Error	Assuming other people's behavior is a result of their personality, while failing to acknowledge potential situational influences

person? Logically, perhaps they should have, but the primacy effect biased their interpretations, and they formed negative impressions of the person instead. Both groups gave more weight to the first characteristics they knew about the person. Numerous similar studies confirm this general finding, strongly supporting the importance of the primacy effect. We do tend to form impressions of people based on how we perceive them the first time we meet.

Why do we do this? The answer is consistent with our earlier explanation of the human need to understand things. When we first meet someone, we don't know anything about the person; we don't have any idea what to expect. Thus, we are motivated to gather information about the person quickly and form an initial judgment as a way of determining whether the person is (in a general sense) a friend or foe. Although this is an extreme type of judgment today (and hopefully we don't make such judgments so quickly and blindly in everyday situations), you can see how it has been a critical asset in an evolutionary sense. Once we have some initial information, further information seems less important, so we pay less attention to it—our busy minds have moved on to something else. Hence, first impressions tend to be lasting impressions.

Is it possible to overcome the primacy effect? Unfortunately, it may be impossible to eliminate it entirely, although we can certainly make efforts to diminish its impact. The key lies in being mindful of its existence and its power over our judgment. When you first meet a person or acquaint yourself with a new situation (such as a new class at school or a new job), take a moment afterwards to examine your first impressions. Were they generally positive or negative? How strong were they? Make a mental note of them and remind yourself that they may or may not turn out to be completely accurate. Plan to keep an open mind as you learn more about the person or situation, and as you continue to gather impressions, compare them to your earlier ones. Do your best to be objective; don't reject or discount something just because it doesn't fit with earlier impressions. Then, after you've had longer-term exposure to the person or situation, you'll be in a better position to form a more accurate impression.

False Consensus Bias

A second perceptual error we tend to make is called the **false consensus bias**. Essentially, this is our mistaken assumption that others see things the same way we do. If we thought a movie was a good one, others must have liked it too, for example; or if we make a certain judgment about a person, we assume others drew the same conclusion. This bias was first demonstrated in a study conducted on a college campus (Ross, Greene, & House, 1977), which asked students to put on a sandwich-board sign that said "Repent" and walk around campus for 30 minutes. Students received credit for participation in the experiment whether they agreed to wear the sign or not. Students were also asked to estimate what percentage of other students would agree to wear the sign. In reality, 50% of the students agreed to wear the sign, but without knowing this, students incorrectly predicted that up to 77% would make the same decision they had made.

> **False consensus bias** Our mistaken assumption that others see things the same way we do.

By now, you're probably realizing the error in this assumption. Why do we do this? Research has found several likely reasons. First, we tend to associate more with people who are similar to us and who also share our beliefs. Thus, when we wonder how many other people think the way we do, it is only natural that our estimate would be skewed by the fact that our perception of "other people" relies heavily on our own experiences and our own social groups (Kunda, 1999). Also, as we will learn in the next chapter, assuming that others believe the way we do strengthens our own confidence in our beliefs (Sherman, Presson, & Chassin, 1984).

There is one interesting exception to this false consensus bias. When we are considering one of our talents, abilities, or positive qualities, we tend to see ourselves as more unique than we actually are. In other words, instead of assuming others are similar to us in these respects, we assume they are not. This phenomenon is known as the **false uniqueness bias**. For example, one study asked people whether they would stop to help someone whose car had broken down, and also what percentage of other people would do the same thing. People who said they would stop to help tended to underestimate the likelihood of others helping (Goethals, 1986).

> **False uniqueness bias**
> When we are considering our talents, abilities, or positive qualities, we tend to see ourselves as more unique than we actually are.

Critical Thinking **QUESTION** For any two of the three biases just discussed, give an example from your own life of a time that each bias contributed to a misunderstanding in a work or personal relationship.

The Confirmation Bias: Seeing What We Expect to See

Once we have gathered initial information about a person or situation and formed a judgment about it (often influenced by the primacy effect), a second type of bias takes effect and influences our perception of subsequent information. The **confirmation bias** involves our tendency to seek out and pay attention to information that supports our preexisting notions, and also to ignore or discount contradictory information. The unfortunate result of this bias is that our initial judgment, even if incorrect, is strengthened, because we pay attention only to information that supports it. Intricately linked to our need to find causal connections for events is our need to be right about our conclusions. The sooner we figure out the connection and form a conclusion, the sooner we can cross that concern off the list and turn our attention to the next issue. As a result, we sometimes rush to judgment without knowing it. Rapidly becoming a classic example of confirmation bias are the beliefs people formed in the O.J. Simpson case.

> **Confirmation bias** Our tendency to seek out and pay attention to information that supports our preexisting notions, and also to ignore or discount contradictory information.

Most people remember the case. In 1994, O.J. Simpson's wife and her friend were brutally murdered, and several days later O.J. was on the run in a white Bronco. In the months leading up to the trial, hundreds of details regarding the case and the evidence being collected were "leaked" to the press, and by the time the trial began it was a national television event. Most people made up their minds about O.J.'s guilt or innocence early on, without knowing very much about the evidence. People who remembered Simpson's great football career or his affable presence as a football commentator or rental car spokesperson were initially shocked. They couldn't believe that an American icon could commit such an unspeakable act. Once that initial conclusion was formed, it was easy to find reasons to reject the notion of Simpson's guilt; all they had to do was turn on the television and listen to his attorneys or other spokespeople for his defense. On the other hand, people who had strong feelings about the prevalence of domestic violence in our society and were aware of Simpson's history of such behavior had an easier time accepting Simpson's guilt. Once their initial conclusion was formed, all they had to do was turn on the television and listen to attorneys for the prosecution to find support for their beliefs. In both cases, people were seeking information to support the conclusions they had already drawn.

That is one key component in confirmation bias—*we look for evidence to confirm our existing beliefs.* When we find this confirming evidence, we grab it and remember it. When we encounter evidence to the contrary or something that doesn't fit, we tend to ignore or reject it. For example, people believing in Simpson's innocence, upon hearing that the infamous glove didn't fit, said, "See, I knew he didn't do it." Faced with DNA evidence from the crime scene that matched Simpson's DNA, though, Simpson supporters explained it away, suggesting that a racist cop planted the evidence.

The second component in confirmation bias is *the tendency to interpret ambiguous information in a manner consistent with your own beliefs.* The cut on Simpson's finger that was noticed by law enforcement two days after the murders is an example of ambiguous information. The cut appeared to be just a couple of days old, so those convinced of Simpson's guilt were sure he had accidentally cut himself while slashing the victims' throats. But Simpson's supporters pointed out that Simpson had a reasonable explanation for the cut: He said he was so upset when he heard of his wife's death, he had cut himself on a broken hotel glass. There was no way to prove where the cut actually came from, but people on both sides of the issue interpreted the evidence in a manner consistent with their preexisting beliefs and thus were certain the evidence supported their side.

To sum up, confirmation bias is an error we make in perception as we strive to determine the "right answer" to a problem or situation. We form an initial conclusion, often under the influence of the primacy effect, then the confirmation bias steps in to help us along our misguided way. The confirmation bias strengthens existing perceptions, whether they are right or wrong, by focusing our attention and memory on information that supports our original position. This protects us from the discomfort and anxiety caused by the possibility that we could be wrong, or that the answer is unknown. Working together, the primacy effect and confirmation bias can have substantial effects on our judgments and misjudgments of others. Once our minds are made up, we are often blind to new, conflicting information. As with the other cognitive biases we have discussed, the key to reducing the impact of the confirmation bias lies in continually being aware of it and remaining open to other viewpoints.

Sorry, Steve. I'll always think of you as the slimy, creepy
caterpillar I used to know.

FIGURE 5.1 | Which cognitive bias seems to be operating here?

Critical Thinking **QUESTION** Think of a recent news event (political, social, religious, etc.) about which you had a strong opinion. Identify at least one specific way you might have overlooked competing information in your effort to seek corroborating information.

The Fundamental Attribution Error

Have you ever been driving down the road, minding your own business, when suddenly another driver cut in front of you, causing you to hit your brakes? Or what about the driver who, on a highway or freeway, suddenly swerves across several lanes to make an offramp, rather than gradually moving from lane to lane as the law requires? And what about tailgating—don't you hate it when somebody tailgates you? What do you do in these situations? Most people find themselves calling the other driver some pretty rude names, thinking, "What a jerk! Who lets these idiots on the road, anyway?" It seems obvious that these drivers are reckless maniacs who shouldn't be on the road, doesn't it? But wait a minute—have *you* ever cut someone else off while driving or followed someone too closely? Sure, you probably have. Does that make you an idiot or a maniac? Of course not. You probably had a very good reason. Maybe you needed to get in the other lane, and traffic was so thick you had to cut it pretty close. Or maybe you were tailgating because you were running late and the driver in front of you was going too slow to be in that lane. Or maybe you were just a little distracted and didn't realize what you were doing. You're a good driver, but nobody's perfect.

Why is it, then, that when other people do these things they are maniacs, but when we do them, we're not? Are we all hypocrites? No, we are simply committing an error in perception known as the **fundamental attribution error**, which is our human tendency to assume that other people's behavior is due to something about their personality, while at the same time failing to consider possible situational influences. Unfortunately, as its name implies, we make this basic mistake in perception rather frequently as we strive to determine the cause of others' behavior. As a result, we often jump to a negative conclusion when, for example, someone is late or hurts our feelings. We may decide the other person is irresponsible, inconsiderate, or self-centered, thus making a general assumption about the person's character. We temporarily forget that we may have done this same thing at some point, and in our case there may have been a situational cause. It's easy for us to recognize something in *our* situation that caused us to be late, and we certainly didn't hurt someone's feelings intentionally. Maybe we were upset and said something hurtful in the heat of the moment, or maybe we didn't know it would hurt their feelings. It doesn't make us an inconsiderate or irresponsible person.

> **Fundamental attribution error** Our human tendency to assume that other people's behavior is due to something about their personality, while at the same time failing to consider possible situational influences.

Clearly, then, we're being a bit one-sided when we routinely see situational factors involved in our own slip-ups, but don't extend the same courtesy to others when they make the same mistakes. The reason this is such an easy trap to fall into has to do with the focus of our attention. When we are focusing on another person, what we notice most is the person himself. What is going on around the person, in his environment or situation, is peripheral to our view. Thus, when this other person does something that catches our attention, it stands to reason that we attribute his behavior to him, not his situation. This is known as an **internal attribution**, when we attribute a person's behavior to something about the person, his character, or his personality. When we are focusing on ourself, though, what we notice most is our surroundings—our environment or our situation—because that is what we see. As a result, when we do something slightly out of the ordinary, we explain our behavior in terms of a situational influence. This is known as an **external attribution**, when we attribute behavior to an external or situational factor. Basically, it's easy for us to see situational influences on our own behavior because we notice the situation more readily than we do when we're observing someone else's behavior. It follows, then, that we might unintentionally judge others more harshly than we judge ourselves.

> **Internal attribution** When we attribute a person's behavior to something about the person, his character, or his personality.

> **External attribution** When we attribute behavior to an external or situational factor.

Interestingly, people who live in cultures that value interdependence more than independence seem to be less likely to make the fundamental attribution error. One study that demonstrated this asked Americans and Hindu Indians to describe a situation in which someone they knew did something either good or bad to another person. Then they were asked to explain why the person did the good or bad act. Americans tended to attribute the behavior to the person's character (thus making the fundamental attribution error). Hindu Indians were more likely to explain the behavior in terms of situational forces, such as the person's role or responsibilities (Miller, 1984).

Overcoming the Fundamental Attribution Error

Understanding why we commit this error, though, doesn't absolve us of responsibility for it. Clearly, this mistake poses a threat to good relations with others. Fortunately, there are some easy steps we can take to overcome the fundamental attribution error and be more accurate in our explanations for others' behavior. Based on a formula developed by Harold Kelley (1967), we simply ask ourselves three questions that, when answered, will give us the information we need to determine whether our attribution is correct. This process will be easier to understand with an example, so let's imagine that your friend Jan borrowed your favorite CD and hasn't returned it, even though she was supposed to give it back the next day. If you jump to the conclusion that Jan is forgetful, you might be making the fundamental attribution error, because forgetfulness is a personality characteristic (an internal attribution). To be fair, you need to find out if there might be something in Jan's situation that is influencing her behavior. What three questions do we need to ask to make this determination? (See Figure 5.2).

First, *we need to know if the person has exhibited this particular behavior before in this situation*. Kelley calls this component **consistency**—in other words, is this a consistent behavior for this person in this situation? In this example, have there been other times Jan has borrowed things and not returned them promptly? If the answer is no, then making an internal attribution (calling her forgetful) is premature, because this is the first time she has done this. Something about her situation probably affected her behavior—maybe she's been studying for a big exam and forgot she had the CD. If the answer is yes, then perhaps an internal attribution is correct—maybe Jan *is* forgetful—but we still need more information.

> **Consistency** Whether a particular behavior typically occurs in that situation.

Next, we need to know if the person has exhibited this behavior in other situations. Kelley calls this component **distinctiveness**—in other words, is this behavior distinct to this situation? In this example, does Jan forget things in other situations, such as important dates, or does she just forget to return borrowed items? The answer to the distinctiveness question is tricky, because if you can say that *yes*, Jan is often forgetful in other situations, then the answer is *no* in terms of distinctiveness: Jan's forgetful behavior is *not* distinct to borrowing situations. If this is the case, then you have two pieces of information indicating that an internal attribution may be correct. Maybe Jan is indeed forgetful. She's forgotten to return things before and has also forgotten important dates. To confirm your impression, you can then go on to the third question. But, if you can't think of other situations in which Jan has been forgetful, then the situation is

> **Distinctiveness** Whether a particular behavior typically occurs in other situations.

FIGURE 5.2 | Avoiding the Fundamental Attribution Error

Event

Jan borrowed your CD and hasn't returned it.

Initial Attribution

Jan is a forgetful person. (An internal attribution)

Is this correct, or are you making the fundamental attribution error?

1. **Consistency:** *Has Jan been forgetful in this situation before? (Has Jan borrowed things and failed to return them in the past?)*

| **YES** | **NO** → You have insufficient evidence to conclude that Jan is a forgetful person; this may be an isolated incident. |

↓

2. **Distinctiveness:** *Has Jan been forgetful in other situations? (Has Jan forgotten other things, such as important dates?)*

| **YES** | **NO** → Although Jan has failed to return borrowed items in the past, she doesn't forget other things, so calling her forgetful is an overgeneralization. What is it about borrowing things that might lead to her forgetting? |

↓

3. **Consensus:** *Do others do this, too? (When you lend things to others, do they fail to return them, too?)*

| **YES** | **NO** → This behavior seems limited to Jan; she does indeed seem to have a pattern of forgetfulness. |

↓

If others also fail to return borrowed items to you, perhaps you are doing something to influence their behavior; for example, do you give any signals that returning them isn't urgent (i.e., "*Don't worry about it*" or "*It's no big deal*")?

---

distinctive, so the answer to this question is yes, and you must recognize that calling Jan forgetful is an overgeneralization and that you have made the fundamental attribution error. At this point, it would be a good idea to look for situational explanations for Jan's behavior. In this case, what is it about borrowing things that might be affecting Jan's memory? For example, maybe she remembers important dates by writing them down, but forgets about things she borrows because she didn't make a note of it.

> **Consensus** Whether other people typically exhibit this behavior in this situation.

The third question to ask is *whether others exhibit this behavior in this situation.* Kelley calls this component **consensus**, because it seeks to determine whether this behavior is common among other people. Think back and ask yourself if others who borrow your CDs also tend to keep them for too long. If the answer is no, then this is not a common behavior, so you do not have consensus; thus, it seems this behavior is limited to Jan. If you have already determined that Jan has forgotten to return your CDs before, and that she has often forgotten other things, too, then your internal attribution of Jan's behavior appears to be correct: Jan does seem to be forgetful. On the other hand, if others who have borrowed your CDs also keep them too long, then you can't assume that this forgetful behavior is due to something about Jan. In fact, it may be something about you—maybe you tend to give your friends the impression that returning things promptly is no big deal to you (see Figure 5.2).

At first, this formula may seem rather cumbersome. We make many attributions about others' behavior every day, so often that we typically aren't even aware that we're doing it. In light of this, asking yourself these three questions each time is unrealistic, because it would take too much attention away from other things you are trying to accomplish in your busy life. But you can use the formula in those instances when a meaningful person in your life does something that bothers you. Before you jump to a conclusion and make the fundamental attribution error, take a moment to ask yourself these three questions. In many cases, you'll realize that your initial judgment is premature or an overgeneralization. Reversing the error and recognizing the situational influences on the other person's behavior can go a long way in keeping relationships healthy.

To test your understanding of the fundamental attribution error in your own life, turn now to Activity 5.1.

Interim SUMMARY #1

Cognitive errors play a major role in our misperceptions and subsequent misunderstandings. These errors are the natural by-product of our sophisticated brain, but nonetheless can lead us astray in our interpretations and relations with others. The primacy effect is our tendency to pay more attention to initial information we have about a person or event than we do to information that comes along later. The false consensus bias is our erroneous assumption that others must see a person or situation the same way we do. The confirmation bias reinforces the primacy effect by predisposing us to pay more attention to information that confirms our preexisting beliefs, while simultaneously discounting or ignoring information to the contrary.

The fundamental attribution error, another powerful cognitive bias, is our tendency to assume that others' behavior is a consequence of their personality, rather than recognizing the many ways in which situational factors may be influencing their behavior. Fortunately, this can be overcome by a three-question process that includes a closer, more rational look at the consistency, consensus, and distinctiveness of the behavior in question.

INDIVIDUAL AND GROUP DIFFERENCES THAT AFFECT PERCEPTION

PREVIEW QUESTIONS

(1) In what ways does our physiology influence our perceptions of others?

(2) What are three ways that our cultural norms influence our perception of others and the world?

(3) What is perception-checking, and how can it help us avoid misunderstandings?

unaware of the effects of his or her stature on others, he or she may misunderstand their reactions.

Research shows some interesting findings about the effects of beauty. In general, people respond more favorably to others whom they find physically attractive. Also, people judged to be physically attractive are assumed to be more socially competent, smarter, and happier than less attractive people (Eagly, Ashmore, Makhijani, & Longo, 1991). In reality, though, there is no relation between physical attractiveness and happiness or psychological adjustment. Why? Because not all attractive people consider themselves to be attractive; attractiveness is subjective. What makes the difference is their own perception of their physical attractiveness. People who believe themselves to be more attractive do report higher self-esteem, however, than people who do not consider themselves as particularly attractive (Feingold, 1992).

Finally, being exposed to beauty influences our mood. The mere act of seeing others whom we perceive as attractive has the power to make us feel better or worse. When we see attractive people of the opposite sex, our mood becomes more positive, but when we see attractive others of the same sex as ourselves, we feel less positive (Kenrick, Montello, Gutierres, & Trost, 1993).

To explore the ways in which biological factors have played a role in your own perceptions and in others' perceptions of you, turn now to Activity 5.2 at the end of this chapter.

Special Topic
BEAUTY AND BODY IMAGE: A CULTURAL OBSESSION

Physical attractiveness has long been considered important in Western culture. It may surprise you, however, to know that definitions of attractiveness vary over time and among various cultural groups. The current Western standard of beauty for women prefers extreme slimness, in contrast to standards just a few decades ago. Recent studies comparing Playboy Playmates of the Year, Miss America Pageant winners, and fashion models over the last 80 years found the BMI (body mass index, which essentially measures your lean-fat ratio) in these women declined significantly over the past few decades, to a point where many of the models currently meet weight standards for anorexia (Owen & Laurel-Seller, 2000; Byrd-Bredbenner, Murray, & Schlussel, 2005).

Fifty years ago, for example, the average weight of the woman crowned Miss America was 134 pounds; in the 1990s her average weight was just 117 pounds. Similarly, fashion models in the 1960s weighed about 8% less than the average female, but by 1992 the difference had tripled, with models averaging a weight that was 25% less than the average woman. This pursuit of the ultra-thin body has become an obsession for many American women, beginning in their early years. One study reported that 56% of teenage girls had tried to lose weight because they perceived themselves to be too heavy; in reality, most of these dieting teens were within a normal weight range (Patton et al., 1997).

Interestingly, this perception of beauty is not shared by all cultures of the world, and not even all cultures within the United States. A study comparing British and Ugandan perceptions of beauty, for example, showed participants a set of drawings of both female and male bodies. The body sizes ranged from anorexic to obese, with more average sizes in between. The Ugandan participants rated the larger female figures higher than the British participants did (Furnham & Baguma, 1994). In traditional African cultures, larger bodies are symbolic of wealth, prosperity, and high status. Also, African American women in the United States have been less likely than white women to feel pressured by the ultra-thin standard of beauty, although this pattern may be changing. A 1994 study published by *Essence* magazine reported that, although wealthy African American women and poor African American women still were unconcerned with the pursuit of thinness, middle-class African American women reported feeling more pressure to be thin.

 **Critical Thinking QUESTION** What reasons can you think of that might explain the pressure to be thin felt by middle-class African American women, but not by their wealthier or poorer counterparts?

Cultural Influences on Perception

A couple of years ago, Catherine, one of my students, told this story about the time she met her fiancé's best friend, David. David was from France; Marco (the fiancé) had met him on a student exchange program, and they had been good friends ever since. Marco and Catherine's wedding was approaching, and they were both excited that David had agreed to fly over and be Marco's best man. On the day he was to arrive, both Marco and Catherine had planned to meet him at the airport, but Marco got called in to work at the last minute, so Catherine went to the airport alone. She and David had never met before, but both had seen pictures of each other, so Catherine was sure she and David would recognize each other when he got off the plane. Sure enough, they did, and as she held out her hand to greet him, she was taken aback when he wrapped his arms around her and kissed her with great enthusiasm. What a slime, she thought—she had never met this guy before, and moreover, she was about to marry his best friend, yet he was coming on to her! She was too embarrassed to say anything to him, though, and was really upset at the dilemma it put her in: Should she tell Marco the truth about his lecherous friend, or should she just pretend it never happened?

Well, fortunately for all of them, Catherine soon found out that David wasn't coming on to her at all—when he hugged her and kissed her on both cheeks, he was simply greeting her in the way that was customary in his culture. You can imagine Catherine's relief when she realized she had made a mistake in her interpretation of David's behavior. This is just one example of how easy it is to misunderstand things people say or do when their culture differs from your own. And because we don't know all the different customs of the many cultures in the world, we often have no way of knowing when we do make a mistake. As a result, we may end up misjudging someone completely, and we all know how frustrating and even hurtful being misunderstood can be.

What can we do about it? Well, the first thing we can do is to continue to educate ourselves about different cultural norms and beliefs. When necessary, we can use the Pillow Method (which we learned in Chapter 4) to develop a deeper understanding of and empathy for those beliefs that really differ from our own. Remember, gaining a deeper understanding of someone else's belief and accepting it as valid doesn't mean you are sacrificing your own belief. Later in this chapter, we'll learn a communication technique that we can use in situations when we aren't sure if our interpretation is correct. For now, though, let's work on the educational component and take a closer look at some of the most common cultural differences we encounter that influence our perception.

Personal Space   Have you ever been talking to a person who seemed to want to stand closer to you than you thought was appropriate or comfortable? What did you do? Did you casually take a step back, trying to make it look as if you were just shifting your weight from one foot to the other? Did you merely lean back slightly, so your faces weren't so close together? Or did you cut the conversation short and get away as soon as possible?

If you've ever been in this situation, you probably remember how uncomfortable it was. What was happening was that your personal space boundary was being violated. In the United States, research indicates that there are at least three categories of **personal space** boundaries (Hall, 1966), which identify what most Americans perceive as the comfortable amount of distance required in various types of situations. The "intimate zone," which is zero to 18 inches, is reserved for our closest friends and loved ones, often in private conversations. The "personal zone," 18 inches to 4 feet, typically denotes casual interactions with friends, acquaintances, and familiar coworkers. From 4 to 12 feet is the "social zone," a space boundary we usually need for professional interactions with people we do not know well or at all.

Personal space   The comfortable amount of distance between people in conversation.

Consequently, our urge to back up when someone comes too close is simply our effort to reestablish a comfortable distance. If we cannot do that, then we feel discomfort or even anxiety, which interferes with our communication ability. Our interpretation of someone who stands too close is likely to be a negative one, because the person's behavior is causing us discomfort.

On the other hand, what if someone were trying to have a one-on-one conversation with you from a distance of about 6 feet? Wouldn't that seem like a little too much space? Consequently, wouldn't you feel compelled to move a little closer? Many North Americans and northern Europeans would, which illustrates the relatively narrow margin of error in personal space boundaries. You may not have found this to be much of an issue if you spend most of your time with people from your own culture. When you interact with people from different cultures, though, you might encounter different personal space boundaries.

For example, people from Italy, Greece, and other southern European cultures (as well as Middle Eastern cultures) have a closer personal space boundary than Americans do, so their comfort zone is going to propel them to stand closer to an American than the American is probably going to be comfortable with. Imagine that you are talking with someone from one of these other cultures. This other person moves in close—say, about 1½ to 2 feet away, so you back up a little to reestablish your own comfort zone of 3 to 4 feet. The other person then moves in closer, trying to find a comfortable space again. What are you both thinking? The other person is probably thinking you are rude, or not interested in the conversation, or maybe that they smell bad, since you keep backing off. You may be thinking the other person is rude or pushy, since they're trying to invade your space (you think).

What's really happening, though, is that 2 feet of space to the other person is equivalent to 3 or 4 feet to you, so when you move farther away, it feels to the other person the way you would feel trying to talk to someone about 6 feet away. Both of you are misjudging the other as a result of interpreting their behavior based on your own cultural norms. Once you understand each other's behavior more accurately, you realize that you're both doing the same thing for the same reasons.

Eye Contact　　Imagine that you are going to an interview for an important job that you really want. What will you do to make a good impression? Many people list eye contact at or near the top of the list. Eye contact, in white American culture, signals honesty, interest, and sincerity. When we're talking with someone who doesn't maintain eye contact, but instead looks down or away while talking and listening, we might wonder what the person is hiding, or assume lack of interest, low self-esteem, or lack of confidence.

Here again, though, this is a Western cultural norm—norms are different in many other cultures. In Asian cultures, for example, it is *disrespectful* to look a potential employer in the eye—the employer is considered more of an authority figure, and many Asian cultures have strong rules about the importance of respecting authority. To look an authority figure (whether it be an employer, parent, or teacher) in the eye is to signal that you think you are of the same status, which is interpreted as disrespect. So, if someone from a traditional Asian culture is applying for a job with a traditional American company, the Asian applicant might avoid eye contact as a show of respect, but be interpreted by the American employer to be dishonest or lacking confidence. You can see, then, how important it is to be aware of different eye contact norms, since mistakes can have a significant impact on our relations with others.

Eye contact norms differ in some less formal interactions, as well. In much of the United States, for example, if a woman makes casual eye contact and perhaps smiles or says "hello" as she passes by someone on a sidewalk or in a hallway, she is considered polite. If a woman does this as she passes by a man in Mexico, South America, or many areas of southern Europe or the Middle East, however, she risks being considered brazen, and the man may interpret her eye contact as sexual interest. This is a very important rule for American women to remember if they are planning to travel to any of these areas, because women have sometimes been followed, harassed, and even assaulted by men in this situation.

Talking Rules　　Rules of conversation—**talking rules**—also differ among various cultures in a number of ways. One difference has to do with the general value placed on talking. In the United States, for example, talking is one of the dominant means of connecting with others; hence, a conversation that has many periods of silence is usually considered to be an uncomfortable situation. We've even developed a range of "filler words" such as "um," "you know," and "like" to use when we're searching for the right word or phrase.

> **Talking rules**　Rules of conversation.

Many Asian cultures, along with Native American cultures, have the opposite view: Silence is valued more highly than talking. To people from these cultures,

Americans seem like chatterboxes. Furthermore, cultures that value silence perceive silence as a time when a person is thinking deeply and thoughtfully; if you are talking, then you can't be thinking. Americans, on the other hand, tend to "think out loud." Once again, these two opposing viewpoints can interfere with our human relations if we don't understand that they are rooted in equally valid cultural values.

Another interesting difference with regard to conversational rules has to do with what some people would call interrupting. This is humorously illustrated by one of my former students, who told the story of the time she first met her future husband's family. She was at their home for a holiday meal, and in telling our class about it she said, "I couldn't get a word in edgewise!" She said his family members just kept talking and talking, interrupting each other and talking over each other, and there was never a pause in the conversation that would have given her a chance to say anything. Consequently, she didn't say much the entire evening, and her fiancé's family later remarked to him that she seemed rather aloof and uninterested in their family. She, ironically, had left thinking *they* weren't very interested in *her!*

Well, as you might have guessed, that wasn't the case at all. Her fiancé's family was of Italian descent and lived in New York, and their conversational style was rapid and emotional, with the expectation that others just jump right in; several people talking at once was no problem. She, however, was of German descent and lived in the Northwest, and her family's conversational style was slower, with the expectation that one person speaks at a time, followed by a short pause in the conversation to signal that it's okay for someone else to speak. In her family, two or more people talking at the same time was considered rude, whereas in his family it was considered normal and a sign of closeness. Fortunately, each of them was able to adapt to the other's family, and after figuring out what their differences were, they got along very well.

One other difference regarding conversational rules deals with the use of "small talk." Typically, Americans take pride in efficiency and place great value on getting a job done well and quickly. Thus, when people meet in some type of business environment, Americans often get right to the point, immediately bringing up the relevant topic. If the other person tries to engage in some "chit-chat," perhaps commenting on the weather, sports, or some other nonrelated subject, the traditional American might perceive the other person as avoiding the issue. If the other person is a subordinate in some way (such as an employee), the American might even think the employee is unprepared or trying to schmooze.

Once again, though, not all cultures share American beliefs and values about efficiency. Many Asian, southern European, and Middle Eastern cultures, for example, value relationships over efficiency, and thus wouldn't think of talking business until they had exchanged some small talk, thus creating a comfortable rapport. Someone who tried to avoid small talk and jump right into a discussion of business would appear rude and inconsiderate.

Clearly, then, we can see how easy it is to misjudge someone based on cultural differences. All of us, regardless of our own culture, interpret others' behavior through the lenses of our own cultural norms, and when someone "breaks a rule," we perceive the person to be rude or lacking in some way. Ironically, they

(handwritten note in top margin: "where we left off 5-8-14")

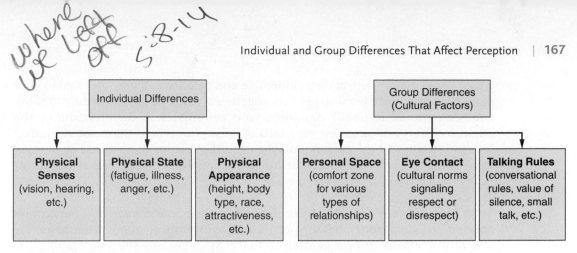

FIGURE 5.3 | Individual and Group Differences Affecting Perception

are usually thinking the same thing about us, and these misperceptions can wreak havoc on our human relations. Knowing some of these more common differences is a great start to better understanding of other cultures. Figure 5.3 summarizes differences affecting perception.

To explore ways in which cultural factors have influenced your own relationships and experiences, turn now to Activities 5.3 and 5.4 at the end of the chapter.

Perception-Checking: A Remedy for Misjudgments

We can see, then, that numerous physiological and cultural factors influence our perception, and the impact is doubled by the fact that perception is a two-way street. Any of these factors can alter our perception of someone else, while at the same time alter others' perception of us. In addition, there are numerous situational influences on a person's behavior, which increase our odds of drawing the wrong conclusion. One remedy for this potential minefield of misjudgments is to simply recognize the many ways our perception can differ from others', and make it a practice to give others the benefit of the doubt. Sometimes, though, we feel a need to get some specific clarification of the reasons behind another person's behavior. We may acknowledge the possibility of a misjudgment on our part, but not know how to correct it. For these situations, there is a simple communication tool we can use called perception checking.

Perception-checking is a three-part statement you make to another person when you need clarification of something the person said or did. Essentially, you describe what you noticed, then offer a couple of different interpretations that come to mind, asking which interpretation is the correct one.

> **Perception-checking** A three part statement you make to another person when you need clarification of something the person said or did.

For example, imagine that you are out at a club with the person you are romantically involved with, and you come back from the restroom to see this person standing very close to the person you know he or she had been dating before you. Their heads are close together, and they are laughing and looking into each other's eyes. It would be easy in this situation to jump to the conclusion that they want to get back together, which could make you feel very vulnerable and defensive. If you later said to your date, "You obviously want to get back together with your ex," how do you think your date would respond? Assuming your assumption is incorrect, he or she might feel hurt and angry at your lack of trust. The whole thing could escalate into a big fight, and the evening (maybe even the relationship) would be in trouble. Wouldn't it be better to handle it more rationally with perception-checking? Let's give it a try.

Steps in Perception-Checking ⎛*The first step in the process is to describe the person's behavior.*⎞ In other words, tell the person what you noticed about what he or she said or did, and do it in a neutral, factual way. *Make sure you aren't substituting your interpretations for the facts,* which is an easy mistake to make. In our example, if you said, "I saw you with your ex, and it was obvious that you want to get back together," you would be describing your interpretation of the facts, instead of the facts themselves. That would be a mistake, because it implies that you can read the other person's mind, which often puts the other person on the defensive. Instead, just state the facts: "I noticed that you were talking with your ex earlier, and you were standing pretty close together." The key to delivering this description of behavior successfully is to make sure your nonverbal communication signals your sincere attempt to understand what was going on. If you make this statement in an accusatory tone of voice, accompanied by a glare, it won't work.

⎛*The second step in perception-checking is to offer a couple of different ways you think you could interpret the behavior.*⎞ In this example, after saying, "I noticed you talking with your ex earlier, and the two of you were standing pretty close together," you could follow it with, "I didn't know if you were feeling interested in him (or her) again, or if you were just trying to hear each other over the band, or if it was something else."

By doing this, you are conveying your concern to your date, while at the same time acknowledging that there might be a simple, innocent explanation. This approach tends to reduce the possibility of the other person becoming defensive, which in turn increases the likelihood of getting the truth and of keeping your relationship stable.

⎛*The third step in perception-checking is asking the other person which interpretation is correct.*⎞ Sometimes you won't even need this step, because many people will respond after you've described the behavior and offered a couple of different interpretations. At times, though, you'll need to be more direct and follow up with something like, "Why were you standing so close together?" or "What was going on?" Alternatively, you can phrase the second part of your perception-checking statement in the form of a question: "Are you still interested in her (or him), or were you just trying to hear each other over the band?" Either way, your nonverbal signals must signal sincerity and open-mindedness as you use perception-checking, or else your carefully worded effort will be wasted. If you are feeling strong emotions, it is usually a good idea to wait until you are feeling calmer before talking to the other person about the situation and using perception-checking. Table 5.2 summarizes the use of perception-checking.

TABLE 5.2 | Applying Perception-Checking

DESCRIBE BEHAVIOR	OFFER POSSIBLE INTERPRETATIONS	ASK FOR CLARIFICATION
I noticed that you were talking with your ex earlier, and you were standing pretty close together.	I didn't know if you were feeling interested in him (or her) again, or if you were just trying to hear each other over the band.	What was going on?

Tips for Using Perception-Checking   This technique works best in cultures that prefer direct communication, such as American culture. Many other cultures, such as Asian and Middle Eastern cultures, feel offended by such directness and prefer a more indirect way of communicating. In these instances, perception-checking would probably embarrass the other person and thus would not be effective. We'll go into more detail about cultural differences in communication in Chapters 8 through 10.

One final note on perception-checking: When first exposed to it, people often have one of two reactions. One reaction is that it simply isn't necessary—that you can understand what people mean just fine without asking. After reading and absorbing the first part of this chapter, hopefully you know better than to fall into that trap! The other common reaction accepts that perception-checking is a useful tool and thinks it will be easy to use. But although this technique is simple, it takes practice to use it gracefully and effectively on the spur of the moment.

The best way to learn a new communication technique is to practice it in hypothetical situations at a time when you aren't feeling the stress of an emotional situation. That way, you can become more skilled at using it, so that when you need it in a real-life situation, you can use it with ease, thus avoiding a potential misunderstanding. Toward that end, each time a new communication technique is introduced in this book, there will be an accompanying worksheet with hypothetical situations to help you practice using that new technique. To help learn perception-checking, turn now to Activity 5.5 at the end of the chapter.

Interim SUMMARY #2

Both internal and external factors influence our perception of events. Internal factors, called physiological factors, include our physical senses (sight, hearing, etc.), our physical state (whether we are fatigued, etc.), and our physical attributes (such as height, attractiveness, etc.). Each of these factors can influence our perception of a person or situation and can also affect another person's perception of us.

External factors that influence perception are rooted in cultural norms. Personal space boundaries set the appropriate distance to be maintained between people in a conversation, and in some cultures depend on the nature of the relationship between the persons. Norms regarding eye contact also vary widely among cultures, with some Western cultures interpreting direct eye contact as a show of respect and some Eastern cultures interpreting direct eye contact as a sign of disrespect. Talking rules also vary cross-culturally: Some cultures prefer structured conversations in which one person speaks at a time, whereas others prefer more flexible conversation patterns in which several people may talk simultaneously. Understanding these differences is important to accurately interpret behavior that is different from our own.

Perception-checking is an excellent tool that can help us clarify another person's behavior when we aren't sure how to interpret it. It is a three-step statement that includes a factual description of the behavior or event, two alternate interpretations for it, and a request for clarification.

MEMORY AND PERCEPTION

PREVIEW QUESTIONS

(1) How accurate are our memories? How do memory errors influence our human relations?

(2) What perceptual errors can skew our memories and lead to misunderstandings with others?

Memory Is Reconstructive

True or false: Memory is like a tape recorder in the brain: It records events and information, so that we can retrieve it when we need it.

Answering "true" to this statement is not unusual—this is often how memory is perceived. We talk about retrieving a memory, or make reference to "filing" information away in our brain in case we need it later. These images of memory lend themselves well to the "memory is like a tape recorder" analogy, and until fairly recently, even scientists thought this to be correct. Over the past few decades, though, there has been a great surge of research on memory, and our understanding of memory has vastly improved as a result. We now know, for example, that memory is not like a tape recorder in the brain, and rather than retrieve information, it is more accurate to say we *reconstruct* it.

Therefore, memory is more accurately made up of perceptions, and thus it is subject to the same perceptual errors we have been discussing in this chapter. Memory is also vulnerable to an additional set of errors that result from the ways it is encoded and retrieved, and there are numerous opportunities for these errors to occur. What are some of these errors, and how can we use this information to improve our relations with others? To answer these questions, we must first develop a general understanding of how memory works.

The Stages of Memory

The memory process has three stages: encoding, storage, and retrieval. Essentially, we take information in, store it, and retrieve it later as needed. Although memories left "in storage" are subject to decay and interference, it is the encoding and retrieval phases in which perceptual errors are most likely to occur, thus modifying our memories. It is through these errors that our perceptions of past events become distorted. Let's examine these interesting processes more closely.

Encoding and Schemas   In the **encoding** stage, we take information in and organize it in a way that is meaningful to us, so that we can store it for later retrieval. This organizational process leaves much room for various perceptions. One dominant model of memory, called the *three-box model* (see Figure 5.4), suggests that the first step in this encoding process is a type of memory called **sensory memory**. When we are exposed to a situation or event, our five senses, through which we gather information, are flooded with input. How can we remember it all? We can't. In fact, research on sensory memory has indicated that although we have the capacity to take in a large amount of sensory information, we can only retain it for a second or two. Anything that grabs our attention may then continue on to the second step in the encoding process, known as **working memory**. Working memory can hold information for about 30 seconds, according to research findings, after which anything still retained might finally make it to the last stop in the encoding process, known as **long-term memory**. During the brief period of retention afforded by sensory and working memory, we must make determinations about what information (if any) is important enough to retain more permanently in long-term memory.

> **Encoding** Taking in information and organizing it in a way that is meaningful to us, so that we can store it for later retrieval.

> **Sensory memory** 1-2 second time frame during which we encode information from our immediate sensory experiences.

> **Working memory** A time frame of about 30 seconds during which we either use and dispose of the information, or work to retain it.

> **Long-term memory** Relatively permanent storage of information.

Different people in the same situation, then, might naturally focus on different pieces of information—thus, the first opportunity for differing perceptions occurs. Say, for example, that you and a friend witness a car accident. The accident happens in the span of just a few seconds. What images impact you most during the 1 second or less of your sensory memory? And in the ensuing 30 seconds following the accident, what details will seem most relevant to you? Research on working memory suggests that it is limited in capacity to between five and nine pieces of information, so some details will naturally have to be filtered out prior to the information making it to long-term memory. Do you think you'll both notice the same things in the initial second, and also filter out the same things in the next 30 seconds? Probably not; it is more likely that your impressions will have some things in common, but there will also be some differences. Remember the various physiological factors that influence our

---

FIGURE 5.4 | The Three-Box Model of Memory

Sensory Memory	$\rightarrow$	Working Memory	$\rightarrow$	Long-Term Memory
(1–2 seconds)		(About 30 seconds)		(Relatively permanent)

perception. Any of these factors can play a role in what we notice and how we interpret a situation.

> **Schemas** Sets of beliefs and expectations each of us has about certain concepts, events and situations.

At this point, as we are forming our memories to transfer to long-term storage, another opportunity for error presents itself. **Schemas** are sets of beliefs and expectations each of us has about certain concepts, events and situations. They typically consist of all the related pieces of information you have about something, such as various occupations, types of people, and social or environmental situations, and the information about each one clusters together for easy access in your mind. They include the various images that come to mind, along with the various rules that fit the situation. For example, we all have schemas for being in school that involve appropriate classroom etiquette, where people sit, patterns of speaking, and so forth, which are based on our own experience in school. People who have attended colleges that emphasize traditional modes of education would probably have a schema that reflected students sitting in rows of desks, taking notes, and not speaking very often, while the professor stands in the front of the classroom and lectures. On the other hand, students who have attended colleges that rely on more interactive modes of education would likely have a different schema, perhaps picturing students sitting in small groups or in a circle, discussing issues and theories, moving about the room, or participating in some other hands-on type of project. Thus, it becomes clear that different people can have different schemas for the same thing, depending on individual past experiences.

Schemas influence our encoding because they can modify the way we interpret or perceive a situation. Remember that sensory memory can only hold images and sounds for 2 seconds or less. Since it is impossible to catalog all of the sensory information available in any given situation, we grab onto whatever gets our attention and lose the rest. Then the sensory information that makes it into working memory must be organized to be retained in long-term storage. Studies indicate that we must organize the information in a meaningful way—if it doesn't make sense to us, we are likely to lose the information before it gets to long-term memory. During this processing, if there are gaps in the information we were able to hold on to, we fill in those gaps based on our available schemas.

This is not generally a deliberate process, but one that goes on without intention or awareness. In the earlier example of witnessing a car accident, for example, imagine that as you are rounding a corner at an intersection, you see two cars slam into each other ahead on the street. As you take in and process what you saw, your schemas about the drivers might influence your perception of who was at fault for the accident, especially since you turned the corner just as they hit each other and only got a glimpse of what happened. If one driver is a young teenage boy driving a flashy sports car, and the other driver is a responsible-looking, well-dressed businessperson in a four-door sedan, which driver will witnesses more likely indicate is the driver at fault? Many witnesses in this situation would probably assume the teenage boy was at fault. Their schemas of young teenage boys in sports cars might include recklessness and inexperience, whereas if the other driver "looks like a responsible person," he or she will be presumed to be a responsible person and thus probably not at fault. Witnesses will encode the information as they perceive it with the help of their schemas, but because they aren't aware that their schemas are operating to modify the encoding, they will "remember" the incident as they *think* they saw it, rather than as it actually happened.

Finally, we must recall the physiological and cultural influences on perception discussed earlier in this chapter, because they can also influence memory via our perception. For example, a hearing-impaired person might remember different images at the scene of an accident than would a person who had auditory information coming in along with other sensory information. Similarly, culture would influence your perception: If you are a teenager who identifies with the teenage driver, you would probably have different schemas of the drivers involved and assume the older driver to be at fault. This principle was evident in the O.J. Simpson case as well, when a Gallup poll revealed that whereas only 42% of whites approved of the "not guilty" verdict, 78% of blacks thought it was appropriate (1995). The primacy effect can also play a role in encoding. Because our sensory and working memories are limited, the things we notice first are more likely to be retained.

Identify a schema of your own—it might be your set of expectations about some aspect of school, work, or relationships. Next, consider how your schema might be influencing what you pay attention to in that situation, and ultimately how it might affect what you remember or forget.

So far, we have learned that as we encode events, we operate within a three-step process. In sensory memory we only have a second or two to grab onto whatever catches our attention most strongly; then we have about 30 seconds available in working memory to process that information and try to make it meaningful enough so that we can retain it in long-term memory. Factors that can influence our perception during this process include attention and schemas, along with the physiological and cultural factors discussed earlier in this chapter, and the primacy effect. These perceptual influences allow numerous opportunities for unintentional encoding errors.

Retrieval and Reconstruction   Perception can play a role in the retrieval of memory, too, and once again, schemas can be heavily involved. Just as we use our existing schemas to fill in the gaps of what goes into memory, we also use schemas to fill in the gaps of what we recall from memory. Because a schema represents our accumulation of images and experiences regarding a person, topic, or situation, you can imagine how easy it can be to get one memory mixed up with a related memory. Can you think of a time you were remembering something and got it mixed up with something similar? Most likely you can. It happens not just with events, people, and situations, but (unfortunately) on exams, too!

Memory retrieval is also influenced by cues that are present at the time of our retrieval attempt. This is a critical factor involved in eyewitness testimony. Imagine that, after witnessing the car accident, a police officer interviews you about what you saw and asks, "About how fast do you think the cars were going when they smashed into each other?" Does it seem as if the officer is trying to influence your answer in any way? Unintentionally, perhaps, that is exactly what this question does: Using the word "smashed" instead of the more neutral word "hit" was found to increase witness estimates of a car's speed by 20% in a study conducted by Elizabeth Loftus, one of today's leading researchers in memory (Loftus & Palmer, 1974). The word "smashed" served as a cue to indicate a higher speed, and the witnesses incorporated this bias into their memory of what they saw—without ever realizing it.

Cues can also influence our memories of people. One study, for example, had participants engaging in conversations with someone they hadn't met before. Later, the participants were told either that the person they'd conversed with had liked them, or that the person had disliked them. Finally, participants were asked to reflect back on their conversations and describe their conversational partner's behavior. Participants who had been told their partner had liked them rated their partner's behavior in positive terms, such as comfortable and relaxed. Participants who had been told that their conversational partner had disliked them, on the other hand, rated their partner's behavior in more negative terms, such as nervous and uncomfortable (Croxton, Eddy, & Morrow, 1984). The partner in each case was a research associate trained to act the same way in each encounter (unbeknownst, of course, to the participants). Positive or negative cues, though, influenced the participants' memories of the conversations and thus their perceptions of reality.

Our recollections of past events appear to be subject to error as well. People who have taken a vacation, for example, were asked by researchers to rate their enjoyment of the vacation while they were on it. Later, after the vacation had faded into the past, they were asked again to rate their enjoyment of the vacation, and in their recollections they reported much greater enjoyment of the vacation than they had when they were actually on the vacation (Mitchell, Thompson, Peterson, & Cronk, 1997). This phenomenon has been labeled **rosy retrospection**—apparently, as time passes, we tend to forget the minor annoyances and remember the pleasures more vividly.

Rosy retrospection Our tendency to forget minor annoyances and remember pleasures of a positive experience more vividly over time.

Interestingly, we also tend to modify our recollections of people as our experiences with them change. Married couples, for example, were surveyed just after marriage, and then again after two years. At the two-year mark, couples whose marriages were going well remembered being very happy as newlyweds. Couples who were experiencing marital difficulties after two years, remembered having problems even as newlyweds. In reality, though, both groups of couples—happy and unhappy—had reported great happiness as newlyweds; the unhappy ones just didn't remember it that way (Holmberg & Holmes, 1994).

Schemas, cues, rosy retrospection, and reconstructing memories to fit current perceptions are just a few of the ways that our recollections of a person or event can differ from someone else's perception of the same person or event. Understanding these processes and realizing that they are normal, human, and unintentional can reduce the friction experienced when our memories don't match those of someone else.

Critical Thinking QUESTION Compare your memory of a recent event with the memory of someone else who also experienced that event. Note the differences in your perceptions and identify how at least one of the concepts in this section contributed to your different perceptions and memories.

Interim SUMMARY #3

Our complex memory system also contributes to misperceptions. Memories are recon-structed, not retrieved. In other words, we remember things the way we think they were, rather than the way they actually were. Schemas, cues, and rosy retrospection all influence this reconstruction process. During encoding, storage, and retrieval, numerous opportuni-ties exist for perceptual input, which helps explain why our memory of an event is sometimes different from that of someone else.

Critical Thinking QUESTION Now, take another look at the introduction to this chapter. In reviewing the various explanations students gave for why Princess Diana's death was such a notable international event, can you explain their differing percep-tions in terms of a few of the concepts you learned in this chapter?

CHAPTER TERMS

Primacy effect
False consensus bias
False uniqueness bias
Confirmation bias
Fundamental
  attribution error
Internal attribution

External attribution
Consistency
Distinctiveness
Consensus
Physiological factors
Personal space
Talking rules

Perception-checking
Encoding
Sensory memory
Working memory
Long-term memory
Schemas
Rosy retrospection

ACTIVITY 5.1

OVERCOMING THE FUNDAMENTAL ATTRIBUTION ERROR

1. What is the fundamental attribution error?

_____

_____

2. Describe a situation from your own life when you made an internal attribu-tion about someone's behavior, potentially committing the fundamental attri-bution error.

_____

_____

_____

_____

3. What internal attribution did you make in that situation?

_____

_____

4. What three questions would you have to ask yourself to see if your internal attribution was correct?

_____

_____

_____

_____

_____

_____

5. To the best of your knowledge, what is the answer to each of the three questions you identified in Question 4?

_____

_____

_____

_____

_____

6. Did you make the fundamental attribution error in this situation? Explain your answer.

_____

_____

_____

_____

_____

_____

_____

ACTIVITY 5.2

WHEN PHYSIOLOGY INTERFERES WITH PERCEPTION

INSTRUCTIONS: *In this chapter, you learned numerous ways that physiological factors can influence your perception of people and events, as well as others' perceptions of you. Think about times in your own life when these factors played a role in your own relationships (personal or professional), and choose three examples to discuss in the following spaces. Two examples should illustrate ways that any two of these factors influenced your perception of another person or an event; the third example should illustrate a time that you think one of these factors influenced someone else's perception of you. Each example should have three parts:*

1. *A short (3–4 sentences) description of the situation*

2. *Identification of the physiological factor that influenced perception in that situation*

3. *A short explanation of how it influenced perception and the potential misunderstanding it might have caused*

Example 1:

1. _____

_____

_____

2. _____

_____

_____

3. _____

_____

_____

_____

_____

Example 2:

1. _____

_____

_____

2. _____

_____

_____

3. _____

_____

_____

_____

_____

Example 3:

1. _____

_____

_____

2. _____

_____

_____

3. _____

_____

_____

_____

_____

REFLECTIONS

As you think about your examples, what would you say is the "take-home lesson" of this section?

_____

_____

_____

_____

_____

ACTIVITY 5.3

PERSONAL EXPERIENCE WITH CULTURAL FACTORS IN PERCEPTION

INSTRUCTIONS: *In this chapter, you learned numerous ways that cultural factors can influence your perception of people and events, as well as others' perceptions of you. Think about times in your own life when these factors played a role in your own relationships (personal or professional), and choose three examples to discuss in the following spaces. Two examples should illustrate ways that any two of these factors influenced your perception of another person or an event; the third example should illustrate a time that you think one of these factors influenced someone else's perception of you. Each example should have three parts:*

1. *A short (3–4 sentences) description of the situation*
2. *Identification of the cultural factor that influenced perception in that situation*
3. *A short explanation of how it influenced perception in that situation and the potential misunderstanding that it might have caused*

Example 1:

1. _____

_____

_____

2. _____

_____

_____

3. _____

_____

_____

_____

_____

Example 2:

1. _____

2. _____

3. _____

Example 3:

1. _____

2. _____

3. _____

REFLECTIONS

As you think about your examples, what would you say is the "take-home lesson" of this section?

_____

_____

_____

_____

ACTIVITY 5.4

ENHANCING AWARENESS OF CULTURAL DIFFERENCES

INSTRUCTIONS: *Chapter 5 included a discussion of several cultural differences that influence perception, along with how those differences can set up potential misunderstandings in our relations with diverse others. In addition to those differences discussed in the chapter, there are a multitude of others. For this assignment, research and discuss two additional cultural differences that could lead to misunderstandings in our human relations. If you have experiences of your own to draw from, you may use them; if not, you can either interview someone with more extensive multicultural experience or use the Internet or the library to gain your information.*

Then, write a 1-2 page paper describing your findings. For each cultural difference you discuss, you should include:

1. A complete description of the cultural behavior
2. The culture in which the behavior is common
3. What the behavior means in its native culture
4. How the behavior could be misperceived in other cultures
5. The source of your information

In class, you may be asked to share your findings with other students in a small group or large group discussion.

ACTIVITY 5.5
DEVELOPING YOUR PERCEPTION-CHECKING SKILLS

PART 1

Following are some hypothetical situations in which one person does or says something that may be misperceived by another. Imagine yourself in each situation. Write a perception-checking statement that you could use to clarify what the other person meant. In each statement, remember to:

1. Describe the other person's behavior specifically yet tactfully.
2. Offer two possible interpretations of the behavior.
3. Request clarification.

Example:

Situation: You're having trouble in your biology class. A couple of weeks ago, one of your classmates who is acing the class offered to study with you, and you gratefully agreed. You didn't set up a specific time, though, and now a couple of weeks have passed and he hasn't said anything else about it.

Perception-Checking Statement: "A couple of weeks ago, we were talking about how I was having trouble in biology, and you offered to study with me. You haven't said anything about it since then, and I was wondering if you'd gotten too busy, or if you were just waiting for me to say something?"

1. For her birthday a couple of months ago, you gave your friend Sharon a gift certificate to the store where you work. She seemed to really like it, but you haven't seen her come into the store to use it yet.

_____

_____

_____

2. You're getting ready to apply to another school and have requested a letter of recommendation from one of your teachers. He agreed to write it and was supposed to call you when it was ready to be picked up. The deadline for applications is now just five days away, and he hasn't called you yet.

_____

_____

_____

3. You are dining at a nice restaurant with your significant other, who seems unusually quiet.

_____

_____

_____

4. You play on your school's soccer team, which requires you to have a minimum 2.0 GPA. Several times lately, your coach has asked how your classes are going.

_____

_____

_____

5. One of your best friends moved to a different state last year, and the two of you planned to go on a vacation together this summer. You've left her several messages over the last few weeks, but she hasn't returned your calls.

_____

_____

_____

6. Several times lately, your employer has told you to go home early or not to come in at all. The time off was nice at first, but now you're starting to worry about your paycheck.

_____

_____

_____

manner consistent with real-life prison rules. The "guards" would work in shifts, just as real prison guards did.

On the day of the experiment, Zimbardo enlisted the aid of the local police department in picking up the participants who had been assigned to the role of "prisoner." A real squad car, lights blazing, arrived in front of the "prisoner's" home, read him his rights, handcuffed him, and drove him to the basement of the Stanford University psychology building. There, he was fingerprinted, strip-searched, de-loused, and given his prison garments to wear, which consisted of a one-piece dresslike garment with a number sewn on it, and a stocking cap. A chain was locked around each prisoner's ankle as a symbol of his status. He was then escorted to his "cell," which was a small room with bars on the front that he would share with two other "prisoners."

After all the "prisoners" had arrived and been incarcerated in their cells, the "guards" began their jobs. They, too, had been outfitted with clothing symbolic of their status: They wore khaki uniforms with black belts and badges, and carried nightsticks. To familiarize their "prisoners" with their numbers and roles, a roll call was performed. The prisoners, not taking their roles too seriously, began goofing off and making mocking remarks to the guards. This behavior annoyed the guards, who then escalated their demands in an attempt to establish their authority. A power struggle had begun, and over the next several days, this battle for control between guards and prisoners intensified. Guards put prisoners in "solitary confinement" for such small crimes as refusing to eat cold sausages at a meal. Prisoners retaliated by barricading themselves in their cells, and guards responded by taking away their beds and their bathroom privileges, making them sleep on the floor and urinate in a bucket in their cells.

The behavior of the participants in the experiment, playing their roles as "guards" and "prisoners," was changing rapidly. Because no physical punishment was allowed, guards became increasingly inventive in their attempts to control the prisoners as the experiment progressed, resorting to increasingly cruel means of humiliation and derogation. Similarly, prisoners, who at first had banded together in a show of solidarity with one another, soon abandoned their "all for one and one for all" approach as each began looking out solely for himself. According to the prison consultant, everything was happening just as it did in real-life prison situations.

Zimbardo himself, playing the role of prison warden, admits to being excited about how well the simulation was going, when just 6 days into the experiment a graduate student assistant told him she thought that what he was doing to the participants was terrible. Zimbardo took a fresh look at what had transpired and realized to his dismay that he had gotten caught up in the simulation and had lost sight of his ethics. At that point, he ended the experiment and began a series of debriefings for all the participants. What was revealed in the debriefings is sobering.

In the short 6 days of the experiment, average college boys who were initially very similar developed startling changes in their outlooks. "Prisoners" were shaken by the experience, suddenly aware of how depersonalized they had become, and how that experience had led them to abandon their concern for others and look out only for themselves. They were also struck by the fact that their dignity and firm grasp on reality could be endangered by just a few days in a disempowered role. One prisoner even went on to pursue graduate work in psychology, eventually becoming a prison psychologist.

"Guards" in the experiment demonstrated an even greater change. Faced with the reality of the cruelty they had inflicted on people who were similar to themselves, they began to adjust their thinking in order to justify the behavior that they couldn't otherwise explain. They had abused their power, which didn't fit with their perceptions of themselves as "nice guys." Since that abusive behavior was now in the past, it couldn't be changed. Therefore they were faced with a choice: They could change their perceptions of themselves and begin to think of themselves as cruel and abusive people, or they could change their perceptions of the situation. To keep their positive perception of themselves intact, they began to explain their behavior as a necessary response to that of the prisoners and the roles in which they found themselves. Simply put, they blamed their victims.

Why did these normal, well-adjusted college boys behave the way they did in this experiment? Why did the people who were peripherally involved with the experiment, such as the research assistants, the prison consultant, the local priest who paid a visit, and even the participants' parents, allow the experiment to go on? And how did Dr. Zimbardo, a respected professional, become blinded to the realities of what was happening in his experiment?

We live in social worlds, constantly interacting with others in our environment. Our interactions themselves are a dynamic process, with each successive action building on and responding to the previous ones. In Chapters 1 through 3, we explored elements of culture, the self, personality, and development that lay the foundations in helping us understand why people do what they do. In Chapters 4 and 5, we learned the many ways in which emotion and perception influence our interactions with others. In this chapter, we will fill in a few more pieces of this puzzle by exploring the principles of social influence, deepening our understanding of the power of the situation in explaining why people do what they do.

CONFORMITY

PREVIEW QUESTIONS

(1) Why do people conform?

(2) In what situations are people more likely to conform?

(3) How does conformity improve human relations? How does it hinder good human relations?

Do you consider yourself a conformist? Most people in the United States would answer "No!" to this question. On the contrary, the United States was built on a foundation of rugged individualism, a value that is essentially the opposite of conformity. We even have a number of different expressions that encourage individualism: "Dare to be different!" "Be yourself!" "Follow your own path!" But wait . . . don't we also have expressions telling us to conform? How about "Don't rock the boat!" "Don't

FIGURE 6.1 | "Berkeley's Naked Guy"

Andrew Martinez, a student of the University of California at Berkeley, broke social norms by routinely going to school naked (although in this photo, he wore shoes and a sweat shirt due to cold weather). What do you think were the consequences—positive and/or negative—of his actions?

upset the apple cart!" "Don't make waves!" So which advice do we tend to follow? If you're confused, you are not alone. Many Americans struggle to assert their individuality, while simultaneously being rewarded for conformity (Figure 6.1).

Before we go any further, we should clarify our meaning of **conformity**: a voluntary change in a belief or behavior with the intent to follow a perceived social norm. Social norms are simply rules, usually unspoken, about the appropriate way to think or behave in a culture or subculture. For example, when we're at a movie theater or in a store, and we're ready to pay for our movie or groceries, there are certain rules we follow. Do we just charge up to the counter, pushing people out of the way so we don't have to wait? Of course not—we wait in line until it's our turn. This is a social norm in Western culture; it is considered polite behavior. Norms can also be specific to *subcultures*, or smaller groups within a culture, which might have norms such as body piercing, food preferences, smoking, or gun ownership. There are a multitude of ways in which we conform. Remember our discussion of self-monitoring in Chapter 2? When we alter our behavior, dress, or talk a certain way to fit in, we are managing our identity and thus conforming.

> **Conformity** A voluntary change in a belief or behavior with the intent to follow a perceived social norm.

Is conformity necessary in a society? Of course it is. At the very least, it helps maintain a sense of order. Beyond that, it can also enhance feelings of belonging and cooperation, which we'll address in the next section. On the other hand, we in Western culture also like to assert our individuality. So how much conformity is appropriate? This is a more complex question, and one on which different cultures have different perspectives. Think about that question as you read the next section and decide where you stand on this interesting issue.

Motives for Conformity

Why do we conform? Research has identified two basic motives at the heart of our tendency to conform. When we conform in order to "fit in" with a certain group, **normative social influence** is at work. Peer pressure is a classic example of normative social influence. It is common among teens to go along with what their friends are doing, even if it is something an individual might not otherwise want to do. This type of conformity isn't limited to just teens. Adults find themselves doing this as well, for better and for worse. "Dressing for success" when you want to fit in with others at your new

> **Normative social influence** When we conform in order to "fit in" with a certain group.

job is probably a positive example of normative social influence, because it will enhance your sense of belonging and probably help your coworkers see you as "one of the gang" more quickly. On the other hand, letting your friends convince you to party with them all night just before an important exam is probably a less beneficial example of normative social influence. Normative social influence affects people in cultures all around the world: Riding a moped in Italy is cool, whereas in some parts of the United States it is not. Smoking has become less socially acceptable among many U.S. cultures than it remains in many European and Asian societies. And topless or nude beaches in Spain and France, although not considered out of the ordinary in Europe, continue to be "tourist attractions" for more conservative American travelers.

On the other hand, when conformity helps us make the right decision in a situation where we aren't sure what to do, **informational social influence** is at work. For example, imagine the first-time college student who notices some classmates quizzing each other with index cards that have terms or concepts written on one side and the definition or explanation written on the other side. These students seem confident about the upcoming exam, and the "flash cards" seem to be a useful tool. The new college student might make some flash cards of her own, hoping

> **Informational social influence** When conformity helps us make the right decision in a situation where we aren't sure what to do.

they will help her learn the course material. Informational social influence has provided her with information about what to do in an unfamiliar situation. Watching others when we ride public transportation for the first time in a new city can help us figure out how it works. Similarly, informational social influence was at work in the wake of the September 2001 attack on the World Trade Center and Pentagon. People who had travel plans paid attention to what other travelers were doing as they tried to decide whether they felt safe enough to travel.

 Apply these motives for conformity to your relationships, either at work, at school, or interpersonally. Which type (informational or normative) tends to influence you the most? Does it vary from situation to situation?

Situational Conditions Influencing Conformity

Research has identified several factors that influence the likelihood of conformity. For example, we are more likely to conform when the task or situation seems unclear or is difficult. In one of the classic studies on conformity by Solomon Asch (1955), participants were shown a set of vertical lines and asked which line was the same length as the comparison line (see Figure 6.2). As you can see, the answer is pretty obvious, but when others in the group gave the wrong answer, 37% of the participants conformed and gave the wrong answer at least once.

In similar studies, where the answer was less obvious (see Figure 6.3), conformity increased to 46% (Crutchfield, 1955). Although American society has become less conforming in the years since these studies (Bond & Smith, 1996), current studies still indicate moderate levels of conformity. Ambiguity of the situation tends to produce greater conformity.

The power of conformity in ambiguous situations was also found in a 1996 study of eyewitness identification. Participants were first shown a drawing of a person, then shown drawings of several people, including the one they had already

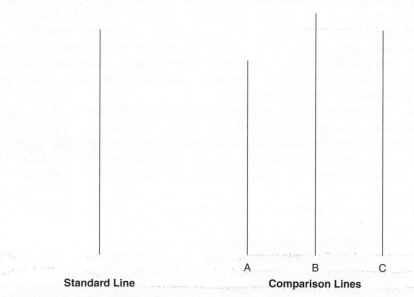

Standard Line   **Comparison Lines**

FIGURE 6.2 | Asch's Vertical Line Test of Conformity

Sample Question: Which of the comparison lines is the same length as the standard line?

Source: Adapted from Social Psychology, *by D. G. Myers, 1999, Boston: McGraw-Hill.*

FIGURE 6.3 | Crutchfield's Test of Conformity

Sample Question: Which figure is larger?

Source: Adapted from "Conformity and Character," by R. A. Crutchfield, 1955, American Psychologist, 10, pp. 191–198.

seen, in a hypothetical "lineup," and asked to pick out the one they'd originally seen from the lineup. Some had seen the first drawing for 5 seconds, and others had seen it for only half a second. In some cases, participants heard other "eyewitnesses" identify the wrong person first. In the more difficult task, where participants had seen the original drawing for only half a second, would they be more likely to conform and give the incorrect answer than participants who had seen the original drawing for a full 5 seconds? As predicted, indeed they were (Baron, Vandello, & Brunsman, 1996). This clearly has sobering implications for our legal system.

Ambiguity of the situation affected my own conformity recently while on vacation. I was snorkeling alone in an unfamiliar area when I noticed most other snorkelers in the area swimming back to shore. I wasn't sure why everyone was leaving the water, but thought if they knew something I didn't about some kind of danger (Yikes! Was there a shark in the area?), it would be a good idea to pay attention, so I swam back to shore, too. As it turned out, most of them were simply trying to get their snorkel gear back to the rental shop before it closed. My need for self-protection in an unfamiliar situation led me to conform that day, because I decided it was better to be safe than sorry!

Group size also influences conformity, but not in the way you might think. In another of the classic experiments on conformity, a group of people stopped on a busy sidewalk in New York City and looked up, pretending to be looking at something. Would other people passing by also stop and look up, and did that depend on how many were already looking? Yes, and no. When just one person was looking up, other passers-by stopped and looked up about 40% of the time; that number increased to about 50% when two people were looking up, and continued increasing to over 75% when 5 people were looking up. As the group size grew beyond 5, though, the conformity rate remained about the same (Milgram, Bickman, & Berkowitz, 1969). Other studies have produced similar results, indicating that group size does increase conformity as the group grows to about 5; beyond that, size makes little or no difference.

Culture has a strong influence on conformity as well, via the values embraced by that culture. As we noted earlier, Americans seem to have almost a knee-jerk negative reaction to the idea of conformity, which is understandable given the importance of individualism in our culture. Conforming behavior is assumed to be mindless behavior, which flies in the face of the independent thought embraced by Western individualists. Not all cultures on our planet share these views, however. As we learned in Chapter 1, collectivistic cultures consider group harmony, cooperation, and respect to be of greater importance than independent thought. Group well-being is of greater value than individual well-being. So it follows that one would expect greater conformity in collectivistic cultures, a prediction that has been supported in various cross-cultural studies. For example, Japanese, Indonesians, and Arabians have been found to be more conforming than Americans. Research has also found greater incidence of conformity in Puerto Rican and Italian subjects (Matsumoto, 2000). In these and other collectivistic cultures, conformity is considered a positive behavior, and one that is necessary and helpful in a peaceful and productive society.

We can also apply these principles of conformity to the Stanford Prison Experiment, described at the beginning of this chapter. Given ambiguous instructions about how to control the "prisoners," students in the role of "guard" probably took their cues from things they had seen on television and eventually from each other. Behaviors of the prisoners were influenced by conformity as well: At one point they were faced with a choice between giving up their blankets to let one of their fellow prisoners out of solitary confinement, or keeping their blankets (in which case the prisoner would remain in solitary confinement). At first there was a little disagreement among some prisoners, but once several of them had chosen to keep their blankets, the rest conformed and expressed the same choice.

Now that we understand the powerful influences that drive us to conform, as well as the potential benefits of conformity, we can better appreciate the nature of our struggle with these conflicting needs in Western culture. In what ways do you conform? When are you affected by normative social influence? By informational social influence? Do you consider your own examples of conformity to be positive or negative behaviors? Explore these questions and other aspects of your own conformity in Activity 6.1 at the end of this chapter.

Interim SUMMARY #1

We live in a social world, and thus we are subject to a constant barrage of forces that have the potential to influence our perceptions and behaviors. These social influences act on us at three different levels of strength. The lowest level is conformity, whereby we voluntarily adapt our behavior to match what others seem to be doing in that situation. When we conform to enhance our sense of belonging to the group, normative social influence is at work. When we conform to increase our chances of accuracy, informational social influence is at work. Conformity is typically greater when the situation is ambiguous, when group size is about 5, and in collectivistic cultures.

COMPLIANCE

PREVIEW QUESTIONS

(1) How is compliance different from conformity?
(2) What are the six basic principles of compliance, and how does each one influence our relations with others?
(3) Which principle(s) of compliance is often found in unhealthy relationships?
(4) Which principle(s) of compliance has interfered most with the effectiveness of your own human relations? How can it be overcome?

Remember, conformity is a voluntary behavior. The next step up on the ladder of social influence is **compliance**, which is agreeing to a specific request. It goes beyond conformity, because when we conform no one has explicitly asked us to do

> **Compliance** Agreeing to a specific request.

so—our motivation comes from within. Compliance is still a voluntary behavior, but it is in response to an overt request. If a friend asks to borrow some money, for example, and you agree, you are complying with your friend's request. We see examples of compliance not only in our personal relationships and the workplace, but in the marketplace as well. In general, how compliant are you? Do you find yourself often going along with what others ask of you? On the other side of the picture, how persuasive are you in influencing others to go along with you?

Basic Principles of Compliance

According to Arizona State University Professor Robert Cialdini, extensive research on compliance has discovered that there are six basic psychological principles that underlie most means of compliance (Cialdini, 2001). Let's explore these principles and learn how you can use them to improve your own relations with others, as well as to become more aware of your own response patterns.

Reciprocity   Imagine a friend is asking to borrow some money from you. In considering your friend's request, you might think about how often she has borrowed money before, and whether you've ever borrowed from her, or might do so in the future. These thoughts illustrate the first principle of compliance: the **principle of reciprocity**, which is based on the powerful social norm of reciprocity. In other words, we are more likely to agree to someone's request if we feel we "owe" them, perhaps because they've done us a favor in the past.

> **Principle of reciprocity** Belief that it is important to reciprocate, or "pay back" favors.

If this isn't the case, we might comply anyway to build a kind of reciprocity "savings account"—thus increasing the likelihood that if we need something from that person in the future, he or she will remember our compliance and return the favor.

One of the earliest studies on reciprocity demonstrated its powerful effect. Participants in an "art appreciation" study, working in teams of 2, were asked to rate the quality of some paintings. During a short break period partway through the experiment, some of the participants were unexpectedly offered a Coke by their teammate. (In reality, this teammate was an assistant to the researcher, just pretending to be a participant. These assistants are called "confederates.") This other "participant" said he'd asked the experimenter if it was okay to go get a Coke, and since the experimenter had said it was okay, he'd brought one back for his teammate, too. Later, after the experiment was over, the confederate mentioned to the real participant that he was selling tickets to a raffle, and that there was a prize for the person who sold the most tickets. Would he help him out and buy some? Participants who had been given the Coke by the confederate bought, on average, twice as many raffle tickets as those who had not, demonstrating the principle of reciprocity: Those who felt they "owed" the seller a favor paid up, thus balancing the social scales.

The principle of reciprocity is alive and well in retail sales as well, perhaps most noticeably in grocery stores when free samples of a product are offered. When the silver-haired lady with the kind face offers you a slice of warm buttered bread, "hot out of the oven," how can you refuse? Then, wouldn't you feel just a little bit rude if you walked away without putting a loaf of that bread in your basket? Evolutionary psychology suggests that one reason we feel such a strong obligation to reciprocate is that this type of social exchange has been a crucial component in individual and group survival. People who violate the rule of reciprocity, taking but not giving back, are often called "moochers" or other negative labels. Interestingly, this rule works in reverse as well: A cross-cultural study has found that people who give without accepting anything in return are also disliked (Gergen, Ellsworth, Maslach, & Seipel, 1975). Perhaps this explains why people sometimes avoid asking for a favor when they know they cannot repay it (Riley & Eckenrode, 1986).

A common sales tactic called the "door in the face" technique can be linked to this principle of reciprocity and was demonstrated in an Arizona study. College students were approached by a person who claimed to be from the "County Youth Counseling Program" and asked if they'd be willing to volunteer to help chaperone a group of troubled youths on a day-trip to the local zoo. Only 17% agreed to this request. Other students were approached by the same person, but asked if they'd be interested in being a volunteer counselor for the "County Youth Counseling Program," a position that required a minimum commitment of 2 hours per week for at least 2 years. When students said "no" to this request for a long-term commitment, the recruiter responded in an understanding manner, then asked if the student would instead be willing to volunteer on a one-time basis to help chaperone a day-trip to the zoo with these youths. A whopping 50% agreed to this request when it followed the more extreme request! Why did three times as many people comply in the second situation? Because by backing off and accepting the students' refusal of the request for the 2-year commitment, the recruiter put the students in a position where they felt obligated to reciprocate the concession. This strategy is also used effectively in business negotiations when a negotiator asks for more than what she really wants, so that she can trigger the reciprocity norm in her target by accepting his refusal, ultimately increasing the odds of getting what she really wanted in the first place.

 In what situations has the principle of reciprocity influenced you to go along with something? Were you glad you complied, or did you have mixed feelings about it?

Before you start thinking that the reciprocity principle is all about manipulation, remember its evolutionary value. Honest reciprocation of good deeds can be a strengthening factor in relationships; using it to manipulate people, on the other hand, ultimately undermines the strength of a relationship. Unfortunately, some people do take advantage of this principle. If you find yourself feeling suspicious of someone's motive for offering you a favor, research has found an effective solution: Simply refuse the favor. By saying "no, thanks," you're avoiding the consequent obligation. This is not to suggest that we should never accept favors or kindnesses from others, or that we should generally be suspicious of them. Indeed, what a sad world that would be. This does suggest, however, that we remain aware of this potential dilemma: We don't want to go through life feeling suspicious, never building fulfilling relationships, but at the same time we don't want to be taken advantage of by tricksters. Perhaps the best we can do is to go on faith and give others the benefit of the doubt. If we become aware that someone is abusing our trust, we can then opt out of the reciprocity expectation. If someone *was* using it to manipulate us, we have no obligation to reciprocate the favor or concession, since that isn't what this norm is about.

Commitment The second principle of compliance is the **principle of commitment**, which indicates that we are more likely to agree to something if we have already made a smaller commitment to it. To understand this principle, we must first understand our human need for consistency, which is driven by both internal and external forces. First, in our busy lives, thinking and acting in ways that are consistent with our previous thoughts and actions gives us a sense of stability, and also helps simplify matters by reducing the amount of time we must spend considering the issue, thus freeing us to get more accomplished. Second, we prefer others to be consistent. Consistency leads to predictability, and for the most part, we feel more comfortable when we know what to expect from someone. This reliability is a critical part of a relationship, because it helps form the basis of trust. Our strong preference for consistency is at the heart of the principle of commitment.

> **Principle of commitment**
> A small initial commitment to a person or idea increases the likelihood that we will make a more significant commitment later.

Now, imagine that you live in a quiet residential neighborhood, and that there are a lot of young children in your neighborhood. As your city has grown, traffic on your street has gotten busier and busier, to the point that you and your neighbors worry that the cars are going too fast and could accidentally hit one of the children. One day, a volunteer worker comes to your door, asking if you would help make drivers more aware by displaying a sign in your yard that says "Drive Carefully." The volunteer's request isn't as harmless as it sounds, though. The volunteer shows you a picture of the sign, and it is hideous! It looks crudely built, poorly lettered, and so large that it almost completely obstructs the view of the nice home at which it is displayed in the picture. This was the scenario in the study that established the principle of commitment as such a powerful influence (Freedman & Fraser, 1966).

Would you agree to display the sign in your yard? Because it was so ugly, researchers found that only 17% of the residents agreed to display this sign in their yard. In a similar residential neighborhood nearby, though, when homeowners received the same request regarding the same ugly sign, 76% agreed—more than four times as many! What was the difference with this second group of homeowners? Their neighborhood was just as nice, their homes were just as nice, and they didn't differ from the first group in any significant way—except one. About two weeks prior, a different volunteer worker had visited them, asking them to display a small, 3-inch-square sign that said, "Be a safe driver." Almost all had agreed, since it was such a small request. In fact, they probably didn't give it a second thought. And since they had made that first commitment to the "drive safely" cause, they were more than four times as likely to agree to display the large, ugly sign two weeks later. This powerful result of an initial commitment is known as the "foot-in-the-door" technique. Its effectiveness comes from the fact that once we make a small commitment to someone or something, our need for consistency motivates us to remain true to that commitment, even when it asks more of us.

What is even more surprising is the results of the follow-up study done by the same researchers. They visited yet another group of homeowners, this time asking them to sign a petition supporting an effort to "Keep California Beautiful." Two weeks later, the homeowners were approached again and asked to display the large, ugly sign that said, "Drive Carefully." Would the initial commitment to keeping their state beautiful influence their commitment to safe driving? You might not think so, because the two campaigns weren't the same, and the sign was especially ugly. To the surprise of everyone, though, the foot-in-the-door technique worked again: Half of the residents who had signed the "Keep California Beautiful" petition agreed to display the ugly "Drive Carefully" sign! Apparently, signing the beautification petition influenced the signers to think of themselves as responsible, civic-minded people who had the courage to take a stand on important issues. This powerful new image of themselves kicked in when they were asked to display the ugly safe driving sign—they were trying to "do the right thing," because that's the way they saw themselves.

The power of this seemingly insignificant initial commitment is sobering. Think about it—a small act, such as signing a petition or agreeing to a minor request, has the power to influence our self-image, a result that can leave us vulnerable to various types of manipulation by people who want something from us. One all-too-common example of this is demonstrated in abusive relationships (see the Special Topic: "Unhealthy Relationships and the Principle of Commitment"). The fact that this self-image change happens on a subconscious level, without us even being aware of it, is part of what gives it its power. In fact, research in this area indicates that commitments are strongest when they are made without coercion—when we think we're making the decision without others' influence. The reality is, though, that we *are* being influenced; we just don't know it. Learning about this principle can effectively raise our consciousness about it, thus helping us avoid falling into this trap.

Special Topic
UNHEALTHY RELATIONSHIPS AND THE PRINCIPLE OF COMMITMENT

Have you ever been in a relationship that turned out to be unhealthy in some way? A healthy relationship is one that involves mutual trust, open and honest communication, and an environment that supports growth for everyone involved in the relationship. With that definition in mind, chances are good that most of us have had our share of relationships that weren't entirely healthy, whether they were friendships, family relationships, or romantic relationships. How do we find ourselves in this type of relationship when we certainly don't start out looking for it? The principle of commitment often goes a long way toward answering this question.

"We used to have a rule that we would never go to bed mad," says Holly as she reflects on her marriage of 7 years. "That way, whenever we did have a disagreement or conflict about something, we would always talk about it by the end of the day. We didn't always get it resolved right away, but at least we started talking about it, so we were connecting in some way. It helped keep us from building up hard feelings toward each other." After her husband's job moved him into a swing shift, though, their busy lives put them on different schedules, with Holly struggling to keep up her grades, her part-time job, and care for their 3-year-old son. "At some point, we quit sticking to that rule," Holly remembers. "One problem didn't get resolved, then another, and eventually, we both had a bunch of resentment and hurt built up toward each other, and we didn't know how we got there, or how to fix it."

Letitia talks of a relationship with a boyfriend who was abusive. "When we first started going out, he always wanted to know where I was when we weren't together," she recalls. "It made me feel he was really interested in me. He was possessive, but I thought that meant he loved me. The first time we had a fight, he got in my face and was yelling and calling me names—he's a big guy, and it kind of scared me, but after we made up he said that he was just scared to lose me. I can see now that, by accepting those early things he did, I was taking small steps toward the physical abuse that came later." In the next few months, Letitia remembers, there were escalating incidences of verbal abuse, along with the physical abuse that started with him pushing her in the heat of an argument. The next time it was a slap, and eventually he punched her and threw her up against a wall. "I actually had to get stitches on my face," she says, pointing to a scar on the side of her forehead. "The doctor that sewed me up was a woman, and she talked to me about domestic violence. My first reaction was, hey, I'm not in that kind of relationship! But then I saw myself in the mirror, saw the bruises and the stitches, and realized that I was. I never thought I could be one of those women who let themselves be abused, but I also never knew how it could just creep up on you like that." With the support of her sister and a local domestic violence support group, Letitia got out of that abusive relationship and now helps other women who find themselves where she was just 18 months ago.

Although Holly's story doesn't involve abuse, it illustrates the same pattern of deterioration that Letitia's story tells, and the same downward spiral that typifies many unhealthy relationships.

Whether the relationship is characterized by verbal, emotional, or physical abuse, or just by lack of honesty or support, unhealthy relationships often develop through a series of small incidents. The first one doesn't seem like a big deal—in fact, you may not even notice it as a problem at the time. But it leads to the next incident and the one after that, with each one becoming successively worse until, like Holly and Letitia, you find yourself in an unhealthy relationship, with no idea how things became so bad.

Raising our awareness of how easily we can be drawn into a bad relationship or situation is the first step toward guarding against this possibility. Then, learning to take a personal "time out" to assess the current status of the relationship and ask yourself if it feels right, feels safe, and is what you set out to have, can be your best opportunity to stop the process before it goes any further. And if you need help getting out of an abusive relationship, call your local domestic violence hotline, or log on to http://endabuse.org.

Commitment in Everyday Life

The principle of commitment is used in a myriad of ways by people who want us to buy something or donate our time. The classic example is the much-maligned car salesperson, who uses the principle repeatedly. It starts when you respond to an ad that offers the car you want at a price that you know is less than any other competing deals. You race down to the dealership, only to find that that particular deal was for one car only, but they do have a few others that are very similar, and you agree to look at them. You've already made two commitments: the first got you to the car lot and the second was when you agreed to stay and look at the other cars. The salesperson shows you one that is like the one in the ad, but just a few hundred dollars more, "because it has this nice pinstriping." You agree to a test drive (commitment number 3). It feels pretty good (of course it does, it's a brand-new car), and the salesperson tells you it really suits you. You don't want to make a rash decision, though—you know how pushy those salespeople can be—so you tell him that you aren't ready to decide today. Understandingly, he nods and agrees that you wouldn't want to rush such an important decision. To help get all the facts, though, how about sitting down and running the numbers, just so you know what you're looking at if you do buy the car? Here's where the principle of reciprocity kicks in. He was nice to understand you when you said you didn't want to decide today, so you really should reciprocate and let him get you the rest of the information you need—whammo, commitment number 4!

You sit down in his office (now making a public commitment, because everyone in the showroom can see you in there), and he asks you if you would buy the car if he can get it for you for the amount you've discussed. You say you would—if you decided you want it, reminding him you aren't going to be pushed into anything. Again, he understands, thus increasing your psychological debt to him, and he asks you to write the proposed sale price on a piece of paper. Kind of goofy, you think, but harmless, so you comply, and now you're up to commitment number 6 (not so harmless, after all). He asks you to wait while he "gets the manager's okay on this," and leaves you sitting there for a few minutes. You're starting to catch on to his little game, but it would be rude just to leave, so you sit there and wait (commitment number 7). He comes back and—surprise, surprise, the manager won't go for the deal, because they'll lose money (he says), but he will go for a deal just a little higher. . . . And you know how the story goes from there. At this point, you've become so entrenched in the commitment that you're probably going to end up with the darn car, and it'll be today, too. The principle of commitment worked its magic on you, as it has on so many others. As you drive the car home, you soothe yourself with the thought that it really is a great car, and you do look really good in it. Just like the participants in the Stanford Prison Experiment discussed at the beginning of this chapter, you adjust your thinking to justify actions that you're surprised to have taken.

Of course, the principle of commitment can be used in positive ways as well. For example, people trying to lose weight or quit smoking often find that they are more successful when they publicly announce their intentions to their friends and family. Stating their goal in this manner, especially for people who place a high value on others' perceptions of them, seems to help them persevere through the temptations they face in their efforts (Fenigstein, Scheier, & Buss, 1975). A Chicago restaurant owner used this principle to reduce the number of no-shows among people who had made reservations. When a person made a reservation, the receptionist had previously said, "Please call us if you change your plans," and 30% of the reservations never showed up. Instead, receptionists were instructed to ask, "Will you call us if you change your plans?" This simple act of asking for a commitment and waiting for the person to say "Yes" decreased the no-shows by two-thirds, to only 10% (Cialdini, 2001).

Critical Thinking QUESTION Consider ways in which you have used the principle of commitment to influence others to comply with your wishes. Did you use this principle intentionally or unintentionally?

Overcoming the Effects of the Principle of Commitment Given the demonstrated strength of the principle of commitment, is it ever possible to avoid falling into its trap? Cialdini asserts that it is, and he offers two possible aids, both of which involve listening to your inner signals. If, at some point in the escalation of the commitment request, your stomach starts to tighten up or you start to get a funny feeling, Cialdini notes that is a pretty good sign that you're about to do something you don't want to do. A second signal is more cognitive, and involves asking yourself, "If I had this to do over again and knew at the beginning of the process what I know now, would I be doing this?" If the answer is "no," then you should listen to it and refuse to make the next commitment. So, to avoid becoming trapped by the principle of commitment, first we need to learn to take an internal "time out" to check these inner signals. Then we need to be assertive enough to disengage from the process if it doesn't feel rights, (see Figure 6.4). In Chapter 9, you'll learn some tips for gaining the assertiveness and communication skills necessary to extricate yourself from this uncomfortable situation.

Copyright © John Nebraska.

Yeah, I can't stand the sight of you anymore either, but we've sunk so much money into this wedding already....I think we should go with the chicken.

FIGURE 6.4 | Have you ever been in a situation where the principle of commitment carried you far beyond where you wanted to be?

Principle of social proof Going along with a belief or behavior because it looks like many others are doing the same thing.

Consensus Principle of social proof.

Social Proof The third principle of influence identified by Cialdini is the **principle of social proof**, also known as **consensus**. This principle is a lot simpler than the previous two. The principle of social proof points out that we are more likely to agree to something if we think many others have already done so. This principle, like the others, is commonly used by salespeople and promoters of social causes. One common example is the television ad that tells you its computer is the best-selling computer of the year, or that more doctors recommend a certain type of pain reliever than any other. In both cases, the advertiser is trying to convince you that buying the product must be the right choice, because so many other people have already done so. Or perhaps a door-to-door volunteer for a local environmental group asks for your signature on a petition, showing you a list of others in your neighborhood who have already signed; again, this is a way of convincing you that it must be the right thing to do, because others are doing it. In our relationships, social proof influences us heavily by way of peer pressure; in fact, peer pressure is simply social proof. "If everyone else is doing it, then I guess I should, too."

Research on the principle of social proof has found it to be most effective under two conditions. First, we are most influenced by social proof in situations when we are unsure what to do. Young people trying cigarettes for the first time, for example, who may not know the negative health effects of long-term smoking, may feel unsure when someone offers them a cigarette. It looks cool, others are doing it, so why not? The second condition is that we are more likely to be influenced by social proof when we see ourselves as similar to the person or people who are already doing it. For example, television advertisers carefully choose spokespeople or actors who most resemble the group of people they are trying to reach. If they are selling minivans, they will be more successful using actors that look like a typical family than they would be if they used the best-looking people they could find. In handling conflict in relationships, a topic about which many feel unsure, we are most likely to take our cues from our own social group. Unfortunately, many people are not in the habit of openly talking about conflict, so in the absence of real-life models they may take their cues from the relationships they see portrayed on television—for better or for worse, depending on their choice of programming.

Like the principles of reciprocity and commitment, the principle of social proof works, at least in part, because it lulls us into an automatic, unthinking response. The best way to avoid doing something simply because others are doing it is to consciously ask yourself, "Do I really want to do this?"

Liking   The fourth and fifth principles, like the principle of social proof, operate on relatively simple concepts. One is the **principle of liking**. This principle, not surprisingly, suggests that we are more likely to go along with someone when we see him or her as a likeable person. When this is a friend, it doesn't seem unreasonable. It becomes potentially shady when a total stranger tries to activate this principle to get you to buy or agree to something. The classic example of this principle in action is the Tupperware party, and more recently its clones like the candle party, basket party, home interiors party, or Pampered

> **Principle of liking** Agreeing to do something because the person making the request is likable.

Chef party. You know how these work: A friend hosts the party, at which a representative of the company gives the sales pitch. Everyone who is at the party is a friend of the host or hostess and knows that the host will get credit in money or products for whatever guests buy at the party. So it feels as if you're buying things from a friend, to whom you're more likely to be generous than you would be to a total stranger.

Critical Thinking **QUESTION**   Other principles of compliance play a role in these parties, too. Can you identify them and explain how they work in this type of party?

We also see examples of the principle of liking in door-to-door sales and petitions. Who can resist the cute child who lives down the street when he is selling wrapping paper or cookies for his school? Even when he's selling items I'm not really interested in, I always find myself buying something, because he's a nice boy, and I tell myself it's good for his self-esteem and his school! Commercial salespeople and volunteers for charitable organizations may use this principle when they ask potential customers for names of friends who might be interested in their product or services. Then they call on the friends and say, "Your friend Jack (or whoever) gave me your name and thought you'd be interested in hearing about this." This activates the principle of liking, because it sounds as if the recommendation is coming from your friend, whom you're more likely to trust than a total stranger. Even salespeople in stores capitalize on this principle when they smile and make a little conversation with you before trying to sell you something.

Why Liking Works   Research in social psychology has found several factors that influence people to like someone else. Physical attractiveness is one of these factors: Good-looking people are more likely to be voted into public office (Budesheim & DePaola, 1994), hired for jobs (Mack & Rainey, 1990), get lighter sentences in criminal trials (Downs & Lyons, 1991), helped when they are in need, and judged more intelligent by teachers (Ritts, Patterson, & Tubbs, 1992). As is the case with social proof, similarity seems to influence liking as well: Research has found people are more likely to help someone who is dressed in a similar manner and to sign petitions or purchase goods from others who appear similar. Third, we fall prey to compliments: People have been found to like others who praise them. Repeated contact also influences liking. For example, voters may vote for a candidate simply because they recognize her name rather than the opponent's name. The name feels more familiar, so they like it better. Finally, association influences liking. In a now-classic study, men who saw a car ad featuring a beautiful female model rated the car as better designed, faster, and more attractive than did men who saw the same ad without the beautiful female model (Smith & Engel, 1968).

Merely being associated with someone or something likeable can also enhance others' liking of you. Politicians, for example, like to be photographed with noteworthy people; it seems to increase viewers' estimation of the politician. Perhaps the most amusing example of the influence of association on liking is the case of the weather forecaster. Television meteorologists repeatedly report that viewers say positive things to them when the weather is good and seem upset with them when the weather is bad. Clearly, these forecasters don't create the weather, but the simple association people make between the forecaster and the weather is enough to promote liking or disliking. Perhaps our parents' warnings are true after all: It seems we really are judged by the company we keep.

Authority   The fifth principle of compliance is the **principle of authority**. Another simple concept, this principle suggests that we are more likely to agree to something when an authority figure makes the request. For example, when a famous basketball star tells you a particular type of shoe will enhance your performance on the court, you're more likely to be convinced than you would be if the same message came from a nonexpert. Similarly, we are more likely to be swayed by advertisements for medical products when the spokesperson is a doctor, dressed in a white lab coat, with the initials "M.D." prominently displayed after her name. And if the person is a general authority figure, his or her request will be effective in a wide range of situations. The former president

> **Principle of authority** We are more likely to agree to a request made by an authority figure.

of my college, for example, routinely sent out letters each year asking employees to support a particular scholarship fund.

Research has found numerous examples of the authority principle in action. One study chose 12 articles by well-known authors from important universities that had been published in the past three years, changed the names and university affiliations to names that were unknown or obscure, and resubmitted the articles in manuscript form to the original journals that had published them. Only one of the articles was accepted for publication under these circumstances, presenting dismaying evidence of the importance of authority (Peters & Ceci, 1982). Another study examined the effect of clothing on compliance, asking people on the street to comply with a minor request, such as picking up a paper bag that had been left on the sidewalk. Half of the time, the request was made by a person wearing average-looking street clothes; in the other half, the identical request was made by a person in a security guard's uniform. Would you expect the compliance rate to differ based on the clothing of the requestor? If you would, you would be correct: 92% of the sample complied with the request made by the person in the security guard's uniform, whereas only 42% complied when the request was made by the person in street clothes (Bickman, 1974; Bushman, 1988). And a Texas university professor reports that, while grocery shopping in an Italian neighborhood, he saw that canned tomatoes with the brand name "Furmano" were sold out, whereas the same product with the brand name "Furman" was not. Upon closer inspection, he noticed that both were produced by the same company: That market-savvy entity was simply adding the "o" to its name in an attempt to appear more authentic to the Italian population (Cialdini, 2001).

Critical Thinking
QUESTION Can you name at least one situation in which you've gone along with something because the request came from an authority figure?

Scarcity The last of the principles of compliance identified by Cialdini is the **principle of scarcity**, which maintains that people or products seem more attractive when they are unavailable or available for only a limited time or in limited quantity. Retail stores seem to capitalize on this principle frequently, with sales that are billed as "Today Only!" "The 15-Hour Sale," or "The Semi-Annual Sale." Even though our rational brains know that there will be another sale with similar deals soon, we may feel compelled to rush down to that store quickly so as not to miss a great deal. Limited editions are another common example of this principle, whether in art, videos, or collectables. The special membership deal at the health club that is available for a limited time only, and the special deal on that Florida vacation that expires in 72 hours also aim to take advantage of our need to get something that is scarce.

Why does this scarcity principle trigger such a strong urge in otherwise rational people? The answer may be found in the **theory of psychological reactance** developed by psychologist

Principle of scarcity People or products seem more important when their availability seems limited.

Theory of psychological reactance Humans have a strong need to control our own destinies and choices, and when these freedoms are threatened, we exert extra effort to hang onto them.

Jack Brehm (Brehm & Brehm, 1981). This theory suggests that humans have a strong need to control our own destinies and choices, and when these freedoms are threatened, we exert extra effort to hang onto them. This psychological reactance aspect of the scarcity principle seems especially relevant to our personal relationships: Haven't you ever found yourself wanting to be with a person more when that person was unavailable? Perhaps it was because they were with someone else, or maybe they just didn't seem too interested in you—either way, you may feel a greater pull toward that person than you would if they were really hot for you. In this situation, it might pay to ask yourself if you're truly interested in the person, or instead being driven by the scarcity principle—the answer might help you avoid a messy situation.

At this point, we should note that our reliance on the last four principles is rooted in some degree of logic. After all, when many people do something (consensus) or like something or someone (liking), there is an increased chance that we will, too. Similarly, if an authority figure tells us something about her area of expertise, chances are good that she is right. And if something is in short supply, that is often because it is a desirable item. Thus, taking these "shortcuts" isn't always a bad choice. In today's technology- and information-driven world, we often are exposed to far more information than we can possibly process thoughtfully. As a result, we have to make choices about what information is most important, spend our time on that, and use mental shortcuts to make less-important decisions. This is where these compliance principles come in: as tools for our mental shortcuts. The key to using them effectively is to learn to make a distinction in our motivation for going along with the request: Is it honestly something we want to do, or are we being swept along by our unconscious reaction to a principle of compliance?

Table 6.1 summarizes the six principles of compliance.

To test and expand your understanding of these psychological principles of compliance, turn now to Activities 6.2 and 6.3. The first activity challenges you to identify the various principles of compliance at work in a local shopping mall. The second activity offers you an opportunity to examine the ways in which these psychological principles have influenced your choices and actions in your own personal relationships.

Interim SUMMARY #2

Compliance, the second level of social influence, refers to our behavior when we agree to a specific request from someone. Cialdini has identified six different psychological principles that increase compliance. They are the principles of reciprocity, commitment, social proof (or consensus), liking, authority, and scarcity. Although these principles of social influence can work to enhance our relations with others, they can also induce us to act in ways that are not in our best interest or that we might regret later. The best way to avoid being misled by principles of compliance is to learn to recognize them, take a "time out," and consciously ask yourself if the choice you are about to make is a good one.

TABLE 6.1 | Principles of Compliance

PRINCIPLE	DESCRIPTION	EXAMPLE
Reciprocity	Belief that it is important to reciprocate, or "pay back" favors	Taking care of a friend's pet while she is on vacation, because she sometimes gives you rides to work
Commitment	A small initial commitment to a person or idea increases the likelihood that we will make a more significant commitment later	Agreeing to stay at work an extra half-hour increases the chance that we'll agree to greater requests, such as working extra shifts
Social Proof	Going along with a belief or behavior because it looks like many others are doing the same thing	Contributing to a charity you aren't really interested in simply because many others at your workplace are doing so
Liking	Agreeing to do something because the person making the request is likable	Buying a more expensive computer than you planned because you really like the salesperson
Authority	We are more likely to agree to a request made by an authority figure	Volunteering to help with a local political campaign because your teacher said it was important
Scarcity	People or products seem more important when their availability seems limited	Buying more than you need of something because it is on sale for a limited time

OBEDIENCE

PREVIEW QUESTIONS

(1) How is obedience different from conformity and compliance?

(2) What did the Milgram experiment teach us about obedience?

(3) What situational factors affect obedience to authority?

(4) How do these lessons help us improve our relations with others?

A third type of social influence is the strongest of all: *obedience to authority*. **Obedience** can be distinguished from compliance by the addition of a negative consequence for refusal. The power of authority was stunningly demonstrated in a now-classic psychological experiment conducted by a Yale University researcher named Stanley Milgram (1974).

> **Obedience** Agreeing to a request from an authority figure, when there is a negative consequence for refusal.

The Milgram Experiment

In the wake of World War II and the atrocities perpetuated on the Jews by the Nazis, it was the general consensus among citizens worldwide that Hitler's soldiers were just monstrously evil people by nature. How else could their inhumane persecution of innocent people be explained? Certainly no reasonable person would have carried out orders to commit mass executions, onlookers insisted. Milgram agreed, and as a social psychologist decided to conduct a study to prove it. He wanted to demonstrate that Americans would never obey authority if it meant hurting an innocent person; in other words, that "this could never happen to us." He ran an advertisement in the local newspaper asking for volunteers to participate in his study and chose 40 average white men to participate.

As each participant arrived at the lab, he was met by a tall, stern-looking researcher in a crisp grey lab coat. Another person was there, too, who appeared to be another participant, and the researcher explained to them that the study was examining the effects of punishment on learning. One participant would take the role of "teacher" and the other would be the "learner." To determine who did what, the participants each drew a slip of paper out of a hat. Unbeknownst to the real participant, the other "participant" was actually working for Milgram, just pretending to be a participant. The real participant found that his slip said "teacher," while the confederate (the fake participant) said his slip said "learner."

Now that the roles were assigned, the stern-looking researcher asked both men to follow him into the next room, where he strapped the learner into a chair and attached an electrode onto his wrist. He explained that the punishment in the study would be a series of electric shocks at increasingly higher voltages. Expressing some concern at this point, the learner (who, you remember, is really a confederate of the study) mentioned that he had a slight heart condition. The researcher assured him that, although the shocks might be painful, there would be "no permanent tissue damage." The teacher (the real participant) was also a little concerned, so the researcher let him feel a 45-volt shock, which felt something like a moderate sting. Thus reassured, the teacher followed the researcher into the next room where the researcher explained his role in the experiment.

As the teacher, he was to teach a series of word pairs to the learner, and each time the learner made a mistake, the teacher was to deliver an electric shock to the learner. There was a console in front of the teacher's chair with 30 switches from left to right. The switch on the far left was labeled 15 volts, the next switch 30 volts, and so on in 15-volt increments, up to the switch on the far right, labeled 450 volts. Underneath the voltage labels were a series of descriptions of the relative strength of the voltages. On the far left the description read "Slight Shock"; the next description read "Moderate Shock," and so forth to the last few, which read "Danger: Severe Shock" and finally "XXX."

The experiment began. Each time the learner made a mistake, the teacher administered a shock. Each time a shock switch was flipped, a loud buzzer would go off, indicating the shock had been delivered. At the 75-volt shock, the learner made a mild sound of surprise, which got a little louder with each of the next few shocks. At 120 volts, the learner said, "Hey, this really hurts!" When the teacher looked to the researcher for guidance, thinking perhaps they should stop, the researcher first said, "Please go on." At 150 volts, the learner started screaming and pleading to be let out of the experiment, shouting about his heart condition. When the teacher hesitated, the researcher next said, "The experiment requires that you continue." With each successive shock, the learner continued shouting and screaming loudly, begging the experimenter to stop. The next time the teacher hesitated, concerned about the learner's health, the researcher said, "It is absolutely essential that you continue." After the 330-volt shock, the learner's room became strangely silent—there were no more screams. Upset, the teacher looked to the researcher, who told him, "You have no other choice; you must go on." When the learner didn't answer the next question at all, the researcher instructed the teacher to treat a nonresponse as an incorrect answer and deliver the next level of shock.

In reality, the study wasn't about the effects of punishment on learning, but a test to see how obedient these normal, middle-class white men would be when asked by an authority figure to harm another person. What would you predict? Prior to his experiment, Milgram surveyed more than 100 people, asking them how far they thought the participants would go in shocking the learner, and none of the people surveyed thought any participant would shock past 300 volts. Most thought the participants would stop as soon as the learner became distressed. Even a group of psychiatrists Milgram questioned predicted that only 1 person in 1,000 would deliver shocks all the way to the 450-volt level.

To the dismay of Milgram and people everywhere, 63% of the participants shocked the learner all the way to the 450-volt level. The participants *thought* they did, anyway—the only real shock delivered in the experiment was the 45-volt "test" shock the teacher got at the beginning just to see what it felt like. Participants didn't know that until after the experiment was over, though. Milgram's attempt to show the world that "normal" people would never harm others just because they were ordered to do so backfired. It turned out that authority truly has a powerful effect on our behavior.

Does this mean that the participants in Milgram's study were evil people? Not at all. If we draw that conclusion, we are making the fundamental attribution error that we learned about in Chapter 5—assuming people's behavior to be the product of personality factors, without recognizing the enormous power of situational factors. The fundamental attribution error, in fact, is exactly why people were so stunned by the results of this study—because they assumed that most people are "good" people and hence wouldn't intentionally cause harm to another person. They didn't consider the potential strength of the situation, in this case, the power of a legitimate authority figure.

It is also important to note that the participants in Milgram's study did not enjoy their role. On the contrary, many felt considerable anxiety when the experimenter insisted they continue. When the learner began protesting in earnest, many of the participants tried to convince the experimenter that they should stop because the learner was in such pain. When the participants were assured that the experimenter would take complete responsibility for anything that happened, though, participants typically continued to obey the experimenter's demands to continue shocking the learner. As they did so, many sweated profusely, stuttered, or exhibited other signs of stress.

 *Critical Thinking* QUESTION Compare the findings and factors involved in the **Milgram Experiment** to the recent situation in Abu Ghraib (Figure 6.5). What similarities do you note?

Milgram Experiment A classic study of obedience to authority.

FIGURE 6.5 | Based on what you know about the behavior of some military personnel at the Abu Ghraib prison, what principles of social influence discussed in this chapter may have contributed to their behavior?

Situational Factors in Obedience

The findings of Milgram's original study clearly demonstrated the power of situational factors to influence people's behavior. The next question, then, had to be, "What are the specific situational factors at work in obedience situations?" Milgram and numerous others set out to determine the answer, and they identified several key components.

First, proximity of the victim played a role. In the original study, the "learner" was in a separate room from the "teacher," which had the effect of allowing some psychological (as well as physical) distance between the two. In later studies that put them in the same room, teachers delivered fewer shocks. When the participant had to actually place the learner's hand on a shock plate to deliver the shock (rather than simply flipping a switch), the obedience level dropped to 30%.

Second, proximity of the experimenter influenced obedience. In the original study, the experimenter stood next to the participant as he delivered instructions. When the experimenter was not in the room, but giving instructions by telephone, many participants pretended to obey, but actual obedience dropped to 21%.

Perhaps the most influential situational factor in obedience was observed when Milgram had three participants working together. (Only one was the real participant—the other two were confederates working for Milgram and were just pretending to be participants.) When these two other teachers defied the experimenter's request to continue and refused to deliver any more shocks, obedience dropped to 10%. This obedience level has been replicated in other studies, which have also determined that when in the presence of dissenters, only about 10% of research subjects obey an order with which they do not agree (e.g., Gamson, Fireman, & Rytina, 1982). An example of a disobedient subject seems to liberate another subject from the social expectation of obeying authority, perhaps by offering an alternate acceptable norm to which to conform.

Gender and Culture in Obedience

Did you notice that in Milgram's original study, the participants were all white men? If you did, you may be wondering if the results would have been different if he had used women, or people of other races. Researchers wondered the same thing and conducted numerous experiments to find out. What were the results? Interestingly, obedience levels in women and in people from other countries were found to be very similar to those levels originally discovered by Milgram. In replications of Milgram's study in Europe, South Africa, the Middle East, and Australia, obedience rates in Jordan and Australia were almost identical to U.S. rates, and German subjects demonstrated even higher obedience rates of 85% (Mantell, 1971). People in collectivistic cultures tended to be influenced by others more than did people in individualistic cultures (Bond & Smith, 1996).

More recently, a Dutch study set up a similar moral dilemma, asking men and women to make a series of 15 negative and derogatory comments to a job applicant who was taking a test that would determine whether he got an important job or not. (Of course, unbeknownst to the participants, the "job applicant" was actually a confederate of the researchers.) As the comments got worse, the job applicant became increasingly distressed, going from nervous to angry to complete despair. Would the participants stop making the comments as the applicant became more upset? Control-group participants, who did not have an experimenter ordering them to continue, all stopped making the comments before the end of the experiment. When the experimenter asked them to continue, though, 92% of the participants did so, delivering all 15 derogatory comments to the distressed applicant (Meeus & Raaijmakers, 1995).

What experiences have you had with authority, either in a position of authority or in a subordinate position? Explore the links between your own experiences and the information in this chapter in Activity 6.4 at the end of the chapter.

REFLECTIONS ON THE STANFORD PRISON EXPERIMENT

Each type of social influence examined in this chapter played a role in the events of the Stanford Prison Experiment, which was described at the beginning of this chapter. Conformity was involved when, finding themselves in the unfamiliar positions of "prison guard" and "prison inmate," participants in both roles naturally looked to others in the same role for cues as to how they were supposed to act. They followed one another's lead, partly because they wanted to play their role effectively (informational social influence) and partly because they wanted to fit in with the others in the same role (normative social influence).

Principles of compliance were involved as well. When the prisoners started goofing off in the first roll call at the beginning of the experiment, guards reciprocated by toughening up their demeanor and their demands. In turn, the prisoners reciprocated by taunting the guards and starting to misbehave even more, to which the guards reciprocated by becoming more demanding, and so on. The principle of reciprocity, in this case of negative actions, influenced participants in both roles to "pay each other back" for the negativity they were experiencing. By the same token, some guards tried to convince a few of the prisoners to give them "inside information" about what the prisoners were planning next, in return for which they offered special meals and other comforts.

The principle of commitment was perhaps the most powerful principle of compliance in the experiment. Six days into it, just prior to Zimbardo's realization of what was happening and his subsequent termination of the experiment, conditions were so bad that one prisoner had been released from the experiment due to serious concerns about his psychological state. Other prisoners, having been forced to urinate in a bucket in their cells, had withdrawn their support from a fellow prisoner in solitary confinement, just so that they could have their blankets back. Guards had resorted to extreme derogatory treatment of the prisoners, robbing them of their dignity and even of their identities. How did it get so far out of hand? One step at a time, then a little more, and a little more, until after just a few days, things had gone far beyond what anyone ever thought possible. This "foot-in-the-door" aspect of the commitment principle even affected Zimbardo. He became so involved in his role as "prison warden" that he completely lost sight of the big picture and his ethics.

Of course, obedience to authority was at the heart of the whole situation. Zimbardo was a well-respected psychologist at a renowned university. Participants, as well as research assistants, went along with the escalating situation because of the legitimacy of the authority over the experiment. Parents who, on "visiting day," visited their "prisoner" sons, raised no objections to what they saw—after all, it was a Stanford University experiment, so they must know what they're doing, right? (Of course, the guards cleaned things up nicely prior to visiting day, so parents weren't aware of how bad things really were.) If anyone—participants, assistants, parents—thought that things had gotten a little out of hand, they probably looked around and saw that no one else was objecting, so it must be okay. The principle of consensus thus played a role, too.

Yet all it took to stop the spiraling chain of events was one person, a research assistant who noticed that it didn't feel right, and that conditions were far different from what she had expected coming into the experiment. She had the courage to speak her mind to Zimbardo, telling him that she thought he was putting the participants through too much. Zimbardo then looked at the situation from the perspective of principal investigator (rather than "prison warden") and realized that she was right. Since that fateful day, Zimbardo and psychology teachers everywhere have used the Stanford Prison Experiment as a powerful example of the sometimes insidious nature of social influence. Our lack of awareness is what gives it its power.

Interim SUMMARY #3

The most powerful level of social influence is obedience to authority, which distinguishes itself from compliance by the nature of its negative consequences for refusal. Milgram's classic studies on obedience laid the groundwork for our understanding of this powerful influence, and subsequent research has demonstrated that men and women alike followed instructions and carried out acts they thought were harmful to another person when the instructions came from a legitimate authority figure. In these situations, obedience was maximized when the victim was distant, when the authority figure was in close proximity, and when there were no examples of disobedience. The strength of the authority figure has been demonstrated in numerous cultures worldwide, with the general finding that people from collectivistic cultures tend to exhibit slightly higher rates of obedience than those in individualistic cultures.

The key to avoiding undue influence of these principles in our own behavior and our relationships is to raise our level of awareness of them. Understanding their power and becoming more conscious of their presence can help us to act in ways that are truly consistent with our intentions and our values.

CHAPTER TERMS

Stanford Prison Experiment
Conformity
Normative social influence
Informational social influence

Compliance
Principle of reciprocity
Principle of commitment
Principle of social proof
Consensus
Principle of liking

Principle of authority
Principle of scarcity
Theory of psychological reactance
Obedience
Milgram Experiment

ACTIVITY 6.1

EXPLORING YOUR OWN CONFORMITY

INSTRUCTIONS: *Consider the various situations in which you conform. Identify four personal examples of your own conformity and answer the following questions for each one:*

A. Briefly describe (in a sentence or two) the situation in which you conform.

B. Is your motive for this conformity informational or normative social influence? Briefly justify your answer.

C. Are any situational influences (for example, ambiguity, group size, culture) on conformity present in this example? Explain your answer.

D. Do you consider this example to be a positive or a negative example of conformity? In other words, is this conformity beneficial to you or not?

Example 1:

    a. _____

    _____

    b. _____

    _____

    c. _____

    _____

    _____

    d. _____

    _____

    _____

Example 2:

    a. _____

    _____

    b. _____

    _____

    c. _____

    _____

    _____

    d. _____

    _____

    _____

Example 3:

    a. _____

    _____

    b. _____

    _____

    c. _____

    _____

    _____

    d. _____

    _____

    _____

Example 4:

a. _____
_____

b. _____
_____

c. _____
_____
_____

d. _____
_____
_____

SUMMARY AND CONCLUSIONS

What insights have you gained from this exercise? What conclusions can you draw from your answers?

_____
_____
_____
_____
_____
_____
_____
_____
_____
_____
_____

ACTIVITY 6.2

COMPLIANCE PRINCIPLES AT THE MALL

INSTRUCTIONS: *Take a trip to a nearby shopping mall and visit some of the department stores and smaller retail stores. Pretend to be shopping, so that salespeople treat you like an average customer. Bring a small notepad with you and keep a sharp eye out for the principles of compliance that are in action all around the mall. Each time you find one, make some notes about what it is, how it works, and any "gut" reactions you have to it. Then, in the following space, discuss your findings about any four of the principles you found in your investigation. Your discussion of each principle should include:*

1. *A description of how the principle was used, along with the name of the principle*
2. *Any "gut" reactions you had to it*

3. Conclude your discussion with your reflections on this experience.

ACTIVITY 6.3

PRINCIPLES OF COMPLIANCE IN PERSONAL
RELATIONSHIPS AND THE WORKPLACE

INSTRUCTIONS: *Consider the various ways that the principles of compliance have influenced your own choices in your relationships or your actions in the workplace. For example, when did they play a role in your choice to pursue a relationship or a job? How have they influenced the continuing development of your relationships or work habits, and/or your decisions to stay in relationships or jobs that aren't ideal? Have they also influenced decisions you've made to leave relationships or jobs? Identify two or three examples that seem to best illustrate the impact of these psychological principles on your relationships and discuss them in a 2-3 page paper. Your discussion of each example should include:*

1. The name of the principle that affected you

2. How it played a role in that relationship or workplace choice

3. Your reflections on that choice, knowing what you know now about how your choice was influenced by a principle of compliance

ACTIVITY 6.4

ESSAY: PERSONAL EXPERIENCES WITH POWER
AND POWERLESSNESS

INSTRUCTIONS: *This chapter revealed the strength of an authority figure as an influence our behavior. For this exercise, choose one of the following options to explore your own experiences with authority. Your instructor will tell you whether you should write a paper on this topic, or instead discuss your experience with others in a small group.*

A. Think of a time that you were in a fairly long-term position of authority.

1. Describe your role, along with the number and roles of the people over whom you had authority.

2. How did you exert your authority? In other words, how did you get people to do what you wanted them to do? If you used principles of compliance, discuss which ones, how you used them, and how people responded to them. If you enforced your authority with negative consequences for disobedience, describe how you did this and how people responded. Give an example or two to illustrate your description.

3. Describe the hardest situation you faced during your time in that authority position, along with how you dealt with it. Upon reflection, how well do you think you handled it, and why?

4. In what ways did your experience as an authority figure affect your concept of yourself? In other words, what new facets of yourself (positive and/or negative) did you uncover as a result of your experiences?

B. Think of a time you were in a fairly long-term subordinate position.

1. Describe your role, along with your relationship to the authority figure.

2. How did your authority figure exert his or her authority over you? In other words, how did the person get you to do what she or he wanted you to do? If the person used principles of compliance, discuss which ones, how they were used, and how you responded to them (in terms of your actions, as well as your feelings about them). If the person enforced authority with negative consequences for disobedience, describe how this was used and how it affected you. Give an example or two to illustrate your description.

3. When the authority figure did something that frustrated, angered, or hurt you, how did you respond (both publicly and privately)? What are your reflections on that situation and your response to it?

4. In what ways did your experience in a subordinate position affect your concept of yourself? In other words, what new facets of yourself (positive and/or negative) did you uncover as a result of your experience?

PREJUDICE: FOUNDATIONS, CAUSES, EFFECTS, AND REMEDIES

7

CHAPTER

Your greatness is measured by your kindness; your education and intellect by your modesty; your ignorance is betrayed by your suspicions and prejudices; and your real caliber is measured by the consideration and tolerance you have for others.

—WILLIAM J. H. BOETCKER

On the morning of September 11, millions of Americans got up and went about their business as usual, thinking it was just another day. In New York City, it was a particularly beautiful day, with late summer sunshine lighting the clear blue sky. At 8:46 A.M., that sense of normalcy and peace was shattered when a hijacked airliner carrying 92 people and 20,000 gallons of jet fuel slammed into the North Tower of New York's World Trade Center. Minutes later, a second jet crashed into the South Tower, and with it came a dawning awareness that what had been thought to be a terrible accident was instead an unimaginable act of terror. In the next hour, a third hijacked plane hit the Pentagon, and a fourth crashed into a field in Pennsylvania, diverted from what was thought to be a fourth target in Washington, D.C. by a group of heroic passengers. Some 3,000 people, including firefighters and rescue personnel, financial wizards and janitors, mothers and children, were killed in the attacks of what has come to be known universally as simply "9/11".

In the aftermath of this horrific tragedy, Americans and friends around the world have faced a new set of questions centered on the struggle to understand the causes of 9/11. What kind of person would commit such an atrocious act against innocent people? Why? And what can we do to keep such a thing from ever happening again? In our effort to understand and cope with this unforeseen attack, these questions and our increased vigilance seem reasonable and necessary. But when we learned that the attack was masterminded and carried out by a group of Islamic fundamentalist terrorists, an unfortunate outgrowth of our newfound vigilance became increased suspicion of Arab Americans and people of the Muslim faith. A spurt of hate crimes ensued, such as the September 15, 2001 killing of gas station attendant Balbir Singh Sodhi in Mesa, Arizona, who was guilty of nothing more than having a beard and wearing a turban. He was neither Muslim nor of Arab descent, but his killer felt angered by the attack on America and threatened by Sodhi's superficial resemblance to the perpetrators of the terrorist attack. What Sodhi's murderer didn't understand was that his act of vengeance made him no different than the terrorists he was seeking to punish.

This chapter will examine the roots of the prejudices with which all humans struggle and the suspicions that, for some, became more pronounced in the wake of 9/11. We will seek to understand the universal causes of these attitudes and behaviors, and to learn how some of them may be overcome with education and ongoing effort.

THE FOUNDATIONS OF PREJUDICE

PREVIEW QUESTIONS

(1) How strongly must we identify with a group to be biased in its favor? How does this bias influence outgroups?

(2) What is flexible ethnocentrism, and how can we develop it in ourselves?

(3) Do all people stereotype? What factors influence stereotyping?

(4) Are the foundations of prejudice found in all cultures? Why or why not?

Cross-cultural research over the past half-century has identified several key factors that contribute to prejudice. Most recently, studies have begun to indicate that whereas some of these factors are probably unavoidable, others can be overcome. Our discussion of prejudice, then, will take a two-tiered approach that parallels the research. First we will examine the factors that appear to be inevitable, which we will call the foundations of prejudice. Because there are three of them, we can visualize these three foundations of prejudice as the three legs of a stool (Figure 7.1).

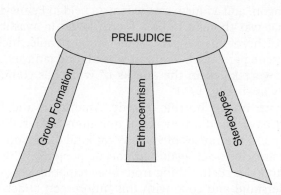

FIGURE 7.1 | Principles of group formation, ethnocentrism, and stereotypes are the basic human foundations of prejudice.

The First Leg: Group Formation

Throughout our history, humans all over our planet have formed themselves into groups. Early civilizations lived in bands and tribes, working together to feed and protect themselves. More modern civilizations are not that different from our early ancestors in that we, too, typically band together with others in families or similar social groups to feed and protect ourselves. From an evolutionary standpoint, group membership has facilitated our very survival. From a psychological standpoint, group membership has an array of advantages and disadvantages, which we are about to explore.

One key factor in understanding the psychological importance of groups in human behavior is social identity, which (as you may recall from Chapter 2) contributes to our self-concept. Our social identity includes the various groups with which we feel connected; for example, you might identify yourself as a student at your school, a musician, a member of your race and/or religion, a dad, and so forth with regard to people you spend time with and things you like to do. In other words, social identity is the "we" part of our self-concept (Myers, 1999). **Social identity theory** includes the idea that, in our efforts to maintain positive self-esteem, we may develop bias that favors our own groups over other groups. Thus, liking our own groups more than other groups contributes to a higher sense of self-esteem.

> **Social identity theory** The idea that, in our efforts to maintain positive self-esteem, we may develop bias that favors our own groups over other groups.

The classic experiment that demonstrated our strong tendency to form groups and to identify with them was conducted in 1971 by European psychologist Henri Tajfel. In his study, participants were shown a series of slides, each containing a number of dots. Each slide was flashed very briefly, without sufficient time to count the dots, and the participants were asked to estimate the number of dots on that slide. Participants worked alone. At the end of the testing session, each participant met with someone on Tajfel's lab team to hear the results. Some were told that they were "underestimators," and the others were told they were "overestimators." Later in the experiment, the same participants, still each working alone, were told they must divide 15 points (each point worth money) among 9 randomly selected participants of the experiment. The participants, whom they had never met, were identified on their worksheet by only a coded participant number, and the designation "overestimator" or "underestimator." Participants who had been told they were "underestimators" awarded the majority of points to other "underestimators"; participants told they were "overestimators" similarly rewarded other "overestimators" with the lion's share of the available points. Furthermore, when each participant completed his or her work and joined the other participants, someone in the group inevitably asked, "Which were you?" The answer was met by cheers from the like group and boos from the other (Tajfel, Billig, Bondy, & Flament, 1971).

Numerous other studies have retested Tajfel's findings with similar results. Typically, people assign about two-thirds of the rewards to their own group and about one-third to the other, and this finding holds true for women and men alike, as well as for various age groups. This favoritism is known as **ingroup bias**, and Tajfel demonstrated how easily we tend to demonstrate this

> **Ingroup bias** Favoring others with whom we identify over those whom we perceive as different.

bias, even when the groups are defined in a meaningless way. When our group affiliation is based on something that is actually meaningful to our self-concept, such as political and social beliefs, ethnicity, religion, or gender, you can imagine how much stronger the bias becomes. Research in this area indeed finds that the more strongly we identify with a group, the more ingroup bias we demonstrate toward it (Crocker & Luhtanen, 1990). Also, when our group is a minority group, our bias is stronger than when we perceive our group to be in the majority (Ellemers, Rijswijk, Roefs, & Simons, 1997). If, for example, you are a political liberal in a town that is largely conservative, your bias in favor of your liberal viewpoints and against the opposition will be stronger than it would be if most people around you were also liberals.

Critical Thinking
QUESTION

What ingroup biases do you see in your own relationships? How are these biases beneficial? How are they harmful?

Ingroup bias has a flip side, though, which is **outgroup bias**, or downgrading others who are different or not in your group. Ingroup bias and outgroup bias apply not just to the people in the group, but to the norms and customs in the group as well. For example, people tend to believe that the rules and norms of their own culture represent the right way to do things; conversely, they often see behaviors of other cultures as strange or even wrong. Ingroup and outgroup bias have been found in cultures all over the world and appear to be inextricably linked to our need to belong to a group. We can see how these biases have been beneficial from an evolutionary standpoint, because they promote and strengthen the bond among people in the same group. In our increasingly multicultural world, however, ingroup and outgroup bias can easily evolve into prejudice and discrimination.

Outgroup bias Downgrading others who are different or not in your group.

Just as the complexity of our self-concept can help protect us against loss and threat to our self-concept (remember that from Chapter 2), the complexity of our social identity affects our ingroup bias. Interesting new research has found that people who identify with a diverse set of social groups (in other words, have more complex social identities) exhibit less outgroup bias than people whose social identities connect only to groups that are very similar to one another (Brewer & Pierce, 2005). It seems, then, that by developing connections to a broader, more diverse representation of the people in our environment, we will automatically be taking a step toward reducing our own biases.

The Second Leg: Ethnocentrism

The next component that serves as a foundation for prejudice is **ethnocentrism**, or our tendency to see the world through the lenses of our own culture. Professor David Matsumoto of San Francisco State University, who has been an important contributor to our understanding of how psychological principles can be used to improve multicultural relations, suggests that ethnocentrism is a phenomenon that can have two different outcomes. One outcome is the ingroup and outgroup biases discussed earlier, which Matsumoto (2000) calls

Ethnocentrism Our tendency to see the world through the lenses of our own culture.

inflexible ethnocentrism, or judging others as wrong simply because they are different. This negative outcome, in fact, is the outcome typically associated with ethnocentrism. A more positive outcome is **flexible ethnocentrism**, which involves a less judgmental perspective toward unfamiliar cultures and leads to better human relations. Let's examine Matsumoto's ideas in more depth.

> **Inflexible ethnocentrism**
> Judging others as wrong simply because they are different.

In a departure from the traditional view of ethnocentrism (which argues that we should not be ethnocentric), Matsumoto suggests that ethnocentrism is an inevitable by-product of our upbringing, regardless of our culture. As we grow up within a society, we learn the rules of our society and the expected behaviors, beliefs, and values that go along with them. These rules and norms define a culture, and are integral to successful adaptation to its social group. We learn to expect others in our social group to think and act in similar ways, and subsequently we notice whether people fulfill these expectations by acting appropriately. When we see people acting in ways that fit our expectations, their behavior seems "normal," and when their behaviors do not fit what we have learned to expect, it strikes us as "abnormal" or odd. This sequence of events (developing expectations, noticing others' behavior, and judging its fit with our expectations) is all accomplished automatically, without conscious thought. In this way, we learn to see others' behavior through the lenses of our own culture, judging whether it fits or it doesn't based on our own norms and expectations. This ethnocentrism, present in all cultures, is not only inevitable, but is necessary, for if we don't value the rules and norms of our culture, what motivation do we have to uphold them? Ethnocentrism, then, helps keep a society functioning smoothly, avoiding mass chaos.

> **Flexible ethnocentrism**
> Recognizing our own tendency toward ethnocentrism, and working toward a deeper understanding and empathy for norms of different cultures.

Becoming More Flexibly Ethnocentric   The key to avoiding the negative outcome of ethnocentrism (inflexible ethnocentrism) lies in our *awareness* of our own ethnocentrism. We must recognize that we are ethnocentric, and that it is a natural condition. Then we can follow a series of steps to help ensure that ours is a flexible ethnocentrism.

The first step toward flexible ethnocentrism is to become consciously aware of the rules of our own cultural group, and to recognize how these rules affect our perceptions and judgments of others. Western culture, for example, places a high value on beauty, especially in women: Women are supposed to do their best to look as attractive as possible at all times. Toward this end, women spend an enormous amount of money on cosmetics, clothing, and ongoing attention to their hair. Enhancement and exhibition of physical beauty, then, is a cultural rule for Western women. This norm affects Westerners' perceptions and judgments of others in that women who do not adhere to this norm are looked down on and often criticized with derogatory language. Becoming aware of norms such as these, and the judgments that often arise from them, is the first step toward flexible ethnocentrism.

 *Critical Thinking* QUESTION   Identify one norm that you adhere to from one of your own cultural groups.

The next step is to recognize that other cultures have their own set of rules, beliefs, and behaviors that, although they may be very different from our own, are just as important to their own society as ours are to us. Continuing with the same example, one group of women that does not adhere to the Western value on exhibition of female beauty is Muslim women. Instead of showing off the latest hairstyle, it is Muslim custom for a woman to cover her head with a scarf, called a *hijab*. In addition, a traditional Muslim woman may also shun slacks and wear only loose-fitting dresses or similar garments. This custom is at odds with the Western custom of showing off one's physical attributes. When a Muslim woman adheres to Muslim custom by wearing a hijab and traditional dress in a Western country such as the United States, Westerners need to remember that she is doing so because it is important to her belief system. Too often, we react instead by thinking how different she looks and assuming that she must be different from us in many other ways as well.

 *Critical Thinking* QUESTION Continuing with the example from the norm you identified previously, name one variation you've noticed. In other words, describe what people do or exhibit that differs from your own norm.

The third step on the path to flexible ethnocentrism is to learn about other cultures' specific beliefs and norms, so that we can better understand them in their own context. For example, most Westerners are aware that Muslim women traditionally wear a headscarf and loose clothing, but few understand why they would want to cover themselves up in that way. Talking to a Muslim woman or even conducting a quick Internet search reveals the reasons behind her attire. The Qur'an, which is the Muslim equivalent of the Christian Bible, decrees that women should cover their heads and let their bodies be known only to their husbands. In addition, it emphasizes modesty for both women and men, so that they will be evaluated on the basis of their intelligence and abilities instead of their physical attributes. Interestingly, the Qur'an offers guidelines for men as well: They are not supposed to wear tight-fitting clothes, either, and they are also prohibited from wearing silk or gold. Women, on the other hand, can wear silk and gold. These guidelines stem from Allah's statement that men and women should not appear like each other. Adhering to these rules is considered a sign of dignity and good moral character, both of which are highly valued in Muslim society. Understanding the origin of these Muslim customs helps us make sense of them and to recognize that although they may be different from our own beliefs and customs, they work just as well for the Muslim people as ours do for us. (And when you think about it, women in Western culture didn't typically wear slacks, either, until partway into the twentieth century.)

Critical Thinking QUESTION Based on what you identified in the previous two critical thinking questions, do a little research and try to determine what drives the different norm you've observed in others.

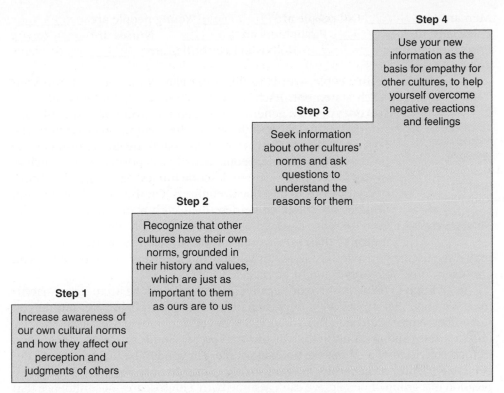

Step 4

Use your new information as the basis for empathy for other cultures, to help yourself overcome negative reactions and feelings

Step 3

Seek information about other cultures' norms and ask questions to understand the reasons for them

Step 2

Recognize that other cultures have their own norms, grounded in their history and values, which are just as important to them as ours are to us

Step 1

Increase awareness of our own cultural norms and how they affect our perception and judgments of others

FIGURE 7.2 | Steps to Flexible Ethnocentrism

The fourth and final step in becoming flexibly ethnocentric is this: As you continue to learn more about other cultures, keep filing your new information away in your brain, so that you build an ever-broadening set of perspectives from which to draw when you encounter someone behaving in a way unfamiliar to you. Matsumoto emphasizes that flexible ethnocentrism is not about forsaking your own cultural beliefs and values, but about adding knowledge of other cultures to your set of expectations of others' behavior. By doing so, you'll increase the chances that you will be able to understand the meaning of their behavior and how it fits into their belief system, which can ultimately lead to better human relations. Figure 7.2 summarizes the steps to flexible ethnocentrism.

One way to further develop flexible ethnocentrism is to spend a little time with someone who seems very different from you. Talk to the person about his or her background, beliefs, and interests to develop an understanding of the person's viewpoint. Activity 7.1 offers you an opportunity to try this out.

The Third Leg: Stereotypes

For the short statements that follow, fill in the blanks with the first things that come to mind, without second-guessing or censoring yourself: Women are _____.

Men are _____. Old people are _____. Young people are _____. Politicians are _____. Firefighters are _____. Nurses are _____. Prison inmates are _____. Hollywood celebrities are _____. Students are _____.

If you're like most people, words to fill in the blanks just popped into your head as you read each statement. Each of your completed statements reflects a **stereotype**, or a generalization about a group of people that assumes that members of the group share common characteristics. Some of your stereotypes were probably negative, others were positive. For example, people usually use positive words such as caring or compassionate to describe nurses, and words like brave or courageous to describe firefighters. On the other hand, prison inmates are likely to be described with a negative label. Also, you are more likely to use positive words to describe your own ingroups than you would for outgroups. If you are young, you may have used a positive stereotype for young, and a negative one for old; if you are older, those stereotypes might be reversed.

> **Stereotype** A generalization about a group of people that assumes that members of the group share common characteristics.

In addition to being positive or negative, stereotypes can be accurate or inaccurate. We hope that nurses are compassionate, and many probably are, but do you remember Nurse Ratched from the classic novel and movie *One Flew Over the Cuckoo's Nest?* She certainly didn't fit the stereotype! Some prison inmates, even though convicted of a crime, are not bad people. They might be loving parents, dependable friends, or generous to strangers. Because stereotypes are a general impression of a group of people, we can't assume with a high degree of confidence that a particular person from the group will fit our stereotype.

Critical Thinking **QUESTION** Think about the stereotypes you identified at the beginning of this section. Can you think of one or two examples of people you know (or know of) that do *not* fit the stereotype you wrote in the blank?

Why We Stereotype If stereotyping can't be relied on for accuracy, why do we engage in it? Interestingly, research indicates that stereotyping is a natural part of our thinking process, just like the other cognitive biases we learned about in Chapter 5. At any given moment, we are bombarded by so much information from our five senses that we cannot even begin to pay close attention to all of it. So we take mental shortcuts, one of which is to categorize and classify things. When we come into contact with a new person, we activate stereotypes based on the small amount of information we have about that person, such as how he or she looks, acts, talks, or the role in which we see him or her (like nurse, teacher, or politician). The goal of the stereotype, or mental shortcut, is to give us something to go on or to help us be prepared to interact effectively with that person. One researcher called them a "cognitively inexpensive way of understanding others" (Kenrick, Neuberg, & Cialdini, 1999, p. 414). When they are accurate, stereotypes can help us be more efficient, saving time and effort as we navigate through the day. For example, when I hired a housepainter from Jamaica to paint my house, we agreed that he would arrive and begin work between 8 and 9 every morning. Without fail, he showed up around 11 or noon, seemingly unaware that he was late. We've all heard jokes about "Jamaica time," and in this case, the stereotype that Jamaicans are less concerned about punctuality than Americans turned out to be useful, because it helped me recognize that he wasn't irresponsible, he was just "on Jamaica time, mon!" Like others from *polychronic cultures*, Jamaicans *value relationships over time efficiency*; this painter spent time with his wife and children each morning before coming to work and didn't like to rush through that important family time.

All too often, though, stereotypes are not accurate. Instead, they are overgeneralized or blown out of proportion, in which case they can do much more harm than good. One man tells the story of his wife, an educated white woman, who took a wrong turn in her city and ended up driving through an unfamiliar black neighborhood. She noticed quite a few people she passed staring and gesturing at her, which made her nervous, and she locked her car doors. A few blocks later, she realized she was driving the wrong way on a one-way street. She had activated negative stereotypes about the "outgroup," which led her to misinterpret their actions as threatening, when in fact they were trying to help her (Kenrick et al., p. 414).

Inaccurate stereotypes can also lead to **self-fulfilling prophecies**, which occur when a person begins to act in a manner consistent with the expectations placed upon him or her by others. Consider, for example, Tara, a black student in a predominantly white school, who isn't doing very well in her social studies class. Her teacher, familiar with the numerous statistics demonstrating that blacks, on average, perform less well in school than whites, assumes that Tara is less intelligent than her fellow students and is probably doing her best. Not wanting to embarrass Tara, the teacher calls on her less and less often and expects less from her than he does from the other students. This teacher is operating on a stereotype that comes from accurate data (blacks do perform less well in school than whites, on average), but that is widely interpreted *inaccurately*. To assume that the reason for the performance difference between blacks and whites is due to intelligence is to overlook the fact that whites often have access to better schools and more financial and social resources, as well as the fact that when these mitigating circumstances are controlled for, research has found no significant differences between blacks' and whites' IQ scores. Tara's social studies teacher, although he probably meant well, failed to be an effective teacher for Tara because he relied on his stereotype for black students. Worst of all, his actions may create a self-fulfilling prophecy if Tara, in response to her teacher's apparent lack of interest in her and his failure to engage her in the material, becomes less and less interested in the class, causing her grade to drop even further.

> **Self-fulfilling prophecy** A person begins to act in a manner consistent with the expectations placed upon him or her by others.

Social Contributors to Stereotypes   One of the reasons stereotypes persist is the confirmation bias, which we learned about in Chapter 5. Recall that the confirmation bias is our tendency to notice and remember events that are in line with our expectations and beliefs, whereas we are less likely to remember events that do not fit our existing belief system. One recent study, for example, found that people were more likely to remember positive acts done by members of their ingroup and negative acts done by outgroup members. At the same time, they tended to explain away or trivialize negative acts committed by ingroup members (Sherman, Klein, Laskey, & Wyer, 1998). So, if you come upon the scene of a car accident involving a young person and an older person, your stereotypes will probably affect your assumptions and memories in two ways. First, you're likely to assume that the outgroup member was at fault. Second, if you find that your assumption is incorrect, you will probably make some sort of excuse for your ingroup driver ("Well, in this rain, anyone could get into a fender-bender"). Thus, your stereotypes remain firmly in place.

Outgroup homogeneity effect Our tendency to assume that members of an outgroup are more alike than members of our ingroup.

Another factor that contributes to stereotypes is the **outgroup homogeneity effect**, which is our tendency to assume that members of an outgroup are more alike than members of our ingroup. In other words, we recognize greater diversity among members of our ingroups than among outgroup members. Upon reflection, this bias seems natural, in light of the fact that we probably have more information about ingroup members than outgroup members. For example, as a teacher of psychology, I know that people with advanced degrees in psychology go into many fields other than counseling or teaching: We are writers, researchers, advertisers, child development specialists, organizational consultants, and CIA agents, to name just a few. I also know that psychologists range widely in age, political viewpoints, personalities, and interests. The general population, though, not being psychologists, tends to think we're all alike: We're either the insightful professorial type, a bit stuffy or snooty, who wants to psychoanalyze you, or the supportive, earthy type who wants to give you a hug.

Critical Thinking **QUESTION** Can you think of how the outgroup homogeneity effect plays a role in your own stereotypes?

In addition to outgroup homogeneity and the confirmation bias, stereotypes can be created and perpetuated by several other means. Often, a stereotype will be passed from generation to generation within a family, with subsequent generations being "taught" the stereotype but never even having any actual contact with the object of the stereotype (Brislin, 1993). Also, we must recognize the fact that our own stereotypes are always based on a limited sample: We can never assume that we've interacted with all persons in a particular cultural group. Thus, our observations based on this limited sample must be somewhat inconclusive and open to modification. Figure 7.3 summarizes reasons why we stereotype.

Who Stereotypes More Often, and When? Finally, research has discovered a few personal and situational variables that affect a person's tendency to stereotype. The first is the need for structure. Some people have a greater need for predictability and order in life than others do; they are more bothered by interruptions and unexpected events. These people rank higher on the Personal Need for Structure scale and tend

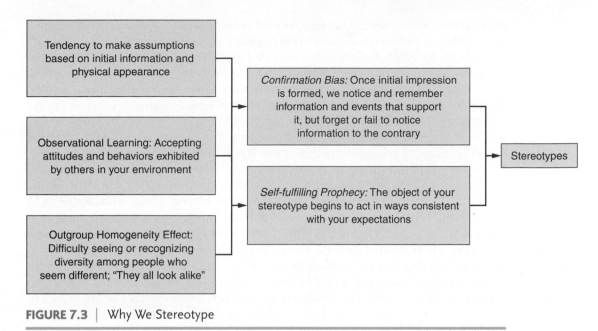

FIGURE 7.3 | Why We Stereotype

to stereotype others more easily (Neuberg & Newsom, 1993). Also, people in more powerful positions tend to stereotype people in less powerful positions more than the less powerful stereotype the powerful (Fiske, 1993). For example, secretaries and assistants in a business organization are less likely to stereotype their managers than their managers are to stereotype them. Both cognitive and social reasons have been suggested for this finding. First, some would argue that people in high-power positions may have more demands on their time and thus, must use stereotyping to maintain cognitive efficiency. Second, people in high power positions may simply have less to lose when they stereotype those with less power, since the less powerful have less opportunity for impact on them (Goodwin & Fiske, 1993).

Situational variables have been found to affect stereotyping as well. People who are in a good mood are more likely to engage in stereotyping, presumably because a good mood makes us a bit complacent (Stroessner & Mackie, 1992). Interestingly, people in certain "emotionally aroused" states such as anger, fear, or anxiety are also more likely to stereotype, in this case because the emotional arousal from that particular mood reduces their resources available for cognitive processing (Wilder, 1993). When these happy or aroused people come in contact with someone for whom they have competing stereotypes, they generally act on the one most consistent with their current mood (Erber, 1991). For example, when I was traveling in Italy one year, I was on my own for a few days. When I arrived at the train station in Milan, which is a large and busy transportation hub, I felt overwhelmed: The physical layout of the station was unfamiliar to me, I don't speak a lot of Italian, I had too much luggage from a shopping binge, and it was noisy and crowded. While hanging on to my bags, I was trying to figure out which direction to go to catch my connecting train, which was scheduled to depart soon. When a group of animated Italian men walked by me, very close, and seemed to be "checking me out," I felt irritated and a little threatened, almost as if my inner voice were snarling, "Sexist hoodlums!" Clearly, the demands of my situation activated my stereotypes of Italian men, and because my mood was more stressed than happy at the time, the stereotypes were negative. Conversely, my positive stereotype of Italian men was activated when I was dining in an open-air Italian restaurant with a female friend, enjoying perfect weather, a great meal and some good wine. The male waiter was overly attentive and when he asked us to meet him and a friend later at a dance club, I merely chuckled inwardly, thinking benevolently that "these Italian guys sure appreciate women!"

We're also more likely to stereotype when there are many demands on our thinking, such as when you are in an unfamiliar or complicated situation. In the example above, the confusion of the Milan train station along with my need to find my connecting train before it departed was causing me to use all my cognitive resources to try to figure out which direction to go. As a result, there were no resources left to make a rational evaluation of the men who bothered me. Imagine your first day at a new school or a new job—did it seem as if there was a lot going on? If so, you were probably more likely to stereotype some of the people you met. Also, an employer who is trying to interview a number of applicants in a short amount of time might find herself engaging in some unconscious stereotyping based on how they look and act, as she tries to make judgments about the applicants with only limited information.

To explore your own stereotypes, how they have developed, and their impact on your relationships, turn now to Activity 7.2.

The Foundations of Prejudice: A Final Word

Group formation and its accompanying ingroup/outgroup biases, ethnocentrism, and stereotyping are not limited to a particular culture. They are universal phenomena that experts agree are probably inevitable, because they grow out of the basic human need for survival. Group affiliation has been part of human survival since our beginning. Ethnocentrism contributes to survival by way of social learning, which is a process that helps us fit into our social group. Stereotyping contributes to survival by acting as a cognitive shortcut to information processing. In their purest form, they are all beneficial. Their value becomes more ambiguous when we allow them to evolve into prejudice, which we will examine next.

Interim SUMMARY #1

Throughout history, prejudice has been a powerful influence on our relations with others. To better understand the complex psychological processes that fuel prejudice, we must begin with its foundations. The important role group membership plays in our physical safety and our psychological well-being drives us to group together with others, and also to value our group over competing groups. Ethnocentrism, our tendency to filter our perceptions through the lenses of our own culture, supports prejudice when we assume that our cultural perceptions are the only correct ones. Increasing our awareness of our tendency to do this, educating ourselves about alternative cultural beliefs and values, and recognizing their validity, are steps we can take toward flexible ethnocentrism and, subsequently, toward a reduction in our own prejudice.

Stereotypes are an outgrowth of our need to mentally classify things. In and of themselves, they can be useful when we need to make a quick assessment of a new situation. Too often, though, they are either inaccurate or overused, both of which contribute to prejudice when we make a generalization about a group of people based on our personal observation in one or a few isolated situations. Confirmation bias, the outgroup homogeneity effect, and the intergenerational effect all strengthen our tendency to stereotype, as does an individual's need for structure and his or her mood and stress level.

PREJUDICE AND DISCRIMINATION

PREVIEW QUESTIONS

(1) What is prejudice, and how prevalent is it in today's society?

(2) What factors influence prejudice, and how?

(3) How do prejudice and discrimination impact our relations with others?

(4) What are some effective strategies for overcoming prejudice?

(5) How can you incorporate these concepts into your own life and relations with others?

Prejudice

Now that we understand the roots of prejudice, let's examine prejudice itself in more detail. Simply put, **prejudice** is a prejudgment about a particular group of people. Typically, we think of prejudice as consisting of negative judgments, but research shows that people can be positively prejudiced as well (Kenrick et al., 1999). Either way, we are prejudiced when we judge a person or group based only on our stereotypes about them, rather than a rational evaluation of the facts available to us. The difference between a stereotype and a prejudice is that a stereotype is

> **Prejudice** Prejudgment, or superficial judgment, about a particular group of people.

strictly a cognitive process, whereas a prejudice is an attitude, which includes an emotional component. Some common prejudices in American culture include those based on race, sex, age, weight, religion, disability, and sexual orientation (see Figure 7.4).

Prejudice is a universal phenomenon, present in cultures all around the world in varying forms and degrees. For example, the English have traditionally been biased against Africans, Russians and Europeans prejudiced against Jews, Japanese against Koreans, and Chinese against Japanese (Taylor, Peplau, & Sears, 2000). Many times, the bias becomes more pronounced when the dominant group begins to feel threatened by an influx of immigrants from another country, such as French prejudice against immigrants from North Africa. In addition to racial and ethnic prejudice, gender bias is prevalent in the world as well. According to a 1991 United Nations report, girls represent two-thirds of the uneducated children in the world, with some regimes (such as the former Taliban regime in Afghanistan) going so far as to forbid women and girls from receiving education.

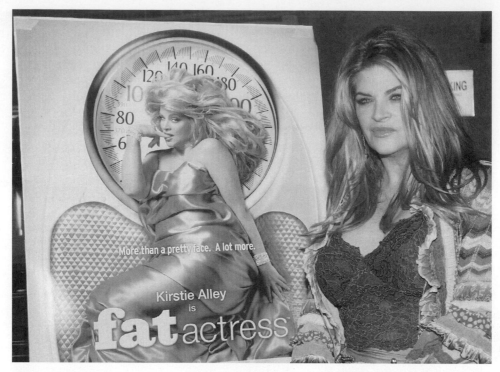

FIGURE 7.4 | The media attention and negative judgments Kirstie Alley has received about her weight are powerful indicators of our continued prejudice towards people who are overweight.

In the United States, some prejudices appear to have dramatically declined over the last 50 years. Whereas a large majority of whites favored school segregation based on race in the 1940s, almost none express support for segregation today. Similarly, the percentage of men expressing prejudice toward women executives in the workplace declined from 41% in 1965 to 5% in 1985 (Tougas, Brown, Beaton, & Joly, 1995). Implementation and enforcement of equal rights legislation have played a key role in reducing prejudice and discrimination, yet although Americans are less likely to openly admit prejudice, carefully designed research reveals that prejudice still exists. Essentially, two strong forces conflict with each other: The increasing value placed on equality in the United States (supported in many cases by laws) is in direct conflict with the extremely persistent nature of long-standing prejudices. As a result, modern prejudice has become more and more subtle; you could perhaps say it has "gone underground." For example, many whites feel comfortable working with blacks, but may express discomfort with more intimate contact such as interracial dating and marriage. Similarly, while people may express support for women in roles that are not traditionally feminine, their emotional reactions to and judgments of women in these roles may remain negative (see Figure 7.5). The effects of prejudice are still pronounced. In a nationwide study of college students, students of African

FIGURE 7.5 | Despite outward statements to the contrary, many people still have prejudice against those who seek non-traditional roles.

American, Asian American, and Mexican American descent felt socially isolated up to 9 times more often than did students of European American descent (Myers, 1999).

It is important to note that, in contrast to the foundations of prejudice discussed in the first part of this chapter, prejudice itself is not inevitable. There is growing evidence that prejudice can be overcome. We'll discuss ways of overcoming prejudice in the last part of this chapter; for now, keep that possibility in mind as we seek to understand the causes of prejudice.

Causes of Prejudice

Realistic Group Conflict Theory Several key factors have been identified that promote the formation and maintenance of all types of prejudice. One of the most widely discussed factors is the **realistic group conflict theory**, which argues that people become prejudiced against others with whom they must compete for limited resources such as jobs, money, or status. This theory helps explain why, for example, African American shopowners in Los Angeles felt prejudice against Asian Americans who began to buy the shops in the neighborhoods that had traditionally been dominated by African Americans. Similarly, white Americans' prejudice against Americans of other races may result partly from affirmative action, when whites perceive a threat to their jobs or admission to their chosen university. In both of these cases, the group that has traditionally held the dominant position feels threatened, and the other group has long-held feelings of frustration over

> **Realistic group conflict theory** People become prejudiced against others with whom they must compete for limited resources such as jobs, money, or status.

the lower status they have traditionally held. Both of these emotions play a significant role in the development and maintenance of prejudice.

The realistic group conflict theory as a contributor to prejudice was dramatically demonstrated in a landmark study called the Robbers' Cave experiment (Sherif, 1966). With their parents' permission, 22 well-adjusted, middle-class 11-year-old boys from Oklahoma were selected to participate in a study of conflict and cooperation (although the parents knew it was an experiment, the boys, of course, did not). Randomly divided into two groups of 11 boys each, the boys were taken in their separate groups to a Boy Scout camp in the woods for a 2-week camping trip. For the first week, neither group knew of the others' existence; their separate camps were over half a mile apart, and camp counselors kept each group busy with swimming, games, and other camp activities. During this first week, the boys formed a bond with other boys in their group, resulting in each group developing a group identity and deciding on a name for themselves. One group named themselves the Eagles and prided themselves on clean language (they instituted a ban on profanity); the other group, in contrast, established more of a "tough-guy" image, naming themselves the Rattlers.

Then the counselors began the second phase of the experiment. They arranged for the two groups to discover one another, when one group found the other group playing baseball on "their" baseball field. From the outset of their discovery of one another, the groups demonstrated bias, with each calling the other derogatory names. Each perceived the other group as a threat to their space and their resources. Next, the counselors suggested the boys compete in a tournament, with the winners getting medals and a trophy, and the boys enthusiastically agreed. Over the next few days, the teams competed against each other in 10 games, including football, baseball, tug-of-war, treasure hunts, and various other activities. As the competition continued, with each team winning some of the games and the tournament championship at stake, hostility between the groups escalated. In addition to name-calling, teams began to ransack each other's cabins, vandalizing them and burning each other's flags. When the Eagles eventually won the tournament, the hostility culminated with the Rattlers stealing the winners' medals and trophy. In just a few days, competition for resources had created strong prejudice in well-adjusted middle-class boys.

Critical Thinking **QUESTION** Think about one of the types of prejudice you see most often in your own environment. Has realistic group conflict theory played a role in facilitating the development of that prejudice? If so, how?

Social Learning Theory Social learning also plays a role in prejudice. As you recall from Chapter 3, **social learning theory** demonstrates the many ways our development is influenced by our family and friends. Just as we learn mannerisms, communication styles, how to play sports or to paint, and fashion sense from people around us, we also learn belief systems, including prejudice. As children and teens, when we hear our parents, teachers, or friends express viewpoints, we emulate them; they are our role models (for better or for worse), and we conform because we want to belong and because we

Social learning theory Developing behaviors and attitudes based in role models in our environment.

FIGURE 7.6 | Children often learn prejudices from the important people in their environments. This process typically happens without awareness of the consequences.

want to be "right." These viewpoints sometimes contain prejudices, and thus these prejudices become ingrained in us, often without our awareness (see Figure 7.6). One study revealed the disturbing finding that by age 7, most urban white children in the United States exhibited some signs of racial prejudice (Aboud, 1988). The mass media play a role in our social learning as well. With the average American watching four hours of television each day, television and other media sources often serve as a guide for our beliefs and behavior.

 Think about what prejudices you learned as a child from your family and social group. Understanding that in many cases these prejudices are unintentional, which of the foundations of prejudice do you think contributed to development of them?

Relative Deprivation   Another contributing factor in prejudice is **relative deprivation**, which is the perception that others have more than you do, or that another group is better off than your own group. Have you ever felt good about your job, your earnings, your clothes, or your life, only to have the wind let out

> **Relative deprivation** The perception that others have more than you do, or that another group is better off than your own group.

of your sails when you see someone else whose job, paycheck, clothes, or life is better than yours? Because we gauge our self-worth partly by social comparisons, which we discussed in Chapter 2, when our comparisons reveal us to be inferior, our self-worth suffers a blow. And because we need a target for the frustration that results from the feeling of relative deprivation, the person or group that seems to have it better than you becomes a scapegoat for your hostility, which in turn fuels negativity and prejudice against them. The media contribute to relative deprivation as well, because it is difficult to turn on the television or open a magazine without being bombarded by images of glamorous people with lots of money living exciting lives. Relative deprivation helps explain why employees at one retail store might be quite satisfied with their wages, until they learn that employees at a neighboring store earn more. Similarly, a female executive might feel good about her salary, until she learns that male executives doing the same job are earning 25% more.

Emotions Prejudice has an *emotional component* as well. In the previous examples, we can see the point at which emotions become involved and prejudice develops. In the Robbers' Cave experiment, when the groups first came in contact with each other, the fact that each group had already formed a group identity led the boys to perceive the other group as the outgroup, and they stereotyped their "rivals" with name-calling. Once they began to compete, however, the stakes were raised, emotions got involved, and prejudice evolved. In situations of relative deprivation, feelings of resentment are the natural outgrowth of perceived unfairness, in which case the dominant group becomes the scapegoat, or the target of that resentment. In both cases, the strong emotional component strengthens the prejudice and makes it more resistant to change.

Discrimination

Many people think that discrimination is the same thing as prejudice, and although it is true that they are often related, they are not the same thing. **Discrimination** is the unfair treatment of a person or group solely on the basis of their group membership. In many cases, discrimination is the behavioral component of prejudice: A person feels prejudiced (an attitude), which leads him or her to discriminate against the object of the prejudice (behavior). Discrimination can sometimes be unrelated to prejudice, however, in one of two ways. The first situation is when we unknowingly discriminate, as in the case of the business that spreads the word of a new job opening by word-of-mouth. If everyone who already works there is of the same race, age group, or sex, chances are the people who hear about the job will be, too. In this case, the employer may not be prejudiced against a particular group, but may discriminate simply by unwittingly excluding that group from the hiring process. Second, people who are prejudiced may refrain from discriminatory behavior when they abide by laws prohibiting discrimination.

> **Discrimination** The unfair treatment of a person or group solely on the basis of their group membership.

Effects of Prejudice and Discrimination

Effects on Self-Esteem   Prejudice and discrimination can affect a person in several different ways, according to research in this area. Two of these possible effects were illustrated in a carefully controlled study by Jennifer Crocker and her associates (Crocker, Joekl, Testa, & Major, 1991). In the study, black students filled out a questionnaire about themselves and were told that a white student in a nearby room was going to read the information they had provided and give them some feedback on it. Following the feedback, which was either negative or positive, the black students took a self-esteem test. In looking at the differential effects of negative and positive feedback on the black students' self-esteem, two different test conditions were compared. In the first condition, the black student thought that his or her race was not known to the white student, and in the second condition, the black student thought the white student could see him or her through a one-way mirror and thus did know his or her race. When they thought their race was unknown to the white evaluator, both positive and negative feedback affected the black students' self-esteem in predictable ways: Positive feedback increased self-esteem, and negative feedback decreased self-esteem. But when they thought the white student could see them and thus know they were black, negative feedback did not have a damaging effect on self-esteem, because the student attributed the negative feedback to racism. Most interesting of all was the effect of positive feedback when the black student thought the white student evaluator knew his or her race: Self-esteem actually decreased, because the student perceived the positive feedback as condescending.

So the black students' perception of discrimination had both a positive and a negative effect. On the one hand, it helped them maintain their self-esteem in the face of negative feedback, and subsequent research has confirmed this finding. On the other hand, it also kept them from internalizing the positive feedback, thus denying themselves a self-esteem booster. In discussing the results, Crocker suggests a further possible drawback to assuming that feedback is influenced by prejudice: If that perception is inaccurate, and the feedback really is authentic, an opportunity for learning and growth is lost, because authentic feedback is a valuable tool for self-knowledge.

Effects on Sense of Control   People who perceive themselves to be the target of discrimination feel less personal control over their lives as a result (Ruggiero & Taylor, 1997). This discovery helps explain a curious finding among many people who belong to groups that traditionally have been the target of prejudice and discrimination. Most women, for example, believe that a gender bias exists and express awareness of the wage differential in the United States. When asked if they personally have experienced this discrimination, though, most of these same women say no; they believe that they are an exception to the rule, even when they work in an organization known for its discriminatory practices (Crosby, Pufall, Snyder, O'Connell, & Whalen, 1989). This discrepancy between personal and group discrimination exists among persons in other targeted groups as well. It seems, then, that this may be a way of acknowledging discrimination while at the same time maintaining a sense of personal control over one's life, work, and relationships.

Stereotype Threat   Another effect of prejudice is a phenomenon known as **stereotype threat**, a condition identified by researcher Claude Steele (1997).

> **Stereotype threat** When an individual's identity is heavily based on a characteristic for which there are strong stereotypes, that individual will maintain a heightened awareness of the likelihood of being stereotyped and feel afraid of that possibility.

Steele suggests that when an individual's identity is heavily based on a characteristic for which there are strong stereotypes, that individual will maintain a heightened awareness of the likelihood of being stereotyped and feel afraid of that possibility. One study that demonstrated stereotype threat gave a difficult test of verbal ability to both black and white students at a prestigious university. Half the students were told it was a test of their academic ability, and the other half were told it was merely a lab test. When told it was a lab test, there were no differences between the scores of the black students and the white students. When told it was a test of academic ability, however, black students performed only half as well as their white counterparts. The idea that their academic ability was being tested triggered the black students' awareness of the stereotype that black students are less intelligent than white students, and the resulting anxiety interfered with their ability to do as well on the test as they were capable of doing (Steele & Aronson, 1995).

Steele suggests that persons who experience stereotype threat may eventually begin to avoid situations where anxiety from the threat is activated as a means of protecting their self-esteem. Thus, the stereotype becomes a sort of self-fulfilling prophecy. Imagine, for example, a man who has always wanted to be a nurse. He passes the entrance exams with high scores and enrolls in the nursing program at a local college as one of only two men in the freshman class of this traditionally female-dominated profession. As he interacts with patients during his training, his stereotype threat (that men aren't as well suited to nursing as women are) is activated, and when a patient snaps at him, his anxiety level increases as he worries that patients will never accept him as a nurse because he is a man. This anxiety level could interfere with his concentration, leading to mistakes on the job. Eventually, he might quit the program to avoid failing.

Once the powerful effects of stereotype threat were demonstrated, researchers wondered if it could be reduced or eliminated. Researcher Steven Spencer (Spencer, Steele, & Quinn, 1999) tested this hypothesis in a study of male and female students who were good at math and for whom their mathematical ability was a strong part of their identity. Participants in the study were given an extremely difficult math test, one so difficult that (unbeknownst to them) researchers expected all of them to do very poorly on it. Half the students were told that there were no gender differences in how well people performed on the test, while the other half were told that there *were* gender differences in test scores. Researchers knew that the women in the experiment would normally feel stereotype threat based on the stereotype that women aren't as good at math as men are, and they wondered if the announcement that there were no gender differences would reduce the stereotype threat, thus reducing the anxiety level of the female participants. Their results

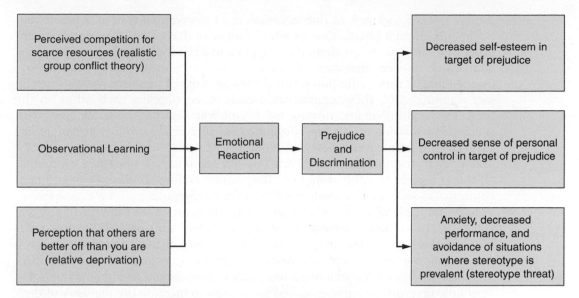

FIGURE 7.7 | Causes and Consequences of Prejudice and Discrimination

were as they had hoped: Although the announcement that there *were* gender differences activated the anxiety level consistent with stereotype threat and resulting in poorer performance among the female participants, when told there were *no* gender differences, the stereotype threat seemed to disappear, because women and men performed equally well on the test.

Figure 7.7 summarizes the causes and consequences of prejudice and discrimination. To explore your own experiences with prejudice and discrimination, turn now to Activity 7.3 at the end of this chapter.

Overcoming Prejudice

Superordinate Goals   Fortunately, research is increasingly focusing on effective means of overcoming prejudice. One of the earliest indications that prejudice could be reversed came from the Robbers' Cave experiment discussed earlier. When we left off with our discussion of the experiment, intergroup hostility had been firmly established, with the two teams of boys having engaged in numerous hostile acts against each other. At this point, phase 3 of the experiment began. Sherif and his associates wanted to try to establish friendly relations between the two groups. They began with the counselors saying nice things to each group about the other group; not surprisingly, perhaps, this had no effect on the boys' hostility. Then, they arranged for the groups to spend noncompetitive time together, such as eating meals together. Not only did this not work, but it resulted in very messy food fights. Finally, they tried implementing a **superordinate goal**: a problem that could only be solved if the two

> **Superordinate goal** A goal, shared by conflicting groups, that can only be attained if the groups work together.

groups worked together. In one instance, the boys wanted to rent a movie, but could only afford it by combining their money with that of the other group. In another, the camp truck "accidentally" got stuck in a mudhole, and when one of the counselors "noticed" that there was a tug-of-war rope in the back of it, the boys decided maybe they could pull it out if they all worked together. When their effort was successful, they congratulated each other, slapping each other on the back and laughing about winning the tug-of-war "against the truck." So, with successful achievement of a superordinate goal, intergroup hostility and prejudice evolved into friendly and peaceful relations. Attitudes had changed drastically, and when the camping trip ended and boys prepared to go home, they insisted on all riding together on the same bus. The "happy ending" to Sherif's experiment continues to serve as a template for conflict resolution today.

The principle of cooperation that lies at the heart of the superordinate goal was tested in a different setting by psychologist Eliot Aronson (1978) some years later. Working with Alex Gonzalez in a Texas school district, Aronson's research was a response to the increased racial tensions being experienced as a result of school integration. Prior to integration, student populations in public schools had very little diversity; integration called for schools to increase the diversity of their students, thus mixing various races and social classes. Early results of the new policy were disheartening: Students continued to associate only with others of their own race and class, and prejudice among the students seemed to be growing. Aronson wondered if, by creating an environment of cooperation where students had to work together to do well in school, prejudice could be reduced and students of all races and classes would get along.

> **Jigsaw classroom** Where students work together to learn, rather than compete against each other.

Aronson's plan was to implement a new technique called the *jigsaw classroom*, where students would work together to learn, rather than compete against each other for grades and the teacher's attention. The jigsaw classroom was a learning process that had two phases. In the first phase, students got into small groups called "expert groups" where they were responsible for learning a particular portion of the day's lesson. For example, if the class was studying the Middle Ages, one expert group might learn about the feudal system, another about the plague, another about the Crusades, and so forth. When all members of each expert group had mastered their group's material, they went into phase 2, which moved them into different groups called "jigsaw groups." Jigsaw groups were made up of one student from each of the expert groups, and each of these students was responsible for teaching their "expert" material to the other students in their jigsaw group. The only way, then, to learn the complete lesson was to rely on one another for the various portions of the lesson. At the end of the "jigsaw" group's session, all students would have learned the complete lesson and would have done so by sharing their expertise.

The jigsaw classroom proved to be a great success. Prior to its implementation, students who had been the objects of prejudice had little confidence in their learning and speaking abilities, and thus rarely spoke up in class. As a result, they got less feedback and learned less. The jigsaw classroom created instant equality between races and classes, because students had to rely on each other to learn the material and thus had to help each other to do so. As a result, minority students learned more, which increased their self-confidence, which in turn had a positive effect on their speaking ability, which increased their self-confidence even more in a self-perpetuating cycle. Students of different races and classes began to see each other as individuals, rather than as colors or classes, thus reducing the prejudice and discrimination that had previously been so problematic. In addition to liking each other more, students of all groups reported liking school more. In his excellent book *Nobody Left to Hate*, Aronson (2000) applies 30 years of research in the jigsaw classroom to the ongoing and disturbing trend of school violence, making a strong case that such incidents as those at Columbine and Springfield high schools could be avoided with careful implementation (beginning in grade school) of the basic philosophies and practices of the jigsaw classroom.

To try your hand at using superordinate goals to overcome prejudice, turn now to Activity 7.4.

Changing Social Norms Through Mindfulness   Social norms are influencing the decline of prejudice as well, because each generation is born into an increasingly multicultural world with slightly less prejudice than the one before. Psychologist Patricia Devine (e.g., Devine & Monteith, 1999) argues that we can speed up this process on a personal level by making a conscious effort to challenge our stereotypes. The effort she proposes must begin with an awareness of one's own prejudices and the stereotypes that fuel them. Then, when we come into contact with an object of our prejudice, we must consciously activate our stereotype and challenge it. For example, if we have a prejudice against older people because our stereotype of them is that they aren't mentally sharp anymore, we can challenge that by taking some time to talk to someone who is older. Chances are, we can learn a lot from that person, which will challenge our stereotype and help us overcome the prejudice that results from it. It takes a strong and ongoing commitment, but Devine's research has demonstrated that it can be successful in helping people "unlearn" their prejudices. Her work fits nicely with that of David Matsumoto and his theory of flexible ethnocentrism. Matsumoto adds that, in order to be successful in overcoming one's prejudices, we must also learn to control the negative emotions that accompany them. The valuable work of these researchers and others like them offer hope that we can overcome some of the cultural divides that plague our generation and our world, and learn to live and work together with an appreciation of both our similarities and our differences.

Interim SUMMARY #2

Prejudice is a universal phenomenon that, although on the decline in some areas, still persists. Realistic group conflict theory, social learning, relative deprivation, and emotions all fuel prejudice, and when prejudicial attitudes begin to affect behavior, discrimination occurs. Perceptions of discrimination influences people's interpretation of feedback and their sense of personal control. It can also create stereotype threat, which can be reversed under certain conditions.

Psychological research has identified several strategies that can successfully combat prejudice. When two or more groups are in conflict with each other, prejudice can be reduced by the implementation of superordinate goals. One type of superordinate goal was demonstrated in Aronson's jigsaw classroom, whereby students in racially diverse classrooms had to rely on each other to fully and accurately learn each day's lessons. Increasing their reliance on each other created a sense of support and interdependence that replaced intergroup hostility and also increased students' personal self-esteem and overall classroom performance levels.

Although social norms change slowly, they do become adjusted with each new generation. Patricia Devine suggests that the social norms of prejudice can be changed if we make a personal commitment to become aware of our stereotypes and actively challenge them as often as possible. In this way, we will become more aware of their inaccuracies and work towards reducing them, and over time, each successive generation will exhibit less prejudice

CHAPTER TERMS

Social identity theory
Ingroup bias
Outgroup bias
Ethnocentrism
Inflexible
  ethnocentrism
Flexible ethnocentrism
Stereotype

Self-fulfilling
  prophecies
Outgroup homogeneity
  effect
Prejudice
Realistic group conflict
  theory
Social learning theory

Relative deprivation
Discrimination
Stereotype threat
Superordinate goal
Jigsaw classroom

ACTIVITY 7.1

BECOMING MORE FLEXIBLY ETHNOCENTRIC

INSTRUCTIONS: *Identify a cultural group that seems very different from your own and that you don't know much about. It could be an age group that is much older or younger than your own, a religious or political group that you don't understand, or an ethnic or racial group you don't know much about, just to name a few possibilities. Next, follow the steps in part 1 to create some interview questions geared toward increasing your understanding of that culture. Then, seek someone of that culture and ask if you might talk for a while to learn more about each other. Use the questions you've developed as you talk with that person. Finally, reflect on the experience by answering the questions in part 2 of this activity.*

PART 1: DEVELOPING INTERVIEW QUESTIONS

Develop some interview questions by asking yourself what it is about the culture that seems so different from your own culture. This may include behavior patterns, styles of dress, the basis of belief systems, and so on. Brainstorm a list of things you've noticed, then turn those factors into questions. Your questions should be as diplomatic and respectful as possible.

_____

_____

_____

_____

_____

_____

_____

_____

_____

PART 2: REFLECTING ON THE EXPERIENCE

1. Whom did you choose to interview and why? Attach a list of the questions you asked to this assignment when you turn it in.

_____

_____

_____

_____

_____

_____

_____

_____

_____

2. What assumptions did you have about the person and about his or her culture before you did your interview? Give a few specific examples, along with what you based each assumption on. Be honest!

_____

_____

_____

_____

_____

_____

_____

_____

3. What did you learn about the person and his or her culture as a result of your interview? Discuss three or four of the most interesting and useful ideas you gained.

_____

_____

_____

_____

_____

_____

_____

_____

_____

_____

_____

_____

4. Overall, what did this experience teach you about human relations? How will this experience be helpful to you in the future?

_____

_____

_____

_____

_____

_____

_____

_____

_____

_____

_____

ACTIVITY 7.2

EXPLORING YOUR OWN STEREOTYPES

INSTRUCTIONS: *Answer the following questions about your own stereotypes. Be honest—remember, we all have stereotypes, and if we aren't honest about them, we can't hope to improve our human relations.*

1. Name two or three groups that you tend to stereotype the most.

_____

_____

_____

2. a. For each group named in question 1, brainstorm a list of the assumptions
      you tend to make about that group when you stereotype it.

   _____

   _____

   _____

   _____

   _____

   _____

   _____

   _____

   _____

   b. Which assumptions are positive, and which ones are negative?

   _____

   _____

   _____

   _____

   _____

3. Where do you think your stereotypes came from?

   _____

   _____

   _____

   _____

   _____

4. Give an example of a time when the confirmation bias strengthened one of
   your stereotypes.

   _____

   _____

   _____

   _____

   _____

5. Give an example of a way in which the outgroup homogeneity effect influenced one of your stereotypes.

   _____

   _____

   _____

_____

_____

6. Give an example of a time when your emotional state (happy, stressed, or angry) activated a stereotype, and describe that situation.

_____

_____

_____

_____

_____

7. If someone were to stereotype you, what would that stereotype be, and why?

_____

_____

_____

_____

_____

8. How accurate is the stereotype you described in question 7? Explain your answer.

_____

_____

_____

_____

_____

9. How do you feel when someone stereotypes you? Does it also affect your behavior? Explain your answer.

_____

_____

_____

_____

_____

_____

_____

_____

10. What reflections do you have on this exercise? Discuss one main insight you've developed from it, along with how you will use it to improve your relations with others.

_____

_____

_____

_____

_____

_____

_____

_____

_____

_____

ACTIVITY 7.3

PREJUDICE AND DISCRIMINATION IN YOUR LIFE

1. Identify a prejudice that you have toward another group. Which of the causes of prejudice discussed in this chapter seem to best explain the origin of your prejudice? Explain your answer.

_____

_____

_____

_____

_____

_____

_____

_____

_____

_____

_____

2. Have you ever been the target of prejudice? Describe that situation, along with how it affected you. If feedback was involved from the person you thought was prejudiced against you, how did that feedback affect you?

_____

_____

_____

_____

_____

_____

_____

_____

_____

_____

_____

3. a. What is your biggest fear in terms of how someone might stereotype you? In other words, what stereotype do you fear being labeled as the most? How has this fear affected your choices in terms of interests and opportunities you pursue or don't pursue?

_____

_____

_____

_____

_____

_____

_____

_____

_____

_____

_____

b. Reflect on the stereotype threat you discussed in part a of this question. Do you feel you've missed some opportunities? If you could go back and do things over again, would you do anything differently? What would it would take for you to overcome the stereotype threat that you feel?

_____

_____

_____

_____

_____

_____

_____

_____

_____

ACTIVITY 7.4

OVERCOMING PREJUDICE

INSTRUCTIONS: *Apply the model of superordinate goals to some type of group prejudice that you see in your own life. Use the following steps to help develop your program. For best results, brainstorm with your classmates or other people in your life.*

1. Briefly describe the prejudice you see that you'd like to try to help correct. Who exhibits the prejudice? Who is the target of the prejudice? What behaviors illustrate the prejudice?

_____

_____

_____

_____

_____

_____

_____

_____

_____

2. Applying the theory of superordinate goals, how could you get these two groups together to work toward a goal that (a) is meaningful to both groups, and (b) requires them to work together to achieve it (in other words, neither group could accomplish it alone)?

   a. What goal do you think would be effective? If you can't decide, think about what values are important to both of these groups. They may include family, health, children, and so forth. List as many possibilities as you can think of, then choose the one you think is the most promising.

_____

_____

_____

_____

_____

   b. How can you facilitate these two groups working together to achieve the goal? Remember that the groups need to have equal status and play equal roles in the development and implementation of the plan.

_____

_____

_____

_____

_____

_____

_____

_____

_____

_____

LISTENING

The biggest mistake is believing there is one right way to listen, to talk, to have a conversation—or a relationship.

—DEBORAH TANNEN

My third year in graduate school, my mother was diagnosed with cancer. Surgery was quickly scheduled, but afterwards her doctors admitted they hadn't been able to remove all of the cancerous growth. Her prognosis wasn't good, but they thought she might have a chance with aggressive chemotherapy treatments. The news came as a shock to my family, because Mom had always seemed strong and invincible. As I struggled to comprehend the gravity of the situation, I knew that I needed to be there for her in whatever way she needed. At the time, I didn't really know what all that might involve, but I decided I should tell my graduate advisors what was going on, so that if and when taking care of my mom conflicted with any of my school responsibilities, they wouldn't be caught unaware.

The first advisor I met with was a female professor whom I held in high regard. Not only was she a respected scholar, but she seemed like a nice person, and in our previous meetings we had gotten along very well. I trusted her, which was why I decided to talk to her first. We met in her office, and after exchanging the usual small talk, I told her that I had a concern I needed to share with her. I carefully explained what had happened to my mom, and that the doctors had told us the chemotherapy would take a significant physical toll on her and that she was going to need our help. I said that I wasn't sure yet what that was going to mean in terms of my time, but that since Mom lived several hours away from where I was, I thought that as her treatment progressed it might affect my work at school in some way. I concluded by saying that even though things weren't at that point yet, I wanted to give her (my advisor) a "heads-up" just in case.

Her reply was completely unexpected. In a very matter-of-fact tone, she said, "Well, all I can tell you is that other graduate students have had family crises during their time here—some of them have even had crises of their own. You just have to deal with it. If you're serious about your work, you won't let this get in the way." She went on in the same vein for a few moments while I sat there, stunned into silence. When she finished, I said something like, "Okay, well, I just wanted you to know what was going on . . ." and managed to maintain my composure until I got out of her office and down the hall into my own. Then I broke down, shocked and devastated by her callous response. I had discussed a topic with her that was painful for me, but did so because I wanted to be completely honest and up front about possible changes in my schedule. She had shown absolutely no sensitivity to my situation and in essence had implied that my mom's illness was not important.

After that experience, I approached my next advisor with some trepidation. I didn't know him as well, and I was even more concerned because I was assigned to be his assistant for the coming term, which meant that any absences on my part would have a direct impact on him. Again, we met in his office, and I explained what was happening with my mom and how I was concerned that it might take me away from school from time to time, depending on how she responded to the treatment. His response, like that of my female professor, came as a complete surprise. "I can tell that you're really worried about your mom," he said. "You must be very close." Cautiously, I replied that I came from a small family, and that we'd always been close. He listened attentively, nodding, looking at me in a way that seemed to say, "Go on." I found myself opening up a little about how my mom had always been the heart of our family, the one who mediated when my dad's strong personality clashed with my own, and who worked tirelessly to support the myriad projects and interests of my sister, my dad, and me in every possible way. She'd always been there for me, and now I needed to be there for her. "Of course you do," my professor said. Still a little anxious, I reminded him, "I'm hoping it won't interfere with my work for you next term, but there's no way to predict what might happen." "I understand that," he said gently. "It's clear to me that your primary concern right now is your mother's health, and that's okay. I mean, however important we like to think our work is, it's the people we love and our relationships with them that are really important, right? You've shown yourself to be a conscientious person and a very capable student; if and when the time comes that you have to be away from school to care for your mother, we'll work around it. Try not to let it worry you." Overwhelmed with relief and gratitude for his understanding and support, I thanked him and said I would keep him informed. As I left his office, he offered his best wishes: "I hope your mother's treatment goes well."

One concern presented in a similar way to two different professors had yielded two very different outcomes. As you might imagine, these conversations had a lasting impact on my perception of each professor and on my relationship with each of them. In this chapter, we will begin to examine the ways in which communication affects the development of trust in a relationship and the important role that listening plays in that process. We will then learn a variety of listening styles that can enhance a relationship and apply these listening styles to real-life situations in an effort to improve our ability to be good listeners and build trusting relationships.

RELATIONAL CLIMATE: FEELING VALUED

PREVIEW QUESTIONS

(1) What is a relational climate?

(2) What are the three levels of confirmation that measure the degree of support in a relationship?

(3) How do our behaviors influence how safe others feel in their relationships with us?

Perhaps you have had an experience similar to that just described, in which you talked with two different people about something important to you and received two very different responses. Even if you haven't, you have probably had the two kinds of experiences at different times, and you know what each one feels like. In all of our relationships, personal and professional, a level of comfort develops that dictates the degree to which we feel safe, supported, and understood within that relationship: this comfort level is referred to as the **relational climate**. Just as we use the word *climate* to refer to the comfort level of the physical environment (such as sunny and warm, hot and humid, or cold and wet), the climate of a relationship describes the comfort level of the emotional environment in that relationship. As you might imagine, there are varying degrees of comfort in relationship climates, just as there are varying degrees of comfort in the weather.

> **Relational climate** The degree to which we feel safe, supported, and understood in a relationship.

Confirming and Disconfirming Climates

The best way to conceptualize the climate in a relationship is to think of it as a continuum, with a completely positive climate on one end, a completely negative climate on the other, and varying degrees in between (see Figure 8.1). The positive climate is called a **confirming, or a supportive, climate**. In this type of relationship, we trust the other person and have learned that we can

> **Confirming (supportive) climate** A positive relational climate based on mutual trust, respect, and support.

FIGURE 8.1 | The Relational Climate

Confirming
(Supportive)

Disconfirming
(Defensive)

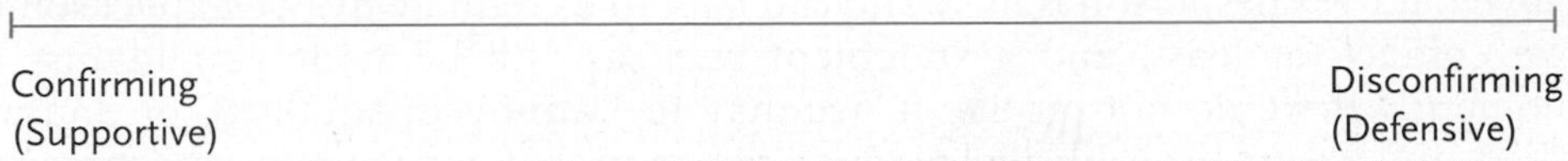

Disconfirming (defensive) climate A negative relational climate, characterized by defensiveness, negative judgments, and mistrust.

count on him or her to listen to us, understand us, and generally be supportive, confirming our thoughts and feelings. The negative climate, on the other hand, is called a **disconfirming, or defensive, climate**. In these relationships, we cannot count on the other person to listen and understand us; on the contrary, the other person in this type of relationship typically imposes his or her judgment on us, rejecting our thoughts and feelings, and leaving us feeling as though we are misunderstood, wrong, or unworthy. As a result, we often fall into a cycle of defensiveness in this type of relationship.

In reality, the climate in most of our relationships is somewhere in the middle area of the continuum; rarely, if ever, is a relationship completely confirming or disconfirming. Even in a very supportive and confirming relationship, there are times when we just don't feel as though the other person really understands completely, or when they simply disagree with us; it is unrealistic to expect complete support and agreement in all things, especially in our individualistic culture. Also, in order to understand and confirm, the other person must be listening very attentively, and as we will see in the upcoming section on listening, it is not possible to always listen attentively to another person. A variety of physical, intellectual, and emotional barriers get in the way. As a result, the climate of a relationship generally evolves, over time and with experience, to a particular place on the continuum that represents the realistic level of support that you have learned to expect from that person. In our most confirming relationships, we feel genuinely valued. And this feeling of acceptance and respect from others contributes to our psychological growth (Buber, 1970) and self-actualization.

Levels of Confirmation

Research on relational climates has identified three specific levels of confirmation in a relationship (Cissna & Sieberg, 1986), along with examples of communication that illustrate each level. The most basic level of confirmation is to simply *recognize another person's existence*, such as by saying hello or making eye contact. When we greet another person, either verbally or nonverbally, we are sending a confirming message that says "I see you." On the other hand, when we encounter another person and either look away or "look right through them," we are failing to recognize that person's existence. Think about it: When you walk around your campus or your workplace, do people generally make eye contact with you and smile, nod, or say hello? In Western culture, this is considered polite and appropriate behavior, making us feel that we belong. We are typically most comfortable in environments that promote this feeling of friendliness and recognition. By the same token, when we go into a restaurant or retail establishment, we expect prompt recognition by an employee. If the salesperson is busy and can't get to us right away, we expect some eye contact, at least, and a statement such as "I'll be with you in just a moment." If we do not receive it, we may feel annoyed, snubbed, or diminished, and we are probably less likely to return to that particular establishment.

Another way that we deny recognition in relationships is by giving the other person "the silent treatment," or simply not talking to the other person as a punishment. This type of withdrawal can be extremely damaging to relationships, because it comes across as a power play. Keeping a balance of power is a key component in successful relationships. We'll address power and conflict in more depth in Chapter 10.

The second level of confirmation is to *acknowledge another person's thoughts, feelings, or actions*. We do this by making appropriate responses, either verbally or nonverbally, in our interactions with them. For example, if your roommate comes home, plops down on the sofa, and says, "Man, what a long day I had!" a supportive response might be "You must be exhausted!" or "You sound really frustrated—want to talk about it?" Responses like this let your roommate know that you heard what she said and that you care. But if you say something like, "I'm glad you're home—what are you making for dinner? I'm starved!" or "It couldn't have been any worse than mine!" you are discounting her feelings and signaling that you only care about your own needs. These types of irrelevant or thoughtless responses usually leave a person feeling unimportant or misunderstood and take away from the general level of trust in the relationship if they become a pattern.

The third and highest level of confirmation is accepting another person's thoughts or feelings as valid; this is known as **endorsement**. The strongest type of endorsement we can provide to another person is to agree with him. For example, imagine that a friend says to you, "I'm really upset about my sister—I think she's making a big mistake by moving in with that guy she's been seeing." If you know the sister and agree that she's making a mistake, you might say something like, "I know what you mean. They've only known each other for two weeks. I'm worried about her, too." This message offers full support to your friend by agreeing that his concern is valid, and also by agreeing that you feel the same way. When we receive this type of confirmation from someone, we feel understood and validated.

> **Endorsement** Accepting another person's thoughts or feelings as valid.

On the other hand, we deny a person endorsement when we signal that his feelings are wrong or unimportant. A response such as, "You worry too much about your sister—you need to let her make her own mistakes and stop trying to run her life" rejects the concern that your friend is sharing with you. It imposes a value judgment on your friend about how involved we should be in the lives of family members, and furthermore says that your friend is wrong for worrying. If you've ever been on the receiving end of this type of message (and most of us have), you know how hurtful it feels. In essence, this message is almost saying, "I don't really want to hear about it—you don't matter enough to me for that."

At the same time, though, what if that is really what you think? You don't want to be dishonest about it, but you do care about your friend and his feelings. Is there a way to provide endorsement if you don't agree with someone? Assuming that we value honesty in a relationship, this can be a challenge, but it is possible. If we can't agree, we can at least try to understand why a person is feeling or thinking a certain way in a particular situation. In the same example with your friend and his concerns about his sister, you could say something like, "It sounds like you're really worried that she'll end up being hurt by this guy. She's your little sister, and you've always tried to protect her from being hurt, so it's scary to have to let go now that she's all grown up." This type of response lets your friend know that you are hearing him, that you care about his feelings, and that you understand how he would feel that way. You stop short of agreeing, thereby maintaining honesty in the relationship, without diminishing the respect and trust you've built up.

At this point, you may be thinking, "Well, this all makes sense, but nobody I know talks that way. I don't think I can do this!" If you are, just hang in there—that's a common feeling at this point. Even though some of the communication skills we will learn may sound unnatural at first, that's only because they are unfamiliar to us. They are almost like a foreign language in that respect. Just try to keep an open mind and give them a fair chance—just as a foreign language becomes easier and more familiar over time, so will this. Effective communication and listening aren't inborn talents that some people magically have; on the contrary, they are made up of a set of skills that we all have to develop and refine throughout our lives. Research demonstrates that, when used artfully, they do work. Next we'll start focusing on these skills and how to develop them.

First, let's sum up. The three levels of confirmation we just discussed (see Table 8.1) all contribute to the climate in a relationship, or the degree to which you feel valued in the relationship. This in turn affects the level of trust in the relationship and ultimately its importance in your life. In my own example with my professors in graduate school (in the chapter opening), both professors met the first level (*recognition*) by meeting with me and giving me an opportunity to speak. The first professor got stuck in the second level: She did respond to what I said (thus signaling that she *heard* my words), but she failed to *acknowledge* my concerns, both about my mother and about the impact of my situation on my work and my colleagues (thus signaling that she didn't really *understand* the meaning of what I was trying to convey to her). The second professor not only heard and understood (thus providing acknowledgment), but rose to the third level when he agreed that my

TABLE 8.1 | Levels of Confirmation

LEVEL	DESCRIPTION	EXAMPLE
Recognition	Verbal or nonverbal behavior signaling that we notice a person	Saying hello, nodding, or smiling in greeting
Acknowledgment	Verbal or nonverbal behavior acknowledging a person's thoughts, feelings, or actions	Expressing sympathy to a person in distress, or showing recognition that a person's perception of a situation is valid
Endorsement	Accepting a person's thoughts or feelings as valid	Agreeing with a person's perception, or expressing understanding (empathy) for someone's emotional response

mother's health took precedence over what was happening in school that term (*endorsement*). Even if he hadn't agreed with my priorities, I suspect that he would have provided endorsement by expressing understanding of how I would feel the way I did, given my family background and value system.

 Think about two contrasting experiences you have had in terms of relational climate. Identify one relationship in which you feel highly valued, respected, and supported, and another relationship in which you often feel disconfirmed. Analyze each relationship in terms of recognition, acknowledgment, and endorsement by giving an example from each relationship of a time you did/didn't receive one or more of these confirming messages.

Turn to Activity 8.1 to gain insight into your own relational climates.

Now that we have a general understanding of relational climate, its pivotal role in the development of relationships, and the basic levels of confirming communication, let's turn our attention to the skill that provides the foundation for the development of a positive relationship climate: listening.

Interim SUMMARY #1

Relationships are heavily influenced by the emotional climate, or general level of trust in that relationship. Confirming climates offer support by recognizing each other's existence, acknowledging each other's thoughts and feelings, and endorsing or accepting these feelings and beliefs as valid. The relationship climate sets the stage for positive or negative relationships and is maintained in part by the listening styles that each partner in the relationship uses.

BASIC ELEMENTS OF LISTENING

PREVIEW QUESTION

In addition to physically hearing, what other elements are necessary for good listening?

Effective communication involves a variety of skills, and the single most important of these skills is listening. Why? Because no matter how effective we are at getting a point across to another person, we can't know *what* point we need to convey until we know what the other person's needs are; and we can't be sure about that if we haven't first listened and understood. Thus, good listening skills involve not just hearing, but understanding, and responding in a way that clarifies and/or confirms your understanding.

The importance of listening skills applies to both our work and our personal lives. Human resource managers seem to know this: When surveyed, they identified listening as the number one skill of effective managers (Winsor, Curtis, & Stephens, 1999). Similarly, adults ranked listening the most important communication skill for effectiveness in both family and broader social settings (Wolvin, 1984).

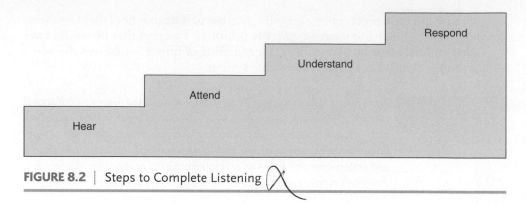

FIGURE 8.2 | Steps to Complete Listening

There are four basic elements of listening, which can be thought of as four incremental steps to complete listening (see Figure 8.2). We'll go over them briefly in the next few paragraphs, then in the following section identify the various barriers that can interfere with each step, and how we can overcome these barriers.

Hearing

The first step is the physical element of listening, which is *hearing*. As we discussed in the perception section of Chapter 5, sometimes we can't physically hear what a speaker is saying; it might be because we have a hearing impairment, or perhaps because the speaker isn't enunciating clearly, is too far away for us to hear, or other sounds in the environment are competing for our attention. One place this commonly happens is in the classroom. Have you ever had trouble hearing what the professor was saying? This is an especially troubling problem if the information you missed shows up on an exam! What are the most common reasons that you fail to hear people, and what can you do about it?

Attending

The second step in listening is *attending*, or actually paying attention to what a speaker is saying. Here again, most of us can think of a time when we weren't really paying attention to what someone was saying, perhaps because we were distracted or not really interested. In our busy lives, all too often we find ourselves "multitasking," or juggling several things at once. If one of these things involves communication, it is doubtful that it will be as effective as it could be. To be an effective listener and communicator, however, we must recognize that *attending is a choice*. Certainly there are barriers that make it more difficult for us to pay attention (which we'll discuss in the next section), but with commitment and practice, we can learn to overcome these barriers and take control of this important element.

Understanding

Once we physically hear a speaker, and have attended to the message, the third step in effective listening is *understanding*. This involves attending not just to what the speaker says, but to the nonverbal aspect of the message and the context of the message. For example, you ask a friend how her day was and she says, "It was fine," but she sighs as she says it and looks downward. How do you interpret her message? Does she mean it wasn't fine, but she isn't sure if you really want to hear about it? If that is the case, knowing something about her, her life, her culture, and her general outlook can help you decide what she's really trying to communicate to you.

Responding

The final step in effective listening is *responding*. At first, this may sound odd, because we typically think of listening as a passive behavior that doesn't involve speaking. Think about it, though: How can we be sure we understand the other person without some kind of response? Even if we do understand without saying anything, how will the other person know this if we don't say anything? For example, if your friend in the previous paragraph says her day was fine but her nonverbal signals seem to say otherwise, you could check out your hunch with a perception-checking statement (such as those we learned in Chapter 5) something like this: "Did something happen that bothered you, or are you just tired?" This type of response signals your friend that you aren't sure what she means, and that you're willing to listen if she wants to talk. There are actually a number of different types of effective listening responses that could be used in this situation or any other, and we'll explore them in more detail later in the chapter.

Overall, then, four steps are involved in the complete listening process. We must first physically hear the message, then pay attention to it, understand it, and respond to it. A breakdown at any of these stages will interfere with your listening effectiveness.

OVERCOMING COMMON BARRIERS TO LISTENING

PREVIEW QUESTIONS

(1) What are three internal barriers to listening, and how can we overcome them?

(2) What are three external barriers to listening, and how can they be overcome?

(3) Describe four counterfeit listening styles and consider how these effect our interactions with others.

As important as listening is, we must also recognize that there are a variety of barriers that interfere with our ability to listen effectively. Some of these barriers are internal, originating in our thoughts or our emotions; others are external and originate in the message, the sender, or the environment. By understanding what these barriers are, we can work toward recognizing when they interfere with our listening goals and learning to overcome them. Let's take a closer look.

Internal Barriers to Listening

Emotional Noise   One common internal barrier is **emotional noise**, which can include stress, anxiety, anger, or any other emotion that interferes with our ability to focus our full attention on the speaker. As we learned in Chapter 4, strong emotions interfere with our ability to cognitively process information accurately and efficiently. Because listening effectively relies on accurate understanding, emotional noise naturally interferes with effective listening.

> **Emotional noise** Stress, anxiety, anger, or any other emotion that interferes with our ability to focus our full attention on the speaker.

The emotion could be coming from one of several different sources. For example, if you are feeling angry about a recent argument with someone, the physiological arousal associated with that anger would probably interfere with your ability to listen well. Or maybe you've had a particularly bad day, and your stomach is in knots; that would also interfere with your listening ability. An extremely positive emotional state could have the same influence: Perhaps you've just fallen blissfully in love with someone, in which case your euphoria would probably keep you from being able to concentrate on what the speaker is trying to communicate to you. Finally, the emotional noise could be triggered by the situation, if you are having strong positive or negative feelings about the speaker, or if the situation provokes some strong emotion in you. In the example at the beginning of this chapter, emotional noise may have accounted for my female professor's ineffective response to my concern. Perhaps she was upset about something unrelated to what I was saying, or possibly the subject of cancer triggered something for her: Maybe someone she loved was fighting cancer, or my situation could have reminded her of a time when she had to choose between work and family. In any case, her emotions could have interfered with her ability to fully understand the concern I was trying to communicate to her.

One way to cope with emotional noise is to use the self-talk skills we learned in Chapter 4, which involve recognizing when an emotion is interfering with our thinking or listening and replacing the emotional thoughts with more rational thoughts. If it has been a while since you studied that chapter and need a refresher, take a few moments now to review that section and the corresponding activity (Activity 4.1).

Cognitive Distractions   A second type of internal barrier is **cognitive distractions**. This is exactly what it sounds like: something that is on our mind (a cognition) that we're having trouble putting aside to focus on the speaker's message. We might be ruminating over a recent exam that didn't go well or over a problem we're having with someone at home or at work. Or it might be a very busy time when we're juggling several things at once, and we just don't have the mental capacity to concentrate on something else, even for a short time. So, when the speaker is talking, we find that our focus keeps slipping away from his or her message and back toward

> **Cognitive distractions** Something that is on our mind (a cognition) that we're having trouble putting aside in order to focus on the speaker's message.

our own issue. As a result, we probably feel as if we're tuning in and out of the message, which puts us at risk for missing key components of it.

When emotional noise or cognitive distractions threaten our ability to listen effectively, the first step in overcoming these barriers is to recognize when they are occurring. Then we can do one of two things. One option is to learn to **compartmentalize**, which involves *mentally "filing away" our own issues temporarily*, knowing that they'll still be there later and we can come back to them when we have time. This is a learned skill, and it comes more easily to some people than it does to others. Developing this skill takes some practice and some trial-and-error periods. As you practice it, you need to tell yourself several things: first, that by putting it away, you aren't going to forget about it, and if you do, then it must not have been that important after all. Second, trying to work it out while someone else is talking to you isn't giving yourself the best chance to work it out successfully, because you can't focus your full attention on it. At the same time, you're causing potential damage to the relationship between you and the speaker by failing to listen effectively. Ultimately, you're cheating yourself and the speaker by trying to divide your attention. Just like other skills, compartmentalization might take some trial and error to learn, but it is possible (Isaacs, 1999).

> **Compartmentalize** Mentally "filing away" our own issues temporarily.

Compartmentalization is a great tool in a variety of situations, so it's worth learning. On the other hand, if you haven't developed that skill yet, or if it isn't working in that situation, your other option is to admit to yourself and to the speaker that your attention is elsewhere. Apologize, and ask if the speaker is willing to give you a little time to sort it out, and then the two of you can talk. Although this might be disappointing or even frustrating to the speaker, he would probably rather you be honest about it than to waste his time and yours with a half-hearted attempt to listen. It's not an ideal solution, but it may be the best available one.

I use both of these options in my own life. Over the years, I've gotten pretty good at compartmentalization, but my efforts to mentally "put things away" don't always work. For example, I came home one day after an especially trying day at work. My computer had crashed, resulting in the loss of some important documents; a different computer glitch had resulted in my getting a particularly undesirable schedule for the next term; and to top it all off, a winter storm had hit and it took me two hours to drive the 25 miles between school and home. I'd left for work at 6 A.M., and by the time I got home, it was 8 P.M., and I was exhausted. As it turned out, my husband had received an interesting job offer that day and wanted to talk about the pros and cons of taking it. He noticed right away how stressed I was, though, and I admitted that I didn't think I could be a very good listener right then. We agreed to wait and talk about his job offer the next morning, after a good night's sleep. He was a little disappointed, because he'd been excited to share his news with me, but he also knew how it felt to be wiped out at the end of a long day. His ability to empathize with me, combined with his recognition of the fact that he'd only end up frustrated if I wasn't giving him my full attention, made it easier for both of us to accept the compromise. After all, we're only human, and we have to acknowledge that we have limits.

Premature Judgment The third internal barrier is the **premature judgment**, which can take one of two forms. The first occurs when, at some point partway through the speaker's message, we think we know where they're going with it, so we stop listening carefully. Mentally, we might be thinking, "Yeah, yeah, yeah, I know what you're saying, wrap it up already!" Obviously, the danger here is that we're wrong, and our premature judgment might cause us to miss important information that the speaker hasn't said yet. We're especially at risk for falling into this trap in our closest relationships, when we know each other well and thus think we can "read each other's minds" to some extent. Because we're sometimes right, these positive experiences reinforce our notion that we know what's coming next, which serves to lure us into a potential trap each time a message starts to sound familiar.

> **Premature judgment** When we stop listening to a message before the speaker is finished, either because we think we know what the speaker is going to say, or because we have already formed an opinion about the speaker or the message.

 *Critical Thinking* **QUESTION** Which cognitive biases from Chapter 5 are likely to facilitate the premature judgment?

A second type of premature judgment comes *when we form an opinion about the speaker or her message*. In some cases, this can be based on a stereotype that we place on the speaker. For example, if someone who strikes you as a "jock" or an "airhead" is trying to talk with you about school or an academic subject, you might not take the person seriously. You might wonder what the agenda really is, or assume that the person doesn't know what she or he is talking about. In other cases, the premature judgment might be related to the topic of the message, especially if the topic is a "hot button" issue for you. It might have to do with a political or social issue that you feel strongly about, such as abortion or gun control. When someone starts talking about the issue, you will probably immediately classify the speaker as "on your side" or not, and that classification subsequently influences how well you actually hear the message. (This ties in with the concept of ingroups/outgroups we learned in the previous chapter.) To overcome this barrier to listening, we need to keep improving our awareness of our stereotypes, and also of our "hot button" issues. Then we can begin to notice when we find ourselves making premature judgments about a speaker or a message based on these triggers, and teach ourselves to halt that process and start listening more carefully instead.

External Barriers to Listening

Noise Just as there are three internal barriers to effective listening, there are also three external barriers to listening (Wood, 2002). The most obvious external barrier to effective listening is *noise*. The noise can come from other conversations in the room, a television or stereo playing, traffic, or any other sound that intrudes while you're trying to listen to someone. In these cases, it's best to try to remove the barrier by eliminating the noise or moving to a quieter location. In other cases, the intrusion may not come from loud sounds, but from unexpected ones.

For example, in a class last week on the second floor of a building, we all heard an unusual and increasingly loud noise coming from the corridor outside. As the noise level peaked, I glanced out the window and noticed—of all things—a fork-lift being driven across the balcony outside. My students looked outside, too, and for a moment, we all lost our train of thought while we pondered the oddity of it.

We do have some ability to filter out unwanted noise, as evidenced in the psychological concepts of *sensory adaptation* and *selective attention*. **Sensory adaptation** refers to our ability to become accustomed to an intrusive stimulus, such as loud music, traffic noise, or the "white noise" put out by a computer. At first, the noise from these stimuli are distracting, but if they remain stable over time, our senses become less responsive to them, which eventually results in our ability to ignore them. **Selective attention** refers to our ability to focus our attention on one incoming stimulus, while filtering out others that are less relevant. These two abilities work together to help us filter out unwanted noise. At a large, noisy party, for example, we might initially have trouble hearing what someone is saying to us, but once our senses adapt to the noise of the party (sensory adaptation) and our hearing becomes attuned to the speaker's voice (selective attention), we can then start understanding what the person is saying without too much trouble.

> **Sensory adaptation** Our ability to become accustomed to an intrusive stimulus.

> **Selective attention** Our ability to focus our attention on one incoming stimulus, while filtering out others that are less relevant.

Interestingly, the personality traits of introversion and extraversion have been found to have an impact on our individual ability to filter out unwanted noise. As you'll recall from Chapter 3, extraverts tend to be high energy and sociable, whereas introverts tend to be more reserved and inwardly focused. A great deal of research has examined other differences between introverts and extraverts, and one of the consistent findings has been extraverts' greater tolerance of noise and other stimuli. Hans Eysenck (1967), one of the most influential contributors to trait theories of personality, argues that these differences are rooted in an area of the brain known as the reticular activating system (RAS). The RAS is responsible for our physiological arousal level, keeping us alert and attentive. Eysenck theorizes that introverts and extraverts have different RAS "settings," so to speak, and that introverts' settings are higher than extraverts', causing introverts to be more sensitive to changes in external stimuli such as noise. Research testing Eysenck's theory has supported the idea: Extraverts prefer higher levels of noise in learning environments than introverts, and extraverts also perform better in noisy environments than do introverts (Geen, 1984). Thus, extraverts are better able to filter out noisy distractions while listening than introverts.

Information Overload   In our fast-paced and busy lives, **information overload** interferes with our listening when we try to process too much information. One situation in which this occurs is at school. An average student who is taking 3–5 classes each term is faced with the daunting task of listening and remembering several hours of incoming academic information each day. In the first hour of class, while your brain is relatively fresh, you can probably listen and process what you learn fairly effectively. Later in the

> **Information overload** Interferes with our listening when we try to process too much information.

day, however, when you're in your third or fourth hour of class, you are more susceptible to information overload. At that point, it is much more difficult to understand and remember information that is presented than it was in the first hour. Therefore, you'll need to work harder at effectively listening and processing that information: For example, you might want to tape record your later classes so you can review the session later on and make sure you didn't miss anything. Alternatively, you might schedule breaks between your classes and use that break time partially to review what you've already learned, so that it is more embedded in your memory, and partially to give your brain a chance to rest before the next class session.

Information overload also occurs when multiple messages come in at once. In our busy lives, we often multitask, or try to accomplish several things at one time: reading the mail, catching up on the daily news on television, and making dinner, for example. Imagine that you're trying to listen to an important news update when a family member walks in the room and starts to tell you something. Will you be able to pay attention to what she is saying, while still keeping an ear to the news? Logic says no, but how often do we try to do just that and end up not getting a complete understanding of either message?

Some research on sex differences in the brain indicates that women may be more likely than men to engage in the sort of multitasking just described, and that their brains are actually designed to facilitate multitasking a bit more than men's brains (Rueckert, Baboorian, Stavropoulous, & Yasutake, 1999; Springer & Deutsch, 1998). Men are more likely to focus intently on one thing at a time. In what ways could these research findings influence sex differences in information overload?

Message Complexity   Whereas message overload involves too many messages, **message complexity** may only involve one message. The problem, though, is that the message itself is too complicated to absorb without turning your focus inward and thus away from the speaker for a time. The complexity of the message may be a result of the language of the message, or simply the level. Again, a common example of message complexity comes from the academic environment. The first class you take in a subject that is new to you often presents the challenge of a new set of terms or vocabulary distinct to that subject. As a result, your ability to listen and process the information in that class will be slower, because you will be spending some of your efforts "translating" the new terms into a language that you understand. We might have the same trouble in a new work environment, or when we learn a new computer program—both situations often have a "language" of their own. And we will experience a similar challenge anytime we are trying to listen to a message in a language that is not our native language.

> **Message complexity** The message itself is too complicated to absorb without turning your focus inward, and thus away from the speaker for a time.

To sum up, six different barriers challenge our efforts to listen effectively. Internal barriers include emotional noise, cognitive distractions, and premature judgments; external barriers include environmental noise, information overload, and message complexity. All of these barriers can be overcome to some

TABLE 8.2 | Barriers to Effective Listening and Strategies for Overcoming Them

BARRIER	COPING STRATEGY
Emotional Noise	Use self-talk or compartmentalization
Cognitive Distractions	Use self-talk or compartmentalization
Premature Judgments	Be aware of stereotypes and hot-button issues; use self-talk to overcome them
Noise	Eliminate the noise or change environments
Information Overload	Take breaks; mentally review
Message Complexity	Take notes; ask questions to clarify

degree. The first step in doing so is raising our level of awareness so that we recognize when one or more of the barriers are interfering with our listening. For a summary of these barriers, along with strategies for overcoming them, see Table 8.2.

Now, turn to Activity 8.2 for an opportunity to identify these barriers in your own life and practice overcoming them.

Counterfeit Listening Styles

So far, we have learned about the importance of climate in a relationship and its effects on listening. We've also identified the four basic elements of listening and examined a variety of barriers that can interfere with our best efforts to listen. Now let's identify several types of **counterfeit listening styles**: behaviors that, on the surface, may look like listening, but in effect are actually counterproductive to good listening.

> **Counterfeit listening styles** Behaviors that, on the surface, may look like listening, but are actually counterproductive to good listening.

Pseudolistening Imagine a friend is telling you about something that recently happened, and you're nodding and saying "um-hum" in all the right places, but your mind is elsewhere. All of a sudden, you become aware that your friend has stopped talking and seems to be waiting for you to say something. You quickly search your memory in a futile attempt to remember what the last thing was that she said, and then, feeling rather embarrassed, ask, "I'm sorry—what was that?" If that sounds familiar, then you are guilty of the counterfeit listening style known as **pseudolistening**. When we pseudolisten, we give the

> **Pseudolistening** Giving only the impression of listening by nonverbal behaviors such as nodding, keeping eye contact, and verbal prompts.

impression of listening by our nonverbal behaviors such as nodding, keeping eye contact, and sometimes even using verbal prompts, such as "yeah" and "really?" In reality, though, we aren't paying close attention to what the speaker is saying. Our pseudolistening might be a result of one of the barriers to listening we discussed earlier, such as information overload or emotional noise, but the presence of a barrier doesn't excuse our failure to listen. Typically, the speaker in this situation feels frustrated, annoyed, or even betrayed by your

FIGURE 8.3 | When was the last time you engaged in pseudolistening?

pseudolistening, which ultimately can deteriorate the quality and climate of your relationship. Furthermore, if you are listening to gain information, such as in a classroom situation, you risk missing something important (see Figure 8.3).

Selective Listening   We **selectively listen** when we screen a message for certain topics or issues, and then either respond only to those aspects of the message or tune those parts out. So, in essence, we are either "tuning in" to what we're interested in or "tuning out" when something bores us or we don't want to hear it. For example, in class, you might find your attention wandering when, all of a sudden, the professor says something about an exam. Exam? All of a sudden she has your attention, and you're listening again! Conversely, if your parent or roommate is talking to you and starts to complain about your lack of housekeeping ability—a topic that he's always griping about—you might tune that part of the message out. Another common situation that may prompt selective listening is an argument: Our emotions kick in, and we may hear only what we expect to hear. In all these cases, when we selectively listen, we are attending only to part of the message.

Selective listening When we screen a message for certain topics or issues, and then either respond only to those aspects of the message or tune those parts out.

Defensive Listening   **Defensive listening** is closely linked to communication climate and is more likely to occur when the climate is less trusting or more threatening. When we defensively listen, we perceive criticism when none is intended. Consider the following example: John and Marta have been married for five years and just recently had their first child. Adjusting to the challenges of parenting has taken its toll on their relationship, and lately it seems they're always arguing about something. Then one day John, who has been working upstairs, comes downstairs and says to Marta, "Did I hear the baby crying?" Marta glares at him and replies, "No, the baby isn't crying—why do you always accuse me of neglecting the baby?" In this example, John was just trying to be helpful, but in light of their deteriorating communication climate, Marta was feeling somewhat fearful about the stability of her marriage. As a result, she interpreted John's question defensively as a criticism of her parenting ability.

> **Defensive listening** We perceive criticism when none is intended.

Defensiveness is something to which we are all susceptible—some of us more than others, or only in certain relationships, and each of us with different "hot-button" issues that are likely to provoke our defensiveness. We'll examine ways of overcoming defensiveness in Chapter 10, but for now, suffice it to say that defensive listening is probably the worst of the counterfeit listening styles, because one defensive response can trigger a downward spiral of increasingly negative communication.

Stagehogging   The fourth counterfeit listening style is **stagehogging**. Stagehogging occurs when someone is talking to us, and we use something the speaker says as an opening to jump in with a story of our own (Vangelisti, Knapp & Daly, 1990). Carly, for example, tells this story: "I was talking to one of my friends about snowboarding and telling him how great the snow is up on Mt. Hood this year. Before I could finish, he jumped in and started telling me all about his trip to Tahoe last month, and how awesome the snow was there, and all about these new jumps he was doing. I never even got to finish my story—all of a sudden, it was all about him."

> **Stagehogging** When someone is talking to us, and we use something the speaker says as an opening to jump in with a story of our own.

Joshua says this about his stagehogging habit: "I am a stagehog. I interrupt frequently. I often feel I am helping, but now I think it's because I want attention. To rectify this I have been very careful to make sure others complete their message. Another benefit is that now I have time to consider the relevance of what I wanted to say."

Although stagehogging is sometimes a deliberate attempt at one-upmanship, it can also result from a sincere attempt to relate to what the speaker is saying. For example, if someone is telling you about how difficult their math class is, you might respond by saying something like, "Oh, I know what you mean—my math class was really hard, too." If you stop there, your response will probably sound sincere and supporting. If, on the other hand, you go on to talk about how hard the teacher was to understand, how confusing the tests were, and all the other reasons your class was hard, you've gone too far, and you've fallen into the counterfeit listening style of stagehogging. There is often a fine line between supporting and stagehogging, and we really need to apply our understanding of the person, their culture, and their situation to find the right balance. If you go over the line, stagehogging leaves the speaker feeling let down, because it sends the message that what he's saying isn't interesting or important. As a result, it detracts from the relationship climate and the overall quality of a relationship.

To identify your own weaknesses in the counterfeit listening styles, turn now to Activity 8.3.

Interim SUMMARY #2

The process of listening involves four steps: hearing, attending, understanding, and responding. Internal and external barriers can interfere with our listening efforts. They include emotional noise, cognitive distractions, premature judgments, physical noise, information overload, and message complexity. All of these barriers can be overcome, but it takes time, effort, and ongoing practice to achieve this goal.

Counterfeit listening styles include pseudolistening, selective listening, defensive listening, and stagehogging. These listening behaviors are counterproductive. They promote disconfirming, rather than confirming or supportive relationship climates. We are all susceptible to these ineffective listening styles at different times and in different situations, and therefore we must monitor ourselves to keep them from creeping in. Otherwise, they can chip away at the climate of our relationships.

AUTHENTIC LISTENING STYLES

PREVIEW QUESTIONS

(1) Which two listening styles are controversial, and why?

(2) Describe five more helpful listening styles, along with tips for effective use of each one.

> **Authentic listening styles**
> Ways of responding to a speaker that show genuine interest in and empathy for the person and situation.

Now that we've learned about ineffective styles of listening, let's turn our attention to listening styles that work. **Authentic listening styles** are ways of responding to a speaker that show genuine interest and empathy for the person and situation. We will explore seven styles of authentic listening, all of which are also active listening styles. Active listening is simply engaged listening, when we show our interest through verbal and nonverbal responses. Of the authentic listening styles, five of them tend to be helpful in many situations, and two are helpful only occasionally and thus should be used sparingly. Let's look at the latter two first.

Controversial Listening Styles

Advising In Western culture, the listening response used most frequently is the **advising** response (Notarius & Herrick, 1988). In fact, many people who consider themselves good listeners pride themselves on the quality of advice they offer to friends and loved ones who confide in them. Ironically, though, advising is typically the *least* helpful response we can give (Goldsmith & Fitch, 1997). Think about it: In our individualistic culture, we like to do things our own way, and that includes solving our own problems and figuring things out for ourselves. Most of us don't like to be told what to do, which in essence is what advising does.

> **Advising** A listening response that offers advice.

The only time advising might be useful is if and when the person specifically asks for your advice, and even then, it may not be the best response. For example, a friend says, "I have a paper due tomorrow and there's no way I'm going to have it done on time. What do you think I should do?" Before you offer advice, ask yourself if you want to be responsible for the success or failure of your suggestion if the person follows your advice. Without knowing the circumstances, the late-paper policies of the professor in question, and any history between the student and professor, how can you be sure your advice is the best plan? Initially, at least, other response styles (discussed in the following paragraphs) might be more helpful to your friend.

Evaluating Even less helpful is the response style of evaluating. **Evaluating** is a response that makes a judgment about the person or situation. The only time evaluating is appropriate is when you are truly in a position of authority with the person and situation—if, for example, you are an academic advisor and a student is asking you which courses to take to complete his or her major. In that case, the choices may be fairly clear cut, and stating those options to the student would probably be helpful—assuming, of course, that you are certain you're right. In other situations, such as the one in the previous paragraph (where your friend is concerned about a paper that isn't done), an evaluating response might be, "Well,

> **Evaluating** A response that makes a judgment about the person or situation.

you just have to find a way to get it done!" This is similar to the response in the first section of this chapter, in the example of the friend who was worried about his sister. Saying "You worry too much . . . (and so on)" is an evaluating response, because it implies a judgment about your friend. In both of these examples, even though you may mean well, your friend may feel you don't understand, or that you aren't interested enough in him to spend any additional time listening. Evaluating responses, used inappropriately, pose a real threat to the climate of our relationships. When we do use them, it is important to do so tactfully and with good intentions. Regardless of our intent, however, rarely are we in a truly authoritative position that may be appropriate for the evaluating response.

If evaluating responses sound familiar to you, you are not alone! Adrianna has this to say about her tendency to evaluate: "I find myself judging instead of being supportive. I think if I can be more supportive instead, my friends and family will confide in me more. As it stands, people are afraid of what I might think or say."

Alanna adds this: "I have strong opinions and tend to tell others exactly what I think. Obviously, this is not helpful because I don't have all the answers, and it doesn't leave a lot of room for discussion. I would love to try to listen to what others say without judgment. I am very curious, so I am trying to ask more questions and actually listen to the responses."

Helpful Listening Styles

When we truly want to be a good listener and to help someone, the best thing we can do is to encourage the person to talk it out and explore his or her own thoughts and feelings about the issue. This philosophy may remind you of that old proverb that asks, "Which is better: to give a person a fish, or teach him to fish?" Advising is analogous to giving the fish, which feeds the person for one meal—or, in listening, solves one problem for them. Teaching a person to fish, on the other hand, helps a person become self-sufficient and have a lifetime of meals; this is what we are aiming to do with the following listening styles. All five of them can be useful, so becoming familiar with all of them will increase our versatility and effectiveness as a listener with a variety of people and situations.

Analyzing   One effective listening style is **analyzing**, which we use when we want to offer a different perspective on the issue, or perhaps help the person figure out what might be at the heart of their concern. To be effective, an analyzing response must be phrased in a tentative manner, starting with a word or phrase like "maybe" or "I wonder if . . . " For example, imagine that a friend says to you, "I don't know what's going on with my roommate. She hardly ever talks to me or just hangs out anymore." An analyzing response might be, "Maybe she's preoccupied with school and feels too busy and stressed to relax and take any breaks." An advantage of this type of response is that it offers the person a possible explanation or an alternative viewpoint. On the other hand, it may not be what the person is looking for. In this example, your friend may have more unexpressed thoughts or feelings about the situation, and an analyzing response runs the risk of shutting them down. Overall, analyzing responses work best with people who like to look at all sides of an issue before forming a conclusion. When someone just needs to get something off their chest, your analysis may be irrelevant.

> **Analyzing** To offer a different perspective on the issue.

Questioning   A second type of effective listening response is the **questioning** response, which is simply asking a question geared toward either clarifying your understanding of the speaker, or helping him or her work through the issue. In the example from the previous paragraph, a questioning response might be, "How long has your roommate been acting that way?" or "Has anything happened between the two of you that might be bothering her?" Either of these questions encourages your friend to continue talking about her concern and shows that you're interested in trying to help her understand what's going on. For this reason, questioning responses are

> **Questioning** Asking a question geared toward either clarifying your understanding of the speaker, or helping him or her work through the issue.

often effective, especially when the questions are open-ended (such as "How are you feeling about your new relationship?") rather than closed-ended ("Are you having fun in your new relationship?"). Open-ended questions tend to promote greater disclosure and consequently, better intimacy.

In fact, there are only two general situations in which questioning responses are ineffective. One of these situations is when your question is aimed at satisfying your personal curiosity rather than helping your friend sort through her issue. A personal curiosity question could be a gossipy question such as, "Oh, I remember her—is her hair still purple?" or even more tangential such as, "How much do you guys pay for your apartment?" Questioning responses are also ineffective in those situations where someone has a lot they need to get off their chest, and they need to just spill it all out without any interruptions. In this situation, asking a question runs the risk of distracting the speaker from her train of thought and also may be perceived as an interruption.

Minimally Encouraging   So, what listening styles *are* effective when someone has a lot to get off their chest? One useful style is **minimally encouraging**, which is just what it sounds like. It involves encouraging the speaker to continue by giving short and unintrusive responses both verbally and nonverbally. Verbal encouragers include such phrases as "uh-huh," "yeah," "wow, "no kidding," "really," or "go on." Nonverbal encouragers include nodding your head, leaning forward a bit, and maintaining eye contact. This type of listening response works best with people who like to give lots of detail when they talk, or when someone just needs to "vent." When using the minimal encourager, though, be careful not to fall into pseudolistening—stay focused on what the person is saying.

> **Minimally encouraging** Encouraging the speaker to continue by giving short and unintrusive responses both verbally and nonverbally.

Supporting   Another effective listening style is the **supporting** response, which involves saying something intended to validate the speaker's thoughts or feelings, let the speaker know that you understand what he is thinking or feeling, or express support and concern for him as a person. Continuing with the example of the friend whose roommate isn't talking to her much, a supporting response could take several forms, such as, "Gee, that's awful—I can't imagine having a roommate who doesn't talk," or "That must be really disconcerting for you—I know that you've always been friends with your roommates in the past." Responses like this signal to the speaker that you care and are really listening (Figure 8.4). As is the case with the other listening styles, though, there is one thing to be careful of with supporting responses: In this case, we don't want to sound as if we're brushing off the speaker. If we said something like, "Well, I'm sure you'll work it out—you're good with people," we might mean well, but in essence we are shutting down the conversation and discouraging the speaker from saying any more about it.

> **Supporting** Saying something intended to validate the speaker's thoughts or feelings, let the speaker know that you understand what he is thinking or feeling, or express support and concern for him as a person.

Paraphrasing   Paraphrasing is the most broadly effective of all the authentic listening styles, but also the most difficult to master artfully. Unfortunately, this is

EAR

EYES

UNDIVIDED
ATTENTION

HEART

FIGURE 8.4 | This Chinese character that refers to listening nicely illustrates the important components of authentic listening.

Calligraphy by Angie Au

one of those skills that has sometimes become misinterpreted in mainstream culture; some classes teach that paraphrasing involves repeating back what the speaker said, word for word. This is not paraphrasing, and it is not effective! True paraphrasing goes far beyond that in both depth and effectiveness. So, if you have encountered that incorrect style of paraphrasing prior to this class, try to forget it so it doesn't interfere with what you're about to learn.

Paraphrasing is sometimes called "reflective listening," and the word "reflective" can be a useful image in helping us grasp what a good paraphrasing response does. When you think about something that is reflective, what object comes to mind? A mirror, right? A mirror provides us with information about our appearance that can be useful in several ways. One thing a mirror does, at its most basic level, is to confirm what we already suspect about how we look—for example, that we have a good haircut or that we look good in green. Even though we already know these things, confirmation can be reassuring. Similarly, the most basic goal of paraphrasing is to reflect back to the speaker what we think they are saying, so that we confirm for them that they are getting their message across to us. A good paraphrasing response doesn't stop there, though.

Continuing with the mirror analogy, sometimes our reflection tells us something about how we are feeling that day—tired and run down, perhaps, or maybe excited and happy. By the same token, a good paraphrasing response reflects the emotion we think the speaker is feeling about her situation. In the example with the untalkative roommate, we might say, "It sounds like you're feeling confused (or upset, or frustrated, or disappointed, or whatever word seems to describe what you think the speaker is feeling)."

Finally, a mirror sometimes provides us with new information or a different view of ourselves—perhaps we forgot to zip up our pants, didn't realize our hair was looking a bit shaggy, or hadn't noticed that this style of shirt really makes us look hot! In the same way, the most complete paraphrasing responses try to "read between the lines" of what the speaker is saying, helping them to recognize thoughts or ideas they might have about the issue that they weren't yet aware of. In this example, perhaps you think your friend is especially frustrated with her roommate situation, since she just moved into town, hadn't met a lot of people yet, and was hoping that her roommate would also be her friend.

All in all, a complete **paraphrasing** response *reflects back to the speaker what you are hearing and includes three components: (1) how it sounds as if the speaker is feeling, (2) what you think the speaker might be thinking that she hasn't yet said, and (3) delivered in a way that encourages the speaker to continue* by ending with a phrase such as "Is that right?" "Am I understanding you correctly?" or something similar. Putting all these elements together, in the roommate example, you might say something like, "Gee, you sound like you're disappointed, because you really thought you guys had hit it off and were hoping that you'd be able to be friends, not just roommates—am I understanding you?"

> **Paraphrasing** A listening response that reflects what the speaker is feeling and thinking, expressed tentatively.

This paraphrasing response reflects back to your friend the message you think she is trying to convey, including how she's feeling about the situation, and an attempt to read between the lines to try to understand the issue more clearly. By phrasing it in a tentative way (ending with "am I understanding you?") you are signaling that you think you understand, but aren't sure, and you want the speaker to continue. If you're right about the speaker's thoughts and feelings, your friend will feel really understood—and there are few better feelings in the world than the feeling that somebody really "gets" you. She might say, "You know, you're right—I didn't realize it, but I think I did expect that we'd hang out together—maybe that was unrealistic." Even if you're wrong, your attempt to read between the lines can still be useful in helping your friend work through the issue. She might say, "I am disappointed, and I'm also frustrated—but I don't think I expected us to become good friends. I think what's really bothering me is that she doesn't do her share of the chores around here. Since she's never around, I can't seem to bring the subject up, so I just end up doing everything!" In either case, your paraphrasing response showed your friend that you're really listening, and encouraged her to work through the issue by identifying the thoughts and feelings she was having about it.

Using Paraphrasing Effectively Do we always need to include all these elements in a paraphrasing response? The answer is no. Sometimes a partial paraphrase—

which is either a reflection of the speaker's feelings or of her thoughts, but not both—will do just fine.

Also, the effectiveness of the paraphrasing response is not limited to situations in which we are listening to help someone. Paraphrasing responses can be equally useful when we are listening to gain information, and in that type of situation, they need not include the feeling. Imagine, for example, that your boss says, "That new person we hired isn't working out very well, so I'll need you to work this weekend." On the surface, that message may seem clear, but on closer inspection, there is room for misunderstanding. Before reading on, see if you can identify the ambiguous parts of the message.

What did you come up with? For starters, what does the boss mean by "this weekend?" Saturday, Sunday, or both? Is she including Friday in that? And just a few hours each day, or the entire day? The day shift or the night shift? What does she mean by "not working out" when she refers to the new hire? Is she firing him, and if so, will she expect you to work weekends from now on? Or is she saying that she wants you to help train the new hire this weekend, and after that your schedule will be back to normal? What sounded like a clear message turns out to be potentially confusing after all. So you can use a paraphrasing statement to get clarification: "So, you're firing the new guy, and I'll need to pick up his Saturday shift until you find a replacement—is that right?" Or, "Do you mean that you want me to work both days this weekend to help the new guy learn the ropes, and then I'll be back to my regular schedule?" Either way, you're showing an effort to understand and diplomatically giving her a chance to clarify her message for you.

At this point, you might be wondering, "Can't I just ask a question for clarification instead of using paraphrasing?" In some cases, yes, but be careful. Often, the speaker isn't aware that he is being unclear, and a question might trigger a defensive response—"What do you mean, you don't understand—I just spelled it out for you!" he might think, not realizing that wasn't the case. In the previous example, if you ask the boss, "Do you mean I need to work Saturday, Sunday, or both, and how long will this go on?" your boss might interpret your questions as challenges. Also, when more than one thing needs to be cleared up, a litany of questions can start to sound like an attack. Paraphrasing responses soften that effect by showing an effort to understand, and then just asking if your current understanding is correct. On the other other hand, in close relationships with a supportive communication climate, a question often works just fine for clarification. As is the case with other response styles, there is no "one size fits all" formula for success. When in doubt, it is probably best to err on the side of caution and use paraphrasing. Then, over time and with practice, you'll get a better feel for what is likely to be effective in various situations.

Shamika says this about her new paraphrasing skills: "I have never tried using this approach before, but the other day my friend was upset about her boyfriend. When I paraphrased what she said in my own words, it really helped both of us to better understand the problem. I love this method now."

Overall, paraphrasing responses tend to be the most useful of the authentic listening responses, but that doesn't mean we should always use them. On the contrary, we'd sound a bit repetitive if we always did. Also, paraphrasing responses

TABLE 8.3 | Listening Styles

A friend says to you, "I don't know what to do this summer. I need to decide whether I'm going to keep taking classes, or work full-time."

STYLE	POSSIBLE RESPONSE
Advising	Well, given that money has been tight for you lately, you probably ought to work so you can save up for next year.
Evaluating	You definitely need to work—otherwise, you'll just end up farther in debt!
Analyzing	Hmmm . . . in the past you've said you do better in school when you get that mental break during the summer; maybe you're just anxious to get your degree and that's why you're feeling uncertain this year.
Questioning	What do you think the advantages and disadvantages are of each option?
Minimally encouraging	(nodding, with full eye contact and a look of concern) Hmmm . . .
Supporting	As close as you are to finishing school, I can see how you'd be anxious to finish, but at the same time worried about getting farther in debt if you don't work for a while.
Paraphrasing	You sound really worried, like maybe you're afraid that if you take time off school you might get so used to the nice money that you won't go back to school in the fall . . . is that what's stressing you out?

require more time and effort than the other response types, and we don't always have the time, or care enough to make the effort. So paraphrasing responses are best suited to situations or people who are important to you and for when you can take or make the time necessary to really focus on the conversation.

Table 8.3 summarizes the listening styles. Turn now to Activity 8.4 to practice applying these listening styles to real-life situations.

GENDER AND LISTENING STYLES

PREVIEW QUESTIONS

(1) How are the communication goals of men and women different from each other?

(2) How do these differences affect listening style, and what can we do about it?

Now that we have a thorough understanding of the various elements of listening, barriers to listening, and counterfeit and authentic listening styles, let's look at how gender influences our listening patterns. One of the most widely recognized cultural differences in listening is the difference between traditional masculine and feminine listening styles. In general, men tend to communicate to gain status, and women tend to communicate to create harmonious relationships (Tannen, 1990). Even though not all men and all women fall into the traditional categories, these research-based generalizations have been tremendously useful in understanding some common problems in male-female communication. Listening styles is a prime example.

Because men often communicate to gain status, effective listening must work toward that goal by demonstrating authority and competence. Thus, men are more likely to take a problem-solving approach to listening, offering advice and suggestions in a genuine attempt to help. Women, on the other hand, in their efforts to create harmonious relationships, take a more empathy-oriented approach to listening, expressing support and understanding for the speaker. Research indicates they are also more likely to give verbal and nonverbal signals of listening, such as eye contact, head nods, and minimal encouragers (Tannen, 1990). When the cultures collide, the stage is set for frustration and misunderstanding. Marital therapists, in fact, report that their women clients often complain that their husbands don't listen to them. When the husbands hear this, they often feel bewildered because they *do* think they listen.

Consider this classic example: A woman is experiencing some frustrations at work and starts to tell her male partner about it. Several sentences into her story, he jumps in with a suggestion of what she should do about the problem. She's not looking for advice; she just needs to "vent" and to feel understood, so she ignores his suggestion and continues with her story. Not sure why she didn't respond to his suggestion, he listens a little more, then offers a second idea of how she could handle the situation. The pattern repeats itself, with her becoming increasingly frustrated because (a) she hasn't finished telling him about it yet, and thus some of his suggestions aren't relevant, and (b) she wants to know he understands how she's feeling—she's a smart girl and can solve her own problems! Why won't he just listen to me, she wonders? He also becomes increasingly frustrated—after all, she always says she wants him to listen, and hasn't he been doing just that? If he wasn't listening, then how would he be able to offer these good ideas, which by the way she didn't even acknowledge? It seems to him that she says she wants him to listen, but when he does, it doesn't help her, so what's the point? Both end up frustrated and feeling that their partner isn't listening, when in reality, they both mean well; they just have different needs and expectations of the listening process.

By learning about this gender difference in listening, and recognizing that our different listening styles come from both nature and nurture and that they are perfectly understandable and reasonable given our backgrounds, you've already taken the first step to resolving the potential conflict that can arise when they clash. The next step is to share this information with significant others in your life, so that they, too, understand the basis of your differences. Then you can all work toward a compromise. For example, if you want to be heard and supported when you talk to a problem-solving friend, tell the friend what you want. Say something like, "I need to tell you about something, and it's kind of long and complicated, so I just need to get it all off my chest and for you to just listen and try to understand." Or, if you want advice, ask for it. By being specific about what we need from a listener, we can avoid this type of listening-style misunderstanding.

Also, don't expect that just learning about this listening style difference will result in a magical change. It takes time, effort, and practice for men and women to learn to overcome this long-standing difference. Many couples successfully navigate through the trial-and-error period by agreeing that it's okay to gently remind each other when they fall into old habits. Also, couples who enjoy humor might engage in some playful teasing when they catch each other at it—humor can be a great way to diffuse any building tension and remind you that you're in this together.

TIPS FOR SUCCESSFUL APPLICATION OF THE PRINCIPLES OF LISTENING

PREVIEW QUESTION

(1) Now that we have developed a variety of listening tools, what else can we do to improve our effectiveness in listening?

Before we leave the topic of listening, let's touch on a few final tips that can aid in our effective application of these principles.

Consider Your Listening Goals and Your Limits

In any listening situation, the response styles you choose should be geared toward your goals. The two basic categories of listening goals are listening to help and listening for information. When we listen to help, we usually have some type of personal or professional relationship with the speaker, and he or she is turning to us for support or advice. Thus, listening for feelings as well as for thoughts is generally appropriate and effective. On the other hand, when we listen for information, our needs are usually more self-oriented. We might be in a classroom situation, at work, or in a conversation with someone who is providing a service, such as an auto mechanic or bank loan officer. In these situations, listening for feelings isn't very relevant; instead, we want to listen carefully for details and ambiguities, and rely on the listening styles of questioning and paraphrasing to clarify our understanding of the message.

Effective listeners must also consider their own limits in terms of time and interest. Engaged, authentic listening takes mental and emotional effort, as well as time. Realistically, we don't always have those resources available or want to expend them on just anyone in any situation. If we do try to help everyone, we won't have any resources left for those who truly matter, so be honest with yourself about your limits and learn to set boundaries around your listening.

Consider the Speaker's Needs

To be an effective listener, it is also important to consider the speaker and what he or she seems to need from you. Knowing what we know about gender differences in listening styles, for example, it may be reasonable to assume that a woman is looking for support and understanding. Exceptions to this general rule certainly apply, however—some women are more task-oriented and hence may feel frustrated with a listener's attempts to empathize. Of course, our ability to be effective listeners is at its best with those whom we know well. And, any time we are in doubt about what the speaker needs, we can ask: "Are you wanting some advice, or just needing support?"

Minimize Distractions

In important conversations, do your best to eliminate potential barriers that threaten your listening effectiveness. Turn off the television or stereo, turn off your cell phone, close the door, and do whatever else you can do to eliminate external distractions. Also, remember that if your internal barriers are interfering with your focus, either compartmentalize or ask for some time to work through your own issue before you tackle someone else's. In the long run, your relationships will be stronger as a result.

Mentally Summarize Key Ideas

When someone has a lot to get off their chest, we can sometimes feel challenged to keep it all straight without jumping in and responding. Interestingly, differences in speaking and thinking speeds can help with this challenge: The average person speaks about 125 words per minute, whereas we can mentally process four to five times that amount, or up to 800 words per minute. We can use this difference to our advantage by using our extra brain resources to mentally summarize and review what the speaker has already said. In doing so, however, be careful not to prematurely judge what the person is saying or assume you know where she's going and tune out. Instead, keep listening for new information and details, so you end up with a clear picture of the speaker's message.

Molly says this about her experiences applying these principles of communication: "In the past I would have made fun of such approaches to communication. But through trying it out I have found how incredibly beneficial it is to my friendships and other relationships. People respond to me with far more openness and trust than ever before!"

Interim SUMMARY #3

In total, there are seven different types of authentic listening responses. Paraphrasing is probably the most effective and is useful in a wide variety of listening situations, including listening to help and listening for information. Analyzing is a useful method of offering a different perspective to someone, whereas questioning can help clarify an issue. Supportive responses and minimal encouragers both offer acceptance to the speaker, while simultaneously inviting them to continue. All five of these listening responses typically enhance the climate of our relationships. Advising, on the other hand, is only helpful when someone specifically asks for your opinion, and even then can be risky if your advice doesn't work for the other person. Evaluative responses should be reserved only for those situations in which you are truly an authority figure and your expert opinion is being sought.

Gender affects listening styles via the different communication goals often found in men and women. Men often communicate to gain status; women more often communicate to build consensus. As a result, men often listen with the goal of problem-solving, and women are more likely to be seeking empathy and understanding. Understanding these differences can help us be more sensitive to potential misunderstandings, especially when we clarify what we want from a listener.

In applying the principles of listening, it is important to consider our goals and limits, as well as the speaker's needs. We also must learn to minimize distractions and to mentally summarize key ideas. All of these skills help us utilize the various principles of listening more effectively, and in turn build stronger relationships.

A LOOK BACK AT THE LISTENING STYLES OF MY GRAD SCHOOL PROFESSORS

At the outset of this chapter, I recounted a real-life example of how listening styles and relationship climate had affected my own life when I was in graduate school. Now that we've identified and learned about the various listening styles, let's re-examine those conversations to see what style each professor used.

The first professor used an evaluating response, which, as we have learned is often the case, was ineffective and hurtful. The second professor used several of the authentic listening styles, beginning with a partial paraphrase, followed by minimal encouragers, and finally a supporting response. At the end of my conversation with him, I felt understood, validated, and safe. These two conversations proved to be pivotal in my relationship and trust in each of these professors. Not surprisingly, perhaps, I approached future interactions with the first professor with great caution, and never trusted her any more than I had to. The second professor became one of my most trusted and valued mentors, and to this day, I remember him with respect and gratitude. This example also serves as a reminder to me how interactions that may seem inconsequential to us can have a great impact on someone else. No matter how busy or complicated our lives get, I don't think any of us would want to be remembered as the person who judged others with apparent disregard for their feelings. We can't be perfect listeners, but we can try to be aware of our strengths and limitations, and honor others' trust in us with honesty and authenticity.

CHAPTER TERMS

Relational climate
Confirming
   (supportive) climate
Disconfirming
   (defensive) climate

Endorsement
Emotional noise
Cognitive distractions
Compartmentalize
Premature judgment

Sensory adaptation
Selective attention
Information
   overload
Message complexity

Counterfeit listening styles	Stagehogging	Analyzing
Pseudolistening	Authentic listening styles	Questioning
Selective listening	Advising	Minimally encouraging
Defensive listening	Evaluating	Supporting
		Paraphrasing

ACTIVITY 8.1

RELATIONAL CLIMATES IN YOUR LIFE

PART 1: LEVELS OF CONFIRMATION

A. The simplest level of confirmation is to recognize another person's existence. Think about the degree to which you do this, and how it varies in different environments you are in. For example, what do you do to acknowledge people when you see them? How does it differ at school? At work? At a party? With your family? In the following space, discuss your strong points in this area, as well as at least one specific example of where you might improve on this.

_____
_____
_____
_____
_____
_____
_____
_____
_____

B. The middle level of confirmation involves acknowledging another person's feelings, thoughts, or actions. Consider your own patterns of this, again noting how they differ in the different environments you live and work in. Then, in the following space, write several specific examples of how you succeed in this area, as well as at least one example of how you might improve in this area.

_____
_____
_____
_____
_____
_____
_____
_____

C. The highest level of confirmation involves accepting another person's thoughts or feelings as valid. Once again, consider what you do to endorse others. Whom do you endorse the most? The least? How does this endorsement affect your relationships with these individuals? Discuss these questions in the following space.

_____

_____

_____

_____

_____

_____

_____

_____

_____

PART 2: YOUR RELATIONAL CLIMATES

A. Identify the person whom you trust the most. Then, consider what that person does to build your relational climate, specifically using the three levels of confirmation. Elaborate on their behaviors in this area in the following space.

_____

_____

_____

_____

_____

_____

_____

_____

B. Identify a person in your life with whom you have a difficult, less supportive relationship. Consider what this person does (in the way of confirming behaviors) to contribute to the status of your relationship. Then, consider what you do (in terms of confirming behaviors) to contribute to the status of your relationship. Write about both of these contributors in the following space.

_____

_____

_____

_____

_____

_____

_____

_____

——— ACTIVITY 8.2 ———
BARRIERS TO EFFECTIVE LISTENING

INSTRUCTIONS: *In this section of the chapter, we identified six different barriers to effective listening, along with some suggestions for overcoming each one. In this activity, you will identify the three barriers that you struggle with the most and generate at least one specific idea to try to overcome each one.*

1. Of the six barriers to effective listening, the three that I have the most trouble with are:

   a. _____

   b. _____

   c. _____

2. For what you wrote on line a, give a specific example of how you do this, along with the impact it had on the listening situation and/or relationship.

   _____

   _____

   _____

3. Based on the suggestions in the text for overcoming this barrier, write one specific thing you can try to help yourself overcome it. (Note: Don't just write the name of the strategy, for example, self-talk. Instead, apply it to the situation, writing specifically what you could tell yourself in the self-talk.)

   _____

   _____

   _____

4. For what you wrote on line b, give a specific example of how you do this, along with the impact it had on the situation and/or relationship.

   _____

   _____

   _____

5. Based on the suggestions in the text for overcoming this barrier, write one specific thing you can try to help yourself overcome it.

_____

_____

_____

6. For what you wrote on line c, give a specific example of how you do this, along with the impact it had on the listening situation and/or relationship.

_____

_____

_____

7. Based on the suggestions in the text for overcoming this barrier, write one specific thing you can try to help yourself overcome it.

_____

_____

_____

8. Finally, team up with one or a few other members of your class and compare your answers. Offer one another at least one additional suggestion for overcoming your barriers, and write one of the suggestions you get from a classmate in the following space.

_____

_____

_____

ACTIVITY 8.3

COUNTERFEIT LISTENING IN YOUR LIFE

1. Think of a recent time when you were talking with someone about something important to you, and that person engaged in some form of counterfeit listening. Describe what they did and how you felt as a result in the following space.

_____

_____

_____

2. Now, think about your own listening habits. Which one or two counterfeit listening styles do you use the most?

One counterfeit listening style I use a lot is _____.
An example of when/how/with whom I use this is:

_____

_____

_____

Another counterfeit listening style I use a lot is _____.
An example of when/how/with whom I use this is:

_____

_____

_____

3. Have you gotten caught using counterfeit listening? Think about your most important relationships. How has counterfeit listening affected the development of these relationships?

_____

_____

_____

ACTIVITY 8.4

AUTHENTIC LISTENING RESPONSES

INSTRUCTIONS: *In this exercise, you will practice constructing and using effective listening responses. You may work on these individually or in small groups. For each of the following statements, write effective listening responses that you could use that fit each of the listening styles.*

1. *A coworker says to you, "I'm really upset with our new boss. He just came in and changed a bunch of rules without even paying any attention to how well the old rules were working!"*

Advising Response: _____

_____

Evaluative Response: _____

_____

Supportive Response: _____

_____

Analyzing Response: _____

_____

Questioning Response: _____

_____

Paraphrasing Response: _____

_____

Which of these responses would you use, and why?

_____

_____

_____

2. *Your significant other says to you, "It seems like we never spend any time together anymore."*

Advising Response: _____

_____

Evaluative Response: _____

_____

Supportive Response: _____

_____

Analyzing Response: _____

_____

Questioning Response: _____

_____

Paraphrasing Response: _____

_____

Which of these responses would you use, and why?

_____

_____

_____

3. *A close friend says to you, "I'm worried about my mom. She's been yelling at everyone a lot lately, and that's really out of character for her."*

Advising Response: _____

_____

Evaluative Response: _____

_____

Supportive Response: _____

_____

Analyzing Response: _____

_____

Questioning Response: _____

_____

Paraphrasing Response: _____

_____

Which of these responses would you use, and why?

_____

_____

_____

4. Finally, write your own example of something someone said to you recently that was important. Then, write what you could have said using any three of the listening response styles.

Someone said to you:_____

_____

Listening Response 1: Type of response _____

How you could say it:_____

_____

Listening Response 2: Type of response _____

How you could say it:_____

_____

Listening Response 3: Type of response _____

How you could say it:_____

_____

What type of response *did* you use? What did you say, and what effect did it have?

_____

_____

_____

Was there a better type of response you could have used? If so, explain.

_____

_____

_____

VERBAL AND NONVERBAL COMMUNICATION

> The real art of conversation is not only to say the right thing at the right place but to leave unsaid the wrong thing at the tempting moment.
>
> —DOROTHY NEVILL

In the previous chapter, we introduced the issue of trust in a relationship, and the importance of listening in the development of a supportive and trusting relational climate. Prior to that, in Chapters 5 and 6, we examined the role of perception in our relationships, recognizing both internal and external factors that have an impact on our perception, as well as several common perceptual errors that lead to misunderstandings. As a result, we now know how easily misunderstandings develop, and how we can apply various listening styles to try to clarify others' messages and intentions. In this chapter, we will take an additional step toward better communication as we examine the ways that our words influence relationships: or, you might say, the uses and abuses of language.

VERBAL COMMUNICATION

Dorothy Nevill's insightful statement at the beginning of this chapter really underscores the complex nature of effective communication: It involves not only knowing what to say, but the best way to say it, and also the best time to say it. Meeting this high standard requires knowledge and practice in several key areas, which can be organized around four guiding principles of effective verbal communication.

First, *language must be clear:* We must learn to choose our words carefully and specifically, so that we avoid common misunderstandings that occur when we use vague language. Second, *language must be responsible:* When we express our opinions, we must acknowledge that they are opinions, rather than present them as fact. Third, *language must be context-sensitive:* In other words, we must have knowledge and understanding of gender and other cultural variables that influence people's varying expectations of communication, and we must apply that understanding to our language so that the listener will accurately understand our meaning. Finally, *language must be congruent*: We must be aware of the nonverbal signals that we use (often unknowingly) when we speak and ensure that they support the message we are trying to send, rather than undermine it. Development of these skills goes a long way toward reducing defensiveness in relationships and replacing it with a climate of trust. Now, let's examine each principle in greater detail.

LANGUAGE MUST BE CLEAR

PREVIEW QUESTIONS

(1) What is abstract language, and how does it interfere with our human relations?

(2) Describe two specific types of abstract language and give examples of how each one can be overcome.

The first principle of effective verbal communication is that language must be clear and specific. **Abstract language** is language that is vague, a condition that forms the basis for many misunderstandings. Abstract language is often conceptualized as a ladder, with highly abstract language on the top rung and increasingly more specific language on the progressively lower rungs (see Figure 9.1).

> **Abstract language**
> Language which is vague.

As you can see from Figure 9.1, making the transition from highly abstract language to very specific language is a multistep process. Often the use of abstract language isn't intentional; instead, it may stem from a perceptual bias that we learned about in Chapter 5—the **false consensus bias**, or our assumption

> **False consensus bias** Our assumption that others see things the same way we do.

that others see things the same way we do. This mistaken assumption lures us into using a kind of verbal shorthand, where we say things that are vague or general, with the assumption that others will know what we mean. Sometimes we get lucky and they do understand. In our closest relationships, for example, abstractions may be interpreted accurately because of our shared history and in-depth knowledge of each other. Too often, however, others misunderstand, and the stage is set for a potential problem.

A good example comes from Patricia, one of my former students, who says this about her tendency to use abstract language: "I told my roommate that I needed her to respect my privacy. Several days later, I noticed that she seemed to be avoiding me—she was never around in the evenings when we used to talk. Instead, she'd either be gone or in her room with the door closed. Also, she wasn't bringing in the mail or taking phone messages like we always used to do for each other. I asked her what was wrong, and she said she was just trying to respect my privacy. I realized then that I'd been way too vague—all I meant was that I didn't

FIGURE 9.1 | Levels of Abstraction in Language

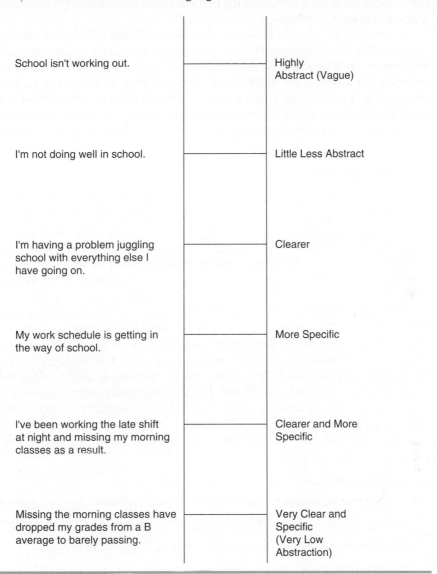

School isn't working out. — Highly Abstract (Vague)

I'm not doing well in school. — Little Less Abstract

I'm having a problem juggling school with everything else I have going on. — Clearer

My work schedule is getting in the way of school. — More Specific

I've been working the late shift at night and missing my morning classes as a result. — Clearer and More Specific

Missing the morning classes have dropped my grades from a B average to barely passing. — Very Clear and Specific (Very Low Abstraction)

want her to come into my room without knocking first. Instead, I hurt her feelings, and it led to a big misunderstanding."

In fact, abstract language is such a common source of confusion that it was immortalized in a classic episode of the sitcom *Friends*, when Rachel told Ross they needed to "take a break." Thinking they had broken up, he was devastated, drowned his sorrows in a bar, and ended up spending the night with another woman. When Rachel showed up the next morning to talk to him, though, he realized he'd misunderstood, and that she really wanted to work things out. Unfortunately, when she realized what he'd done, she felt betrayed, and then it really was all over (until a few seasons later, anyway).

How often do you find yourself using abstract language? Perhaps you've recommended that someone should be more organized, more responsible, or lead a healthier lifestyle. Or maybe you've asked a roommate to help more around the house, or suggested to a significant other that the two of you needed more variety in your relationship. Consider the various ways you could decrease the level of abstractions in your own language by replacing abstract terms with specific, concrete examples. For practice building this skill, turn to Activity 9.1 at the end of this chapter.

Relative Language

Now that we understand what abstract language is, let's examine two specific types of abstract language. The first is **relative language**, which refers to the use of words or phrases that "gain their meaning by comparison" (Adler & Towne, 2003, p. 181). In other words, relative terms will be interpreted in different ways by different people, based on each person's own experiences and preferences, which provide the basis for comparison. Have you ever taken a class, for example, that you heard was an interesting class, but when you took it you found it to be boring? Or maybe you saw a movie that you thought was excellent, but when you recommended it to some friends, they later told you it was awful. Other common examples of relative terms include beautiful/ugly, smart/dumb, nice/mean, fun/dull, and clean/dirty. When we use relative words to describe something, we run the risk of the other person misinterpreting our meaning, which in turn sets up a potential conflict. We can avoid this danger with the same solution that we used for abstract language: Give a specific, concrete description that states the facts, and let the other person form his or her own interpretation. Consider these examples:

> **Relative language** Words or phrases that "gain their meaning by comparison".

> **Relative statement:** "We won't stay for very long."
>
> **Descriptive statement:** *"We'll only stay for half an hour."*
>
> **Relative statement:** "I've been doing pretty well in school lately."
>
> **Descriptive statement:** *"I got two A's and two B's last term in school."*
>
> **Relative statement:** "Southern California weather is so boring!"
>
> **Descriptive statement:** *"The temperature in San Diego averages between 60 and 80 degrees year-round, and it's sunny 345 days of the year!"*

Relative language may be most risky when we are asking someone to do something. Ann provides this example: "When I left the house yesterday morning, I asked my husband if he would 'clean up a little.' When I got home, he'd cleaned the bathroom, which was nice, but the house was still really cluttered, and that was what had been bothering me. To be more clear, I should have said, 'Will you please put away your golf clubs that are in the family room, throw away the old newspapers, and vacuum the family room and the living room?'"

Static Language

A second type of abstract language is **static language**, or language that implies that a situation or person is always the same. For example, we might say that Shane is quiet, or that Tamira is obnoxious. In Chapters 5 and 6, we learned many ways that our behavior is influenced by situational forces, so we know that a person's behavior won't be consistent all the time. On the contrary, our behavior is influenced by our moods and other internal states, as well as by the people around us and our interpretations of a situation. In addition, you may also remember that we tend to assume that others' behavior is a result of their personality, rather than their situation, and this mistake promotes the conclusion that others' behavior is more consistent than it actually is.

> **Static language** Language that implies that a situation or person is always the same.

(Do you remember the term for this error in judgment? Think about it for a moment, then look at the bottom of the next page to see if you're right.)

Examples of static language abound. Like other types of abstractions, static language can be clarified with a specific, factual statement. Consider these examples, along with their more descriptive replacements:

Static language: "She has a hot temper!"

Descriptive language: *"Yesterday when we were talking about parenting, she raised her voice and pounded her fist on the table."*

Static statement: "That restaurant is terrible!"

Descriptive statement: *"When I went to that restaurant last week, I found a hair in my food!"*

Static statement: "Steven is lazy."

Descriptive statement: *"When we were at a barbecue last night, we ran out of aluminum foil, and Steven drove his car one block to the store instead of walking."*

These examples clearly show how our use of static language can mislead others about a person or situation. Like other types of abstractions, though, static language causes even bigger problems when we use it to express concerns or complaints to others. The situation only gets worse when, in our frustration, we commit the *fallacy of overgeneralization* (which, as you remember from Chapter 4, is when we exaggerate the frequency of a behavior, such as when we use the words "always" or "never"). Jenna provides this example: "Last week, my little sister refused to take out the trash, even though it was her week to do it. Frustrated, I said to her, 'You never do your share!' She got defensive, and we got into a shouting match about who did more around the house. It would have been better if I'd said, 'I noticed that the trash can is full. Have you been busy, or did you just forget to take it out?'" Jenna's analysis is especially good because, in addition to noting how she could have described her sister's behavior rather than overgeneralizing about it, she ended her description with a *perception-checking statement* (from Chapter 4) that shows empathy and recognition that her sister's mistake might have been unintentional.

As you read the section on static language, you might have noticed that some static statements also include relative language. The one about the restaurant, for example, uses the word "terrible," which we could interpret to mean bad food, bad service, uncomfortable environment, or something else unpleasant. It also used the word "is," which implies that the situation at the restaurant is unchanging. The more descriptive alternative clarifies what the speaker meant by "terrible" (the hair in the dish), and also specifies exactly when it happened. This illustrates the primary rule for overcoming abstractions: Replace abstract terms with concrete terms, and try to include a specific example that describes exactly *what* happened and *when* it occurred.

To build your own skills at identifying the various types of abstract language and replacing abstractions with descriptions, turn to Activity 9.2 at the end of this chapter.

LANGUAGE MUST BE RESPONSIBLE

PREVIEW QUESTIONS

(1) What do we mean by "responsible language"?

(2) What are the three components of an effective I-statement?

(3) Describe two additional important points about using I-statements effectively.

The second principle of effective communication is that language must be responsible: In other words, when we express our opinion, we must make it clear that it is an *opinion* and avoid presenting it as fact. We took the first step toward this principle in the previous section, when we learned how to replace abstract terms, which usually reflect opinions or judgments, with more concrete terms, which usually reflect the facts. The other key element in the language of responsibility involves taking responsibility for our own feelings, which may remind you of something you learned in Chapter 4. As you recall from that chapter, the **fallacy of causation** occurs when we blame someone else for our own feelings, such as when we say "You make me so mad!" Committing that fallacy has two negative outcomes: First, we feel helpless to change the feeling; and second, the other person feels blamed, which often leads to defensiveness. In Chapter 4, we learned how to use self-talk to reverse the first negative outcome of that fallacy; in this section, we will address the second.

> **Fallacy of causation** We blame someone else for our own feelings.

I-Language vs. You-Language

One of the biggest threats to positive relationship climates occurs when we have a complaint or concern. Perhaps you say to a friend, "You need to be more responsible," or tell a significant other, "You're getting on my nerves!" In either situation,

Answer to question on previous page: The *fundamental attribution error* is assuming that other people's behavior, rather than a situational factor, must reflect their personality.

the receiver may hear your message as criticism, which may feel like a threat to the relationship, which in turn may promote defensiveness in the receiver. This type of message is known as **you-language**, because it tends to cast blame on the other person. What can we do to avoid this? Are we supposed to keep quiet about our concerns? No! The remedy comes in the form of a type of language known as **I-language**, so called because it sends the message in a manner that takes responsibility for the impact the other person's behavior has on you, rather than simply scolding or casting blame.

> **You-language** Language that implies blame on the other person.

> **I-language** Language that takes responsibility for the impact the other person's behavior has on you, rather than simply scolding or casting blame.

The Three Components of an Effective I-Statement

Effective I-statements consist of three basic elements: a behavioral description, an emotional descriptor, and a consequence. Let's examine each element more closely. The **behavioral description** relies on the clear and specific descriptions we learned as alternatives to abstract language (including relative and static language). A behavioral description often works well at the beginning of the I-statement. If, for example, you are tempted to tell a significant other "You're too clingy!" the first step in replacing this you-statement with an I-statement is to describe exactly what the other person is doing that is bothering you. Using the word "clingy" is relative language, because your idea of clingy may not match theirs. Also, saying the person is "too" clingy implies a judgment, and no one likes to be judged—in fact, it's one of the things that contribute to a defensive relational climate. Instead, we need to replace the abstract language with clear and specific language, often by giving an example. For instance, you could describe a situation that illustrates what you mean by clingy without using that label, such as, "In the past week, you've called me several times a day." If you say this behavioral description in a sincere, nonaccusatory tone of voice, then you're letting the other person know what you've noticed, and by being so factual, you're describing it in a way with which they are unlikely to disagree. *This is a key element of an effective I-statement: If you exaggerate or use judgmental or abstract language in your behavioral description, you're setting yourself up for disagreement or even argument.* It is critical to describe the behavior in language with which the other person will agree, so that the person will "get on the same page" with you.

> **Behavioral description** Clear, specific, and factual description of a person's behavior.

Then, once the groundwork is laid with a *specific, nonjudgmental behavioral description,* you can go on to the second component, which is to state the emotion you felt when the behavior occurred—the **emotional description**. In doing so, be sure that you choose a word that accurately expresses how you felt, such as "I'm feeling *pressured,*" or, "I'm starting to feel a little *overwhelmed.*" Choosing a word that accurately describes your emotion fosters empathy in the other person, because it helps the person to know exactly how you felt. And as we learned in Chapters 4 and 8, empathy brings people closer together and

> **Emotional description** To state the emotion you felt when the behavior occurred.

FIGURE 9.2 | Examples of Emotion Words

afraid	concerned	exhausted	hurried	nervous	sexy
aggravated	confident	fearful	hurt	numb	shaky
amazed	confused	fed up	hysterical	optimistic	shocked
ambivalent	content	fidgety	impatient	paranoid	shy
angry	crazy	flattered	impressed	passionate	sorry
annoyed	defeated	foolish	inhibited	peaceful	strong
anxious	defensive	forlorn	insecure	pessimistic	subdued
apathetic	delighted	free	interested	playful	surprised
ashamed	depressed	friendly	intimidated	pleased	suspicious
bashful	detached	frustrated	irritable	possessive	tender
bewildered	devastated	furious	jealous	pressured	tense
bitchy	disappointed	glad	joyful	protective	terrified
bitter	disgusted	glum	lazy	puzzled	tired
bored	disturbed	grateful	lonely	refreshed	trapped
brave	ecstatic	happy	loving	regretful	ugly
calm	edgy	harassed	lukewarm	relieved	uneasy
cantankerous	elated	helpless	mad	resentful	vulnerable
carefree	embarrassed	high	mean	restless	warm
cheerful	empty	hopeful	miserable	ridiculous	weak
cocky	enthusiastic	horrible	mixed up	romantic	wonderful
cold	envious	hostile	mortified	sad	worried
comfortable	excited	humiliated	neglected	sentimental	

Source: From Looking Out, Looking In (with CD-ROM and InfroTrac) 11th edition by ALDER/PROCTOR/TOWNE. 2005 Reprinted with permission of Wadsworth, a division of Thomson Learning: www.thomsonrights.com. Fax 800-730-2215.

promotes supportive relational climates. Figure 9.2 suggests some words you can use to describe your feelings.

The third component of an effective I-statement is to state the **consequence** that behavior has or will have on your own thinking or actions, or in other words,

> **Consequence** The impact the behavior has on you.

why it is an issue for you. In this case, you might say, "I think our relationship might be moving too fast," or "That's why I haven't been returning your calls." This might seem to you to be stating the obvious, but remember the false consensus bias? Describing the consequence in this way helps the other person see the logical connection between his or her behavior and the consequence, and in turn helps the person understand why you're bringing this issue up.

By using all three of these elements, then, we've replaced the judgmental you-statement "You're too clingy!" with the more responsible and descriptive: "In the past week, you've called me several times a day. I'm feeling a little overwhelmed, and that's why I haven't returned your calls." Although the other person still may not be happy to hear it, he or she is much more likely to understand your feelings, and thus is less likely to respond defensively. Therefore, you have accomplished the

FIGURE 9.3 | Anatomy of an I-Statement

Behavioral Description (using clear, specific, and factual language)	In the past week, you've called me several times a day.
How you feel about it (using an emotion word)	I'm feeling a little overwhelmed;
State the consequence (the impact the other person's behavior has or may have on you)	that's why I haven't been returning your calls.

daunting task of expressing a concern, and you've done so in a manner that is honest, clear, responsible, and sensitive to the other person's feelings (see Figure 9.3).

While these three elements of an effective I-statement are fresh in our minds, let's consider a few more examples of how you-statements can be transformed into I-statements:

> *You-statement:* "You are so unreliable!"
>
> *I-statement:* "*You said you'd have my car detailed by this afternoon, but it still isn't done. I'm upset, because I have a potential buyer coming to look at it in 15 minutes.*"
>
> *You-statement:* "You're so self-absorbed!"
>
> *I-statement:* "*Jim, when we went to dinner last night, you talked about your basketball performance for almost an hour. I felt insignificant, and I wondered if you were interested in what's happening in my life.*"
>
> *You-statement:* "You always try to solve my problems!"
>
> *I-statement:* "*Yesterday when I told you I was late for work, you told me I should get up earlier. I felt frustrated, and I wondered if you thought I wasn't able to figure simple things out for myself. I'm worried that if this continues, I won't feel comfortable being open with you.*"

These last two examples illustrate two more important points about effective I-statements. First, in both situations the speaker was making a statement about an *ongoing pattern* in the relationship. In one, she'd noticed Jim frequently monopolizing their conversation with tales of his own life, and in the other, the speaker had noticed her partner habitually offering advice on simple issues. For the I-statement, though, the speaker chose to give just the most recent example, rather than reciting a list of examples, which would most likely raise defensiveness in the receiver. This illustrates the first important point: *It's unrealistic to expect one I-statement to be a cure-all for significant or ongoing relationship concerns. Instead, think of it as a conversation-starter*, or a method to bring up your concern that is most likely to lead to a productive and nondefensive discussion.

Second, did you notice how the last two examples ended? Both times, the speaker had a "consequence" that was fairly extreme. In the first case, she thought her partner didn't care about the goings-on in her life, and in the second, the speaker felt she was on the verge of just not talking openly with her partner anymore. Presenting these consequences as foregone conclusions, though, would raise defensiveness in the other person. Imagine if instead the last speaker had said, "I'm just not going to talk to you anymore!" This leads to the second key

I admire your strong decision-making in this time of peril, but you're making me feel like a terrible girlfriend and I may throw-up.

FIGURE 9.4 | What is wrong with this attempt at an I-statement? As you can see, effective I language is more difficult than it may seem!

point: *When we have a serious consequence that needs to be aired, we can soften it with a phrase such as "I'm worried that . . ." or "I'm wondering if . . . ."* By doing this, we transmit the gravity of our concern to our partner, but do so in a manner that feels less threatening, because it demonstrates that we haven't yet reached that conclusion. Thus, the receiver still feels some control over the issue, which is more likely to lead to a productive discussion.

Essentially, then, what we're accomplishing with I-language is communication that is balanced in power, and this balance in power is a critical factor in maintaining healthy relationships (see Figure 9.4). To start building your own I-language skills, turn now to Activity 9.3 at the end of this chapter.

Interim SUMMARY #1

Clear communication relies on four basic principles; thus far in this chapter, we have discussed two of them. First, language must be clear. Clear language uses words that are concrete and specific, rather than vague or abstract. Often, we use abstract language unknowingly, assuming that the other person will know what we mean; this is the false consensus bias, which can contribute to serious misunderstandings. The two most common types of abstract language are relative language and static language. Relative language uses words that are only meaningful if the listener knows exactly what you are comparing them to—good or bad, fun or boring, and so forth. Static language implies that the situation is always the same, such as when we say "School is boring," which implies not only that it is always boring, but also uses a relative term (*boring* means different things to different people). Abstract language can be remedied by using more concrete, descriptive terms, or by giving a specific example of what you are talking about. For example, you might say, "I have trouble staying awake in class when the professor just lectures for an hour without taking questions."

The second principle of effective communication is that language must be responsible. Responsible language avoids the fallacy of causation by taking responsibility for the impact someone else's behavior has on our own emotions and/or thinking. It also incorporates the concrete and specific language we use to avoid abstractions. This type of statement is called an I-statement, and it includes three components: a specific description of the situation, a statement of how you felt when it happened, and the consequences the situation has for you. For example, rather than telling your roommate, "You never do anything around here!" (which would promote defensiveness and interfere with a productive relationship with the roommate), you could say, "I've noticed that you've had your school stuff on the kitchen table for the last week. I'm feeling stressed, because there's no room to eat at the table, or for me to do my own work."

Incorporating these principles into our communication patterns will help build supportive and trusting relationships.

LANGUAGE MUST BE CULTURALLY SENSITIVE

PREVIEW QUESTIONS

(1) What do we mean by high-context and low-context communication?

(2) What are elaborate, exact, and succinct communication styles?

(3) What is the difference between instrumental and affective communication, and what are four specific communication differences that can arise from these diverse styles?

(4) How do the worldviews of men and women typically differ, and how do these differences in perspective promote communication differences?

Thus far in this chapter, our discussion of communication has relied on the assumption that both communicators share the same culture—specifically, mainstream Western culture. In our increasingly diverse world, this assumption is often false. To truly become effective communicators, then, we must become fluent in multiple communication styles. Fortunately, fluency in communication styles is much easier to develop than fluency in another language! Let's examine the basic types of cultural communication styles and consider how we can adapt our language to fit each type.

High- and Low-Context Cultures

In Chapter 1, you learned about individualism and collectivism, a framework used to illustrate the core value system of the many cultures of our world. Individualist cultures, you recall, value independence and individual achievement most highly, whereas collectivist cultures value interdependence and needs of the group over individual goals. An additional concept that is relevant to our discussion of culture is the relativity of time: *Monochronic* cultures, which are often individualist in nature, value time efficiency most highly, whereas *polychronic* cultures, which are often collectivist, value interpersonal relationships most highly. Weaving these two cultural concepts together helps us understand the next cultural concept we will address: high- and low-context cultures.

> **High-context communication**
> Communication that relies more heavily on attention to contextual details and less on explicit language to transmit its message.

As we learned in the first few pages of this book, *context* refers to the various elements of the situation, which can include the relationship between the communicators, their past history, the location and topic of their discussion, and conversational goals, just to name a few. **High-context communication**, then, is communication that relies more heavily on attention to these contextual details and less on explicit language to transmit its message. Essentially, high-context communication is indirect (abstract), rather than direct, trusting that the listener will be able to interpret the vague language of the speaker based on an in-depth understanding of the context.

If this is confusing to you at this point, don't worry! The probable reason for any confusion is that this is completely at odds with the principles of clear communication we've just been learning. Remember that even though we're including cultural context in our general study of human relations, we are learning communication primarily from a Western, or individualist perspective. And the reason is simple: A majority of the people with whom we communicate in the Western world operate on this level, so we're focusing on this "mainstream" approach. To be effective with the diverse people we'll meet in life, however, we also need to learn about alternate approaches, and high-context communication is an important one.

Now, back to the indirect language style of the high-context culture. An interesting example of this comes from sociologist Sumiko Iwao. In her book, *The Japanese Woman: Traditional Image and Changing Reality* (1993), she notes the value placed on intuitive understanding in Japan. The ability to understand someone without words is a sign of intimacy between two people. In fact, speaking openly about deep feelings in Japanese culture diminishes those feelings. Instead, *isshin denshin* is prized, a term that means "traditional mental telepathy" (Matsumoto, 2000). Other high-context cultures include Arab and, to a lesser degree, Mediterranean cultures.

High-context, or indirect, communication is the preferred style of language in most collectivistic cultures, which makes perfect sense given the high value placed on group harmony in collectivistic society. Communicating in this "verbal shorthand" reinforces the closeness of the relationship between the two speakers. Also, indirect communication allows a speaker to communicate a subtle message, which in some cases might save a listener from embarrassment. "Saving face" is a high priority in collectivist cultures, and that goal is supported by indirect communication.

Imagine, for example, that a friend borrowed some money from you and didn't pay it back by the agreed-upon time. You need it repaid in order to register for your classes, and the deadline is just a few days away. Rather than directly asking your friend about the money, which might embarrass him, a communicator in a high-context culture might say something like, "Tuition has gotten so expensive." Assuming that the borrower is also a high-context communicator, we can be fairly sure he would read between the lines and understand the unspoken meaning of your statement. By communicating indirectly, you've gotten your message across without shaming your friend, and harmony between you has been preserved.

Low-context communication, on the other hand, is much more direct and relies on clear, concrete, and explicit language. Communicators in low-context cultures do not pay the close attention to contextual detail that their high-context counterparts do; instead, they depend on a speaker to "say what you mean, and mean what you say." Other common American phrases that typify this approach to communication include "Don't beat around the bush" and "Get to the point." Surprisingly, perhaps, American culture isn't the lowest-

> **Low-context communication** Relies on clear, concrete, and explicit language.

context culture; Scandinavian, German, and Israeli cultures have been found to rely on even more direct communication (Harris, 1974, Gudykunst & Ting-Toomey, 1988) (see Figure 9.5).

FIGURE 9.5 | High- and Low-Context Cultures

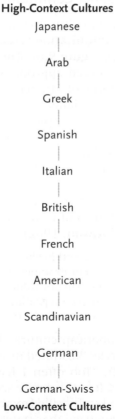

High-Context Cultures

Japanese

Arab

Greek

Spanish

Italian

British

French

American

Scandinavian

German

German-Swiss

Low-Context Cultures

Source: Samovar & Porter, 1997. Used with permission.

High Value on Achievement and Status
(traditional male worldview)

High Value on Equality and Connection
(traditional female worldview)

FIGURE 9.7 | Gendered Worldviews

That said, our study of male and female communication differences begins with their differences in worldview (Tannen, 1986). Men tend to see the world in a hierarchical way, focusing on status and power, and employing aggression to compete their way to a higher status. Women prefer an egalitarian viewpoint that focuses on equality and a balance of power, and employs cooperation in the goal of achieving empathy and harmony in relationships (Figure 9.7). Can you see how each of these viewpoints would naturally lead to the divergent styles of instrumental and affective communication? A worldview that focuses on getting ahead must rely on task-oriented (instrumental) communication to be as efficient as possible. An equality-oriented worldview, on the other hand, relies on mutual understanding (affective communication) to maintain good feelings in a relationship.

Sociolinguist Deborah Tannen, in her book *You Just Don't Understand* (1990), details some of the ways that these divergent communication styles "trickle down" into specific types of misunderstandings in communication between women and men. Following is an overview of some of the most common differences. (Remember as we go over these that, once again, we are making generalizations; the traditional "men's style" discussed will apply to many men, but not all, and similarly, the traditional "women's style" will apply to many women but not all.)

Problem-Solving vs. Empathy   Tannen notes that men's conversation revolves around problem-solving, whereas women's is an effort to develop empathy. This ties directly into the instrumental/affective dichotomy, and the result is often frustration when the two styles collide. Imagine, for example, a man and a woman having a discussion about her new job that is all the way across town. She says something like, "I didn't realize traffic was so bad on that road—it took me 45 minutes to get there, and I was almost late on my first day!" According to Tannen, he might respond with the suggestion, "You need to get up earlier, then, so you can be sure to get there on time." Feeling annoyed, she might retort, "Duh! Like I can't figure that out for myself!" and withdraw, wondering why she ever bothered trying to talk to him at all. He, on the other hand, might feel rejected and confused—after all, he was just trying to help!

An analysis of this conversation through the lenses of gendered communication styles reveals that each person meant well, but because their partner's communication goals were different from their own, they ended up at odds with each other. She was sharing her information about the traffic in an attempt to establish a connection with him; essentially just making conversation, because that's how you build a relationship in a world of empathy. For his part, he offered a solution to what he thought was her dilemma, because in his world, the purpose of communication is to accomplish tasks, which includes problem-solving. They misunderstood each other's intentions: She thought he was trying to control her, which is directly at odds with her value of equality, and he didn't know what to think when she rejected his perfectly logical solution.

Details vs. Big Picture   A second common misunderstanding in communication between men and women centers around the issue of details vs. big picture. Who tends to give and expect more details? Yes, you guessed it—women. And that makes sense, argues Tannen, because details are necessary in order to truly *understand* or empathize with a person. On the other hand, in a world where efficiency and problem-solving are the goals, the "big picture" is what's most important; details are not only distracting, but slow things down.

Consider this example: A man and a woman sit down to have dinner together at the end of the day. She asks, "So, how was your day?" "Fine," he replies. Not satisfied with the brevity of his response, she follows up with, "Well, what did you do?" "I worked," he says with a questioning look on his face, "like I always do." This she already knew, so she still feels as though she has no sense of what his day was like. Persisting, she says, "Isn't there a new employee that you're training? How is that going?" "It's going just fine!" he replies with a bit of exasperation. "Well," she shouts back, "tell me about it—what is this person like?" "There's nothing to tell," he exclaims, "just a normal person, doing a normal job!" "Oh!" she declares, "Why won't you ever talk to me?" Stunned, he looks at her and says, "I *am* talking to you—what do you want?"

What does she want? She wants details! She wants him to paint a verbal picture for her that will allow her to imagine what his day was like—not just whether it was good or bad, but what was typical and/or unusual about it, how he felt about things that happened or didn't happen, what was interesting or dull, and so forth. These details help her empathize with him and feel more connected. His failure to understand what seems like her constant questioning is based in his "big picture" philosophy—it was good or it was bad, and that's all that's important. For her part, the frustration she feels when he doesn't respond to her questioning results from her lack of understanding how, in his world, details only cloud the bottom line.

Asking for Help   A third gender-based difference in communication found by Tannen in her research is the acceptability of asking for help. When we consider what we already understand about the relationship between gendered worldviews and the communication styles associated with them, it stands to reason that in a world where achievement and status is valued highly, asking for help would send the message that someone else must know more than you, and thus be smarter (and ultimately have a higher status). This is why men are often uncomfortable asking for help. Women, on the other hand, are taught to believe that asking for help is perfectly acceptable: After all, it builds a connection between you and the person who is helping, and that's what it's all about in that world.

Most people don't have too much trouble thinking of examples of this in their own life. In fact, this gender difference is so common that stand-up comics sometimes even use stories about it in their routines. One common example has to do with asking for directions to a new store, restaurant, or other location. When they're having trouble finding it, women are much more likely to stop at a corner gas station and ask the attendant for help than men are. And who hasn't heard a story (or lived it!) about assembling a new bicycle, shelving unit, or other type of product for which "some assembly is required"? Women tend to rely on the manual, whereas men scoff at the thought! Once again, the reason is simple: In a world of achievement, a person gains a real sense of accomplishment from solving a problem all by himself. And while this is not *un*important in the traditional female world, the potential connection formed by working with someone else on a problem overrides the need for individual achievement.

Use of Questions   Men and women also use questions differently, according to Tannen. For men, a question is just that: a question that needs to be answered. Women, though, use questions more indirectly—specifically, to make requests or to state needs. For example, in the workplace, a female supervisor might say to a subordinate, "Can you have that project done by Friday?" If her subordinate is male, he might think about her request, consider the other things he has to do by Friday, then say something like, "Probably not by Friday, but I'll have it done by Tuesday." To him, this answer reflects his honest viewpoint, and he states it in an attempt to be cooperative and straightforward. If the supervisor doesn't understand the different ways men and women use questions (and why), she might feel insulted, disrespected, or think her authority was being questioned. Because even though she asked a question, what she really meant was, "I need this project done by Friday."

Why didn't she just say that, then? The answer can again be traced back to the differences in gendered worldviews. For a woman, in the pursuit of equality, it's much more polite to ask if the project can be done by Friday—her assumption, of course, is that the listener will understand that's what she needs, and agree. This particular difference in communication styles is exacerbated by gender stereotypes and expectations in general: Women are (traditionally) supposed to be polite. Thus, if she says, "I need that done by Friday" in an assertive manner, she risks being labeled demanding, domineering, or just plain mean.

Men, though, have different expectations placed upon them. Traditionally, they are supposed to be assertive and strong, so a person would expect that if (as a supervisor) he needed something done by Friday, he would say, "I need it done by Friday." Moreover, if he said, "Can you have that done by Friday?" when he really *needs* it done by then, he'd risk being labeled as spineless, weak, or ineffective. In this way, we Westerners truly are guilty of a double standard in our expectations of clear communication.

This gender difference in communication styles can be found in personal relationships as well as in the workplace. Consider the woman who says to her male partner, "When you get a minute, could you take out the trash?" Two hours later, she notices that he hasn't taken out the trash, and she gets annoyed and says to him, "Why don't you respect me enough to do something around here once in a while!"

Describe the reason for the misunderstanding in the preceding situation.

How could you replace her you-language with a more responsible I-statement?

Overcoming Gendered Differences in Communication Even in the "liberated" 21st century, traditional patterns of gender socialization, which directly influence gendered communication, are alive and well. So, to communicate effectively, we must treat these gender differences like any other cultural element in communication. We must first acknowledge that they exist; second, do our best to understand the value systems from which they derive; and finally, recognize that both styles are equally valid and make perfect sense in the context of their divergent value systems. Doing this will help us respect communication styles that differ from our own, which is key to a positive communication climate.

In respecting different communication styles, we must also let go of the need to make others conform to our own style. This is harder than it might seem, since our styles are so firmly rooted in us. Instead, when we find ourself confused and frustrated by a miscommunication with someone of the opposite gender (or someone of the same gender who might have the opposite worldview), we need to think about how their gender role might be influencing the way they are communicating and/or interpreting what we are trying to communicate. Then we can be more understanding and forgiving, and think about how we might modify our message so that it is "heard" accurately. Sometimes this involves "speaking the other language"—or, in other words, a woman forgoing her need for details in a particular situation, or a man restraining himself from offering solutions to a woman who is discussing a concern.

Finally, for this type of cross-cultural communication to be effective, we need to share what we've learned about it with others in our life. That way, we can work together toward overcoming the differences, rather than one person bearing sole responsibility for it. A skill we learned in Chapter 5 is especially useful for this: the skill of perception-checking. For example, if a man and his female friend are talking, and she is telling him about some problem she is having, rather than immediately offering advice, he could use perception-checking to find out what she does want. "Are you asking me what I think you should do, or are you just venting?" he might ask. Similarly, when he asks how her day was and she starts to give him a minute-by-minute description, she shouldn't feel too annoyed if his eyes start to glaze over! Instead, she can either give him what he needs—the bottom line of how her day was—or, if she needs to get the details off her chest, she can ask for that: "I know you might've been hoping for a short answer, but I need to get some things off my chest—can you humor me?" When both partners are working together to overcome these differences, requests like this are easily understood, and differences can even become a source of "inside jokes" that bring the two people closer together.

To understand the specific ways gendered communication affects your own life, turn to Activity 9.4.

Interim SUMMARY #2

The third principle of effective communication is that language must be culturally sensitive. There are several ways researchers have categorized cultures with the goal of understanding similarities and differences among them. Low-context cultures, for example, rely heavily on the spoken word and place a high value on the first two principles of communication we have learned (clear and responsible language). High-context cultures are quite the opposite, focusing instead on the nonverbal cues of the situation, as well as the relationship and shared knowledge between the two communicators. As a result, high-context communicators prefer more indirect styles of communicating, the accurate interpretation of which reinforces the connection between the communicators.

Cultural communication styles can also be grouped according to the degree of verbosity of the speech used by each culture, or according to the goals of the communication. Elaborate language is very colorful and wordy; exacting language says what needs to be said—no more and no less; and succinct language uses few words. Instrumental communication uses language to accomplish tasks, and affective communication uses language to build relationships.

Although men and women are certainly more alike than they are different—there is much less than 1% difference in our DNA—identifying the differences helps us become more effective communicators. In general, men in traditional Western cultures are socialized to be dominant, assertive, and to see the world and their role in it as a race to the finish line. Therefore, men tend to use communication in instrumental ways—to accomplish tasks and to maintain status and power. Women are traditionally socialized to be cooperative and kind, and to see their role in the world as one that promotes harmony and equality. Therefore, women tend to use communication in affective ways—to build relationships, make people feel comfortable, and maintain harmony.

Research by Deborah Tannen has identified several specific ways these gender differences affect communication between the sexes. Women tend to give and expect more detail in communication, because details promote empathy and understanding. Men, conversely, tend to focus on the big picture and problem-solving in communication, because these goals promote task accomplishment and achievement. Also, women are more comfortable than their male counterparts asking for help when they need it. Finally, women tend to make requests or demands in the form of a question, which in their mind is polite, but can lead to misunderstandings if the receiver doesn't recognize that it is indeed a demand masquerading as a request.

As with all other cultural differences in communication that we are studying, it is imperative to recognize that we are speaking in generalities: These principles will be true for a majority of people, but not for all. To overcome gender differences in communication styles and goals, we can educate our friends and family about the differences, so that we can work together to overcome them and take turns accommodating each other.

LANGUAGE MUST BE CONGRUENT: THE IMPORTANCE OF NONVERBAL COMMUNICATION

PREVIEW QUESTIONS

(1) What is meant by "congruence" in language, and what three cautions must we be aware of in understanding nonverbal communication?

(2) Describe eight different types of nonverbal communication, along with how each one affects your relations with others.

(3) Give some examples of cultural differences in nonverbal communication.

Thus far, we have focused our study of language in human relations exclusively on verbal language, or what is spoken. A large portion of the messages we send when communicating, though, is transmitted nonverbally. In fact, research has found that nonverbal communication accounts for at least 65% of the interpretation of a message, and may even be as high as 90% (Burgoon, 1994). In this section, we will explore some of the most common types of nonverbal communication, as well as how culture affects the meaning and interpretation of nonverbal cues.

Before we examine the specific types of nonverbal communication, though, a few notes of caution are necessary. *First, nonverbal signals in communication are often unintentional, and also unconscious.* In other words, many times we are unaware of the nonverbal cues we are sending in our communication. Therefore, they have great power to either reinforce our spoken message, or to undermine it. Increasing our awareness of the types of nonverbal cues we use, as well as when we tend to use them, can help us work toward more congruence (similarity) between our spoken and unspoken language. It can also help us be more accurate interpreters of others' communication to us.

The second important note is that *one single nonverbal cue cannot be reliably interpreted to mean the same thing across situations.* For example, we often hear that crossed arms signal impatience, or a "closed" mind. This may sometimes be the case, but they can also mean that the person is tired, or it may just be the way the person likes to stand. When interpreting nonverbal cues, then, we need to look for *patterns* of cues, rather than a single cue, to more accurately decode the unspoken message.

Third, we must also recognize that other cultures may have different interpretations of the same nonverbal cue: For example, as we learned in Chapter 5, looking someone in the eye is a positive characteristic in Western culture, but considered a sign of aggressiveness or disrespect in many other cultures. Cross-cultural proficiency is a very complicated task, because there are so many differences in nonverbal cues across cultures. In fact, there are far too many to include in this book. Instead, we will present the major types of nonverbal cues for Western culture, then address some of the more common cultural differences that we are likely to encounter.

Types of Nonverbal Communication

Body Posture and Orientation   When you were growing up, did anyone ever tell you to "stand up straight"? Most of us have heard this before. In Western culture erect posture signals confidence and honesty, whereas someone who is slouching is often assumed to lack confidence or self-esteem. When a person's posture is *rigidly* erect, though, it may convey tension. Generally, then, an upright but relaxed posture is considered the best way to convey confidence in our culture. Interestingly, it also signals status: Research has found that in communication between two people of unequal status (for example, a boss and employee), the higher status person can be identified by her relaxed posture, whereas the lower status person can be recognized by his more rigid posture. The next time you're in a crowded public place, observe some of the interactions of others and see if you can spot the higher status person by the nonverbal cues.

Body orientation The direction your body is facing relative to those with whom you are interacting.

Body orientation refers to the direction your body is facing. This may seem like a less obvious aspect of nonverbal communication than posture, and since we are often not aware of it, it has the power to send revealing messages about how we feel when communicating with someone. When we are facing a person directly—not just with the head, but with the body— it conveys a sense of directness and genuine interest in the conversation and the other person. On the other hand, if we are trying to end a conversation or get away, we might continue looking at a person with the head and face, but turn the body away to signal that we need to leave.

Touch   In general, touch is used by a communicator to help build rapport or trust with the person with whom they are speaking. Research supports its effectiveness in many situations. For example, waiters in restaurants get higher tips when they lightly touch the patron on the arm or shoulder (Crusco & Wetzel, 1984). Touch also increases cooperation, as found in several studies where research subjects were asked to sign a petition or complete some other small act. They were more likely to agree to do so when they were touched lightly by the requestor.

In some cases, though, touch is unwanted, and in these situations it decreases trust and comfort. Consider, for example, when it comes from someone with whom you are not interested in developing or pursuing a relationship. Unwanted touch from a higher status person in the workplace is one form of sexual harassment.

Gender has a significant impact on patterns of touch, because men and women in Western culture are socialized to use touch differently. For women, touching indicates warmth and intimacy, whereas men use touch to assert status or power.

One fascinating aspect of touch as a nonverbal signal is demonstrated in Arab and Middle Eastern culture. In much of that region, smell is an important element of nonverbal communication. Just as the personal space norms are closer in these regions than they are in the United States, one of the benefits afforded by closer personal space is the ability to smell the other person.

> To the Arab, to be able to smell a friend is reassuring. Smelling is a way of being involved with another, and to deny a friend his breath would be to act ashamed. [Additionally], the Burmese show their affection during greeting by pressing mouths and noses upon the cheek and inhaling the breath strongly. The Samoans show affection by juxtaposing noses and smelling heartily. (Almaney & Alwan, 1982, p. 17)

Physical Appearance   Western culture places much importance on physical appearance. For better or worse, people who are more attractive (according to cultural standards) are assumed to have a wide variety of positive characteristics: They are judged to be friendlier, more intelligent, easier to get along with, more caring, and to have higher self-esteem, to name a few of the most common assumptions about attractive people. This finding is so widely supported by research that it has a name. In social psychology it is called the "What Is Beautiful Is Good" phenomenon. This affects communication in that better-looking people are assumed to be more honest. They are also more likely to receive promotions in the workplace, and to get more dates as singles.

The way we dress and adorn ourselves also influence the messages we send. People in professional environments, for example, are taken more seriously when they dress in a manner that conforms to the expectations of their profession. In the corporate environment, people attain greater credibility when they wear business suits or other tailored attire, whereas someone who dressed that way to go to a football game would look foolish. Muslim women wear the hijab to symbolize their faith, and the Masai women of Kenya must wear specific jewelry to indicate their marital status; to do otherwise risks harsh punishment.

Critical Thinking QUESTION   Consider the way you present your physical appearance, including dress, hairstyle, body adornments such as jewelry and body art, and so forth. In what ways do you think your physical presentation influences others' perceptions of you, your own sense of confidence, and ultimately your communication with others?

Personal Space   In Chapter 5, we learned about personal space norms and their impact on perception. All of that applies to nonverbal communication as well, because perception plays a major role in how we decode messages. (Take a quick look back at that section of Chapter 5 to review.) Added to the personal space expectations discussed in that chapter, it is also important to note that personal space boundaries are related to a person's status, with higher status people commanding greater amounts of personal space (Henley, 1977). Higher status individuals are also more likely to invade a person's space. Finally, gender affects reactions to personal-space invasions, in that men are prone to responding aggressively when their space is invaded, whereas women are more likely to accommodate the intrusion (Fisher & Byrne, 1975).

Paralanguage and Silence We also discussed talking rules in Chapter 5 (again, take a quick look back at that section to review the main points). **Paralanguage** is communication that is verbal, but wordless, such as a person's tone of voice, sighs, murmurs of agreement or dismay, volume, inflections, and rate of speech (fast or slow). With our tone, we can convey warmth and sincerity, uncertainty, confidence, anger, or a wide range of other messages. In fact, marriage researcher John Gottman (whose work we will examine in more detail in the next chapter) has found that a negative tone of voice, such as sarcasm or derisiveness, is one of the most powerful signals of dissatisfaction among married couples.

> **Paralanguage**
> Communication that is verbal, but wordless.

There are many other examples of the impact of paralanguage on messages. People who speak more rapidly are assumed to be more knowledgeable, people who speak hesitantly are interpreted as being less sure of themselves, and people who talk loudly may seem angry or obnoxious. We also use inflections to emphasize what we consider to be the most important part of a message ("I'd *never* go there!"). And recently, gender studies have noted women's tendency to raise the pitch of their voice near the end of a sentence—for example, a student calling her professor on the phone might say, "Professor Hamilton, this is your student, Maddi Salazar?" Her tone indicates a question, but clearly she isn't asking if her name is correct! Instead, her raised pitch near the end of the sentence signals the unspoken words, "Do you know who I am?" and/or "Do you have time to talk to me?" This is congruent with the traditional female worldview that values connection, but it can be misunderstood if one doesn't know this is the basis of that paralanguage. Instead, it might be misconstrued as lack of confidence.

Eye Contact and Facial Expressiveness Have you ever heard the expression, "If looks could kill!" or "The eyes are the windows to the soul"? These age-old phrases underscore the importance of how we use our facial features to transmit unspoken messages. In Chapter 5, we learned how rules of eye contact vary culturally (once again, take a quick look back to review), and we can add to that a wide variety of facial expressions. Would you believe that research has found more than one thousand different expressions that can be formed from various combinations of facial movements (Ekman, 1971), ranging from the simple to the complex? A wrinkled nose, for example, can indicate disgust; a compressed-lips smile combined with raised eyebrows can signal hope for a longshot. Our facial expressions can be subtly modified to send messages of anger, love, invitation, challenge, or scorn. Take a moment now to look around your environment. Zero in on one person's facial expression, and ask yourself what it is signaling.

Gestures Gestures, which are movements of the hands, arms, or other parts of the body, fall into several categories, and their meaning is most often unique to each culture. One category, known as *emblems,* is made up of gestures that have a direct verbal translation—for example, in the United States, spreading the first two fingers into a V-shape is widely recognizable as the "peace" sign. It was originally used to mean "victory," though, and if you turn your palm backwards instead of forward, in some countries it is an insult. Similarly, pointing your first finger toward your temple (the side of your forehead) means you are smart in the United States, but that you are stupid in parts of Asia and Europe!

Another category—illustrators—is gestures that do not function on their own, but serve instead to underscore the importance of what a person is saying. Some cultures tend to use illustrators a great deal, whereas others use them only minimally. Italian and other southern Mediterranean cultures make great use of illustrators: They might wave their hands or arms around to emphasize their point, pound on a table to show anger, or hit themselves on the head to illustrate their stupidity in a situation. At the other end of the spectrum, Japanese culture is much more reserved in its use of illustrators. Both emblems and illustrators are generally used unconsciously.

Physical Environment   We often think of nonverbal communication as something we do with our bodies, but it includes the way we structure our physical environment as well. The way we decorate our homes, the cars we drive, and the places we hang out all give important clues about who we are, and thus influence our communication and relations with others. Retail establishments use research in this area to influence their patrons. One interesting study found that the speed of the music played in a restaurant influenced the pace at which diners ate. When no music was played, diners averaged 3.23 bites of food per minute. That figure went up to 3.83 bites per minute when slow music was played, and 4.4 bites per minute when fast music was played. Other studies have confirmed that slower music and softer lighting tend to create more relaxed moods, whereas faster or louder music and brighter lighting tend to speed people up. This is useful information in communication; we can use the physical environment to increase the chances of attaining our communication goals.

Critical Thinking QUESTION   Think about the living room (or similar space) in your home and how the seating, technology (television, etc.), and other items are arranged. What type of communication does this physical environment promote, and what messages does it send to people?

Before going on, turn to Activity 9.5 to examine your own uses and interpretations of nonverbal communication.

Culture and Nonverbal Communication

As stated earlier, nonverbal communication is unique to each culture; therefore, to try to list all the differences is far too great a task for this short section of a book. Instead we will look at some general differences that have been documented among different categories of culture. Table 9.1 lists some interesting differences in the way certain nonverbal cues are interpreted cross-culturally.

Contact Cultures   Cross-cultural research has found that, worldwide, certain cultures tend to be much more expressive than others in their communication

TABLE 9.1 | Examples of Cross-Cultural Differences in Nonverbal Cues

Greetings	Korea	*Bowing. The bow is lower and lasts longer with a person of higher status; bows between friends are generally short.*
	Kenya	*Handshake with right hands. The lower status person also, with his left hand, grips his own right forearm during the shake.*
	Saudi Arabia	*Men kiss each other on both cheeks.*
	Sri Lanka	*Hands are placed palms together, at chin level, while the person bows and states a traditional greeting*
Obscenities	Australia	*Making a "V" with the first two fingers, with the palm facing inward (this applies also in England)*
	Guatemala	*Making a fist, with the thumb between the first two fingers (applies also in other South and Central American areas)*
	Peru	*Mimicking a pistol with each hand and pointing them at someone from waist level*
	Iran	*Rubbing your open hand down your face, as if stroking a beard*
Closeness	United States	*Crossing the first two fingers*
	China	*Clasping the index fingers of each hand together*
	Thailand	*Pressing palms together and placing them against a cheek*
	Japan	*Tapping the tips of the index fingers together*

Contact cultures Tend to engage in more open contact with each other and use nonverbal cues to signal warmth, closeness, and availability.

behaviors. These cultures have been labeled **contact cultures** (Hall, 1966), because they tend to engage in more open contact with each other and use nonverbal cues to signal warmth, closeness, and availability more than their "low-contact" counterparts. They touch each other more often, maintain closer personal space boundaries, and are generally more expressive with their nonverbal behaviors. Contact cultures include the Arab regions, North Africa, southern European countries, eastern Europe and Russia, and Latin America. Interestingly, these cultures are mostly located in warm climates. Cross-cultural researchers have theorized that warmer climates allow people to be outside and interact with each other year-round more than cold-climate regions, and thus they have developed more expressive communication patterns.

Low-contact cultures include the regions of northern Europe, Great Britain and the United Kingdom, North America, and virtually all Asian cultures. A study of university students (Anderson, Lustig, & Anderson, 1990) even found a relationship between the latitude (north/south) of the university and the degree of touch avoidance of its students.

Individualism–Collectivism (IC) Cross-cultural research into nonverbal dimensions of communication has also found differences between individualistic and collectivistic cultures. People in collectivistic cultures, for example, tend to coordinate their schedules and actions with those in their family group (such as having dinner together, making efforts to be on similar work schedules), whereas individualists in the same family are much more likely to do as they please, coming and going according to the demands of their own personal schedule. This pattern has even been found in the singing and dancing patterns of collectivistic cultures—their dance styles, for example, exhibit much greater synchrony than the dance styles of individualistic residents.

Social norms in individualistic cultures promote greater freedom of emotional expression than the norms in collectivistic cultures. This makes sense, argue cultural researchers, because in collectivistic cultures people have built-in networks of affiliates (family, friends, etc.), whereas in individualistic countries, the individual bears primary responsibility for creating and sustaining networks of relationships. Thus, individualists must express emotions more freely as they work toward developing their desired relationships. Collectivists are more likely to inhibit their emotional expression unless it supports the needs of the group.

Power Distance (PD)   The cultural dimension of power distance is also a useful lens to identify some cultural differences in nonverbal communication. As you recall from Chapter 1, high PD cultures tend to prefer greater status differences among people and work to maintain these status differentials. Low PD cultures prefer equality to status differentials.

In terms of nonverbal communication, high PD cultures encourage emotions that promote and maintain status differences. For example, it would be appropriate to show positive emotion to a high-status person and negative emotion to a low-status person. Also, low-status individuals in high PD cultures have been found to smile more often than subordinates in low PD cultures, perhaps in an effort to keep relations positive with higher status people. Finally, people in low PD cultures are less sensitive than those in high PD cultures to the impact of their paralanguage on others. Americans, for example, high in individualism, tend to speak more loudly and assertively than people in many other cultures—but since we are also low in PD, we tend *not* to be aware of this impact on different cultures, and thus risk being thought of as insensitive or even obnoxious.

Interim SUMMARY #3

The fourth and final principle of effective communication is that language must be congruent; in other words, the nonverbal cues we use—often unconsciously—must support, rather than undermine, the words of our message. There are many types of nonverbal language, including body posture and orientation, touch, physical appearance, personal space, paralanguage, eye contact and facial expressions, gestures, and physical environment. All of these types of communication combine to create literally thousands of different types of messages we can send nonverbally. In fact, nonverbal cues make up between 65% and 90% of the interpretation of a message. Thus, we must learn to become more aware of our own nonverbal cues, so that we can use them more consciously to support our verbal messages.

Nonverbal communication varies widely from culture to culture. Contact cultures tend to be more expressive nonverbally than low-contact cultures, and also tend to be located in warmer climates. Differences in the usage patterns of nonverbal communication have also been found for the individualism–collectivism dimension, as well as the power distance continuum.

CHAPTER TERMS

Abstract language
False consensus bias
Relative language
Static language
Fallacy of causation
You-language
I-language
Behavioral description

Emotional description
Consequence
High-context
  communication
Low-context
  communication
Elaborate language
Exacting communication

Succinct communication
Instrumental
  communication
Affective communication
Body orientation
Paralanguage
Contact cultures

ACTIVITY 9.1

ABSTRACTION LADDERS

Using the ladder model of abstract language, build ladders that show increasingly concrete language for the following examples.

1. Highly Abstract   We need to make some changes in this relationship!
   Less Abstract   _____

   _____

   _____

   Clearer   _____

   _____

   _____

   Clearest   _____

   _____

   _____

2. Highly Abstract   That is a hard class.
   Less Abstract   _____

   _____

   _____

   Clearer   _____

   _____

   _____

Clearest _____
_____
_____

3. Highly Abstract (Write your own example) _____
_____
_____

Less Abstract _____
_____
_____

Clearer _____
_____
_____

Clearest _____
_____
_____
_____

ACTIVITY 9.2

IDENTIFYING AND REPLACING ABSTRACT LANGUAGE

INSTRUCTIONS: *For the following statements, first identify whether the statement uses relative language, static language, or both. Then correct the problem by replacing the abstract language with language that is clearer and more specific. (Hint: Using specific examples is a great way to be clear!)*

1. *My job stinks!*   Relative   Static   Both   (circle one)

   Rewrite more clearly: _____
   _____

2. *I had a great weekend!*   Relative   Static   Both   (circle one)

   Rewrite more clearly: _____
   _____

3. *That was an excellent movie!*   Relative   Static   Both   (circle one)

   Rewrite more clearly: _____
   _____

4. *She is so rude!*   Relative   Static   Both   (circle one)

   Rewrite more clearly: _____
   _____

5. Write your own: _____

                            Relative   Static   Both   (circle one)

Rewrite more clearly: _____

_____

ACTIVITY 9.3

PRACTICING I-LANGUAGE

INSTRUCTIONS: *Rewrite each of the following you-statements with more responsible I-language. For best results, imagine yourself in a specific situation where you might say this, and then use the situational elements to provide a behavioral description, a statement of emotion, and the consequences. You may also work on these statements in groups if your instructor allows it.*

1. I can't take your whining anymore!

   _____

   _____

2. You're so sweet!

   _____

   _____

3. We need to come to some agreement about our workload.

   _____

   _____

4. Can you please just be responsible for once?

   _____

   _____

5. I'm worried.

   _____

   _____

6. I don't think we communicate very well.

   _____

   _____

7. You make me really happy.

   _____

   _____

8. I've had it with that class.

_____

_____

9. It seems like we never agree on what we want to do.

_____

_____

10. I don't think you appreciate what I do around here.

_____

_____

11. I can tell you really respect me—thanks.

_____

_____

12. (Write your own)

_____

_____

13. (Write your own)

_____

_____

14. (Write your own)

_____

_____

REFLECTIONS

Now that you've worked with I-language, in what ways, situations, or relationships do you think it will help you? Also, is there a specific aspect of it that still is troublesome for you? If so, explain.

_____

_____

_____

_____

_____

_____

—— **ACTIVITY 9.4** ——————————————

GENDERED COMMUNICATION IN YOUR LIFE

1. The text describes two different worldviews that tend to apply to men and women. Which applies to your own worldview and communication goals: the traditional "male" viewpoint, or the traditional "female" viewpoint? Give an example to illustrate your answer.

_____

_____

_____

_____

_____

_____

_____

2. The text also describes several specific differences in gendered communication (big picture vs. details, problem-solving vs. empathy, use of questions, asking for help). Choose any two of these that especially relate to your own life and relationships, and for each one, describe a specific situation where this difference led to a misunderstanding.

   a. Describe the situation:

_____

_____

_____

_____

_____

Name the difference (e.g., use of questions, etc.)

_____

_____

How it led to a misunderstanding:

_____

_____

What you could do differently next time to overcome the potential misunderstanding:

_____

_____

b. Describe the situation:

_____

_____

_____

_____

_____

_____

_____

Name the difference (e.g., use of questions, etc.)

_____

_____

How it led to a misunderstanding:

_____

_____

_____

_____

What you could do differently next time to overcome the potential misunderstanding:

_____

_____

3. Reflections: Now that you have learned about these gender differences in communication and examined how they have affected your own human relations, what are your thoughts and/or feelings about it?

_____

_____

_____

_____

_____

_____

4. Exchanging thoughts with classmates: Discuss your examples and reflections with several other class members in a group situation. Then, based on what you hear from your classmates, write one additional thought here that you think is interesting and/or important.

_____

_____

_____

_____

_____

_____

_____

── **ACTIVITY 9.5** ──────────────────────

YOUR NONVERBAL COMMUNICATION:
What Works, and What Doesn't

INSTRUCTIONS: *The text discusses eight different types of nonverbal communication, along with examples of each, and ways that they are typically interpreted in Western culture. For this exercise, examine your own nonverbal cues, as well as those of others, to increase your awareness of the impact of this type of language on our relationships.*

1. First, apply each of the types of the nonverbal communication to your own life by giving a real example of how you or someone who was communicating with you used it, along with its impact on the message.

   a. Body Posture or Orientation:

   _____

   _____

   _____

   b. Touch:

   _____

   _____

   _____

   c. Physical Appearance:

   _____

   _____

   _____

   d. Personal Space:

   _____

   _____

   _____

   e. Paralanguage and Silence:

   _____

   _____

   _____

    f. Eye Contact and Facial Expressiveness:

_____

_____

_____

    g. Gestures:

_____

_____

_____

    h. Physical Environment:

_____

_____

_____

2. Now, pair up with one of your classmates, and go to a public place (a public place on campus is fine, such as the cafeteria). As unobtrusively as possible, look around and (together) identify a group of two or three people who are talking together. Observe the group for about 5 minutes. Each of you (privately) form some interpretations about status, relationships, and so on, based on the nonverbal communication that you observe. Once each of you has formed your own opinions, share your viewpoints with your partner. In what ways were your interpretations similar? In what ways were they different?

    a. Identify the group of people you observed (for example, you might say "We observed a group of three people, sitting at a table together with their books open. It looked like they might be studying together. There were two women and one man." _____

_____

    b. Record your impressions about who had the most power in the group, what the relationships were between them, and so forth, along with the specific nonverbal behaviors you saw that led you to your impressions.

    Nonverbal behavior: _____   Impression: _____

    _____   _____

    _____   _____

    Nonverbal behavior: _____   Impression: _____

    _____   _____

    _____   _____

    Nonverbal behavior: _____   Impression: _____

    _____   _____

    _____   _____

    Nonverbal behavior: _____   Impression: _____

    _____   _____

    _____   _____

Nonverbal behavior: _____   Impression: _____

_____   _____

_____   _____

c. Share your findings with your partner.

Did you come to any similar interpretations? If so, describe one.

_____

_____

_____

_____

Did you have any different interpretations? If so, describe one.

_____

_____

_____

_____

CONFLICT AND CONFLICT RESOLUTION

Peace is not the absence of conflict, but the presence of creative alternatives for responding to conflict.

—DOROTHY THOMPSON

CONFLICT: MYTHS, MISPERCEPTIONS, AND FACTS

PREVIEW QUESTIONS

(1) How do we define interpersonal conflict, and what are the most important aspects of the definition?

(2) Discuss three myths about conflict, and how they can be overcome.

What's the first thing that comes to mind when you think of conflict?

"Fighting."

"It makes me tense."

"Arguments."

"Not getting along."

"Yelling, then crying, then silence."

The above responses are a sampling of what students typically reply to this question. What did you think of? For many people, *conflict* conjures up negative images, like the ones listed above. Indeed, even Webster's dictionary begins its definition of conflict with "a fight, battle, or struggle . . . ." Furthermore, we typically think of conflict as a situation in which there is only one winner. And when the conflict is between two people who care about each other, or two colleagues in the workplace, the investment both parties have in the relationship makes the outcome of the conflict pretty significant, a fact that fuels the conflict with emotion.

Does this all sound depressingly familiar? If it does, hang in there! The issue of conflict is not nearly as grim as we tend to think it is—in fact, it can even be positive. If you're skeptical, that's okay—most of us have some pretty strong preconceptions about conflict. Just keep an open mind as you read on, and this chapter will help you see conflict in a brand-new light.

Let's begin by defining **interpersonal conflict** as a situation in which two or more people in an interdependent relationship perceive themselves to have different viewpoints or goals, which are incompatible. A couple of aspects of this definition merit further attention: first, by *interdependent relationship*, we mean that both or all parties have a stake in continuing the relationship, or that they depend on the other person in some way. Second, note the last part of the definition: *perceive themselves* to have different viewpoints or goals. This is an important point, because conflict often occurs based on misunderstanding or miscommunication, rather than true differences in goals or viewpoints. So, if we can clarify our goals early, the conflict often diminishes, or even disappears altogether. In doing so, we may also find that goals that seemed incompatible may not necessarily be. We'll discuss an excellent method to do this later in this chapter.

> **Interpersonal conflict**
> Situation in which two or more people in an interdependent relationship perceive themselves to have different viewpoints or goals, which are incompatible.

Before we embark on our study of conflict styles and resolution methods, we must first debunk a few common myths about conflict. By doing so, we can reduce some of the tension people often feel when dealing with conflict, and thus put ourselves in a better position to approach it effectively and with realistic expectations.

Myth #1: Healthy Relationships Have Little or No Conflict

This is simply not true. Numerous studies of friendships as well as intimate relationships have demonstrated that virtually all relationships have conflict. Think about it: What are the odds that any two people are going to agree on everything, all the time? It's a little silly when you look at it that way, isn't it—especially in our individualistic culture, where we are encouraged to have our own opinions and follow our own paths. Conflicts can be large or small, ranging from issues such as how to spend money or time, to whether there is a right way to load the dishwasher. One study of friendships found that virtually *all* of the participants acknowledged conflicts in their relationships with each other (Samter & Cupach, 1998). And marriage researcher John Gottman, who is the leading researcher in the United States on the dynamics of happy relationships, has consistently found that there is *no* relationship between the amount of conflict in a relationship and the overall health of the relationship. Healthy relationships have just as much conflict as unhealthy relationships. The key lies in how we deal with the conflicts, which takes us to our next myth.

Myth #2: Conflict Is Always Destructive

Looking back at the responses at the beginning of this chapter, it is clear that many people equate conflict with negative outcomes. Fortunately, research has demonstrated that this is untrue also. In fact, conflict can actually be constructive, or helpful, to a relationship. One interesting study of relationship development studied couples who had just had their "first big fight (FBF)" and found that "survivors" of

Danger   Opportunity

FIGURE 10.1 | Chinese Character for Crisis

the FBF experienced a number of benefits, including a greater sense of mutual commitment to the relationship (Siegert & Stamp, 1994). Dealt with constructively, conflict also helps us clarify our own needs and values, understand more about the needs and values of the other person, and develop increasingly effective conflict resolution skills, which can then be applied to other relationships and situations. Simply put, we get better with practice. Most importantly, perhaps, constructive conflict increases trust in a relationship: Each time we get through a difficult situation intact, it strengthens our commitment, increases the sense of "being in this together," and reminds us of how much we are valued by the other person (Figure 10.1).

Myth #3: In Any Conflict, There Can Only Be One Winner

This myth may be more applicable in individualist cultures that emphasize competing, rather than collectivist cultures that emphasize harmony and cooperation. When we accept this myth, though, it increases the distance between the persons having the conflict and creates a "win-lose" perspective that can easily become a self-fulfilling prophecy. In a sense, it makes us fight harder to defend our own viewpoint, at the expense of hearing the other person's viewpoint, so that we "don't give an inch." Instead, recognizing that conflict can be resolved in ways that support all parties' needs or goals can help us reframe the way we perceive conflict and work harder to finding creative ways to make this happen.

Overcoming the Myths

Recognizing the degree to which we buy into these myths is an essential first step in improving our own patterns of conflict resolution. The study previously discussed of couples who survived their first big fight (FBF) revealed that the biggest differences between the survivors and nonsurvivors were in their perceptions and expectations of conflict. "The survivors generally believed that a successful relationship required a joint effort in problem-solving, some sacrifice from both parties, and the ability and/or willingness to adjust one's own ways of doing things in order to mesh with the partner's way of doing things" (Siegert & Stamp, 1994, p. 357).

Remember that, just like other myths, these myths gain their power from their place in our *unconscious* (rather than our conscious awareness). Once we

TABLE 10.1 | Myths and Facts about Conflict

MYTH	FACT
Healthy relationships have little or no conflict.	Virtually all relationships have conflict; the closer two people become, the more they share with each other, which increases the opportunity for conflict.
Conflict is always destructive.	Conflict can be constructive; it can improve relationships by increasing commitment, trust, and mutual understanding.
A conflict can have only one winner.	Managed constructively, conflicts can have outcomes that support the needs of all parties.

acknowledge the ways each of us has let these myths influence our attitudes toward conflict, we can then work toward noticing when they start to do it again, and using self-talk (learned in Chapter 4) to remind ourselves that we're acting on a myth rather than the facts. In this way, we can learn to overcome the myths and replace them with realistic expectations.

After reviewing this section and Table 10.1, turn to Activity 10.1 to explore how myths about conflict have affected your own relationships.

PERSONAL CONFLICT STYLES: THE GOOD, THE BAD, AND THE UGLY

PREVIEW QUESTIONS

(1) Describe the two main factors in the dual-concern model of conflict.

(2) How do these two factors combine to create five specific conflict styles?

(3) What are the strengths and weaknesses of each of the five conflict styles in the dual-concern model?

(4) What is passive-aggressive behavior, and why is it so harmful?

Think about the last time you had a conflict with someone at work or in your personal life. How did you handle it? Did you keep quiet and hope it would work itself out, or did you confront it head on? More than 40 years of research on how people handle conflict has revealed that, although the particular situation can influence how we respond, each of us has a preferred **conflict style** (e.g., Blake & Mouton, 1964; Rubin, Pruitt, & Kim, 1994; Thomas & Kilmann, 1974). In other words, we each have a tendency to respond to conflict in a manner that is fairly consistent over time and across situations. Our personal conflict style has been shown to be influenced by our personality, the patterns we observed growing up in our own family environment, and our larger cultural perspective. We'll discuss these influences in more detail a little

Conflict style An individual's typical method of responding to conflict.

later, but first let's develop an understanding of what the basic conflict styles are, and which one tends to be your preference.

Before continuing, complete the Conflict Style Inventory in Part 1 of Activity 10.2.

The Dual-Concern Model (The Good and the Bad)

Overall, research has found that there are five general conflict styles. These conflict styles are characterized by two distinct factors: **assertiveness**, or the degree to which we are interested in pursuing our own goals and interests; and **cooperativeness**, which is the degree to which we are interested in maintaining the relationship or supporting the goals of the other person. Because these two concerns—for self and other—have been found to be at the heart of conflict style, it is known as the **dual-concern model** (Blake & Mouton, 1964; Pruitt & Rubin, 1986). Our general interest—low or high—in each of these two distinct goals combines to form our personal conflict style.

As you read about each one, keep in mind that there are two important uses for this information. First, try to determine which style tends to be the one you use the most, and what is effective and ineffective in that pattern. Second, recognize that different situations often call for different styles; so, to maximize your effectiveness at dealing with interpersonal conflict, consider how and when you might use each of these different styles.

Accommodating Let's examine each of these conflict styles in more detail. The **accommodating** style is characterized by a high degree of interest in the relationship, and a low degree of concern about one's own interests. If this is your style preference, you probably prefer harmony to conflict, want to be liked, and perceive conflict to be damaging to relationships. As a result, when conflict arises, you tend to sacrifice your own needs or goals in order to preserve the relationship—at least, that's what you *think* you are doing. Although this style is certainly useful in certain situations, when it is used too much the accommodator often ends up feeling used or unappreciated, which ultimately breeds resentment in a relationship. Clearly, then, frequent accommodating only gives one the illusion of preserving the relationship—in the long run, it actually creates an imbalance of power, which is destructive.

In what situations can accommodating be an effective strategy? In long-term relationships, whether business or personal, there are times when one person's desire for something is much stronger than the other person's competing desire. Imagine, for example, that you and a close friend are getting together this Friday night. You've talked about several options, including a movie, going to a huge party you've heard about, or just hanging out. You're somewhat interested in the

Assertiveness The degree to which we are interested in pursuing our own goals and interests.

Cooperativeness The degree to which we are interested in maintaining the relationship or supporting the goals of the other person.

Dual-concern model A framework for understanding conflict style that is based on the degree of assertiveness and cooperativeness that motivates an individual's response to conflict.

Accommodating Characterized by a high degree of interest in the relationship, and a low degree of concern about one's own interests.

movie, since you've heard it's pretty good, and you aren't that much of a partier. Your friend, though, really wants to go to the party. She's been really stressed out lately with 18 credits at school and extra hours at work, and she thinks that a huge party with lots of people and music will be a good way for her to destress and blow off some steam. In this case, her interest in going to the party is much stronger than your interest in the movie. Also, you can catch the movie another time, and this *is* supposed to be the party of the year. Assuming that there have been times in the relationship when *she* accommodated *you*, it makes good sense to support her needs instead of yours in this situation. This type of reciprocity helps preserve a sense of equality and mutuality in relationships.

Dominating   The **dominating** style is based on a high degree of interest in one's own goals, and a low degree of interest in the relationship or goals of the other person. This is the direct opposite of the accommodating style and is the most confrontational style in the dual-concern model. Dominating behaviors may range from aggressive tactics such as threats and insults, to blaming, to such nonverbal tactics as stonewalling, which is withdrawing from the conversation either physically (leaving the room, for example) or psychologically (giving "the silent treatment"). Stonewalling is destructive because by ignoring the other person, you are taking his or her power away and essentially communicating that the person is irrelevant. Dominators tend to be goal-oriented, competitive, and perceive conflict as a situation in which only one person can win and others must lose. This set of beliefs drives them to pursue winning without regard to its impact on the relationship or the other person.

> **Dominating** Based on a high degree of interest in one's own goals, and a low degree of interest in the relationship or goals of the other person.

Given the "win-lose" nature of the dominating style, is there ever a time when it is an effective strategy? Communication expert David DeCenzo (1997) suggests that dominating may have a positive outcome in the workplace if used by a legitimate authority figure when a difficult decision must be made quickly. In this type of situation, perhaps the best solution is one that is unpopular, and the supervisor bears the responsibility for implementing that decision even if it means others won't like it. In addition, it may be used (for better or worse) in situations where the other person seems likely to give in (Pruitt & Rubin, 1986).

Avoiding   The **avoiding** style is characterized by a low degree of interest in pursuing one's own goals, as well as a low degree of interest in supporting the relationship or the other person's goals. People who routinely avoid conflict may do so because their experiences with conflict have been negative (a behavioral explanation), or because they have a lower biological tolerance for the emotional stress that conflict often carries with it (a personality/emotional stability explanation). Either way, when a potential conflict arises, avoiding may take one of several forms.

> **Avoiding** Characterized by a low degree of interest in pursuing one's own goals, as well as a low degree of interest in supporting the relationship or the other person's goals.

One common type of avoiding behavior is to *downplay the significance* of the issue. Take, for example, a married couple having a conflict about whether to spank their children: The wife thinks it is okay when necessary, but the husband has strong concerns about its potential long-term impact.

If he were an avoider, he might tell himself, "It isn't that big of a deal—what do psychologists really know, anyway? The media just tends to blow everything out of proportion." Alternatively, he might choose a *distracting* technique, perhaps by going outside or shutting himself into his office with a video game when his wife is going to spank one of the children. He might even *deny* the actual existence of the conflict, perhaps by abdicating the role of authority figure to his wife and focusing on carrying out a different role in the family. All of these strategies enable a person to avoid confronting a conflict head-on.

If you are individualistic, you're probably noticing how wrong this type of behavior seems—it flies in the face of our cultural messages about asserting ourselves. Surprisingly, though, research on the long-term effects of an avoiding pattern are mixed. On one hand, there is a well-documented connection between suppression of negative emotions and decreased immune-system activity. In other words, people who do not express their negative emotions may suffer health consequences (Petrie, Booth, & Pennebaker, 1998). So, if avoiders are suppressing their negative emotions, this may be a negative effect.

We can't be sure, though, whether avoiders are suppressing their negative emotions about the conflict, or actually avoiding the negative emotions by avoiding the conflict. If that is the case, their conflict style may be health-promoting. Marriage researcher John Gottman, for example, has discovered that partners who withdraw from conflict often do so as a reaction to a rapidly rising blood pressure—essentially, they are calming themselves down by withdrawing. One of his additional findings is that some happily married couples deal with conflict via avoidance, and if both partners exhibit this style, it can work for them.

Other psychologists feel compelled to point out the long-term risks of avoidance in a relationship. By never confronting conflict, you never build your conflict resolution skills and, eventually, the odds are you'll encounter a conflict that can't be dealt with effectively by avoidance. At that point, the avoider has much less chance of getting through the conflict effectively than someone with more experience in confronting conflict. Also, remember the benefits of constructive conflict resolution: increased awareness of your own goals and feelings, increased awareness of your partner's goals and feelings, and an increased sense of mutuality and commitment in the relationship. Avoiders miss these relationship-sustaining benefits.

There may, however, be certain situations in which avoiding is an effective strategy. Perhaps the benefit of engaging in the conflict is minimal—for example, if it is a temporary issue, or one that won't have much of an impact on you or your needs. Conversely, the risk of engaging in the conflict may be too high, such as if your conflict is with your boss at work and others who have had conflict with her have been fired. If you need your job and can deal with the consequences, sometimes avoidance is a reasonable choice.

Compromising The fourth conflict style is the **compromising** style, characterized by a moderate degree of interest in one's own goals, and an equally moderate degree of interest in the relationship and/or goals of the other person. Compromisers value harmony as well as individual satisfaction and pursue solutions that are agreeable to both parties. Typically, these solutions take the

Compromising Characterized by a moderate degree of interest in one's own goals, and an equally moderate degree of interest in the relationship and/or goals of the other person.

form of "meeting in the middle," or each person getting part of what they want, but giving up a little something as well in the interest of a mutually satisfactory outcome. The obvious advantage of this style is that each party gains some satisfaction; the disadvantage is that each also has to make some sacrifice.

Examples of compromise abound. For example, imagine you and friend are going to dinner: You want Mexican food, but your friend wants something Italian. Instead of going to a restaurant specializing in either Mexican food or Italian food, you might choose a "bistro" or "bar and grill" type of restaurant that has some kind of quesadilla or burrito on the menu, but also a pasta dish like fettucine. The sacrifice is that it might not offer as many choices or be as authentic as a restaurant that specializes in one type of food, but the benefit is that you both get something fairly close to what you wanted. Or consider the roommates who are having a conflict about getting a pet. One really wants a cat or small dog, but the other is adamantly opposed to the idea. A compromise might involve getting a pet, but either keeping it in the pet-lover's room or outside so that the other roommate doesn't have to deal with it. This solution gives each of them part of what they want, but also requires that they make some sacrifice for the sake of equality.

The required sacrifice is the element of compromise that keeps it from being the best overall conflict style. There is a better option, which we'll discuss in a moment. Overall, though, compromising is a conflict style that values equality in a relationship, and it can be an effective solution in certain situations. When time is short and a solution must be reached, compromise is often the best we can do. Also, if the issue isn't one that goes to the core of the relationship or that repeatedly surfaces in the relationship, compromise is often just fine.

Integrating   The final conflict style in the dual-process model is the **integrating** style, in which a person has a strong interest in pursuing their own goals, and an equally strong interest in supporting the relationship and/or the goals of the other person. Integrating goes beyond compromising, in that the goal of integrating is for each person to get *all* of what they want, without the sacrifice that comes with compromise. This may sound like an awfully high standard, and it definitely requires more time and effort than compromise. It tends to be motivated by the belief that conflict is normal, healthy, and necessary for personal growth as well as relationship development and satisfaction.

> **Integrating** Characterized by a strong interest in pursuing one's own goals, and an equally strong interest in supporting the relationship and/or the goals of the other person.

This positive view of conflict fuels integrators' response to conflict: When they encounter it, they openly disclose their viewpoints, listen carefully to others' viewpoints, and put a great deal of effort into developing a creative solution that meets both parties' needs completely (Pruitt & Carnevale, 1993).

Are you skeptical? If you are, you are probably not alone. True integration requires a well-developed set of communication and conflict resolution skills, which many people lack, as well as a high level of creative thinking (see Figure 10.2). However, remember that you have already begun to work toward developing many of these skills, including active listening and principles of effective verbal and nonverbal communication. You've also learned many of the psychological concepts that influence people's behavior. A little later in this chapter, we will explain how these principles and concepts can be combined into something called

Pas

As y
mod
depe
that
is in

outs
othe
thing
thing
reall
it ca
tain
who

with
passi
or ur
exam
perha
than
every
phon
about
she a
the r

P
passi
realiz
back,
and u

W
of the
out m
cultur
expec
behav
Wome
seem i
havio
comm
or con

Pa
conflic

Who knew that Grizzlies liked to play poker?

FIGURE 10.2 | Creative problem-solving can play a key role in effective conflict resolution.

the "win-win" conflict resolution method, which is a technique geared specifically toward collaborative solutions to conflict. At that point, you'll have the basic tools necessary to try integration in your own life. So, given what you've learned already, integration isn't out of reach.

Just so we have a true understanding of how integration differs from compromise, let's go back to the example above of the roommates with the conflict about getting a pet. If the issue were really important to their relationship and they had the time and skills to do it, they could try an integrated approach. To do this, they'd each have to openly talk about their needs as well as their concerns, and actively listen to each other. As they do this, they might discover that what is motivating one or both of them is something different from what they originally thought. For example, maybe the roommate who wants a pet realizes (as she talks about why she wants a pet) that what's really motivating her is her awareness of the many pets who are strays or unwanted, and so her first thought was to adopt one from the local humane society. Her primary goal, then, was to help animals rather than to share her life with one. With this new understanding, she might realize that she could do more good by volunteering at the humane society, rather than adopting a single pet.

As you can see from Figure 10.4, a person who has high collectivistic values but low individualistic values would be said to have an **interdependent self-construal**. Conversely, a person with high individualistic values but low collectivistic values would have an **independent self-construal**. These two identities are similar to the concepts of individualism/collectivism that we've already studied. The other two identities are the new concepts. Some people have both high individualistic values *and* high collectivistic values: *They value pursuing their own goals, but place an equally high value on connection to their social group*. This is known as a **biconstrual identity**. Finally, a person could have little sense of individuality, as well as little sense of connection to the larger group. This is called the **ambivalent identity**.

> **Interdependent self-construal** High collectivistic values but low individualistic values.

> **Independent self-construal** High individualistic values but low collectivistic values.

> **Biconstrual identity** Value pursuing their own goals, but place an equally high value on connection to their social group.

> **Ambivalent identity** Little sense of individuality, as well as little sense of connection to the larger group.

In examining whether these four types of self-construals were related to conflict style, researchers noted several major findings. First, independents, interdependents, and biconstruals all used integrating and compromising more than ambivalents. Also, biconstruals were found to use a wider variety of conflict styles than any other identity group. This makes sense, given their strong connection with both self-goals and relationship goals. At the other extreme, ambivalents had a very narrow range of styles. In fact, they tended to use the passive-aggressive style more than any other group. Researchers suggested this may be the result of a less well-defined identity: If you don't feel a sense of individuality or a sense of connection to others, you might feel less secure, and consequently feel it necessary to use passive-aggressive conflict behaviors rather than the more solution-focused choices.

Culture and Conflict Style: The Bottom Line

The research findings presented here are indeed complicated. But stay with it; in our increasingly multicultural world, the reality is that we are going to be interacting with a wide variety of people who will have different cultural backgrounds and identities. The more information we have about how culture and identity influences conflict style and other communication behaviors, the better our chances of getting along well and interacting effectively with our diverse communities.

Interim SUMMARY #2

Personality, as measured by the Big Five inventory, is related to conflict style. Four of the five conflict styles have unique personality trait combinations.

Culture and cultural identity have much more complicated connections with conflict style. First, it is important to note that collectivist cultures assign different meanings to avoiding and accommodating than their individualist counterparts. The importance placed by collectivists on group harmony and concern for others' feelings promotes a positive outlook on avoiding and accommodating, rather than the negative outlook seen by individualists.

The most progressive approach taken to examining the relationship between culture and conflict style involves the concept of self-construal, which describes a person's identity based on their sense of individuality as well as their sense of connection to others. Of the four self-construals, biconstruals (who have a strong sense of individuality as well as a strong connection to others) employ the widest variety of conflict styles, making them potentially the most effective across a variety of conflict situations. Ambivalents, conversely, tend to rely on passive-aggressive behavior in conflict situations.

Understanding the complexities of culture's impact on conflict style is critical to effectively interacting with the diverse population with which we live.

REDUCING DEFENSIVENESS IN CONFLICT RESOLUTION

PREVIEW QUESTIONS

(1) Describe six common types of defense-arousing communication, along with a more supportive alternative for each one.

(2) What is the most effective type of response when someone is criticizing us and the criticism is accurate? How should we respond when it is not accurate?

(3) When criticism is unclear, or you don't understand how it is relevant to the other person, what are several options for responding nondefensively?

(4) What is an effective nondefensive response style that can be used in many different situations?

We began this chapter by debunking some common myths about conflict to prepare for a more realistic approach toward conflict resolution. Our second step was to develop a solid working knowledge of the various conflict styles, so we can recognize that different people tend to approach conflict in different ways, and also so we could increase the number of strategies available to us in any given conflict situation. We now move on to the third step in our study of conflict resolution—reducing defensiveness—which will help us create less threatening environments when we do engage in conflict. And the more you can reduce defensiveness in conflict situations, the better your chances of resolving the conflict in a manner that is satisfying to all parties.

In Chapter 8, we learned about relational climate, which is the degree to which a person feels either supported and understood (a supportive climate), or judged and misunderstood (a defensive climate). The authentic listening skills we learned in that chapter, as well as the verbal and nonverbal communication skills we learned in Chapter 9, all contribute greatly to creation and maintenance of a supportive climate. In listening supportively, we signal to the other person that we care, which increases trust. By giving feedback responsibly (through use of I-language, for example), we signal respect to the other person, and also do what we can to keep them from feeling judged, which also builds trust. In this section, we will add two final components to those skills that will be the "icing on the cake" in terms of our ability to keep defensiveness at a minimum in our relationships, so that we can enjoy the benefits of a truly trusting and supportive relational climate.

Reducing Defensiveness in Others

When I ask my students, "How many of you have problems with defensiveness in your relationships—either you are frequently defensive, your partner is, or you both are?" at least 80% of the class raise their hand. Defensiveness is extremely destructive to relationships—when one person gets defensive, it's easy to lash out or withdraw, either of which is likely to put the other person on the defensive, and then off you go into what feels like the land of no return! This pattern has been termed a **defensive spiral**: One negative comment tends to be reciprocated, then each provokes another, getting worse as you go along, and the downward spiral that is created is very difficult to turn around (Wilmot, 1987). Fortunately, some excellent techniques have been developed specifically to reduce defensiveness, both in others and in ourselves.

> **Defensive spiral** One negative comment tends to be reciprocated, then each provokes another.

Reducing defensiveness in others is an area of research led by communication expert Jack Gibb (1961), who spent a number of years observing communication in groups to determine which types of comments promoted defensiveness and which did not. Gibb found that the defense-arousing types of comments could be summarized into six categories. He also identified ways that each type of comment could be rephrased to send a more supportive (less defense-arousing) message. Let's examine each of these categories and consider which tend to be the biggest problems for each of us.

Evaluation vs. Description   The first defense-provoking category is when we use language that evaluates or judges another person. We talked about this in Chapter 9: **Evaluative language** is also known as you-language. Examples are statements such as, "You're such a penny-pincher," "You need to take better care of yourself," or "That was a dumb thing to do." This type of message implies that something is wrong with the other person, which makes him or her feel less safe and ultimately less trusting in that relationship.

> **Evaluation** Language which evaluates or judges another person.

> **Description** Fact-based, nonjudgmental description of the other person's behavior.

The remedy for evaluation is **description**. Does this remind you of anything you learned in the last chapter? Yes—I-language. As you recall, an essential component of a good I-statement is a fact-based, nonjudgmental description of the other person's behavior. The you-statements in the last paragraph, for example, could be revised into these more descriptive statements: "I noticed that you flinched when the waiter brought the check at dinner last night"; "I'm worried that you've been eating fast food every day lately"; or "I saw the dent in your new car where you ran into that bus." All of these statements simply acknowledge a fact by describing it; in many cases, you'd follow up the statement with other components of I-language, like how you felt about it and/or why you're concerned.

Certainty vs. Provisionalism   Gibb's second category describes a situation in which a person implies that she is "the last word" on a subject, that her opinion is the only important one, or that she's made up her mind based on what she already knows and nothing you can say will change it. This is what Gibb called **certainty**, and as you know if you've been on the receiving end of this type of statement, it tends to create defensiveness in the recipient. Imagine, for example, that you're looking for your first job. You are going to apply at a cool new store in the mall. You're telling your friend about it, and your friend says, "They're not going to hire anyone without retail experience—why are you wasting your time?" Essentially, your friend sends a message that he is the last word on the subject, and any thoughts you have about the issue are irrelevant.

> **Certainty** A defense-arousing message that signals closed-mindedness.

Certainty messages can be replaced by **provisional** ones, which instead imply that there may be more to the situation than you know, or acknowledge that not all situations are the same. Really, isn't that almost always the case? In the previous example, your friend could instead say, "Wow—good for you! Are you concerned that they'll want someone with experience, or did the ad say they were willing to train?" This message retains its honesty by asking about the experience component, but comes across as more supportive by recognizing that experience may not be a requirement in this situation.

> **Provisionalism** A supportive message that signals open-mindedness.

Control vs. Problem Orientation   The third category tends to surface in situations where we are working with another person or people in some type of collaborative effort. It might be a school or work project, dividing up the household chores with roommates, or figuring out how you and your partner are going to afford the tuition increase at school. The defense-arousing approach basically tells the other person what to do, or sends a **controlling** message in some other way. For example, in a school project, a controller might say, "I'll do the first part; Ted, you do the graphics; and Misha, you write the last section." The speaker might feel good about this, but the other two people probably won't like it much.

> **Control orientation** Making decisions for other people.

The defense-reducing alternative is to take a collaborative, problem-focused approach (a **problem orientation**). Instead of sending a message that "I'm the smartest, so I'll make the decisions!" it signals respect for others and places a value on equality. For the school project, a person might say, "How do we want to divide this up? I'm terrible at graphics, so that would be my last choice—what parts are you guys interested or not interested in?" This is much more likely to keep relations positive in the group.

> **Problem orientation** Working collaboratively with partners to share decision-making.

Strategy vs. Spontaneity   The defense-arousing behavior called **strategy** refers to communicating in a way that is meant to manipulate the other person, or influence him or her indirectly to do or say something. It also refers to people who seem to have "hidden agendas"—they're after something but they aren't being completely

> **Strategy** Communicating in a way that is meant to manipulate the other person, or influence them indirectly to do or say something.

honest about it. This promotes defensiveness because it goes right to the heart of trust: In individualistic cultures, we rely on directness as a signal of trust, so if someone isn't direct, it seems as if they have something to hide, which increases suspicion and puts a person on the defensive.

This category is a little more difficult to recognize than the other categories are. In face-to-face situations, strategy is often more apparent in the nonverbal element of communication, or in what a person *doesn't* say, than in the actual words. It also is more likely to show up in a pattern over time with a particular person, rather than in one single interaction. For example, Cathy, one of my students, talked about her sister's use of strategy. The sister routinely asked Cathy how she was doing in school, what she was doing in her spare time, and so forth, and gave the impression that she was genuinely interested. Cathy responded by revealing quite a bit to her sister over time. Later, she found out that her sister was using some of what she learned against her when she talked to their parents. When Cathy found out, she felt really betrayed, and she didn't trust her sister much after that.

There are other, shorter-term examples. A person who needs help moving might ask a friend, "Hey, do you still have that nice truck?" Then, when she says yes, the strategic communicator follows up with, "Can I borrow it to move some stuff this weekend?" Or have you ever had someone say to you, "If I asked you a personal question, would you answer it honestly?" This is almost guaranteed to make the listener a little wary! Instead, Gibb recommends a more direct, or what he calls spontaneous approach. You could replace the first example with, "I'm moving this weekend—could I possibly borrow your truck for some of the big stuff?" As for the second example, if it's a sensitive issue, it's a sensitive issue, and beating around the bush is probably only going to make it worse. Try to wait for the right time and place, then just ask, "Could we talk about the previous relationship you were in?"

Neutrality vs. Empathy

This category involves communicating genuine interest in the other person. When a person seems disinterested, Gibb calls it **neutrality**.

> **Neutrality** Apparent lack of concern or feeling, sending a message that the other person is unimportant.

Neutrality, or apparent lack of concern or feeling, sends a message that the other person is unimportant, which creates a disconfirming or defensive climate. Take, for example, the daughter who is talking to her mom about a fight she had with her boyfriend. As she is talking, her mom doesn't respond much, either verbally or nonverbally. Eventually Mom shrugs and says matter-of-factly, "I told you not to get involved with him; you aren't right for each other." This response is likely to leave the daughter feeling misunderstood, and less likely to trust her mom with her feelings in the future.

As we learned in Chapter 4, empathy is when we imagine ourselves in the other person's position and how they might be feeling. Research has demonstrated that empathy is an important factor in building healthy relationships. Several of the listening responses we learned in Chapter 8 could be used to do this. A supportive response by the mother might be, "I'm so sorry you're having problems, honey." Even better would be a paraphrasing response, such as, "You sound more upset than I've heard you in a long time; are you worried that this is the end of the relationship?" Either of these responses would let the daughter know that her mom is really listening, cares about her, and is trying to understand what she's going through.

Superiority vs. Equality   The final category is based on messages that signal **superiority**, or convey that the speaker is smarter, knows more, or is better in some other way than the listener. This promotes feelings of judgment and unworthiness in the other person in a relationship, or at the very least resentment. In any case, it creates a defensive climate. Take, for example, Damon, the youngest boy in a family, whose three older brothers have all excelled at baseball. Damon went out for baseball this year, but didn't make the team. When he told his older brother, his older brother said, "Dude, what do you mean you didn't make the team? Baseball runs in the family—what's your problem?"

> **Superiority** Defense-arousing message that conveys that the speaker is smarter, knows more, or is better in some other way than the listener.

Ouch! Damon was already feeling down about the situation, and now he feels worse. Will he ever be as good as his brothers, he wonders? A more supportive response would have been, "That's a total bummer—I feel for you. I remember when I went out for soccer but didn't make it. It's not the end of the world, though—different people are good at different things—you'll find something that works for you." This message is geared toward demonstrating to Damon that they're all equal—they aren't the same, they may have different strengths and weaknesses, but no one's strength is any more valuable than another's.

Defense-Arousing Communication: The Bottom Line

As you learned about six common ways we use language that raise defensiveness in others, did you notice a common theme among them? Each defense-arousing category seems to create an imbalance in the relationship—one that places the speaker in power and consequently disempowers the receiver. Maintaining a balance of power is critical in personal relationships, because it helps both partners feel a sense of equity and equal value in the relationship. Thus, learning to replace our own patterns of defense-arousing communication with more supportive alternatives will help us develop and strengthen our close relationships.

But what about relationships where there is a clear power differential, such as in the workplace, or other relationships where there is a mutually accepted authority figure? Is it still important to use supportive communication? The answer is yes. In situations where one person has authority over another, the subordinate is usually quite aware of this power differential. Being constantly reminded of it via defense-arousing, power-flexing communication is only going to create resentment. Using supportive alternatives, on the other hand, will make the subordinate feel more valued and increase his or her respect for the authority figure. It's a win-win solution.

Table 10.3 summarizes these six categories of defense-arousing communication.

Turn now to Activity 10.3 to practice identifying defense-arousing messages and replacing them with more supportive alternatives.

TABLE 10.3 | Reducing Defensiveness in Others

CATEGORY	INSTEAD OF . . .	SAY THIS:
Evaluation vs. Description	You aren't doing very well in school this term.	I've noticed that you've missed more classes than usual this term.
Certainty vs. Provisionalism	You're going to flunk out if you don't get your act together.	I'm concerned that you might not be able to catch up on everything you've missed.
Control vs. Problem Orientation	You need to get a second job.	We need to figure out a way to get our bills paid on time.
Strategy vs. Spontaneity	Do you think it's important to help others out when they're in a bind?	I missed class yesterday; could I please borrow your notes to see what I missed?
Neutrality vs. Empathy	I'm tired of hearing you complain about your lack of a social life.	It sounds like you're feeling really lonely, but don't know what to do about it.
Superiority vs. Equality	I don't understand how you can be struggling in English; when I took it I got an A.	We all have strengths and weaknesses; sure, I did well in English, but I still have a hard time with math!

Reducing Our Own Defensiveness

Now that we've learned how we can reduce defensiveness in others, let's turn our attention to our own patterns of defensive communication. When a person says something to you that sounds critical, insulting, or diminishing, do you tend to respond defensively? If so, you are not alone. These types of comments, especially when they come from someone we value, can cut right to the core of our self-image. (Remember the sociometer theory of self-esteem from Chapter 2?) And when our self-image is threatened, it is quite natural to defend it. So, even though defensiveness is a natural response, unfortunately it is not a productive one. As we noted earlier, once we respond defensively, it tends to provoke a reciprocal type of comment, and the downward spiral begins.

What can we do about it? Research in this area has identified a number of nondefensive response-types, which are useful in responding to criticism without beginning the downward spiral. The type we choose depends on the specifics of the situation. First, is the criticism justified? As much as we may hate to admit it, sometimes criticism is right on target, and in these cases, the best thing we can do is just to accept it and agree. In other situations, we may disagree with the criticism, but it is still possible to respond nondefensively. Finally, often criticism doesn't follow the rules of clear communication we've been learning about in this book—after all, many of the people we talk with will not have taken this class! As a result, the criticism may use you-language or be vague. When this happens, we have several choices in how we respond. Let's examine these options in more detail.

If the Criticism Is Accurate   This may be the hardest situation to deal with, so let's talk about it first and get it over with. When someone criticizes you about something you know to be true, the easiest way to deal with it is just to *agree*. This may seem like a difficult proposition, but try it—it gets much easier with practice!

Imagine that you are working on a class assignment with a partner from the class; each of you is responsible for half the work. Two days before the project is due, your partner e-mails you her part of the project. You've agreed to put it together with yours, make sure everything looks nice, and print out the final product. On the morning of the day the project is due, you sit down to do all this, but just as you finish, your computer crashes—and you hadn't saved the project yet. You realize that there's no way you can recreate everything before the deadline, so you're going to get marked down for being late. When you call your partner to let her know, she gets really upset and says, "Why did you wait until the last minute? I gave you my part two days ago! Your irresponsibility is going to screw up my grade!" Clearly, your friend is using you-language and violating several of Gibb's principles, but responding defensively is only going to make things worse. Instead, if you just agree and admit that you made a mistake, it will diffuse the tension immediately. "You're right; I shouldn't have waited until the last minute. I'm really sorry."

Critical Thinking **QUESTION**   When was the last time someone criticized you and was right? How did you handle it?

If the Criticism Isn't Accurate   This is a more difficult situation, but if you disagree with the criticism, sometimes saying so just builds tension. Granted, in some relationships, disagreeing is a mutually acceptable option, and in those relationships you may be able to disagree without sounding defensive. In many relationships, though, disagreeing is interpreted as an affront. In that case, how can you honestly respond to the critic without sounding defensive? *By recognizing how they might have come to see it the way they do.*

Jesse did a nice job with this type of response when his girlfriend told him, "You think too much." He replied, "I *have* been spending a lot of time thinking lately; this decision I have to make about where to go to school next year feels like a really important thing." By responding this way, he's acknowledging that he has been thinking a lot; in his mind, though, it isn't too much, since he's making a big decision. By saying this to her in a sincere and even tone of voice, he's validating her perception without giving up his own voice.

If the Criticism Isn't Clear   Many times, someone voicing criticism will use relative or static language. As you recall from Chapter 9, these are both types of abstract language that are not specific enough to convey a message that is likely to be interpreted accurately. In these cases, you have three choices.

The simplest choice is to *ask for clarification*. In Jesse's example, if he didn't know what his girlfriend was talking about, he could ask. "What are you seeing that makes you think that?" Of course, this needs to be done in a nondefensive tone of voice and with other congruent nonverbal behaviors. Remember how important it is for our nonverbal signals to support our words, rather than contradict them. Shon offers an additional example. When his roommate said, "I sure wish you would help me around the house more," he asked for clarification by responding, "Could you please be more specific about what it is that you'd like me to help you with?" And it worked—she smiled and said, "It'd be great if you'd do the laundry!"

Either way, asking the critic to specify exactly what he or she means is a very direct way of getting clarification. The only potential barrier to effective use of this strategy is the nonverbal component. Keep in mind that the critic has a clear idea of what he wants, but is probably completely unaware of how vague his communication really is. So, in asking what he means, it's important to be sincere with your words and your nonverbal signals, so he doesn't misinterpret you as being sarcastic.

Because of the risk sometimes involved in asking for clarification, often a better option is to *guess about the specifics*—*if* you think your guess has a decent chance of being correct. In Shon's example, if he remembered his roommate complaining about his failure to do the laundry in the past, he might have been better off saying, "Are you wanting me to do the laundry, or is it something else?" Fortunately, he and his roommate had a pretty supportive communication climate already, so there was little risk of *her* getting defensive when he asked (instead of guessing) about her specific concern.

Jennifer's example was when her dad said to her, "You've been too loud lately!" She had a feeling he was talking about the night before, when she had some friends over, so this is what she said: "When you say I've been too loud lately, is it because I had some people over last night and we distracted you from your work?" By guessing about the specifics (when you can), you're showing a real effort to understand what the other person means, or trying to empathize, which as we know builds trust.

A third, related option is to find out exactly what the person *does* want from you. In other words, *what do they want you to do about it?* In Jennifer's case, she could say, "I did have friends over last night, Dad—do you have any ideas about what we could do to keep from distracting you when I have friends over on a night that you're working?" This signals that she shares his concern and is open to suggestion. Rob, another student, was able to use this response style at work, when his boss said, "You're doing that all wrong!" He simply replied, "Can you show me how you'd like me to do it?"

Of course, this sounds so simple. In reality, though, it can be difficult—at first, anyway. As mentioned earlier, criticism often puts us on the defensive, and if we're accustomed to responding defensively, it might seem impossible to change that. But remember what we learned about operant conditioning and positive reinforcement in Chapter 3? That principle tells us that we learn to do things faster and more repeatedly when we get positive reinforcement for them. Learning these nondefensive response styles is a great example of positive reinforcement in action: The first time you use one (assuming it comes out right), you will be truly amazed at how well it works. If things are tense when the critic says what she says, your nondefensive response will be like throwing a pitcher of water on a piece of paper that has caught fire—it will extinguish the blaze immediately! It takes all the hostility away. Add to this the fact that the other person probably isn't enjoying the tension any more than you are, so he'll be relieved and grateful that you took it so well. These two "reinforcements" will make it so much easier to respond nondefensively the next time, and pretty soon nondefensive responses will be your norm.

When You Don't Know Why the Critic Is Bringing This Up Finally, there will be situations when you have no idea why the person is criticizing you about this. In these cases, you have two options. First, you could *ask about the consequences of your behavior*. Maria used this type of response when her mom said to her, "You're getting too serious too fast with that guy!" Impressively, Maria was able to respond nondefensively (after some practice in class!) by replying, "What do you think might happen, Mom?"

Another option is to *ask if something else is wrong*. This doesn't mean you should invite more criticism! This is a good choice in a particular type of situation: when you think the critic is lashing out at you *not* because of a legitimate problem she has with you, but because she's stressed about something else, and you just happen to be in the wrong place at the wrong time. In Maria's example, if that were the case, she might have replied, "Gosh, Mom, we've been seeing each other almost a year now, and I thought you really liked him. Is there something else you're worried about?"

Another example to which you could apply this option goes back to Jesse's case (his girlfriend criticized him for thinking too much). If that seemed really out of character for her, it might be useful to say something like this: "Yeah, I know I tend to overanalyze, but I didn't think that bothered you—is there something going on that you want to talk about?"

One of the ironies of close relationships is that, the more we trust someone, the more we let our guard down with that person. Consequently, we're not on our "good behavior" as much, and that person is likely to get the fallout when we're having a tough time. Remember the defense mechanism of displacement from Chapter 3? This is bound to happen in any relationship, and it's important to recognize that so you can keep it in its proper perspective. Rather than letting the situation escalate into a fight about something you don't need to fight about, these nondefensive replies are much more compassionate and healthier for your relationships.

A Multipurpose, Nondefensive Response Option

There is one additional type of nondefensive response that is effective across a wide variety of the types of situations we've been discussing, and that is paraphrasing. As you'll remember from Chapter 8, paraphrasing is reflecting back to the speaker what it sounds as if they're feeling, as well as what you think is going on in their head. The goal is to do this in your own words and to do your best to read between the lines, rather than simply repeating their words. (Take a quick look back at that section of Chapter 8 if you need a brief review.) In addition to being a great supportive listening technique, paraphrasing is an excellent all-purpose, nondefensive response style.

To see how it can be effective, let's apply paraphrasing to some of the examples we've already used. When Shon's roommate criticized him for not helping around the house, he might have said, "You sound really upset; is it because your parents are coming to visit this weekend and you want everything to look really nice?" This validates her feeling and makes a reasonable guess about why she is upset. By keeping it in the form of a question, he's giving her a chance to confirm his guess, or to provide additional clarification. Either way, he's keeping a positive tone in the discussion, rather than letting it spiral downward.

Here are a few additional paraphrasing responses to these examples:

Jesse's example (about thinking too much): "You sound sad, like you might be worried that we're growing apart because we haven't been talking as much lately—is that what's on your mind?"

Jennifer's example (about being loud): "You seem really frustrated, Dad, almost as if you don't know how we can continue to coexist with our totally different schedules—am I getting what you're saying?"

Maria's example (about her boyfriend): "It sounds like us being so serious is freaking you out, Mom . . . maybe because it's hard to see me growing up and thinking of moving out?"

All of these examples show compassion for the critic and a genuine attempt to empathize and understand the concern so that you can work toward resolving it together. Each time you do this successfully, you'll build additional trust in each other, gain more skill at artfully utilizing these response styles, and continue to improve the overall quality of your important relationships. Table 10.4 summarizes the nondefensive responses to criticism.

Next, turn to Activity 10.4 to practice developing your own skills at responding nondefensively to criticism.

TABLE 10.4 | Responding Nondefensively to Criticism

TYPE	WHEN TO USE	EXAMPLE
Agree	If the criticism is accurate	You're right: I am a bad driver.
Understand the critic's perception	If the criticism is clearly communicated, but you don't agree with it	I can see how you would think I'm a bad driver, since I have gotten three tickets this year.
Ask for clarification	When the criticism is unclear	When you say I'm a bad driver, what exactly are you referring to?
Guess about specifics	When the criticism is unclear but you think you might know what the critic is talking about	When you say I'm a bad driver, are you talking about the fact that I've gotten three tickets this year?
Ask what the critic wants you to do differently	When you don't know what the critic wants	Do you have any suggestions about how I could improve my driving?
Ask about the consequences of your behavior	When you don't know how the issue is relevant to the critic	What are you afraid might happen?
Ask if something else is wrong	When you think the critic is displacing anger onto you	You've never been concerned about my driving record before; has something happened recently that is bothering you?
Paraphrasing	In any situation where you want to diffuse the tension	It sounds like you're worried for me, maybe because you think my insurance will get canceled?

Interim SUMMARY #3

Defensiveness is a dangerous and destructive pattern in relationships. Although it is a *natural* response to a perceived threat (such as to your self-concept), it is not a *productive* response. On the contrary, it tends to be reciprocated and to create a downward spiral of negativity in a relationship. Therefore, it is important to learn to send messages in a way that is least likely to create defensiveness in others, and also to respond nondefensively when we are criticized.

There are six categories of defense-reducing communication styles. The first is to use descriptive terms instead of evaluative ones. Also, we should focus on problem-solving instead of controlling, being provisional (open-minded) to others' ideas, and showing empathy. Finally, it is important to avoid being manipulative and acting superior. All of these supportive behaviors help create a power balance in relationships.

When we are the target of criticism, we can employ numerous nondefensive response styles to keep the situation from escalating. We can agree, if the criticism is true, or agree with the critic's perception if that makes sense to us. If the criticism is unclear, we can ask for or guess about specifics, or ask what we should do differently. If you don't know what the critic is worried about, ask what they think the consequences are. If you think they're displacing their own worry about something else onto you, gently suggest that. Finally, paraphrasing is an excellent multipurpose, nondefensive response style.

RESOLVING CONFLICT: AN INTEGRATIVE APPROACH

PREVIEW QUESTIONS

(1) When you want to resolve an important conflict with someone, what are five important steps to take toward an integrative solution?

(2) What is one current conflict you are facing in your own life for which the integrative approach might be useful?

In the early part of this chapter, we learned about five basic conflict styles, along with the strengths and weaknesses of each, and when each style might be useful. Of the five conflict styles, the integrative style is the most challenging to put into action, but also the most important for healthy long-term relationships (whether business or personal). We discussed an overview of integrated conflict resolution in that section and used the example of the two roommates who initially disagreed about getting a pet. Now, as we wrap up this chapter, let's examine it in more detail so we can be prepared to try it out the next time we have an important issue to resolve.

In books and articles about conflict resolution, this style is known as the **win-win method**, since its goal is to meet the needs of each party fully, without making sacrifices such as are required by the compromise solution. Although this is an optimal solution, it also can take a good deal of time and energy

> **Win-win method** To meet the needs of each party fully, without making sacrifices.

from all parties, so it is essential that each of you is committed to a win-win solution before you embark on the process. The process recommended here is a step-by-step process; when you use it, follow each step carefully and don't be tempted to skip anything. Because the win-win solution can be a challenge to create, you want to do everything you can to put the odds in favor of a happy outcome. These guidelines will help you keep from sabotaging yourselves in the process.

As we go through each of the steps, we will also see how it applied to a real-life situation faced by Pam and her husband. Pam, a former student in this class, used the integrative approach to address an issue that was becoming a real conflict in her marriage. Her 11-year-old daughter Jessica wanted to go to church. The family wasn't a church-going family, so this represented something new. Pam thought they should let Jessica go, and her husband strongly disagreed. As you may have noticed in your own environment, conflicts over religion can be explosive and very threatening to relationships. Read on to see how Pam and her family dealt with their situation.

Step One: Identify the Problem

Win-win problem solving, or the integrative approach, begins with some honest thinking about what the problem really is. This is something you should do on your own, before bringing up the issue to the other person in the conflict. Be careful *not* to assume that you already know what the problem is and don't need this step. Why not? Because, by the time an issue gets to the point where it's important enough to call for an integrative solution, chances are your emotions have gotten involved and may even be pretty strong. When this happens, as we learned in Chapter 4, our strong emotions can skew our perception of the issue, and it's critical to have a clear and accurate picture of what the issue really is in order to truly solve it.

So, to clarify the crux of the issue for yourself, spend some time thinking about what you need that you aren't getting in this situation. It can even be useful to try putting it into an I-statement, to be sure you are (a) describing the current status or situation clearly and factually; (b) identifying the emotional impact it is having on you; and (c) able to state the consequences the situation has for you in a manner that takes responsibility for your thoughts and feelings, rather than blaming them on the other person. This I-statement will also be useful in the next step.

As Pam thought about the issue, her initial thoughts were that there was no reason not to let Jessica go to church if she wanted to. In Pam's mind, it was important to let her daughter try things out and form her own opinions. She thought her husband was against the idea for a couple of reasons: first, that he didn't want to have to deal with taking her to church, and also that he'd never gone to church and had turned out fine, so Jessica didn't need to go either.

The I-statement she wrote that clarified her ideas went like this: I'm concerned (feeling) about our disagreement over Jessica's desire to go to church (stating the facts). In my viewpoint, it is important for Jessica to try things out and form her own opinions about things now, so she'll be better prepared to take charge of her life as she gets older (her perception of the consequences).

Step Two: Set a Time and Place to Discuss the Issue

Once you've accurately identified what the problem is for you and how it's affecting you, it's time to let the other person know, give him or her a chance to have some thinking time about it, and set up a time to try the integrative method. Timing is critical here—don't ambush the other person with it! Choose a moment to bring up the issue when neither of you is stressed or in a hurry to get somewhere. You can use the I-statement you crafted in Step One, and/or incorporate whichever of Gibb's categories of non–defense-arousing communication seem appropriate. Let the other person know you've been thinking a lot about it, have some ideas, and would like to set up a time that works for you both to talk about it and try to reach a win-win solution. This gives him some time to prepare himself—which builds a sense of equality and trust, because you've had some time to think about it already—and reinforces that equality through the mutual choice of a good time and place.

As you make the date, be sure not to sabotage yourselves by trying to squeeze it into a short time period; choose a time when neither of you has anything you must do for an hour or two. If you end up with extra time, you can just hang out and celebrate your success! Also, think about your environment. Choose a place where you won't be distracted by other people or too much noise from your surroundings. That way, you'll be able to concentrate on what each of you is saying, which will increase the chances of a successful outcome.

One last tip: If it is a complex issue, as is often the case, consider suggesting that it is okay for either of you to bring some notes to the discussion. That may sound a little dorky, but think about it: You probably have a lot riding on the outcome, so why not do everything you can to increase the chances of success? Because you might feel a little uncomfortable, at least early on, it might help to have written down the way you want to present some things. That will help keep you both on track, and also help keep you from using defense-arousing types of communication.

In this step, Pam chose to mention the issue to her husband one night after Jessica had gone to bed. She said: "I've been feeling stressed about our lack of agreement on whether Jessica should be allowed to go to church. I learned this new conflict-resolution approach in my human relations class—it's called the win-win method, because the goal is for both people to feel good about the solution. I was thinking maybe we should try it out and see if it helps us figure out what to do about the church thing." Her husband was willing, so they decided they'd have time the following Saturday afternoon. Jessica would be at a birthday party, so they could talk about it at home without distractions.

Step Three: Exchange Viewpoints

When the time comes for your discussion, the best way to start out is for each of you—one at a time—to describe your viewpoint. Doing it one at a time will help keep you from arguing or getting derailed. If you like, you can flip a coin to decide who goes first; or you can start out by describing what the issue is for you. (By going first, you can use your communication skills to set a positive tone for your discussion.) This will probably build on the I-statement you came up with earlier; typically, issues that need a win-win solution are too complex to fit neatly into one simple I-statement. Ideally, you'll have thought about the best ways to state all this to your partner, and maybe even have some notes to guide you. Include the facts of the situation, how you feel about it, and the consequences it has for you. If you have additional concerns or perceptions you want to check, you can include those as well, as long as you present them as the perceptions they are rather than fact. The goal here is to get all aspects of your concern and unmet needs on the table, and to get to a point where you both feel as though your partner truly understands your viewpoint.

While you are describing the situation, work toward observing your partner's responses, both verbal and nonverbal. Hopefully, by this time, you'll have shared some of what you've learned about effective listening responses, and he will use them to clarify his understanding of what you're saying. If not, help him out by asking him what seems to make sense about what you're saying, and what doesn't.

Once you are both satisfied that your partner truly understands your viewpoint and concerns, it's your partner's turn to do the same thing: share his viewpoint, feelings, and consequences it has for him. This is your turn to really listen supportively, to try to understand not only *what* he thinks and feels, but *why* he thinks and feels what he does. Keep in mind that your partner hasn't had the communication training you've had in this class, so if he uses you-language or other defense-arousing communication, do your best to be graceful and not respond in kind. Instead, practice the nondefensive responses and accept the lion's share of the responsibility for keeping the discussion productive. Falling into a downward spiral will only end up hurting you both.

Most times, a sincere and honest discussion utilizing clear communication and supportive listening results in a greatly enlightened understanding of the issue for both of you. Remember how we learned that one of the benefits of good paraphrasing is that the paraphraser's interpretation can often give new insight into the other person's own understanding of the issue? That can be a huge benefit in problem-solving, so do your best to include some of that.

Once you've both gotten everything out, feel understanding for the other, and feel understood by the other, you might realize that the issue is a little different than you thought. If this is the case, take a moment to restate the problem with your new information: Identify what you agree on and what you don't agree on, and what each of you needs to feel good about the outcome.

Pam had actually taught the effective listening responses to her husband for an earlier class assignment, so that gave them an advantage. She started out with the I-statement she'd crafted in Step One, but added a little to it: "I'm concerned about our disagreement over Jessica's desire to go to church. In my view, it is important for Jessica to try things out and form her own opinions about things now, so she'll be better prepared to take charge of her life as she gets older. As I've thought about this, it's occurred to me that our differences might be based in our own childhoods: I went to church and you didn't. I wonder if that's why you're against it: because you didn't go and you turned out fine, so Jessica doesn't need to go either. Do you think that's part of it?"

As their discussion progressed, several new parts of the issue came to light. First, as Pam elaborated on why she felt it was important for Jessica to try things out so she would be capable of choosing a good path for herself, her husband realized that he agreed with this viewpoint. For her part, Pam came to understand that a majority of her husband's issue was that he felt she gave Jessica too much freedom to do what she wanted to do, and that they were in danger of spoiling her. In his view, Jessica needed to learn that in real life, sometimes you don't get what you want. That made sense to Pam. Interestingly, once she said that to her husband, it didn't seem like a big deal to him anymore. That helped them realize that the "spoiling" thing wasn't really an issue after all, but a power struggle.

Her husband's other concern was his perception—admittedly based on stereotypes and lack of personal experience—that churches pretty much told a person how to think and believe, and also that they fostered prejudice against those who didn't share their beliefs. He wanted Jessica to think for herself, and also felt it was important to teach Jessica that it doesn't matter how you look or if you have an alternate lifestyle—people are people, and differences are okay. Pam strongly agreed with these goals, which was an excellent insight for both of them: They realized they were essentially in agreement on how to raise their daughter. That gave them a sense of relief and diffused much of the tension.

At this point, they restated the issue with the new information they'd uncovered. They both wanted Jessica to learn to think for herself and accept people's differences. They both didn't want her in an environment that encouraged prejudice. The conflict was how to meet Pam's need of letting Jessica try things out, without violating the legitimate concerns they both had about the way they wanted to raise her.

Step Four: Brainstorm and Analyze Options

Once you've gotten all sides of the issue out in the open and clarified the true nature of the conflict, the next step is to brainstorm potential solutions and write them down. The first couple of options that come to mind will probably be familiar ones that you've already thought about. That's as good a place as any to start, so go ahead and write them down. The key to success in this step is to push beyond the familiar and not hold anything back, no matter how crazy it might sound. Believe it or not, the things that seem crazy or impossible often lead to true win-win solutions. Don't shoot anything down at this stage—first you need to give it a chance.

Once you've written down as many options as you can, go back and consider the advantages and disadvantages of each one (in terms of how it does or doesn't meet the needs you each have). Quite a few may end up being crossed off the list once you've done this, but hopefully you'll have a few options left that you can explore. At that point, think about how you'd implement them, and mutually choose the best option to try out.

This is the list Pam and her husband came up with:

1. *Let Jessica pick a church and just go. (Meets Jessica's need, but both parents would worry about what the church was teaching.)*
2. *Go with Jessica to church. (Neither parent was very enthusiastic about this; Pam wouldn't mind going for a while, but her husband absolutely did not want to go.)*
3. *Tell Jessica she can't go to church, but she can join a club of some kind that fosters the principles Pam and her husband believe in. (Keeps them from worrying about prejudice, but restrains Jessica from making her own decisions, which is important to both of them.)*
4. *Watch a religous TV show together. (Lets parents monitor what Jessica is being exposed to, but restrains her choices and keeps her from trying out what she wants to try out.)*
5. *Read the Bible together. (Doesn't really meet anyone's need: not Jessica's because she wants the whole church experience, and not the parents because they aren't interested in reading the Bible.)*
6. *Find someone they trust to go with Jessica to church. (At first this seemed odd, because they didn't feel it was someone else's responsibility. It led to another option, though . . . see #7.)*
7. *Talk to neighbors, coworkers and other people they know about various churches to see if there are some that don't fit the stereotypes they have about churches. (If they could find one that fit with their beliefs, they could let Jessica go without the concerns they previously had.)*

Once they got to #7, they realized they might be onto something workable, so they stopped there and agreed to try it. They both felt excited that they'd come up with an idea they actually thought might work, and also relieved that they'd done it together. Additionally, they reported feeling much closer, because they had reinforced the agreement they had on how to raise their daughter, which increased their trust in each other and their sense of connection.

Step Five: Set a Time to Follow Up

At this point, you've done the hard work and you are probably feeling pretty good about it. And that's okay—enjoy and appreciate your success! But there is one last pitfall you need to avoid: Don't blindly assume it's going to work. Plan to give it your best shot, but also recognize that you can never know with certainty what the future holds. So, think about how long a good trial period would be for your solution, and mutually agree on a time to check back in with each other to talk about how well it is or isn't working. That way, you make it "safe" for each of you to be honest about any difficulties you might encounter in implementing the solution.

When you do get back together to follow up, be honest. Sometimes the solution will be working just fine. More often, though, it will need a little adjustment here and there, and once in a while, you may have to start back at the beginning. Don't let this scare you away from this last step, though. After all that effort, what would be the point of continuing with something that wasn't working very well? The trust you built up in each other through the win-win process will carry you through whatever changes you need to make to it, as long as you continue to be honest and listen to each other.

Pam and her husband asked around and found a friend who went to a church that encouraged acceptance of everyone, regardless of how they looked or what their lifestyle was. This was what they had been hoping for, so they told Jessica she could go and check it out. Pam went with her the first two times, and came away feeling that it was going to be okay. They agreed that after two months, they'd talk to Jessica about what she was learning and gaining from going to church, and reevaluate things then.

Win-win solutions are entirely possible, but they do take commitment, honesty, and good communication and listening skills. Consider how you can try this in your own life. Are you currently dealing with a conflict that is significant to a work or personal relationship? If so, give this a try. If not, think about the conflicts you are currently facing. It's not a bad idea to try this out for the first time on something that is of only moderate importance. That way, you can become familiar with it and work out any little difficulties you might encounter in its implementation, so that you're more prepared to use it effectively when something big does come up. Table 10.5 summarizes the steps in the win-win method of problem solving.

TABLE 10.5 | Steps to Win-Win Problem Solving

STEP	KEYS TO SUCCESS
Identify the Problem	Think carefully and get to the root of the issue. What are your unmet needs? To help gain focus, try writing an I-statement that accurately captures your thoughts and feelings about the issue.
Set a Time and Place to Discuss the Issue	Decide together with the other person when you both have adequate time to talk about the issue without interruptions or distractions.
Exchange Viewpoints	One at a time, share all of your thoughts and feelings about the issue. When hearing your partner's perceptions, listen carefully and nondefensively. Use the communication and listening techniques from previous chapters to clarify and support each other.
Brainstorm and Analyze Options	While brainstorming, don't stop to analyze or critique anything; just let the ideas flow, no matter how crazy they seem. When you have a long list of options, identify the pros and cons of each one. Decide together which option to pursue.
Set a Time to Follow Up	Don't assume the plan will work flawlessly. Decide how long the trial period should be, and when you will meet again to talk about what is working and what is not.

Interim SUMMARY #4

When you are facing an important conflict in an important relationship, the best method to resolve the conflict is often the integrative approach. Also known as the win-win method, this approach involves five distinct steps: identifying the problem, setting a time and place to discuss the issue, exchanging viewpoints, brainstorming and analyzing options, and setting a time to follow up on the final decision. The integrative approach is a time-consuming process that involves a good deal of commitment and honesty from everyone involved, but which pays off in the effectiveness of the outcome, both in the immediate situation as well as in the strength of the long-term relationship.

EFFECTIVE CONFLICT RESOLUTION: SOME FINAL WORDS

We've learned a lot about conflict in this chapter. You may have noticed that much of this chapter builds on what we learned in previous chapters. After all, the more you know about yourself, your personality, and your emotions, the better you can regulate your interactions with others. Also, the more you know about the social and cultural factors that influence our perceptions and prejudices, the more understanding you can be of others who have different viewpoints. Finally, communication skills—clear verbal and nonverbal language, supportive relational climates, and effective listening—all help reduce the likelihood of conflict, and at the same time make us better prepared to effectively resolve conflict when we do encounter it (see Figure 10.5).

FIGURE 10.5 | Learning to confront conflict head-on can be a scary and intimidating experience at first. Going through it together, though, using the effective skills you've learned, increases trust in a relationship and reduces fear of conflict.

CHAPTER TERMS

Interpersonal conflict
Conflict style
Assertiveness
Cooperativeness
Dual-concern model
Accommodating
Dominating
Avoiding
Compromising
Integrating

Passive-aggressive
 behavior
Self-construals
Interdependent
 self-construal
Independent
 self-construal
Biconstrual identity
Ambivalent identity
Defensive spiral

Evaluation
Description
Certainty
Provisionalism
Control orientation
Problem orientation
Strategy
Neutrality
Superiority
Win-win method

ACTIVITY 10.1

CONFLICT MYTHS IN YOUR LIFE

INSTRUCTIONS: *This chapter began by discussing three predominant myths about conflict which, when believed, interfere with our ability to effectively resolve conflict. Which of these myths has been the biggest factor in your life (preferably for you, but if not for you, for someone close to you)?*

Write a couple of paragraphs that (1) identify the myth that has been most problematic, (2) give a specific example of a time that this myth influenced your approach or perception of a conflict, and (3) state the consequence this myth had in that situation. (4) End your discussion with some thoughts about what you might have done differently in that situation, knowing what you know now.

_____

_____

_____

_____

_____

_____

_____

_____

_____

_____

ACTIVITY 10.2

CONFLICT STYLE INVENTORY

PART 1

INSTRUCTIONS: *For each of the following statements, choose a number between 1 and 7 that represents the degree to which you agree or disagree with the statement.*

(1 = strongly disagree, 7 = strongly agree)

_____ 1. I generally try to satisfy the needs of my peers.

_____ 2. I try to work out a compromise that gives both of us some of what we want.

_____ 3. I try to work with my peers to find solutions that satisfy our expectations.

_____ 4. I usually avoid open discussions of differences with my peers.

_____ 5. I exert pressure on my peers to make decisions in my favor.

_____ 6. I try to find a middle course or compromise to resolve an impasse.

_____ 7. I use my influence to get my ideas accepted.

_____ 8. I use my authority to get decisions made in my favor.

_____ 9. I usually accommodate the wishes of my peers.

_____10. I give in to the wishes of my peers.

_____11. I bargain with my peers so that a middle ground can be reached.

_____12. I exchange information with my peers to solve a problem together.

_____13. I sometimes bend over backwards to accommodate the desires of my peers.

_____14. I sometimes take a moderate position so that a compromise can be reached.

_____15. I usually propose a middle ground for breaking deadlocks.

_____16. I negotiate with my peers so that a compromise can be reached.

_____17. I try to stay away from disagreement with my peers.

_____18. I avoid conflict situations with my peers.

_____19. I use my expertise to make others decide in my favor.

_____20. I often go along with the suggestions of my peers.

_____21. I try to give and take so that a compromise can be made.

_____22. I try to bring all our concerns out in the open so that the issues can be resolved in the best possible way.

_____23. I collaborate with my peers to come up with decisions acceptable to us.

_____24. I try to satisfy the expectations of my peers.

_____25. I sometimes use my power to win a competitive situation.

_____26. I try to keep my disagreement with my peers to myself in order to avoid hard feelings.

_____27. I try to avoid unpleasant exchanges with my peers.

_____28. I keep disagreements with my peers to myself to prevent disrupting our relationship.

_____29. I try to work with my peers for a proper understanding of a problem.

Source: Deborah Cai and Edward L. Fink, "Conflict Style Differences Between Individualists and Collectivists" _Communication Monographs_ 69, pp. 67–87. Copyright 2002 Reprinted by permission of Taylor & Francis and the authors.

PART 2: SCORING

INSTRUCTIONS: _Score your inventory by adding up sets of numbers as follows:_

A. Add up your scores for 1, 9, 10, 13, 20, and 24; then divide the total by 6. This is your Accommodating Score.

B. Add up your scores for 2, 6, 11, 14, 15, 16, and 21; then divide the total by 7. This is your Compromising Score.

C. Add up your scores for 3, 12, 22, 23 and 29; then divide the total by 5. This is your Integrating Score.

D. Add up your scores for 4, 17, 18, 26, 27, and 28; then divide the total by 6. This is your Avoiding Score.

E. Add up your scores for 5, 7, 8, 19, and 25; then divide the total by 5. This is your Dominating Score.

PART 3

Based on your final scores, answer the following questions:

1. What was your highest score? Name the style and discuss how it explains your general approach to conflict.

   _____

   _____

   _____

2. What was your second-highest score? Was it very close to your highest score, or significantly lower? Discuss how it interacts with your highest score to influence your general approach to conflict.

   _____

   _____

   _____

3. Discuss one thing that works pretty well about your preferred conflict style; in other words, what is one advantage for you about it?

   _____

   _____

   _____

4. Discuss one disadvantage you've found in using your preferred conflict style.

   _____

   _____

   _____

5. Finally, what is one specific way you could improve your general approach to conflict? (This answer might include incorporating more of one of your lower scores, etc.)

   _____

   _____

   _____

ACTIVITY 10.3

PREVENTING OR REDUCING DEFENSIVENESS IN OTHERS

INSTRUCTIONS: *For each of the following scenarios, identify at least one of Gibb's categories of defense-arousing communication. Then rewrite the original statement in a way that replaces the defense-arousing statement with more supportive language. Following are Gibb's categories:*

Evaluation vs. Description	Control vs. Problem Orientation
Strategy vs. Spontaneity	Neutrality vs. Empathy
Superiority vs. Equality	Certainty vs. Provisionalism

Example: Girl to her older brother: "You don't have a life. All you do is play on the computer!"

Types of defense-arousing communication: evaluation, certainty

More supportive way of communicating: "I've noticed that you've been playing on your computer several hours a day lately. I'm concerned that you might be neglecting the other aspects of your life. Can we talk about this?"

1. Girl to her ex-boyfriend: "You're never going to graduate from high school, and you'll just end up in a blue-collar job for the rest of your life!"

   Types of defense-arousing communication: _____

   More supportive way of communicating: _____

   _____

2. Guy to his roommate: "You're too condescending!"

   Types of defense-arousing communication: _____

   More supportive way of communicating: _____

   _____

3. One person to roommate: "If you're going to charge me for gas money every time we do anything together, then I'll just take the bus."

   Types of defense-arousing communication: _____

   More supportive way of communicating: _____

   _____

4. One person to a coworker: "You keep whining about missing your girlfriend, and we're tired of listening to you. Why don't you just move to Arizona so you can be with her?"

   Types of defense-arousing communication: _____

   More supportive way of communicating: _____

   _____

5. Girl to her brother: "If I thought about business half as much as you do, I'd be 10 times more successful than you."

   Types of defense-arousing communication: _____

   More supportive way of communicating: _____

   _____

6. One person to a friend: "You've got to get your drinking under control."

Types of defense-arousing communication: _____

More supportive way of communicating: _____

_____

7. One person to her brother: "All you do is party. You're wasting the money Mom and Dad are spending to put you through school."

Types of defense-arousing communication: _____

More supportive way of communicating: _____

_____

8. A woman to her ex-husband: "You always take what I say the wrong way. I think we should just communicate in writing from now on."

Types of defense-arousing communication: _____

More supportive way of communicating: _____

_____

9. One friend to another: "That class wasn't hard when I took it. I'm tired of hearing about all the problems you're having with it."

Types of defense-arousing communication: _____

More supportive way of communicating: _____

_____

10. A boss to an employee: "You're always having to take time off work to take care of your baby. I'm going to have to let you go if this continues."

Types of defense-arousing communication: _____

More supportive way of communicating: _____

_____

ACTIVITY 10.4

RESPONDING NONDEFENSIVELY TO CRITICISM

INSTRUCTIONS: *For each of the following scenarios, identify two different ways you could respond nondefensively to the speaker. In your responses, choose from the following nondefensive response styles:*

Ask for specifics	Guess about specifics
Paraphrase speaker's ideas	Ask what the critic wants
Ask about the consequences of your behavior	Ask what else is wrong
Agree with the truth	Agree with the critic's perception

Example: A boss says to an employee: "Don't ever treat a customer that way again."

One type of nondefensive response: Ask what the critic wants

How you could say it: "What would you like me to do differently next time?"

Second type of nondefensive response: Agree with the truth

How you could say it: "You're right; I lost my temper. I'm sorry."

1. A mom says to her daughter: "If you move in with those other girls you'll just end up fighting with them because you have a hard personality to live with."

Nondefensive response type: _____

How you could say it: _____

_____

Nondefensive response type: _____

How you could say it: _____

_____

2. A husband to his wife: "Must be nice to have a day off to just do whatever you want."

Nondefensive response type: _____

How you could say it: _____

_____

Nondefensive response type: _____

How you could say it: _____

_____

3. A guy to his girlfriend: "You spend way too much money on clothes."

Nondefensive response type: _____

How you could say it: _____

_____

Nondefensive response type: _____

How you could say it: _____

_____

4. One person to his friend: "You should invest in a better car. Your car seems like it is really falling apart."

Nondefensive response type: _____

How you could say it: _____

_____

Nondefensive response type: _____

How you could say it: _____

_____

5. One roommate to another: "You're neurotic!"

Nondefensive response type: _____

How you could say it: _____

_____

Nondefensive response type: _____

How you could say it: _____

_____

6. A mother to her daughter: "It's almost impossible to get a book of poetry published. You won't be able to do it."

Nondefensive response type: _____

How you could say it: _____

_____

Nondefensive response type: _____

How you could say it: _____

_____

7. A mother to her son: "You never do anything unless I tell you to!"

Nondefensive response type: _____

How you could say it: _____

_____

Nondefensive response type: _____

How you could say it: _____

_____

8. A girl to her boyfriend: "Your life is out of control—you have no direction!"

Nondefensive response type: _____

How you could say it: _____

_____

Nondefensive response type: _____

How you could say it: _____

_____

Key Concepts in Intimate Relationships

CHAPTER 11

Love doesn't make the world go 'round; love is what makes the ride worthwhile.

—Franklin P. Jones

Turn on the television, listen to some music, open a magazine, watch a movie, check your Internet homepage . . . what do all these things have in common? Very often the songs, articles, movies, and programs are dealing with some aspect of relationships and love. This is not strictly a Western cultural phenomenon, nor is it a recent development: Loving and being loved has been dreamed about, fought for, and relentlessly pursued throughout the history of humankind. Our innate need to belong and be connected to others permeates our lives, and the stories it creates are woven through our histories and cultures like rich tapestries. These stories perpetuate the value we place on love and teach us about love.

But are these lessons we learn about love necessarily *good* lessons? Do they adequately prepare us for healthy love relationships, or do they set us up for pain and heartache? Are the expectations they create in us realistic, and do they model the skills and behaviors necessary to sustain long-term relationships? Or do they instead consist of too much myth and fantasy, minimizing the hard work and dedication to growth it takes to sustain healthy, long-term relationships? Unfortunately, the latter seems to be the case, and this leaves us ill-prepared to achieve the long-term love that we so desire. The divorce rate in the United States continues to hover around 50%.

The psychological principles and communication skills discussed in the previous chapters of this book will go a long way toward helping you develop and maintain healthy relationships in both your personal and professional life. In this chapter, we will focus specifically on love relationships. What influences them? How can we avoid common problems and pitfalls that threaten them? And what can we do to keep them strong and healthy throughout our lives?

WHAT IS LOVE?

PREVIEW QUESTIONS

(1) What are the three main elements in Sternberg's love theory, and how do they combine to form four additional combinations?

(2) What are the primary styles of loving in Lee's theory, and how do they combine to form three secondary styles?

Take a moment and ask yourself: What is love? How would you define it? Write your thoughts in the margin of the page. Let them take whatever form they will, whether it be a string of words or complete sentences, lines from a poem or song, or whatever comes to mind when you think about what love is.

Defining love isn't an easy task. We all seem to know it when we find it, but it takes different forms in different relationships. Let's take a look at how the most popular theories in psychology and sociology conceptualize love. As you learn about them, consider how they fit, deviate from, or complement your own definition of love.

Sternberg's Triangle Theory of Love

The most robust psychological theory of love comes from Yale professor Robert Sternberg (1986, 1987), who postulates that love relies on three primary elements, from which several combinations can result. This triangle theory works much like the primary colors (red, yellow, and blue) in that each is a color by itself, but it can also combine with one or more of the others to make a different color, such as combining yellow and blue to make green. What are the three primary elements of love according to this theory, and what types of love do various combinations produce? (See Figure 11.1.)

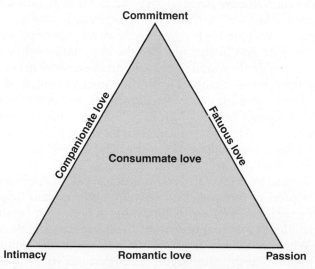

FIGURE 11.1 | Sternberg's Love Triangle

Primary Elements: Intimacy, Passion, and Commitment **Intimacy** is the first of the primary elements of love. Intimacy includes trust, caring, warmth, honesty, and a deep level of understanding and knowledge about each other. The key to developing and maintaining intimacy is open, clear, and honest communication. (Note that intimacy, as it is defined here and in most psychological contexts, is not sexual intimacy, but emotional intimacy.) **Passion**, the second primary element, refers to the sexual desire and physical attraction one person feels for another in a love relationship. In other words, this is the "chemistry" we feel when we are with the other person. **Commitment** is the third primary element. It is the conscious decision that one loves the other person and is willing to make certain sacrifices to maintain that relationship over the long term. These three primary elements are sometimes thought of as the emotional, physical, and cognitive aspects of love, with intimacy representing the emotional component, passion the physical component, and commitment the cognitive component (Brehm, Miller, Perlman, & Campbell, 2002).

According to Sternberg, each of these primary elements can constitute a love relationship all by itself. Intimacy by itself is referred to as **liking**, such as a friendship that is developing, but may not be at the point of long-term commitment. Passion, without intimacy or commitment, Sternberg calls **infatuation** (perhaps for obvious reasons), and commitment in the absence of intimacy and passion is called **empty love**.

Combining the Elements Thus far, the types of love composed solely of a primary element probably don't closely match your own definition of love. The combinations possible when combining the primary elements, though, are likely to look more like the types of love relationships we see around us. For example, **romantic love** is the combination of intimacy and passion; you might see this type of love in a relationship where the lovers haven't yet decided if they want to make a long-term commitment. Alternatively, romantic love could characterize a relationship where a long-term commitment isn't possible for some reason, such as if the partners meet at a summer internship in a distant city and plan to return to their respective hometowns at the end of the summer. Romantic love might also be found in an extramarital affair, when one or both partners is already committed to someone else.

Companionate love is love that includes intimacy and commitment, but no passion. This type of love relationship might commonly be found in a long-term couple who still maintain a close sense of intimacy and a strong commitment to each other, but for whom the passion has subsided.

Intimacy Includes trust, caring, warmth, honesty, and a deep level of understanding and knowledge about each other.

Passion Sexual desire and physical attraction.

Commitment The conscious decision that one loves the other person and is willing to make certain sacrifices to maintain that relationship over the long term.

Liking Intimacy by itself.

Infatuation Passion, without intimacy or commitment.

Empty love Commitment in the absence of intimacy and passion.

Romantic love The combination of intimacy and passion.

Companionate love Love that includes intimacy and commitment, but no passion.

Fatuous love is made up of commitment and passion, without intimacy. This might strike you as odd—why or how could this happen, you might be wondering. Sternberg notes this type of relationship might be that of a couple who meet, feel instant passion, and make a quick decision to marry or otherwise commit—before intimacy has had a chance to develop, or before the couple even know if they will be able to develop intimacy.

> **Fatuous love** Made up of commitment and passion, without intimacy.

> *Critical Thinking* **QUESTION** Can you think of any situations that might promote fatuous love, or influence a couple to marry or commit almost immediately in a relationship?

Finally, **consummate love** is love that is made up of all three elements: intimacy, passion, and commitment. This type of love is generally what people in Western cultures idealize—a relationship based on closeness and intimacy, but filled with passion, and with a solid commitment to each other.

> **Consummate love** Love that is made up of all three elements: intimacy, passion, and commitment.

In considering all these possible combinations, it is important to recognize that they don't typically consist of a perfect balance of the various components. In other words, consummate love (for example) probably won't have identical amounts of passion, intimacy, and commitment, but instead would probably be weighted toward one or another of the components. The same would be true for romantic love, or any of the other combination types. Relationships go through stages and cycles in which the degree of passion, intimacy, and commitment naturally fluctuates. We'll discuss these fluctuations in more detail a bit later in this chapter.

Before continuing, turn to Activity 11.1 to examine how Sternberg's Triangle Theory might explain some of the love relationships in your own life, or in those you see around you.

Lee's Love Styles

A different model for understanding love has been proposed by John Lee (1977, 1988). Rather than identifying types of love relationships, like Sternberg's theory, Lee's theory aims to pinpoint individual styles of loving another person. Like Sternberg's theory, though, Lee's theory involves both primary and secondary styles.

> **Eros** Erotic love, or love that is based primarily on physical attraction and a strong sense of passion toward the love object.

Before reading on, turn to Activity 11.2 and complete part 1, the Love Attitudes Survey.

Lee's Primary Styles **Eros**, the first of Lee's primary styles, refers to erotic love, or love that is based primarily on physical attraction and a strong sense of passion toward the love object. In eros love, a person typically falls in love quickly based on instant chemistry, is preoccupied with constant thoughts of the other person, and wants to be with him or her all the time. **Ludus**, the second

> **Ludus** Game-playing love, in which a person sees love as a game of skill and strategy.

primary style, refers to game-playing love, in which a person sees love as a game of skill and strategy. In this type of love, a person often dates several people at the same time, with no intention or interest in any type of commitment with any of them. The ludus lover is interested primarily in the sense of excitement that comes from juggling several relationships simultaneously, and sees lies or deception as a necessary and useful tool in the game. He or she also is very good at maintaining control of his or her emotions (which, of course, would be necessary to succeed in this type of pursuit). The third primary style, **storge** love, is a stable love, typically deep and long-term, in which the relationship is based on strong friendship and mutual respect. In this type of love, strong emotions and even sex are not highly valued elements in the relationship. Instead, storge lovers prefer talking and doing things together that both enjoy.

> **Storge** Stable love, typically deep and long-term, in which the relationship is based on strong friendship and mutual respect.

Lee's Secondary Styles   In general, each secondary style combines two of the primary styles, but the resulting style also has unique characteristics of its own. **Pragma** love is a practical love that results from an objective evaluation of the advantages and disadvantages of a particular love relationship or love object, and which seems to make sense from a logical, "cost vs. benefit" standpoint. Pragma is a combination of storge and ludus; its goal is a long-term friendship-based love that doesn't prioritize passion, but the strategy involved in the balance-sheet approach to choosing a partner is one type of the game-playing aspect of ludus.

> **Pragma** Practical love that results from an objective evaluation of the advantages and disadvantages of a particular love relationship or love object.

The **mania** love style combines the passion of eros with the game-playing of ludus. However, the eros lover is typically self-confident and secure—qualities lacking in the mania lover. The emotional self-control of the ludus lover is also missing in the mania lover. The end result is an obsessive, desperate, and possessive type of love, in which jealousy and doubt prevail. Finally, **agape** love combines eros and storge, resulting in a deep abiding love that is not without passion, and that is also selfless. The agape lover believes that love should be unconditional, and loves and gives to the partner without concern for reciprocity.

> **Mania** An obsessive, desperate, and possessive type of love, in which jealousy and doubt prevail.

Table 11.1 summarizes Lee's love styles. Research has generated a good deal of support for the existence of these love

> **Agape** Deep abiding love that is not without passion, and that is also selfless.

TABLE 11.1 | Lee's Love Styles

Eros	Passion-based love
Ludus	Game-playing love
Storge	Calm, stable love
Pragma	Practical love
Mania	Obsessive love
Agape	Selfless love

styles. In addition, findings indicate that an individual's love style may change over time, and also may vary as a function of the particular relationship he or she is in at a given time.

Gender and Cultural Differences in Love Styles Numerous studies have been conducted using Lee's typology, and findings indicate that women are more likely to illustrate the pragma and storge love styles, whereas men are more likely to favor ludus (e.g., Hendrick & Hendrick, 1995). Also, Asian Americans seem to prefer storge and pragma styles more than Latinos, African Americans, or European Americans; Latino Americans are more likely to exhibit ludus than European Americans (Contreras, Hendrick, & Hendrick, 1996; Hendrick & Hendrick, 1986). Finally, an international study found that agape was more prevalent among French participants than Americans, and storge and mania were found more often in American individuals than French individuals (Murstein, Merighi, & Vyse, 1991).

Before continuing, turn back to Activity 11.2 and complete the scoring and reflection sections of this self-assessment.

Interim SUMMARY #1

Two predominant theories have emerged to try to define and explain love. Sternberg's triangle theory suggests that passion, intimacy, and commitment are the three basic elements of any love relationship, and that any of these alone or in combination with others can comprise love. Intimacy alone is known as liking, passion alone is infatuation, and commitment alone is empty love. Secondary love types include romantic love (intimacy and passion), companionate love (intimacy and commitment), and fatuous love (passion and commitment). Consummate love includes all three primary elements. In any of the combinations, it is important to note, the various elements may be present in varying or unequal amounts.

Lee's love styles theory looks instead at an individual's predominant ideas and expectations about love. Eros (passionate love), storge (stable love), and ludus (game-playing love) are the three primary elements of this typology. Pragma combines ludus and storge, mania combines eros and ludus, and agape combines eros and storge. These preferences have been found to differ among various gender and cultural groups, and also vary within an individual over his or her lifetime.

FALLING IN LOVE: ATTRACTION AND MATE SELECTION

PREVIEW QUESTIONS

(1) What is proximity, and how does it influence the relationships we develop?

(2) What are three common ways of measuring physical attractiveness? To what extent do standards for physical attractiveness vary cross-culturally? Overall, how important is physical attractiveness in relationships?

(3) What aspects of similarity are important in relationships?

(4) When people develop online relationships, do these same factors apply?

Now that we've considered various ways of defining love, let's examine the factors that influence us to fall in love. What makes us attracted to one person, but not another? Once we get past initial attraction, what other factors play a role in our decision to make a long-term commitment? The concepts of attraction and mate selection have been studied for more than 60 years, and results indicate that proximity, physical attractiveness, and certain types of similarity are the most powerful influences on the mate selection process. Let's explore each of these in more depth.

Proximity

Attraction must logically start with exposure. **Proximity** refers to geographical closeness to another person, and research over the past 50 years demonstrates the power of proximity. One early study (Festinger, Schachter, & Back, 1950) examined the role of proximity in friendship development. Students at the Massachusetts Institute of Technology were randomly assigned to apartments around campus and later surveyed to determine which students ended up becoming friends. Forty-one percent of the time, students named the person living next door to them as one of their three closest companions. Moreover, there was a direct linear relationship between proximity and friendship: The person two doors away was named as one of their three closest companions 22% of the time; the person three doors away 16% of the time; and the person four doors away 10% of the time.

> **Proximity** Geographical closeness to another person.

What explains the powerful effect of proximity? Both convenience and exposure contribute to it. In our busy lives, it is much easier to get to know someone we frequently see. After all, the more often we see the person, the more likely we are to exchange greetings, chat about things, and so forth, and this is how relationships begin. It is also much easier to find time to spend together when you eliminate the need for one person to travel a great distance to meet the other. And time together fosters relationships, even in established ones like marriage. Married people who live apart (for employment reasons, for example) are more likely to divorce than couples who live together (Rindfuss & Stephen, 1990).

Convenience aside, research indicates that repeated exposure, in and of itself, seems to increase attraction. This **mere exposure effect** finds that people tend to like others more when they have seen them more frequently, even if they have not spoken to the person. One clever study of this phenomenon had female students attend certain college classes (in which they were not enrolled) 5, 10, or 15 times during the term. They did not talk to anyone during the times they attended. At the end of the term, other students who were actually enrolled in the class were shown photos of the women who had attended, along with a photo of a woman who had not. Students reported more positive attitudes toward the women who had attended, even though they had not had any interactions with them. What's more, positive attitudes and liking were greatest for the women who had attended class

> **Mere exposure effect** People tend to like others more when they have seen them more frequently, even if they have not spoken to the person.

more frequently (Moreland & Beach, 1992). Exposure increases familiarity, and we like what is familiar more than what is not.

Although the power of proximity may seem like common sense, take a moment to consider its implications for our own relationships. If we are most likely to develop relationships with those we see most often, who are these people in your own life? Are you in an environment that suits you, with people who truly interest you and share your values? Or did you choose your school, classes, workplace, or neighborhood based on convenience or necessity? Knowing the potential long-term impact of proximity, are you satisfied with your choices? If not, what is one adjustment you might make?

Physical Attractiveness

Have you ever heard the phrase, "Beauty is only skin deep"? Or "You can't judge a book by its cover"? We tend to give a great deal of lip-service to the idea that looks can be deceiving, but research, surprisingly, shows that we don't really live by these principles. On the contrary, we form quick judgments of people based on how they look. We discussed this to some degree in Chapter 7 in our discussion of stereotyping, and research on attraction indicates that it applies to love relationships as well.

In general, we tend to assume that "what is beautiful is good." In study after study, participants judge attractive people to be more socially skilled, intelligent, and well-adjusted than their less-attractive counterparts (e.g., Eagly et al., 1991). These judgments influence our behavior: Physically attractive people get hired sooner and earn higher salaries in the workplace (Hamermesh & Biddle, 1994), and conversely are less likely to be convicted of certain crimes (e.g., Downs & Lyons, 1991). These findings apply cross-culturally as well, with one slight modification: The qualities assumed to be possessed to a greater degree in attractive people seem to depend on the values of the culture. In other words, attractive people in any culture are assumed to have more of the desired qualities of that culture (e.g., Wheeler & Kim, 1997). For example, attractive people in individualistic cultures would be assumed to be high achievers, whereas attractive people in collectivistic cultures would be assumed to take good care of their families.

But what constitutes attractiveness or beauty? Even though it may seem that definitions of beauty depend entirely on individual preferences, research shows surprising similarities in who is considered attractive, even cross-culturally. These similarities are found in facial features, as well as body shapes and proportions, for both men and women. Let's explore these similarities in greater detail.

Facial Features   Think for a moment of the women and men in your culture considered to be the most attractive (see Figure 11.2). Chances are they have certain facial features in common. The women probably have big eyes, full lips, a small chin and nose, well-defined cheekbones with narrow cheeks, and a broad smile. The men probably have strong jaws and broad foreheads. Both the men and women most likely have clear skin and strong, white teeth. Around the world, women and men

FIGURE 11.2 | Brad Pitt and Halle Berry both exemplify the facial features and symmetry that are considered attractive cross-culturally.

who possess all these features are considered to be more attractive than those who do not (Cunningham, Druen, & Barbee, 1997; Jones, 1995). Even babies as young as 3 months old demonstrate a preference for faces with these features (Langlois, Ritter, Roggman, & Vaughn, 1991), which strongly suggests that there is more to these preferences than cultural norms—after all, an infant hasn't had time to learn about cultural norms. This is an intriguing idea that we will return to shortly.

Symmetry   A second factor that influences a person's degree of attractiveness is the symmetry in his or her face and body, according to several new studies (Honekopp, Bartholome, & Jansen, 2004; Rhodes, Roberts, & Simmons, 1999). **Symmetry** refers to how symmetrical, well-matched, or balanced one side of a person's face and body are, compared to the other. You might initially think that we're all perfectly symmetrical, but in truth we are not. One eye might be a little lower than the other, one ear a little longer or wider, and so forth. Many times these differences are too subtle for the naked eye to really notice, but it appears that on some level, we are indeed aware of them.

> **Symmetry** Refers to how symmetrical, well-matched, or balanced one side of a person's face and body are, compared to the other.

In examining this factor, researchers first measure symmetry in faces and bodies with specialized instruments designed to detect even small differences. Then pictures of these same people are shown to raters who know nothing about the measures of symmetry. When asked to rate the attractiveness of the people in the photos, raters invariably assign the highest ratings to the most symmetrical faces (Grammer & Thornhill, 1994).

Waist-Hip Ratio

Waist-hip ratio is a third factor found to be predictive of ratings of attractiveness. **Waist-hip ratio (WHR)** is determined by a person's proportions: specifically, how big is the waist as compared to the hips? For women, the ideal WHR in terms of defining beauty is 0.7, which means that her waist measurement would be 70% the size of her hip measurement. Cross-cultural research has found that women with this WHR are considered more attractive than women whose ratios are higher or lower (Singh & Luis, 1995). There is a preferred WHR for men as well: Men whose waists are 90% the size of their hips are rated most attractive (a WHR ratio of 0.9).

> **Waist-hip ratio (WHR)**
> Determined by a person's proportions: specifically, how big is the waist as compared to the hips.

A Logical Explanation

By now, you're probably thinking that this is curiously interesting, but how can it be explained? How can it be that preferences for facial features, symmetry, and waist-hip ratio are such defining factors in physical attractiveness, and moreover that they are so in virtually all cultures? Here are a few hints that might help you figure it out:

First, people with the above-mentioned WHRs tend to be healthier than those whose ratios are larger or smaller. Specifically, women with a 0.7 WHR and men with a 0.9 WHR are less likely to develop heart disease and diabetes than other men and women.

Second, women with a WHR of 0.7 are actually more fertile than women with higher or lower ratios. Studies find they get pregnant more easily (e.g., Singh, 1994).

Third, consider what clear skin and eyes might indicate. If you're thinking "good health," you are exactly right.

Fourth, the preferred facial features for women tend to represent youth and vitality. The preferred facial features for men indicate strength and power. Decades of research supports the idea that men are attracted to youth in women, while women prize strength in men. In addition, higher testosterone levels seem to promote the development of strong jaws and broad foreheads.

Have you figured it out yet? Overall, the physical traits found to influence physical attractiveness are the same traits that indicate good health and fertility. And healthier mates are more likely to produce healthy offspring and to pass along their healthy genetic predispositions to them. It seems that, somehow, we humans have a way of detecting which potential mates are most likely to contribute to healthy offspring.

And, the most recent research indicates that women's preferences for men with the above characteristics are strongest when a woman is fertile! Creative new studies have tracked women's attraction to various men, both symmetrical and asymmetrical, over several months, and compared their daily records of attraction to where they are in their menstrual cycle. Findings revealed that women are most attracted to symmetrical men when the women are fertile. At other times in their cycle, this preference disappears (e.g., Gangestad, Thornhill, & Garver-Apgar, 2005). What's more, research finds that women are more likely to achieve orgasm with a symmetrical male partner than with an asymmetrical one, which in turn increases the chances of conception. It seems, then, that we are engineered to seek out and procreate with mates who have the best genes.

Cultural Norms and Attraction   All in all, physical attractiveness plays a strong role in attraction, and we have seen some striking similarities in cross-cultural definitions of beauty. Once the basic physical standards (facial features, symmetry, WHR) have been met, though, cultural and societal norms influence certain defining features of beauty as well. For example, the current Western standard of beauty for women is thinner than in previous decades. Several decades ago, the standard was more voluptuous. We can see the trend if we look at photos of models in older magazines, or go online and compare current Miss America winners to those 20, 30, 40, and 50 years ago. This differential grows even greater if we compare the current standard to, for example, paintings of Renaissance women, or even women in later 19th-century Europe. At those times, the standard of beauty for women dictated a larger size (although still adhering to the correct WHR, symmetry, and facial features we discussed).

This trend has been explained in terms of the prevalence of food in a culture and its general economic prosperity. When times are tough and food more scarce, the preference seems to be for heavier women. Conversely, in times of plenty and economic prosperity, the preference shifts toward thinner women (Anderson, Crawford, Nadeau, & Lindberg, 1992).

Critical Thinking QUESTION   The preceding paragraphs have explained our preference for attractive mates in two ways: for biological/evolutionary reasons, and as a result of sociocultural influence. Challenge yourself to identify at least one other possible explanation. Hint: Consider the theories discussed in Chapter 3 to see which one might best explain our interest in attractive mates.

Matching in Physical Attractiveness   Of course, not everyone meets the standards for beauty we have been describing, but most people eventually pair off with someone. How do we reconcile this with the strong preference for physical attractiveness we undeniably have? Simple: We tend to seek the most attractive mate we think we can get (Carli, Ganley, & Pierce-Otay, 1991). In other words, most of us have a sense of our own level of attractiveness, and we tend to pursue others we think are in about the same category, as long as they show reciprocal interest in us.

There is one exception to the general "matching" rule in physical attractiveness. **Social exchange theory** (Blau, 1964; Sprecher, 1998) is based on the general principle that, in relationships, we want the best we can get for what we have to offer,

> **Social exchange theory** The general principle that, in relationships, we want the best we can get for what we have to offer, and we might "exchange" what we have for something a potential partner is offering.

and we might "exchange" what we have for something a potential partner is offering. Specifically, research supporting this theory indicates that two people who have different "good qualities" to offer might get together in a relationship if each places a high value on what the other has. A classic example of this explains why we sometimes see an older man who isn't particularly handsome, but is wealthy and powerful, with a beautiful younger woman: He is "exchanging" his wealth and status for her youth and beauty. This makes sense because the qualities he has to offer are those that women value in male partners, and the qualities she has to offer are important in men's search for female partners.

Individual and Group Differences in the Value of Attractiveness Given the preponderance of research underscoring the importance of physical attraction in mate selection, you might be wondering if we're all a bit shallow! Relatively speaking, just how important is physical attractiveness? In general, it tends to rank among the top preferences, but it is not necessarily the highest. Kindness, trustworthiness, and dependability tend to matter more in the long run, both for men and women, as well as cross-culturally (Buss, 1989; Regan, 1998). Table 11.2 lists these findings.

TABLE 11.2 | Buss's Cross-Cultural Findings of Preference in Mate Selection

MEN'S RANKING OF VARIOUS TRAITS	WOMEN'S RANKING OF VARIOUS TRAITS
1. Mutual attraction—Love	1. Mutual attraction—Love
2. Dependable character	2. Dependable character
3. Emotional stability and maturity	3. Emotional stability and maturity
4. Pleasing disposition	4. Pleasing disposition
5. Good health	5. Education and intelligence
6. Education and intelligence	6. Sociability
7. Sociability	7. Good health
8. Desire for home and children	8. Desire for home and children
9. Refinement, neatness	9. Ambition and industriousness
10. Good looks	10. Refinement, neatness
11. Ambition and industriousness	11. Similar education
12. Good cook and housekeeper	12. Good financial prospect
13. Good financial prospect	13. Good looks
14. Similar education	14. Favorable social status or rating
15. Favorable social status or rating	15. Good cook and housekeeper
16. Chastity (no previous experience in sexual intercourse)	16. Similar religious background
17. Similar religious background	17. Similar political background
18. Similar political background	18. Chastity (no previous experience in sexual intercourse)

Source: Buss's Cross-Cultural Findings of Preference in Mate Selection by David Buss in Adjustment and Human Relations *by Patricia Alexander (New Jersey: Pearson Education, 1999).*

In addition, research finds that physical attractiveness in a mate is more important to some individuals than it is to others. Overall, studies that ask participants to rank various characteristics of their ideal mate in order of importance find that men rank physical attractiveness higher than women do (e.g., Kenrick, Groth, Trost, & Sadalla, 1993). Self-monitoring also influences the importance of attraction in a mate. (As you recall from Chapter 2, self-monitoring refers to the degree to which we adjust our behavior to fit a particular social situation. High self-monitors are more likely to alter their behaviors to "fit in," whereas low self-monitors are more concerned with presenting their "true self" regardless of the demands of the social situation.) Men who are high self-monitors place greater importance on physical attractiveness in their female partners, and in one study even said they would prefer to date a beautiful woman who was rude over an unattractive woman with a very nice personality (Snyder, Berscheid, & Glick, 1985).

Attractiveness in Long-Term Relationships   We have seen that physical attractiveness is one of the most important factors influencing initial attraction. But is it also important in long-term relationships? The evidence indicates that it is, although to a lesser extent. Emotional stability, an agreeable personality, and trustworthiness consistently emerge as three more important factors in long-term relationships (Kenrick, Groth, et al., 1993), although physical attractiveness generally follows close behind—and again, typically ranks higher for men than for women.

A recent large-scale study in Spain (Sangrador & Yela, 2000) found that physical attractiveness was the single most important predictor of initial attraction, but only the ninth-most important in established relationships. Interestingly, though, physical attractiveness of the partner was related to satisfaction with the relationship, with greater attractiveness predicting greater satisfaction. Of course, as the authors of the study note, we cannot be sure whether relationship satisfaction is truly a product of attractiveness, or if a person sees his partner as more attractive when he is happy in the relationship. In other words, do I love you because you are beautiful, or are you beautiful because I love you?

Similarity

A third factor that influences attraction is similarity: We are more attracted to similar others than those who seem different. Does this surprise you? After all, we get a mixed bag of expectations from our culture. We hear that "birds of a feather flock together," but we also hear that "opposites attract." You might be thinking of a relationship you know of (maybe even one of your own) in which the two partners seem like opposites. If that's the case, and you feel a little skeptical of this similarity factor, keep in mind a couple of things as we examine this trend. First, remember that your own experiences are not necessarily the norm—research findings report averages for a majority of people, to which there are always exceptions. Also, remember the power of perceptions. What specific characteristics are you thinking about when you label a couple as "opposites"? Their physical appearance? Their political viewpoints? Their degree of extraversion? As you will see in a moment, the role similarity plays in attraction is more powerful for some characteristics than others.

Demographic Similarity   One type of similarity that promotes attraction is demographic similarity. **Demographic** refers to population statistics, such as age, race, religion, income level, educational level, and other basic types of information you might find on a census report. We tend to be attracted to others of a similar age, race, religion, and so forth. One recent large-scale study found that, for dating couples, demographic factors with the greatest similarity were age and scores on the verbal SAT. For married couples the list was similar, with a few additions: Married couples were more likely to be of the same religion and similar in educational level and high school and/or college GPA (Botwin, Buss, & Shackelford, 1997).

> **Demographic** Refers to population statistics, such as age, race, religion, income level, educational level, and other basic types of information you might find on a census report.

Similarity in Attitudes and Values   The degree to which we share general attitudes and values with our partner plays a role as well; for example, we are more likely to be interested in others who share similar viewpoints on issues and beliefs that are important to us. These first two types of similarity are typically explained in terms of validation (Duck, 1972); spending time with people who share our beliefs validates or confirms our sense of being right, and thus is comfortable and affirming. (Remember the self-verification function of the self-concept that we learned about in Chapter 2?) People who are demographically similar to us are more likely to share our values and beliefs.

Personality Similarity   Research examining the role of personality similarity reveals a more complex picture. Studies have focused primarily on personality attributes in married couples, but evidence also supports the role of personality similarity in attraction. For example, one study found that people were attracted to others with similar temperaments: Happy people were more likely to be attracted to other happy people (Locke & Horowitz, 1990).

Among married couples, similarity in personality traits has a consistent but fairly weak impact on relationship satisfaction. One study, for example, found similarity in two traits predict marital satisfaction. Pleasantness (a general measure of tendency toward a positive mood) and dominance (a general measure of tendency to feel in control of one's life) both increased satisfaction with the relationship when partners were similar in these dimensions (Blum & Mehrabian, 1999). These findings are generally consistent with findings of previous studies.

Final Thoughts on Similarity   In reviewing differences in similarity between dating couples and married couples, two important points are worth noting. First, we must recognize that a greater degree in similarity of married couples (as compared to dating couples) on a particular dimension (such as religion) does not necessarily mean that similarity will make a couple more likely to marry. It could also be true that, by the time a decision to marry has been made, partners have become more similar in their religious viewpoints. The same, of course, could be true for many factors: As a couple's relationship develops and grows, they are more likely to become similar in their viewpoints.

Second, we must consider the issue of perceptions versus reality. In other words, can we be sure two partners are as similar to each other as they think they are? Remember the various cognitive biases we learned about in Chapter 5, and how these biases influence our perception. For example, the confirmation bias influences us to remember the things that fit our current beliefs and forget or fail to notice the ones that don't. In a happy relationship, it would be normal for the partners to notice and remember the ways they are similar (as well as other positive events and aspects of their relationship) more than they would notice or remember anything negative. (Remember the concept of "rosy retrospection" we learned about near the end of Chapter 5?) This "positive illusion" (Taylor, 1989) can actually help sustain long-term relationships when they encounter stresses (Brehm & Kassin, 1990).

Attraction on the Internet: Do the Same Factors Apply?

Clearly, there has been a great deal of research on attraction that teaches us what tends to attract one person to another. The Internet is increasingly playing a role in dating and romance. Web sites such as Match.com get an average of four million visitors each month, each of whom spends (on average) close to an hour per visit (Greenspan, 2003). Is there any information available about whether online attraction operates on the same principles as in-person attraction?

The answer is yes. Although research is just beginning on this interesting topic, several intriguing sets of findings have emerged. When looking for love on the Internet, people have greater control over their self-presentation, as well as the pace of the relationship (Cooper & Sportolari, 2003). For example, you can choose when to exchange photos, which gives the relationship a chance to develop prior to physical attractiveness exerting any influence. As a result, physical attractiveness may be less important; as we just learned, it may be that people perceive their mates to be more attractive because they love them (rather than vice versa). Also, self-disclosure is easier on the Internet than in person, which typically results in faster development of relationships, but may also be subject to dishonesty (Levine, 2000) (see Figure 11.3). Finally, flirting and erotic activities may be easier to engage in in a virtual environment, and are usually exciting; on the other hand, they may also create unrealistic expectations in one or both partners if the relationship develops offline (Levine, 2000).

Use of the Internet to seek dates or romance is on the rise. One large study that included only people with access to the Internet found that 41–45% of them used the Internet "at least occasionally" to seek dates or romance (dates were defined as casual encounters; romance was defined as a long-term relationship). Some research indicates that men are more likely than women to look online for dates or romance, and age plays a role as well. People in their early 40s look for dates on the Internet more than any other age group; people in their late 40s look for romance on the Internet more than other age groups (Greenspan, 2003). Another factor found to prompt Internet dating is the perceived availability of potential dates in a

Online you said you were tall, lean and muscular
with a wild side, but I had no idea.

FIGURE 11.3 | Although online dating may help a couple get to know each other before they actually meet, there is still plenty of room for surprises.

person's social circle: People surrounded by couples and uninteresting singles expect to find a greater pool of possibilities online (Valkenburg & Peter, 2005). People who have experienced recent breakups of long-term relationships also tend to be heavier Internet dating users. Researchers suggest that in these cases, the Internet may be helping people reacclimate themselves to the idea and realities of dating after having been in a long-term relationship.

Overall, it appears that cyberspace might be a very useful "training ground" for people who are learning about their own relationship interests, exploring their sexuality, readjusting to single life, or having difficulty finding potential partners in their physical environment. Having greater control over when and what to self-disclose may make a person feel psychologically safer; as one researcher put in, the Internet allows a relationship to develop in a way that is "intimate yet separate" (Cooper & Sportolari, 1997). For people interested in taking their online romances offline, though, experts recommend doing so within one month in order to decrease the risk of unrealistic expectations (Levine, 2000).

Interim SUMMARY #2

Proximity, physical attractiveness, and similarity are powerful factors in attraction and mate selection. Proximity influences attraction in that we are more likely to develop relationships with the people who live and work near us. Physical attractiveness plays a powerful role in attraction, and is consistently near the top of the list in what both men and women seek in an ideal mate. Surprisingly, there are more similarities than there are differences in how people define beauty. For both men and women, certain facial features, symmetry, and an ideal waist-hip ratio predict attractiveness cross-culturally. Evolutionary psychology suggests that this is true because of the health and fertility benefits associated with these characteristics. Once these standards have been met, however, culture and individual preference do play a role in what each of us finds attractive in potential mates. Nonetheless, partners are likely to be similar to each other in their attractiveness level, unless one partner is exchanging a more important quality (such as status) for beauty.

Similarity is the third factor influencing attraction and mate selection. Demographic similarity and similarity in attitudes and values predicts both attraction and long-term relationship satisfaction. We must question, however, if similarity in attitudes and values causes a couple to get together, or if spending a great deal of time together causes their attitudes and values to become more similar. Personality similarity has a small but measurable impact on relationship satisfaction, especially if both partners are agreeable and feel in control of their lives. Finally, cognitive biases such as the confirmation bias have been found to influence couples' perceptions of partner similarity.

Online dating services and Web sites are used by almost half the single adult population. Benefits of online dating include greater control over self-presentation and pace of the relationship; one drawback is the possibility of unrealistic expectations. People in their 40s use the Internet more than any other age group to seek dates and romance, especially if they have experienced a recent breakup of a long-term relationship. Experts recommend meeting an online connection after no more than a month of online relationship development if both parties are interested in a long-term relationship.

MAKING RELATIONSHIPS WORK: KEYS TO HEALTHY LONG-TERM RELATIONSHIPS

PREVIEW QUESTIONS

(1) How does love typically change over the course of a long-term relationship?

(2) What are love maps, and how do they influence long-term relationships? How are attributions, an emotional bank account, and shared power important in long-term relationships?

(3) What are the Four Horsemen, and how do they affect conflict resolution?

(4) Describe five tools that help a couple manage conflict effectively.

And now . . . the moment you've been waiting for . . . you've found the person with whom you want to spend the rest of your life. You are deliriously happy. But on some level, danger lurks in the form of awareness that it might not always be that way. Immersed in a culture of instant gratification, surrounded by once-happy couples who found themselves overcome by "irreconcilable differences," what are the odds of keeping your relationship and your love alive over the long term? (As you know, current divorce statistics indicate that they're not in your favor.) Is there anything you can do to increase the chances of overcoming the odds and becoming one of those happy old couples? Fortunately, the answer is yes. Let's find out how.

Realistic Expectations

At the beginning of this chapter, we talked about how messages about love permeate our culture, and questioned whether the stories they told were realistic or not. In many ways, they are not realistic, and instead create in us a set of expectations about long-term relationships that is overly idealistic. As a result, when we encounter difficulties or unexpected changes in our relationship, we might conclude that it isn't the "right" relationship for us, because if it were, we wouldn't have this problem. The truth is, though, all relationships encounter problems, and all relationships change over time in various ways. Knowing what to expect and how to cope with it constructively makes a world of difference in how problems and changes affect a couple's relationship. And although we can't predict all the issues we might encounter, we can predict one that may be the most important. Let's take a look.

Passionate and Companionate Love   One change that occurs in almost every long-term relationship has to do with the nature of the love the partners feel for each other. When we first "fall in love" with someone, we are usually overwhelmed with **passionate love**. Characterized by "intense arousal and absorption with a partner" (Hendrick, 2004), passionate love is fueled by

> **Passionate love** Intense arousal and absorption with a partner.

both physiological and cognitive factors. When we feel this intense attraction, our brains produce several neurochemicals, such as dopamine and PEA (phenylethylamine), which stimulate us and promote feelings of excitement and happiness. Every time we are with the object of our attraction or even think about him or her, our brains become flooded with these pleasure chemicals, which is what makes us feel so intensely aroused and keeps us coming back for more. It is, quite literally, a natural high, and an addictive one.

Like any other addictive substance, though, we eventually need more and more of it to feel the same "high." Since our bodies are not capable of continuing to produce these chemicals in such abundance, over time the "high" we feel starts to diminish. What once was enough to "turn us on" isn't quite the same anymore; we become habituated to that level and want more, but our bodies can't produce more. And the amount we are getting isn't producing the same degree of euphoria as it previously did. This is when the intensity of passion starts to drop off gradually. When we start to notice the decrease we might start to question whether we are really "in love" with this person. If we define love as passion-based, then as the passion drops our conclusion might be that we are not.

As if the neurochemical aspect of passion weren't enough, there is also a cognitive factor that contributes to the intensity we feel early in a relationship. Because it is a new relationship, there is much we don't know about the other person, which allows us to fill in the blanks with fantasy. We let our imaginations run wild, and without evidence to the contrary, it is easy to hope that our assumptions might be true. Remember the "what is beautiful is good" phenomenon? This is one way it fuels passion, but it can ultimately set us up for disappointment. As we learn more about our new partner, there are bound to be things about him or her that didn't fit our fantasies (and vice versa). Ultimately, then, the intensity of passionate love tends to be fairly short-lived, as our neurochemical level slowly returns to normal and we get to know our partner better and more realistically.

Companionate love is a strong friendship-based love that tends to be much more stable than passionate love (Sprecher & Regan, 1998). Rather than the intense feelings of arousal and euphoria, companionate love is characterized as a relationship based on trust, mutual respect, affection, honesty, communication, happiness, and sharing (e.g., Castaneda, 1993; Sprecher & Regan, 1998). This fits with Sternberg's conception of companionate love as a combination of intimacy and commitment. Companionate love does not appear to diminish over time in healthy relationships; on the contrary, by its very nature it seems to increase over time. As a couple continue to build a relationship, they learn more about each other and become more connected, which increases all the "intimacy" components of companionate love.

> **Companionate love**
> Relationship based on trust, mutual respect, affection, honesty, communication, happiness, and sharing.

Typically, then, passionate love may be what gets us into long-term relationships, but it is companionate love that sustains them. This is critical knowledge for couples. Otherwise, they may find themselves surprised, upset, and bewildered when the passion starts to die down in their relationship. They may misinterpret this change in their emotional intensity as a sign that something is wrong in the relationship, which may turn the tide from positive to negative. Once we start looking for problems, it is very easy to find them—or create them. They may conclude that they didn't really love each other after all and go their separate ways, cheating themselves out of the opportunity to find out if they could have had a happy long-term relationship. Moreover, they risk dooming themselves to a never-ending series of short-term relationships if they continue to end each new relationship when the passion starts to fade.

Does this mean we must resign ourselves to long-term relationships that are without passion? No! It just means that passion will diminish, but it doesn't have to disappear entirely. Earlier research and theory suggested that a shift from passionate love to companionate love was a natural developmental change in relationships, but newer research indicates that as one increases, the other doesn't necessarily decrease at the same pace. One study of married couples (Tucker & Aron, 1993) found that passionate love continued throughout the relationship, although it did have ups and downs, such as the decrease that typically coincides with the arrival of children. A cross-cultural study of married couples between the ages of 20 and 60 found that the most satisfied couples also reported feeling passionate love for their mates (Contreras, Hendrick, & Hendrick, 1996).

On the other hand, expressed affection and frequency of sex, two important indicators of passionate love, do have a strong tendency to decline fairly rapidly after the first year or two of marriage. But what might surprise you is that long-term married couples don't usually see this as a bad thing: On the contrary, companionate love is associated with high levels of happiness and satisfaction in these relationships (Hecht, Marston, & Larkey, 1994). Companionate love, with its emphasis on intimacy, feels stable, warm, dependable, and emotionally supportive.

The Big Picture   At this point, then, we know that passionate love is a function of the intense emotional arousal we feel early in a romantic relationship, and that our brain chemistry can only sustain that high level for a fairly short period of time. We also know that companionate love is based on the more gradual development of true intimacy over time, and as such, it is more stable than passionate love. Most couples experience a decline in passion that begins shortly after marriage and continues throughout the length of the relationship, but they don't seem upset about it. Instead, they value and appreciate the warmth and closeness of the companionate love that characterizes most long-term relationships. The fact remains, though, that many of us do value passion and feel at least a small amount of disappointment at the thought that it might not last. Add this feeling to the findings that some couples do indeed seem to experience higher and longer-lasting levels of passion than others, and we are left with a question: Are these couples doing anything differently from their less-passionate counterparts, or are they just lucky?

Research has only recently begun to examine this interesting question, but we do have a few early findings that seem to fit with what we know about what causes passion. As you recall, passion is characterized by emotional intensity, which in turn is fueled by brain chemicals that are responding, in part, to the *novelty* of the situation. Over time, what causes passion to decline is our habituation to the same stimulus. So, by engaging in new and interesting experiences with our partner, we can rejuvenate the brain chemistry that fires our passion. Too often, couples fall into a rut, doing the same thing over and over with their free time. To some degree, this predictability is comforting, but at a certain point the comfort is outweighed by feelings of boredom or lack of stimulation. Even though it takes some effort and energy, couples who manage to balance the familiar with the unfamiliar report more passionate love in their relationships (Aron, Norman, Aron, KcKenna, & Heyman, 2000).

A related perspective on passion and intimacy has been proposed by Roy Baumeister and his colleagues (Baumeister & Bratslavsy, 1999). Building on the work cited above, they suggest that passion is a function of *change* in emotion (rather than simply emotion), and thus passionate love can be sustained by change in the *relationship,* especially changes in intimacy that foster greater emotional connection. Baumeister provides some provocative evidence for his supposition, and that evidence supports and strengthens what we've already learned about the value of novelty in a relationship. Several studies have found that engaging in novel and exciting situations increases relationship satisfaction (e.g., Norman & Aron, 1995; Reissman, Aron, & Bergen, 1993); and although passion has not been specifically measured in these studies, Baumeister notes that, because it has been found to be a strong indicator of relationship satisfaction, a rise in relationship satisfaction is likely indicative of a rise in passion.

Probably the most powerful evidence for an increase in intimacy leading to an increase in passion comes from a fascinating study of birthing practices among married couples. It has been well documented for several decades that the arrival of children typically has a negative impact on relationship satisfaction, measured specifically by decreased intimacy and less frequent sex (e.g., Belsky & Isabella, 1985; Call, Sprecher, & Schwartz, 1995). One study, however, wondered if couples who give birth at home might have different experiences (Moran, 1992), and compared these couples to those who gave birth in a more traditional hospital environment surrounded by medical personnel. The results were significant: 85% of couples who gave birth at home reported greater frequency of sex 4 months after their child was born, as well as greater intimacy with their partners. Couples who gave birth in hospitals did not experience these increases. In explaining the findings, researchers suggest that the decision to give birth at home may be reflective of a particularly strong value on intimacy, which is then enhanced by the intimacy of the birthing experience. These findings support Baumeister's proposition that a change in intimacy can promote greater passion.

Finally, our neurochemistry may play a role. Mounting evidence finds that the hormone oxytocin is released in both women and men during sex (e.g., Hiller, 2004), and that it functions also to increase pair bonding (Uvnas-Moberg, 1998). In other words, when we have sex with someone, we get a surge of oxytocin, which (among other things) increases our desire for emotional connection with that person. The initial passion in a relationship, then, may foster the development of a deeper, companionate love, via biological mechanisms as well as emotional and cognitive ones. And the emotional closeness, in turn, might continue to provide motivation for sex with one's partner, ultimately resulting in a "feedback loop" in which sex fuels intimacy, which in turn refuels the desire for sex.

Gottman's Seven Principles

Finally, let's examine evidence from some recent, groundbreaking research that reveals the keys to successful long-term relationships. John Gottman, professor of psychology at the University of Washington, has studied couples for more than 20 years in an effort to figure out what makes some couples' marriages succeed and others fail. His work goes far beyond any other research in this field in that his methods are more scientifically sound than any others. His findings shatter some long-held myths about what makes relationships work and also provide new hope to couples desiring long-term happiness together. He discusses his findings, along with their implications, in his best-selling book, *The Seven Principles for Making Your Marriage Work* (Gottman & Silver, 1999).

At the core of Gottman's principles for success is the need to create and nurture intimacy in your relationship. One of the great ironies of close relationships is that the very trust that we so value often leads us to take these relationships for granted—for example, sacrificing quality time with our partner, trusting that your relationship is strong enough to handle it. Although this is true to a certain extent, Gottman's research has found that a relationship cannot run on residual intimacy for very long. Like anything else, it becomes depleted and needs nurturing and sustenance to remain strong. His seven principles all revolve around specific ways to nurture the precious intimacy that is at the heart of healthy and happy long-term relationships. Interestingly, many of the ideas inherent in his principles are consistent with other research we have reviewed throughout this book. As such, they function as additional and converging evidence of their power to create healthy relationships.

The Importance of Communication

Healthy couples, according to Gottman, have detailed **love maps** that are created out of a deep and broad awareness of their partner. They include the partner's likes and dislikes, fondest hopes and dreams as well as deepest fears, significant memories, closest friends, and preferences about everything from food and entertainment to politics and heroes. These love maps are developed as a result of self-disclosure by one partner, and careful listening and attending by the other partner. Many couples develop love maps early in a relationship, but this information needs constant updating to remain accurate, because people are constantly accumulating new experiences and evolving from them. Unfortunately, many couples assume they know all there is to know about each other, and in the face of competing demands from work and other priorities, they unknowingly sabotage their relationship by failing to stay connected to this degree.

> **Love maps** Created out of a deep and broad awareness of their partner.

Powerful evidence for the importance of love maps comes from a study of couples who just had their first child. As previously noted, this is a time when couples typically experience a drop in intimacy and marital satisfaction. In fact, 67% of the couples in this study experienced a dramatic drop in marital satisfaction after the birth of their first child. The remaining 33%, however, did not—on the contrary, half of them experienced greater marital satisfaction. Researchers traced the difference to the couples' love maps. Those who had richer, more detailed maps sustained their intimacy and relationship satisfaction through this upheaval, whereas those who had less detailed maps did not.

For a sample activity on building a love map, turn now to Activity 11.3.

The Importance of Positive Attributions

In Chapter 5, we noted the power of perceptions in shaping and changing our attitudes and beliefs; additionally, in Chapter 8 we learned about relationship climates (defensive vs. supportive). This research extends to our romantic relationships, in that as long as we are feeling generally positive about the relationship, we give our partner the benefit of the doubt in potentially negative situations, and we interpret positive situations as normal for our happy relationship. This builds and maintains supportive climates. Unfortunately, though, we can be very vulnerable to perceived changes in our relationships, and the climate can shift quickly from positive to negative (e.g., Huston & Chorost, 1994).

> **Positive attributions** Interpreting positive experiences as normal in a relationship, and giving your partner the benefit of the doubt in negative situations.

Research by Gottman and others finds that, as couples begin to take each other for granted and communicate less, small misunderstandings begin to occur. As these misunderstandings start to accumulate, tension rises, and the climate shifts toward defensiveness. That defensiveness fuels more overtly negative communication behaviors, which ultimately extinguish the warm feelings and respect the couple initially relied upon. At this point, the marriage is in trouble, unless time and energy is specifically directed toward rebuilding the positive feelings and regard that are so critical to relationship success.

Gottman provides several exercises that couples can do, separately and together, to rebuild these fragile feelings. They include questions geared toward reconnecting with the positive and happy memories the couple experienced earlier in their relationship, as well as opportunities to challenge the current negative interpretations of the relationship and replace them with more generous-minded interpretations, and "assignments" that remind the couple to prioritize time together doing things that are enjoyable for both of them. Overall, Gottman reports that some couples whose relationships have severely deteriorated are able to revive it by engaging in these activities.

Build an "Emotional Bank Account"   Building on the concept of relationship climate, Gottman further notes the importance of general goodwill and positive feelings in a relationship, and how easy it is to take this for granted and stop doing the little "extra" things that foster this sense of connection. Paying attention to the countless small things you do for each other helps remind each partner of their importance to each other; and on the opposite end of the spectrum, forgetting to do little things for each other or neglecting to prioritize each other chips away at the sense of constancy and support in the relationship. Gottman suggests that the **emotional bank account** created by continuing to make small, everyday sacrifices and by making efforts to notice and appreciate the kindnesses of your partner helps sustain couples through more demanding times in which these efforts may fall a bit short.

> **Emotional bank account**
> Created by continuing to make small, everyday sacrifices and by making efforts to notice and appreciate the kindnesses of your partner.

Critical Thinking QUESTION   Think of a close relationship of your own; it can be a romantic relationship, a close friendship, or a family relationship. In this relationship, identify at least five things that you do to foster goodwill in the relationship, and five things the other person does for you that make you feel valued. Remember to include the "little things."

The Importance of Shared Power   Gottman's work also provides strong evidence for the importance of shared power in a relationship. Noting the long-standing cultural tradition of male dominance and patriarchy in the United States, Gottman further specifies that the challenge here is primarily to the male partner in the relationship. Examinations of couples in conflict reveal that, although the female partner may express negative emotions or anger, she is rarely the one to escalate the anger in a conflict situation. Instead, escalation usually comes from the male partner, whereas the woman is much more likely to keep her negativity at the same level or even attempt to reduce it. Gottman suggests that this male tendency reflects a basic male need to dominate and that, whether its origins are biological or cultural, the evidence unequivocally demonstrates its debilitative effect on marriage. Eighty-one percent of the time, men who cannot overcome this tendency end up divorced (Gottman & Silver, 1999).

Gottman goes on to note the advantage women seem to have over men in basic communication skills, as well in sharing power. Girls grow up playing games that rely on communication, whereas boys' games focus on dominance and can succeed quite well with little or no discussion whatsoever. Additionally, girls' games often involve power sharing and reciprocity (such as in taking turns being the hostess or the leader), whereas boys' play is often consistently led by the dominant boy in the group. As adults, then, it makes sense that women would be more comfortable discussing relationship issues: indeed, Gottman's research finds that 80% of the time, discussions about conflict issues are initiated by the female partner in a relationship. This holds true for all couples, regardless of happiness or conflict levels in the relationship. And, it also makes sense that men—as a result of their early experiences (which is probably fostered greatly by biological factors)—are not well versed in listening to others' perspectives or showing openness to others' suggestions. Unfortunately, this resistance to influence from others is directly at odds with the need for mutual respect and power-sharing in modern romantic relationships.

Conflict Management Skills: Avoiding the Four Horsemen
Gottman's work focuses extensively on how couples handle conflict in their relationship and has discovered some surprising trends. First, the amount of conflict in a relationship is not a good predictor of overall relationship health. Some couples who seem to fight all the time can have a relationship that is just as healthy (or in some cases more so) as that of a couple who rarely fights. *The key to relationship health lies instead in the ratio of positive interactions to negative interaction in the relationship: As long as a couple has five positive interactions for every negative interaction, their relationship will be healthy.* Interactions can be big or small. "Small" positive interactions include such things as a smile, touch, or compliment; "small" negative interactions might include glares or snapping at each other. Essentially, an "interaction" is any moment the couple shares, good or bad. This 5:1 ratio is a very powerful finding that has revolutionized the way relationship experts think about conflict in a relationship. It provides solid evidence for the idea that conflict by itself does not hurt a relationship, as long as the couple compensates for it with positive interactions. This ties back to the idea of an emotional bank account we discussed a bit earlier.

Second, there is no "one size fits all" method of conflict resolution. Even though such techniques as the win-win method of conflict resolution discussed in Chapter 10 can be very effective, Gottman's research has found that some successful couples use methods like this, while other successful couples do not. Some couples, or partners, are simply not well suited to this highly rational and systematic approach toward conflict. Although this may not be surprising, the fact that couples who can't do this *can* still resolve conflict effectively is quite a departure from previous findings and thinking on the subject. To really understand conflict management, and the various ways this can be achieved, we must first understand the key factors that make conflict escalate, or in Gottman's words, the Four Horsemen.

The Four Horsemen are metaphoric phases in what Gottman sees as the apocalyptic demise of many marriages. The first horseman is **criticism**. Gottman recognizes the need to express concern over issues in relationships, but he makes an important distinction between criticism and complaint. A complaint expresses concern about a behavior or situation. Criticism is more broadly directed at the person (rather than the behavior) and includes blame and negative judgment. A complaint is legitimate and constructive, whereas criticism is judgmental and destructive. This is exactly what we learned in Chapter 9 is called I-language. As you recall, I-language expresses concern by stating the behavior, along with the emotional impact and the consequence the behavior has for you. It specifically avoids making judgments or casting blame on the other person. Gottman calls I-language a "soft startup" to conflict discussions, and his research indicates that couples who are able to begin conflict discussions in this manner are much more likely to emerge from the conflict discussion with the relationship and good feelings intact.

> **The Four Horsemen** Metaphoric phases in what Gottman sees as the apocalyptic demise of many marriages.

> **Criticism** Directed at the person (rather than the behavior) and includes blame and negative judgment.

On the other hand, when conflicts begin with criticism, that signals a "harsh start-up." Couples whose discussions begin in this manner are likely to quickly progress to the second horseman, which is **contempt**. Contemptuous behaviors include sarcasm, mocking, name-calling, eye-rolling, and other verbal and nonverbal signals of disgust. Contempt conveys a strong message of disrespect and superiority, which Gottman believes develops from long-simmering resentment in a relationship, fueled by negative thoughts and a negative climate. It is, in his words, poisonous to relationships, and typically leads almost instantly to the third horseman: **defensiveness**.

> **Contempt** Conveys a strong message of disrespect and superiority.

We have already examined defensiveness in fairly great detail in Chapter 10, so by now you should have a solid understanding of what defensive responses sound like, as well as their tendency to increase hostility in a conflict situation. Essentially, defensive responses avoid taking any responsibility for the problem, and instead deflect it back toward the other person. Defensiveness, contempt, and criticism tend to work together, interacting and feeding each other over time in a relationship, until enough negativity builds up to bring on the fourth and final horseman: **stonewalling**. Stonewalling occurs when one partner withdraws from a conversation, either by clamming up or by physically leaving the room and the discussion. This is a way of retaining power, because it leaves the other person completely helpless and devoid of information regarding the partner's feelings and intentions about the conflict and the issue. Gottman's research indicates that stonewalling doesn't usually occur early in a relationship, but instead tends to emerge after repeated and prolonged unresolved conflict. Eighty-five percent of the time, the stonewaller in a relationship is the male partner, and Gottman's research suggests a powerful biological reason for this behavior.

> **Defensiveness** Avoiding taking any responsibility for the problem, and instead deflecting it back toward the other person.

> **Stonewalling** When one partner withdraws from a conversation, either by clamming up or by physically leaving the room and the discussion.

Some Final Words on Conflict Gottman's final key to effective conflict management is both novel and surprisingly obvious: Some conflicts are not going to be resolved. This is true for any couple, but not does necessarily have to signal relationship stress. Instead, couples need to learn to recognize when a conflict is unresolvable (at least, at that time), and to develop ways to accept the situation without getting into a repeating cycle of unproductive and frustrating conflict about it—a pattern Gottman calls **gridlock**.

> **Gridlock** Getting into a repeating cycle of unproductive and frustrating conflict about a currently unresolvable issue.

To overcome gridlock, we must recognize that what appears to be the conflict isn't usually the root of the problem. Instead, one person's seemingly stubborn and irrational position on something is probably just the external manifestation of a long-standing and deeply valued dream or need. For example, one person's need to save a lot of money might reflect a deep need for security, while their partner's need to accumulate material things could reflect a similar need for security. Different needs or dreams show up in habits and patterns that may be obvious or obscure. The key to dealing with the conflict that arises from them lies in first trying to understand where they come from, and then in respecting and honoring your partner enough to accept them—even if they seem unreasonable or irrational.

This doesn't mean you should sacrifice your own needs or values, though. One way to cope with conflict, once you've both shared and understood your respective feelings about the issue, is to each create two lists: one list of your core areas in which you cannot give in, and a second list of the areas in which you can be flexible. Gottman cautions that partners should take all the time they need to create these lists and really dig deeply into themselves to make both areas accurate, honest, and as open as possible. Then, after sharing your lists, try to reach a temporary compromise that you can try out for a few months. Later, revisit the issue, see how you're both feeling about it, and make some adjustments if you need to. This strategy for dealing with seemingly unresolvable conflicts is similar to the integrative approach we learned in Chapter 10.

Finally, Gottman notes the importance of saying thank you to each other in a meaningful way, by expressing what each has contributed that they feel appreciative of.

Creating Shared Meaning By incorporating these principles, behavior patterns, and priorities into a relationship, Gottman believes that a couple develops an ever-increasing closeness and intimacy. This, in turn, creates a sense of shared meaning that permeates the couple's lives and their sense of unity and identity. Ultimately, these principles and the shared meaning they help create continue to work together in a constant feedback loop that makes the relationship grow stronger and more enriching with each passing year.

All in all, Gottman's principles may be the most comprehensive and valid set of recommendations for successful relationships that we have available to us (see Figure 11.5). His book also includes a number of well-crafted and effective exercises that partners can use to develop the various principles and strengths, and thus is highly recommended reading.

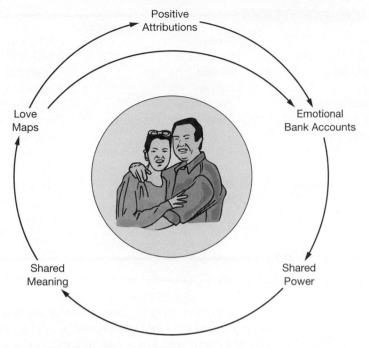

FIGURE 11.5 | Tips for Keeping Romantic Relationships Strong

Interim SUMMARY #3

A variety of useful principles that help sustain healthy long-term relationships has been found by research. First, it is critical to understand the difference between passionate love and companionate love, and the biological and cognitive forces that naturally influence the transition of passionate love to companionate love over time in a relationship. Couples who value passion can use these same biological and cognitive principles to keep their passion alive over the long-term.

John Gottman's groundbreaking studies of married couples has revealed many important keys to keeping marriage relationships positive. First, couples need to prioritize time together and communication, in order to stay connected and nurture their intimacy levels. This facilitates positive attributions and helps couples build emotional bank accounts, both of which help couples cope effectively with difficult times. It is also important that couples share power, a requirement that Gottman notes is typically more difficult for men than for women in our culture.

Conflict management skills include the soft startup, repair attempts, soothing themselves and each other, learning to compromise, and also accepting each other's quirks and flaws. It is also crucial in conflict to avoid the Four Horsemen, which are criticism, contempt, defensiveness, and stonewalling. These destructive conflict behaviors tend to feed each other and create a cycle of negativity that often spells doom for a couple. Finally, effective conflict management includes the recognition that all conflict isn't necessarily resolvable, and that couples must learn to dig deep within themselves to uncover the roots of their issues and to accept each other's sticking points.

Incorporating all of Gottman's principles for healthy relationships helps couples create shared meaning, which fosters unity and an ever-stronger sense of identity in the couple.

CHAPTER TERMS

Intimacy	Storge	Love maps
Passion	Pragma	Positive attributions
Commitment	Mania	Emotional bank
Liking	Agape	account
Infatuation	Proximity	The Four Horsemen
Empty love	Mere exposure effect	Criticism
Romantic love	Symmetry	Contempt
Companionate love	Waist-hip ratio	Defensiveness
Fatuous love	Social exchange theory	Stonewalling
Consummate love	Demographic	Soft start-up
Eros	Passionate love	Repair attempts
Ludus	Companionate love	Gridlock

ACTIVITY 11.1

THE LOVE TRIANGLE IN YOUR LIFE

INSTRUCTIONS: *For this exercise, apply Sternberg's triangle theory of love to a relationship of your own, or to a relationship that you have in-depth knowledge of (e.g., your parents' relationship or the relationship of a couple who is very close to you).*

1. Briefly state the relationship you will analyze, identifying whose relationship it is and how long this couple has been together.

   _____

   _____

   _____

   _____

   _____

2. On a scale of 1–5 (1 = lowest, 5 = highest), how much intimacy does this couple have? Give an example or two to support your answer.

   _____

   _____

   _____

   _____

3. On a scale of 1–5, how much passion does this couple seem to have? Give an example (keeping it G-rated) to support your answer.

   _____

   _____

   _____

_____

_____

4. On a scale of 1–5, how committed to each other does this couple seem? Give an example or two to support your answer.

_____

_____

_____

_____

5. Based on the information you have provided, what type of love does this couple have, according to Sternberg's model?

_____

_____

_____

_____

6. How satisfied is this couple with their relationship? To what extent do you think their love style influences their satisfaction level?

_____

_____

_____

_____

ACTIVITY 11.2
LOVE ATTITUDES SURVEY

PART 1

INSTRUCTIONS: *As you read the following items, think about your current love relationship, or a particular one from your past. Otherwise, answer in terms of what you think your response would most likely be. Then rate your agreement with each statement on a scale of 1–5, with 1 as strong disagreement, and 5 as strong agreement.*

_____ 1. My partner and I have the right physical "chemistry" between us.

_____ 2. I feel that my partner and I were meant for each other.

_____ 3. My partner and I really understand each other.

_____ 4. My partner fits my ideal standards of physical beauty/handsomeness.

_____ 5. I believe that what my partner doesn't know about me won't hurt him/her.

_____ 6. I have sometimes had to keep my partner from finding out about other lovers.

_____ 7. My partner would get upset if he/she knew some of the things I've done with other people.

_____ 8. I enjoy playing the "game of love" with my partner and a number of other partners.

_____ 9. Our love is the best kind because it grew out of a long friendship.

_____10. Our friendship merged gradually into love over time.

_____11. Our love is really a deep friendship, not a mysterious mystical emotion.

_____12. Our love relationship is the most satisfying because it developed from a good friendship.

_____13. A main consideration in choosing my partner was how he/she would reflect on my family.

_____14. An important factor in choosing my partner was whether or not he/she would be a good parent.

_____15. One consideration in choosing my partner was how he/she would reflect on my career.

_____16. Before getting very involved with my partner, I tried to figure out how compatible his/her hereditary background would be with mine in case we ever had children.

_____17. When my partner doesn't pay attention to me, I feel sick all over.

_____18. Since I've been in love with my partner, I've had trouble concentrating on anything else.

_____19. I cannot relax if I suspect that my partner is with someone else.

_____20. If my partner ignores me for a while, I sometimes do stupid things to try to get his/her attention back.

_____21. I would rather suffer myself than let my partner suffer.

_____22. I cannot be happy unless I place my partner's happiness before my own.

_____23. I am usually willing to sacrifice my own wishes to let my partner achieve his/hers.

_____24. I would endure all things for the sake of my partner.

PART 2

INSTRUCTIONS: _Score this scale as follows. First, divide the scale into 6 sets of 4: 1–4, 5–8, 9–12, 13–16, 17–20, 21–24. Second, add up your scores for each set. The first set represents your eros score. The second set represents your ludus score. The third set represents your_ *storge score. The fourth set represents your pragma score. The fifth set represents your mania score. The sixth set represents your agape score.*

My scores are:

Eros _____

Ludus _____

Storge _____

Pragma _____

Mania _____

Agape _____

PART 3: REFLECTIONS

1. What was your highest score? If you scored very highly on two styles, name them both.

   _____

   _____

   _____

   _____

2. Does this score seem to accurately reflect the way you feel about the person you were thinking of when you completed the survey? Write a few sentences that explain your answer.

   _____

   _____

   _____

   _____

3. How satisfied are you with the love style revealed by this survey? Write a few sentences that explain your answer.

   _____

   _____

   _____

   _____

4. a. In what ways does this love style meet your relationship needs?

   _____

   _____

   _____

   _____

   b. How do you think this love style affects your relationship partner?

_____

_____

_____

_____

Source: Adapted from Hendrick, C., Hendrick, S. S., & Dicke, A. (1998). *The Love Attitudes Scale: Short Form. Journal of Social and Personal Relationships,* 15, 147–159.

ACTIVITY 11.3

BUILDING A LOVE MAP

INSTRUCTIONS: *Following are some questions from "The 20 Questions Game," created by John Gottman. Try this with your current partner, or a close friend. First, randomly choose about 10 numbers between 1 and 20, and circle those numbers in the list. Then, ask each other the questions attached to each number. The goal of the game is to learn more about each other.*

1. Name my two closest friends.
2. What stresses am I facing right now?
3. What was I wearing when we first met?
4. Who is my favorite relative?
5. What kinds of books do I like to read?
6. What was one of my best childhood experiences?
7. What is my favorite meal?
8. What do I fear the most?
9. What is my favorite TV show?
10. What makes me feel the most competent?
11. What do I most like to do with time off?
12. Name one of my major rivals or "enemies."
13. What am I most sad about?
14. What are two of my aspirations, hopes, wishes?
15. What is my favorite song?
16. What foods do I hate?
17. Name two of the people I most admire.
18. What personal improvements do I want to make in my life?
19. What is my favorite holiday?
20. Describe in detail what I did today, or yesterday.

REFLECTIONS

A. Overall, how much did you know about your partner? How did it make you feel? How did it make your partner feel?

_____

_____

_____

_____

_____

_____

B. Overall, how much did your partner know about you? How does that make you feel? How does it make your partner feel?

_____

_____

_____

_____

_____

_____

C. How satisfied are you with your current level of intimacy? What are some specific things you can do to increase or maintain it?

_____

_____

_____

_____

_____

_____

ACTIVITY 11.4

TRUTH OR FICTION IN HOLLYWOOD? A FILM REVIEW

INSTRUCTIONS: *For this assignment, choose a recent or classic Hollywood film that centers around a couple in a romantic relationship. Review these questions before watching the film, then write your responses based on your analysis of the relationship portrayed in the film.*

1. Name the film, and name the characters involved in the relationship you will analyze. Briefly describe (in a sentence or two) a bit about each character.

2. What love style(s) seem to best capture the nature of the love you saw between these two characters (you may use Sternberg's theory and/or Lee's theory). Did the love style(s) change or evolve as the film went on? Discuss your

observations, and give a specific example or two of scenes from the film that illustrate your points.

3. Assess the relationship in terms of various concepts involved in attraction and mate selection. Choose any three findings from this chapter to apply to the relationship in the film, and discuss how each one applied (or did not apply).

4. Analyze the relationship in terms of Gottman's seven principles. Choose any three of the principles and discuss how they affected the relationship in the film.

5. Overall, how accurate was the portrayal of this couple's relationship in the film? What is one final thought you are left with after completing this assignment?

SURVIVING AND THRIVING IN THE WORKPLACE

Work and play are the words used to describe the same thing under differing conditions.

—MARK TWAIN

Work . . . what images and feelings come to mind? What does "going to work" mean to you? Is work a means to an end—in essence, something you must do to keep a roof over your head? Or do you think of it more as an end in itself—something that can provide deep and meaningful satisfaction, and a feeling of time well spent? These are important questions to consider, because most of us will spend a majority of our adult lives at work.

In this chapter, we will explore some of the key issues in finding or creating a healthy work life: leadership, motivation, and creativity. We will also consider the meaning of work in a broader sense, and how our individual and cultural values may affect our perceptions and expectations about work. Ultimately, this information will help you begin to clarify the role of work in your own life and set about achieving the vision that you create.

LEADERSHIP

PREVIEW QUESTIONS

(1) Describe six characteristics of effective leaders.

(2) What is the interactionist perspective on leadership? Under what circumstances is task-oriented leadership most effective, and when is relationship-oriented leadership most effective? What is follower readiness, and how can a leader adapt to various levels of follower readiness?

(3) Describe the differences between consensus and charismatic leaders, and the situations in which each is effective.

(4) Discuss the difference between transactional and transformational leadership. How do these two types of leaders develop, and how is each style effective?

(5) How do gender and culture influence leadership effectiveness?

What makes a great leader? Are great leaders born, or they made? Can anyone be a great leader, given the right skills and/or the right situation? Or are there certain people who just have a knack for leadership, and who would probably rise to a position of leadership in most any situation? These are questions that have fascinated humans for centuries and have been the source of debate among some of humankind's greatest thinkers.

Leadership Influencing others to voluntarily accept and pursue goals and challenges that may be difficult, but which are in accord with the values of both the leader and the followers.

More recently, research has attempted to answer these questions in a more systematic way, to determine whether great leaders share certain characteristics and leadership styles, and what it takes for successful leadership in any organization or endeavor. In doing so, a variety of definitions of what exactly constitutes leadership have emerged. For our purposes, we will define leadership rather broadly: **Leadership** is influencing others to voluntarily accept and pursue goals and challenges that may be difficult, but which are in accord with the values of both the leader and the followers.

The most prominent leadership theories tend to support two clusters of answers: the trait theories, which argue that leadership is based on a constellation of personal characteristics; and the interactionist theories, which assert that great leaders are the product of certain personality characteristics combined with the right situational factors. Let's look at these theories in greater detail.

Trait Theory: The Great Person Theory of Leadership

The **Great Person theory of leadership** contends that certain people are born with a set of personality traits that make them destined to become great leaders. Some recent studies have indeed found that leaders tend to score higher than others on certain measurements, which include some of the personality traits we learned about in Chapter 3. One large-scale study that incorporated data from more than 70 individual studies of leadership traits found that leaders were more likely to score high on extraversion, openness to experience, and conscientiousness than people who were not leaders (Judge, Bono, Ilies, & Gerhardt, 2002).

Great Person theory of leadership Certain people are born with a set of personality traits that make them destined to become great leaders.

Drive A multifaceted component that includes achievement motivation, ambition, energy, tenacity, and initiative.

Six Characteristics of Leaders In addition to these personality traits, leadership experts Shelley Kirkpatrick and Edwin Locke (1996) note that research on leadership has identified six characteristics commonly found in leaders. First, leaders possess high levels of **drive**, a multifaceted component that includes achievement motivation, ambition, energy, tenacity, and initiative. People high in achievement motivation especially enjoy taking on and succeeding at challenging tasks, and those high in ambition continually set goals designed to push themselves a little further than before. To reach ever higher goals, a great deal of energy and tenacity is required. One must devote many hours to reaching the goal and have the ability to persist in the face of obstacles and setbacks. Finally, initiative refers to a proactive approach that anticipates problems and takes advance action to avoid them, as well as having the courage to make changes.

Leadership motivation, the second characteristic identified by Kirkpatrick and Locke, is defined as the desire to influence others and to accept the responsibilities that come with this type of power. This includes being comfortable giving direction to others, as well as providing and implementing consequences—both positive and negative—for subordinates' success or failure. Honesty and integrity comprise the third component of effective leaders. **Honesty** refers to open and clear communication, and **integrity** involves consistency between what a person says and what she or he does. This component may be the most important, in that lack of it seriously undermines a leader's effectiveness, even when he or she demonstrates a great deal of the other components.

Self-confidence is the fourth characteristic of good leaders. Taking responsibility for others, including the difficult decisions a leader must make, requires a strong belief in oneself and one's ideas, as well as the emotional stability to remain calm and retain one's composure in difficult and challenging circumstances. Fifth, leaders tend to have above-average intelligence. Part of being an effective leader requires the ability to process large amounts of information, often very quickly, and then to make sound decisions based on critical analysis of that information. And finally, good leaders have a great deal of expertise in their field, which includes knowledge of the industry in general, as well as the niche in which that particular company fits.

All in all, then, research does support the notion that great leaders share some common characteristics (Figure 12.1). But are these characteristics enough, in and of themselves, to propel a person into a leadership position? Or are other factors involved?

> **Leadership motivation** The desire to influence others and to accept the responsibilities that come with this type of power.

> **Honesty** Open and clear communication.

> **Integrity** Consistency between what a person says and what she does.

> **Self-confidence** Strong belief in oneself and one's ideas, as well as emotional stability.

Critical Thinking **QUESTION** Think of someone you know (or know of) who is a leader. To what extent does this person have these six characteristics?

Interactionist Theories of Leadership

An alternative perspective on leadership proposes that great leaders emerge from circumstances that combine an individual with leadership potential with certain situational factors. In other words, becoming a great leader also means being in the right place at the right time. These **interactionist theories**, then, suggest

> **Interactionist theories of leadership** Great leaders emerge from circumstances that combine an individual with leadership potential with certain situational factors.

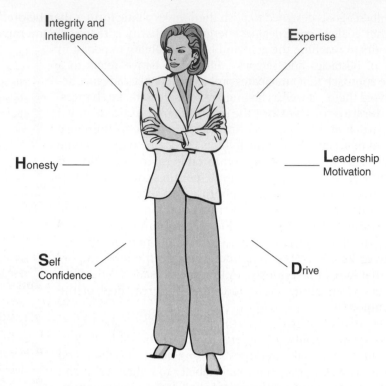

Integrity and
Intelligence

Expertise

Honesty ——

—— Leadership
Motivation

Self
Confidence

Drive

FIGURE 12.1 | The "Shield" of Leadership: Six Characteristics of Leaders

that one type of leader might be effective in one situation, whereas a different type of leader would be effective in a different situation. Several credible theories fit into this category.

> **Task-oriented leaders** Most concerned with productivity, and focus on providing direction and specific instructions for staff members.

> **Relationship-oriented leaders** More concerned with morale, and focus on building good interpersonal relationships and positive feelings among staff members.

Fiedler's Contingency Model of Leadership The first interactionist theory is that of Fred Fiedler (1967, 1987), who proposes that successful leadership relies on the right combination of leadership style and situational control. Fiedler characterized leadership style as either task-oriented or relationship-oriented. **Task-oriented leaders** are most concerned with productivity, and focus on providing direction and specific instructions for staff members. **Relationship-oriented leaders** are more concerned with morale, and focus on building good interpersonal relationships and positive feelings among staff members.

Situational control is measured by a combination of three factors: the leader's degree of power, his or her relationship with staff members, and the clarity of the task. High situational control occurs when a leader is a true authority figure with legitimate power over staff members (in other words, power to hire, fire, and promote), has a positive relationship with staff members, and has a clearly defined task. *Low situational control* occurs when the leader has little power, is not well liked by the staff, and the task is unclear or ambiguous. *Moderate situational control* occurs when one or two of these factors fit the "high" category, with the remaining one or two in the "low" category. In other words, high situational control refers to a great deal of external structure that holds the organization together, whereas low situational control occurs in less stable environments.

> **Situational control** Measured by a combination of three factors: the leader's degree of power, his or her relationship with staff members, and the clarity of the task.

Fiedler predicts that a task-oriented leadership style would be most effective in both high- and low-situational control environments, whereas a person-oriented leader would be best suited to a moderate control environment. The reasoning behind these predictions is a bit complicated. First, in low-control situations, where conditions are unstable, staff members need a great deal of guidance and direction, which makes the task-oriented leader perfect for that environment; a relationship-oriented leader would put too much emphasis on fostering good relations, which wouldn't help people figure out the task or get it accomplished. In high-control situations, the task is clearly defined and relations are positive, and in this situation a task-oriented leader will continue to push staff members to achieve, whereas the relationship-oriented leader may be seen as meddlesome and risks interfering. Moderate-control situations, on the other hand, provide the perfect environment for the relationship-oriented leader, because his or her open communication will foster creative solutions as well as keeping morale high. Table 12.1 summarizes these findings.

Research in a wide variety of workplaces, including the military, hospitals, schools, and sports teams, has demonstrated moderate support for Fiedler's theory (Fiedler & House, 1994). Although the most recent research on leadership has shifted in direction, Fiedler's concepts of task-oriented and relationship-oriented leadership, as well as his basic premise— that effective leadership depends on the right match between the leader and situation—remain widely accepted.

As you think about your own leadership style, are you more relationship-oriented or task-oriented? Turn now to Activity 12.1 to take a quiz designed to give you the answer to this question.

TABLE 12.1 | Fiedler's Recommended Leadership Styles

USE TASK-ORIENTED LEADERSHIP WHEN:	USE PERSON-ORIENTED LEADERSHIP WHEN:
Poor leader/staff relations + unclear task; leader may be powerful or weak	Good leader/staff relations + unclear task + weak leader
Good leader/staff relations + clear task; leader may be powerful or weak	Poor leader/staff relations + clear structure; leader may be powerful or weak
Good leader/staff relations + unclear task + powerful leader	

The Hersey-Blanchard Model of Leadership   An alternate model of the interactionist perspective on leadership has been proposed by Paul Hersey and Kenneth Blanchard (1993). This model adds a new ingredient to the leader-situation recipe: **Follower readiness** is a component that combines the expertise level of staff members with their general motivation to accomplish a task.

Follower readiness A component that combines the expertise level of staff members with their general motivation to accomplish a task.

There are four categories of readiness, seen as increasing degrees of development of a person in a particular type of work. At first, in Stage 1, you know nothing about what to do or how to do it, thus you are unable and also lack the self-efficacy to be willing to jump right in. Next, in Stage 2, you've been there long enough to have general sense of what the work involves and thus you are willing to jump in and give it a try, but you still lack the necessary expertise to do well. Then, by Stage 3, you've developed enough expertise to be feeling a bit *over*confident—hence you feel unwilling to accept direction from your leader, who can see that you have a little learning left to do. Finally, by Stage 4, your expertise has caught up to your confidence level, and you've learned from having experienced Stage 3 that your leader might still know a little more than you do; thus you are both capable and willing.

According to this model, people need different types of leadership at each stage. Certain stages require greater task-oriented leadership, others rely on greater relationship-oriented leadership. This model further specifies that in task-oriented leadership, communication is one-way (from leader to follower), whereas relationship-oriented leadership involves two-way communication and includes good listening behavior on the part of the leader. As an employee progresses through the stages, optimal leader behavior progresses from telling, to selling, to participating, to delegating (see Figure 12.2).

In Stage 1, the staff member is both unskilled and uncertain about the goals; thus, what he needs most is the clear direction and detailed instruction of task-oriented leadership. This leadership style is known as **telling**. When he reaches Stage 2, he has developed a general sense of the goals of the work, and thus the leader should begin to answer questions and listen to her staff member's ideas, incorporating relationship-oriented leadership as well (but still maintaining a high degree of task-oriented leadership to help the staff member continue to learn the specifics of the work). This is the **selling** style of leadership.

Telling Providing task-oriented leadership.

Selling Providing high degrees of both task-oriented and relationship-oriented leadership.

When the staff member reaches Stage 3, his self-efficacy may outpace his expertise, making him think he doesn't need any further instruction. The best type of leadership at this point, according to the model, is high relationship orientation, so that when the employee makes a mistake or runs into a problem, his leader is there as a mentor. This is known as the **participating** style of leadership. Finally, when an employee is highly skilled and also has a strong sense of awareness regarding the goals of the work, the best leader provides little leadership of any kind, and merely backs away and trusts the employee to know what to do and how to do it.

Participating Providing relationship-oriented leadership.

FIGURE 12.2 | Hersey-Blanchard Recommended Leadership Styles

LEADERSHIP STYLE	LEADERSHIP BEHAVIOR	FOLLOWER READINESS
Telling	High Task-Oriented Leadership and Low Relationship-Oriented Leadership	Inexperienced follower needs clear instructions to perform task
Selling	High Task-Oriented Leadership and High Relationship-Oriented Leadership	Follower with some experience needs clear instructions and relational support
Participating	High Relationship-Oriented Leadership and Low Task-Oriented Leadership	Follower with more experience benefits from mentoring
Delegating	Low Task-Oriented Leadership and Low Relationship-Oriented Leadership	Expert follower needs little or no instruction or relational support

This final stage is the **delegating** style of leadership. Overall, according to this model, an effective leader must be able to adjust his or her leadership style to fit the particular stage of development of each employee.

Now, return to Activity 12.1 and complete the section on interpreting your score.

Delegating Providing low levels of both task-oriented and relationship-oriented leadership.

Critical Thinking
QUESTION Think of the last time you were in a follower position, either at work or in another group environment. What stage of follower readiness do you think best characterized you when you first started in that position? Were you in that position long enough for your readiness stage to advance? Finally, in what ways did your leader provide (or not provide) appropriate leadership behavior, according to this model?

to join the leader in what ultimately becomes their collective pursuit of what is now their shared vision and goal. In doing so, their own values and beliefs become transformed as they begin to mirror the leader's guiding principles, and the followers are often transformed into leaders themselves.

Transformational leadership includes four specific types of leader behaviors (Bass, 1985). *Idealized influence* refers to the high moral standards embodied by the leader, which inspire loyalty and admiration in followers. *Inspirational motivation* includes the vision put forth by the leader, as well as his or her keen ability to communicate it effectively and persuasively. *Intellectual stimulation* involves the leader's encouragement of followers to think creatively and to challenge existing norms; the leader also acts as a role model for these behaviors. *Individual consideration* is the leader's attention to the individual needs of the followers, and his or her facilitation of their continued development. By employing all four of these types of behaviors, the leader not only inspires followers to join the cause, but leads by example, through which followers often learn to become leaders in their own right.

Charismatic leaders, discussed in the previous section, seem especially suited to transformational leadership. Their unique and powerful ability to motivate others to work toward goals that transcend self-interest and instead aim for a higher, more collective purpose corresponds closely with the goal of transformational leadership. But whereas the charismatic leader does seem to meet the first two behavioral criteria we described (idealized influence and inspirational motivation), she or he does not necessarily fulfill the latter two (intellectual stimulation and individual consideration). Thus, it would seem that some, but not all, charismatic leaders may also be transformational leaders; the concepts do overlap, but are not identical.

Is One Style Better Than the Other?

Overall, research strongly supports the advantages of transformational leadership over transactional leadership, both in productivity and in follower satisfaction (e.g., Lowe, Kroeck, & Sivasubramaniam, 1996). However, a closer look indicates that transactional leadership sometimes serves an important purpose as well. Transactional leadership operates within an existing organizational structure and with an eye toward existing goals and current performance levels. Within this framework, the transactional leader's pattern of monitoring and controlling followers' behavior through use of rewards and other exchanges has been found to be effective at maintaining performance levels and job satisfaction.

Its effectiveness is limited, however, in comparison to that of transformational leadership. Research that measures both transactional and transformational leadership behaviors in the same organization demonstrates that the highest levels of performance, motivation, and job satisfaction occur when both transactional *and* transformational leadership behaviors are present. One interpretation of this finding is that transactional methods are useful in maintaining the status quo in a group, but transformational methods are necessary to keep moving forward and to experience growth, both for individuals within the organization and for the organization itself.

What Influences Leadership Style?   Finally, a very interesting perspective on how a person becomes a transactional or transformational leader has been proposed by developmental psychologist Robert Kegen (1982). You might recall from Chapter 2 that human development is often conceptualized as a series of stages. In keeping with that framework, Kegen's work suggests that transactional and transformational leadership behaviors evolve out of different stages of development of a person's view of the self and the world (see Table 12.2). This theory also fits nicely with the research indicating two specific levels of exchange within the transactional leadership style.

Transactional leaders who rely on low-level exchanges, such as money or other tangible resources, tend to be motivated primarily by their own agendas. In other words, these leaders are most interested in achieving their own goals and needs, and thus they make decisions that rely on their own perceptions and beliefs. These perceptions and beliefs include the assumption that others are motivated by their own personal agendas as well. In other words, this leader's worldview seems to be very individualistic, operating from the core assumption that each person must look out for himself. Although this leader may say that he is interested in higher goals, such as morale and community building, he doesn't possess a cognitive framework that can really embrace this concept.

Transactional leaders who rely on high-level exchanges, such as the exchange of emotional resources like trust or respect, are operating at a higher level of development, according to Kegen. These leaders are motivated primarily by the desire for positive relationships with their followers. In their decision making, they are able to consider the needs of others in addition to their own needs and goals, and in fact they might sacrifice their own needs in order to maintain positive relationships with others. These leaders recognize that some followers are more interested in mutually satisfying work relationships than in concrete rewards, and in communicating this understanding they motivate their followers more effectively than they would with the use of concrete rewards. Their ultimate goal is to achieve mutual trust and respect.

Whereas this relationship orientation is often effective, it is also a double-edged sword. Sometimes a leader must make tough decisions that end up siding with one constituent over another, and this type of leader may become immobilized in this

---

TABLE 12.2 | Kegen's Developmental Model of Transactional and Transformational Leaders

STAGE	WHAT MOTIVATES THE LEADER (UNCONSCIOUSLY)	WHAT THE LEADER FOCUSES ON IN DECISION MAKING
Lower-Order Transactional	Personal goals and agendas	Personal beliefs, feelings, needs
Higher-Order Transactional	Positive relationships built on mutual trust and respect	Needs of group and of self; fairness to everyone
Transformational	Strongly held guiding principles	How can strong relationships move group toward embracing and achieving vision?

situation, unable to make a decision that doesn't preserve all existing loyalties. When this happens, the very principle that created his effectiveness—his interest in loyalty and mutuality—can lead to his downfall.

Transformational leaders, according to Kegen's model, are operating at the highest level of development. These leaders have developed a strong internal sense of their values and use it as the guiding force of their leadership and their decision making. Whereas the high-quality-exchange transactional leader has difficulty resolving conflict when competing loyalties are involved, the transformational leader is not similarly bound. Instead, he is able to transcend the personal needs of himself and others, and to make a decision that is consistent with the strong value system that began with him but became the value system of the group. In other words, this leader possesses a wisdom that allows him to see beyond some of the immediate negative consequences of a decision and focus instead on the greater positive consequences that the decision will ultimately promote. This same unwavering commitment to the value system inspires followers to embrace the value system as their own.

It is important to note that this developmental model of leadership aims to explain the boundaries of a leader's cognitive viewpoint, and that boundaries decrease with each higher level of development. For example, a leader at the lowest level is confined to personal agenda-oriented decisions and must rely on the low-level exchange system of rewards for services. A leader at a higher level, however, although capable of utilizing other forms of motivation, in certain situations may choose to utilize the reward system of low-level exchange to meet a relational or value-driven goal. So, just because a leader is utilizing a reward-for-service system in one instance, observers should not conclude that he is necessarily stuck in a low developmental stage; instead, observers should look for long-term patterns of decision making to ascertain a leader's developmental stage.

Finally, Kegen theorizes that, just as individuals are capable of expanding their cognitive frameworks as they grow older and wiser, leaders are capable of progressing from a lower stage to a higher stage as they develop and grow. In reflecting on this assertion, it would stand to reason that personality traits might influence the degree to which a person is capable of growth. A leader with a high degree of openness to experience, for example, would probably be more likely to experience greater growth than one without as much of this trait.

Cultural Issues in Leadership

Now that we have an in-depth understanding of the various qualities and behaviors associated with leadership, as well as several major theories of leadership, the final question is this: Are leadership styles, preferences, and values consistent across cultures, or does culture play a significant role in determining leadership effectiveness?

Culture and Leadership   To what extent does culture, and the different values associated with various cultures, influence leadership styles and preferences? As you might guess, much of the work conducted (and therefore, cited in this book thus far) has been among individualistic cultures, which, as you know, tend to place a higher value on achievement than on relationships in the workplace. Thus, we might have predicted the Western preference for task-oriented leadership. Collectivistic cultures, on the other hand, show greater preference for relationship-oriented leadership. One study in Iran identified good leaders as being nurturing, supportive, and "like a father" (Ayman & Chemers, 1983). Another study, this one in India, found that the most effective leaders begin by nurturing relationships and then give task-oriented direction (Sinha, 1986).

Leadership preferences, then, are clearly influenced by culture and its associated values. "Asking people to describe the qualities of a good leader is in fact another way of asking them to describe their culture," says noted cultural researcher Geert Hofstede (2001, p. 388). Power distance (PD) is an additional cultural dimension that predicts differences in leadership styles and preferences. Power distance, as you recall from Chapter 1, refers to the way a culture deals with inequality: High PD cultures have stricter boundaries between status groups and value inequality as a means for maintaining order and structure. Low PD cultures, on the other hand, strive to reduce inequality and are less comfortable with status and power differences.

The United States, for example, as a relatively low PD culture, has strong preferences for more democratic, participative leadership. Although this might work well in the United States and other low PD cultures, it is vital to recognize that, in high PD cultures, this emphasis on two-way communication between leader and subordinate is very uncomfortable for both parties. In one Greek study, for example, a Greek employee's boss—who was American by birth and education—asked him how long he thought a job he was working on should take. The Greek subordinate felt embarrassed, and reported to the researcher, "He is the boss. Why doesn't he tell me?" (Triandis, 1973). This is an eloquent illustration of how a leadership practice that is valued and appreciated in one culture can be completely ineffective in another.

Gender and Leadership   Numerous studies have examined gender issues in leadership. Overall, it seems that there are more similarities than there are differences between the leadership styles of men and women (Powell, 1993). The differences that do exist, however, are worth noting, and also not surprising, given what we know about gender roles and stereotypes.

In general, men are more likely to rely on task-oriented leadership, whereas women are more likely to combine task- and relationship-oriented leadership styles (Eagly & Johnson, 1990; Helgeson, 1990). To clarify, men and women are equally task-oriented, but women tend to be more democratic and participative in their leadership style. This finding—that women in leadership roles are just as task-oriented as their male counterparts—does not seem to have had an impact on gender role stereotypes, however. In a study that required group members to rate each other's leadership abilities, then elect a leader, men were elected to the leadership positions in 67% of the cases (Eagly & Karau, 1991); on the small number of leadership ability items that tapped into relationship-oriented leadership skills, women received higher ratings than their male counterparts. Overall, though, men were rated better task-oriented leaders, and thus better leaders overall.

If women are equally task-oriented as men and have the advantage of greater relationship orientation, why, then, are there still far fewer women than men in leadership positions? One researcher cites the deep conflict many women feel about juggling the conflicting demands of work and family (Crosby, 1991). Other research underscores the powerful and pervasive nature of gender role stereotypes. For example, one study noted that, in same-sex work groups, the person who was randomly seated at the head of the table was often considered to be the leader; in mixed-sex groups, though, this rule only applied when the person at the head of the table was male (Porter, Geis, & Jennings (Walstead), 1983). Another study found that both men and women were more likely to be perceived as leaders when they were assertive, but the nonverbal behaviors of group members reflected subtle differences: Members were less likely to smile and nod, and instead more likely to frown in response to verbal assertiveness, when the leader was female (Butler & Geis, 1990).

Overall, it seems that group members are more likely to be approving and value their leaders when the leader fits their preconceived notions—in other words, their stereotypes—of a leader (Eagly, Makhijani, & Klonsky, 1992). This might seem to make sense, but it also threatens our abilities and efforts to think more rationally and grow beyond our stereotyped expectations.

Understanding Leadership Styles: Some Final Words

We've covered a great deal of information in this section, with the goal of understanding the most useful models of leadership. How can we use this information?

First, and perhaps most obvious, this information can be useful to anyone who is currently in a leadership position, or who may be in a leadership position in the future. Having an understanding of what different followers need at different stages of development, as well as what your own strengths are as a leader, is critical to effective functioning for both you and your group.

Remember, too, that there are many different kinds of leaders, some of whom have titles that designate them as leader and some of whom do not. Leaders are not only presidents and managers of organizations; they are also coaches, teachers, community activists, parents, and role models. They are also those individuals in any group who are seen as the "go to" person, or someone who can be relied on to stand up and voice an opinion. With this in mind, reconsider yourself in terms of leadership: Can you identify leadership positions you hold in any ways you did not recognize prior to studying this section?

Finally, consider those who lead you, in all the various dimensions identified in the previous paragraph. To what extent do these leaders make effective use of the principles of leadership? In what ways do they fall short? Can you identify the charismatic leader and the consensus leader? The transactional leader and the transformational leader? Understanding the leadership style and behaviors of the leaders in your world can help you be more effective in your own role.

As we have seen, leaders take many forms in many different situations. Turn now to Activity 12.2 for a chance to interview a leader in your own life and learn what makes this leader effective or not.

Interim SUMMARY #1

A variety of personality and situational factors have been put forth as predictors of leadership effectiveness. The Great Person theory argued in favor of personality characteristics being the dominant force in determining who becomes a leader. Research utilizing the Big Five personality framework does indeed note that leaders are more likely to be extraverted, open to experience, and conscientious. Other research in this area finds that leaders score higher than followers on six additional characteristics: Drive, leadership motivation, honesty and integrity, self-confidence, intelligence, and expertise have been found to characterize leaders.

Interactionist leadership theories argue that great leaders are a combination of personality and situational variables. Fiedler's contingency model contributed the concepts of task orientation and relationship orientation, and also the notion that effective leadership behavior depends on the degree of environmental control available in a situation. The Hersey-Blanchard model added the concept of follower readiness and applied it to the equation of leader effectiveness: In that model, effective leaders must use different combinations of task orientation and relationship orientation with different levels of follower readiness. The third interactionist approach distinguishes between consensus leaders, whose effectiveness grows out of their ability to negotiate compromise, and charismatic leaders, whose effectiveness comes from their personal ability to inspire great loyalty. Research suggests that charismatic leaders may be more likely to emerge and gain success in times of crisis, whereas stability is maintained well by the consensus-building tactics of the consensus leader.

A broader view of leadership style includes the models of transactional and transformational leadership. Transactional leaders' effectiveness results from their use of rewards: Low-level exchanges offer an equitable exchange of productivity for pay raises or other tangible rewards; high-level exchanges rely on the exchange of more mutual and/or relational rewards such as respect or trust. Transformational leaders' effectiveness grows out of their ability to communicate a vision powerful enough to inspire followers to embrace it as their own. Transformational leaders also model their behavior to followers, which in turn often promotes the development of similar leadership abilities in the followers.

Transformational leadership tends to produce higher job satisfaction and productivity than transactional leadership, although transactional leadership can sustain the status quo in an organization. Also, a leader's transactional or transformational style may be influenced by his or her stage of development. Finally, leadership behaviors are influenced by both gender and culture. Women utilize as much task orientation as men and more relationship orientation, but they still battle obsolete stereotypes about women as leaders. Culture is a powerful predictor of leadership preferences and is influenced by individualism–collectivism and power distance orientations.

MOTIVATING PEOPLE IN THE WORKPLACE

PREVIEW QUESTIONS

(1) Why are some people more motivated than others?

(2) What is the difference between intrinsic and extrinsic motivation, and how are they affected by a person's goals? Describe three ways of fostering intrinsic motivation.

(3) What important steps are involved in effective goal setting?

Now that we understand some basic principles of leadership, let's take a broader look at the workplace. In addition to the right leadership style, what other factors influence a person's motivation to work? This topic has been studied by psychologists for more than 100 years, and the results can help us understand why we are motivated in some situations more than others, as well as how motivation varies among different people.

Achievement motivation, or the desire to attain a high standard of excellence in one's life pursuits, seems to vary among individuals. As you have probably observed in your own life, some people are driven to succeed and do well in whatever they attempt, whereas others appear to drift along, placing a higher value on different goals. What influences a person's level of achievement motivation and helps explain these differences we have observed?

> **Achievement motivation**
> The desire to attain a high standard of excellence in one's life pursuits.

Studies indicate that, although a person's general level of achievement motivation tends to be fairly stable over time, it is influenced by situational factors. For example, one study gave fifth graders a series of learning and problem-solving games. As they worked on the games, some children were praised for "being smart," and others were praised for "working hard." When children were given feedback indicating whether they had "passed" or "failed" a specific game, the children who had been praised for "working hard" were more likely to try the game again when they were told they had failed. Children who had been praised for "being smart," when told they had failed, were more likely to give up and subsequently lie to their peers about how well they did (Mueller & Dweck, 1998).

In explaining these results, researchers suggested that children perceive intelligence as being fixed, so when their achievement level is attributed to intelligence ("being smart"), failure is considered lack of intelligence; subsequently, they feel they have no control over it and might as well quit. Children who are praised for "working hard," on the other hand, feel greater control over their achievement, and therefore are more likely to persist in the face of failure.

How does this help us understand why some people are motivated more than others? We may be born with a genetic predisposition to a certain approach toward life, but our motivation can be increased by the right kind of support in our environment—from our families, teachers, and friends. One type of support, as demonstrated in the previously mentioned study, comes from being encouraged to see yourself as being in control of your efforts and achievement level. We are also influenced by the rewards we perceive from a task, as well as our enjoyment level of that task, which are two different types of motivation that we will explore next.

> **Intrinsic motivation**
> Desire to pursue or engage in something for the internal rewards it brings.

> **Extrinsic motivation**
> Driven by the pursuit of external rewards or the avoidance of external punishments.

Intrinsic and Extrinsic Motivation

In general, there are two basic types of motivation. **Intrinsic motivation** is a desire to pursue or engage in something for the internal rewards it brings, such as an inner sense of fulfillment, enjoyment, or pleasure. **Extrinsic motivation** is driven instead by the pursuit of external rewards (such as money, praise, recognition, or other tangible rewards) or the avoidance of external punishments. In applying these concepts to ourselves, it is important to recognize that we can be intrinsically motivated toward some goals, but extrinsically motivated toward others. For example, you might be intrinsically motivated in your psychology class, because what keeps you coming to class and working hard is the interesting material. You really enjoy learning about it and thinking about how it helps you understand yourself and others better. Your efforts in your math class, on the other hand, might be extrinsically motivated if you are not enjoying the material, but you keep going to class and studying so you will get a decent grade, or so you won't fail the class and have to take it again.

 *Critical Thinking* QUESTION Outside of school, identify one thing you spend time on for which you are intrinsically motivated, and also one thing you spend time on for which you are extrinsically motivated. For each situation, explain your answer.

Intrinsic and extrinsic motivation also differ with respect to the type of goal an individual is pursuing. **Performance goals** focus on a specific level of achievement, such as an A in a class, a promotion at work, or winning a competition. **Mastery goals**, on the other hand, focus on improving one's level of skill or competence at the task. Connecting this information to what you know about the difference between intrinsic and extrinsic motivation, which type of goal do you think is associated with intrinsic motivation, and which with extrinsic? If you associated mastery goals with intrinsic motivation, and performance goals with extrinsic motivation, you were exactly right! When a person is intrinsically motivated toward something, her goals are more likely to be mastery oriented, whereas extrinsic motivation tends to thrive on performance goals. In the study of fifth graders described above, the students who were given feedback about working hard (in other words, encouraged to value hard work rather than intelligence) were much more likely to enjoy the games, and also to choose mastery goals over performance goals.

> **Performance goals** Focus on a specific level of achievement.

> **Mastery goals** Focus on improving one's level of skill or competence at the task.

So what does all this mean? Intrinsic motivation stimulates enjoyment of a task, as well as higher achievement in that area. The intrinsically motivated mastery goals provide a longer-term and more sustainable level of enjoyment for that task, and also provide the resilience to keep us pushing onward when we experience failure. And everyone experiences failure; there is simply no way to excel in something without overcoming a series of failures. Interpreted in the light of performance goals, though, failure has farther-reaching and more debilitating effects, which ultimately undermine both enjoyment of the process and eventual level of achievement.

Fostering Intrinsic Motivation

Given the importance of intrinsic motivation, then, how can we cultivate it in ourselves, as well as in others?

Use Rewards Wisely First, we must note that not all external rewards are created equal. Researchers have identified a distinction between rewards used to control and rewards used to inform (Deci & Ryan, 1987; Pittman, 1980).

The typical type of external rewards associated with performance goals and extrinsic motivation are used to control: for example, telling a student that he will get money for every A he earns, or offering employees cash bonuses if they attain a certain level of performance. Clearly, this type of reward serves to underscore the importance of performance, thus fostering extrinsic motivation. Then, when the reward is no longer offered, the person's performance is likely to drop, since his motivation was reward-based. Research also indicates that overreliance on external rewards actually decreases intrinsic motivation: College football players on a scholarship (thus getting external rewards for playing) report enjoying the game less than their nonscholarship teammates (Ryan, 1980).

Informational rewards To inform a person that he or she has done well at the end of a task.

Control-based rewards Incentives for doing well offered before a task is accomplished.

On the other hand, praising employees for doing well *after* the fact, or taking a student on a surprise weekend trip to celebrate doing well at the end of a semester, are **informational rewards**. In other words, they are given to inform a person that he or she has done well at the end of a task—as opposed to **control-based rewards**, which are offered as incentives for doing well before a task is accomplished. It seems that control-based rewards increase a person's focus on performance and commensurately detract from the inherent enjoyment of the process. Informational rewards, coming after a task has been completed, strengthen the internal sense of satisfaction a person has already gained from mastery of the process.

The Art (and Science) of Goal-Setting Setting goals is another key element in fostering achievement motivation. As it turns out, though, not all goals are created equal, either. Certain goals are much more likely to be attained than others, and by following a series of steps in setting our goals, we can increase our own odds of achieving them (see Figure 12.3).

First, *goals must be specific*. If you want to do better at school, you should identify a specific area where you want to improve and target a specific measure of achievement of the goal. For example, instead of "I'm going to improve at school," tell yourself, "I want to raise my grade from a C to a B in biology." Or, if you're trying to get in better shape, don't just say, "I'm going to get in better shape." Instead, identify a specific way you will do that, such as "I'm going to walk 30 minutes a day at least three times a week." Research strongly

---

FIGURE 12.3 | Cultivating Intrinsic Motivation

- Use rewards to inform, not to control.
- Set goals that are specific, challenging but achievable, and positive.
- Create conditions that support people's values and preferences.

supports the achievement of this type of goal over more generalized, vague goals. In the same way, setting goals for yourself at work must be specific, rather than general.

Second, *goals must be challenging, but achievable*. Here is where the art of goal setting comes in: The most achievable goals are those that push you a little further than you've gone before, but are not so high that you're setting yourself up for failure. So, going from a C to a B in class would be more achievable than, say, raising your GPA from 2.1 to 3.8 in one term. Similarly, if you are not in the habit of exercising, starting out with 30 minutes of walking three times a week will require some determination and effort, but it is achievable, whereas "going to the gym for two hours a day every day of the week" is probably not.

Third, *goals should be framed in positive terms,* or aimed at what you want to achieve, rather than what you want to avoid. These positive goals are called *approach goals,* whereas goals framed in terms of what you're trying not to do are called *avoidance goals.* For example, if you want to eat a healthier diet, telling yourself, "I'm going to eat five servings of fruits and vegetables each day" is an approach goal, whereas "I'm going to go to McDonald's less often" is an avoidance goal.

The problem with avoidance goals is similar to one of the problems with punishment that we discussed in Chapter 3: They don't focus your attention on an alternative, more desirable behavior. As such, they undermine our efforts to change. If we instead focus on what we *will* do, we are taking an automatic step toward success: When we think about stopping at McDonald's but remember that we're trying to quit, we already have an idea of what we can do instead, which increases our chances of doing it. Also, this positive focus may produce more positive emotions, because it shifts your attention to achievement of your goal, rather than letting it linger on what you're missing (Elliot & Sheldon, 1998).

Turn now to Activity 12.3 to apply these goal-setting tips to your own life.

Adapt to the Needs of Your Environment   One additional strategy that helps motivate others has been identified by researchers. As we have noted previously, different people have different values and different goals; thus, they also respond differently to various types of incentives and working conditions. Some people are more collaborative, whereas others have a strong preference for independent decision making. If you know the people for whom you are responsible and need to put some of them into a team to work together, whom will you choose? Let the collaborative people collaborate! Similarly, some people are highly motivated by recognition, so publicly recognize them when they do well. People with strong mastery goals enjoy challenges more than people with performance goals. To the extent possible, creating conditions that work with (rather than against) people's individual preferences and styles fosters greater achievement and has the added benefit of creating a happier workplace environment.

What is one situation in which you could increase motivation (in yourself or in others) by fostering intrinsic motivation? To explore how you can do this, complete Activity 12.4.

Interim SUMMARY #2

Achievement motivation varies among individuals, but can also be shaped by our environment. Intrinsic motivation tends to foster greater and longer-term enjoyment of a task than extrinsic motivation, and thus has a positive impact on achievement motivation. Also, mastery goals promote intrinsic motivation more than performance goals.

Intrinsic motivation can be stimulated by judicious use of rewards, and by using rewards to inform rather than to control. Setting goals that are specific, challenging but achievable, and framed in positive terms increases the likelihood that we will achieve our goals, and thus fosters greater motivation as well. Finally, paying attention to what motivates the various individuals in your environment can be key in creating conditions that encourage people to work harder and develop higher levels of motivation.

CREATIVITY

PREVIEW QUESTIONS

(1) What is creativity?

(2) What are six key components found in creative people?

(3) Can creativity be fostered in anyone, or is creative ability something "you either have or you don't"? Explain your answer.

In this chapter, we are considering various factors that help us gain a better understanding of our workplace, and improve our experiences in the workplace. We have already learned the important role intrinsic motivation plays in our enjoyment of work—intrinsic motivation is essentially synonymous with enjoyment of a task or a type of work. It stands to reason, then, that anything we can do to increase our intrinsic motivation at work will in turn increase our enjoyment of work. And one of the most effective things we can do toward this goal is to exercise our creative powers.

What Is Creativity?

Creativity is defined as producing something that is both novel and useful. In other words, it needs to be something new and previously unknown (at least to the creator), but it also has to have a purpose. Many people think that creativity is associated only with artistic pursuits or with great inventions or discoveries, but creativity can be exercised in any area. Parents are creative when they think of a new and effective way to teach their child an important lesson. Skateboarders or other athletes who develop a new technique that improves the sport or their own performance are exercising creativity. Students are creative when, after struggling to master a subject or concept, they suddenly come up with a method that works. We all have the ability to be creative—some of us are just more experienced at it than others.

> **Creativity** Producing something that is both novel and useful.

Although there are certainly people we think of as creative "geniuses"—perhaps Picasso, Einstein, Beethoven, or the Wright brothers come to mind—most psychologists who study creativity find that a fairly predictable set of common characteristics underlie most creative ideas and discoveries. By identifying these characteristics, we can set about applying them to our own lives and becoming more routinely creative, thus fostering greater intrinsic motivation, enjoyment, and meaningfulness in our work.

The Wright Brothers: A Case Study in Creativity

To set the stage for our discussion of the common characteristics of creativity, let's use the Wright brothers' invention of the airplane as a case study. Many people think the Wright brothers were the first people to "fly," but that isn't actually the case. As early as the 15th century, Leonardo da Vinci was experimenting with a "flying machine"; although his ideas remained on the drawing board, they provided inspiration for several pioneers in flight over the next few centuries. In the middle of the 18th century, Sir George Cayler worked extensively on flying and developed the first glider. One hundred years later, Otto Lilienthal modified Cayler's ideas and actually made more than 2,000 flights in what was essentially a hang glider. He also used mathematics and aerodynamics to make extensive calculations for weight and wind velocity. Around the same time, Samuel P. Langley developed the first powered flying machine, which had two sets of wings with propellers between each set and used a miniature steam engine to power the propellers; and Octave Chanute was modifying Lilienthal's hang glider to include two wings on each side as well.

The Wright brothers were fascinated by the work of Lilienthal, Langley, and Chanute, and pored over published reports of their experiments. As children, Orville and Wilbur had played with a toy helicopter that used rubber bands to power its propellers, and had experimented themselves with building similar contraptions. As they grew older, they also developed expertise in building other structures and in the mechanics and engineering of bicycles. So, when they began the process of what would eventually become the "invention" of the first airplane, they were building on discoveries that had already been made as well as their own expertise in mechanics and engineering.

Their first attempt didn't work. On the contrary, it took more than five years of trial and error, patience and perseverance, and continual modification before they took their famous "first flight" at Kitty Hawk. Thus, what observers often see as a rather instantaneous discovery, based on a sudden insight, is in truth very often the result of a much more extensive and complicated process. In addition, the Wright brothers' story nicely illustrates the characteristics commonly found in creative people.

Characteristics of Creative People

Expertise　First, creative people have expertise in their area. The more a person knows about a concept, business, sport, art, or other area, the greater and broader her range of experiences in that area. Think about it. In what area are you most creative? Chances are, it's something that you've been doing for some time and for which you have developed expertise.

Divergent Thinking Many times a creative effort is the result of *recombining existing ideas or ingredients in a new, untried combination.* The more a person knows about the various ingredients and how they work together, the greater the potential for a creative new discovery with those ingredients. This **divergent thinking**, or the ability to generate many ideas, or more complex ideas from a single starting point, is another characteristic of creativity. We can see how our ability to think this way would be enhanced in our own areas of expertise.

> **Divergent thinking** The ability to generate many ideas, or more complex ideas from a single starting point.

Divergent thinking can be developed by frequent *brainstorming*, wherein one or more people generate as many ideas, thoughts, or solutions as possible in a short period of time. In doing so, their ideas build off each other, or "piggyback" on each other, which helps stimulate the continued flow of thoughts. The key to successful brainstorming is to write down every idea, no matter how crazy or impossible it might seem. It is crucial to avoid the temptation to start evaluating the ideas or thinking about why one would or would not work. Instead, stay focused on the "storming" aspect of the task. Later there will time for evaluation of the strengths and weaknesses of the various ideas you generated, but getting sidetracked by that different type of brain activity too early inhibits the "storming" phase.

To try out brainstorming for yourself, turn to Activity 12.5.

Risk Taking and Its Components Third, creative people are risk-takers, although not necessarily in terms of risking accidental death like the Wright brothers! Risk-taking stems from an adventurous personality, and we expect that people who score higher on the Big Five trait of openness to experience would be more inclined to take risks than people with lower scores on that trait (McAdams, 1994).

Even though this characteristic has genetic roots, our individual risk-taking abilities can be increased with practice and the right attitude. What is the right attitude? It is both cognitive and emotional in nature, and centers around the old adage, "Nothing ventured, nothing gained." In other words, it relies on the *awareness that risks are inherent in growth*—if we never step out of our comfort zone, how can we ever progress forward? This awareness is the cognitive component. Reminding ourselves of this can help us overcome our fear of risk taking. The other element—*self-confidence*—is both emotional and cognitive in nature; it takes a fairly hardy sense of self-confidence to move ahead in the face of the unknown. Every time we do this, though, it adds to our self-confidence, so this is where practice becomes important, because it gets a little easier each time. As E. Paul Torrance put it, "It takes courage to be creative: Just as soon as you have a new idea, you're in the minority of one."

Our abilities to engage in risk taking rely on two additional cognitive components: *the ability to be critical of one's own work*, and a *willingness to learn from one's mistakes*. The trial-and-error involved in most creative developments is only successful when the creator is willing and able to step back from the project and objectively assess what is working and what is not. This type of analysis is made much easier by the perception of mistakes as a normal part of learning and growth. Rather than judging ourselves as "wrong" or "inferior" in some way when an attempt doesn't succeed the way we had hoped, it is vital that we remove the emotional negativity from the experience, and replace it with a positive emotionality based on the courage we showed in the attempt. Giving ourselves a mental "pat on the back" for trying can give us the boost we need to get past any feelings of failure, and instead to focus on learning from the experience so we can improve on it the next time.

A Creative Environment   All these characteristics lead us to the next component in creativity: a creative environment. Studies of creative people find that they establish environments for themselves that foster their creativity. The specifics of the environment vary with individual needs and the particular nature of the work—sometimes it involves removing distractions, sometimes it relies on the right type of technical and/or esthetic elements in the work space, and sometimes it involves collaboration with others. The Wright brothers, as well as many other famous inventors, exchanged ideas with others who were working on similar inventions, asking questions and learning from one another's experiences. This has the added benefit of helping a person *see an idea or problem from an alternate perspective*. Similarly, research on creativity finds that *creative people tend to surround themselves with other creative people*, which effectively creates an environment in which the norms themselves foster greater creativity. As psychologist Robert Sternberg noted, "The most powerful way to develop creativity in your students is to be a role model. Children develop creativity not when you tell them to, but when you show them." This concept applies to adults as well. Creative environments are filled with role models for creativity.

Patience and Its Components   Another component of creativity is patience. Creative discoveries, as we have learned, are more typically the result of extensive and effortful processes rather than sudden flashes of insight. As such, it takes time and persistence to achieve them. It also requires the creator to develop a greater *tolerance for uncertainty*—an ability that can be enabled by self-confidence as a person uses her self-confidence to remain strong and focused even when she doesn't know what the next step will be.

In addition, research finds that the creative process often includes one or more periods of **incubation**, when the creator walks away from the project for a time and lets the ideas and discoveries made thus far develop naturally and without conscious effort. Becoming impatient with the process, or overly focused on meeting a deadline, can influence a creator to eliminate the incubation period, and ultimately risk missing out on the potential fruits of that phase.

> **Incubation** The creator walks away from the project for a time and lets the ideas and discoveries made thus far develop naturally and without conscious effort.

Passion   Finally, creative people do what they love. Passion for your work may be the most critical element in creativity, in that without it, even the most expert, patient, self-confident, and divergent-thinking individual may not have the drive necessary to sustain a long-term effort. In the words of Oprah Winfrey, "Passion is energy. Feel the power that comes from focusing on what excites you."

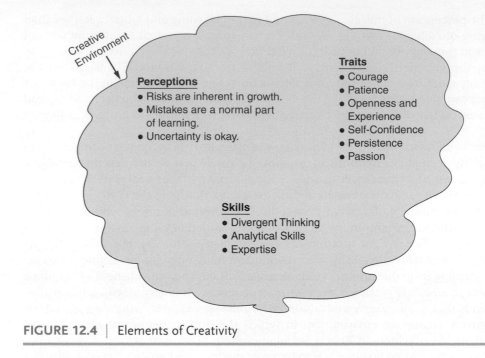

FIGURE 12.4 | Elements of Creativity

Overall, research strongly supports the notion that people enjoy their work more when they are able to exercise creativity in it. Creativity fosters intrinsic motivation, which in turn promotes greater enjoyment of the process. Creativity, as we have learned, is not limited to the arts or to great inventions, but can be applied to any endeavor or pursuit. Figure 12.4 summarizes the elements of creativity.

What ways can you find to exercise creativity in your own work? Turn now to Activity 12.6 to apply what you've learned about creativity to this important question.

PUTTING IT ALL TOGETHER: THE ROLE OF WORK IN A MEANINGFUL LIFE

PREVIEW QUESTIONS

(1) Describe three dimensions of cultural values, and how each one affects the role of work in a meaningful life.

(2) How do individual values influence the meaning of work?

If you won the lottery, would you keep working, or would you quit? Surprisingly, 86–89% of American lottery winners have continued working, even when they won average amounts of over three million dollars (Arvey, Harpaz, & Hui, 2001; Kaplan, 1985). This fits with, and in some cases even exceeds, predictions people make when asked, "If there were no financial reasons to carry on working, would you stop or continue working?" (e.g., Harpaz, 1989). What's more, the findings are relatively similar around the world, ranging from a low of 65% in Germany (Ruiz-Quintanilla & Wilpert, 1991), to a high of 93% in Japan (Harpaz, 1989). Women's responses to this question are similar to men's responses, in most cases only a few percentage points lower, indicating that this apparent need to work is largely universal.

What motivates this strong drive to work? If it isn't money, is it power or prestige, personal achievement, the need for connection with others, or perhaps just habit? If it is true that humans are driven by a need to find meaning in our lives, then how is work helping us fulfill this need? Recently, large-scale research including populations from all inhabited continents has begun to examine this question. Here, we will report the preliminary findings, along with posing a few questions for continued deliberation.

Individual and Cultural Values

In Chapter 1, we explored the topic of values and discussed how a culture's values influence its perceptions of the world, as well as relations among its people. Cross-cultural research in this area has identified 10 core values that underlie people's behavior all around the world (Schwartz, 1992; 1994). These values are power, achievement, hedonism, stimulation, self-direction, universalism, benevolence, tradition, conformity, and security (see Figure 12.5 for a description of

---

FIGURE 12.5 | Schwartz's Values   Definitions of motivational types of values in terms of their goals and the single values that represent them.

Power: Social status and prestige, control or dominance over people and resources (Social Power, Authority, Wealth).

Achievement: Personal success through demonstrating competence according to social standards (Successful, Capable, Ambitious, Influential).

Hedonism: Pleasure and sensuous gratification for oneself (Pleasure, Enjoying Life).

Stimulation: Excitement, novelty, and challenge in life (Daring, a Varied Life, an Exciting Life).

Self-Direction: Independent thought and action-choosing, creating, exploring (Creativity, Freedom, Independent, Curious, Choosing Own Goals).

Universalism: Understanding, appreciation, tolerance, and protection for the welfare of all people and for nature (Broadminded, Wisdom, Social Justice, Equality, a World at Peace, a World of Beauty, Unity with Nature, Protecting the Environment).

Benevolence: Preservation and enhancement of the welfare of people with whom one is in frequent personal contact (Helpful, Honest, Forgiving, Loyal, Responsible).

Tradition: Respect, commitment, and acceptance of the customs and ideas that traditional culture or religion provides (Humble, Accepting My Portion in Life, Devout, Respect for Tradition, Moderate).

Conformity: Restraint of actions, inclinations, and impulses likely to upset or harm others and violate social expectations or norms (Politeness, Obedient, Self-Discipline, Honoring Parents and Elders).

Security: Safety, harmony, and stability of society, of relationships, and of self (Family Security, National Security, Social Order, Clean, Reciprocation of Favors).

Source: Schwartz et al. (1999) Basic Individual values, Psychology: An International Review 48, 49–71 Copyright 1999 Reprinted by permission of Blackwell Publishers.

Conservatism Represents the priority of maintaining the status quo in a society, in order to keep group relations stable.

Autonomy Represents the cultural priority of pursuing individual freedoms, both intellectual and emotional, and a general value of openness to change.

Hierarchy Represents the belief that socially responsible behavior involves respecting status differences and adhering to the rules attached to one's own status in society.

Egalitarianism Represents the belief that socially responsible behavior involves respecting each individual as an equal.

Mastery Represents the belief that humans should seek to control whatever they can.

Harmony Represents the belief that humans should try to fit into the environment without changing it.

each value). These core values can be divided into three broad categories, each of which can be seen as a continuum, with polar opposites on either end. Each category represents a major issue that all societies must resolve; the way each society chooses to resolve it dictates where on the continuum that particular society is placed.

Conservatism vs. Autonomy The first category seeks to determine how a culture defines the relationship between the individual and the group. This is similar to the dimension of individualism–collectivism that we have already learned, but goes a bit beyond it. **Conservatism**, on one end of this continuum, represents the priority of maintaining the status quo in a society, in order to keep group relations stable. **Autonomy**, on the other end of this continuum, represents the cultural priority of pursuing individual freedoms, both intellectual and emotional, and a general value of openness to change. The values of social order, respect for tradition, family security, and wisdom are associated with conservatism, whereas autonomy is linked to the values of curiosity, broadmindedness, creativity, pleasure, an exciting life, and a varied life.

Hierarchy vs. Egalitarianism The second category defines the rules by which people in the society should interact. **Hierarchy**, on one end of this continuum, represents the belief that socially responsible behavior involves respecting status differences and adhering to the rules attached to one's own status in society; this is essentially a position that legitimizes inequality in a society. **Egalitarianism** is the polar opposite of hierarchy, and represents the belief that socially responsible behavior involves respecting each individual as an equal. This perception of equality promotes transcendence of selfish interests in favor of spending time on improving the overall societal conditions. On the Schwartz value survey, hierarchy is linked to the values of social power, authority, humility, and wealth. Egalitarianism is represented by equality, social justice, freedom, responsibility, and honesty.

Mastery vs. Harmony The third category deals with how humans interact with the world around them, both physical and social. **Mastery** represents the belief that humans should seek to control whatever they can, whereas **harmony** represents the opposite perspective that humans should try to fit into the environment without changing it. On the Schwartz values survey, mastery values are ambition, success, daring, and competence; harmony values are unity with nature, protecting the environment, and a world of beauty.

Research on how various countries around the world fit into this model find that English-speaking countries tend to score highest on mastery and emotional autonomy. Western European countries score highest on egalitarianism and autonomy, whereas eastern European countries score highest on conservatism and harmony. Asian and Islamic countries value hierarchy and conservatism; Latin American countries and Japan score about in the middle of the continuums, though are slightly closer to hierarchy, mastery, and emotional autonomy.

Applying Cultural Values to Work

These general cultural values can be used to predict how individuals in a culture think and feel about work. Research in this area is currently underway. What do researchers expect to find?

Work Centrality   **Work centrality**, or the significance of work in a person's life, is one of the main dimensions we can use to assess this issue. To make this determination, researchers ask people a general question about the importance of work in their life, as well as questions about how important work is compared to four other key areas (family, community, religion, and leisure).

> **Work centrality** The significance of work in a person's life.

Researchers expect that higher work centrality scores will be found in cultures that place a high value on mastery and hierarchy. The reasoning behind their hypothesis is that mastery, or control, is primarily achieved through work, and that hierarchy is generally very prevalent in work as well. On the other hand, the values of autonomy, egalitarianism, harmony, and conservatism may conflict with the centrality of work in a person's life.

Societal Norms about Work   Another way to measure the meaning of work in a culture is to examine societal norms about work. To assess this, researchers ask a series of questions that reveal whether people in the culture perceive work as something meaningful to which all persons in a society are entitled, or whether people instead perceive work as an obligation that must be met, even if it is unpleasant.

Researchers expect that cultures that place a high value on egalitarianism and autonomy will perceive work as entitlement, whereas cultures that value conservatism and hierarchy are more likely to perceive work as an obligation. Early results of work in this area support the hypothesis. Germany—which is one of the two highest scoring countries on egalitarianism and intellectual autonomy—scored very highly on the entitlement norm as well. In contrast, the United States—which scored extremely high on hierarchy—was found to have a societal norm of obligation (England & Quintanilla, 1994). Further research is needed to continue to develop our understanding in this area.

Individual Motivations to Work   Finally, numerous studies reveal that four basic values influence our individual motivation to work. These **work values** are intrinsic, extrinsic, power, and social.

> **Work values** Intrinsic, extrinsic, power, and social.

Researchers expect that a culture that values autonomy will see intrinsic work values among its people, whereas a culture that values conservatism and hierarchy will see extrinsic motives. Power motives are hypothesized to be more prevalent in cultures driven by values of hierarchy and mastery; social motives are expected to drive work goals in egalitarian and harmony-oriented cultures (Ros, Schwartz, & Surkiss, 1999).

Individual Values and the Meaning of Work

Cultural values often influence the values of individuals within that culture, but the degree to which they influence them depends both on the individual and the values of the culture itself. Earlier in this book, we saw how personality and other internal factors influence a person's goals and life choices: Individuals who score high on extraversion, for example, might be more motivated by social work goals, whereas an individual who scores high on openness to experience might be more driven by intrinsic work goals. The value system of the culture itself also plays a role in determining the degree to which individuals in that culture conform to societal values: Individuals in cultures that value conservatism will more likely express work goals consistent with the prevailing cultural value system, whereas individuals in cultures that value autonomy are more likely to deviate from societal norms.

The four basic work values outlined in the previous section also help us understand individual motivations to work. People who work primarily for intrinsic reasons tend to value personal growth, autonomy, interest, and creativity, whereas people who work primarily for extrinsic reasons value such things as pay and security. People who work primarily to meet their needs for social contact value contributions to society and contacts with people, and people whose primary work goal is power value prestige, authority, and influence.

To assess your own motivations for work, turn now to Activity 12.7 and complete the short questionnaire (Work Value Survey from Ros et al., 1999).

The Meaning of Work: A Summary

What have we learned, then, about the meaning of work in people's lives? Clearly it plays a primary role in the structure of our lives; if it didn't, the vast majority of people wouldn't expect to continue working if their financial need disappeared. Beyond that, we have learned that the very value of structure itself is higher among some cultures than others: Cultures that prize hierarchy and conservatism rely on work to meet these basic value goals and to maintain social order. Finally, we have learned that individuals work to meet one of four basic needs: intrinsic, extrinsic, power, or social needs.

Research on the meaning of work in our lives is in its infancy. At present, we have far more questions than we do answers. Until more results are in from current studies and additional studies are conducted, we are left to ponder the meaning of work in our lives. Would you continue working if you had no financial need? If so, why? If not, what would you do instead? You might be tempted to think, "I'd be on vacation for the rest of my life!" But do you really think that would be fulfilling in the long term? What other pursuits would interest you, such

FIGURE 12.6 | Too often, we look for easy answers to life's complicated questions.

as learning a different kind of work, or working in an area that made social contributions, such as volunteer work of some kind?

Contemplating these questions and letting your mind explore the possibilities of this "what-if" scenario can provide some useful insight into how well your current work and work goals really match your overall life goals. If they are relatively congruent, chances are you are generally satisfied with your work life. If, they are not, you might try applying the principles of creativity we learned earlier in this chapter to consider how you might transition out of what you are currently doing and into a direction that suits you better, keeping in mind also what you've learned about yourself, your personal values, and your work values. After all, we spend a majority of our waking lives working—let's make that time count! (See Figure 12.6.)

Interim SUMMARY #3

Creativity can enhance our enjoyment of the work in which we engage, and everyone has the ability to be creative. A number of characteristics seem to promote creativity in individuals: expertise in the subject area, divergent thinking, risk taking, a creative environment, patience, and passion for the work. There are several cognitive and emotional elements inherent in these characteristics.

Values—both cultural and individual—also affect the way a person perceives work in his or her life. Cultural values tend to center around three broad categories: conservatism/

autonomy, hierarchy/egalitarianism, and mastery/harmony. A culture's prevailing value system on these dimensions is thought to influence the centrality of work in their lives, as well as their perception of work as entitlement or obligation. Individual work values tend to fall into one of four categories: intrinsic, extrinsic, power, or social. Most people around the world assert that they would continue working even if they had no financial need, a finding that strongly supports the role of work in our lives.

A FINAL THOUGHT

All in all, I hope this textbook has helped you improve your understanding of yourself and others, as well as become more effective in your interactions, both personally and professionally.

We have taken in-depth looks at internal factors in human relations, external influences on human relations, and specific skills involved in communication and conflict resolution, and zeroed in on key concepts in personal relationships and our work lives. We've examined the role of personality, the self, and our life stage, as well as our emotions, cognitions, and societal forces in influencing the way we think, feel, and act in a variety of situations. We have also learned much about developing positive relationship climates, and how to listen and communicate effectively and nondefensively.

In summing up, I cannot help but be reminded of a poster I saw once entitled, "Everything I Need to Know About Life I Learned in Kindergarten." (It's okay to chuckle about that—I always do!) It had a list of things like, "Play fair," "Clean up your own mess," and "Say you're sorry when you hurt somebody." At the risk of being reductionist, these tenets really are at the core of good human relations. Playing fair implies respect and the value of equality; cleaning up your own mess is about taking responsibility for our own beliefs and actions; and apologizing when we hurt somebody communicates empathy. Taken together, they all build respect and trust in relationships.

So, as you go through life, I wish you well in your personal relationships, your professional relationships, and in your own personal growth. If you have any feedback about this book or any part of it, I welcome your comments—whether they be now or even years from now. And here's one final critical thinking question for you:

 If you were to create a poster that summed up what you learned in this class, what would it say?

CHAPTER TERMS

Leadership

Great Person theory of
  leadership

Drive

Leadership motivation

Honesty

Integrity

Self-confidence

Interactionist theories of
  leadership

Task-oriented leaders

Relationship-oriented
  leaders

Situational control

Follower readiness

Telling   Intrinsic motivation   Conservatism
Selling   Extrinsic motivation   Autonomy
Participating   Performance goals   Hierarchy
Delegating   Mastery goals   Egalitarianism
Charismatic leader Informational rewards Mastery
Consensus leader   Control-based rewards Harmony
Transactional leaders Creativity   Work centrality
Transformational leaders Divergent thinking   Work values
Achievement motivation Incubation

ACTIVITY 12.1

ASSESSING YOUR LEADERSHIP STYLE

INSTRUCTIONS: *The following 35 statements describe various aspects of leadership behavior. Think about a work group that you are currently leading, or a work group that you have led in the past. It could be at your workplace, or for a school project, or as a leader or coach of some community group or team. Keep that group in mind, and answer the following questions based on how you would be likely to act as the leader for that group. (If you have never been a leader, answer the questions as you imagine you would if you were in a leadership position at your workplace, school, or community.)*

 For each item, check whether you would be likely to behave in the described ways Always (A), Frequently (F), Occasionally (O), Seldom (S), or Never (N).

If I Were the Leader of a Work Group: (A) (F) (O) (S) (N)

1. I would most likely act as the spokesperson of the group. ☐ ☐ ☐ ☐ ☐
2. I would encourage overtime work. ☐ ☐ ☐ ☐ ☐
3. I would allow members complete freedom in their work. ☐ ☐ ☐ ☐ ☐
4. I would encourage the use of uniform procedures. ☐ ☐ ☐ ☐ ☐
5. I would permit the members to use their own judgment in solving problems. ☐ ☐ ☐ ☐ ☐
6. I would stress being ahead of competing groups. ☐ ☐ ☐ ☐ ☐
7. I would speak as a representative of the group. ☐ ☐ ☐ ☐ ☐
8. I would needle members for greater effort. ☐ ☐ ☐ ☐ ☐
9. I would try out my ideas in the group. ☐ ☐ ☐ ☐ ☐
10. I would let the members do their work the way they think best. ☐ ☐ ☐ ☐ ☐
11. I would be working hard for a promotion. ☐ ☐ ☐ ☐ ☐
12. I would be able to tolerate postponement and uncertainty. ☐ ☐ ☐ ☐ ☐

	(A)	(F)	(O)	(S)	(N)
13. I would speak for the group when visitors were present.	☐	☐	☐	☐	☐
14. I would keep the work moving at a rapid pace.	☐	☐	☐	☐	☐
15. I would turn the members loose on a job and let them go to it.	☐	☐	☐	☐	☐
16. I would settle conflicts when they occur in the group.	☐	☐	☐	☐	☐
17. I would get swamped by details.	☐	☐	☐	☐	☐
18. I would represent the group at outside meetings.	☐	☐	☐	☐	☐
19. I would be reluctant to allow the members any freedom of action.	☐	☐	☐	☐	☐
20. I would decide what shall be done and how it shall be done.	☐	☐	☐	☐	☐
21. I would push for increased production.	☐	☐	☐	☐	☐
22. I would let some members have authority to make certain decisions.	☐	☐	☐	☐	☐
23. Things would usually turn out as I predict.	☐	☐	☐	☐	☐
24. I would allow the group a high degree of initiative.	☐	☐	☐	☐	☐
25. I would assign group members to particular tasks.	☐	☐	☐	☐	☐
26. I would be willing to make changes.	☐	☐	☐	☐	☐
27. I would ask the members to work harder.	☐	☐	☐	☐	☐
28. I would trust the group members to exercise good judgment.	☐	☐	☐	☐	☐
29. I would schedule the work to be done.	☐	☐	☐	☐	☐
30. I would refuse to explain my actions.	☐	☐	☐	☐	☐
31. I would persuade others that my ideas are to their advantage.	☐	☐	☐	☐	☐
32. I would permit the group to set its own pace.	☐	☐	☐	☐	☐
33. I would urge the group to beat its previous record.	☐	☐	☐	☐	☐
34. I would act without consulting the group.	☐	☐	☐	☐	☐
35. I would ask that group members follow standard rules and regulations.	☐	☐	☐	☐	☐

SCORING INSTRUCTIONS

The scoring for this assessment is complicated, so please follow the instructions carefully.

1. Circle statement numbers 8, 12, 17, 18, 19, 30, 34, and 35. For each of these statements that you checked S (seldom) or N (never), place a number 1 in the left margin next to the circled number.

2. For the 27 statements not circled, place a 1 in the left margin next to the statement number for each statement that you checked A (always) or F (frequently).

3. You should now have 1's in the left margin of many of the 35 statements.

4. Circle the 1's in the margin you have written in front of the following statements: 3, 5, 8, 10, 15, 18, 19, 22, 24, 26, 28, 30, 32, 34, and 35. Count the number of circled 1's you have and write it here: R = _____. This is your relationship-oriented leadership score.

5. Count the number of 1's you have that are not circled for the remaining statements, and write that number here: T = _____. This is your task-oriented leadership score.

Interpreting Your Score

Complete this section after you have read about the Hersey-Blanchard Model of leadership.

1. Which of the following best characterizes your scores on this assessment? (check one)

_____ High T and High R

_____ High T and Low R

_____ Low T and High R

_____ Low T and Low R

2. Review the Hersey-Blanchard Model of leadership, which suggests that optimal leadership behavior varies based on follower readiness. Consider the work group you had in mind when you completed the questionnaire. Was the group in Stage 1, Stage 2, Stage 3, or Stage 4 in terms of readiness? Explain your answer.

_____

_____

_____

_____

_____

3. Based on your score, is your leadership style telling, selling, participating, or delegating?

_____

4. How well does your leadership style match up with the readiness level of your work group? What modifications should you make, according to this model, to increase your effectiveness as a leader of this group? Give a specific example of one thing you could do that would fit the recommendations of this model.

_____

_____

_____

_____

_____

5. Overall, what did you learn from this assessment? What thoughts or questions do you have about it?

_____

_____

_____

_____

_____

Source: Adapted from *A Handbook of Structured Experiences for Human Relations Training,* vol. 1, by J.W. Pfeiffer and J.E. Jones (eds.). Copyright 1974 by Pfeiffer & Company, San Francisco, CA. Used with permission. The T-P Leadership Questionnaire was adapted from Sergiovanni, Metzcus, and Burden's revision of the Leadership Behavior Description Questionnaire, *American Educational Research Journal* 6 (1979), pp. 62–79.

ACTIVITY 12.2
LEADERSHIP IN ACTION

INSTRUCTIONS: *Interview a leader in your own life—it could be a leader at your workplace, your school, or your community. Sample questions will be provided by your instructor. Then, write a 3–4-page paper that describes this leader's leadership style and its effectiveness in the context of at least three leadership principles from this chapter.*

ACTIVITY 12.3
GOAL-SETTING YOUR WAY TO SUCCESS

INSTRUCTIONS: *For this assignment, apply the three keys to effective goal setting to a goal of your own. Identify something you would like to achieve (it could be in school, at work, in a personal relationship, for your health, etc.), and create a step-by-step plan that specifically addresses each of the three keys to effective goal setting.*

ACTIVITY 12.4
BUILDING INTRINSIC MOTIVATION

INSTRUCTIONS: *Consider how intrinsic motivation affects your own life, either in a setting where you are trying to motivate others, or in a setting where others are trying to motivate you.*

1. In a few sentences, describe the setting you will analyze for this assignment (be sure to state who is the motivator in the setting).

2. What kinds of rewards are offered for achievement in this setting? Give a few examples. How are the rewards used: as informational rewards, or control-based rewards? Currently, how effective is the reward system? Identify at least one specific improvement that could be made.

3. Overall, to what extent do the goals in your setting follow the three rules of effective goal setting? What is one thing that is working well in terms of these goals? What is one specific improvement that could be made?

4. Overall, to what extent are the people in your setting well suited to their environment? Give one example of something that seems to fit, and one example of a specific way this aspect of intrinsic motivation could be improved.

5. In summary, how well is the current setting fostering intrinsic motivation?

ACTIVITY 12.5

CREATIVITY AND BRAINSTORMING

INSTRUCTIONS: *In groups of about four, practice brainstorming by coming up with as many answers to the following questions as you can. Remember that the key to good brainstorming is to say whatever comes to mind, no matter how crazy it might sound. Write it down and keep going! There is always time later to analyze the pros and cons of the answers, so don't let that get in the way of the "storming" process. As a group, aim for at least 15 answers to each question.*

1. How many different uses can you think of for a paper clip?

_____

_____

_____

_____

_____

2. If you were traveling around the world, what would you take with you?

_____

_____

_____

_____

_____

3. If you had an unlimited money supply, what would you do with it?

_____

_____

_____

_____

_____

4. How many different forms of transportation can you think of?

_____

_____

_____

_____

_____

5. Imagine that you had no clothes, but needed to go out in public. Assuming the cultural norms prohibit nudity, what other items commonly found in and around your house could you use as clothing?

_____

_____

_____

_____

_____

ACTIVITY 12.6
EXERCISING YOUR CREATIVE POWERS

INSTRUCTIONS: *Identify at least three ways you can apply the principles of creativity discussed in this chapter to your workplace and/or other pursuits in your life. For each one, write a paragraph or two that includes specific ideas of how you can integrate that principle and expand your creativity.*

ACTIVITY 12.7
WORK VALUE SURVEY

INSTRUCTIONS: *The following 10 items represent a variety of values that influence people in their work. For each item, consider this question: How important is this to you in choosing an occupation? Rate each item on a scale from 1 (very important) to 4 (not at all important).*

_____ 1. Good salary and work conditions

_____ 2. Job security (permanent job, pension)

_____ 3. Interesting and varied work

_____ 4. Work with people

_____ 5. Prestigious, highly valued work

_____ 6. Work in which you are your own boss

_____ 7. Contributing to people and society

_____ 8. Authority to make decisions over people

_____ 9. Social contact with coworkers

_____10. Opportunities for occupational advancement

SCORING

First, add up your scores for items 4, 7, and 9, then divide the total by 3. This is your Social Values score. Second, add up your scores for items 1 and 2, then divide the total by 2. This is your Extrinsic Values score. Third, add up your scores for items 5 and 8, then divide the total by 2. This is your Power Values score. Finally, add up your scores for items 3 and 6, then divide the total by 2. This is your Intrinsic Values score.

My Social Values score is _____.

My Extrinsic Values score is _____.

My Power Values score is _____.

My Intrinsic Values score is _____.

REFLECTIONS

A. What was your highest score? (If two were very close, name them both). What is your first reaction to this?

_____

_____

_____

_____

B. Does your highest score fit with researchers' predictions about the connection between culture and individual motivations to work? Explain.

_____

_____

_____

_____

C. Overall, how well is your current value system toward work functioning in your life? Is it creating a high degree of satisfaction with your work, or inhibiting your satisfaction with your work? Explain.

_____

_____

_____

_____

D. Would you say that your high score on this scale accurately represents your overall values in life? Why or why not?

_____

_____

_____

_____

Source: From "Basic Individual Values, Work Values, and the Meaning of Work," by M. Ros, S. H. Schwartz, and S. Surkis, 1999, *Applied Psychology: An International Review, 48.*

GLOSSARY

Abstract language   Language which is vague.

Accommodating   A conflict resolution style characterized by a high degree of interest in the relationship, and a low degree of concern about one's own interests.

Achievement motivation   The desire to attain a high standard of excellence in one's life pursuits.

Activating event   Event that is meaningful to the person experiencing it.

Acute stressors   Stressful situations that require immediate response and are short-term.

Advising   A listening response that offers advice.

Affective communication   Person-oriented, and focuses on building and maintaining good relations between the communicators.

Agape   Deep abiding love that is not without passion, and that is also selfless.

Age of Mastery   Characterized by renewed vigor and purpose, from about ages 45–65.

Age 30 transition   According to Levinson a period of four to five years when a man questions the choices he has made so far, considering what modifications he might make to build a more stable and fulfilled life.

Aggression   A behavior that is destructive or hostile.

Agreeableness   A personality trait which includes behaviors such as kind, sincere, courteous, helpful, patient, honest, and cooperative.

Alarm phase   Fight or flight response.

Ambivalent identity   Little sense of individuality, as well as little sense of connection to the larger group.

Analyzing   To offer a different perspective on the issue.

Anger   A normal human emotion that provides a signal that something is wrong.

Assertiveness   The degree to which we are interested in pursuing our own goals and interests.

Authentic listening styles   Ways of responding to a speaker that show genuine interest in and empathy for the person and situation.

Autonomy   Represents the cultural priority of pursuing individual freedoms, both intellectual and emotional, and a general value of openness to change.

Avoiding   A conflict resolution style characterized by a low degree of interest in pursuing one's own goals, as well as a low degree of interest in supporting the relationship or the other person's goals.

Behavioral description   Clear, specific, and factual description of a person's behavior.

Behaviorist theory   The theory which suggests that our personality is shaped exclusively by our experiences.

Biconstrual identity   Value pursuing their own goals, but place an equally high value on connection to their social group.

Big Five theory   A theory which suggests that personality can be measured on five major dimensions.

Body orientation   The direction your body is facing relative to those with whom you are interacting.

Catastrophizing Exaggerating the importance of a negative event.

Catharsis The theory that releasing pent-up hostilities will return us to a peaceful state.

Certainty A defense-arousing message that signals closed-mindedness.

Charismatic leader Engaging personality fuels his or her success.

Chronic stressors Stressful situations not resolved quickly that are long-term.

Classical conditioning A type of learning that relies on associating a neutral stimulus with a natural, biological stimulus.

Cognitive appraisal Interpretation of an event in the context of our individual belief system, expectations, needs, and past experiences.

Cognitive distractions Something that is on our mind (a cognition) that we're having trouble putting aside in order to focus on the speaker's message.

Cohort A group of people born at about the same time in history, so that they share common experiences in society at about the same time and age.

Commitment The conscious decision that one loves the other person and is willing to make certain sacrifices to maintain that relationship over the long term.

Companionate love Love that includes intimacy and commitment, but no passion. (Sternberg's Model)

Companionate love Relationship based on trust, mutual respect, affection, honesty, communication, happiness, and sharing.

Compartmentalize Mentally "filing away" our own issues temporarily.

Compensatory self-improvement Identifying something related to the stressor that was previously ignored, and taking action in that related area.

Compliance Agreeing to a specific request.

Compromising A conflict resolution style characterized by a moderate degree of interest in one's own goals, and an equally moderate degree of interest in the relationship and/or goals of the other person.

Conditional positive regard Giving positive regard and acceptance only in certain conditions.

Conditioned response (CR) A learned response to conditioned stimulus.

Conditioned stimulus (CS) A previously neutral stimulus that has become associated with an unconditioned stimulus.

Conditioning Learning from our experiences.

Confirmation bias Our tendency to seek out and pay attention to information that supports our preexisting notions, and also to ignore or discount contradictory information.

Confirming (supportive) climate A positive relational climate based on mutual trust, respect, and support.

Conflict style An individual's typical method of responding to conflict.

Conformity A voluntary change in a belief or behavior with the intent to follow a perceived social norm.

Conscientiousness A personality trait characterized by dependability, efficiency, persistence, and a strong sense of order.

Conscious The portion of our mind that we are aware of at any given time.

Consensus Whether other people typically exhibit this behavior in this situation.

Consensus leader Succeeds based on his or her centrist position and skills at mediation.

Consequence The impact the behavior has on you.

Conservatism Represents the priority of maintaining the status quo in a society, in order to keep group relations stable.

Consistency Whether a particular behavior typically occurs in that situation.

Consummate love Love that is made up of all three elements: intimacy, passion, and commitment.

Contact cultures Tend to engage in more open contact with each other and use nonverbal cues to signal warmth, closeness, and availability.

Contempt Conveys a strong message of disrespect and superiority.

Context The personalities, cultural backgrounds, and situational factors involved in each interaction.

Control The general belief that you can influence your life and your situations.

Control orientation Making decisions for other people.

Control-based rewards Incentives for doing well offered before a task is accomplished.

Cooperativeness The degree to which we are interested in maintaining the relationship or supporting the goals of the other person.

Counterfeit listening styles Behaviors that, on the surface, may look like listening, but are actually counterproductive to good listening.

Creativity Producing something that is both novel and useful.

Criticism Directed at the person (rather than the behavior) and includes blame and negative judgment.

Culture A set of values, shared by a group of people, which shape and influence the norms, attitudes, beliefs, expectations, perceptions, and behaviors of the group members.

Defense mechanisms Strategies our unconscious uses to resolve anxiety.

Defensive listening We perceive criticism when none is intended.

Defensive spiral One negative comment tends to be reciprocated, then each provokes another.

Defensiveness Avoiding taking any responsibility for the problem, and instead deflecting it back toward the other person.

Delegating Providing low levels of both task-oriented and relationship-oriented leadership.

Demographic Refers to population statistics, such as age, race, religion, income level, educational level, and other basic types of information you might find on a census report.

Description Fact-based, nonjudgmental description of the other person's behavior.

Direct expression of anger Expressing your anger directly toward the object of your anger.

Disconfirming (defensive) climate A negative relational climate, characterized by defensiveness, negative judgments, and mistrust.

Discrimination The unfair treatment of a person or group solely on the basis of their group membership.

Displacement Redirecting a negative feeling toward a "safe" target.

Distinctiveness Whether a particular behavior typically occurs in other situations.

Divergent thinking The ability to generate many ideas, or more complex ideas from a single starting point.

Dominating A conflict resolution style based on a high degree of interest in one's own goals, and a low degree of interest in the relationship or goals of the other person.

Downward comparisons Identifying and acknowledging situations in which people are worse off than you are.

Drive A multifaceted component that includes achievement motivation, ambition, energy, tenacity, and initiative.

Dual-concern model A framework for understanding conflict style that is based on the degree of assertiveness and cooperativeness that motivates an individual's response to conflict.

Early adult transition According to Levinson, completion of the major task of adolescence—forming an identity—and working toward becoming an independent, self-reliant person.

Egalitarianism Represents the belief that socially responsible behavior involves respecting each individual as an equal.

Ego The part of personality concerned with meeting the needs of the id in a way that is realistic, and fits with the laws or rules of society.

Elaborate language Uses many words to convey its message and is very colorful and expressive.

Emotional bank account Created by continuing to make small, everyday sacrifices and by making efforts to notice and appreciate the kindnesses of your partner.

Emotional description To state the emotion you felt when the behavior occurred.

Emotional intelligence Self-awareness, emotional self-control, persistence, empathy, and social competence.

Emotional noise Stress, anxiety, anger, or any other emotion that interferes with our ability to focus our full attention on the speaker.

Emotion-focused coping An attempt to regulate the emotional impact of the stress.

Empathy Feeling and understanding the emotions of another person.

Empirical evidence Based on data that has been collected through precise measurement under carefully controlled conditions.

Empty love Commitment in the absence of intimacy and passion.

Encoding Taking in information and organizing it in a way that is meaningful to us, so that we can store it for later retrieval.

Endorsement Accepting another person's thoughts or feelings as valid.

Eros Erotic love, or love that is based primarily on physical attraction and a strong sense of passion toward the love object.

Ethnocentrism Our tendency to see the world through the lenses of our own culture.

Evaluating A response that makes a judgment about the person or situation.

Evaluation Language which evaluates or judges another person.

Exacting communication Clear and specific language that states the facts, and no more.

Exhaustion phase Our resistance levels drop to a point that is below normal, because our resources have been depleted and can no longer combat the threat.

External attribution When we attribute behavior to an external or situational factor.

Extinction The phase of classical conditioning that involves eliminating the conditioned response.

Extraversion/introversion A personality trait based on a person's preferences for social or contemplative environments.

Extrinsic motivation Driven by the pursuit of external rewards or the avoidance of external punishments.

Fallacy of causation We blame someone else for our own feelings.

False consensus bias Our assumption that others see things the same way we do.

False uniqueness bias When we are considering our talents, abilities, or positive qualities, we tend to see ourselves as more unique than we actually are.

Fatuous love Made up of commitment and passion, without intimacy.

Feminine culture Expects and accepts overlapping roles for men and women.

Flaming Fifties A time to build on and enjoy pursuit of the new goals set during middlescence.

Flexible ethnocentrism Recognizing our own tendency toward ethnocentrism, and working toward a deeper understanding and empathy for norms of different cultures.

Flourishing Forties Characterized by the recognition that 40 doesn't feel old, which prompts middlescence.

Focusing Digging deep into feelings about a situation in search of new insights that may lie at the heart of what is causing the stress.

Follower readiness A component that combines the expertise level of staff members with their general motivation to accomplish a task.

Fully functioning person One who gets along well with others by offering unconditional positive regard and genuinely caring about them.

Fundamental attribution error Our human tendency to assume that other people's behavior is due to something about their personality, while at the same time failing to consider possible situational influences.

Gender The *social* or *cultural* differences between masculinity and femininity.

General adaptation syndrome (GAS) The human body's response to stressful or threatening situations.

Generalization When a conditioned response occurs upon exposure to a stimulus that is similar to the original conditioned stimulus.

Generativity vs. stagnation Erikson's second stage of adult development, which is to nurture the next generation, or to raise children in a way that helps them master their environments and establish their own identities.

Great Person theory of leadership Certain people are born with a set of personality traits that make them destined to become great leaders.

Gridlock Getting into a repeating cycle of unproductive and frustrating conflict about a currently unresolvable issue.

Hardiness A personality style that consists of three components: control, commitment, and challenge.

Harmony Represents the belief that humans should try to fit into the environment without changing it.

Hierarchy Represents the belief that socially responsible behavior involves respecting status differences and adhering to the rules attached to one's own status in society.

High power distance cultures Stricter hierarchies with greater distance between each level.

High uncertainty avoidance culture Perceive uncertainty as an ongoing threat to be resisted.

High-context communication Communication that relies more heavily on attention to contextual details and less on explicit language to transmit its message.

Honesty Open and clear communication.

Human relations The ability to interact effectively with diverse others in a variety of situations.

Humanists theory The theory which suggests we are all born with an innate drive to reach our potential as good, contributing persons to our society.

Id The part of personality concerned with satisfying our basic instincts and urges.

Identity The unique sense of self which requires individuating from the family.

I-language Language that takes responsibility for the impact the other person's behavior has on you, rather than simply scolding or casting blame.

Incubation The creator walks away from the project for a time and lets the ideas and discoveries made thus far develop naturally and without conscious effort.

Independent self-construal High individualistic values but low collectivistic values.

Indirect expression of anger   Channeling your anger in a direction other than toward the object of your anger.

Individualism–Collectivism (IC)   A value system based on the relative importance of the individual versus the group or family.

Infatuation   Passion, without intimacy or commitment.

Inflexible ethnocentrism   Judging others as wrong simply because they are different.

Information overload   Interferes with our listening when we try to process too much information.

Informational rewards   Rewards given to inform a person that he or she has done well at the end of a task.

Informational social influence   When conformity helps us make the right decision in a situation where we aren't sure what to do.

Ingroup bias   Favoring others with whom we identify over those whom we perceive as different.

Instrumental communication   Task-oriented, and focuses on achieving the speaker's goal.

Integrating   A conflict resolution style characterized by a strong interest in pursuing one's own goals, and an equally strong interest in supporting the relationship and/or the goals of the other person.

Integrity   Consistency between what a person says and what she does.

Integrity vs. despair   Erikson's third stage of adult development, which is the challenge of looking back on one's life and feeling a sense of satisfaction at a life lived well.

Interactionist theories of leadership   Great leaders emerge from circumstances that combine an individual with leadership potential with certain situational factors.

Interdependent self-construal   High collectivistic values but low individualistic values.

Internal attribution   When we attribute a person's behavior to something about the person, his character, or his personality.

Interpersonal conflict   Situation in which two or more people in an interdependent relationship perceive themselves to have different viewpoints or goals, which are incompatible.

Intimacy   Includes trust, caring, warmth, honesty, and a deep level of understanding and knowledge about each other.

Intimacy vs. isolation   Erikson's first stage of adult development, which is to establish and maintain an intimate relationship with a life partner.

Intrinsic motivation   Desire to pursue or engage in something for the internal rewards it brings.

Jigsaw classroom   Where students work together to learn, rather than compete against each other.

Johari Window   A visual representation of the parts of yourself that are known to you and known to others.

Law of effect   Behaviors followed by positive consequences are more likely to be repeated, and behaviors followed by negative consequences are less likely to be repeated.

Leadership   Influencing others to voluntarily accept and pursue goals and challenges that may be difficult, but which are in accord with the values of both the leader and the followers.

Leadership motivation   The desire to influence others and to accept the responsibilities that come with this type of power.

Liking   Intimacy by itself.

Long-term memory　Relatively permanent storage of information.

Love maps　Created out of a deep and broad awareness of their partner.

Low power distance cultures　De-emphasize hierarchies and strive to reduce distance between the various levels.

Low uncertainty avoidance cultures　Perceive uncertainty as normal and non-threatening.

Low-context communication　Relies on clear, concrete, and explicit language.

Ludus　Game-playing love, in which a person sees love as a game of skill and strategy.

Mania　An obsessive, desperate, and possessive type of love, in which jealousy and doubt prevail.

Masculine culture　Expects a high degree of separation between men's and women's role.

Masculinity-Femininity (MAS)　The degree of differentiation between the roles of men and women in a culture.

Maslow's need hierarchy　A model which suggests that lower-order needs must be met before we can focus on higher-order needs.

Mastery　Represents the belief that humans should seek to control whatever they can.

Mastery goals　Focus on improving one's level of skill or competence at the task.

Mere exposure effect　People tend to like others more when they have seen them more frequently, even if they have not spoken to the person.

Message complexity　The message itself is too complicated to absorb without turning your focus inward, and thus away from the speaker for a time.

Middlescence　A time of reflection on life so far and reassessment of goals, values, and identity. Signals the transition from First Adulthood to Second Adulthood.

Midlife transition　A period of reflection and questioning regarding the life choices he has made so far.

Milgram Experiment　A classic study of obedience to authority.

Minimally encouraging　Encouraging the speaker to continue by giving short and unintrusive responses both verbally and nonverbally.

Myth of causation　Belief that one person's emotions are the direct result of another person's actions.

Myth of helplessness　Assuming that you are stuck in a bad situation and cannot do anything about it.

Need for approval　Belief that you are okay only if everyone else approves of you.

Negative reinforcement　A consequence that increases likelihood of a behavior by taking away or avoiding something unpleasant.

Neuroticism　A personality trait characterized by anxiety, nervousness, self-consciousness, and moodiness.

Neutral stimulus (NS)　A stimulus which is not meaningful.

Neutrality　Apparent lack of concern or feeling, sending a message that the other person is unimportant.

Normative social influence　When we conform in order to "fit in" with a certain group.

Obedience　Agreeing to a request from an authority figure, when there is a negative consequence for refusal.

Observational learning　The process by which we learn behaviors by watching others engage in them. Also known as modeling.

Openness to experience　A personality trait characterized by originality, imagination, independence, curiosity, and broadmindedness.

Operant conditioning   A type of learning based on associating behaviors with the consequences they have previously produced.

Optimism   The tendency to focus on the positive aspects of a situation.

Outgroup bias   Downgrading others who are different or not in your group.

Outgroup homogeneity effect   Our tendency to assume that members of an outgroup are more alike than members of our ingroup.

Overgeneralization   Exaggerating the frequency of an event, or making broad assumptions based on limited evidence.

Paralanguage   Communication that is verbal, but wordless.

Paraphrasing   A listening response that reflects what the speaker is feeling and thinking, expressed tentatively.

Participating   Providing relationship-oriented leadership.

Passion   Sexual desire and physical attraction.

Passionate love   Intense arousal and absorption with a partner.

Passive-aggressive behavior   When a person acts passive on the outside, but secretly commits some type of aggression against the other person.

Perception-checking   A three part statement you make to another person when you need clarification of something the person said or did.

Perfectionism   Expecting yourself to achieve perfection in tasks, relationships, communication, or other goals.

Performance goals   Focus on a specific level of achievement.

Persistence   Continuing to work toward goals despite setbacks and frustration.

Personal space   The comfortable amount of distance between people in conversation.

Personality   The unique pattern of thoughts, feelings, and behaviors in an individual that is consistent over time and across situations.

Personality traits   Characteristics that predict a person's behavior consistently across a wide range of situations.

Phobias   Irrational fears.

Physiological factors   Biological factors.

Positive attributions   Interpreting positive experiences as normal in a relationship, and giving your partner the benefit of the doubt in negative situations.

Positive regard   Positive feedback, good feelings, and acceptance.

Positive reinforcement   A consequence that increases likelihood of a behavior by adding something pleasant.

Possible selves   Visions, both positive and negative, of who and what we might become someday.

Power Distance (PD)   Examines how a culture deals with the basic issue of human inequality.

Pragma   Practical love that results from an objective evaluation of the advantages and disadvantages of a particular love relationship or love object.

Preconscious   The part of the unconscious that can be brought into consciousness by focusing on it.

Prejudice   Prejudgment, or superficial judgment, about a particular group of people.

Premature judgment   When we stop listening to a message before the speaker is finished, either because we think we know what the speaker is going to say, or because we have already formed an opinion about the speaker or the message.

Primacy effect   People pay more attention to initial information they receive about a person or situation than they do to later information.

Principle of authority   We are more likely to agree to a request made by an authority figure.

Principle of commitment   A small initial commitment to a person or idea increases the likelihood that we will make a more significant commitment later.

Principle of liking   Agreeing to do something because the person making the request is likable.

Principle of reciprocity   Belief that it is important to reciprocate, or "pay back" favors.

Principle of scarcity   People or products seem more important when their availability seems limited.

Principle of social proof   Going along with a belief or behavior because it looks like many others are doing the same thing.

Private self   The part of our self that is known only to us.

Problem orientation   Working collaboratively with partners to share decision-making.

Problem-focused coping   Taking specific action geared toward reducing the threat presented by the stressor.

Projection   Having an unacceptable impulse or thought, but instead of seeing it in ourselves, we think we see it in others.

Provisionalism   A supportive message that signals open-mindedness.

Proximity   Geographical closeness to another person.

Pseudolistening   Giving only the impression of listening by nonverbal behaviors such as nodding, keeping eye contact, and verbal prompts.

Psychoanalytic theory   The theory which suggests that our personality is shaped by an ongoing internal struggle between two or more conflicting needs.

Psychology   The scientific study of thoughts, feelings, and behaviors.

Public self   The image we present to the world.

Punishment   Anything that decreases the chances of the behavior being repeated.

Questioning   Asking a question geared toward either clarifying your understanding of the speaker, or helping him or her work through the issue.

Rationalization   Creating a rational explanation or justification for our behavior.

Reaction formation   Acting in a way that is completely opposite to an unacceptable thought or impulse.

Realistic group conflict theory   People become prejudiced against others with whom they must compete for limited resources such as jobs, money, or status.

Regression   Psychologically retreating to an earlier, less mature time.

Regulating emotions   Managing the intensity and duration of feelings and the ability to delay gratification.

Reinforcement   A consequence that increases the likelihood of the behavior being repeated.

Relational climate   The degree to which we feel safe, supported, and understood in a relationship.

Relationship-oriented leaders   More concerned with morale, and focus on building good interpersonal relationships and positive feelings among staff members.

Relative deprivation   The perception that others have more than you do, or that another group is better off than your own group.

Relative language   Words or phrases that "gain their meaning by comparison".

Repair attempts   Anything—verbal or nonverbal—that a partner does to try to make things a little more positive and less tense during a conflict.

Repression   Completely suppressing a feeling which is unacceptable.

Resistance phase   Our bodies work to keep our immune systems at a peak and to repair damage while we continue to combat the threat.

Romantic love   The combination of intimacy and passion.

Rosy retrospection Our tendency to forget minor annoyances and remember pleasures of a positive experience more vividly over time.

Sage Seventies Successful 70-somethings stay mentally and physically in shape and continue to find missions in life.

Schemas Sets of beliefs and expectations each of us has about certain concepts, events and situations.

Selective attention Our ability to focus our attention on one incoming stimulus, while filtering out others that are less relevant.

Selective listening When we screen a message for certain topics or issues, and then either respond only to those aspects of the message or tune those parts out.

Self The sum total of who and what you are, both consciously and unconsciously.

Self-actualization When an individual has developed a complete sense of who she is and what her strengths are, and routinely acts in a way that is consistent with that.

Self-awareness An ongoing attention to one's internal states.

Self-concept The relatively stable set of perceptions you have about yourself.

Self-confidence Strong belief in oneself and one's ideas, as well as emotional stability.

Self-construals Pertain to the way we perceive, or construe, our self.

Self-efficacy The extent to which we believe we are capable of achieving our goals.

Self-enhancement The basic human need to feel good about ourselves.

Self-esteem How we feel about ourselves, or the degree to which we are satisfied with our self-concept.

Self-fulfilling prophecy A person begins to act in a manner consistent with the expectations placed upon him or her by others.

Self-knowledge The conscious knowledge you have about your motivations, beliefs, expectations, values, strengths, and weaknesses.

Self-monitoring We utilize different parts of our self, or different public selves, in different situations.

Self-perception Assumptions about ourselves based on our own observations of our behavior, thoughts, and feelings.

Self-talk Internal thoughts that reinforce our interpretation of an activating event.

Self-verification The human tendency to seek out and retain information that confirms or verifies our self-concept.

Selling Providing high degrees of both task-oriented and relationship-oriented leadership.

Sensory adaptation Our ability to become accustomed to an intrusive stimulus.

Sensory memory 1-2 second time frame during which we encode information from our immediate sensory experiences.

Serene Sixties Characterized by a sense of inner harmony, usually a result of a sense of living in a manner consistent with one's ideal self.

Sex The *biological* differences between men and women.

Situational control Measured by a combination of three factors: the leader's degree of power, his or her relationship with staff members, and the clarity of the task.

Situational reconstruction Imagining ways the situation could be worse, ways the situation could be better, and forming an action plan that lists steps to take to improve the stressful situation.

Social comparison Evaluating yourself based on how you think you compare to others.

Social exchange theory The general principle that, in relationships, we want the best we can get for what we have to offer, and we might "exchange" what we have for something a potential partner is offering.

Social identity theory   The idea that, in our efforts to maintain positive self-esteem, we may develop bias that favors our own groups over other groups.

Social learning theory   Developing behaviors and attitudes based in role models in our environment.

Social support   The awareness that one is cared for, valued, and part of a network of communication and mutual support.

Sociometer theory   Self-esteem acts as a gauge, or monitor, that measures the level of acceptance a person feels from his or her social environment.

Soft start-up   Begining a conflict discussion with I-language.

Spontaneous recovery   Occasional, unpredictable recurrence of a conditioned response that has become extinct.

Stagehogging   When someone is talking to us, and we use something the speaker says as an opening to jump in with a story of our own.

Stanford Prison Experiment   A classic study of social influence on behavior and perceptions.

State self-esteem   The type of self-esteem which is vulnerable to momentary fluctuations.

Static language   Language that implies that a situation or person is always the same.

Stereotype   A generalization about a group of people that assumes that members of the group share common characteristics.

Stereotype threat   When an individual's identity is heavily based on a characteristic for which there are strong stereotypes, that individual will maintain a heightened awareness of the likelihood of being stereotyped and feel afraid of that possibility.

Stonewalling   When one partner withdraws from a conversation, either by clamming up or by physically leaving the room and the discussion.

Storge   Stable love, typically deep and long-term, in which the relationship is based on strong friendship and mutual respect.

Strategy   Communicating in a way that is meant to manipulate the other person, or influence them indirectly to do or say something.

Stress   The feeling of arousal and the resulting physiological and psychological effects of being exposed to the stressor.

Stressors   Stressful events or situations.

Sublimation   Channeling an unacceptable feeling or urge into a positive, or more socially acceptable direction.

Succinct communication   Understated language that says very little and relies on the listener to understand the unspoken meaning.

Superego   The part of personality concerned with making sure the id and the ego function in a way that is consistent with the person's own moral code.

Superiority   Defense-arousing message that conveys that the speaker is smarter, knows more, or is better in some other way than the listener.

Superordinate goal   A goal, shared by conflicting groups, that can only be attained if the groups work together.

Supporting   Saying something intended to validate the speaker's thoughts or feelings, let the speaker know that you understand what he is thinking or feeling, or express support and concern for him as a person.

Symmetry   Refers to how symmetrical, well-matched, or balanced one side of a person's face and body are, compared to the other.

Talking rules   Rules of conversation.

Task-oriented leaders   Most concerned with productivity, and focus on providing direction and specific instructions for staff members.

Telling Providing task-oriented leadership.

The Four Horsemen Metaphoric phases in what Gottman sees as the apocalyptic demise of many marriages.

Theory of psychological reactance Humans have a strong need to control our own destinies and choices, and when these freedoms are threatened, we exert extra effort to hang onto them.

Trait self-esteem An individual's general pattern of self-esteem over a lifetime.

Transactional leader Base success on a series of equitable exchanges with followers.

Transformational leader Ignites the energies and interest of followers to the point where they become united with the leader in values and pursuit of the vision.

Tryout Twenties A feeling of freedom to "try out" different roles in life, both occupationally and in close relationships.

Turbulent Thirties A time in which young adults are juggling multiple roles, often including raising children, building a career, and maintaining an intimate relationship with a partner.

Tyranny of shoulds Belief that other people, or the world in general, ought to think and act in a way that fits your belief system.

Uncertainty Avoidance (UA) The extent to which the members of a culture feel threatened by uncertain or unknown situations.

Unconditional positive regard Giving positive regard and acceptance at all times and in all situations.

Unconditioned response (UR) A natural, biological response to a stimulus with no prior learning.

Unconditioned stimulus (US) A stimulus which produces a natural, biological response with no prior learning.

Unconscious The large portion of our mind including thoughts, feelings, memories, and expectations, that we are not aware of.

Values Guiding principles.

Waist-hip ratio (WHR) Determined by a person's proportions: specifically, how big is the waist as compared to the hips.

Win-win method A conflict resolution style aims to meet the needs of each party fully, without making sacrifices.

Work centrality The significance of work in a person's life.

Working memory A time frame of about 30 seconds during which we either use and dispose of the information, or work to retain it.

Work values Intrinsic, extrinsic, power, and social.

You-language Language that implies blame on the other person.

REFERENCES

Aboud, R. (1988). *Children and prejudice.* New York: Basil Blackwell.

Adler, R. B., & Towne, N. (1996). *Looking out/looking in* (8th ed.). Fort Worth, TX: Harcourt Brace.

Adler, R. B., & Towne, N. (2003). *Looking out/looking in* (10th ed.). Belmont, CA: Wadsworth/Thomson Learning.

Almaney, A. & Alwan, A. (1982). *Communicating with the Arabs.* Prospect Heights, IL: Waveland Press.

Anderson, J. L., Crawford, C. B., Nadeau, J., & Lindberg, T. (1992). Was the Duchess of Windsor right? A cross-cultural review of the socioecology of ideals of female body shape. *Ethology & Sociobiology, 13,* 197–227.

Anderson, P. A., Lustig, R., & Andersen, J. F. (1990). Changes in latitude, changes in attitude: The relationship between climate and interpersonal communication predispositions. *Communication Quarterly, 38,* 291–311.

Aron, A., Norman, C. C., Aron, E. N., McKenna, C., & Heyman, R. E. (2000). Couples' shared participation in novel and arousing activities and experienced relationship quality. *Journal of Personality and Social Psychology, 78,* 273–284.

Aronson, E. (1978). *The jigsaw classroom.* Beverly Hills, CA: Sage.

Aronson, E. (2000). *Nobody left to hate.* New York: W. H. Freeman.

Arvey, R. D., Harpaz, I., & Hui, L. (2001). Work centrality and post-award work behavior of lottery winners. *Journal of Psychology: Interdisciplinary and Applied, 138,* 404–420.

Asch, S. E. (1946). Forming impressions of personality. *Journal of Abnormal and Social Psychology, 41,* 258–290.

Asch, S. E. (1955, November). Opinions and social pressure. *Scientific American,* 31–35.

Astin, J. (1993). *What matters in college? Four critical years revisited.* San Francisco, CA: Jossey-Bass.

Ayman, R., & Chemers, M. M. (1983). Relationship of supervisory behavior ratings to work group effectiveness and subordinate satisfaction among Iranian managers. *Journal of Applied Psychology, 68,* 338–341.

Baker, H. D. R. (1979). *Chinese family and kinship.* London: Macmillan.

Bandura, A. (1977). Self-efficacy: Toward a unifying theory of behavioral change. *Psychological Review, 84,* 191–215.

Bandura, A., & Walters, R. H. (1959). Adolescent aggression: A study of the influence of child-training practices and family interrelationships. Oxford, England: Ronald.

Baron, R. S., Vandello, J. A., & Brunsman, B. (1996). The forgotten variable in conformity research: Impact of task importance on social influence. *Journal of Personality and Social Psychology, 71,* 915–927.

Bass, B. M. (1985). Leadership: Good, better, best. *Organizational Dynamics, 13,* 26–40.

Bateson, M. C. (1994). *Peripheral visions: Learning along the way.* New York: HarperCollins.

Baumeister, R. F., & Bratslavsky, E. (1999). Passion, intimacy, and time: Passionate love as a function of change in intimacy. *Personality and Social Psychology Review, 3,* 49–67.

Baumeister, R. F., Campbell, J. D., Krueger, J. I., & Vohs, K. D. (2003). Does high self-esteem cause better performance, interpersonal success, happiness, or healthier lifestyles? *Psychological Science in the Public Interest, 4,* 1–44.

Beauregard, K. S., & Dunning, D. (1998). Turning up the contrast: Self-enhancement motives prompt egocentric contrast effects in social judgments. *Journal of Personality and Social Psychology, 74,* 606–621.

Beck, A. T. (1987). Cognitive therapy. In J. K. Zeig (Ed.), *The evolution of psychotherapy.* New York: Brunner/Mazel.

Belsky, J., & Isabella, R. A. (1985). Marital and parent-child relationships in family of origin and marital change following the birth of a baby: A retrospective analysis. *Child Development, 56,* 342–349.

Bem, D. J. (1972). Self-perception theory. In L. Berkowitz (Ed.), *Advances in experimental social psychology* (Vol. 6, pp. 1–62). New York: Academic Press.

Berkman, L., & Syme, S. L. (1979). Social networks, host resistance, and mortality: A nine-year follow-up study of Alameda County residents. *American Journal of Epidemiology, 109,* 186–204.

Bickman, L. (1974). The social power of a uniform. *Journal of Applied Social Psychology, 4,* 47–61.

Blake, R. R., & Mouton, J. S. (1964). *The managerial grid.* Houston, TX: Gulf.

Blau, P. M. (1964). *Exchange and power in social life.* New York: Wiley.

Blum, J. S., & Mehrabian, A. (1999). Personality and temperament correlates of marital satisfaction. *Journal of Personality, 67,* 93–125.

Bond, R., & Smith, P. B. (1996). Culture and conformity: A meta-analysis of studies using Asch's (1952b, 1956) line judgment task. *Psychological Bulletin, 119,* 111–137.

Botwin, M. D., Buss, D. M., & Schackelford, T. K. (1997). Personality and mate preferences: Five factors in mate selection and marital satisfaction. *Journal of Personality, 65,* 107–136.

Bouchard, G., Lussier, Y., & Sabourin, S. (1999). Personality and marital adjustment: Utility of the five-factor model of personality. *Journal of Marriage & the Family, 61,* 651–660.

Brehm, S., & Brehm, J. W. (1981). *Psychological reactance: A theory of freedom and control.* New York: Academic Press.

Brehm, S. S., & Kassin, S. M. (1990). *Social psychology.* Boston: Houghton Mifflin.

Brehm, S. S., & Kassin, S. M. (1996). *Social psychology* (3rd ed.). Boston, MA: Houghton Mifflin.

Brehm, S. S., Miller, R. S., Perlman, D., & Campbell, S. M. (2002). *Intimate relationships* (3rd ed.). Boston: McGraw-Hill.

Brewer, M. B., & Pierce, K. P. (2005). Social identity complexity and outgroup tolerance. *Personality and Social Psychology Bulletin, 31,* 428–437.

Brislin, R. (1993). *Understanding culture's influence on behavior.* Fort Worth, TX: Harcourt Brace Jovanovich.

Brown, J. D. (1998). *The self.* New York: McGraw-Hill.

Buber, M. (1970). *I and thou* (Walter Kaufmann, Trans.). New York: Scribner.

Budesheim, T. L., & DePaola, S. J. (1994). Beauty or the beast? The effects of appearance, personality, and issue information on evaluations of political candidates. *Personality and Social Psychology Bulletin, 20,* 339–348.

Burgoon, J. K. (1994). Nonverbal signals. In M. L. Knapp & G. R. Miller (Eds.), *Handbook of Interpersonal Communication.* Newbury Park, CA: Sage.

Burman, B., & Margolin, G. (1992). Analysis of the association between marital relationships and health problems: An interactional perspective. *Psychological Bulletin, 112,* 39–63.

Burns, J. M. (1978). *Leadership.* New York: Harper & Row.

Bushman, B. J. (1988). The effects of apparel on compliance: A field experiment with a female authority figure. *Personality and Social Psychology Bulletin, 14,* 459–467.

Buss, D. M. (1989). Sex differences in human mate preferences: Evolutionary hypotheses tested in 37 cultures. *Behavioral and Brain Sciences, 12,* 1–14.

Butler, D., & Geis, F. L. (1990). Nonverbal affect responses to male and female leaders: Implications for leadership evaluations. *Journal of Personality and Social Psychology, 58,* 48–59.

Byrd-Bredbenner, C., Murray, J., & Schlussel, Y. R. (2005). Temporal changes in anthropometric measurements of idealized females and young women in general. *Women & Health, 41,* 13–30.

Cai, B. A., & Fink, E. L. (2002). Conflict style difference between individualist and collectivists. *Communication Monographs, 69,* 67–87.

Call, V., Sprecher, S., & Schwartz, P. (1995). The incidence and frequency of marital sex in a national sample. *Journal of Marriage & the Family, 57,* 639–652.

Carli, L. L., Ganley, R., & Pierce-Otay, A. (1991). Similarity and satisfaction in roommate relationships. *Personality and Social Psychology Bulletin, 17,* 419–426.

Castaneda, D. M. (1993). The meaning of romantic love among Mexican-Americans. *Journal of Social Behavior & Personality, 8,* 257–272.

Chaikin, A. L., Derlega, V. J., Bayma, B., & Shaw, J. (1975). Neuroticism and disclosure reciprocity. *Journal of Consulting and Clinical Psychology, 43,* 13–19.

Chemers, M. M., & Fiedler, F. E. (1978). The effectiveness of leadership training: A reply to Argyris. *American Psychologist, 33,* 391–394.

Chung, T., & Mallery, P. (2000). Social comparison, individualism-collectivism, and self-esteem in China and the United States. *Current Psychology: Developmental, Learning, Personality, Social, 18,* 340–352.

Church, A. T., & Katigbak, M. S. (2000). Trait psychology in the Philippines. *American Behavioral Scientist, 44,* 73–94.

Cialdini, R. B. (2001). *Influence: Science and practice* (4th ed.). Boston: Allyn & Bacon.

Cissna, K. N. L., & Sieberg, E. (1986). Patterns of interactional confirmation and disconfirmation. In J. Steward (Ed.), *Bridges, Not Walls* (4th ed.) New York: Random House.

Collins, N. L., Dunkel-Schetter, C., Lobel, M., & Scrimshaw, S. C. (1993). Social support in pregnancy: Psychosocial correlates of birth outcomes and postpartum depression. *Journal of Personality and Social Psychology, 65,* 1243–1258.

Contreras, R., Hendrick, S. S., & Hendrick, C. (1996). Perspectives on marital love and satisfaction in Mexican American and Anglo-American couples. *Journal of Counseling & Development, 74,* 408–415.

Cooper, A., & Sportolari, L. (2003). Romance in cyberspace: Understanding online attraction. In M. Coleman & L. Ganong (Eds.), *Points & counterpoints: Controversial relationship and family issues in the 21st century (an anthology).* Los Angeles, CA: Roxbury.

Coyne, J. C. (1987). Depression, biology, marriage and marital therapy. *Journal of Marital & Family Therapy 13,* 393–407.

Crocker, J., Joelkl, K., Testa, M., & Major, B. (1991). Social stigma: The affective consequences of attributional ambiguity. *Journal of Personality and Social Psychology, 60,* 218–228.

Crocker, J., & Luhtanen, R. (1990). Collective self-esteem and ingroup bias. *Journal of Personality and Social Psychology, 58,* 60–67.

Crosby, F. J. (1991). *Juggling.* New York: Free Press.

Crosby, F., Pufall, A., Snyder, R. C., O'Connell, M., & Whalen, P. (1989). The denial of personal disadvantage among you, me, and all the other ostriches. In M. Crawford and M. Gentry (Eds.), *Gender and thought.* New York: Springer-Verlag.

Crosby, F. J., Williams, J. C., & Biernat, M. (2004). The maternal wall. *Journal of Social Issues, 60,* 675–682.

Croxton, J. S., Eddy, T., & Morrow, N. (1984). Memory biases in the reconstruction of interpersonal encounters. *Journal of Social & Clinical Psychology, 2,* 348–354.

Crusco, A. H., & Wetzel, C. G. (1984). The Midas touch: The effects of interpersonal touch on restaurant tipping. *Personality and Social Psychology Bulletin, 10,* 512–517.

Crutchfield, R. A. (1955). Conformity and character. *American Psychologist, 10,* 191–198.

Csikszentmihalyi, M. (1997). *Finding flow: The psychology of engagement with everyday life.* New York: Basic Books.

Cunningham, M. R., Druen, P. B., & Barbee, A. P. (1997). Angels, mentors, and friends: Trade-offs among evolutionary, social, and individual variables in physical appearance. In J. A. Simpson & D. T. Kenrick (Eds.), *Evolutionary social psychology* (pp. 109–140). Mahwah, NJ: Erlbaum.

DeCenzo, D. A. (1997). *Human relations: Personal and professional development.* Upper Saddle River, NJ: Prentice-Hall.

Deci, E. L., & Ryan, R. M. (1987). The support of autonomy and the control of behavior. *Journal of Personality and Social Psychology, 53,* 1024–1037.

Devine, P. G., & Monteith, M. J. (1999). Automaticity and control in stereotyping. In S. Chaiken & Y. Trope (Eds.), *Dual-process theories in social psychology.* New York: Guilford Press.

Digman, J. M. (1989). Five robust trait dimensions: Development, stability, and utility. *Journal of Personality, 57,* 195–214.

Downs, A. C., & Lyons, P. M. (1991). Natural observations of the links between attractiveness and initial legal judgments. *Personality and Social Psychology Bulletin, 17,* 541–547.

Duck, S. W. (1972). Friendship, similarity and the Reptest. *Psychological Reports, 31,* 231–234.

Eagly, A. H., Ashmore, R. D., Makhijani, M. G., & Longo, L. C. (1991). What is beautiful is good, but . . .: A meta-analytic review of research on the physical attractiveness stereotype. *Psychological Bulletin, 110,* 109–128.

Eagly, A. H., & Johnson, B. T. (1990). Gender and leadership style: A meta-analysis. *Psychological Bulletin, 108,* 233–256.

Eagly, A. H., & Karau, S. J. (1991). Gender and the emergence of leaders: A meta-analysis. *Journal of Personality and Social Psychology, 60,* 685–710.

Eagly, A. H., Makhijani, M. G., & Klonsky, B. G. (1992). Gender and the evaluation of leaders: A meta-analysis. *Psychological Bulletin, 111,* 3–22.

Ekman, P. (1971). Universals and cultural differences in facial expressions of emotion. *Nebraska Symposium on Motivation,* 207–283.

Ellemers, N., Rijswijk, W. V., Roefs, M., & Simons, C. (1997). Bias in intergroup perceptions: Balancing group identity with social reality. *Personality and Social Psychology Bulletin, 23,* 186–198.

Elliot, A. J., & Sheldon, K. M. (1998). Avoidance personal goals and the personality-illness relationship. *Journal of Personality and Social Psychology, 75,* 1282–1299.

Ellis, A. (1962) Rational psychotherapy. Journal of General Psychology, *59,* 35–49.

Ellis, A. (1962). *Reason and emotion in psychotherapy.* Oxford, England: Lyle Stuart.

Ellis, A. (2001). *Overcoming destructive beliefs, feelings, and behaviors: New directions for rational emotive behavior therapy.* Amherst, NJ: Prometheus Books.

England, G. W., & Quintanilla, S. A. R. (1994). *Work meanings: Their structure and stability.* WORC Paper 94.11.046/6. Tilburg University, The Netherlands.

Erber, R. (1991). Affective and semantic priming: Effects of mood on category accessibility and inference. *Journal of Experimental Social Psychology, 27*, 480–498.

Erikson, E. H. (1963). *Childhood and society.* New York: Norton.

Eysenck, H. J. (1967). *The biological basis of personality.* Springfield, IL: Thomas.

Feingold, A. (1992). Good-looking people are not what we think. *Psychological Bulletin, 111*, 304–341.

Fenigstein, A., Scheier, M. F., & Buss, A. H. (1975). Public and private self-consciousness: Assessment and theory. *Journal of Consulting and Clinical Psychology, 43*, 522–527.

Festinger, L., Schachter, S., & Back, K. (1950). *Social pressures in informal groups; a study of human factors in housing.* Oxford, England: Harper.

Fiedler, F. H. (1987). A theory of leadership effectiveness. In F. H. Fiedler & J. E. Garcia (Eds.), *Leadership: Cognitive resources and performance.* New York: Wiley.

Fiedler, F. A., & House, R. J. (1994). Leadership theory and research: A report of progress. In C. L. Cooper & I. T. Robertson (Eds.), *Key reviews in managerial psychology: Concepts and research for practice.* Oxford, England: Wiley.

Fisher, J. D., & Byrne, D. (1975). Too close for comfort: Sex differences in response to invasions of personal space. *Journal of Personality and Social Psychology, 32*, 15–21.

Fiske, S. T. (1993). Controlling other people: The impact of power on stereotypes. *American Psychologist, 48*, 621–628.

Folkman, S., & Lazarus, R. S. (1980). An analysis of coping in a middle-aged community sample. *Journal of Health and Social Behavior, 21*, 219–239.

Freedman, J. L., & Fraser, S. C. (1966). Compliance without pressure: The foot-in-the-door technique. *Journal of Personality and Social Psychology, 4*, 195–202.

Furnham, A., & Baguma, P. (1994). Cross-cultural differences in the evaluations of male and female body shapes. *International Journal of Eating Disorders, 15*, 81–89.

Gabrielidis, C., Stephan, W. G., Ybarra, O., Pearson, V. M. D., & Villareal, L. (1997). Preferred styles of conflict resolution: Mexico and the United States. *Journal of Cross-Cultural Psychology, 28*, 661–677.

Gamson, W. A., Fireman, B., & Rytina, S. (1982). *Encounters with unjust authority.* Homewood, IL: Dorsey Press.

Gangestad, S. W., Thornhill, R., & Garver-Apgar, C. E. (2005). Adaptations to ovulation: Implications for sexual and social behavior. *Current Directions in Psychological Science, 14*, 312–316.

Geen, R. A. (1984). Preferred stimulation levels in introverts and extraverts: Effects on arousal and performance. *Journal of Personality and Social Psychology, 46*, 303–1312.

Gergen, K. J., Ellsworth, P., Maslach, C., & Seipel, M. (1975). Obligation, donor resources, and reactions to aid in three cultures. *Journal of Personality and Social Psychology, 31*, 390–400.

Gibb, J. (1961). Defensive communication. *Journal of Communication, 11*, 141–148.

Gibbs, J. L., Ellison, N. B., & Heino, R. D. (2006). Self-presentation in online personals: The role of anticipated future interaction, self-disclosure, and perceived success in Internet dating. *Communication Research, 33*, 152–177.

Gillham, J. E., Reivich, K. J., Jaycox, L. H. & Seligman, M. E. P. (1995). Prevention of depressive symptoms in schoolchildren: A two-year follow-up. *Psychological Science, 6*, 343–351.

Goethals, G. R. (1986). Social comparison theory: Psychology from the lost and found. *Personality and Social Psychology Bulletin, 12*, 261–278.

Goldberg, L. R. (1990). An alternative "description of personality": the Big-Five factor structure. *Journal of Personality and Social Psychology, 59*, 1216–1229.

Goldsmith, D. J., & Fitch, K. (1997). The normative context of advice as social support. *Human Communication Research, 23,* 454–476.

Goleman, D. (1995). *Emotional intelligence.* New York: Bantam Books.

Goodwin, S. A., & Fiske, S. T. (1993). *Impression formation in asymmetrical power relationships: Does power corrupt absolutely?* Unpublished manuscript, University of Massachusetts, Amherst.

Gottman, J. M., & Silver, N. (1999). *The seven principles for making marriage work.* New York: Crown.

Graen, G. B., Liden, R. C., & Hoel, W. (1982). Role of leadership in the employee withdrawal process. *Journal of Applied Psychology, 67,* 868–872.

Grammer, K., & Thornhill, R. (1994). Human (Homo sapiens) facial attractiveness and sexual selection: The role of symmetry and averageness. *Journal of Comparative Psychology, 108,* 233–242.

Greenspan, R. (2003). Socializing surfers shop for friends, dates. *ClickZ Network,* November 26.

Greenwald, A. (1980). The totalitarian ego: Fabrication and revision of personal history. *American Psychologist, 35,* 603–618.

Gudykunst, W. B., & Ting-Toomey, S. (1988). *Culture and interpersonal communication.* Newbury Park, CA: Sage.

Gudykunst, W., Yang, S., & Nishida, T. (1987). Cultural differences in self-consciousness and self-monitoring. *Communication Research, 14,* 7–36.

Hall, E. (1959). *The silent language.* Garden City, NY: Doubleday.

Hall, E. T. (1966). *The hidden dimension.* Garden City, NY: Doubleday.

Hamermesh, D. S., & Bidle, J. E. (1994). Beauty and the labor market. *American Economic Review, 84,* 1174–1195.

Harpaz, I. (1989). Non-financial employment commitment: A cross-national comparison. *Journal of Occupational Psychology, 62,* 147–150.

Harris, M. (1974). *Cows, pigs, wars, and witches: The riddles of culture.* New York: Random House.

Hecht, M. L., Marston, P. J., & Larkey, L. K. (1994). Love ways and relationship quality in heterosexual relationships. *Journal of Social and Personal Relationships, 11,* 25–43.

Helgeson, S. (1990). *The female advantage: Women's ways of leadership.* New York: Doubleday Currency.

Hendrick, C., & Hendrick, S. (1986). A theory and method of love. *Journal of Personality and Social Psychology, 50,* 392–402.

Hendrick, S. S. (2004). *Understanding close relationships.* Boston: Pearson Education.

Hendrick, S. S., & Hendrick, C. (1995). Gender differences and similarities in sex and love. *Personal Relationships, 2,* 55–65.

Henley, N. (1977). *Body politics: Power, sex, and nonverbal communication.* Englewood Cliffs, NJ: Prentice Hall.

Hersey, P., & Blanchard, K. H. (1993). *Management of organizational behavior* (6th ed.). Englewood Cliffs, NJ: Prentice Hall.

Hiller, J. (2004). Speculations on the links between feelings, emotions and sexual behaviour: Are vasopressin and oxytocin involved? *Sexual and Relationship Therapy, 19,* 393–429.

Hofstede, G. (1980). *Culture's consequences: International differences in work-related values.* Beverly Hills, CA: Sage.

Hofstede, G. (1991). *Cultures and organizations: Software of the mind.* London: McGraw-Hill.

Hofstede, G. (2001). *Culture's consequences.* Thousand Oaks, CA: Sage.

Holden, G. (1991). The relationship of self-efficacy appraisals to subsequent health related outcomes: A meta-analysis. *Social Work in Health Care, 16,* 53–93.

Holmberg, D., & Holmes, J. G. (1994). Reconstruction of relationship memories: A mental models approach. In N. Schwarz & S. Sudman (Eds.), *Autobiographical memory and the validity of retrospective reports.* New York: Springer-Verlag.

Honekopp, J., Bartholome, T., & Jansen, G. (2004). Facial attractiveness, symmetry, and physical fitness in young women. *Human Nature, 15,* 147–167.

Horney, K. (1950). *Neuroses and human growth.* New York: Norton.

Horowitz, I. A., & Bordens, K. S. (1995). *Social psychology.* Mountain View, CA: Mayfield.

Hughes, M., & Demo, D. H. (1989). Self-perceptions of Black Americans: Self-esteem and personal efficacy. *American Journal of Sociology, 95,* 132–159.

Huston, T. L., & Chorost, A. F. (1994). Behavioral buffers on the effect of negativity on marital satisfaction: A longitudinal study. *Personal Relationships, 1,* 223–239.

Isaacs, W. (1999). *Dialogue and the art of thinking together.* New York: Doubleday.

Iwao, S. (1993). *The Japanese woman: Traditional image and changing reality.* New York: Free Press.

Jamieson, D. W., Lydon, J. E., Stewart, G., & Zanna, M. P. (1987). Pygmalion revisited: New evidence for student expectancy effects in the classroom. *Journal of Educational Psychology, 79,* 461–466.

Johnson, D. W. (1997). *Reaching out: Interpersonal effectiveness and self-actualization* (7th ed.). Needham Heights, MA: Allyn & Bacon.

Joiner, T. E. (1994). Contagious depression: Existence, specificity to depressed symptoms, and the role of reassurance seeking. *Journal of Personality and Social Psychology, 67,* 287–296.

Jones, D. (1995). Sexual selection, physical attractiveness, and facial neotony: Cross-cultural evidence and implications. *Current Anthropology, 36,* 723–748.

Judge, T. A., Bono, J. E., Ilies, R., & Gerhardt, M. W. (2002). Personality and leadership: A qualitative and quantitative review. *Journal of Applied Psychology, 87,* 765–780.

Kaplan, H. R. (1985). Lottery winners and work commitment: A behavioral test of the American work ethic. *Journal of the Institute for Socioeconomic Studies, 10,* 82–94.

Kegan, R. (1982). *The evolving self: Problems and process in human development.* Cambridge, MA: Harvard University Press.

Kelley, H. H. (1967). Attribution theory in social psychology. *Nebraska Symposium on Motivation, 15,* 192–238.

Kenrick, D. T., Groth, G. E., Trost, M. R., & Sadalla, E. K. (1993). Integrating evolutionary and social exchange perspectives on relationships: Effects of gender, self-appraisal, and involvement level on mate selection criteria. *Journal of Personality and Social Psychology, 64,* 951–969.

Kenrick, D. T., Montello, D. R., Gutierres, S. E., & Trost, M. R. (1993). Effects of physical attractiveness on affect and perceptual judgments: When social comparison overrides social reinforcement. *Personality and Social Psychology Bulletin, 19,* 195–199.

Kenrick, D. T., Neuberg, S. L., & Cialdini, R. B. (1999). *Social psychology: Unraveling the mystery.* Needham Heights, MA: Allyn & Bacon.

Kirkpatrick, S. A., & Locke, E. A. (1996). Direct and indirect effects of three core charismatic leadership components on performance and attitudes. *Journal of Applied Psychology, 81,* 36–51.

Kitayama, S. (2000). Collective construction of the self and social relationships: A rejoinder and some extensions. *Child Development, 71,* 1143–1146.

Kitayama, S., Markus, H. R., Matsumoto, H., & Norasakkunkit, V. (1997). Individual and collective processes in the construction of the self: Self-enhancement in the United States and self-criticism in Japan. *Journal of Personality and Social Psychology, 72,* 1245–1267.

Kobasa, S. C., Maddi, S. R., & Puccetti, M. C. (1982). Personality and exercise as buffers in the stress-illness relationship. *Journal of Behavioral Medicine, 5,* 391–404.

Kobasa, S. C., & Puccetti, M. C. (1983). Personality and social resources in stress resistance. *Journal of Personality and Social Psychology, 45,* 839–850.

Kunda, Z. (1999). *Social cognition: Making sense of people.* Cambridge, MA: The MIT Press.

Langlois, J. H., Ritter, J. M., Roggman, L. A., & Vaughn, L. S. (1991). Facial diversity and infant preferences for attractive faces. *Developmental Psychology, 27,* 79–84.

Leary, M. R., Tambor, E. S., Terdal, S. K., & Downs, D. L. (1995). Self-esteem as an interpersonal monitor: The sociometer hypothesis. *Journal of Personality and Social Psychology, 68,* 518–530.

Lee, J. A. (1977). A typology of styles of loving. *Personality and Social Psychology Bulletin, 3,* 173–182.

Lee, J. A. (1988). Love-styles. In R. J. Sternberg & M. I. Barnes (Eds.), *The psychology of love,* pp. 38–67. New Haven, CT: Yale University Press.

Levine, D. (2000). Virtual attraction: What rocks your boat. *CyberPsychology & Behavior, 3,* 565–573.

Levinson, D. J., Darrow, C. N, Klein, E. B., Levinson, M. H., & McKee, B. (1978). *The seasons of a man's life.* New York: Alfred A. Knopf.

Lichtman, R. R., Taylor, S. E., & Wood, J. V. (1987). Social support and marital adjustment after breast cancer. *Journal of Psychosocial Oncology, 5,* 47–74.

Linville, P. W. (1985). Self-complexity and affective extremity: Don't put all of your eggs in one cognitive basket. *Social Cognition, 3,* 94–120.

Linville, P. W. (1987). Self-complexity as a cognitive buffer against stress-related illness and depression. *Journal of Personality and Social Psychology, 52,* 663–676.

Locke, K. D., & Horowitz, L. M. (1990). Satisfaction in interpersonal interactions as a function of similarity in level of dysphoria. *Journal of Personality and Social Psychology, 58,* 823–831.

Loftus, E. F., & Palmer, J. C. (1974). Reconstruction of automobile destruction: An example of the interaction between language and memory. *Journal of Verbal Learning & Verbal Behavior, 13,* 585–589.

Lowe, K. B., Kroeck, K. G., & Sivasubramaniam, N. (1996). Effectiveness correlates of transformation and transactional leadership: A meta-analytic review of the MLQ literature. *Leadership Quarterly, 7,* 385–425.

Lykken, D., & Tellegen, A. (1996). Happiness is a stochastic phenomenon. *Psychological Science 7,* 186–189.

Mack, D., & Rainey, D. (1990). Female applicants' grooming and personnel selection. *Journal of Social Behavior & Personality, 5,* 399–407.

Maddi, S. R. (1998). Creating meaning through making decisions. In P. T. P. Wong & P. S. Fry (Eds.), *The human quest for meaning: A handbook of psychological research and clinical applications* (pp. 3–26). Mahwah, NJ: Lawrence Erlbaum.

Maddi, S. R., & Khoshaba, D. M. (2003). Hardiness training for resiliency and leadership. In D. Paton, J. M. Violanti, & L. M. Smith (Eds.), *Promoting capabilities to manage posttraumatic stress: Perspectives on resilience* (pp. 43–58). Springfield, IL: Charles C Thomas.

Maier, S. F., Watkins, L. R., & Fleshner, M. (1994). Psychoneuroimmunology: The interface between behavior, brain, and immunity. *American Psychologist, 49,* 1004–1017.

Mantell, D. M. (1971). The potential for violence in Germany. *Journal of Social Issues, 27,* 101–112.

Markus, H. (1990). Unresolved issues of self-representation. *Cognitive Therapy and Research, 14,* 241–253.

Markus, H. R., & Kitayama, S. (1991). Culture and the self: Implications for cognition, emotion, and motivation. *Psychological Review, 98,* 224–253.

Markus, H., & Nurius, P. (1986). Possible selves. *American Psychologist, 41,* 954–969.

Martin, R. A., & Lefcourt, H. M. (1983). Sense of humor as a moderator of the relation between stressors and moods. *Journal of Personality and Social Psychology, 45,* 1313–1324.

Maslow, A. H. (1968). *Toward a psychology of being* (2nd ed.). Oxford, England: D. Van Nostrand.

Maslow, A. H. (1971). *The farther reaches of human nature.* New York: Viking Press.

Matsumoto, D. (2000). *Culture and psychology: People around the world* (2nd ed.). Belmont, CA: Wadsworth/Thomson Learning.

McAdams, D. P. (1994). *The persons: An introduction to personality psychology* (2nd ed.). Fort Worth, TX: Harcourt Brace.

McCann, C. D., & Hancock, R. D. (1983). Self-monitoring in communicative interactions: Social cognitive consequences of goal-directed message modification. *Journal of Experimental Social Psychology, 19,* 109–121.

McCrae, R. R., & Costa, P. T., Jr. (1986). Personality, coping, and coping effectiveness in an adult sample. *Journal of Personality, 54,* 385–405.

McCrae, R. R., & Costa P. T., Jr. (1987). Validation of the five-factor model of personality across instruments and observers. *Journal of Personality and Social Psychology, 52,* 81–90.

McCrae, R. R., & Costa, P. T., Jr. (1991). Adding Liebe und Arbeit: The full five-factor model and well-being. *Personality and Social Psychology Bulletin, 56,* 586–595.

Meeus, W. H. J, & Raaijmakers, Q. A. W. (1995). Obedience in modern society: The Utrecht studies. *Journal of Social Issues, 51,* 155–175.

Milgram, S. (1974). *Obedience to authority.* New York: Harper & Row.

Milgram, S., Bickman, L., & Berkowitz, L. (1969). Note on the drawing power of crowds of different size. *Journal of Personality and Social Psychology, 13,* 79–82.

Miller, J. G. (1984). Culture and the development of everyday social explanation. *Journal of Personality and Social Psychology, 46,* 961–978.

Mitchell, T. R., Thompson, L., Peterson, E., & Cronk, R. (1997). Temporal adjustments in the evaluation of events: The "rosy view." *Journal of Experimental Social Psychology, 33,* 421–488.

Moberg, P. J. (2001). Linking conflict strategy to the five-factor model: Theoretical and empirical foundations. *International Journal of Conflict Management, 12,* 47–68.

Montagliani, A., & Giacalone, R. A. (1998). Impression management and cross-cultural adaptation. *Journal of Social Psychology, 138,* pp. 598–608.

Moran, M. A. (1992). Attachment or loss within marriage: The effect of the medical model of birthing on the marital bond of love. *Journal of Prenatal & Perinatal Psychology & Health, 6,* 265–279.

Moreland, R. L., & Beach, S. R. (1992). Exposure effects in the classroom: The development of affinity among students. *Journal of Experimental Social Psychology, 28,* 255–276.

Mueller, C. M., & Dweck, C. S. (1998). Praise for intelligence can undermine children's motivation and performance. *Journal of Personality and Social Psychology, 75,* 33–52.

Mulder, M. (1977). *The daily power game.* Leiden, Netherlands: Martinus Nijhoff.

Multon, K. D., Brown, S. D., & Lent, R. W. (1991). Relation of self-efficacy beliefs to academic outcomes: A meta-analytic investigation. *Journal of Counseling Psychology, 38,* 30–38.

Murstein, B. I., Merighi, J. R., & Vyse, S. A. (1991). Love styles in the United States and France: A cross-cultural comparison. *Journal of Social & Clinical Psychology, 10,* 37–46.

Myers, D. G. (1993). *The pursuit of happiness.* New York: Avon Books.

Myers, D. G. (1999). *Social psychology.* Boston: McGraw-Hill.

Myers, D. G. (2001). *Psychology* (6th ed.). New York: Worth.

National Association of Colleges and Employers. (2003). *Job Outlook Survey.* Bethlehem, PA: NACE.

Nealey, S. M., & Fiedler, F. E. (1968). Leadership functions of middle managers. *Psychological Bulletin, 70,* 313–329.

Neuberg, S. L., & Newsom, J. T. (1993). Personal need for structure: Individual differences in the desire for simple structure. *Journal of Personality and Social Psychology, 64,* 409–420.

Norman, C., & Aron, A. (June, 1995). *The effect of exciting activities on relationship satisfaction: A laboratory experiment.* Paper presented at the International Network Conference on Personal Relationships, Williamsburg, VA.

Notarius, C., & Herrick, L. R. (1988). Listener response strategies to a distressed other. *Journal of Social and Personal Relationships, 5,* 97–108.

Oettingen, G. (1995). Cross-cultural perspectives on self-efficacy. In A. Bandura (Ed.), *Self-efficacy in changing societies* (pp. 149–176). New York: Cambridge University Press.

O'Leary, A. (1992). Self-efficacy and health: Behavioral and stress-physiological mediation. *Cognitive Therapy and Research, 16,* 229–245.

Owen, P. R., & Laurel-Seller, E. (2000). Weight and shape ideals: Thin is dangerously in. *Journal of Applied Social Psychology, 30,* 979–990.

Ozer, E. M., & Bandura, A. (1990). Mechanisms governing empowerment effects: A self-efficacy analysis. *Journal of Personality and Social Psychology, 58,* 472–486.

Patterson, G. R., Chamberlain, P., & Reid, J. B. (1982). A comparative evaluation of parent training procedures. *Behavior Therapy, 13,* 638–650.

Patton, G. C., Carlin, J. B., Shao, Q., Hibbert, M. E., Rosier, M., Selzer, R., et al. (1997). Adolescent dieting: Healthy weight control or borderline eating disorder? *Journal of Child Psychology and Psychiatry and Allied Disciplines, 38*(3), 299–306.

Peters, D. P., & Ceci, S. J. (1982). Peer-review practices of psychological journals: The fate of published articles, submitted again. *Behavioral and Brain Sciences, 5,* 187–255.

Petrie, K. J., Booth, R. J., & Pennebaker, J. W. (1998). The immunological effects of thought suppression. *Journal of Personality and Social Psychology, 75,* 1264–1272.

Pittman, T. S. (1980). Informational versus controlling verbal rewards. *Personality and Social Psychology Bulletin, 6,* 228–233.

Porter, N., Geis, F. L., & Jennings (Walstead), J. (1983). Are women invisible as leaders? *Sex Roles, 9,* 1035–1049.

Powell, G. N. (1993). *Women and men in management.* Thousand Oaks, CA: Sage.

Pruitt, D. G., & Carnevale, P. J. (1993). *Negotiation in social conflict.* Pacific Grove, CA: Brooks/Cole.

Pruitt, D. G., & Rubin, J. Z. (1986). *Social conflict.* New York: McGraw-Hill.

Rathus, S. A., & Nevid, J. S. (1995). *Adjustment and growth: The challenges of life* (6th ed.). Fort Worth, TX: Harcourt Brace.

Regan, P. C. (1998). Of lust and love: Beliefs about the role of sexual desire in romantic relationships. *Personal Relationships, 5,* 139–157.

Reifman, A., Klein, J. G., & Murphy, S. T. (1989). Self-monitoring and age. *Psychology and Aging, 4,* 245–246.

Reissman, C., Aron, A., & Bergen, M. R. (1993). Shared activities and marital satisfaction: Causal direction and self-expansion versus boredom. *Journal of Social and Personal Relationships, 10,* 243–254.

Rhodes, G., Roberts, J., & Simmons, L. W. (1999). Reflections on symmetry and attractiveness. *Evolution and Gender, 1,* 279–296.

Riley, D., & Eckenrode, J. (1986). Social ties: Subgroup differences in costs and benefits. *Journal of Personality and Social Psychology, 51,* 770–778.

Rindfuss, R. R., & Stephen, E. H. (1990). Marital cohabitation: Separation does not make the heart grow fonder. *Journal of Marriage & the Family, 52,* 259–270.

Ritts, V., Patterson, M. L., & Tubbs, M. E. (1992). Expectations, impressions, and judgments of physically attractive students: A review. *Review of Educational Research, 62,* 413–426.

Rokeach, M. (1967). *Value survey.* Sunnyvale, CA: Halgren Tests.

Ros, M., Schwartz, S. H., & Surkis, S. (1999). Basic individual values, work values, and the meaning of work. *Applied Psychology: An International Review, 48.*

Ross, L., Greene, D., & House, P. (1977). The false consensus phenomenon: An attributional bias in self-perception and social-perception processes. *Journal of Experimental Social Psychology, 13,* 279–301.

Rubin, J. Z., Pruitt, D. G., & Kim, S. H. (1994). *Social conflict: Escalation, stalemate, and settlement.* New York: McGraw-Hill.

Rueckert, L., Baboorian, D., Stavropoulous, K., & Yasutake, C. (1999). Individual differences in callosal efficiency: Correlation with attention. *Brain and Cognition, 41,* 390–410.

Ruggiero, K. M., & Taylor, D. M. (1997). Why minority group members perceive or do not perccive the discrimination that surrounds them: The role of self-esteem and perceived control. *Journal of Personality and Social Psychology, 72,* 373–389.

Ruiz-Quintanilla, S. A., & Wilpert, B. (1991). Are work meanings changing? *European Work and Organizational Psychology, 1,* 91–109.

Ruvolo, A., & Markus, H. (1992). Possible selves and performance: The power of self-relevant imagery. *Social Cognition, 9,* 95–124.

Ryan, E. D. (1980). Attribution, intrinsic motivation, and athletics: A replication and extension. In C. H. Nadeau, W. R. Halliwell, K. M. Newell, & G. C. Roberts (Eds.), *Psychology of motor behavior and sport—1979.* Champaign, IL: Human Kinetics Press.

Samovar, L. A., & Porter, R. E. (1997). *Intercultural communication: A reader* (8th ed., p. 24). Belmont, CA: Wadsworth/International Thomson.

Samter, W., & Cupach, W. R. (1998). Friendly fire: Topical variations in conflict among same- and cross-sex friends. *Communication Studies, 49,* 121–139.

Sangrador, J. L., & Yela, C. (2000). "What is beautiful is loved": Physical attractiveness in love relationships in a representative sample. *Social Behavior and Personality, 28,* 207–218.

Scheier, M. F., & Carver, C. S. (1985). Optimism, coping, and health: Assessment and implications of generalized outcome expectancies. *Health Psychology 4,* 219–247.

Scheier, M. F., Matthews, K. A., Owens, J. F., Magovern, G. J., et al. (1989). Dispositional optimism and recovery from coronary artery bypass surgery: The beneficial effects on physical and psychological well-being. *Journal of Personality and Social Psychology, 57,* 1024–1040.

Schlenker, B. R., Dlugolecki, D. W., & Doherty, K. (1994). The impact of self-presentations on self-appraisals and behavior: The power of public commitment. *Personality and Social Psychology Bulletin, 20,* 20–33.

Schwartz, S. H. (1992). Universals in the content and structure of values: Theoretical advances and empirical tests in 20 countries. In M. Zanna (Ed.), *Advances in experimental social psychology* (Vol. 25, pp. 1–65). New York: Academic Press.

Seligman, M. E. P., & Schulman, P. (1986). Explanatory style as a predictor of productivity and quitting among life insurance sales agents. *Journal of Personality and Social Psychology, 50*, 832–838.

Selye, H. (1976). *The stress of life*. New York: McGraw-Hill.

Sheehy, G. (1995). *New Passages*. New York: Random House.

Sheldon, K. M., Elliot, A. J., Kim, Y., & Kasser, T. (2001). What is satisfying about satisfying events? Testing 10 candidate psychological needs. *Journal of Personality and Social Psychology, 80*, 325–339.

Sherif, M. (1966). *In common predicament: Social psychology of intergroup conflict and cooperation*. Boston: Houghton Mifflin.

Sherman, J. W., Klein, S. B., Laskey, A., & Wyer, N. A. (1998). Intergroup bias in group judgment processes: The role of behavioral memories. *Journal of Experimental Social Psychology, 34*, 51–68.

Sherman, S. J., Presson, C. C., & Chassin, L. (1984). Mechanisms underlying the false consensus effect: The special role of threats to the self. *Personality and Social Psychology Bulletin, 10*, 127–138.

Shoda, Y., Mischel, W., & Peake, P. K. (1990). Predicting adolescent cognitive and self-regulatory competencies from preschool delay of gratification: Identifying diagnostic conditions. *Developmental Psychology, 26*, 978–986.

Siegert, J. R., & Stamp, G. H. (1994). "Our first big fight" as a milestone in the development of close relationships. *Communication Monographs, 61*, 345–360.

Singh, D. (1994). Body fat distribution and perception of desirable female body shape by young Black men and women. *International Journal of Eating Disorders, 16*, 289–294.

Singh, D. (1994). Is thin really beautiful and good? Relationship between waist-to-hip ratio (WHR) and female attractiveness. *Personality and Individual Differences, 16*, 123–132.

Singh, D. (1995). Female judgment of male attractiveness and desirability for relationships: Role of waist-to-hip ratio and financial status. *Journal of Personality and Social Psychology, 69*, 1089–1101.

Singh, D., & Luis, S. (1995). Ethnic and gender consensus for the effect of waist-to-hip ratio on judgment of women's attractiveness. *Human Nature, 6*, 51–65.

Singh, D., & Young, R. K. (1995). Body weight, waist-to-hip ratio, breasts, and hips: Role in judgments of female attractiveness and desirability for relationships. *Ethology & Sociobiology, 16*, 483–507.

Sinha, P. (1986). Factors for job satisfaction: For a quality of work. *Indian Journal of Behaviour, 10*, 24–36.

Skinner, B. F. (1953). *Science and human behavior*. Oxford, England: Macmillan.

Smith, G. H., & Engel, R. (1968). Influence of a female model on perceived characteristics of an automobile. *Proceedings of the Annual Convention of the American Psychological Association, 3*, 681–682.

Snyder, M. (1987). *Public appearances/private realities: The psychology of self-monitoring*. New York: Freeman.

Snyder, M., Berscheid, E., & Glick, P. (1985). Focusing on the exterior and the interior: Two investigations of the initiation of personal relationships. *Journal of Personality and Social Psychology, 54*, 972–979.

Snyder, M., & Gangestad, S. On the nature of self-monitoring: Matters of assessment, matters of validity. *Journal of Personality and Social Psychology, 51*, 125–139.

Snyder, M., & Simpson, J. (1985). Orientations toward romantic relationships. In S. Duck & D. Perlman (Eds.), *Understanding personal relationships*. Beverly Hills, CA: Sage.

Spencer, S. J., Steele, C. M., & Quinn, D. M. (1999). Stereotype threat and women's math performance. *Journal of Experimental Social Psychology, 35,* 4–28.

Sprecher, S. (1998). The effect of exchange orientation on close relationships. *Social Psychology Quarterly, 61,* 220–231.

Sprecher, S., & Regan, P. C. (1998). Passionate and companionate love in courting and young married couples. *Sociological Inquiry, 68,* 163–185.

Springer, S. P., & Deutsch, G. (1998). *Left brain, right brain: Perspectives from cognitive neuroscience* (5th ed.). New York: Freeman.

Steele, C. M. (1988). The psychology of self-affirmation: Sustaining integrity of the self. In L. Berkowitz (Ed.), *Advances in experimental social psychology* (Vol. 21, pp. 261–302). New York: Academic Press.

Steele, C. M. (1997). A threat in the air: How stereotypes shape intellectual identity and performance. *American Psychologist, 52,* 613–629.

Steele, C. M., and Aronson, J. (1995). Stereotype vulnerability and the intellectual test performance of African Americans. *Journal of Personality and Social Psychology, 69,* 797–811.

Sternberg, R. J. (1986). A triangular theory of love. *Psychological Review, 93,* 119–135.

Sternberg, R. J. (1987). *The triangle of love: Intimacy, passion, commitment.* New York: Basic Books.

Stroessner, S. M., & Mackie, D. M. (1992). The impact of induced affect on the perception of social variability in social groups. *Personality and Social Psychology Bulletin, 18,* 546–554.

Swann, W. (1997). The trouble with change: Self-verification and allegiance to the self. *Psychological Science, 8,* 177–180.

Tajfel, H., Billig, M. G., Bundy, R. P., & Flament, C. (1971). Social categorization and intergroup behaviour. *European Journal of Social Psychology, 1,* 149–178.

Tannen, D. (1986). *That's not what I meant! How conversational style makes or breaks your relations with others.* New York: William Morrow.

Tannen, D. (1990). *You just don't understand: Women and men in conversation.* New York: William Morrow.

Taylor, D. N. (1995). Effects of a behavioral stress-management program on anxiety, mood, self-esteem, and T-cell count in HIV-positive men. *Psychological Reports, 76,* 451–457.

Taylor, S. E. (1989). *Positive illusions: Creative self-deception and the healthy mind.* New York: Basic Books.

Taylor, S. E. (1999). *Health psychology* (4th ed.). New York: McGraw-Hill.

Taylor, S. E., Peplau, L. A., & Sears, D. O. (2000). *Social psychology.* Upper Saddle River, NJ: Prentice Hall.

Thomas, K. W., & Kilmann, R. H. (1974). *Thomas-Kilmann conflict MODE instrument.* Tuxedo, NY: Xicom.

Thompson, S. C., & Spacapan, S. (1991). Perceptions of control in vulnerable populations. *Journal of Social Issues, 47,* 1–21.

Ting-Toomey, S., Oetzel, J. G., & Yee-Jung, K. (2001.) Self-construal types and conflict management styles. *Communication Reports, 14,* 87–105.

Ting-Toomey, S., Yee-Jung, K. K., Shapiro, R. B., Garcia, T. J., & Oetzel, J. G. (2000). Ethnic/cultural identity salience and conflict styles in four U.S. ethnic groups. *International Journal of Intercultural Relations, 24,* 47–81.

Tougas, F., Brown, R., Beaton, A. M., & Joly, S. (1995). Neosexism: Plus ça change, plus c'est pareil. *Personality and Social Psychology Bulletin, 21,* 842–849.

Triandis, H. C. (1973). Subjective culture and economic development. *International Journal of Psychology, 8,* 163–180.

Triandis, H. C., & Suh, E. M. (2002). Cultural influences on personality. *Annual Review of Psychology, 53,* 133–160.

Trzesniewski, K. H., Donnellan, M. B., & Robins, R. W. (2003). Stability of self-esteem across the life span. *Journal of Personality and Social Psychology, 84,* 205–220.

Tucker, P., & Aron, A. (1993). Passionate love and marital satisfaction at key transition points in the family life cycle. *Journal of Social and Clinical Psychology, 12,* 135–147.

Uvnas-Moberg, K. (1998). Oxytocin may mediate the benefits of positive social interaction and emotions. *Psychoneuroendocrinology, 23,* 819–835.

Valkenburg, P., & Peter, J. (2005). Who looks for dates and romance on the Internet? An exploratory study. *International Communication Association Annual Meeting,* pp. 25–50.

Valkenburg, P. M., Schouten, A. P., & Peter, J. (2005). Adolescents' identity experiments on the Internet. *New Media & Society, 7,* 383–402.

Van de Vliert, E., Schwartz, S. H., Huismans, S. E., Hofstede, G., & Daan, S. (1999). Temperature, cultural masculinity and domestic political violence: A cross-national study. *Journal of Cross-Cultural Psychology, 30,* 291–314.

Vangelisti, A. L., Knapp, M. L., & Daly, J. A. (1990). Conversational narcissism. *Communication Monographs, 57,* 251–274.

Wade, C., & Tavris, C. (1998). *Psychology* (5th ed.). New York: Addison Wesley Longman.

Watson, J. B. (1924). *Behaviorism.* New York: W.W. Norton.

Wheeler, L., & Kim, Y. (1997). What is beautiful is culturally good: The physical attractiveness stereotype has different content in collectivistic cultures. *Personality and Social Psychology Bulletin, 23,* 795–800.

Widom, C. S. (1989). Does violence beget violence? A critical examination of the literature. *Psychological Bulletin, 106,* 3–28.

Wilder, D. A. (1993). The role of anxiety in facilitating stereotypic judgments of outgroup behavior. In D. M. Mackie and D. J. Hamilton (Eds.), *Affect, cognition, and stereotyping: Interactive processes in intergroup perception* (pp. 87–109). New York: Academic Press.

Wilmot, W. W. (1987). *Dyadic communication.* New York: Random House.

Winsor, J. L., Curtis, D. B., & Stephens, R. D. (1999). National preferences in business and communication education: An update. *Journal of the Association for Communication Administration, 3,* 170–179.

Wolfson, N. (1981). Compliments in cross-cultural perspective. *TESOI Quarterly, 15,* 117–124.

Wolvin, A. D. (1984). Meeting the communication needs of the adult learners. *Communication Education, 33,* 267–271.

Wood, J. T. (2002). *Interpersonal communication: Everyday encounters* (3rd ed.). Belmont, CA: Wadsworth/Thomson Learning.

Wood, J. V., Taylor, S. E., & Lichtman, R. R. (2003). Social comparison in adjustment to breast cancer. In P. Salovey & A. J. Rothman (Eds.), *Social psychology of health* (pp. 151–165). New York: Psychology Press.

Zaleznik, A. (1989). The leadership gap. In W. E. Rosenbach & R. L. Taylor (Eds.), *Contemporary issues in leadership.* Boulder, CO: Westview Press.

Zich, J., & Temoshok, L. (1987). Perceptions of social support in men with AIDS and ARC: Relationships with distress and hardiness. *Journal of Applied Social Psychology, 17,* 193–215.

Zimbardo, P. G. (1972). *The Stanford prison experiment: A slide/tape presentation.* Produced by Philip G. Zimbardo, Inc., P.O. Box 4395, Stanford, CA 94305.

NAME INDEX

SUBJECT INDEX